DOCUMENTS TO ACCOMPANY

America's History

Volume 1: To 1877

SIXTH EDITION
Henretta Brody Dumenil

DOCUMENTS TO ACCOMPANY

America's History

Volume 1: To 1877

Melvin Yazawa
University of New Mexico

Bedford / St. Martin's
Boston   •   New York

Cover art: Penn's Treaty with the Indians, 1771–1772. Benjamin West. Oil on canvas. 75 × 107 in, 191.8 × 273.7 cm. Gift of Mrs. Sarah Harrison (The Joseph Harrison Jr. Collection). Pennsylvania Academy of the Fine Arts; Map of the Province of Pensilvania. © www.mapsofpa.com / Harold Cramer.

Manufactured in the United States of America.

2 1 0 9 8
f e d c b

For information, write: Bedford/St. Martin's, 75 Arlington Street, Boston, MA 02116 (617-399-4000)

ISBN-10: 0-312-45442-2
ISBN-13: 978-0-312-45442-5

Preface

What is history? Contrary to conventional wisdom, history is not simply everything that happened in the past; rather history is the *recoverable* past rendered orderly and meaningful by historians. The adjective *recoverable*, which is defined principally by the existence of primary sources, that is, records or artifacts generated by the participants themselves or their observers, thus effectively limits the past available to historical researchers. Without primary sources there is a past but there can be no history. The second part of the definition above suggests that the study of history is a creative exercise, requiring the active intervention of the historian as interpreter of available sources. The researcher must first identify a topic worthy of investigation, then formulate questions that might illuminate that topic. Next he or she must seek out the appropriate primary sources, order them in a meaningful way, and construct a narrative that offers some probable (as opposed to merely possible) answers to the analytical questions posed at the outset. Clearly, even when primary sources are available, the entire process is fraught with potential pitfalls: What is worthy of investigation? Where might the sources be found? How might the sources be arranged? What are some probable answers? But precisely because it relies so heavily on the judgment of the historian, the subject retains a freshness and vitality that persists over time. No two researchers will ask the same questions and come up with the same answers because no two minds are identical. The history you read is perforce only as good as the historian who produced it and whose judgment acted as an invisible hand constantly sifting through the available evidence in search of answers.

Volume I of *Documents to Accompany America's History* brings together nearly two hundred pieces of evidence. It is our hope that this array of documents and illustrations will not only deepen the students' historical understanding and bring them closer to the people and subjects they are studying but also prompt them to hone their analytical skills by confronting aspects of the recoverable past. The inclusion of private as well as public documents—letters, journals, and diary entries along with speeches, resolutions, and legal opinions—rests on the related hope that they reveal something of the diversity of sources extant and therefore something about the variety of histories capable of being undertaken. To be sure, the recoverable past is by definition limited, but there are no set limits to curiosity, creativity, and imagination. Indeed, even our notions of what is recoverable are continuously being expanded by new generations of inspired historical researchers. If in the end *Documents to Accompany America's History* leaves readers with more questions than answers, it will have achieved perhaps its most important function.

The chapters and main headings of this volume correspond exactly to those in *America's History*, Sixth Edition. Introductions to each set of selections and headnotes before individual documents help to establish their proper historical context. In addition, every document is followed by a set of questions, and each section concludes with some Questions for Further

Thought. This organizational arrangement gives instructors the flexibility of singling out a particular selection for examination or exploring an entire section in depth. Regardless of the approach taken, students are encouraged to draw comparisons among the documents themselves and between the documents and the textbook discussions. By making such comparisons they will gain further insight into the larger themes of American history.

A regular part of my teaching load for the past twenty years has been a course on U.S. history to 1877. Working on this volume has given me yet another opportunity to revisit substantive and pedagogical questions. I have benefited from the experience, and for this I wish to thank Joan E. Feinberg, president of Bedford/St. Martin's, William J. Lombardo, Senior Editor for History, and Helene Williams. The contributions of David L. Carlton, Cathy Matson, John K. Alexander, and Louis S. Gerteis have made this volume far better than it would be otherwise. As always, my wife, Jennifer, has been a model of patience and good humor; I feel blessed.

Mel Yazawa

Contents

PART TWO
The New Republic, 1763–1820

DOCUMENTS TO ACCOMPANY

America's History

Volume 1: To 1877

CHAPTER ONE

Worlds Collide: Europe, Africa, and America

1450–1620

Native American Societies

Until late in the fifteenth century, Europeans were separated from the rest of the world by unbreachable oceans. Totally unknown to them were the two continents of the Western Hemisphere with their more than 40 million inhabitants. Those indigenous peoples were the descendants of Asian migrants who had traveled across the temporary land bridge spanning the Bering Strait during the last great Ice Age (see text pp. 6–7).

After 1492, contact with Europeans proved devastating to the inhabitants of the "New World." Lacking a natural immunity to European diseases such as smallpox, measles, and influenza, Native Americans were powerless to resist them. Document 1-1, Graph 1, shows the precipitous decline in the American Indian population north of Mexico in the five centuries after contact with the Europeans. From an estimated 5 to 7 million people, the Native American population shrank to about a quarter million by 1900.

Disease made it easier for the Spanish to conquer the indigenous civilizations of Mesoamerica, but technological superiority was equally important, as the classic eyewitness account of Bernal Díaz del Castillo (Document 1-2) demonstrates.

Well before 1492, Native Americans had developed civilizations and societies of great complexity and variety (see text pp. 6–14). Europeans were amazed—and often affronted—by the sharp cultural differences they encountered, but they also made some effort to understand these differences (Document 1-3). In fact, Europeans often found the indigenous cultures admirable in their differences from the less attractive features of Old World culture (Document 1-4).

1-1   Indian and Non-Indian Population Charts (1492–1980)

Two parabolic lines on Graphs 1 and 2 tell the story of North American population trends after 1492. One part of the story is tragic: the calamitous decline in Native American numbers primarily as a result of the impact of European disease. The other part could be deemed a success story: the startling increase in the population of non-Indian peoples, which was due primarily to high fertility rates and massive immigration. These graphs refer only to populations in what is now the United States. There is no full consensus among scholars regarding the figures underlying Graph 1; in particular, the size of the indigenous population of the New World at the time of contact is a matter of dispute, and indeed may be unknowable. Nonetheless, no adjustments to Graph 1 would alter the fundamentals of the story it tells. This is the greatest known demographic catastrophe in human history.

Source: From Russell Thornton, *American Indian Holocaust and Survival: A Population History since 1492.* Copyright © 1987 by the University of Oklahoma Press. Reprinted by permission.

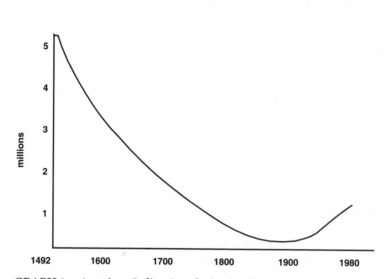

GRAPH 1 *American Indian Population Decline and Recovery in the United States, 1492–1980*

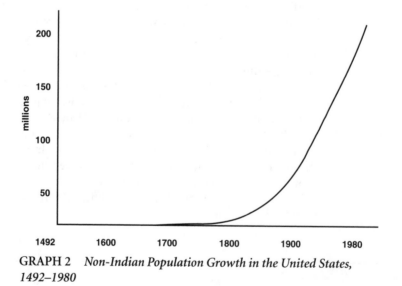

GRAPH 2 *Non-Indian Population Growth in the United States, 1492–1980*

Questions

1. Put this rate of decline in perspective by thinking about a family, a clan, or a tribe. Speculate about the social impact. Imagine a state — say, Wisconsin, with a population of about 5 million in 1990 — losing 95 percent of its people. How would the survivors feel? How could they maintain their economic activities?

2. In which years were Indian and non-Indian populations even? Why did rapid Indian decline occur *before* the arrival of many non-Indians?

3. The non-Indian population rose dramatically after 1800, and the Indian population recovered after 1900. Why?

1-2   The Discovery and Conquest of Mexico (1517–1521)

Bernal Díaz del Castillo

Most of the precontact hieroglyphic writings of the Aztec and Maya were destroyed by Spanish priests, and we have learned about these cultures mainly through European eyes. Bernal Díaz del Castillo, who was born in 1492, accompanied Hernán Cortés on the march to Tenochtitlán and the conquest of Mexico. His firsthand account offers many glimpses of Mexican customs and societies and fascinating hints about Cortés's military strategies. Most subsequent histories of the conquest employ Díaz's reminiscences (see text pp. 23–28, and especially Map 1.5).

Cacique is a Caribbean term, adopted by the Spanish, meaning a native chief. For Díaz's *Montezuma*, read *Moctezuma*.

Source: Excerpts from Bernal Díaz del Castillo, *The Discovery and Conquest of Mexico, 1517–1521*, trans. A. P. Maudslay, 102–105, 119, 156–157. Copyright © 1956 by Farrar, Straus & Cudahy. Copyright renewed 1984 by Farrar, Straus & Giroux, Inc. Reprinted by permission of Farrar, Straus & Giroux, LLC.

We slept the night in those huts, and all the caciques bore us company all the way to our quarters in their town. They were really anxious that we should not leave their country, as they were fearful that Montezuma would send his warriors against them, and they said to Cortés that as we were already their friends, they would like to have us for brothers, and that it would be well that we should take from their daughters, so as to have children by them; and to cement our friendship, they brought eight damsels, all of them daughters of caciques, and gave one of these cacicas, who was the niece of the fat cacique, to Cortés; and one who was the daughter of another great cacique was given to Alonzo Hernández Puertocarrero. All eight of them were clothed in the rich garments of the country, beautifully ornamented as is their custom. Each one of them had a golden collar around her neck and golden earrings in her ears, and they came accompanied by other Indian girls who were to serve as their maids. When the fat cacique presented them, he said to Cortés: "Tecle (which in their language means Lord)—these seven women are for your captains, and this one, who is my niece, is for you, and she is the señora of towns and vassals." Cortés received them with a cheerful countenance, and thanked the caciques for the gifts, but he said that before we could accept them and become brothers, they must get rid of those idols which they believed in and worshipped, and which kept them in darkness, and must no longer offer sacrifices to them, and that when he could see those cursed things thrown to the ground and an end put to sacrifices that then our bonds of brotherhood would be most firmly tied. He added that these damsels must become

Christians before we could receive them. Every day we saw sacrificed before us three, four or five Indians whose hearts were offered to the idols and their blood plastered on the walls, and the feet, arms and legs of the victims were cut off and eaten, just as in our country we eat beef brought from the butchers. I even believe that they sell it by retail in the *tianguez* as they call their markets. Cortés told them that if they gave up these evil deeds and no longer practised them, not only would we be their friends, but we would make them lords over other provinces. All the caciques, priests and chiefs replied that it did not seem to them good to give up their idols and sacrifices and that these gods of theirs gave them health and good harvests and everything of which they had need. . . .

When the Caciques, priests, and chieftains were silenced, Cortés ordered all the idols which we had overthrown and broken to pieces to be taken out of sight and burned. Then eight priests who had charge of the idols came out of a chamber and carried them back to the house whence they had come, and burned them. These priests wore black cloaks like cassocks and long gowns reaching to their feet, and some had hoods like those worn by canons, and others had smaller hoods like those worn by Dominicans, and they wore their hair very long, down to the waist, with some even reaching down to the feet, covered with blood and so matted together that it could not be separated, and their ears were cut to pieces by way of sacrifice, and they stank like sulphur, and they had another bad smell like carrion, and as they said, and we learnt that it was true, these priests were the sons of chiefs and they abstained from women, and they fasted on certain days, and what I saw them eat was the pith of seeds of cotton when the cotton was being cleaned, but they may have eaten other things which I did not see. . . .

I remember that in the plaza where some of their oratories stood, there were piles of human skulls so regularly arranged that one could count them, and I estimated them at more than a hundred thousand. I repeat again that there were more than one hundred thousand of them. And in another part of the plaza there were so many piles of dead men's thigh bones that one could not count them; there was also a large number of skulls strung between beams of wood, and three priests who had charge of these bones and skulls were guarding them. We had occasion to see many such things later on as we penetrated into the country for the same custom we observed in all the towns, including those of Tlaxcala. . . .

Cortés then took these Caciques aside and questioned them very fully about Mexican affairs. Xicotenga, as he was the best informed and a great chieftain, took the lead in talking, and from time to time he was helped by Mase Escasi who was also a great chief.

He said that Montezuma had such great strength in warriors that when he wished to capture a great city or make a raid on a province, he could place a hundred and fifty thousand men in the field, and this they knew well from the experience of the wars and hostilities they had had with them for more than a hundred years past.

Cortés asked them how it was that with so many warriors as they said came down on them they had never been entirely conquered. They answered that although the Mexicans sometimes defeated them and killed them, and carried off many of their vassals for sacrifice, many of the enemy were also left dead on the field and others were made prisoners, and that they never could come so secretly that they did not get some warning, and that when they knew of their approach they mustered all their forces and with the help of the people of Huexotzingo they defended themselves and made counter attacks. That as all the provinces which had been raided by Montezuma and placed under his rule were ill disposed towards the Mexicans, and that as their inhabitants were carried off by force to the wars, they did not fight with good will; indeed, it was from these very men that they received warnings, and for this reason they had defended their country to the best of their ability.

The place from which the most continuous trouble came to them was a very great city a day's march distant, which is called Cholula, whose inhabitants were most treacherous. It was there that Montezuma secretly mustered his companies and, as it was near by, they made their raids by night. Moreover, Mase Escasi said that Montezuma kept garrisons of many warriors stationed in all the provinces in addition to the great force he could bring from the city, and that all the provinces paid tribute of gold and silver, feathers, stones, cloth and cotton, and Indian men and women for sacrifice and others for servants, that he [Montezuma] was such a great prince that he possessed everything he could desire, that the houses where he dwelt were full of riches and [precious] stones and chalchihuites which he had robbed and taken by force from those who would not give them willingly, and that all the wealth of the country was in his hands.

Then they spoke of the great fortifications of the city, and what the lake was like, and the depth of water, and about the causeways that gave access to the city, and the wooden bridges in each causeway, and how one can go in and out [by water] through the opening that there is in each bridge, and how when the bridges are raised one can be cut off between bridge and bridge and not be able to reach the city. How the greater part of the city was built in the lake, and that one could not pass from house to house except by draw-bridges and canoes which they had ready. That all the houses were flat-roofed and all the roofs were provided with parapets so that they could fight from them.

They brought us pictures of the battles they had fought with the Mexicans painted on large henequen cloths, showing their manner of fighting. . . .

Questions

1. What "unusual" customs or rituals did Díaz del Castillo observe?

2. Díaz del Castillo emphasized the strange and the bizarre. Can you spot any similarities between the Native American and Spanish cultures?

3. Do you think Cortés could have conquered Mexico without Indian allies? Why or why not?

1-3   Cortés and the *Requerimiento* (1519–1521)

Hernán Cortés

Hernán Cortés (1485–1547) led the expedition that conquered the Aztec empire of Mexico in 1519–1521. In five graphic "letters" to Charles I, the Spanish king, Cortés recorded his observations and sought to justify the actions he had taken among the indigenous populations of the region. The excerpt that follows is taken from his second letter. The *requerimiento* was a declaration of papal dominion drawn up by the jurist Palacios Rubios of the Council of Castile in 1510. In accordance with prescribed practice, Cortés claimed he tried to read this one-thousand-word legal document to an assembled audience of Indians. Had they accepted its provisions and converted to Catholicism, Cortés would have been duty bound to allow them to retain all of their possessions. Their refusal thus supposedly freed Cortés and his men to "make war against . . . [them] in all ways and manners."

Source: Excerpts from "Second Letter," in *Hernando Cortés: Five Letters, 1519–1526*, trans. J. Bayard Morris (New York: Norton, 2006), 43–47. Reprinted with permission.

I began to deliver my *requerimiento* in due form by means of the interpreters with me and in the presence of a notary: but the more I endeavoured to admonish them and treat them with peaceable words, the more fiercely they attacked us. Seeing then that demands and protestations were alike useless we began to defend ourselves as we could, and thus they continued attacking us until we were surrounded on all sides by more than a hundred thousand men, with whom we contended throughout the day until an hour before sunset when they retired. In this battle, with the half dozen cannon which I had, five or six muskets and the thirteen horsemen who remained, I did them great damage, without suffering anything worse than the toil and weariness of long hours of fighting without food.

And in this it was plainly manifest that God was fighting on our side, that among so great a multitude of people of such fury and skill in war and with such various arms with which to attack us, we came off so free. That night we made ourselves secure in a small tower containing their idols which stood on a slight eminence and then at very early dawn I sallied out leaving two hundred men in the camp and all the guns, and since I was now attacking I took with me the horsemen and a hundred Spaniards on foot together with four hundred Indians from among those whom I brought from Cempoal and three hundred from Ixtacamaxtitlan. And before they had time to gather together I burnt some five or six little villages, each of about a hundred inhabitants, took about four hundred prisoners both men and women, and regained the camp fighting with them but without receiving any casualties. Next day at daybreak more than a hundred and thirty-nine thousand men advanced upon our camp, so many that they seemed to cover the whole plain, and with such determination that several of them succeeded in forcing an entrance and came to handgrips with my men: we marched out against them and by the good will of our Lord helping us in four hours we had cleared a space so that they could not attack the camp directly although they still made a few charges in other parts of the field. And so we were fighting until darkness came and they retired.

Next day I again sallied out in a different direction before daybreak without being perceived by them and with my horsemen, a hundred foot and my faithful Indians, burnt

more than ten townships, in some of which there were over three thousand houses, and the inhabitants there fought against me, for no other Indians came up. And as we bore the banner of the cross and were fighting for our faith and in the service of your Majesty, God gave us such victory in your Majesty's cause that we killed many Indians without ourselves receiving any hurt: and shortly after noon, by which time the forces of the Indians had gathered together from all sides, we were back again in camp with the victory already won.

On the following day messengers came to me from the chieftains saying that they desired to be vassals of your Majesty and my friends, and begging me to forgive their past evil doing. They brought food and certain feather ornaments which they wear and value highly. I told them in reply that they had done very wrong but that it pleased me to be their friend and pardon them what they had done. On the morrow nearly fifty Indians came up who, it appeared, were men of some importance among them, saying that they were bringing us provisions, but paying close attention to the exits and entrances of the camp and certain huts in which we were living. . . . I took one of them carefully aside without the others perceiving it and closeting him with myself and one or two interpreters threatened him that I might get the truth from him: upon which he confessed that Sicutengal who is the captain of this province was stationed with a large force beyond the range of hills which fronts the camp in order to fall upon us that night. . . . He confessed further that they had been sent to spy out our camp and those places in which it could be entered and in what way our straw huts might be set alight and burnt. Forthwith I took another of the Indians and questioned him in like manner, upon which he confessed almost in the same words, and I proceeded thus to threaten five or six, and they all confirmed these words. Seeing this I ordered the whole fifty to be arrested and their hands cut off, which done I sent them back to tell their lord that night and day whenever and however many times he should come against us he should see what manner of men we are.

With this I fortified the camp as strongly as I could, placed my men at such posts as seemed best and remained thus on guard until sunset: and as night was falling the

Indians began to descend the valleys on either side of us, thinking that their advance to surround us and thus be nearer to execute their plan was unperceived. But as I was forewarned I saw them, and it occurred to me that to allow them to approach the camp would be extremely dangerous, for in the night being unable to see my preparations they would approach without fear, and moreover, the Spaniards being unable to see them might in certain instances lack their usual courage in fighting; above all I was afraid lest they should set fire to any part of the camp: for any such accident would have been so damaging to us that not one of us would have escaped: accordingly I determined to go out against them with all my horse either to await them or put them to rout in such wise that they should not reach the camp. And thus it fell out that when they learnt that we were advancing on horseback to attack them, without a moment's delay or so much as a cry they took to the cornfields which covered the whole country and lightened themselves somewhat of the provisions they were carrying for feasting and triumphing over us if they should succeed in obtaining a complete victory: thus they retreated that night and left us unharmed. For several days after this I did not leave camp save to visit the immediate neighbourhood in order to prevent the advance of certain Indians who engaged in shouting and some slight skirmishing.

Having thus rested somewhat I rode out one night, after going the rounds of the first guard, with a hundred foot, the Indians and my own horsemen as before, and a league from the camp no less than five of the horses and mares fell and could in no wise proceed further, upon which I had to send them back to camp: and although all my companions urged me to turn back on account of the evil omen yet I held on my course, considering that God is more powerful than nature. Before dawn I lighted upon two towns in which I killed many people, but abstained from burning houses, since the flames would have betrayed my presence to other towns which were hard by: and just as dawn was breaking I fell upon another town so great that, as I afterwards found by a later examination, it contained more than twenty thousand houses. I attacked it so suddenly that all rushed out unarmed, the women and children naked, into the streets, and I was beginning to do them no small hurt. Upon this, seeing that they could make no resistance certain chieftains of the town came running up to me begging me to do them no more harm, for they were willing to be vassals of your Majesty and my friends, and saw plainly that they were to blame in having refused to believe me; but from that time onward I should see that they would always do what I should bid them in your Majesty's name, and they would be your Majesty's very loyal subjects.

Questions

1. Did Cortés genuinely expect the Indians to understand, let alone accept, the terms of the *requerimiento*? If not, what was its intended purpose?

2. There is more than a hint of self-promotion in Cortés's letter to the king. Was he simply bragging? What other motives might have inspired such a tone in his letter?

3. What impressions did Cortés convey to his readers with regard to the native population? How might the victims of his assault have described these same encounters?

1-4 The Role of Women in Huron Society (1721)

Pierre de Charlevoix

Pierre de Charlevoix, a Jesuit, came to New France as a French spy in 1720. He traveled up the St. Lawrence River, through the Great Lakes, and down the Mississippi to New Orleans. During his travels he kept a journal, cast in the form of letters, that was first published in 1744. Charlevoix's careful observations reveal a social structure that seemed extraordinary to Europeans (see text pp. 9–14). Among the Hurons, he tells us, women played an important role in a democratic decision-making process. The historian James Axtell calls Huron society a "gynecocracy," or a government ruled by women.

Source: From Pierre de Charlevoix, "An Account of Huron Society," in *The Indian Peoples of Eastern America: A Documentary History of the Sexes*, ed. James Axtell. Copyright © 1981 by Oxford University Press. Used by permission of Oxford University Press, Inc.

In the northern parts, and wherever the Algonquin tongue prevails, the dignity of chief is elective; and the whole ceremony of election and installation consists in some feasts, accompanied with dances and songs; the chief elect likewise never fails to make the panegyrick [eulogy] of his predecessor, and to invoke his genius. Amongst the Hurons, where this dignity is hereditary, the succession is continued through the women, so that at the death of a chief, it is not his own, but his sister's son who succeeds him; or, in default of which, his nearest relation in the female line. When the whole branch happens to be extinct, the noblest matron of the tribe or in the nation chuses the person she approves of most, and declares him chief. The person who is to govern must be come to years of maturity; and when the hereditary chief is not as yet arrived at this period, they appoint a regent, who has all the authority, but which he holds in name of the minor. These chiefs generally have no great marks of outward respect paid them, and if they are never disobeyed, it is because they know how to set bounds to their authority. It is true that they request or propose, rather than command; and never exceed the boundaries of that small share of authority with which they are vested. Thus it is properly reason which governs, and the government has so much the more influence, as obedience is founded in liberty; and that they are free from any apprehension of its degenerating into tyranny.

Nay more, each family has a right to chuse a counsellor of its own, and an assistant to the chief, who is to watch for their interest; and without whose consent the chief can undertake nothing. These counsellors are, above all things, to have an eye to the public treasury; and it is properly they who determine the uses it is to be put to. They are invested with this character in a general council, but they do not acquaint their allies with it, as they do at the elections and installations of their chief. Amongst the Huron nations, the women name the counsellors, and often chuse persons of their own sex.

This body of counsellors or assistants is the highest of all; the next is that of the elders, consisting of all those who have come to the years of maturity. I have not been able to find exactly what this age is. The last of all is that of the warriors; this comprehends all who are able to bear arms. This body has often at its head, the chief of the nation or town; but he must first have distinguished himself by some signal action of bravery; if not, he is obliged to serve as a subaltern, that is, as a single centinel; there being no degrees in the militia of the Indians.

In fact, a large body may have several chiefs, this title being given to all who ever commanded; but they are not therefore the less subject to him who leads the party; a kind of general, without character or real authority, who has power neither to reward nor punish, whom his soldiers are at liberty to abandon at pleasure and with impunity, and whose orders notwithstanding are scarce ever disputed: so true it is, that amongst a people who are guided by reason, and inspired with sentiments of honour and love for their country,

independence is not destructive of subordination; and, that a free and voluntary obedience is that on which we can always rely with the greatest certainty. Moreover, the qualities requisite are, that he be fortunate, of undoubted courage, and perfectly disinterested. It is no miracle, that a person possessed of such eminent qualities should be obeyed.

The women have the chief authority amongst all the nations of the Huron language; if we except the Iroquois canton of Onneyouth [Oneida], in which it is in both sexes alternately. But if this be their lawful constitution, their practice is seldom agreeable to it. In fact, the men never tell the women any thing they would have to be kept secret; and rarely any affair of consequence is communicated to them, though all is done in their name, and the chiefs are no more than their lieutenants. . . . The real authority of the women is very small: I have been however assured, that they always deliberate first on whatever is proposed in council; and that they afterwards give the result of their deliberation to the chiefs, who make the report of it to the general council, composed of the elders; but in all probability this is done only for form's sake, and with the restrictions I have already mentioned. The warriors likewise consult together, on what relates to their particular province, but can conclude nothing of importance which concerns the nation or town; all being subject to the examination and controul of the council of elders, who judge in the last resource.

It must be acknowledged, that proceedings are carried on in these assemblies with a wisdom and a coolness, and a knowledge of affairs, and I may add generally with a probity, which would have done honour to the areopagus of Athens, or to the senate of Rome, in the most glorious days of those republics: the reason of this is, that nothing is resolved upon with precipitation; and that those violent passions, which have so much disgraced the politics even of Christians, have never prevailed amongst the Indians over the public good. Interested persons fail not, however, to set many springs in motion, and apply an address in the execution of their designs, we could hardly believe barbarians capable of; they also all of them possess, in the most sovereign degree, the art of concealing their real intentions: but generally speaking, the glory of the nation and motive of honour, are the chief movers in all enterprizes. What can never be excused in them is, that they often make honour consist in satiating a revenge which knows no bounds; a fault which Christianity alone is able to correct, and in which all our politeness and religion are often unsuccessful.

Each tribe has an orator in every town, which orators are the only persons who have a liberty to speak in the public councils and general assemblies: they always speak well and to the purpose. Besides this natural eloquence . . . they have a perfect knowledge of the interests of their employers, and an address in placing the best side of their own cause in the most advantageous light, which nothing can exceed. On some occasions, the women have an orator, who speaks in their name, or rather acts as their interpreter.

Questions

1. What role did women play in Huron decision making?

2. Was their power real or merely a mask for male supremacy?

3. Ideally, Hurons suppressed their "violent passions" for the sake of the public good. How realistic does this sound for a society?

Questions for Further Thought

1. A demographic catastrophe and a brutal conquest of another culture: should we pay more attention to American history before European settlement? Why or why not?

2. Note that the three preceding accounts were all by Europeans and based on European observations. Do they nonetheless contain reliable information about the peoples they discuss? How do you judge?

3. Do these authors *uniformly* assume superiority to their subjects? Or are they ambivalent about them, in some ways even admiring of them? Explain.

Europe Encounters Africa and the Americas, 1450–1550

Even before 1450 "traditional" European society was growing and changing. The population increased, farming techniques improved, and towns and trade expanded. Europe flexed its muscles by looking outward to the Holy Land, which it sought to re-Christianize by conquest, and to new trade routes to Africa and the East. At the same time many Europeans worked toward the spiritual purification of the continent. Much still remained "traditional," including the ties of most people to the land and the supremacy of the Christian faith. Secular rulers rose and fell; wars and anarchy occurred frequently; famine and disease remained an omnipresent threat; and the Black Death, or bubonic plague (roughly 1347–1400), seemed to be an example of God's inexplicable ways. Social conditions changed everywhere, although not at the same time.

The Renaissance, which began early in the fourteenth century in Italy, transformed Europe, and a transformed Europe discovered America (text pp. 19–20). This rebirth, or renewal of intellectual inquiry and human knowledge, offered limitless possibility for learning and creativity. Renaissance humanism liberated Europeans from the spiritual and hierarchical dogmas of the past. It celebrated secular and individual characteristics: willpower, activity, the unlimited potential of human nature, creative talent, and *virtù*. By *virtù*, Italian scholars meant the application of the "manly" powers in the secular pursuits of war, statecraft, and the arts.

Portugal, a small and remote European nation that for fifty years had set its sights on the East, paved the way for the discovery of America (see text pp. 19–20). The Portuguese pioneered new navigational techniques that were eagerly studied by the young Christopher Columbus, who lived in Portugal from 1476 to 1485. Columbus was looking for a quick route to the East when he encountered the unknown American landmass in 1492. The Atlantic Ocean, long a barrier to Europeans, became a bridge to the New World.

Quickly Portugal and Spain began Europeanizing the globe, dividing the new lands between them. In 1498 Vasco da Gama landed on the Malabar Coast of India, establishing an Asian empire of trade and commerce backed by sea power, war, and plunder. Spain established sugar plantations in the Caribbean that soon were worked by African slaves. Hernán Cortés conquered the Aztecs in Mexico; Francisco Pizarro, the Incas in Peru.

The documents in this section explore both continuity and change from the eleventh century through the Renaissance. Document 1-5 recounts the French interest in North America. Document 1-6 deals with Portuguese involvement in the slave trade. Document 1-7 describes the moment of first contact between Europeans and Native Americans.

1-5   Indian Populations of New France (1611)

Father Pierre Biard

By the early seventeenth century, the economic benefits of a burgeoning trade in furs rejuvenated French interest in establishing a commercial colony in North America. In 1604 Pierre De Gua, sieur de Monts, accompanied by Samuel de Champlain, who later founded Quebec, set up a base camp at Port Royal, Acadia. De Monts's settlement proved to be short-lived and never very successful; maintenance costs alone exceeded the total value of the furs obtained in the Indian trade. In 1613 Virginia governor Thomas Dale, worried about the presence of European rivals to the north, commissioned Samuel Argall to lead an expedition against the Acadian settlement. Argall destroyed Port Royal and took most of its inhabitants back to Virginia as prisoners. Among those taken was Pierre Biard, a Jesuit priest, who had arrived at Port Royal in 1611 as part of the missionary vanguard of the Society of Jesus. The following excerpt is taken from a letter written by Biard on June 10, 1611, to Father Christopher Baltazar in Paris.

Source: Excerpts from "Letter from Father Biard, to Reverend Father Christopher Baltazar, Provincial of France, at Paris," in *Jesuit Relations and Allied Documents*, ed. Reuben Gold Thwaites (Cleveland, OH: Burrows Brothers, 1896), 1:173–183.

. . . The nation is savage, wandering and full of bad habits; the people few and isolated. They are, I say, savage, haunting the woods, ignorant, lawless and rude: they are wanderers, with nothing to attach them to a place, neither homes nor relationship, neither possessions nor love of country; as a people they have bad habits, are extremely lazy, gluttonous, profane, treacherous, cruel in their revenge, and given up to all kinds of lewdness, men and women alike, the men having several wives and abandoning them to others, and the women only serving them as slaves, whom they strike and beat unmercifully, and who dare not complain; and after being half killed, if it so please the murderer, they must laugh and caress him.

With all these vices, they are exceedingly vainglorious: they think they are better, more valiant and more ingenious than the French; and, what is difficult to believe, richer than we are. They consider themselves, I say, braver than we are, boasting that they have killed Basques and Malouins, and that they do a great deal of harm to the ships, and that no one has ever resented it, insinuating that it was from a lack of courage. They consider themselves better than the French; "For," they say, "you are always fighting and quarreling among yourselves; we live peaceably. You are envious and are all the time slandering each other; you are thieves and deceivers; you are covetous, and are neither generous nor kind; as for us, if we have a morsel of bread we share it with our neighbor."

They are saying these and like things continually, seeing the above-mentioned imperfections in some of us, and flattering themselves that some of their own people do not have them so conspicuously, not realizing that they all have much greater vices, and that the better part of our people do not have even these defects, they conclude generally that they are superior to all Christians. It is self-love that blinds them, and the evil one who leads them on, no more nor less than in our France, we see those who have deviated from the faith holding themselves higher and boasting of being better than the catholics, because in some of them they see many faults; considering neither the virtues of the other catholics, nor their own still greater imperfections; wishing to have, like Cyclops, only a single eye, and to fix that one upon the vices of a few catholics, never upon the virtues of the others, nor upon themselves, unless it be for the purpose of self-deception.

Also they consider themselves more ingenious, inasmuch as they see us admire some of their productions as the work of people so rude and ignorant; lacking intelligence, they bestow very little admiration upon what we show them, although much more worthy of being admired. Hence they regard themselves as much richer than we are, although they are poor and wretched in the extreme.

Cacagous [a local chief], of whom I have already spoken, is quite gracious when he is a little elated about something; to show his kindly feelings toward the French he boasts of his willingness to go and see the King, and to take him a present of a hundred beaver skins, proudly suggesting that in so doing he will make him richer than all his predecessors. They get this idea from the extreme covetousness and eagerness which our people display to obtain their beaver skins.

Not less amusing is the remark of a certain Sagamore, who, having heard M. de Potrincourt [de Monts's assistant] say that the King was young and unmarried: "Perhaps," said he, "I may let him marry my daughter; but according to the usages and customs of the country, the King must make me some handsome presents; namely, four or five barrels of bread, three of peas or beans, one of tobacco, four or five cloaks worth one hundred sous apiece, bows, arrows, harpoons, and other similar articles."

Such are the marks of intelligence in the people of these countries, which are very sparsely populated. . . . It is maintained that they have thus diminished since the French have begun to frequent their country; for, since then they do nothing all summer but eat; and the result is that, adopting an entirely different custom and thus breeding new diseases, they pay for their indulgence during the autumn and winter by pleurisy, quinsy and dysentery, which kill them off. During this year alone sixty have died at Cape de la Hève, which is the greater part of those who lived there; yet not one of all M. de Potrincourt's little colony has even been sick, notwith-standing all the privations they have suffered; which has caused the Savages to apprehend that God protects and defends us as his favorite and well-beloved people.

What I say about the sparseness of the population of these countries must be understood as referring to the people who live upon the coast; for farther inland, principally among the Etechemins, there are, it is said, a great many people. All these things, added to the difficulty of acquiring the language, the time that must be consumed, the expenses that must be incurred, the great distress, toil and poverty that must be endured, fully proclaim the greatness of this enterprise and the difficulties which beset it. Yet many things encourage me to continue in it. . . .

. . . . [W]e are encouraged by the situation and condition of this place, which, if it is cultivated, promises to furnish a great deal for the needs of human life; and its beauty causes me to wonder that it has been so little sought up to the present time. From this port where we now are, it is very convenient for us to spread out to the Armouchiquois, Iroquois, and Montagnais, our neighbors, which are populous nations and till the soil as we do; this situation, I say, makes us hope something for the future. For, if our Souriquois are few, they may become numerous; if they are savages, it is to domesticate and civilize them that we have come here; if they are rude, that is no reason that we should be idle; if they have until now profited little, it is no wonder, for it would be too much to expect fruit from this grafting, and to demand reason and maturity from a child.

Questions

1. Was Pierre Biard ethnocentric? Is it fair to charge him with ethnocentrism? Why or why not?

2. Is the native voice, as presented by Biard's narrative, too distorted to be of any use to modern readers who want to understand the encounter between Europeans and Indians? Explain.

3. Biard's letter was addressed to his clerical superiors in France but probably reached a much larger audience of interested laypersons, especially potential donors to the Jesuit missions. How did Biard appeal to these disparate audiences? Would clerical and lay readers have responded differently to Biard's observations?

1-6   Prince Henry and the Slave Trade (1444)

Gomes Eannes de Azurara   Well before Europeans first encountered the native populations of the Americas, they made contact with the peoples of West Africa. In the first half of the fifteenth century, Prince Henry "the Navigator" (1394–1460) led Portuguese mariners on a systematic exploration of the African coast in search of wealth and an oceanic route to Asia. Henry's voyages were funded largely by the Order of Christ, an international military order with its roots in the Crusades that sought to protect Christian interests around the globe. Sailing under a royal decree that guaranteed him one-fifth of wealth accumulated on his trips, Prince Henry sought to gain profit and save souls in the African slave trade. The following excerpt, taken from an account by Gomez Eannes de Azurara, the chronicler of Henry's voyages, illustrates this dual mission. The word *Infant* in this text is a translation of Prince Henry's Portuguese title, *Infante*, or "(royal) child."

Source: From Gomez Eannes de Azurara, "Prince Henry and the Slave Trade," in *Documents Illustrative of the History of the Slave Trade to America*, ed. Elizabeth Donnan, vol. 1. Copyright 1930 by the Carnegie Institution of Washington.

Very early in the morning, by reason of the heat, the seamen began to make ready their boats, and to take out those captives, and carry them on shore, as they were commanded. And these, placed all together in that field, were a marvellous sight, for amongst them were some white enough, fair to look upon, and well proportioned; others were less white like mulattoes; others again were as black as Ethiops, and so ugly, both in features and in body, as almost to appear (to those who saw them) the images of a lower hemisphere. But what heart could be so hard as not to be pierced with piteous feeling to see that company? For some kept their heads low and their faces bathed in tears, looking one upon another; others stood groaning very dolorously, looking up to the height of heaven, fixing their eyes upon it, crying out loudly, as if asking help of the Father of Nature; others struck their faces with the palms of their hands, throwing themselves at full length upon the ground; others made their lamentations in the manner of a dirge, after the custom of their country. And though we could not understand the words of their language, the sound of it right well accorded with the measure of their sadness. But to increase their sufferings still more, there now arrived those who had charge of the division of the captives, and who began to separate one from another, in order to make an equal partition of the fifths; and then was it needful to part fathers from sons, husbands from wives, brothers from brothers. No respect was shewn either to friends or relations, but each fell where his lot took him.

O powerful Fortune, that with thy wheels doest and undoest, compassing the matters of this world as pleaseth thee, do thou at least put before the eyes of that miserable race some understanding of matters to come, that they may receive some consolation in the midst of their great sorrow. And you who are so busy in making that division of the captives, look with pity upon so much misery; and see how they cling one to the other, so that you can hardly separate them.

And who could finish that partition without very great toil? for as often as they had placed them in one part the sons, seeing their fathers in another, rose with great energy and rushed over to them; the mothers clasped their other children in their arms, and threw themselves flat on the ground with them, receiving blows with little pity for their own flesh, if only they might not be torn from them.

And so troublously they finished the partition, for besides the toil they had with the captives, the field was quite full of people, both from the town and from the surrounding villages and districts, who for that day gave rest to their hands (in which lay their power to get their living) for the sole purpose of beholding this novelty. And with what they saw, while some were weeping and others separating the captives, they caused such a tumult as greatly to confuse those who directed the partition.

The Infant was there, mounted upon a powerful steed, and accompanied by his retinue, making distribution of his favours, as a man who sought to gain but small treasure from his share; for of the forty-six souls that fell to him as his fifth, he made a very speedy partition of these . . . for he reflected with great pleasure upon the salvation of those souls that before were lost. . . .

Although the sorrow of those captives was for the present very great, especially after the partition was finished and each one took his own share aside (while some sold their captives, which they took to other districts); and although it chanced that among the prisoners the father often remained in Lagos, while the mother was taken to Lisbon, and the children to another part (in which partition their sorrow doubled the first grief)—yet this sorrow was less felt among those who happened to remain in company. For as saith the text, the wretched find a consolation in having comrades in misfortune. But from this time forth they began to acquire some knowledge of our country, in which they found great abundance, and our men began to treat them with great favour. For as our people did not find them hardened in the belief of the other Moors, and saw how they came in unto the law of Christ with a good will, they made no difference between them and their free servants, born in our own country. But those whom they took while still young, they caused to be instructed in mechanical arts, and those whom they saw fitted for managing property, they set free and married to women who were natives of the land, making with them a division of their property, as if they had been bestowed on those who married them by the will of their own fathers, and for the merits of their service they were bound to act in a like manner. Yea, and some widows of good family who bought some of these female slaves, either adopted them or left them a portion of their estate by will, so that in the future they married right well, treating them as entirely free. Suffice it that I never saw one of these slaves put in irons like other captives, and scarcely any one who did not turn Christian and was not very gently treated. . . .

And so their lot was now quite the contrary of what it had been, since before they had lived in perdition of soul and body; of their souls, in that they were yet pagans, without the clearness and the light of the Holy Faith; and of their bodies, in that they lived like beasts, without any custom of reasonable beings — for they had no knowledge of bread or wine, and they were without the covering of clothes, or the lodgment of houses; and worse than all, through the great ignorance that was in them, in that they had no understanding of good, but only knew how to live in a bestial sloth.

But as soon as they began to come to this land, and men gave them prepared food and coverings for their bodies, their bellies began to swell, and for a time they were ill, until they were accustomed to the nature of the country, but some of them were so made that they were not able to endure it and died, but as Christians.

Questions

1. How did Azurara perceive the newly enslaved Africans? Was his professed sympathy for the suffering of the captives deeply felt or superficial? Explain.

2. Is it possible to say anything about Henry's perceptions? Why or why not?

3. How would you describe the contact between cultures in this instance? In what ways was it similar to or different from contact between Europeans and natives in the Americas? What role did religion play in both cases?

1-7   Columbus's Landfall (1552)

Bartolomé de las Casas

In 1492 a Genoese mariner in the pay of Spain set out from Palos for the Canary Islands and thence for Asia (see text pp. 23–24). He had accepted early Renaissance miscalculations of the width of the Eurasian continent, the distance from China to Japan, and the breadth of a degree of longitude. At the end of his 3,000-mile voyage, Columbus thought he had reached Asia; instead, he had landed in the Bahamas. However, great events are measured by their consequences. Christopher Columbus "discovered" America for the Europeans, and the world has not been the same since.

The following passage from Columbus's journal, which includes the brief remarks on the native Bahamians appearing in the text on p. 23, describes the first recorded encounter of Europeans with "America." The journal, you will note, is not Columbus's own, but rather the work of the Dominican missionary and historian Bartolomé de las Casas (see also Document 2-1), who quoted parts of Columbus's log, paraphrased others, and inserted new information.

Source: From *The Journal of Christopher Columbus,* trans. Cecil Jane, rev. and annotated by L. A. Vigneras. Copyright © 1960 by The Hakluyt Society, 19–41. Reprinted by permission of David Higham Associates.

Thursday, October 11th. He navigated to the west-southwest; they had a rougher sea than they had experienced during the whole voyage. They saw petrels and a green reed near the ship. Those in the caravel *Pinta* saw a cane and a stick, and they secured another small stick, carved, as it appeared, with iron, and a piece of cane, and other vegetation which grows on land, and a small board. Those in the caravel *Niña* also saw other indications of land and a stick loaded with barnacles. At these signs, all breathed again and rejoiced. On this day, to sunset, they went twenty-seven leagues. After sunset, he steered his former course to the west; they made twelve miles an hour, and up to two hours before midnight they had made ninety miles, which are twenty-two leagues and a half. And since the caravel *Pinta* was swifter and went ahead of the admiral, she found land and made the signals which the admiral had commanded. This land was first sighted by a sailor called Rodrigo de Triana, although the admiral, at ten o'clock in the night, being on the sterncastle, saw a light. It was, however, so obscured that he would not affirm that it was land, but called Perro Gutierrez, butler of the King's dais, and told him that there seemed to be a light, and that he should watch for it. He did so, and saw it. He said the same also to Rodrigo Sanchez de Segovia, whom the King and Queen had sent in the fleet as *veedor* [comptroller], and he saw nothing since he was not in a position from which it could be seen. After the admiral had so spoken, it was seen once or twice, and it was like a small wax candle, which was raised and lowered. Few thought that this was an indication of land, but the admiral was certain that they were near land. Accordingly, when they had said the *Salve*, which all sailors are accustomed to say and chant in their manner, and when they had all been gathered together, the admiral asked and urged them to keep a good look out from the forecastle and to watch carefully for land, and to him who should say first he saw land, he would give at once a silk doublet apart from the other rewards which the Sovereigns had promised, which were ten thousand maravedis annually to him who first sighted it. Two hours after midnight land appeared, at a distance of about two leagues from them. They took in all sail, remaining with the mainsail, which is the great sail without bonnets, and kept jogging, waiting for day, a Friday, on which they reached a small island of the Lucayos, which is called in the language of the Indians "Guanahaní." Immediately they saw naked people, and the admiral went ashore in the armed boat, and Martin Alonso Pinzón and Vicente Yañez, his brother, who was captain of the *Niña*. The admiral brought out the royal standard, and the captains went with two banners of the Green Cross, which the admiral flew on all the ships as a flag, with an F and a Y, and over each letter their crown, one being on one side of the . . . and the other on the other. When they had landed, they saw very green trees and much water and fruit of various kinds. The admiral called the two captains and the others who had landed, and Rodrigo de Escobedo, secretary of the whole fleet, and Rodrigo Sanchez de Segovia, and said that they should bear witness and testimony how he, before them all, took possession of the island, as in fact he did, for the King and Queen, his Sovereigns, making the declarations which are required, as is contained more at length in the testimonies which were there made in writing. Soon many people of the island gathered there. What follows are the actual words of the admiral, in his book of his first voyage and discovery of these Indies.

"I," he says, "in order that they might feel great amity towards us, because I knew that they were a people to be delivered and converted to our holy faith rather by love than by force, gave to some among them some red caps and some glass beads, which they hung round their necks, and many other things of little value. At this they were greatly pleased and became so entirely our friends that it was a wonder to see. Afterwards they came swimming to the ships' boats, where we were, and brought us parrots and cotton thread in balls, and spears and many other things, and we exchanged for them other things, such as small glass beads and hawks' bells, which we gave to them. In fact, they took all and gave all, such as they had, with good will, but it seemed to me that they were a people very deficient in everything. They all go naked as their mothers bore them, and the women also, although I saw only one very young girl. And all those whom I did see were youths, so that I did not see one who was over thirty years of age; they were very well built, with very handsome bodies and very good faces. Their hair is coarse almost like the hairs of a horse's tail and short; they wear their hair down over their eyebrows, except for a few strands behind, which they wear long and never cut. Some of them are painted black, and they are the colour of the people of the Canaries, neither black nor white, and some of them are painted white and some red and some in any colour that they find. Some of them paint their faces, some their whole bodies, some only the eyes, and some only the nose. They do not bear arms or know them, for I showed to them swords and they took them by the blade and cut themselves through ignorance. They have no iron. Their spears are certain reeds, without iron, and some of these have a fish tooth at the end, while others are pointed in various ways. They are all generally fairly tall, good looking and well proportioned. I saw some who bore marks of wounds on their bodies, and I made signs to them to ask how this came about, and they indicated to me that people came from other islands, which are near, and wished to capture them, and they defended themselves. And I believed and still believe that they come here from the mainland to take them for slaves. They should be good servants and of quick intelligence, since I see that they very soon say all that is said to them, and I believe that they would easily be made Christians, for it appeared to me that they had no creed. Our Lord willing, at the time of my departure I will bring back six of them to Your Highness, that they may learn to talk. I saw no beast of any kind in this island, except parrots." All these are the words of the admiral.

Questions

1. What personal characteristics of Christopher Columbus are revealed in this excerpt?

2. Why did Columbus believe he was in Asia?

3. Can you discover Columbus's motives for making his journey? What were they?

Questions for Further Thought

1. The slave trade flourished in a world supposedly transformed by Renaissance humanism. How was this possible? (See Document 1-6.)

2. Was Europe in 1492 modern or medieval? Progressive or backward? Explain your answer.

3. We know that Columbus's landfall (Document 1-7) was disastrous for Native Americans. Should we celebrate it? Why or why not?

The Protestant Reformation and the Rise of England

In the sixteenth century Catholicism helped fuel the Spanish conquest of America, but the Protestant Reformation reshaped England and delayed that country's exploration of the New World. When Martin Luther published his Ninety-five Theses in 1517 (see text p. 29), England was not prepared politically or economically to join the Iberian countries in the race for empire. John Calvin's emphasis on predestination and congregationalism (see text p. 29) appealed to many people in England and Scotland. When Henry VIII declared himself the head of the Church of England (see text pp. 29), he inaugurated more than a half century of religious turmoil. During the long reign of Elizabeth I (r. 1558–1603), the compromise later known as Anglicanism was hammered out, considerably Protestant in content but unacceptable to either Roman Catholics or ardent Calvinists (see text pp. 29–31). Many religious dissenters sought refuge in America.

Not only religion but also economics reshaped England. A series of economic changes, including a massive rise in inflation, the beginnings of capitalism, and the transition from a local to a national economy, affected the island (see text pp. 32–34). Spain imported vast amounts of gold from America, which it then spent in Europe. The resulting inflation benefited merchants and landowners who were dependent on rents. Mercantilism brought an emphasis on payment in bullion and government aid to merchants. The English colonies became sources of raw materials, conveniently distant havens for political and religious dissenters, and markets for manufactured goods. England's new wealth made possible a military buildup that led to the defeat of a Spanish invasion in 1588 (see text p. 31).

Document 1-8 addresses the serious social difficulties created by enclosure in England. Document 1-9 reproduces Richard Hakluyt's arguments in favor of colonization in America. Documents 1-10 and 1-11 illustrate the initial contact between the English and Native Americans at Roanoke.

1-8   Objections Against Enclosure (1548)

John Hales

Two economic factors challenged sixteenth-century England: a dramatic rise in population and a shortage of agricultural jobs. England's population had shrunk drastically during the Black Death in the fourteenth century. By 1550 it had made good the loss; after that time, people increased their numbers faster than the economy was able to absorb them. The shortage of agricultural jobs was caused partly by enclosure, the large-scale conversion of arable land to sheep pasturage, and the consequent eviction of tenant farmers (see text pp. 32–34). Modern scholarship has minimized the actual extent of enclosure, but to contemporaries it symbolized all the economic problems they had to endure. In 1548 John Hales, an opponent of enclosure, conducted a commission of inquiry in the Midlands (central England) and vented his wrath.

Source: From *Ecclesiastical Memorials* (London, 1721), vol. 2, Appendix of Documents, Document Q, in *Renaissance and Reformation, 1300–1648*, ed. G. R. Elton. Copyright © 1963 by MacMillan, an imprint of Simon & Schuster, Inc. All rights reserved.

As by natural experience we find it to be true that if any one part of man's body be grieved . . . it is a great pain to all the whole body . . . so ought we to consider and remember in the state of the body of the realm. If the poorest sort of the people, which be members of the same body as well as the rich, be not provided and cherished in their degree, it cannot but be a great trouble of the body and a decay of the strength of the realm. Surely, good people, methinks that if men would know how much this ungodly desire of worldly things, and the unlawful getting and heaping together of riches, were hated of God, how hurtful and dangerous for the commonwealth of the realm it is, and what a virtue the mean in all things is, these laws nor a great many more that be needed not. God's Word is full of threats and curses against these kind of greediness. . . . When men in a commonwealth go about to gather as much as they can, and to get it they care not how; not considering whether by their gain any hurt should come to their neighbours or to the commonwealth; not only others, but they themselves should shortly perish. What avails a man to have his house full of gold and be not able to keep it with his force against his enemies? So what shall all our goods avail us if we be not able to defend us from our enemies?

The force and puissance [power] of the realm consists not only in riches but chiefly in the multitude of people. But it appears, good people, that the people of this realm, our native country, is greatly decayed through the greediness of a few men in comparison, and by this ungodly means of gathering together goods, by pulling down towns and houses, which we ought all to lament. Where there were [a few years ago] ten or twelve thousand people, there be now scarce four thousand. Where there were a thousand, now scarce three hundred, and in many places, where there were very many able to defend our country from landing of our enemies, now almost none. Sheep and cattle, that were ordained to be eaten of men, has eaten up the men, not of their own nature but by the help of men. Is it not a pitiful case that there should be so little charity among men? Is it not a sorrowful hearing that one Englishman should be set to destroy his countrymen? The places where poor men dwelt clearly destroyed; lands im-

proved to so great rents, . . . that the poor husbandman cannot live. All things at this present . . . be so dear as never they were—victual and other things that be necessary for man's use. And yet, as it is said, there was never more cattle, specially sheep, than there is at this present. But the cause of the dearth is that those have it that may choose whether they will sell it or not, and will not sell it but at their own prices. . . .

To declare unto you what is meant by this word, enclosures. It is not taken where a man does enclose and hedge in his own proper ground where no man has commons. For such enclosure is very beneficial to the commonwealth: it is a cause of great increase of wood. But it is meant thereby when any man has taken away and enclosed any other men's commons, or has pulled down houses of husbandry and converted the lands from tillage to pasture. This is the meaning of the word, and so we pray you remember it.

To defeat these statutes [laws banning enclosure] as we be informed, some have not pulled down their houses but maintain them; howbeit, no person dwells therein, or if there be it is but a shepherd or a milkmaid; and convert the lands from tillage to pasture. And some about one hundred acres of ground, or more or less, make a furrow and sow that, and the rest they till not but pasture with their sheep. And some take the lands from their houses and occupy them in husbandry, but let the houses out to beggars and old poor people. Some, to colour the multitude of their sheep father them on their children, kinsfolk and servants. All which be but only crafts and subtleties to defraud the laws, such as no man will use but rather abhor. . . .

Besides, it is not unlike but that these great fines for lands and improvement of rents shall abate, and all things wax better cheap—20 and 30 eggs for a penny, and the rest after the rate as has been in times past. And the poor craftsmen may live and set their wares at reasonable prices. And noblemen and gentlemen that have not improved nor enhanced their rents, nor were sheepmasters nor graziers but lived like noblemen and gentlemen, shall be the better able to keep good hospitality among you, and keep servants about them, as they have done in time past. . . .

Questions

1. In Hales's opinion, was enclosure a religious or an economic problem? Why?

2. Do you think moral strictures alone would have been sufficient to reverse the enclosure movement? Why or why not?

3. Did Hales elucidate any underlying economic reasons for enclosure? If so, what were those reasons?

1-9   A Discourse to Promote Colonization (1584)

Richard Hakluyt

By the end of the sixteenth century, England's economic and imperial aspirations had led inexorably to colonization. Explorers such as Martin Frobisher and Humphrey Gilbert had reconnoitered the Atlantic coast of North America. The first Roanoke voyage took place in 1584 (see text p. 46), the year in which Richard Hakluyt (1552–1616) issued his *Discourse Concerning Western Planting*. Hakluyt, a clergyman and travel writer (although he never traveled), was an effective pamphleteer and propagandist for colonization. The *Discourse* was written at the request of Sir Walter Raleigh and contains virtually every positive argument for settlement that would be advanced over the next century. Its purpose was to persuade Queen Elizabeth I to put the English state squarely behind American ventures.

Source: Richard Hakluyt, *A Discourse Concerning Western Planting*, in *Documentary History of the State of Maine*, ed. Charles Deane et al. (Collections of the Maine Historical Society, 1869–1916), 2:152–161.

Chapter XX. A brief collection of certain reasons to induce her Majesty and the state to take in hand the western voyage and the planting there.

1. The soil yields and may be made to yield all the several commodities of Europe. . . .

2. The passage thither and home is neither too long nor too short, but easy, and to be made twice in the year.

3. The passage cuts not near the trade of any prince, nor near any of their countries or territories, and is a safe passage, and not easy to be annoyed by prince or potentate whatsoever.

4. The passage is to be performed at all times of the year, and in that respect passes our trades in the Levant Seas within the Straits of Gibraltar, and the trades in the seas within the King of Denmark's Strait, and the trades to the ports of Norway and of Russia, etc. . . .

5. And where England now for certain hundred years last passed, by the peculiar commodity of wool, and of later years, by clothing of the same, has raised itself from meaner state to greater wealth and much higher honour, might, and power than before, to the equalling of the princes of the same to the greatest potentates of this part of the world; it comes now so to pass that by the great endeavour of the increase of the trade of wool in Spain and in the West Indies, now daily more and more multiplying, that the wool of England, and the cloth made of the same, will become base, and every day more base than [the] other; which, prudently weighed it behooves this realm, if it mean not to return to former old means and baseness, but to stand in present and late former honour, glory, and force, and not negligently and

sleepingly to slide into beggary . . . were it not for anything else but for the hope of the sale of our wool. . . .

6. This enterprise may stay the Spanish king from flowing over all the face of that waste firmament of America, if we seat and plant there in time. . . . And England possessing the purposed place of planting, her Majesty may, by the benefit of the seat, having won good and royal havens, have plenty of excellent trees for masts, of goodly timber to build ships and to make great navies, of pitch, tar, hemp, and all things incident for a navy royal, and that for no price, and without money or request. How easy a matter may it be to this realm, swarming at this day with valiant youths, rusting and hurtful by lack of employment, and having good makers of cable and of all sorts of cordage, and the best and most cunning shipwrights of the world, to be lords of all those seas, and to spoil Philip's Indian navy, and to deprive him of yearly passage of his treasure to Europe, and consequently to abate the pride of Spain and of the supporter of the great Anti-christ of Rome, and to pull him down in equality to his neighbour princes, and consequently to cut off the common mischiefs that come to all Europe by the peculiar abundance of his Indian treasure, and this without difficulty.

7. This voyage, albeit it may be accomplished by bark or smallest pinnace for advice or for a necessity, yet for the distance, for burden and gain in trade, the merchant will not for profit's sake use it but by ships of great burden; so as this realm shall have by that means ships of great burden and of great strength for the defence of this realm. . . .

8. This new navy of mighty new strong ships, so in trade to that Norumbega[1] and to the coasts there, shall never be subject to arrest of any prince or potentate as the navy of this realm from time to time has been in the ports of the empire, in the ports of the Low Countries, in Spain, France, Portugal, etc., in the times of Charles the Emperor, Francis the French king, and others. . . .

9. The great mass of wealth of the realm embarked in the merchants' ships, carried out in this new course, shall not lightly, in so far distant a course from the coast of Europe, be driven by winds and tempests into ports of any foreign princes, as the Spanish ships of late years have been into our ports of the West countries, etc. . . .

10. No foreign commodity that comes into England comes without payment of custom once, twice, or thrice, before it comes into the realm, and so all foreign commodities become dearer to the subjects of this realm; and by this course to Norumbega foreign princes' customs are avoided; and the foreign commodities cheaply purchased, they become cheap to the subjects of England, to the common benefit of the people, and to the saving of great treasure in the realm; whereas now the realm becomes poor by the purchasing of foreign commodities in so great a mass at so excessive prices.

11. At the first traffic with the people of those parts, the subjects of this realm for many years shall change many cheap commodities of these parts for things of high value there not esteemed; and this to the great enriching of the realm, if common use fail not.

12. By the great plenty of those regions the merchants and their factors shall lie there cheap, buy and repair their ships cheap, and shall return at pleasure without stay or restraint of foreign prince; whereas upon stays and restraints the merchant raiseth his charge in sale over of his ware. . . .

13. By making of ships and by preparing of things for the same, by making of cables and cordage, by planting of vines and olive trees, and by making of wine and oil, by husbandry, and by thousands of things there to be done, infinite numbers of the English nation may be set on work, to the unburdening of the realm with many that now live chargeable to the state at home.

14. If the sea coast serve for making of salt, and the inland for wine, oils, oranges, lemons, figs, etc., and for making of iron, all which with much more is hoped, without sword drawn, we shall cut the comb of the French, of the Spanish, of the Portuguese, and of enemies, and of doubtful friends, to the abating of their wealth and force, and to the greater saving of the wealth of the realm.

15. The substances serving, we may out of those parts receive the mass of wrought wares that now we receive out of France, Flanders, Germany, etc.; and so we may daunt the pride of some enemies of this realm, or at the least in part purchase those wares, that now we buy dearly of the French and Flemish, better cheap; and in the end, for the part that this realm was wont to receive, drive them out of trade to idleness for the setting of our people on work.

16. We shall by planting there enlarge the glory of the gospel, and from England plant sincere religion, and provide a safe and a sure place to receive people from all parts of the world that are forced to flee for the truth of God's word.

17. If frontier wars there chance to arise, and if thereupon we shall fortify, it will occasion the training up of our youth in the discipline of war, and make a number fit for the service of the wars and for the defence of our people there and at home.

18. The Spaniards govern in the Indies with all pride and tyranny; and like as when people of contrary nature at sea enter into galleys, where men are tied as slaves, all yell and cry with one voice, *Liberta, liberta*, as desirous of liberty and freedom, so no doubt whensoever the Queen of England, a prince of such clemency, shall seat upon that firmament of America, and shall be reported throughout all that tract to use the natural people there with all humanity, courtesy, and freedom, they will yield themselves to her government, and revolt clean from the Spaniard. . . .

19. The present short trades cause the mariner to be cast off, and often to be idle, and so by poverty to fall to piracy. But this course to Norumbega being longer, and a continuance of the employment of the mariner, doth keep the mariner of idleness and from necessity; and so it cuts off the principal actions of piracy, and the rather because no rich prey for them to take comes directly in their course or anything near their course.

20. Many men of excellent wits and of diverse singular gifts, overthrown by suretyship, by sea, or by some folly of youth, that are not able to live in England, may there be raised again, and do their country good service; and many needful uses there may (to great purpose) require the saving of great numbers, that for trifles may otherwise be devoured by the gallows.

21. Many soldiers and servitors, in the end of the wars, that might be hurtful to this realm, may there be unladen, to the common profit and quiet of this realm, and to our foreign benefit there, as they may be employed.

22. The fry of the wandering beggars of England, that grow up idly, and hurtful and burdenous to this realm, may there be unladen, better bred up, and may people waste countries to the home and foreign benefit, and to their own more happy state.

23. If England cry out and affirm that there are so many in all trades that one cannot live for another, as in all places they do, this Norumbega (if it be thought so good) offers the remedy.

---

[1] *Norumbega:* A legendary kingdom, reputedly located somewhere along the northeastern seaboard of the present United States and Maritime Canada, and allegedly inhabited by a highly civilized people akin in spirit to the ancient Greeks and Romans. Hakluyt uses this term to suggest that the proposed site for his colony was a land overflowing with milk and honey, an earthly paradise prepared for occupation by Europeans.

Questions

1. What were Hakluyt's arguments for colonization? Do they seem persuasive after four hundred years? Why or why not?

2. Which of Hakluyt's arguments pertained to England's internal conditions? Which had an imperial cast?

3. Were Hakluyt's proposed colonies more important as sources of raw materials or as markets? Why?

1-10   A Briefe and True Report of the New Found Land of Virginia (1588)

Thomas Harriot

The Roanoke voyages of 1584–1588 together constitute England's first major effort to establish a colony in North America. The effort failed, and the famous "lost colony" on Roanoke Island off the Carolina coast has fueled much speculation in the four hundred years since its disappearance. We may never know the fate of the colonists; however, Thomas Harriot's *A Briefe and True Report of the New Found Land of Virginia* (1588) offers some insight into English–Indian interaction in the beginning of the colonial period. Harriot, a scientist of some note and onetime tutor in the household of Sir Walter Raleigh, was a member of the 1585 expedition to Roanoke. In addition to making astronomical observations and providing advice on navigation, Harriot studied the natural life and native inhabitants of the region. The selection here describes the dramatic impact that epidemic diseases had on the Indians' perceptions of the English and their religion.

Source: Excerpt from Thomas Harriot, *A Briefe and True Report of the New Found Land of Virginia.* Copyright © 1972 Dover Publications.

. . . There was no town where we had any subtle devise practiced against us, we leaving it unpunished or not revenged (because we sought by all means possible to win them by gentleness) but that within a few days after our departure from every such town, the people [Native Americans] began to die very fast, and many in short space. [I]n some towns about twenty, in some forty, in some sixty, and in one six score, which in truth was very many in respect of their numbers. This happened in no place that we could learn but where we had been, where they used some practice against us, and after such time; the disease [was] also so strange, that they neither knew what it was, nor how to cure it; the like by report of the oldest men in the country never happened before. . . . A thing specially observed by us as also by the natural inhabitants themselves.

Insomuch that when some of the inhabitants which were our friends and especially the Wiroans [Chief] Wingina had observed such effects in four or five towns to follow their wicked practices, they were persuaded that it was the work of our God through our means, and that we by Him might kill and slay whom we would, without weapons [or] . . . com[ing] near them.

And thereupon when it had happened that they had understanding that any of their enemies had abused us in our journeys, hearing that we had wrought no revenge with our weapons, and fearing upon some cause the matter should so rest: did come and entreat us that we would be a means to our God that they as others that had dealt ill with us might in like sort die; alleging how much it would be for our credit and profit, as also theirs; and hoping furthermore that we could do so much at their requests in respect of the friendship we profess them.

Whose entreaties although we showed that they were ungodly, affirming that our God would not subject Himself to any such prayers and requests of men: that indeed all things have been and were to be done according to His good pleasure as He had ordained: and that we to show our selves his true servants ought rather to make petition for the contrary, that they with them might live together with us, be made partakers of His truth and serve Him in righteousness; but notwithstanding in such sort, that we refer that as all other things, to be done according to His divine will and pleasure, and as by His wisdom He had ordained to be best.

Yet because the effect fell out so suddenly and shortly after according to their desires, they thought nevertheless it came to pass by our means, and that we in using such speeches unto them did but dissemble the matter, and therefore came unto us to give us thanks in their manner that although we satisfied them not in promise, yet in deeds and effect we had fulfilled their desires.

This marvelous accident in all the country wrought so strange opinions of us, that some people could not tell whether to think us gods or men, and the rather because that all the space of their sickness, there was no man of ours known to die, or that was especially sick. [T]hey noted also that we had no women amongst us, neither that we did care for any of theirs.

Some therefore were of opinion that we were not born of women, and therefore [were] not mortal, but that we were men of an old generation many years past . . . [and] risen again to immortality.

Some would likewise seem to prophesy that there were more of our generation yet to come, to kill theirs and take their places, as some thought the purpose was by that which was already done.

Those [of our generation] that [they thought] were immediately to come after us they imagined to be in the air, yet invisible and without bodies, and that they by our entreaty and for the love of us did make the people to die in that sort as they did by shooting invisible bullets into them. . . .

Some also thought that we shot them [the Native Americans] ourselves . . . from the place where we dwelt, and killed the people in any such town that had offended us . . . , how far distant from us [they may be].

And other[s] said that it was the special work of God for our sakes, as we ourselves have cause in some sort to think no less, whatsoever some do or may imagine to the contrary. . . .

[T]heir opinions I have set down the more at large that it may appear unto you that there is good hope they may be brought through discreet dealing and government to the embracing of the truth, and consequently to honor, obey, fear, and love us.

Questions

1. According to Harriot, how did the Indians interpret the deaths that seemed to accompany the arrival of the English? Did the colonists attempt to correct any misperceptions the Indians may have had about whether the English were "gods or men"?

2. Hakluyt argued that one of the purposes of colonization was to "enlarge the glory of the gospel, and from England plant sincere religion" (Document 1-9). How is this sentiment reflected in Harriot's account of Indian–English encounters?

3. What are the strengths and weaknesses of Harriot's observations? How might we deal with the weaknesses inherent in Harriot's account?

1-11   Images of Native Americans from Roanoke Island (1585, 1590)

John White and Theodor de Bry

The English painter John White was a member of the 1585 expedition to Roanoke Island. Whereas Thomas Harriot (Document 1-10) recorded his "scientific" observations of the native inhabitants, White attempted to capture their physical likeness for audiences back home in England. He succeeded in creating a remarkable set of images, but his original paintings went largely unseen. Most of his contemporaries knew of White's work only through the derivative engravings executed by Theodor de Bry for the 1590 reprinting of Harriot's *A Briefe and True Report*. In the following pair of images, White's original painting of the wife of the Pomeiooc chief and her daughter may be compared with de Bry's engraving based on the painting.

Source: Watercolor drawing "Indian Woman and Young Girl" by John White (created 1585–1586). Licensed by the Trustees of the British Museum. Copyright © the British Museum. Engraving "Chieff Ladye of Pomeiooc" by Theodor de Bry (printed 1590), based on watercolor by White. Courtesy of the John Carter Brown Library at Brown University.

(A)   *John White, "Indian Woman and Young Girl"*

(B)   *Theodor de Bry, Engraving based on a watercolor by John White*

Questions

1.   What differences can you observe between these two images? Do you think that de Bry consciously modified White's original? Why might he have done this?

2.   Note that in both images the child is holding a doll in Elizabethan dress. What might the doll signify? What can you infer about Indian–European contact at Roanoke from these images?

3.   What impact might these images have had on Europeans seeing them for the first time?

Questions for Further Thought

1.   In what ways did religious and economic motivations for colonization reinforce each other?

2.   Were English colonists driven out of their country by adverse conditions, or were they drawn to America primarily by the promise of progress? Explain your answer.

3.   According to Harriot, White, and de Bry, how would you characterize England's initial contact with Native Americans?

CHAPTER TWO

The Invasion and Settlement of North America

1550–1700

The Rival Imperial Models of Spain, France, and Holland

Early Spanish efforts at colonization and exploration were centered in the Caribbean and Mesoamerica. The Spanish conquistadors were primarily interested in finding precious metals and establishing domination over subject peoples, although sometimes that led to their extermination (Document 2-1). Few Spaniards were interested in living in the New World; Spain's empire, by and large, did not consist of settler colonies. At first only isolated expeditions penetrated North America, motivated mainly by the search for gold and missionary activity. In the latter part of the fifteenth century, however, the Spanish treasure fleet came under attack from English and French privateers, who used the South Atlantic coast as a base of operations. In response, Spain expanded its military presence in Florida, establishing St. Augustine. Similar security concerns led Spanish friars to the northern borderlands of Mexico, or "New Mexico."

Like the Spanish, the French were uninterested in settling their New World holding, Canada, with colonists. Rather, as French adventurers explored the St. Lawrence and Mississippi waterways, they established an extensive fur trade with the native inhabitants, while Jesuits sought Indian conversions to Christianity.

The English were different. While their earliest colonies, like those of the French and Dutch, were established by private commercial enterprises with support from the crown, the first of these, the Virginia Company, floundered about aimlessly in its first years (Documents 2-2 and 2-4). It soon discovered, though, that the best way to make its enterprise successful was to expand its concerns and become a settler colony of the sort advocated by Richard Hakluyt (Document 1-9). While the company itself subsequently lost control of its creation, Virginia began to prosper as a *settler colony*, in which white planters and their indentured servants expropriated land from the native inhabitants and developed a plantation economy built around tobacco.

2-1 History of the Indies (1552)

Bartolomé de las Casas

Fray Bartolomé de las Casas (1474–1566) was born in Seville; his father, a merchant who fell on hard times, became associated with Christopher Columbus. The younger las Casas went to the New World in 1502 to serve as a priest and missionary to the indigenous peoples. In the following years he both proselytized and prospered as a landowner and gold miner, largely using forced Indian labor. In 1514, however, he experienced a conversion that led him to renounce his old life and dedicate himself to exposing the atrocities visited upon the native peoples. In the remaining half century of his long life, he worked assiduously on both sides of the Atlantic to reform Spanish treatment of the indigenous peoples. Among his numerous writings was *History of the Indies*, begun in Hispaniola in the 1520s and published in Seville in 1552. Las Casas's writings were undertaken in the interest of reform and were animated by his deep Catholic piety; yet they were read all over Europe and unintentionally helped bolster, especially among the English, a "Black Legend" of a peculiarly cruel—and Catholic—Spanish dominion.

Source: Excerpt from Bartolomé de las Casas *History of the Indies*, trans. and ed. Andrée Collard (New York: Harper and Row, 1971), 77–82, 154–159. Copyright © 1971 by Andrée M. Collard. Renewed 1999 by Joyce J. Contrucci. Reprinted by permission of Joyce Contrucci.

Once the two caravels on which Comendador Bobadilla[1] was sending Columbus and his brothers as prisoners to Castile had sailed, he [Bobadilla] tried to please the 300 Spaniards who remained on the island. This was the number Columbus had informed the King as being necessary to subjugate the island and its natives; therefore, the King had ordered the admiral to maintain this force. It was more than enough not only to keep the Indians pacified, had they treated them differently, but also to subdue and kill them all, which is what they did. Indeed, twenty or thirty horses were enough to tear them to pieces, especially since they had trained dogs for this purpose and one Spaniard with one dog felt as safe as if accompanied by fifty or a hundred Christians. This is clear even to the dullest minds. How can a people who go about naked, have no weapons other than bow and arrow and a kind of wooden lance, and no fortification besides straw huts, attack or defend themselves against a people armed with steel weapons and firearms, horses and lances, who in two hours could pierce thousands and rip open as many bellies as they wished? This proves Oviedo's[2] error (*History*, Bk III, Ch. 4) when he says that the Christians would have perished if Columbus, on his way to discover Paria, had not dispatched three ships from La Gomera Island to Hispaniola, and when he presents as a fact that the reinforcement saved the lives of Spanish men as well as their hold on the island, since they said they dared not leave the town or cross the river.

Here and elsewhere Oviedo exaggerates in order to justify Spanish tyranny and accuse the poor and forsaken Indians. Endless testimonies and the above argument prove the mild and pacific temperament of the natives, as well as the fact that we surpassed them in arms so that, had we lived among them as Christians, we would have had no need of weapons, horses or fierce dogs to attract them to us. But our work was to exasperate, ravage, kill, mangle and destroy; small wonder, then, if they tried to kill one of us now and then (the only way to catch a group of even thirty of us was if that group was fast asleep). This is a fact: Indians seldom killed groups of fifty or forty men anywhere in the Indies, especially if they had horses and sentries. So then, a group of 300 could certainly defend itself and kill all the Indians on this island, and this was their number before the arrival of Columbus's reinforcement. He brought more men, not because they were needed, but because he had to dispose of the weak, the sick and those homesick for Castile, as I have already said.

But to return to the point, Comendador Bobadilla wanted to please the 300 men who remained on the island, and his first decision dealt with the trial of those men condemned to be hanged. As far as Francisco Roldán[3] and his followers were concerned, I saw them a few days later, as if nothing had happened, safe and sound, happy and living as honored members of the community. I heard nothing about their having been punished in any way because in those days I took no notice nor did I care to know about them. Comendador Bobadilla granted the 300 men liberties and privileges. He taxed their gold at only 1 peso on 11 and they,

---

[1] *Bobadilla:* Francisco de Bobadilla (d. 1502) was sent by the Spanish crown to Hispaniola (Santo Domingo) in 1500 as chief justice and royal commissioner to deal with grievances of the Spanish colonists against Christopher Columbus and his two brothers. On arrival, Bobadilla found the three brothers brutally suppressing a rebellion; he promptly arrested them and returned them to Spain. He died in a shipwreck two years later.

[2] *Oviedo:* Gonzalo Fernández Oviedo y Valdés (1478–1557), author of *The General and Natural History of the Indies* (1535), a procolonialist work generally regarded at the time as authoritative. Oviedo depicted the Indians as inferior to Europeans and as bloodthirsty savages, leading las Casas to attack the veracity of his work.

[3] *Roldán:* Francisco de Roldán (1462–1502), a Spanish colonist in Hispaniola whom Columbus appointed as chief justice before returning to Spain in 1496. He subsequently led a rebellion against the Columbus brothers that was settled when Christopher Columbus agreed to the *encomienda* system, which granted territory (and the Indians living on it) to each colonist. Bobadilla openly took Roldán's side against Columbus.

having no mind to work and excavate, asked him for Indian labor both for the mines and the making of bread. He ordered—rather, he advised—them to form partnerships of two to share all the profits and assigned Indian tribes to them, thus making them very happy. You should have seen those hoodlums, exiled from Castile for homicide with crimes yet to be accounted for, served by native kings and their vassals doing the meanest chores! These chiefs had daughters, wives and other close relations whom the Spaniards took for concubines either with their own consent or by force. Thus, those 300 hidalgos lived for several years in a continuous state of sin, not counting those other sins they committed daily by oppressing and tyrannizing Indians. They called these women servants and shamelessly spoke of them to one another as "My servant so and so" and "X's servant," meaning "My wife so and so" and "X's wife." The comendador didn't give a straw for all this; at least he took no measures to remedy or avoid the situation. He would frequently tell them: "Take as many advantages as you can since you don't know how long this will last"; he cared even less for the hardships, afflictions and deaths of the Indians. The Spaniards loved and adored him in exchange for such favors, help and advice, because they knew how much freer they were now than under Columbus.

The admiral, it is true, was as blind as those who came after him, and he was so anxious to please the King that he committed irreparable crimes against the Indians. However, if he did not report the harm that certain Spaniards caused them, and if he assigned a tribe of Indians to Francisco Roldán and a few others to do work for them or find gold, it seems the occasions were very, very rare, and he acted as if forced to it by his own men, on account of past rebellions. At least he did abominate the free and easy life of those sinners who called themselves Christians. Sin leads to sin, and for many years they lived unscrupulously, not observing Lent or other fasts and, except at Easter, ate meat on Fridays and Saturdays. They saw themselves as masters of lords, served and feared by tribes of nobles and common people who trembled at the sight of them because of past cruelties renewed in the present whenever they felt the whim, and who especially trembled if the chief's wife, daughter or sister was thought to be a Spaniard's "wife." Thus they grew more conceited every day and fell into greater arrogance, presumption and contempt toward these humble people. They no longer felt like walking any distance. Having neither mules nor horses, they rode the backs of Indians if they were in a hurry; if they had more leisure, they traveled as if by litter, stretched on a hammock carried at a good speed and with relays. In this case they also had Indians carry large leaves to shade them from the sun and others to fan them with goose wings. I saw many an escort follow them loaded like a donkey with mining equipment and food, many of them with scars on their shoulders like working animals. Whenever they reached an Indian village, they consumed what to fifty Indians would represent abundance, and forced the chief to bring them

whatever he had, to the accompaniment of dances. Not only were they exceedingly vain in these matters, but they had other women as well who would serve in other capacities such as chambermaid, cook and similar offices. I once knew an organ maker who had such maids.

There were two kinds of servants. One, all the boys and girls taken from their parents on their plundering and killing expeditions, whom they kept in the house night and day; these were called *naborías*, meaning "servants" in the vernacular. And two, seasonal workers for the mines and the fields, who returned to their own homes starving, exhausted and debilitated. And it was a laughing matter to see the Spaniards' presumption, vanity and air of authority when they had not even a linen shirt to their names, nor cape, coat or trousers but wore only a cotton shirt over another shirt from Castile if they had it; if not, they wore their cotton shirt over bare legs and instead of boots they had sandals and leggings. To console them for their services, they beat and insulted the Indians, hardly calling them anything but "dog." Would to God they treated them as such, because they would not have killed a dog in a million years, while they thought nothing of knifing Indians by tens and twenties and of cutting slices off them to test the sharpness of their blades. Two of these so-called Christians met two Indian boys one day, each carrying a parrot; they took the parrots and for fun beheaded the boys. Another one of these tyrants, angry at an Indian chief, hanged twelve of his vassals and eighteen others all in one house. Another shot arrows into an Indian in public, announcing the reason for punishment as his failure to deliver a letter with the speed he required.

Cases of this sort are infinite among our Christians. Having failed in their attempts to defend themselves, these gentle and patient people fled to the hills but, since experience had taught them the impossibility of escaping from Spaniards anywhere, they suffered and died in the mines and other labors in desperate silence, knowing not a soul in the world to whom they could turn for help. And this is at the root of the doubt as to whether they were animals or human beings. Soulless, blind and godless, these Spaniards killed without restraint and perversely abused the patience, natural simplicity, goodness, obedience, gentleness and services of the Indians. They should have admired and pitied them and tempered their own cruelties; instead, they despised and belittled them, discrediting their humanity and believing them to be nonrational animals, and so it was thought throughout the world. The lamentable error to believe them incapable of Catholic indoctrination sprang from this first error and may he who persists in it burn for such beastly heresy.

There were other improprieties, such as saying the Indians needed tutors like children because they could not govern themselves and because, if left to their own resources, they did not work but died of starvation, and all this was said in order to keep power over them. Since nobody spoke on their behalf, but rather ate of the same dish, this pernicious infamy took such roots that for years

Castilian kings, their councils, and all manner of men believed it and treated them like animals, until God gave them someone [i.e., las Casas] who enlightened them and the world as to the truth that lay behind the lethargy—after he had ascertained the stupidity and falseness of that opinion, as will be shown below.

The falseness in itself was not so obscure as to require miraculous light—any rustic mind could have seen it and taken pride in telling others. But having found greed as the prime mover—vehement greed, blind, wild and the root of all evils—it became apparent that the original tyrants and all who followed in their damnable beliefs, confirmed by dismal actions, had been numbed by greed; and a glimmer of hope of stopping it became possible, what learned person does not know that the minds of the wisest and most generous men can degenerate to pusillanimity when subjected to harsh and lasting servitude? Oppressed, afflicted, threatened, tormented and mistreated in various ways, unable to raise their thoughts above their bitter misery, they can forget their own humanity. And this is the first plan of tyrants: in order to sustain themselves on usurped territory, they continually oppress and cause anguish to the most powerful and to the wisest so that, occupied by their calamities, they lack the time and courage to think of their freedom; thus the Indians degenerated into cowardice and timidity, as I amply demonstrated in Chapters 27 and 36 of my *Apologetical History*. Well then, if the wisest of the wise, whether Greek or Roman (history books are full of this), often feared and suffered from this adversity, and if many other nations experienced it and philosophers wrote about it, what could we expect from these gentle and unprotected Indians suffering such torments, servitude and decimation but immense pusillanimity, profound discouragement and annihilation of their inner selves, to the point of doubting whether they were men or mere cats? And who, down to the lowest idiot, will not think blind and downright malicious those who dared spread this belief and defame so many people, saying Indians need tutors because they are incapable of organization, when in reality, they have kings and governors, villages, houses and property rights, and communicate with one another on all levels of human, political, economical and social relations, living in peace and harmony?

Finally, the following argument makes even more apparent the evil design of those deceivers and counterfeiters of truth. They say that without tutors Indians would not work and would die of starvation; let us ask, then, if Spain sent food to the Indians all those thousands of years people lived there and if, when we got there, we found them wanting and thin? Also, did we give them the means to find food—since they lived on air and we brought food to them all the way from Castile—and did we satiate them or, on the contrary, did they satisfy our own hunger and free us from death many times by giving us not only the bare essentials but many superfluous things as well? Oh, vicious blindness!

Wicked, insensitive and detestable ungratefulness! So consequently, these first sowers of destruction are responsible for the infamous lie which spread throughout the world that harmed the cause of multitudes of men, the sons of Adam, without cause and without reason by misinterpreting their natural goodness, gentleness, obedience and simplicity. They should have loved and praised the Indians, and even learned from them, instead of belittling them by publicizing them as beastly; instead of stealing, afflicting, oppressing and annihilating them, making as much of them as they would a heap of dung on a public square. And let this suffice to account for the state of affairs on this island under Bobadilla's government, after he had sent Admiral Columbus as a prisoner to Castile. . . .

When the Spaniards saw how fast they were killing Indians in the mines, plantations and other endeavors, caring only to squeeze the last effort out of them, it occurred to them to replenish the supply by importing people from other islands and they deceived King Hernando with a crafty argument. They notified him either by letter or by a special court representative, presumably with the comendador's consent, that the Lucayo or Yucayo Islands close to Cuba and Hispaniola were full of an idle people who had learned nothing and could not be Christianized there. Therefore, they asked permission to send two ships to bring them to Hispaniola where they could be converted and would work in the mines, thus being of service to the King.

The King agreed, on the blind and culpable recommendation of the council, acting as if rational beings were timber cut from trees and used for buildings or a herd of sheep or any other animals and nothing much would be lost if they died at sea. Who would not blame an error so great: natives taken by force to new lands 100 and 150 leagues away, however good or evil the reason may have been, much less to dig gold in mines where they would surely die, for a King and foreigners they had never offended? Perhaps they sought justification by deceiving the King with a falsehood, that is, that the Lucayo Indians would be instructed in the Faith: which, even if it were true was not right—and it wasn't true, for they never intended anything of the kind nor did anything in that direction. God did not want Christianity at that cost; God takes no pleasure in a good deed, no matter its magnitude, if sin against one's fellow man is the price of it, no matter how minuscule that sin may be; and this is a fact all sinners, especially in the Indies, deceive themselves into ignoring. In total condemnation of this lie, let it be remembered that the Apostles never expatriated anyone by force in order to convert them elsewhere, nor has the universal Church ever used this method, considered pernicious and detestable. Therefore, the King's council was very blind and, consequently, because its members are scholars, it is guilty before God, since ignorance cannot be adduced.

The King's permission arrived and ten or twelve residents from Concepción and Santiago gathered 10,000 or 12,000 gold pesos, bought two or three ships and fifty to sixty salaried men, and raided the Indians who lived in the Lucayos in peace and security. Those are the Lucayo Indians I spoke of at length in Book I and in my *Apologetical History*, so blessed among all Indians in gentleness, simplicity, humility and other natural virtues, it seems Adam's sin left them untouched. I haven't found any comparable nation in the world in ancient history, except perhaps the Seres of Asia, who are a peace-loving and gentle people (Solinus, Ch. 63), who love justice (Pomponius Mela, III, 6), and who know not how to kill or fornicate, have no prostitutes, adulterers, thieves or homicides and adore no idols (Eusebius, *Praeparatione Evangelica*, VI, 8). To this kind of people the Spaniards did the following. They say that the first harvesters of Lucayo Indians, fully aware of their simplicity and gentle manners (they knew this from the report of Christopher Columbus), anchored their ships and were received as they always are before our deeds prove the contrary, that is, as angels from Heaven. The Spaniards said they came from Hispaniola, where the souls of their beloved ones were resting in joy, and that their ships would take them there if they wanted to see them, for it is a fact that all Indian nations believe in the immortality of the soul. After death, the body joins the soul in certain delightful places of pleasure and comfort; some nations even believe that the souls of sinners first undergo torment. So then, with those wicked arguments, the Spaniards deceived the Indians into climbing on board ship, and men and women left their homes with their scant belongings.

On Hispaniola, they found neither father, mother nor loved ones but iron tools and instruments and gold mines instead, where they perished in no time; some, from despair at seeing themselves deceived, took poison; others died of starvation and hard labor, for they are a delicate people who had never imagined such type of work even existed. Later, the Spaniards used every possible wile and force to trick them into ships. At the landing sites, usually Puerto de Plata and Puerto Real on the north shore facing the Lucayos, men, women, children and old people were thrown helter-skelter into lots; the old with the young, the sick with the healthy—they often fell ill in the ships, and many died of anguish, thirst and hunger in the hottest and stuffiest holds—without any concern for keeping man and wife, father and son together, handled like the basest animals. Thus the innocent, *sicut pecora occisionis*, were divided into groups and those who had contributed their share in the raiding expedition drew lots. When someone drew an old or sick one he protested, "Give that old man to the devil, why should I take him? To feed and bury him? And why give me that sick dog? To cure him?"

Sometimes, it happened that Indians died on the spot either from hunger, debilitation, sickness or the pain of a father seeing his son or a husband seeing his wife bought and

taken away. How could anyone with a human heart and human entrails witness such inhuman cruelty? Where was the principle of charity, "Thou shalt love thy neighbor as thyself," in the minds of those who, forgetting that they were Christians or human beings, performed such "humanity" upon human beings? Finally, to cover the cost and pay the salaried men, they agreed to allow the sale of allotted Indians at not more than 4 gold pesos per piece—they referred to them as pieces as if they were heads of cattle. And they thought selling and transferring so cheaply was an honorable thing to do, while in truth, had the price been higher, the Indians would have received better treatment as valuable items and would have lasted longer.

As I said, the Spaniards used many ways to draw the Lucayos from their homeland where they lived as in the Golden Age, a life of which poets and historians have sung such praise. Sometimes, especially at first, they won their trust because the Indians did not suspect them and, living off guard, received them like angels. Sometimes they raided by night and other times in the open, *aperto Marte* as they say, knifing those who, having more experience of Spaniards, defended themselves with bow and arrow, a weapon ordinarily used for fishing and not for war. They brought more than 40,000 people here in a period of four or five years, men and women, children and adults, as Pedro Martyr[4] mentions in Chapter 1 of the seventh *Decada*. . . .

He also mentions the fact that some killed themselves from despair, while others, who were stronger, hoped to escape and return to their land and thus endured their hopeless lives, hiding in the northern mountains closer to home and hoping to find a way to cross over. Once—and Pedro Martyr records this in the same chapter—one of these Indians built a raft from a very large tree trunk called *yauruma* in the vernacular (the penultimate syllable is long), which is a light and hollow wood, tied logs to it with *liana*, which is a type of extremely strong ropelike root, placed some corn from his harvest in the hollow of the logs and filled gourds with fresh water; then, closing both ends with leaves, he took off with another Indian and a few women of his family, all great swimmers like all the Lucayos. Fifty leagues from the coast, they unfortunately met a ship coming full speed from their place of destination; they were captured and returned to Hispaniola in tears and lamentations and perished there like the rest.

We do not know, but it is believable that others made the same attempt, and if so, it was to no avail, since the Spaniards were continually raiding those islands until not one single Indian remained. They chose the rockiest and most inaccessible island to corral all the Indians taken from

---

[4] *Pedro Martyr:* An Italian by birth, Martyr (1457–1526) became a Spanish courtier, soldier, and academic. He was the earliest historian of what he called the New World, devoting much of his life to a massive chronicle entitled *De Orbe Novo*.

the neighboring islands; and there they left them in charge of a Spanish guard, after breaking their canoes to prevent escape until the ship returned for another load. Once they had 7,000 Indians and seven Spaniards guarding them like shepherds and, the ships being delayed, they ran out of cassava, which is all the food they ever gave Indians. As two ships laden with provisions neared the coast, a terrible gale storm sank them all and the islanders died of starvation; I do not remember what I heard about the fate of those shipwrecked. Nobody thought to attribute these disasters to divine punishment for sins committed here; rather, they attributed them to chance, as if there were no Rector in Heaven to see and register such cruel injustice.

I could have found out, and I could consequently now relate, the particulars of many more cruelties inflicted upon this innocent flock, if in those days of my residence in Hispaniola I had cared to question the men who performed such things. But I want to tell what one of them told me in Cuba. He had come to Cuba in an Indian canoe, perhaps as a runaway from his captain or to escape danger or again from a sense of guilt and a desire to leave such reprobate ways. He told me they used to stuff shipholds with hundreds of Indians of both sexes and all ages, pack them like sardines and close all the hatchways to prevent escape, thus shutting off air and light. And, since ships carried food and water only for the Spanish crew, the Indians died and were thrown into the sea, and the floating corpses were so numerous that a ship could find its course by them alone, without need of a compass, charts or the art of navigation. Those were his words. This is certain: no ship ever raided the Lucayos that did not for the above reasons have to throw overboard one-third or one-fourth of its human cargo, and this inhumanity went on sometimes more and sometimes less but it is a fact that it went on. This arrangement, if such a thing can bear that name, brought to Hispaniola over a million souls over a period of ten years—men, women, children and elderly; a few shipments were made to Cuba also, and they all perished in the mines from overwork, anguish and exhaustion.

Pedro Martyr declares that according to his information there were 406 Lucayo Islands, from which the Spaniards enslaved 40,000 Indians to work the mines, and, from all the islands they had a total of 1,200,000. . . . He adds that the Lucayo Indians sometimes killed Spaniards. This happened when a small group of Spaniards were caught off guard because, when they realized the Spaniards meant to destroy them, the Indians used bows and arrows invented for fishing to kill their killers. But it was all in vain since they never succeeded in killing more than a handful. As to what Martyr says about the number of Lucayo Islands, he is including those called Jardin de la Rena and Jardin del Rey, which is a string of small islands south and north of the Cuban coast. The Indians there shared the natural goodness of the Lucayos. However, by Lucayos we refer only to the larger islands that go from Hispaniola to Florida away from Cuba, and these number between forty and fifty, large and small. Pedro Martyr also adds that he kept his information constantly up to date, and this was possible because at that time he was a member of the council of the Indies which he joined in 1518 and I was there when he presented his credentials to the council. The Emperor gave him this post in Saragossa almost immediately after the coronation ceremonies.

Questions

1. What is las Casas's position on the accuracy of previous accounts of the Spanish settlement of the Americas?

2. According to las Casas, what reasons did the Spanish settlers give to justify their treatment of the Native Americans?

3. Does las Casas believe the Spanish king to be knowledgeable about the behavior of the Spanish settlers? Explain your answer based on your reading of the document.

2-2   A True Relation of Virginia (1608)

John Smith

Governor John Smith (1580–1631) is white America's first authentic hero (see text p. 49). A soldier of fortune in Europe, he arrived in Jamestown in 1607 as one of its seven councillors. Over the next two and a half years he almost single-handedly saved the colony from starvation, served as its virtual dictator, explored and mapped the area, and was supposedly rescued from a death sentence by Pocahontas, the daughter of the Indian chief Powhatan. Smith wrote an account of events in the colony; the "True Relation" brought news of Virginia's early trials to England.

The English built a military fort at Jamestown; Smith described the log walls as "palisadoed." *Aqua vitae* ("water of life") is strong liquor—considered essential for good health.

Source: John Smith, *A True Relation of such occurrences and accidents of noate as hath happened in Virginia since the first planting of that Collony, which is now resident in the South part thereof, till the last returne from thence* (London, 1608), in *English Colonial Documents: American Colonial Documents to 1776*, ed. Merrill Jensen (London: Oxford University Press, 1964), 132–136. Reprinted with permission of Oxford University Press.

Kind Sir, commendations remembered, etc. You shall understand that after many crosses in the downs by tempests, we arrived safely upon the south-west part of the great Canaries. Within four or five days after, we set sail for Dominica the 26 of April. The first land we made, we fell with Cape Henry, the very mouth of the Bay of Chesapeake, which at that present we little expected, having by a cruel storm been put to the northward.

Anchoring in this bay, twenty or thirty went ashore with the captain, and in coming aboard [on land], they were assaulted with certain Indians, which charged them within pistol shot, in which conflict Captain Archer and Matthew Morton were shot, whereupon Captain Newport seconding them, made a shot at them, which the Indians little respected, but having spent their arrows retired without harm. And in that place was the box opened wherein the Council for Virginia was nominated, and arriving at the place [Jamestown] where we are now seated, the Council was sworn and the President elected, which for that year was Master Edmund Maria Wingfield, where was made choice for our situation, a very fit place for the erecting of a great city, about which some contention passed betwixt Captain Wingfield and Captain Gosnold. Notwithstanding, all our provision was brought ashore, and with as much speed as might be we went about our fortification.

[On 22 May, Captain Newport, Smith, and several others set forth to explore the country up the James River. They returned on 27 May.] . . . The first we heard was that 400 Indians the day before [26 May] had assaulted the fort and surprised it. Had not God (beyond all their expectations) by means of the ships (at whom they shot with their ordnances and muskets) caused them to retire, they had entered the fort with our own men, which were then busied in setting corn, their arms being then in dry fats and few ready but certain gentlemen of their own, in which conflict most of the Council was hurt, a boy slain in the pinnace, and thirteen or fourteen more hurt.

With all speed we palisadoed our fort; each other day for six or seven days we had alarms by ambuscadoes, and four or five cruelly wounded by being abroad. The Indians' loss we know not, but as they report three were slain and divers hurt. . . .

The day before the ship's departure the king of Pamaunke [i.e., Opechancanough] sent the Indian that had met us before in our discovery, to assure us peace, our fort being then palisadoed round, and all our men in good health and comfort, albeit that through some discontented humours it did not so long continue. For the President and Captain Gosnold, with the rest of the Council, being for the most part discontented with one another, in so much that things were neither carried with that discretion nor any business effected in such good sort as wisdom would, nor our own good and safety required, whereby, and through the hard dealing of our President, the rest of the Council being diversely affected through his audacious command; and for Captain Martin, albeit very honest and wishing the best good, yet so sick and weak, and myself so disgraced through others' malice, through which disorder God (being angry with us) plagued us with such famine and sickness that the living were scarce able to bury the dead; our want of sufficient and good victuals, with continual watching four or five each night at three bulwarks, being the chief cause. Only of sturgeon we had great store, whereon our men would so greedily surfeit as it cost many their lives; the sack, *aqua vitae*, and other preservatives for our health being kept only in the President's hands, for his own diet, and his few associates.

Shortly after Captain Gosnold fell sick, and within three weeks died. Captain Ratcliffe being then also very sick and weak, and myself having also tasted of the extremity thereof, but by God's assistance being well recovered. Kendall about this time, for divers reasons, deposed from being of the Council, and shortly after it pleased God in our extremity to move the Indians to bring us corn ere it was half ripe, to refresh us, when we rather expected when they would destroy us.

About the tenth of September there was about 46 of our men dead, at which time Captain Wingfield having ordered the affairs in such sort that he was generally hated of all, in which respect with one consent he was deposed from his presidency, and Captain Ratcliffe according to his course was elected.

Our provision being now within twenty days spent, the Indians brought us great store both of corn and bread ready made, and also there came such abundance of fowls into the rivers as greatly refreshed our weak estates, whereupon many of our weak men were presently able to go abroad.

As yet we had no houses to cover us, our tents were rotten, and our cabins worse than nought. Our best commodity was iron, which we made into little chisels.

The President's and Captain Martin's sickness constrained me to be cape merchant and yet to spare no pains in making houses for the company, who notwithstanding our misery, little ceased their malice, grudging, and muttering.

As at this time were most of our chiefest men either sick or discontented, the rest being in such despair as they would rather starve and rot with idleness than be persuaded to do anything for their own relief without constraint. Our victuals being now within eighteen days spent, and the Indian trade decreasing, I was sent to the mouth of the river to Kegquouhtan, an Indian town, to trade for corn, and try the river for fish, but our fishing we could not effect by reason of the stormy weather. The Indians, thinking us near famished, with careless kindness offered us little pieces of bread and small handfuls of beans or wheat for a hatchet or a piece of copper. In like manner I entertained their kindness and in like scorn offered them like commodities, but the children, or any that showed extraordinary kindness, I liberally contented with free gift of such trifles as well contented them. . . .

[In January 1608], by a mischance our fort was burned and the most of our apparel, lodging, and private provision.

Many of our old men [became] diseased, and [many] of our new for want of lodging perished. . . .

[O]ur men being all or the most part well recovered, and we not willing to trifle away more time than necessity enforced us unto, we thought good for the better content of the adventurers, in some reasonable sort to freight home Master Nelson [of the ship *Phenix*, which had arrived on 20 April] with cedar wood. About which, our men going with willing minds, [it] was in very good time effected and the ship sent for England [on 2 June 1608]. We now remaining being in good health, all our men well contented, free from mutinies, in love one with another, and as we hope, in a continual peace with the Indians. Where we doubt not but by God's gracious assistance, and the adventurers' willing minds and speedy furtherance to so honourable an action, in after times to see our nation to enjoy a country not only exceeding pleasant for habitation, but also very profitable for commerce in general; no doubt pleasing to Almighty God, honourable to our gracious sovereign, and commodious generally to the whole kingdom.

Questions

1. Does the early experience at Jamestown support the arguments for colonization that had been offered earlier by Richard Hakluyt (see Document 1-9)?

2. Was there any discernible economic base in Smith's Virginia? Explain.

3. What does Smith tell us about Indian–white relations in the first year of the Jamestown colony?

4. Why did Smith feel that the settlers would "rather starve and rot with idleness than be persuaded to do anything for their own relief"?

2-3   Pocahontas and John Smith (1624)

According to John Smith, he and his exploratory party of Englishmen were captured in 1607 by the "chief King" Powhatan, who ruled over lands that later would constitute the Virginia Tidewater. Facing brutal execution, his life was spared when Pocahontas, the "King's most dear and well-beloved daughter," at the very last moment "hazarded the beating out of her own brains" to save his. Smith's account, pictured in this illustration from his *Generall Historie of Virginia*, however, is as problematic as it is famous. To begin with, he did not mention this episode of dramatic intervention in his early narratives; he first wrote about it years later, only after Pocahontas's celebrated marriage to John Rolfe in 1614. Furthermore, at the time of its supposed occurrence, Pocahontas was eleven or twelve years old, hardly old enough to satisfy any of the later romanticized versions of the relationship between Smith and the Indian "princess." So what motivated Pocahontas to act as she supposedly did? And finally, Smith's own description of his encounter with Pocahontas in London in 1616 conveyed none of the warmth one might expect of a meeting between two old friends whose lives were permanently intertwined as a result of a life-and-death decision made a decade earlier.

Source: From John Smith, *The Generall Historie of Virginia, New-England, and the Summer Isles* (London: Printed by I. D. and I. H. for Michael Sparkes, 1624).

King Powhatan comands C. Smith to be slayne his
daughter Pokahontas beggs his life his thankfullness
and how he Subiecled 39 of their kings reade § histi

Questions

1. This illustration appeared in the 1624 edition of Smith's *Generall Historie of Virginia*. What impressions did it convey to English audiences about Smith, the Powhatans, and Pocahontas?

2. Is Smith's account of the Pocahontas episode simply fictional? If something similar to it did occur in 1607, what might be the reason for it from Powhatan's point of view?

3. Why has the Smith account had such lasting power in American thought and culture? What makes it so popular with modern audiences?

2-4   Checklist for Virginia-Bound Colonists (1624)

John Smith

When John Smith sat down to write his *Generall Historie* in 1624, he had already led Virginians through their "starving times" and the Indian massacre of 1622 (see text pp. 48–49). He also had helped the Virginians overcome their reluctance to work. But it was from London that he kept a keen eye on the colonization of the North Atlantic coastline, including the settlement of New England. Although there is no evidence that John Smith met John Winthrop, the leader of the Puritan exodus to Massachusetts, Winthrop probably was familiar with Smith's *Generall Historie*.

Source: Captain John Smith, *The Generall Historie* (1624), edited by Edward Arber and reprinted in his *Travels and Works of Captain John Smith* (Edinburgh: J. Grant, 1910), book 4.

A particular of such necessaries as either private families, or single persons, shall have cause to provide to go to Virginia, whereby greater numbers may in part conceive the better how to provide for themselves.

Apparel

A Monmouth cap.	1s.	10d.
3 falling bands [collars].	1s.	3d.
3 shirts.	7s.	6d.
1 waistcoat.	2s.	2d.
1 suit of canvas.	7s.	6d.
1 suit of frieze [coarse wool].	10s.	
1 suit of cloth.	15s.	
3 pair of Irish stockings.	4s.	
4 pair of shoes.	8s.	8d.
1 pair of garters.		10d.
1 dozen of points [for lacing clothes].		3d.
1 pair of canvas sheets.	8s.	
7 ells of canvas to make a bed and bolster, to be filled in Virginia, serving for two men.	8s.	
5 ells of coarse canvas to make a bed at sea for two men.	5s.	
1 coarse rug at sea for two men.	6s.	

Victual for a whole year for a man, and so after the rate for more.

8 bushels of meal.	2£.	
2 bushels of peas.	6s.	
2 bushels of oatmeal.	9s.	
1 gallon of aqua vitae.	2s.	6d.
1 gallon of oil.	3s.	6d.
2 gallons of vinegar.	2s.	
	3£.	3s.

Arms for a man; but if half your men be armed it is well, so all have swords and pieces.

1 armor complete, light.		17s.	
1 long piece five feet and a half, near musket bore.	1£.	2s.	
1 sword.		5s.	
1 belt.		1s.	
1 bandolier.		1s.	6d.
20 pound[s] of powder.		18s.	
60 pound[s] of shot or lead, pistol and goose shot.		5s.	
	3£.	9s.	6d.

Tools for a family of six persons, and so after the rate for more.

5 broad hoes at 2s. apiece.		10s.	
5 narrow hoes at 16d. apiece.		6s.	8d.
2 broad axes at 3s. 8d. apiece.		7s.	4d.
5 felling axes at 18d. apiece.		7s.	6d.
2 steel handsaws at 16d. apiece.		2s.	8d.
2 two-handsaws at 5s. apiece.		10s.	
1 whipsaw, set and filed; with box, file and wrest [screw key].		10s.	
2 hammers [at] 12d. apiece.		2s.	
3 shovels at 18d. apiece.		4s.	6d.
2 spades at 18d. apiece.		3s.	
2 augers at 6d. apiece.		1s.	
6 chisels at 6d apiece.		3s.	
2 percers stocked [at] 4d apiece.			8d.
3 gimlets at 2d. apiece.			6d.
2 hatchets at 21d. apiece.		3s.	6d.
2 froes to cleave pale [make staves or shingles] [at] 18d. each.		3s.	
2 hand bills [at] 20d apiece.		3s.	4d.
1 grindstone.		4s.	
nails of all sorts to the value of	2£.		
2 pickaxes.		3s.	
	6£.	2s.	8d.

Household implements for a
family and six persons, and so for
more or less after the rate.

1 iron pot.	7s.	
1 kettle.	6s.	
1 large frying pan.	2s.	6d.
1 gridiron.	1s.	6d.
2 skillets.	5s.	
1 spit.	2s.	
platters, dishes, spoons of wood.	4s.	
1£.	8s.	

For sugar, spice, and fruit, and at sea for six men. 12s.6d.

So the full charge after this rate for each person, will amount to about the sum of 12£.10s.10d.

The passage of each man is 6£.

The fraught of these provisions for a man, will be about half a ton, which is 1£.10s.

So the whole charge will amount to about 20£.

Now if the number be great; [not only] nets, hooks, and lines, but cheese, bacon, kine and goats must be added.

And this is the usual proportion the Virginia Company doe[s] bestow upon their tenants they send.

Questions

1. Can you tell from this list of necessary items what kind of colony Smith hoped Virginia would become?

2. What kind of lifestyle do you imagine early Virginians had?

3. What is missing from this list that colonists might obtain from Virginia's environment?

Questions for Further Thought

1. Based on your reading of these four documents (2-1 through 2-4), which of the New World colonies would seem to have the best prospects for long-term prosperity? Why?

2. Do you see any significant differences among the Spanish and English colonies in their attitudes toward the native inhabitants?

3. Judging from these documents, what would you characterize as the *purpose* of colonies, both in the eyes of the colonists and in those of colonial promoters back in Europe?

The English Arrive: The Chesapeake Experience

Seventeenth-century Virginia was not a happy place for English settlers or Native Americans. The colony that would produce the revolutionary leadership of Patrick Henry, George Washington, and Thomas Jefferson had extremely troubled beginnings. The colony almost did not make it. People died at an astonishing rate: 80 percent in the first generation of settlement and 50 percent in the first half century. England poured thousands of mostly male indentured servants into Virginia to raise the tobacco crop. Many died, few married, and, increasingly, most were unable to obtain land of their own after completing a term of servitude (Document 2-5).

2-5   Notes on Indentured Servitude in Virginia (1640)

The plantation system of agriculture, in which extensive land is worked by groups of (usually forced) laborers to produce a lucrative crop for sale to a (frequently remote) market, did not—indeed, *does* not—need slavery per se to operate. In seventeenth-century

Virginia, for instance, the original plantation workforce consisted largely of white indentured servants, who worked a term of years for a master in exchange for their passage and a chance to pursue their happiness in a country less crowded, and with more accessible land, than was afforded by the England of the enclosure era (see Document 1-8). Life as a servant was not all that easy, though; one revolted ship's captain refused to transport servants to Virginia, charging that they "were sold heere upp and downe like horses." Resistance was punished severely, as the following documents show.

These documents are not original council minutes, as the source citation suggests. The original minute books of the Virginia Council and General Court were destroyed by fire in April 1865 during the evacuation of Richmond. Conway Robinson, a legal reporter, made notes from the originals, and those notes remain among our more important sources of information on seventeenth-century Virginia.

Source: H. R. McIlwaine, ed., *Minutes of the Council and General Court of Colonial Virginia, 1622–1632, 1670–1676* (Richmond: Virginia State Library, 1924), 465–467.

11TH OF DEC., 1640.

Whereas William Huddleston servant unto Mr *Canhow* [or *Cantrow?*] hath complained to the board against his master for want of all manner of apparel, *the court hath therefore ordered* that the said Mr *Canhow* [or *Cantrow?*] shall before *christmas* next provide and allow unto the said Huddleston such sufficient apparel of linen and woollen as shall be thought fit by Captain *John West* Esqr or otherwise that the said Captain *West* shall have power to dispose of the said servant until the said *Canhow* [or *Cantrow?*] do perform this order.

7TH OF OCT., 1640.

Whereas Thos Pursell servant unto *Robt Brassure* for the term of four years hath petitioned to the board for his freedom, it being denied unto him by the said *Brassure* in regard the said *Pursell* has absented himself from his said service for the space of three months or there-about *the Court hath therefore ordered* that the said *Pursell* shall be discharged from his said master but shall loose his right in apparel and corn due unto him at the Expiration of his time in respect of his absence from his service as aforesaid & that the said *Brassure* shall Deliver unto the said *Pursell* such apparel beding and what other goods do already belong unto him and are remaining in the custody of the said *Brassure.*

7TH OF OCT., 1640.

Whereas it appeareth to the Court that *Roger Parke* being bound to serve Capt *Corell* for the space of three Quarters of a year and Thos Loving Being agent for the said Capt *Corell* the said *Parke* was assigned to the said *Loving* to serve the said time which the said *Parke* having not performed *the Court hath ordered* that the said *Parke* shall forthwith put in security for the payment of five pounds *sterling* within twenty days after this order unto the said *Loving* in consider-

ation of his said service being not performed as aforesaid otherwise Execution &c.

JUNE 4, 1640.

Whereas upon Information to this Board of two servants that are run away from *Maryland*, and now at the House of *George Minesye* Esqr one of which said servants doth belong unto Mr *Snow* as he pretendeth, and the other to the governour of the aforesaid *Maryland* as is informed *the court hath therefore ordered* that the said servant belonging to the said *Snow* shall be delivered unto him if upon due prooff he make his right appear and the other servant to be returned with all speed unto the said Governour.

JUNE 4, 1640.

Upon the petition of *Hugh Gwyn* gent wherein he complained to this board of three of his servants that are run away to *Maryland* to his much loss and prejudice and wherein he hath humbly requested the board that he may have liberty to make the sale or benifit of the said servants in the said *Maryland* which the Court taking into Consideration and weighing the dangerous consequences of such pernicious precident *do order* that a letter be written unto the said Governour to the intent the said servants may be returned hither to receive such exemplary and condign punishment as the nature of their offence shall justly deserve and then be to be returned to their said master.

9TH OF JULY, 1640.

Whereas Hugh Gwyn hath by order from this Board Brought back from *Maryland* three servants formerly run away from the said *Gwyn*, *the court doth therefore order* that the said three servants shall receive the punishment of whipping and to have thirty stripes apiece one called *Victor*, a *dutchman*, the other a *Scotchman* called *James Gregory*, shall first serve out their times with their master according to their Indentures, and one whole year apiece after the time of their service is Expired. By their said Indentures in recompense of his Loss sustained by their absence and after that service to their said master is Expired to serve the colony for three whole years apiece, and that the third being a negro named *John Punch* shall serve his said master or his assigns for the time of his natural Life here or elsewhere.

JULY 22, 1640.

Whereas complaint has been made to this Board by Capt *Wm Pierce* Esqr that six of his servants and a negro of Mr *Reginolds* has plotted to run away unto the *Dutch* plantation from their said masters and did assay to put the same in Execution upon *Saturday* night being the 18th day *July* 1640 as appeared to the Board by the Examinations of *Andrew Noxe, Richd Hill, Richd Cookeson* and *John Williams* and likewise by the confession of *Christopher Miller, Peter Wilcocke*, and *Emanuel* the foresaid Negro who had at the fore said time, taken the skiff of the said Capt *Wm Pierce* their master, and corn powder and shot and guns, to accomplish their said purposes, which said persons sailed down in the said skiff to *Elizabeth* river where they were taken and brought back again, the Court taking the same into consideration, as a dangerous precident for the future time (if unpunished) did order that *Christopher Miller* a *dutchman* (a prince agent in the business) should receive the punishment of whipping and to have thirty stripes, and to be burnt in the cheek with the letter R and to work with a shakle on his legg for one whole year, and longer if said master shall see cause and after his full time of service is Expired with his said master to serve the colony for seven whole years, and the said *Peter Wilcocke* to receive thirty stripes and to be Burnt in the cheek with the letter R and, after his term of service is Expired with his said master to serve the colony for three years and the said *Richd Cookson* after his full time expired with his master to serve the colony for two years and a half, and the said *Richd Hill* to remain upon his good behaviour until the next offence and the said *Andrew Noxe* to receive thirty stripes, and the said *John Williams* a *dutchman* and a Chirugeon after his full time of service is Expired with his master to serve the colony for seven years, and *Emanuel* the Negro to receive thirty stripes and to be burnt in the cheek with the letter R and to work in shakle one year or more as his master shall see cause, and all those who are condemned to serve the colony after their times are expired with their masters, then their said masters are required hereby to present to this board their said servants so condemned to the colony.

13TH OF OCT., 1640.

The Court hath ordered that *Wm Wootton* and *John Bradye* as principall actors and contrivers in a most dangerous conspiracy by attempting to run out of the country and Inticing divers others to be actors in the said conspiracy to be whipt from the gallows to the Court door and that the said *Bradye* shall be Branded with an Iron in the shoulder, and *Wotton* in the forehead each of them to serve the Colony seven years, the service due from the said *Wotton* to the said Mr *Sanderson* being first performed, each of them to work in Irons during the time of the said censure for the rest of these that are freemen (*viz*) *John Tomkinson* and *Richr West* for consenting and concealing the said plott that they shall be whipt and serve the colony two years and those that are servants (*viz*) *John Winchester, Wm Drummer Robt Rouse* and *Robt Mosely* to be whipt only as also *Margarett Beard*, and that the masters of the said servants shall pay the fees due from the servants to the sheriffs and the servants shall make good the same, at the Expiration of their time by a years service apiece to their said masters and that none of them shall be released from their Irons without order from this Board.

OCT. 17, 1640.

Whereas we are daily given to understand of divers servants that run away from their masters whereby much loss and prejudice doth ensue to the masters of such servants, the court therefore conceiving it to be the most necessary and speedy course to apprehend the said servants *doth order* that upon complaint thereof made unto the sheriffs of the counties where any such servant or servants doth run away that the sheriff thereof or his deputies shall hereby have power to hire boat and hands to pursue the said runaways and that the charge thereof shall be borne and defrayed by the said county.

Questions

1. How seriously did the court take the issue of runaway servants, and why?

2. Do you see evidence of emerging discrimination in the treatment handed out by the court to white and black servants?

3. On the other hand, what evidence do you see of national divisions among the white servant population?

2-6 Two Fruitfull Sisters (1656)

John Hammond

Ever since the tobacco boom of the 1620s, the Chesapeake economy had been dependent on a steady influx of new immigrants. Tobacco was a labor-intensive staple crop, and mortality rates throughout the seventeenth century were too high to allow for a natural increase in the population to supply the needed labor. Land was cheap and handsome profits could be made with tobacco, but only if the supply of poor Englishmen kept up with constantly escalating labor demands. Not surprisingly, given the sad fate of the vast majority of indentured servants who ventured to Virginia and Maryland, the recruitment of new would-be laborers proved to be increasingly difficult. Promotional tracts written by supposedly knowledgeable people sought to convince the undecided to seek their fortunes across the Atlantic. John Hammond, who had spent some twenty-one years in Virginia and Maryland, wrote *Leah and Rachel, or, the Two Fruitfull Sisters, Virginia and Mary-Land* (1656) in an effort to counter what he perceived to be false reports about life in the Chesapeake colonies.

Source: Excerpt from John Hammond, "Leah and Rachel, or, the Two Fruitfull Sisters, Virginia and Mary-Land," in *Settlements to Society, 1584–1763*, ed. Jack P. Greene, (New York: McGraw-Hill, 1966), 50–52. Copyright © 1966. Reprinted with permission by McGraw-Hill.

Those Servants that will be industrious may in their time of service gain a competent estate before their Freedoms, which is usually done by many, and they gaine esteeme and assistance that appear so industrious: There is no Master almost but will allow his Servant a parcell of clear ground to plant some Tobacco in for himself, which he may husband at those many idle times he hath allowed him and not prejudice, but rejoyce his Master to see it, which in time of Shipping he may lay out for commodities, and in Summer sell them again with advantage, and get a Sow-Pig or two, which any body almost will give him, and his Master suffer him to keep them with his own, which will be no charge to his Master, and with one years increase of them may purchase a Cow Calf or two, and by that time he is for himself; he may have Cattle, Hogs and Tobacco of his own, and come to live gallantly; but this must be gained (as I said) by Industry and affability, not by sloth nor churlish behaviour.

And whereas it is rumoured that Servants have no lodging other than on boards, or by the Fire side, it is contrary to reason to believe it: First, as we are Christians; next as people living under a law, which compels as well the Master as the Servant to perform his duty; nor can true labour be either expected or exacted without sufficient cloathing, diet, and lodging; all which both their Indentures (which most inviolably be observed) and the Justice of the Country requires.

But if any go thither, not in a condition of a Servant, but pay his or her passage, which is some six pounds: Let them not doubt but it is money well layed out (yet however, let them not fail) although they carry little else to take a Bed along with them, and then few Houses but will give them entertainment, either out of curtesie, or on reasonable tearms; and I think it better for any that goes over free, and but in a mean condition, to hire himself for reasonable wages of Tobacco and Provision, the first year, provided he happen in an honest house, and where the Mistresse is noted for a good Housewife, of which there are very many (notwithstanding the cry to the contrary) for by that means he will live free of disbursement, have something to help him the next year, and be carefully looked to in his sicknesse (if he chance to fall sick) and let him so covenant that exceptions may be made, that he work not much in the hot weather, a course we alwayes take with our new hands (as they call them) the first year they come in.

If they are women that go after this manner, that is paying their own passages; I advise them to sojourn in a house of honest repute, for by their good carriage, they may advance themselves in marriage, by their ill, overthrow their fortunes; and although loose persons seldome live long unmarried if free; yet they match with as desolate as themselves, and never live handsomely or are ever respected. . . .

The Country is very full of sober, modest persons, both men and women, and many that truly fear God and follow that perfect rule of our blessed Saviour, to do as they would be done by; and of such a happy inclination is the Country, that many who in *England* have been lewd and idle, there in emulation or imitation (for example moves more then precept) of the industry of those they finde there, not onely grow ashamed of their former courses, but abhor to hear of them, and in small time wipe off those stains they have formerly been tainted with; yet I cannot but confesse, there are people wicked enough (as what Country is free) for we know some natures will never be reformed, but . . . if any be known, either to prophane the Lords day or his Name, be found drunk, commit whoredome, scandalize or disturb his neighbour, or give offence to the world by living suspiciously in any bad courses; there are for each of these, severe and wholesome laws and remedies made. . . .

The profit of the country is either by their labour, their stockes, or their trades.

By their labours is produced corne and Tobacco, and all other growing provisions, and this Tobacco however now low-rated, yet a good maintenance may be had out of it, (for they have nothing of necessity but cloathing to purchasse) or can this mean price of Tobacco long hold, for these reasons, First that in England it is prohibited, next that they have attained of late those sorts equall with the best Spanish, Thirdly that the sicknesse in Holland is decreasing, which hath been a great obstruction to the sail of Tobacco. . . .

Of the increase of cattle and hoggs, much advantage is made, by selling biefe, porke, and bacon, and butter &c. either to shipping, or to send to the Barbadoes, and other Islands, and he is a very poor man that hath not sometimes provision to put off.

By trading with Indians for Skine, Beaver, Furres and other commodities oftentimes good profits are raised; The Indians are in absolute subjection to the English, so that they both pay tribute to them and receive all their severall king from them, and as one dies they repair to the English for a successor, so that none neede doubt it a place of securitie.

Several ways of advancement there are and imployments both for the learned and laborer, recreation for the gentry, traffique for the adventurer, congregations for the ministrie (and oh that God would stir, up the hearts of more to go over, such as would teach good doctrine, and not paddle in faction, or state matters; they could not want maintenance, they would find an assisting, an imbracing, a conforming people.)

It is knowne (such preferment hath this Country rewarded the industrious with) that some from being wool-hoppers and of as mean and meaner imployment in England have there grown great merchants, and attained to the most eminent advancements the Country afforded.

Questions

1. In what ways is Hammond's account congruent with what will later be called the "myth of success" in America? Is his appeal similar to appeals made to immigrants in later times?

2. Do portions of Hammond's description accurately reflect conditions that prevailed in the seventeenth-century Chesapeake? Are there hints in his description that might alert the would-be indentured servant that things were not going well in Virginia and Maryland?

3. Were there, as Hammond claimed, "several ways of advancement" in the seventeenth-century Chesapeake? Explain.

Questions for Further Thought

1. Compare John Hammond's description of the life of "Servants that will be industrious" (Document 2-6) with the Virginia General Court's record of the experiences of "divers servants that run away" (Document 2-5). How do you explain the differences? Are there any underlying similarities?

2. Having lived in Virginia and Maryland for some time, Hammond must have been familiar with the actions of masters and servants. Was he merely ignoring the problem posed by runaways?

3. Based on your reading of these documents and chapter 2 of your text, do you think that life in the seventeenth-century Chesapeake was especially harsh? What points of comparison can you make with the rest of the seventeenth-century colonial world?

Puritan New England

If Virginia was founded primarily as a capitalistic, moneymaking venture, New England was launched primarily to serve religious purposes. Other kinds of colonies would sooner or later appear in the region, but the stamp of Puritanism came first. The Puritans, or non-Separatists (Puritans remained members of the Church of England or Anglican

Church), came to America to perfect the Protestant Reformation, a task they felt had been thwarted at home by the leaders of the Anglican Church. Most of their Calvinist theology had been worked out earlier in England. Puritans believed in "predestination"; only a few—the elect—could expect God's redemption on Judgment Day. While Puritans thus did not believe that one could *achieve* salvation, they did maintain that God's grace was displayed in the life of an individual through his actions (works) and the intensity of his belief (faith).

In many ways, then, Puritans looked both forward and backward. On the one hand, they believed, like their European predecessors, that all human institutions—the church, the state, the family—were ordained of God to keep order among the people and to keep them strong in the faith. Such obedience to the community's leaders was especially important because the Puritans saw themselves as fulfilling a great historical mission (Document 2-7).

In the course of years the Massachusetts Bay colony and the other New England colonies clustering around it grew and prospered, thanks to high birthrates, low mortality rates, and a hardworking and enterprising population. This relatively stable society was both anchored and held together by strong family bonds. Fortunately for historians, New Englanders were dogged record keepers, and as Documents 2-8 and 2-9 illustrate, their records provide fascinating glimpses into the private world of parents and children in early Puritan society.

2-7   A Modell of Christian Charity (1630)

John Winthrop

John Winthrop (1588–1649) was the son of a prosperous member of the English gentry. Educated at Cambridge, as a young man he became a convert to Puritanism. In the 1620s economic depression shrank his farm income, and he moved to London to take a minor position in the court system. While there, he became increasingly distressed at what he viewed as the flagrant corruption and immorality pervading both the court of King Charles I and the Church of England under Archbishop William Laud, and he grew fearful of Charles's moves against leading Puritans and the Parliament. He joined with a small group of Puritans proposing to set up a commonwealth well away from England and its dangers and, after deciding to join the exodus himself, was elected governor. In 1630 he sailed with the first group of settlers on the ship *Arbella*. While en route, he delivered the following sermon to his fellow passengers, warning them that, unlike other colonists, they were not to pursue private gain but to be an example to the world of what a truly godly society should be—in the terms of scripture, a "City upon a Hill" (Matthew 5:14).

Source: John Winthrop, "A Modell of Christian Charity," in *The Puritans*, ed. Perry Miller and Thomas H. Johnson, rev. ed. (New York: Harper and Row, 1963), 1:195–199. Copyright © 1963 by Thomas H. Johnson. Reprinted with permission of HarperCollins Publishers.

Written
On Boarde the Arrabella,
On the Attlantick Ocean.
By the Honorable John Winthrop Esquire.
In His passage, (with the great Company of Religious people, of which Christian Tribes he was the Brave Leader and famous Governor;) from the Island of Great Brittaine, to New-England in the North America.
Anno 1630.

CHRISTIAN CHARITIE
A Modell Hereof

GOD ALMIGHTIE in his most holy and wise providence hath soe disposed of the Condicion of mankinde, as in all times some must be rich some poore, some highe and eminent in power and dignitie; others meane and in subieccion.

The Reason Hereof

1. Reas: *First*, to hold conformity with the rest of his workes, being delighted to shewe forthe the glory of his wisdome in the variety and differance of the Creatures and the glory of his power, in ordering all these differences for the preservacion and good of the whole, and the glory of his greatnes that as it is the glory of princes to haue many officers, soe this great King will haue many Stewards counting himselfe more honoured in dispenceing his guifts to man by man, then if hee did it by his owne immediate hand.

2. Reas: *Secondly*, That he might haue the more occasion to manifest the worke of his Spirit: first, vpon the wicked in moderateing and restraineing them: soe that the riche and mighty should not eate vpp the poore, nor the poore, and dispised rise vpp against their superiours, and shake off theire yoake; 2ly in the regenerate in exerciseing his graces in them, as in the greate ones, theire loue mercy, gentlenes, temperance etc., in the poore and inferiour sorte, theire faithe patience, obedience etc:

3. Reas: *Thirdly*, That every man might haue need of other, and from hence they might be all knitt more nearly together in the Bond of brotherly affeccion: from hence it appeares plainely that noe man is made more honourable then another or more wealthy etc., out of any perticuler and singuler respect to himselfe but for the glory of his Creator and the Common good of the Creature, Man; Therefore God still reserues the propperty of these guifts to himselfe as Ezek: 16. 17. he there calls wealthe his gold and his silver etc. Prov: 3. 9. he claimes theire seruice as his due honour the Lord with thy riches etc. All men being thus (by divine providence) rancked into two sortes, riche and poore; vnder the first, are comprehended all such as are able to liue comfortably by theire owne meanes duely improued; and all others are poore according to the former distribution. There are two rules whereby wee are to walke one towards another: JUSTICE and MERCY. These are allwayes distinguished in theire Act and in theire obiect, yet may they both concurre in the same Subiect in eache respect; as sometimes there may be an occasion of shewing mercy to a rich man, in some sudden danger of distresse, and allsoe doeing of meere Justice to a poor man in regard of some perticuler contract etc. There is likewise a double Lawe by which wee are regulated in our conversacion one towardes another: in both the former respects, the lawe of nature and the lawe of grace, or the morrall lawe or the lawe of the gospell, to omitt the rule of Justice as not propperly belonging to this purpose otherwise then it may fall into consideracion in some perticuler Cases: By the first of these lawes man as he was enabled soe withall [is] commaunded to loue his neighbour as himselfe vpon this ground stands all the precepts of the morrall lawe, which concernes our dealings with men. To apply this to the works of mercy this lawe requires two things first that every man afford his help to another in every want or distresse Secondly, That hee performe this out of the same affeccion, which makes him carefull of his owne good according to that of our Saviour Math: [7. 12.] Whatsoever ye would that men should doe to you. This was practised by Abraham and Lott in entertaineing the Angells and the old man of Gibea.

The Lawe of Grace or the Gospell hath some differance from the former as in these respectes first the lawe of nature was giuen to man in the estate of innocency; this of the gospell in the estate of regeneracy: 2ly, the former propounds one man to another, as the same fleshe and Image of god, this as a brother in Christ allsoe, and in the Communion of the same spirit and soe teacheth vs to put a difference betweene Christians and others. Doe good to all especially to the household of faith; vpon this ground the Israelites were to putt a difference betweene the brethren of such as were strangers though not of the Canaanites. 3ly. The Lawe of nature could giue noe rules for dealeing with enemies for all are to be considered as freinds in the estate of innocency, but the Gospell commaunds loue to an enemy. proofe[:] If thine Enemie hunger feede him; Loue your Enemies doe good to them that hate you Math: 5. 44.

This Lawe of the Gospell propoundes likewise a difference of seasons and occasions there is a time when a christian must sell all and giue to the poore as they did in the Apostles times. There is a tyme allsoe when a christian (though they giue not all yet) must giue beyond theire ability, as they of Macedonia. Cor: 2. 6. likewise community of perills calls for extraordinary liberallity and soe doth Community in some speciall seruice for the Churche. Lastly, when there is noe other meanes whereby our Christian brother may be releiued in this distresse, wee must help him beyond our ability, rather then tempt God, in putting him vpon help by miraculous or extraordinary meanes. . . .

1. For the persons, wee are a Company professing our selues fellow members of Christ, In which respect only though wee were absent from eache other many miles, and had our imploymentes as farre distant, yet wee ought to account our selues knitt together by this bond of loue, and liue in the exercise of it, if wee would haue comforte of our being in Christ, this was notoroius in the practise of the Christians in former times, as is testified of the Waldenses[1] from the mouth of one of the adversaries Aeneas Sylvius, mutuo [solent amare] penè antequam norint, they vse to loue any of theire own religion even before they were acquainted with them.

2ly. for the worke wee haue in hand, it is by a mutuall consent through a speciall overruleing providence, and a more then an ordinary approbation of the Churches of Christ to

---

[1] *Waldenses:* A heretical sect of Christians, dating from the twelfth century but extending into the Renaissance and centered in northern Italy; Protestants of Winthrop's time looked to the Waldenses as precursors of their own challenge to Rome. *Aeneas Sylvius* (1405–1464; later Pope Pius II) was among their great adversaries. The Latin phrase is followed by Winthrop's own translation.

seeke out a place of Cohabitation and Consorteshipp vnder a due forme of Government both ciuill and ecclesiasticall. In such cases as this the care of the publique must oversway all private respects, by which not onely conscience, but meare Ciuill pollicy doth binde vs; for it is a true rule that perticuler estates cannott subsist in the ruine of the publique.

3ly. The end is to improue our liues to doe more seruice to the Lord the comforte and encrease of the body of christe whereof wee are members that our selues and posterity may be the better preserued from the Common corrupcions of this euill world to serue the Lord and worke out our Salvacion vnder the power and purity of his holy Ordinances.

4ly for the meanes whereby this must bee effected, they are 2fold, a Conformity with the worke and end wee aime at, these wee see are extraordinary, therefore wee must not content our selues with vsuall ordinary meanes whatsoever wee did or ought to haue done when wee liued in England, the same must wee doe and more allsoe where wee goe: That which the most in theire Churches maineteine as a truthe in profession onely, wee must bring into familiar and constant practice, as in this duty of loue we must loue brotherly without dissimulation, wee must loue one another with a pure hearte feruently wee must beare one anothers burthens, wee must not looke onely on our owne things, but allsoe on the things of our brethren, neither must wee think that the lord will beare with such faileings at our hands as hee dothe from those among whome wee haue liued. . . .

Thus stands the cause betweene God and vs, wee are entered into Covenant with him for this worke, wee haue taken out a Commission, the Lord hath giuen vs leaue to drawe our owne Articles wee haue professed to enterprise these Accions vpon these and these ends, wee haue herevpon besought him of favour and blessing: Now if the Lord shall please to heare vs, and bring vs in peace to the place wee desire, then hath hee ratified this Covenant and sealed our Commission, [and] will expect a strickt performance of the Articles contained in it, but if wee shall neglect the observacion of these Articles which are the ends wee haue propounded, and dissembling with our God, shall fall to embrace this present world and prosecute our carnall intencions seekeing great things for our selues and our posterity, the Lord will surely breake out in wrathe against vs be revenged of such a periured people and make vs knowe the price of the breache of such a Covenant.

Now the onely way to avoyde this shipwracke and to provide for our posterity is to followe the Counsell of Micah,[2] to doe Justly, to loue mercy, to walke humbly with

our God, for this end, wee must be knitt together in this worke as one man, wee must entertaine each other in brotherly Affeccion, wee must be willing to abridge our selues of our superfluities, for the supply of others necessities, wee must vphold a familiar Commerce together in all meekenes, gentlenes, patience and liberallity, wee must delight in eache other, make others Condicions our owne reioyce together, mourne together, labour, and suffer together, allwayes haueing before our eyes our Commission and Community in the worke, our Community as members of the same body, soe shall wee keepe the vnitie of the spirit in the bond of peace, the Lord will be our God and delight to dwell among vs, as his owne people and will commaund a blessing vpon vs in all our wayes, soe that wee shall see much more of his wisdome power goodnes and truthe then formerly wee haue beene acquainted with, wee shall finde that the God of Israell is among vs, when tenn of vs shall be able to resist a thousand of our enemies, when hee shall make vs a prayse and glory, that men shall say of succeeding plantacions: the lord make it like that of New England: for wee must Consider that wee shall be as a Citty vpon a Hill, the eies of all people are vppon vs; soe that if wee shall deale falsely with our god in this worke wee haue vndertaken and soe cause him to withdrawe his present help from vs, wee shall be made a story and a byword through the world, wee shall open the mouthes of enemies to speake euill of the wayes of god and all professours for Gods sake; wee shall shame the faces of many of gods worthy seruants, and cause theire prayers to be turned into Cursses vpon vs till wee be consumed out of the good land whether wee are goeing: And to shutt vpp this discourse with that exhortacion of Moses that faithfull seruant of the Lord in his last farewell to Irsaell Duet. 30. Beloued there is now sett before vs life, and good, deathe and euill in that wee are Commaunded this day to loue the Lord our God, and to loue one another to walke in his wayes and to keepe his Commaundements and his Ordinance, and his lawes, and the Articles of our Covenant with him that wee may liue and be multiplyed, and that the Lord our God may blesse vs in the land whether wee goe to possesse it: But if our heartes shall turne away soe that wee will not obey, but shall be seduced and worshipp . . . other Gods our pleasures, and proffitts, and serue them; it is propounded vnto vs this day, wee shall surely perishe out of the good Land whether wee passe over this vast Sea to possesse it;

Therefore lett vs choose life,
that wee, and our Seede,
may liue; by obeyeing his
voyce, and cleaueing to him,
for hee is our life, and
our prosperity.

---

[2] *Micah:* One of the minor Old Testament prophets. The "Counsell" Winthrop quotes appears in Micah 6:8.

Questions

1. How do Winthrop's religious views shape his vision of the proper social order for the new colony?

2. Describe the covenant entered into by the colonists aboard the *Arbella*. What obligations do the colonists have to God? What dangers does Winthrop warn his shipmates to watch out for?

3. What does Winthrop mean when he says, "wee shall be as a Citty vpon a Hill, the eies of all people are vppon vs"? Who, in particular, might be watching for the success or failure of the colony, and why?

2-8   Puritan Family Law: The Case of John Porter Jr. (1646, 1664)

The ideal social order described by John Winthrop in Document 2-7 is hierarchical—"some highe and eminent in power and dignitie; others meane and in subieccion." This hierarchy, according to the Puritans, was divinely ordained and manifested itself in the well-ordered family. Children learned very early in life that the "father" and "mother" they were told to honor in the Fifth Commandment included "all our superiors," natural, ecclesiastical, and civil. Indeed, most Puritans believed that good order in the family was a precondition to good order in the church and state; as one of them explained, "Such as families are, such at last the church and commonwealth must be." Not surprisingly, ministers and magistrates made it their business to ensure the stability and order of family life. The first document here is an excerpt from a 1646 Massachusetts law concerning the discipline of children, and the second excerpt is a notorious case of filial misbehavior.

Sources: Robert H. Bremner, ed., *Children and Youth in America: A Documentary History* (Cambridge, MA: Harvard University Press, 1970), 1:38; and Nathaniel B. Shurtleff, ed., *Records of the Governor and Company of the Massachusetts Bay Colony* (Boston: From the Press of William White, Printer to the Commonwealth, 1854) 4, part 2:216–218.

(a) Massachusetts, 1646

If any child[ren] above sixteen years old and of sufficient understanding shall curse or smite their natural father or mother, they shall be put to death, unless it can be sufficiently testified that the parents have been very unchristianly negligent in the education of such children, or so provoked them by extreme and cruel correction that they have been forced thereunto to preserve themselves from death or maiming. . . .

If a man have a stubborn or rebellious son of sufficient years of understanding, viz. sixteen, which will not obey the voice of his father or the voice of his mother, and that when they have chastened him will not harken unto them, then shall his father and mother, being his natural parents, lay hold on him and bring him to the magistrates assembled in Court, and testify to them by sufficient evidence that this their son is stubborn and rebellious and will not obey their voice and chastisement, but lives in sundry notorious crimes. Such a son shall be put to death.

(b) The Case of John Porter Jr., 1664

John Porter, Junior, the sonne of John Porter, Salem, in the county of Essex, in New England, yeoman, being about thirty yeares of age, & of sufficient capacity to understand his duty unto his superiours, according to the fifth commandment, but he, being instigated by the divill, & his currupt heart destitute of the feare of God, did not only prodigally wast & riotuously expend about fower hundred pounds of money & goods committed to him by his Father, for his improvement in two voyages to the Berbadoes, & so for England, where by his evill courses he ran himself further into debt, (& was there imprisoned, from whence being relieved by the charitable assistance of some Friends of his Father,) all which debts his father did voluntarily discharge. After this, returning to New England, his parents entertained him with love & tenderness as their eldest sonne, & provided for him [what] was expedient & necessary. All these things have been clearly demonstrated to the Court: but notwithstanding the said John Porter, Junior, did carry himself very perversly, stubbornely, & rebelliously towards his naturall parents, who are persons of good repute for piety, honesty, & estate.

He called his father theife, lyar, & simple ape, shittabed. Frequently he threatned to burne his fathers house, to cutt downe his house & barne, to kill his catle & horses, & did with an axe cutt downe his fence severall times, & did set fire to a pyle of wood neere the dwelling house, greatly endangering it, being neere thirty roads [rods].

He called his mother Rambeggur, Gammar Shithouse, Gammar Pissehouse, Gammar Two Shoes, & told hir her tongue went like a peare monger, & sayd she was the rankest sow in the towne; & these abusive names he used frequently.

He reviled Master Hawthorne, one of the magistrates, calling him base, corrupt fellow, & said he cared not a turd for him.

He reviled, & abused, & beate his fathers servants, to the endangering of the life of one [of] them.

He was prooved to be a vile, prophane, & common swearer & drunkard; he attempted to stab one of his naturall brethren. All which things are prooved by the oathes of sufficient wittnesses upon record.

In this vile & unsufferable course he continued severall yeares, but more especially the two last yeares, sixty two & sixty three [1662 and 1663]. At length, his father. in the sence of his sonnes wickedness & incorriginlenes, & the dayly danger of himself, his estate, & family, by his meanes, sought releife from authority, first more privately, which was ineffectuall, & afterwards more publickly, before the County Court held at Salem, & by that Court was committed to the house of correction at Ipswich, where he was kept some time; & afterward, being set at liberty, did persist in his former wicked course, & being againe complained of by his father to the said Salem Court the fower and twentieth of the ninth moneth, 1663, where his offences being found to be of a high nature, he was committed to prison at Boston, there to remaine for a triall at the Court of Assistants, where he was called to answer upon the fowerth of March, 1663 [1664].

The complaints against him, the said Porter, were produced, the wittnesses brought face to face, & his charge prooved; also, his owne naturall father openly complained of the stubbornes & rebellion of this his sonne, & craved justice & releife against him, being over pressed thereunto by his unheard of & unparreled outrages before named. Unto which complaints the said John Porter, Junior, had liberty to answer for himselfe. He impudently denied some things, others he excused by vaine pretences, & some he owned, but gave no signe of true repentance; whereupon the said Court proceeded to give sentence against him, the summe whereof is, to stand upon the ladder at the gallowes, with a roape about his neck, for one hower, & afterwards to be severely whipt, & so committed to the house of correction, to be kept closely to worke, with the diet of that house, & not thence to be releast without speciall order from the Court of Assistants or the General Court, & to pay to the country as a fine two hundred pounds.

If the mother of the said Porter had not been over-mooved by hir tender & motherly affections to forebeare, but had joyned with his father in complaining & craving justice, the Court must necessarily have proceeded with him as a capitall offendor, according to our law.

By the Court
EDW: RAWSON, Secret[ary]

Questions

1. Was the intent of the 1646 Massachusetts law merely to frighten children into behaving properly? In what ways might parents have been the primary targets of the law?

2. Was John Porter Jr. punishable under the terms of the 1646 law? In what ways was he a prime candidate for capital punishment?

3. Is the 1646 law indicative of the fact that Massachusetts authorities were devoid of affection for children? How many children would you estimate were executed under the auspices of the 1646 law?

2-9   A Colonial Family's Ordeal (1713)

Cotton Mather

New England, unlike the Chesapeake, New France, and New Spain, was populated primarily by transplanted families. One estimate is that nearly 90 percent of the emigrants to Massachusetts during the Great Migration (1630–1642) traveled with family members. Coupled with high birthrates in a relatively healthy environment—mortality rates were not only conspicuously lower than in the Chesapeake but also lower even than in England itself—this preponderance of families accounted for two characteristics that made New England distinctive. First, it was remarkably stable from the outset; thus the social and political institutions established by the first generation shaped the New England experience for much of the remainder of the seventeenth century. Second, its population grew rapidly through natural increase rather than continued immigration; hence it developed a native-born majority early in its history.

Even New Englanders, however, were not immune to epidemic diseases. The following excerpt, taken from the diary of Cotton Mather in the fall of 1713, shows the struggles of one man to hold his family together in the midst of a devastating measles epidemic. A descendant of the most distinguished line of Puritan preachers and arguably the most influential religious figure of his generation, Mather (1663–1728) was by birth and accomplishment a bona fide member of the colony's elite. But he could not escape the ordeals of everyday life. The father of fifteen children, he outlived all but two.

Source: Cotton Mather, *Diary. 1709–1724* (Boston: Massachusetts Historical Society Collections, 7th Series, 8, 1912).

[October 18] G. D.[1] The Measles coming into the Town, it is likely to be a Time of Sickness, and much Trouble in the Families of the Neighbourhood. I would by my public Sermons and Prayers, endeavour to prepare the Neighbours for the Trouble which their Families are likely to meet withal.

G. D. The Apprehension of a very deep Share, that my Family may expect in the common Calamity of the spreading Measles, will oblige me to be much in pleading the Great Family-Sacrifice, that so the Wrath of Heaven may inflict no sad Thing on my Family; and to quicken and augment the Expressions of Piety, in the daily Sacrifices of my Family; and to lay hold on the Occasion to awaken Piety, and Preparation for Death, in the Souls of the children.

[October 24] On the 18 *d.* 8 *m.* a week ago, my Son *Increase* fell sick; about the Middle of the Week, the sickness appeared to be *Measles*. God graciously carries him thro' a gentle Visitation. But now, what Uneasiness is my Family to look for?

[October 26] G. D. The spreading Malady of the *Measles*, which to many proves a Grievous one, having entred my Family, I must in my Family-Sacrifices have an Eye to the Condition of my Family.

I must quicken the præparation of my Domesticks, for the unknown Issue of their Calamity.

And now, my Son *Increase* is on his Recovery, I must oblige him unto it, as his first Work, to draw up in writing, some special Resolutions, for the future Conduct of his Life.

[October 27] G. D. I have some Relatives at *Medford*, especially one Kinswoman languishing under incurable Sickness. If I can accomplish it, I would give them a Visit; and instruct them, and comfort them, and pray with them.

My desireable Daughter *Nibby*, is now lying very sick of the *Measles*.

[October 30] G. D. The Spreading of the Measles in the Town, which will prove an heavy Calamity, and is much worse to us Americans than it is in Europe, it adds exceedingly to the Difficulties of the Families, where they conflict with Poverty. I must have my Eye much upon these miserable Families, and do my best, that they may be provided for.

30 *d.* 8 *m. Friday*. This Day, my Consort [wife], for whom I was in much Distress, lest she should be arrested with the Measles which have proved fatal to Women that were with child, after too diligent an Attendence on her sick Family, was no doubt something before her Time, surprized with her Travail; But God favored her with a very easy Time; and about the middle of the Afternoon graciously delivered her, of both a Son and a Daughter; perfect and likely children, wherein I receive numberless Favours of God.

My dear *Katy*, is now also down with the *Measles*; in somewhat more favorable Circumstances, than those that have gone before her.

[November 1] *Lords Day.* This Day, I baptised my newborn Twins; and first secretly, then publickly, gave them up unto the Lord, and laid hold on His gracious Covenant for them. My Wife's vertuous Mother having worn the Name of *Martha*, the Relatives were fond of having the Daughter called so; which name also signifying, *Doctrix*, may the better suit (as my Father said) a *Doctor's* Daughter. I then thought, who was *Martha's* Brother; and that *Eleazar* was the same with *Lazarus*; and a priestly Name; and the Child must be led to look for the *Help of God*, which is in the Signification of the Name. I had also an excellent Uncle of that Name. So I called them, ELEAZAR and MARTHA.

[November 4] G. D. I would consider, whether I may not do well, to print a little Sheet, of Advice for sick persons, and Houses, and lodge it in the sick Families, as the Malady spreads, which is now likely to prove so grievous unto the Town. I am afraid, whether I shall gett Time, or no.

In my poor Family, now, first, my Wife has the *Measles* appearing on her; we know not yett how she will be handled.

My Daughter *Nancy* is also full of them; not in such uneasy Circumstances as her prædecessors.

My Daughter *Lizzy*, is likewise full of them; yett somewhat easily circumstanced.

My Daughter *Jerusha*, droops and seems to have them appearing.

My Servant-maid, lies very full and ill of them.

Help Lord; and look mercifully on my poor, sad, sinful Family, for the Sake of the Great Sacrifice!

[November 5] My little Son *Samuel* is now full of the Measles.

---

[1] *G. D.*: Good Device, embodying precepts of kindliness and practical Christianity.

[November 7] I sett apart this Day, as I had much Cause, and it was high Time, to do, for Prayer with Fasting before the Lord. Not only are my Children, with a Servant, lying sick, but also my Consort is in a dangerous Condition, and can gett no Rest; Either Death, or Distraction, is much feared for her. It is also an Hour of much Distress in my Neighbourhood. So, I humbled myself before the Lord, for my own Sins, and the Sins of my Family; and I presented before Him the great Sacrifice of my Saviour, that His wrath may be turned away from me, and from my Family; and that the Destroyer might not have a Commission to inflict any deadly Stroke upon us.

[November 8] This Day, I entertained my Neighbourhood, with a Discourse, on Joh. XVIII. II. *The Cup which my Father has given me shall not I drink it?* And, lo, this Day, my Father is giving me a grievous and bitter Cup, which I hop'd, had pass'd from me.

For these many Months, and ever since I heard of the venemous Measles invading the Countrey sixty Miles to the Southward of us, I have had a strong Distress on my Mind, that it will bring on my poor Family, a Calamity, which is now going to be inflicted. I have often, often express'd my Fear unto my Friends concerning it. And now, *the Thing that I greatly feared is coming upon me!*

When I saw my Consort safely delivered, and very easy, and the Measles appearing with favourable Symptomes upon her, and the Physician her Brother apprehending all to look very comfortably, I flattered myself, that my Fear was all over.

But this Day we are astonished, at the surprising Symptomes of Death upon her; after an extreme Want of Rest by Sleep, for diverse whole Dayes and Nights together.

To part with so desireable, so agreeable a Companion, a Dove from such a Nest of young ones too! Oh! the sad Cup, which my Father has appointed me! I now see the Meaning and the Reason of it, that I have never yett been able to make any Work of it, in Prayers and Cries to God, that such a Cup as this might pass from me. My Supplications have all along had, a most unaccountable Death and Damp upon them!

Tho' my dear Consort, had been so long without Sleep, yett she retain'd her Understanding.

I had and us'd my Opportunities as well as I could, continually to be assisting her, with Discourses that might support her in this Time, and præpare her for what was now before us.

It comforted her to see that her children in law were as fond of her, as her own could be!

God made her willing to Dy. God extinguished in her the Fear of Death. God enabled her to committ herself into the Hands of a great and good Saviour; yea, and to cast her Orphans there too, and to beleeve that He had merciful and wonderful Things to do for them.

I pray'd with her many Times, and left nothing undone, that I could find myself able to do for her Consolation.

[November 9] On Munday, between three and four in the Afternoon, my dear, dear, dear Friend expired.

Whereupon, with another Prayer in the melancholy Chamber, I endeavoured the Resignation to which I am now called, and cried to Heaven for the Grace that might be suitable to the calamitous Occasion, and carried my poor Orphans unto the Lord.

It comforts me to see how extremely Beloved, and lamented a Gentlewoman, I now find her to be in the Neighbourhood.

Much weakness continues on some of my other Children. Especially the Eldest. And the poor Maid in the Family, is very like to dy.

G. D. Oh! the Prayers for my poor Children, oh! the Counsils to them, now called for!

The particular Scriptures, I shall direct them to read! And the Sentences thereof to be gotten by heart.

[November 10] G. D. My Relatives, especially those of my deceased Consort, I will entertain with Books of Piety, that shall have in them a Memorial for her.

10 d. 9 m. This Day, in the midst of my Sorrowes and Hurries, the Lord helped me to præpare no less than two Sermons, for a public Thanksgiving, which is to be celebrated the Day after to morrow.

But I am grievously tried, with the threatning Sickness, on my discreet, pious, lovely Daughter *Katharin*.

And a Feavour which gives a violent Shock to the very Life of my dear pretty *Jerusha*.

Fresh Occasions of Supplication and Resignation!

[November 11] *Wednesday*. This Day, I interr'd the earthly part of my dear Consort. She had an Honourable Funeral.

[November 14] *Satureday*. This Morning, the first Thing that entertains me, after my rising, is, the Death of my Maidservant, whose Measles passed into a malignant Feaver, which has proved mortal to her.

Oh! the Trial, which I am this Day called unto in the threatning, the dying Circumstances of my dear little *Jerusha!* The Resignation, with which I am to offer up that Sacrifice! *Father, Lett that Cup pass from me. Nevertheless—*

The Two Newborns, are languishing in the Arms of Death.

[November 15] G. D. Tis a Time of much Calamity in my Neighbourhood, and a Time of much Mortality seems coming on. My public Prayers and Sermons must be exceedingly adapted for such a Time.

15 d. 9 m. *Lord's-day*. I am this day called unto a great Sacrifice; for so I feel my little *Jerusha*. The dear little Creature lies in dying Circumstances. Tho' I pray and cry to the Lord, for the Cup to pass from me, yett the glorious One carries me thro' the required Resignation. I freely give her up. Lord, she is thine! Thy will be done!

[November 16] Little *Jerusha* begins a little to revive.

[November 17/18] *Tuesday, Wednesday*. About Midnight, little *Eleazar* died.

[November 20] *Friday*. Little *Martha* died, about ten a clock, A.M.

I am again called unto the Sacrifice of my dear, dear, *Jerusha*.

I begg'd, I begg'd, that such a bitter Cup, as the Death of that lovely child, might pass from me. *Nevertheless!*—My glorious Lord, brought me to glorify Him, with the most submissive Resignation.

[November 21] *Satureday.* This Day, I attended the Funeral, of my two: *Eleazar* and *Martha*.

Betwixt 9 h. and 10 h. at Night, my lovely *Jerusha* Expired. She was two years, and about seven Months, old. Just before she died, she asked me to pray with her; which I did, with a distressed, but resigning Soul; and I gave her up unto the Lord. The Minute that she died, she said, *That she would go to Jesus Christ.* She had lain speechless, many Hours. But in her last Moments, her speech returned a little to her.

Lord, I am oppressed; undertake for me!

[November 22] G. D. It will be a great Service unto my Flock, for me to exemplify, a patient Submission to the Will of God, under many and heavy Trials, and a most fruitful Improvement of my Crosses. . . .

[November 23] G. D. My poor Family is now left without any Infant in it, or any under seven Years of Age. I must now apply myself with most exquisite Contrivance, and all the Assiduity imaginable, to cultivate my Children, with a most excellent Education. I have now singular Opportunities for it. Wherefore I must in the first Place, earnestly look up to the glorious Lord, who gives Wisdome, for Direction.

Questions

1. What was the context in which Mather understood the measles epidemic? What lessons did he draw from his family's affliction?

2. How did Mather respond to deaths and the prospect of death within his household? Did he respond differently as a father and as a pastor?

3. Would it surprise you to learn that in the midst of his family's distress Mather found the time to write and publish a medical pamphlet on measles? Why or why not? Mather's chief instruction to caregivers was patient submission and liberal doses of tea and honey. Was this medical or religious advice? Explain.

Questions for Further Thought

1. Some historians argue that the Puritans left a lasting mark on American culture, one that persists to the present day. From your reading of Documents 2-7 through 2-9, what particulars of the Puritan legacy can you identify?

2. Based on your knowledge of other colonial experiments in the Americas, was Puritan New England unique in its emphasis on religion as the guiding force in building a society?

3. Was Puritanism a positive or negative force in the life of the family? Explain.

The Eastern Indians' New World

Even before they began their trek across the Atlantic, European settlers conceived of the New World as a wilderness largely devoid of inhabitants. They were wrong, of course; but the indigenous inhabitants of the Chesapeake and New England colonies made much less intensive use of the land than did Europeans, a fact attributed by such European leaders as John Winthrop to their want of "civilization" (Document 2-10). Having marginalized the natives in their minds, the settlers proceeded to marginalize the Indians in fact, swamping the land with ever-growing numbers of people. Natives occasionally fought back, most fiercely in the cases of Opecananough's war on the Virginia colony in 1622 and Metacom's war on the New Englanders in 1675–1676; but such resistance invariably ended in failure and brutal suppression by the Europeans.

Most native peoples lived initially beyond direct contact with Europeans, but few escaped the consequences of their arrival. European diseases devastated Indian peoples and forced many to abandon their traditional communities and join other tribes. As Indians entered into the fur trade with Europeans, game became depleted and warfare between tribes became more common, fundamentally altering the Indian way of life. Finally, as Europeans penetrated into the interior, those natives who did not flee westward found themselves living among strangers in a land no longer their own, one in which they increasingly were forced to follow alien rules (Document 2-11). For Native Americans, it was as if the world in which they had grown up had been bewitched.

2-10   But What Warrant Have We to Take That Land? (1629)

John Winthrop

As John Winthrop wrestled with the question of whether to join the proposed colony of Massachusetts Bay, he committed his thoughts to paper, circulating them among his associates. These statements, which exist in several versions, are remarkable expositions of both the motives impelling Puritans to leave their homeland and the purposes to which they wished to put what they termed the American wilderness. One objection to their scheme concerned their right to invade a land already occupied by others. Winthrop's response to this objection sets forth, with standard Puritan logic, the dominant view of the English toward the native inhabitants.

Source: From John Winthrop, *General Considerations for the Plantation in New England, with an Answer to Several Objections*, in *Winthrop Papers* (Boston: Massachusetts Historical Society, 1931), 2:120.

Obj. 5. But what warrant have we to take that land, which is and hath been of long tyme possessed of others the sons of Adam?

Ans. That which is common to all is proper to none. This savage people ruleth over many lands without title or property; for they inclose no ground, neither have they cattell to maintayne it, but remove their dwellings as they have occasion, or as they can prevail against their neighbours. And why may not christians have liberty to go and dwell amongst them in their waste lands and woods (leaving them such places as they have manured for their corne) as lawfully as Abraham did among the Sodomites? For God hath given to the sons of men a twofould right to the earth; there is a naturall right and a civil right. The first right was naturall when men held the earth in common, every man sowing and feeding where he pleased: Then, as men and cattell increased, they appropriated some parcells of ground by enclosing and peculiar manurance, and this in tyme got them a civil right. Such was the right which Ephron the Hittite had to the field of Machpelah, wherein Abraham could not bury a dead corpse without leave, though for the out parts of the countrey which lay common, he dwelt upon them and tooke the fruite of them at his pleasure. This appears also in Jacob and his sons, who fedd their flocks as bouldly in the Canaanites land, for he is said to be lord of the country; and at Dotham and all other places men accounted nothing their owne, but that which they had appropriated by their own industry, as appears plainly by Abimelech's servants, who in their own countrey did often contend with Isaac's servants about wells which they had digged; but never about the lands which they occupied. So likewise betweene Jacob and Laban; he would not take a kidd of Laban's without speciall contract; but he makes no bargaine with him for the land where he fedd. And it is probable that if the countrey had not been as free for Jacob as for Laban, that covetuous wretch would have made his advantage of him, and have upbraided Jacob with it as he did with the rest. 2dly, There is more than enough for them and us. 3dly, God hath consumed the natives with a miraculous plague, whereby the greater part of the country is left voide of inhabitants. 4thly, We shall come in with good leave of the natives.

Questions

1. By what right does Winthrop believe the English settlers are entitled to the Indians' lands? What authority does Winthrop invoke?

2. What attitudes toward the Native Americans does Winthrop exhibit? Do you think that these attitudes were typical of all English settlers? Explain.

3. Winthrop (a lawyer) argues that there are two different rights to the use of land: a "natural" right and a "civil" right. What does he mean by this, and how does it affect his response to the question in the title of this document?

2-11   Puritan Attack on the Pequots at Mystic River (1637)

John Underhill

The rapid growth of the colonial settlements in New England initiated a series of contests for land and dominion, pitting the English against the local Indians and altering relations among the natives themselves. The Pequot War in 1637 was the first major conflict involving the Puritan military forces and one of the most powerful Indian tribes of the region. Open warfare had actually begun in September of 1636, when Captain John Endicott, commanding some ninety Massachusetts volunteers, destroyed the Pequot community on Block Island (off the Rhode Island coast). Minor retaliatory skirmishes set in motion plans for a full-scale assault against the Pequots. In April 1637, after securing an alliance with the Narragansetts, another of the powerful New England tribes, the provincial assembly of Massachusetts called for an expedition against the Pequots. But Connecticut had already mobilized a force of Englishmen under the command of Captain John Mason. On May 26, with the assistance of several hundred Narragansetts, Mason's men launched a predawn attack on the Pequots at Mystic River. Because most of the warriors were away at the time, the village was occupied primarily by women, old men, and children. Nevertheless, Mason and his troops encircled the "fort" and proceeded to set fire to the houses. Those who tried to flee the inferno were shot by Mason's men. In less than an hour, all but seven of the villagers were dead. Estimates of the total number of Pequots killed that morning ranged between 300 and 700; two Englishmen were killed and perhaps twenty wounded. Captain John Underhill, who participated in the attack, illustrated the episode for his 1638 publication, *Newes from America*.

Source: John Underhill, *Newes from America; Or, A New and Experimentall Discoverie of New England* (London: Printed by I. D[awson] for Peter Cole, 1638). Library of Congress, Prints and Photographs Division, LC-USZ62-32055.

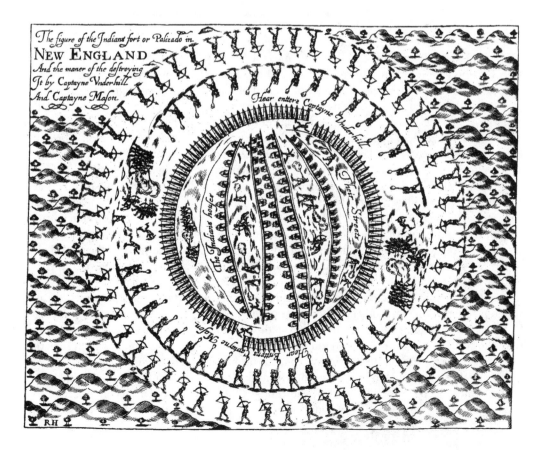

Questions

1.   Based on Underhill's illustration, what are you able to conclude about the attack on the Pequot village? Were unarmed Pequots shot? Was this a massacre?

2.   The Narragansetts formed a second line, or outer circle, of attackers; consequently, most of the killing was probably done by the Connecticut troops. What might explain this arrangement?

3.   Does the fact that Underhill was a participant in the 1637 attack make his illustration more or less credible? Explain.

2-12   Persecutions Excited Against Us (1640)

Jerome Lalemant

The Jesuits were members of the Society of Jesus, a religious order founded by Ignatius of Loyola in 1534, and from the start they were engaged in missionary activities aimed at making converts among "heathen" populations around the world. In New France in the early seventeenth century, the Jesuits lived among the Algonquin and Iroquois peoples, learned the local languages, and made observations that went beyond matters strictly religious. The bulk of these observations were contained in letters written by missionaries in the field which, after being edited by superiors in Quebec and Paris, were published annually in reports known as the *Jesuit Relations*. In the excerpt below, Father Jerome Lalemant describes the Huron response to the devastating impact of the 1639 smallpox epidemic.

Source: Excerpts from Jerome Lalemant, "Of the Persecutions Excited Against Us," in *Jesuit Relations and Allied Documents*, ed. Reuben Gold Thwaites (Cleveland, OH: Burrows Brothers, 1896), 19: 91–97.

The villages nearer to our new house having been the first ones attacked, and most afflicted, the devil did not fail to seize his opportunity for reawakening all the old imaginations, and causing the former complaints of us, and of our sojourn in these quarters, to be renewed; as if it were the sole cause of all their misfortunes, and especially of the sick. They no longer speak of aught else, they cry aloud that the French must be massacred. These barbarians animate one another to that effect; the death of their nearest relatives takes away their reason, and increases their rage against us so strongly in each village that the best informed can hardly believe that we can survive so horrible a storm. They observed, with some sort of reason, that, since our arrival in these lands, those who had been the nearest to us, had happened to be the most ruined by the diseases, and that the whole villages of those who had received us now appeared utterly exterminated; and certainly, they said, the same would be the fate of all the others if the course of this misfortune were not stopped by the massacre of those who were the cause of it. This was a common opinion, not only in private conversation but in the general councils held on this account, where the plurality of the votes went for our death, — there being only a few elders who thought they greatly obliged us by resolving upon banishment.

What powerfully confirmed this false imagination was that, at the same time, they saw us dispersed throughout the country, — seeking all sorts of ways to enter the cabins, instructing and baptizing those most ill with a care which they had never seen. No doubt, they said, it must needs be that we had a secret understanding with the disease (for they believe that it is a demon), since we alone were all full of life and health, although we constantly breathed nothing but a totally infected air, — staying whole days close by the side of the most foul-smelling patients, for whom every one felt horror; no doubt we carried the trouble with us, since, wherever we set foot, either death or disease followed us.

In consequence of all these sayings, many had us in abomination; they expelled us from their cabins, and did not allow us to approach their sick, and especially children: not even to lay eyes on them, — in a word, we were dreaded as the greatest sorcerers on earth.

Wherein truly it must be acknowledged that these poor people are in some sense excusable. For it has happened very often, and has been remarked more than a hundred times, that where we were most welcome, where we baptized most people, there it was in fact where they died the most; and, on the contrary, in the cabins to which we were denied entrance, although they were sometimes sick to extremity, at the end of a few days one saw every person prosperously cured. . . . I will only say in passing,—with reference to the little children who were in danger of death, and who were nowise guilty of the refusal which their parents often made us, to approach them,—that hardly did a dozen of them die without receiving their passport for going to heaven, during the time when we had free access to the villages,—the zeal and the charity of our evangelistic laborers having been more industrious and more active to procure them this happiness than the rage and the hatred of the devil to hinder them.

The reasons which we have thus far adduced, on account of which the barbarians suspect us of being the cause of their diseases, seem to have some foundation; but the devil did not stop there,—it would be a miracle if he did not build the worst of his calumnies on sheer lies.

Robert le Coq, one of our domestics, had returned from Kébec in a state of sickness which caused as much horror as compassion to all those who had courage enough to examine the ulcers with which all his limbs were covered. Never would a Huron have believed that a body so filled with miseries could have returned to health; regarding him then as good as dead, there were found slanderers so assured in their falsehood that they publicly maintained that this young Frenchman had told them in confidence that the Jesuits alone were the authors and the cause of the diseases which from year to year kept depopulating the country; that he had discovered our mysteries, and the most hidden secrets of our enchantments. Some said that we nourished, in a retired place of our house, a certain serpent of which their fables make mention, and that this was the disease. Others said that it was a kind of toad, all marked with pits, and that somebody had even perceived it. Certain ones made out that this disease was a somewhat more crafty demon; and, by what they said, we kept it concealed in the barrel of an arquebus [matchlock gun], and thence it was easy for us to send it wherever we would. They reported a thousand like fables, and all that was held to be true, since it proceeded, they said, from the very lips of a Frenchman, who before his death had rendered this good office to the whole country of the Hurons,—of apprising them of so black a magic, by which in fact all their villages appeared to be desolated. Those were the most powerful weapons with which they combated us; this was the imperative reason which made us all criminals. The surrounding nations were soon informed of this; everybody was imbued with it, and even the children, as well as the fathers, in whatever place we might go to, favored in that matter the definite decree for our death.

Questions

1. Not surprisingly, given the time and its author, Lalemant's account was full of distortions. But what was accurately conveyed in his description of the progress of the epidemic? Why is this significant?

2. What lessons did Lalemant hope to communicate to his readers? To what themes, positive and negative, were they likely to respond?

3. Is it possible to decipher the Indians' voice in Lalemant's report? Were they merely objects acted upon by the Jesuits?

Questions for Further Thought

1. From your reading of Document 2-10, how did the European settlers define the word *property*? How does this compare with the way the Native Americans understood ownership of the land?

2. Was there anything that the Indians could have done to live in peace with the white settlers? Or was the cultural divide too great for finding common ground? Defend your answer.

3. Based on the readings, draw up a list of white cultural attitudes toward the Native Americans. How might Native Americans have seen the white settlers?

CHAPTER THREE

The British Empire in America

1660–1750

The Politics of Empire, 1660–1713

By 1660 England had established a series of colonies in America but did not have a system in place for controlling them. Over the next quarter century, the Stuarts would tighten their control economically and politically. A generous and extravagant man, Charles II rewarded his supporters with millions of acres of land by creating proprietorships in New York, New Jersey, the Carolinas, and Pennsylvania. For example, eight noble supporters of King Charles were granted an extensive tract of land between Virginia and Spanish Florida that they named Carolina after the Latin form (*Carolus*) of the king's name. Except for the requirement that the colonies conform broadly to the laws of England, the proprietors could do as they pleased with their vast domains.

Although the king doled out land liberally to pay his political and financial debts, he kept tight control over colonial trade, which was an important source of royal revenue. Following a pattern established by the Navigation Act of 1651, Charles II and several English governments enacted a series of measures designed to confer on England the full benefit of colonial trade while excluding the Dutch.

The new mercantilism constituted a successful trade policy but was resented as an intrusion into the colonies' internal affairs. The Stuart monarchs then went a step further to establish political control. With the accession to the throne of James II in 1685, the charters of Rhode Island and Connecticut were revoked; the two colonies were merged with the Massachusetts Bay and Plymouth colonies to form a new royal province, the Dominion of New England. Two years later New York and New Jersey were added, creating a political unit that extended from Maine to the Hudson River. The dominion represented a new kind of authoritarian administration that attacked local institutions by abolishing legislative assemblies and town meetings, levying arbitrary taxes, and challenging land titles under the original charters. The Glorious Revolution of 1688 in England triggered a series of insurrections in the colonies (Document 3-2). Local differences, including ethnic rivalry in New York and Protestant–Catholic conflict in Maryland, influenced the causes and outcomes. But everywhere the rebellions marked a turning point in the history of the colonies. They ended authoritarian rule and brought both a new era of political stability and an imperial presence limited mainly to the supervision of colonial trade.

3-1   The Groans of the Plantations (1689)

Edward Littleton

In the second half of the seventeenth century, the sugar-producing islands of the West Indies were the richest colonies in British America, and Barbados was easily the most valuable of them all. It alone accounted for about 60 percent of West Indian sugar exports annually. In 1680, sugar shipments from Barbados to England were worth more than the total exports from all of the North American colonies combined. Not surprisingly, Parliament was keenly interested in maintaining its control over the political and economic affairs of this important source of imperial revenue. Equally unsurprising was the response of the Barbadian planters to what they perceived to be unwarranted impositions on their well-being, especially the heavy taxes levied on sugar. One of these planters, Edward Littleton, who in 1689 had recently settled in England, wrote *The Groans of the Plantations* as a protest against imperial policies. In his pamphlet, Littleton sought an answer to a basic question troubling colonists on the mainland as well: Were transplanted Englishmen entitled to all of the rights of Englishmen at home?

Source: Excerpts from Edward Littleton, "The Groans of the Plantations," in *Great Britain and the American Colonies, 1606–1763*, ed. Jack P. Greene (Columbia: University of South Carolina Press, 1970), 101–112.

In former daies we were under the pleasing sound of Priviledges and Immunities, of which a free Trade was one, though we counted That, a Right and not a Priviledge. But without such Encouragements, the Plantations had been still wild Woods. Now those things are vanisht and forgotten: and we hear of nothing but Taxes and Burdens. All the Care now is, to pare us close, and keep us low. We dread to be mention'd in an Act of Parliament; because it is alwaies to do us Mischief. . . .

The Improvement of the Plantations to the advantage of *England* sounds so bravely, and seems to the Projectors a thing so plausible; that they would have it believed to be their chief Aim and End, in all that they do against us. And then they think they talk very wisely, when they talk of Improving the Plantations to the advantage of *England.* Just as a Landlord would improve his Mannor, by racking his Lands to the utmost Rent. Or as the Masters of Slaves, improve and contrive their Labour to their own best advantage. But it is our misery and ruin to be thus improved. And so it would be to the Counties of Wales, or any *English* Counties, to be improved to the advantage of the rest. . . .

The Projectors might think, in the Naughtiness of their hearts, that many would favour this Project against us, for their owne Ease: and would be willing, or at least content, to have the Plantations bear the whole Burden. Not caring how heavy the burden lay upon others, so they could shift it off from themselves. But this is a thing of so great baseness, that we are very confident, it cannot enter into the heart of any English man, the Projectors themselves excepted. At least there is no English Parliament but will put it far from them. They know that they are entrusted to do equal and righteous Things. They know that the raising of Money is one of the most important things in a State. If it be done equally, though the burden be heavy, yet it is born with cheerfulness.

If otherwise, it occasions furious Discontents, and at last brings all to Confusion. When a Government falls once to shifting and sharking, (pardon the expression, I hope we are not concern'd in it'); it is a great sign that that Government will not stand. No Society of Men can stand without equal Justice, which is the Lady and Queen of all the Vertues. If the equal dividing the common Booties, be necessary to Pirates and *Buccaneers*; the equal distribution of publique Burdens, is much more to a State.

Suppose a Quantity of Land were gain'd here out of the Sea, by private Adventurers, as bigg as two or three Counties. (Never say that the thing is impossible; for we may suppose any thing.) Suppose also, that people went by degrees from all parts of *England*, to inhabit and cultivate this New Country. Would you now look upon these people as Forrainers and Aliens? Would you grudge at their Thriving and Prosperity, and ply them with all the methods of Squeezing and Fleecing? Would you forbid them all forrain Trade; and so burden their Trade to *England*, that their Estates should become worth nothing? Would you make them pay the full value of their Lands in Taxes and Impositions? It cannot be thought that you would do these things. Rather you would esteem the Country a part of *England*, and cherish the People as *English* Men. And why may not the Plantations expect the like Kindness and Favour? If the thing be duly weighed, They also are meer Additions and Accessions to *England*, and Enlargements of it. And our case is the very same with the case supposed. Only herein lies the difference, that there is a distance and space between *England* and the Plantations. So that we must lose our Country upon the account of Space; a thing little more then imaginary: a thing next neighbour to nothing.

Hitherto we have given some account of our deplorable Condition. But to afflict us yet more, we are told that we deserve no better usage, in respect of the great hurt and damage we do to *England*: as all new Colonies do. But then it had been more prudent, and likewise more just and merciful, rather to prevent the settling of the Plantations, then to ruine them now they are settled. The least signification that they were not pleasing, would have kept people at home. People would never have ventured their Estates and Lives, and undergone such Labours; to get the ill will of those, whose Favour they valued. Had this been the opinion alwaies concerning Colonies, it might pass for a Mistake in Judgment. But when We, who had all encouragement at first, shall as soon as we have got something, be accounted pernicious to our Country; we have reason to doubt, that this is only a pretence to oppress us, and not a real belief or sentiment. . . .

But we are very sure, that this Opinion concerning us (if any be really of it) is a great Mistake: and that the Plantations are not only not pernicious; but highly beneficial and of vast advantage to *England*.

We by our Labour, Hazards, and Industry, have enlarged the *English* Trade and Empire. The *English* Empire in *America*, what ever we think of it our selves, is by others esteemed greatly considerable.

We employ seven or eight hundred *English* Ships in a safe and healthy Navigation. They find less danger in a Voyage to our Parts, then in a Voyage to *Newcastle*. And as the Ships come safe, so the Men come sound. Whereas of those that go to the *East-Indies*, half the Ships Company (take one Ship with another) perish in the Voyage.

Let us now consider the further advantages of Trade, though the building, repairing, fitting and furnishing so many Ships, and the finding Cloths and Victuals for the Seamen, is a considerable Trade of it self. But moreover, there is hardly a Ship comes to us, but what is half loaden at least (many of them are deep loaden) with *English* Commodities.

Several Scores of Thousands are employed in *England*, in furnishing the Plantations with all sorts of Necessaries; and these must be supplied the while with Cloths and Victuals, which employs great numbers likewise. All which are paid, out of Our Industry and Labour.

We have yearly from *England* an infinite Quantity of Iron Wares ready wrought. Thousands of Dozens of Howes, and great numbers of Bills to cut our Canes; many Barrels of Nails; many Sets of Smiths, Carpenters, and Coopers Tools; all our Locks and Hinges; with Swords, Pistols, Carbines, Muskets, and Fowling Pieces.

We have also from *England* all sorts of Tin-ware, Earthen-ware, and Wooden-ware: and all our Brass and Pewter. And many a Serne of Sope, many a Quoyle of Rope, and of Lead many a Fodder, do the Plantations take from *England*.

Even *English* Cloth is much worn amongst us; but we have of Stuffs far greater Quantities. From *England* come all the Hats we weare; and of Shoos, thousands of Dozens yearly. The white Broad cloth that we use for Strainers, comes also to a great deal of Money. Our very *Negro* Caps, of Woollen-yarn knit, (of which also we have yearly thousands of Dozens) may pass for a Manufacture.

How many Spinners, Knitters, and Weavers are kept at work here in *England*, to make all the Stockings we wear? Woollen Stockings for the ordinary People, Silk Stockings when we could go to the price, Worsted Stockings in abundance, and Thread Stockings without number.

As we have our Horses from *England*; So all our Saddles and Bridles come from *England* likewise, which we desire should be good ones, and are not sparing in the price.

The Bread we eat, is of *English* Flower: we take great Quantities of *English* Beer, and of *English* Cheese and Butter: we sit by the light of *English* Candles; and the Wine we drink, is bought for the most part with *English* Commodities. Ships bound for the Plantations touch at *Madera*, and there sell their Goods, and invest the Produce in Wines.

Moreover we take yearly thousands of Barrels of *Irish* Beef: with the price whereof those people pay their Rents, to their Landlords that live and spend their Estates in *England*.

But still you persist in the opinion, that the Plantations do more hurt then good, and are pernicious to *England*. Truly if it be so, it were your best way to shake them off, and cleerly to rid your hands of them. And you must not be averse to this motion. For if you cry out that the Plantations do hurt, and yet are not willing to part with them, it cannot be thought that you are in earnest. You will say, this should have been done sooner. But if 'tis fit to be done, 'tis better done late then not at all. Have the Plantations robbed you of your People already? Let them rob you no more. A man will stop a leake in his Vessell, though some be run out.

We of the Plantations cannot hear the mention of being cast off by *England*, without regrett. Nevertheless if it must be so, we shall compose our Minds to bear it. And like Children truly dutifull, we shall be content to part with our dearest Mother, rather than be a burden to her.

Questions

1. What was mercantilism? Were Littleton's arguments squarely in line with mercantilist thought?

2. What assumptions did Littleton make about the establishment of Barbados as an English colony? What was the basis of his objections to parliamentary taxes? Did the North American colonists share Littleton's sentiments?

3. Littleton's pamphlet ended with a thinly veiled threat that Barbados might be forced to consider separating from England. Assuming that other Barbadians agreed with Littleton's appeal, does this suggest that Barbados was latently revolutionary in 1689?

3-2 The Glorious Revolution in Massachusetts (1689)

Thomas Danforth

When the Protestants William and Mary replaced James II as England's monarchs (see text pp. 74–76), New Englanders rebelled against Governor Edmund Andros, an unpopular governor who had been appointed by James II. The author of the following account, Thomas Danforth, had been a leading participant in the uprising. Although he seems to have been apprehensive about prosecution, none of the participants were punished. Danforth's correspondent, Increase Mather, had been sent to London to plead with James II for restoration of the colony's charter; he stayed on to negotiate a new charter with William and Mary.

Source: Thomas Danforth to the Rev. Increase Mather, 30 July 1689, in Thomas Hutchinson, *A Collection of Original Papers Relative to the History of the Colony of Massachusetts-Bay* (Boston, 1769), 567–571.

It is now fourteen weeks since the revolution of the government here. Future consequences we are ignorant of, yet we know that, at present, we are eased of those great oppressions that we groaned under, by the exercise of an arbitrary and illegal commission.

The business [i.e., the seizure of Governor Andros] was acted by the soldiers that came armed into Boston from all parts, being greatly animated by the Prince's [William of Orange] declarations, which about that time came into the country, and heightened by the oppressions of the governor, judges, and the most wicked extortion of their debauched officers. The ancient magistrates and elders, although they had strenuously advised to further waiting for orders from England, were compelled to assist with their presence and counsels for the prevention of bloodshed, which had most certainly been the result if prudent counsel had not been given to both parties. . . .

I am deeply sensible that we have a wolf by the ears. I do therefore earnestly entreat of you to procure the best advice you can in this matter that, if possible, the good intents of the people and their loyalty to the Crown of England may not turn to their prejudice. The example of England, the declarations put forth by the Prince of Orange, now our King, the alteration of the government in England making the arbitrary commission of Sir Edmund [Andros] null and void in the law; these considerations, in conjunction with the great oppressions the people lay under, were so far prevalent in the minds of all, that although some could not advise to the enterprise, yet are hopeful that we shall not be greatly blamed, but shall have a pardon granted for any error the law will charge us with in this matter.

We do crave that the circumstances of our case and condition in all respects may be considered. Nature has taught us self-preservation. God commands it as being the rule of charity toward our neighbor. Our great remoteness from England denies us the opportunity of direction for the regulation of ourselves in all emergencies, nor have we means to know the laws and customs of our nation. These things are our great disadvantage. We have always endeavored to prove ourselves loyal to the Crown of England. And we have also labored to attend the directions of our charter, under which were laid by our fathers the foundation of this His Majesty's colony; and we are not without hopes but that we shall receive from Their Royal Majesties the confirmation of our charter, with such addition of privileges as may advance the revenue of the Crown, and be an encouragement to Their Majesties' subjects here.

Questions

1. What justification does Danforth give for the rebellion?

2. What problems does Danforth fear may result from the rebellion?

3. What does Danforth hope the rebellion will achieve?

Questions for Further Thought

1. Why did the Restoration monarchs attempt to establish tighter control over the American colonies? Why had the crown not attempted this sooner?

2. How might the planters on Barbados have reacted to the Glorious Revolution in Massachusetts? What ideas were apparently held in common by the colonists in these two disparate colonies?

3. Which was more likely to increase the concerns of king and Parliament in 1689: the protests of the planters in the West Indies or the rebellion led by the Puritan establishment in Massachusetts? Explain.

The Imperial Slave Economy

The creation of a new agricultural system in America profoundly affected the history of four continents. Lands seized from Indians in North America and South America were used to raise sugar, tobacco, and other staples. These lands were worked by millions of slaves from Africa and triggered a commercial revolution in Europe. The impact on western Africa and parts of eastern Africa was tragic, as 10 to 12 million people were transplanted, draining Africa of its population and lowering its standard of living. The spiritual and cultural costs may have been higher, disrupting lives, encouraging tribal violence in a struggle for control over the slave trade, and transforming African political structures.

Although there were a few Africans in Virginia as early as 1619, they were not fully defined as slaves until, beginning in the 1660s, new statutes gradually began to designate them as chattel bound for life. Blackness was becoming a mark of inferiority. In the Chesapeake, as in the West Indies and later the Carolinas, the English built an economy based on slave labor (Documents 3-4 through 3-8).

Slavery was a brutal experience, from the initial capture in Africa, to the Middle Passage (Document 3-3), to a degrading life of labor in America. Sugar growing in the West Indies was the worst killer; the loss of life from disease and oppressive labor was staggering. The Chesapeake was less deadly to slaves. The cultivation of tobacco was less physically demanding and only modestly profitable, so planters had neither the need to constantly replace their labor force nor the resources to do so. In South Carolina, however, the death rate was high and the reproduction rate was low, so planters imported large numbers of Africans. Throughout the southern colonies, the growers of staple export crops turned slavery into a central feature of their economic and social systems.

3-3   A Journal of a Voyage Made in the *Hannibal* (1693–1694)

Thomas Phillips

England was a relative latecomer to the transatlantic trade in African slaves. It was only after the restoration of the Stuarts to the throne of England in 1660 that a powerful joint-stock company, known after 1672 as the Royal African Company, could emerge. The Royal African Company, which had a monopoly until 1698, established a network of trading stations along the African coast. In 1693, one Thomas Phillips entered the service of the company and undertook a slave-trading voyage as commander of the ship *Hannibal*. Phillips went first to Guinea, where he collected his cargo at the trading station of Whidaw (or Whydah), then set sail for Barbados. He completed the 4,000-mile journey in

November 1693 with 372 of his original cargo of 700 men and women still alive. Phillips's account of his journey, which follows, is remarkably vivid in its descriptions of both the business of slave trading and the horrors of the Middle Passage.

Source: Thomas Phillips, "A Journal of a Voyage Made in the *Hannibal* of London, Ann. 1693–1694, from England, to Cape Monseradoe, in Africa . . . ," in *Documents Illustrative of the History of the Slave Trade to America,* ed. Elizabeth Donnan (Washington, DC: The Carnegie Institution of Washington, 1930–1935), 1:398–403, 406–410. (Footnotes, except those ending with "Donnan's note," are from the Carnegie Institution edition.) Reprinted with permission.

May the 21st. This morning I went ashore at Whidaw, accompany'd by my doctor and purser, Mr. Clay, the present Capt. of the *East-India Merchant,* his doctor and purser, and about a dozen of our seamen for our guard, arm'd, in order here to reside till we could purchase 1300 negro slaves, which was the number we both wanted, to compleat 700 for the *Hannibal,* and 650 for the *East-India Merchant,* according to our agreement in our charter-parties with the royal African company; in procuring which quantity of slaves we spent about nine weeks. . . .

Our factory [at Whydah] lies about three miles from the sea-side, where we were carry'd in hamocks, which the factor Mr. Joseph Peirson, sent to attend our landing, with several arm'd blacks that belong'd to him for our guard; we were soon truss'd in a bag, toss'd upon negroes heads, and convey'd to our factory. . . .

Our factory built by Capt. Wilburne, Sir John Wilburne's brother, stands low near the marshes, which renders it a very unhealthy place to live in; the white men the African company send there, seldom returning to tell their tale: 'tis compass'd round with a mud-wall, about six foot high, and on the south-side is the gate; within is a large yard, a mud thatch'd house, where the factor lives, with the white men; also a store-house, a trunk for slaves, and a place where they bury their dead white men, call'd, very improperly, the hog-yard; there is also a good forge, and some other small houses. . . . And here I must observe that the rainy season begins about the middle of May, and ends the beginning of August, in which space it was my misfortune to be there, which created sicknesses among my negroes aboard, it being noted for the most malignant season by the blacks themselves, who while the rain lasts will hardly be prevail'd upon to stir out of their huts. . . .

According to promise we attended his majesty with samples of our goods, and made our agreement about the prices, tho' not without much difficulty; he and his cappasheirs[1] exacted very high, but at length we concluded as per the latter end; then we had warehouses, a kitchen, and lodgings assign'd us, but none of our rooms had doors till we made them, and put on locks and keys; next day we paid our customs to the king and cappasheirs, as will appear here-after; then the bell was order'd to go about to give notice to all people to bring their slaves to the trunk to sell us: this bell is a hollow piece of iron in shape of a sugar loaf, the cavity of which could contain about 50 lb. of cowries.[2] This a man carry'd about and beat with a stick, which made a small dead sound. . . .

When we were at the trunk, the king's slaves, if he had any, were the first offer'd to sale, which the cappasheirs would be very urgent with us to buy, and would in a manner force us to it ere they would shew us any other, saying they were the Reys Cosa,[3] and we must not refuse them, tho' as I observ'd they were generally the worst slaves in the trunk, and we paid more for them than any others, which we could not remedy, it being one of his majesty's prerogatives: then the cappasheirs each brought out his slaves according to his degree and quality, the greatest first, etc. and our surgeon examin'd them well in all kinds, to see that they were sound wind and limb, making them jump, stretch out their arms swiftly, looking in their mouths to judge of their age; for the cappasheirs are so cunning, that they shave them all close before we see them, so that let them be never so old we can see no grey hairs in their heads or beards; and then having liquor'd them well and sleek with palm oil, 'tis no easy matter to know an old one from a middle-age one, but by the teeths decay; but our greatest care of all is to buy none that are pox'd, lest they should infect the rest aboard. . . .

When we had selected from the rest such as we liked, we agreed in what goods to pay for them, the prices being already stated before the king, how much of each sort of merchandize we were to give for a man, woman, and child, which gave us much ease, and saved abundance of disputes and wranglings, and gave the owner a note, signifying our agreement of the sorts of goods; upon delivery of which the next day he receiv'd them; then we mark'd the slaves we had bought in the breast, or shoulder, with a hot iron, having the

---

[1] *Cappasheir:* A nobleman. [*Donnan's note.*]

[2] *Cowrie:* A seashell commonly used as money on the African coast. [*Donnan's note.*]

[3] *Reys Cosa,* or slaves of the king. Phillips, engaged in the English trade, Barbot, in the French trade, and Bosman, in the Dutch, all traded on the coast at the end of the seventeenth century and all have left somewhat detailed descriptions of the processes of trade which make possible a comparison of their trade and their dealings with the natives.

letter of the ship's name on it, the place being before anointed with a little palm oil, which caus'd but little pain, the mark being usually well in four or five days, appearing very plain and white after. . . .

When our slaves were come to the seaside, our canoes were ready to carry them off to the longboat, if the sea permitted, and she convey'd them aboard ship, where the men were all put in irons, two and two shackled together, to prevent their mutiny, or swimming ashore.

The negroes are so wilful and loth to leave their own country, that they have often leap'd out of the canoes, boat and ship, into the sea, and kept under water till they were drowned, to avoid being taken up and saved by our boats, which pursued them; they having a more dreadful apprehension of Barbadoes than we can have of hell, tho' in reality they live much better there than in their own country; but home is home, etc: we have likewise seen divers of them eaten by the sharks, of which a prodigious number kept about the ships in this place, and I have been told will follow her hence to Bardadoes, for the dead negroes that are thrown over-board in the passage. I am certain in our voyage there we did not want the sight of some every day, but that they were the same I can't affirm.

We had about 12 negroes did wilfully drown themselves, and others starv'd themselves to death; for 'tis their belief that when they did they return home to their own country and friends again.

I have been inform'd that some commanders have cut off the legs and arms of the most wilful, to terrify the rest, for they believe if they lose a member, they cannot return home again: I was advis'd by some of my officers to do the same, but I could not be perswaded to entertain the least thought of it, much less put in practice such barbarity and cruelty to poor creatures, who, excepting their want of christianity and true religion (their misfortune more than fault) are as much the works of God's hands, and no doubt as dear to him as ourselves; nor can I imagine why they should be despis'd for their colour, being what they cannot help, and the effect of the climate it has pleas'd God to appoint them. I can't think there is any intrinsick value in one colour more than another, not that white is better than black, only we think so because we are so, and are prone to judge favorable in our own case, as well as the blacks, who in odium of the colour, say, the devil is white, and so paint him. . . .

. . . When our slaves are aboard we shackle the men two and two, while we lie in port, and in sight of their own country, for 'tis then they attempt to make their escape, and mutiny; to prevent which we always keep centinels upon the hatchways, and have a chest full of small arms, ready loaden and prim'd, constantly lying at hand upon the quarter-deck, together with some granada shells; and two of our quarter-deck guns, pointing on the deck thence, and two more out of the steerage, the door of which is always kept shut, and well barr'd; they are fed twice a day, at 10 in the morning, and 4 in the evening, which is the time they are aptest to mutiny, being all upon deck; therefore all that time, what of our men are not employ'd in distributing their victuals to them, and settling them, stand to their arms; and some with lighted matches at the great guns that yaun upon them, loaden with partridge, till they have done and gone down to their kennels between decks: Their chief diet is call'd dabbadabb, being Indian corn ground as small as oat-meal, in iron mills, which we carry for that purpose; and after mix'd with water, and boil'd well in a large copper furnace, till 'tis as thick as a pudding, about a peckful of which in vessels, call'd crews, is allow'd to 10 men, with a little salt, malagetta, and palm oil, to relish; they are divided into messes of ten each, for the easier and better order in serving them: Three days a week they have horse-beans boil'd for their dinner and supper, great quantities of which the African company do send aboard us for that purpose; these beans the negroes extremely love and desire, beating their breast, eating them, and crying Pram! Pram! which is Very good! they are indeed the best diet for them, having a binding quality, and consequently good to prevent the flux, which is the inveterate distemper that most affects them, and ruins our voyages by their mortality: The men are all fed upon the main deck and forecastle, that we may have them all under command of our arms from the quarter-deck, in case of any disturbance; the women eat upon the quarterdeck with us, and the boys and girls upon the poop; after they are once divided into messes, and appointed their places, they will readily run there in good order of themselves afterwards; when they have eaten their victuals clean up, (which we force them to for to thrive the better) they are order'd down between decks, and every one as he passes has a pint of water to drink after his meat, which is serv'd them by the cooper out of a large tub, fill'd beforehand ready for them. . . .

When we come to sea we let them all out of irons, they never attempting then to rebel, considering that should they kill or master us, they could not tell how to manage the ship, or must trust us, who would carry them where we pleas'd; therefore the only danger is while we are in sight of their own country, which they are loth to part with; but once out of sight out of mind: I never heard that they mutiny'd in any ships of consequence, that had a good number of men, and the least care; but in small tools where they had but few men, and those negligent or drunk, then they surpriz'd and butcher'd them, cut the cables, and let the vessel drive ashore, and every one shift for himself. However, we have some 30 or 40 gold coast negroes, which we buy, and are procur'd us there by our factors, to make guardians and overseers of the Whidaw negroes, and sleep among them to keep them from quarrelling; and in order, as well as to give us notice, if they can discover any caballing or plotting among them, which trust they will discharge with great diligence: they also take care to make the negroes scrape the decks where they lodge every morning very clean, to eschew any distempers that may engender from filth and nastiness; when we constitute a guardian, we give him a cat of nine tails as a badge of his office, which he is not a little proud of, and will exercise with great authority. We often at sea in the evenings would let the slaves come up into the sun to air themselves, and make them jump and dance for an hour or two to our bag-pipes, harp, and fiddle, by which exercise to preserve them in health; but notwithstanding all our endeavour, 'twas my hard fortune to have great sickness and mortality among them. . . .

Having completed all my business ashore in fourteen days that I lay here, yesterday in the afternoon I came off with a resolution to go to sea. Accordingly about six in the evening we got up our anchors, and set sail for Barbadoes, being forc'd to leave the *East-India Merchant* behind, who could not get ready to sail in nine or ten days; which time I could not afford to stay, in respect to the mortality of my negroes, of which two or three died every day, also the small quantity of provisions I had to serve for my passage to Barbadoes. . . .[4]

We spent in our passage from St. Thomas to Barbadoes two months eleven days, from the 25th of August to the 4th of November following: in which time there happen'd much sickness and mortality among my poor men and negroes, that of the first we buried 14, and of the last 320, which was a great detriment to our voyage, the royal African company losing ten pounds by every slave that died, and the owners of the ship ten pounds ten shillings, being the freight agreed on to be paid them by the charter-party for every negroe deliver'd alive ashore to the African company's agents at Barbadoes; whereby the loss in all amounted to near 6560 pounds sterling. The distemper which my men as well as the blacks mostly die of, was the white flux, which was so violent and inveterate, that no medicine would in the least check it; so that when any of

our men were seiz'd with it, we esteem'd him a dead man, as he generally proved. I cannot imagine what should cause it in them so suddenly, they being free from it till about a week after we left the island of St. Thomas. And next to the malignity of the climate, I can attribute it to nothing else but the unpurg'd black sugar, and raw unwholesome rum they bought there, of which they drank in punch to great excess, and which it was not in my power to hinder, having chastis'd several of them, and flung over-board what rum and sugar I could find. . . .

The negroes are so incident to the small-pox, that few ships that carry them escape without it, and sometimes it makes vast havock and destruction among them: but tho' we had 100 at a time sick of it, and that it went thro' the ship, yet we lost not above a dozen by it. All the assistance we gave the diseased was only as much water as they desr'd to drink, and some palm-oil to anoint their sores, and they would generally recover without any other helps but what kind nature gave them.

One thing is very surprizing in this distemper among the blacks, that tho' it immediately infects those of their own colour, yet it will never seize a white man; for I had several white men and boys aboard that had never had that distemper, and were constantly among the blacks that were sick of it, yet none of them in the least catch'd it, tho' it be the very same malady in its effects, as well as symptoms, among the blacks, as among us in England, beginning with the pain in the head, back, shivering, vomiting, fever, etc. But what the small-pox spar'd, the flux swept off, to our great regret, after all our pains and care to give them their messes in due order and season, keeping their lodgings as clean and sweet as possible, and enduring so much misery and stench so long among a parcel of creatures nastier than swine; and after all our expectations to be defeated by their mortality. No gold-finders can endure so much noisome slavery as they do who carry negroes; for those have some respite and satisfaction, but we endure twice the misery; and yet by their mortality our voyages are ruin'd, and we pine and fret our selves to death, to think that we should undergo so much misery, and take so much pains to so little purpose.

I deliver'd alive at Barbadoes to the company's factors 372, which being sold, came out at about nineteen pounds per head one with another.

---

[4] Here follows a table giving daily observations of wind, weather, and the course of the vessel. Phillips reckoned it 4,075 miles to Barbados. Early in the voyage, fearing that his provisions would become exhausted, he limited the men to "short allowance of provisions, and to two quarts of water per man per day, boiling our provisions in salt water." It is difficult to see why Phillips failed to provide ample provisions unless he found it impossible to barter the goods he carried for food. He makes no mention of such difficulty save at Santiago.

Questions

1. What European attitudes toward black Africans does Thomas Phillips reflect? How might Africans have perceived the Europeans?

2. In what ways do Phillips's religious views affect his decisions aboard the *Hannibal*?

3. Describe the Middle Passage. How did the white slave traders exploit to their advantage the tribal differences among the Africans?

3-4   Slavery and Prejudice: An Act for the Better Order and Government of Negroes and Slaves, South Carolina (1712)

Until the early 1700s most legislation involving African Americans was concerned with the personal status of slaves and was motivated primarily by racial prejudice. Subsequently, another element came into play: fear of their growing numbers. The presence of a servile but potentially rebellious population made it seem necessary to adopt measures of control (see text p. 83). The act passed by South Carolina served as a model for slave codes in the colonial South and later in the southern states.

Source: Thomas Cooper and David J. McCord, eds., *Statutes at Large of South Carolina* (1836–1841), 7:352–357.

WHEREAS, the plantations and estates of this Province cannot be well and sufficiently managed and brought into use, without the labor and service of negroes and other slaves [i.e., Indians]; and forasmuch as the said negroes and other slaves brought unto the people of this Province for that purpose, are of barbarous, wild, savage natures, and such as renders them wholly unqualified to be governed by the laws, customs, and practices of this Province; but that it is absolutely necessary, that such other constitutions, laws and orders, should in this Province be made and enacted, for the good regulating and ordering of them, as may restrain the disorders, rapines and inhumanity, to which they are naturally prone and inclined, and may also tend to the safety and security of the people of this Province and their estates; to which purpose, . . .

II. . . . That no master, mistress, overseer, or other person whatsoever . . . shall give their negroes and other slaves leave . . . to go out of their plantations, except such negro or other slave as usually wait upon them at home or abroad, or wearing a livery; and every other negro or slave that shall be taken hereafter out of his master's plantation, without a ticket, or leave in writing, from his master or mistress, or some other person by his or her appointment, or some white person in the company of such slave, to give an account of his business, shall be whipped; and every person who shall not (when in his power) apprehend every negro or other slave which he shall see out of his master's plantation, without leave as aforesaid, and after apprehended, shall neglect to punish him by moderate whipping, shall forfeit twenty shillings. . . . And for the better security of all such persons that shall endeavor to take any runaway, or shall examine any slave for his ticket, passing to and from his master's plantation, it is hereby declared lawful for any white person to beat, maim or assault, and if such negro or slave cannot otherwise be taken, to kill him, who shall refuse to shew his ticket, or, by running away or resistance, shall endeavor to avoid being apprehended or taken.

III. And be it further enacted by the authority aforesaid, That every master, mistress or overseer of a family in this Province, shall cause all his negro houses to be searched diligently and effectually, once every fourteen days, for fugitive and runaway slaves, guns, swords, clubs, and any other mis-chievous weapons, and finding any, to take them away, and cause them to be secured. . . .

VI. And be it further enacted . . . That every master or head of any family, shall keep all his guns and other arms, when out of use, in the most private and least frequented room in the house, upon the penalty of being convicted of neglect therein, to forfeit three pounds.

IX. And be it further enacted by the authority aforesaid, That upon complaint made to any justice of the peace, of any heinous or grievous crime, committed by any slave or slaves, as murder, burglary, robbery, burning of houses, or any lesser crimes, as killing or stealing any meat or other cattle, maiming one the other, stealing of fowls, provisions, or such like trespasses or injuries, the said justice shall issue out his warrant for apprehending the offender or offenders, . . . he shall commit him or them to prison, or immediately proceed to tryal of the said slave or slaves . . . [and if] they shall find such negro or other slave or slaves guilty thereof, they shall give sentence of death, if the crime by law deserve the same. . . .

X. And in regard great mischiefs daily happen by petty larcenies committed by negroes and slaves of this Province, Be it further enacted by the authority aforesaid, That if any negro or other slave shall hereafter steal or destroy any goods, chattels, or provisions whatsoever, of any other person than his master or mistress . . . [if] adjudged [guilty is] to be publicly and severely whipped, not exceeding forty lashes; and if such negro or other slave punished as aforesaid, be afterwards, by two justices of the peace, found guilty of the like crimes, he or they, for such his or their second offence, shall either have one of his ears cut off, or be branded in the forehead with a hot iron, that the mark thereof may remain; and if after such punishment, such negro or slave for his third offence, shall have his nose slit; and if such negro or other slave, after the third time as aforesaid, be accused of petty larceny, or of any of the offences before mentioned, such negro or other slave shall be tried in such manner as those accused of murder, burglary, etc. are before by this Act provided for to be tried, and in case they shall be found guilty a fourth time of any the offences before mentioned, then such negro or other slave shall be adjudged to suffer death, or other punishment, as the said justices shall think fitting. . . .

XII. And It is Further enacted by the authority aforesaid, That if any negroes or other slaves shall make mutiny or insurrection . . . the offenders shall be tried by two justices of the peace and three freeholders . . . who are hereby empowered and required to . . . inflict death, or any other punishment, upon the offenders . . . if the Governor and council of this Province shall think fitting . . . that only one or more of the said criminals should suffer death as exemplary, and the rest to be returned to the owners.

Questions

1. What is the assumption of this act concerning the cultural level of the slave population?

2. What are the responsibilities and duties of slave owners in regard to governing their slaves?

3. What does the willingness of white South Carolinians to carry out sentences of death or mutilation on slaves, who represented a capital investment, imply about race relations at that time?

3-5   Conflicts between Masters and Slaves: Maryland in the Mid-Seventeenth Century (1658)

Almost from the beginning of Maryland and Virginia's slave history, as the first legislation defined the lifelong condition of slavery, colonists imposed harsher punishments against laborers of African descent than against white servants. Masters could, for example, whip a naked slave without breaking the law, and there were no laws requiring that food and clothing be provided to slaves. But there were limits to punishment and daily mistreatment of slaves, as the following case outlines. In the end, however, the case was referred to a higher court, where testimony was given that the slave, Tony, was a rogue and persistent runaway. At that point the court acquitted Overzee for cruelty against the slave.

Source: "Att a Provincial Court Held att St. Clement's Manor December 2, 1658," Provincial Court Proceedings, *Archives of Maryland* (Baltimore: Maryland Historical Society, 1941), 41:190–191.

ATT A PROVINCIAL COURT HELD ATT ST. CLEMENT'S MANOR DECEMBER 2, 1658

ATTORNEY GENERAL V. [SYMON] OVERZEE

Mr. William Barton informes the court against Mr. Symon Overzee, for that the said Overzee correcting his negro servant the said negro dyed under his said correction.

The examination of Hannah Littleworth aged 27 yeares or thereabouts taken the 27th of November 1658, before Philip Calvert, Esq.

This Examinant sayth that sometime (as shee conseives) in September was two yeares, Mr. Overzee commanded a negro (commonly called Tony) formerly chayned up for some misdemeanors by the command of Mr. Overzee (Mr. Overzee being then abroad) to be lett loose, and ordered him to goe to worke, but instead of goeing to worke the said negro layd himselfe downe and would not stirre. Whereupon Mr. Overzee beate him with some peare tree wands or tweiggs to the bignes of man's finger att the biggest end, which hee held in his hand, and upon the stubberness of the negro caused his dublett to be taken of, and whip'd him upon his bare back, and the negro still remayned in his stubbernes, and feyned himselfe in fitts, as hee used att former times to doe. Whereuppon Mr. Overzee commanded this examinant to heate a fyre shovel, and to bring him some lard, which shee did and sayth that the said fyre shovel was hott enough to melt the lard, but not soe hot as to blister anyone, and that it did not blister the negro, on whom Mr. Overzee powr'd it. Immediately thereuppon the negro rose up, and Mr. Overzee commanded him to be tyed to a Ladder standing on the foreside of the dwelling howse, which was accordingly done by an Indian slve, who tyed him by the wrist, with a piece of dryed hide, and (as she remembers but cannot justly say) that hee did stand uppong the grownd. And still the negro remayned mute or stubborne, and made noe signs of conforming himselfe to his masters will or command. And about a quarter of an howre after, or less, Mr. Overzee and

Mrs. Overzee went from home, and [she] doth not know of any order Mr. Overzee gave concerning the said negro. And that while Mr. Overzee beate the negro and powred the lard on him, there was nobody by, save only Mr. Mathew Stone, and Mrs. Overzee now deceased. And that from the time of Mr. Overzee and his wife going from him, till the negro was dead, there was nobody about the howse but only the said Mr. Mathew Stone, William hewes, and this examinant, and a negro woman in the quartering house, who never stir'd out. And that after Mr. Overzee was gone, upon the relation of Mr. Mathew Stone, in the presence of William Hewes that the negro was dying, this examinant desyred Mr. Mathew Stone to cutt the negro downe, and hee refused to doe it, William Hewes allso bidding him let him alone and within lesse then halfe a howre after the negro dyed, the wind com-ming up att northwest soone after hee was soe tyed, and hee was tyed up betweene three and fowre o'clock in the after-noone, and dyed about six or seaven. . . .

William Hewes sworne in upon court sayth that hee was present, att the time when Mr. Overzee beate the negro, and saw him allso powre lard upon him, and that as hee conceaves and remembers, he saw noe blood drawne of the negro, and this deponent being willing to help the negro from the growd, Mr. Overzee haveing his knife in his hand, cutting the twigs, threatened him to runne his knife in him (or words to that effect) if he molested him, and that the negro (as he think, but cannot justly say) stood up-pon the growd, and sayth further that the negro did com-monly use to runne away, and absent himselfe from his Mr. Overzees service.

Questions

1. What was Symon Overzee tried for? What were the excuses he gave, according to the witnesses?

2. What parts of the witnesses' testimony are unambiguous, and what parts might be dubious?

3. What is the tone of the testimony given? What might Tony have offered as a defense of his behavior?

3-6 An Early Slave Narrative (1734)

Ayubah Suleiman Diallo

Slave narratives before 1750 are rare. One that has survived is that of Ayubah Suleiman Diallo, a priest and merchant of the Senegal region of West Africa. Diallo was captured in 1730 and transported across the Atlantic in a slave ship; he was a slave on a Maryland plan-tation for two years before coming to the attention of Thomas Bluett, an English gentleman, and others, including James Oglethorpe, the philanthropist who played a leading role in the founding of Georgia (see text p. 95). These men took a personal interest in Diallo, with Oglethorpe putting up bond to allow him to leave for England and gentlemen there raising his purchase price and his transportation home to Africa. Clearly Diallo, or "Job" as he was known to his English friends, was a most unusual slave; furthermore, while a learned man, he relied on Bluett to render his story into English. Nonetheless, his story remains an im-portant early look at how the Atlantic slave system dealt with one caught up in its workings.

Source: Thomas Bluett, *Some Memoirs of the Life of Job, the Son of Solomon the High Priest of Boonda in Africa; Who was a slave about two years in Maryland . . .* (London: Printed for Richard Ford, at the Angel in the Poultry, over against the Compter, 1734), 12–24, 54–63.

SECT. I.

An Account of the Family of JOB; *his Education; and the more remarkable Circumstances of his Life, before he was taken Captive.*

JOB's Countrymen, like the Eastern People and some others, use to design themselves by the Names of their Ancestors, and in their Appellations mention their Progenitors several Degrees backward; tho' they also have Sirnames for distinguishing their particular Families, much after the same Manner as in *England.* JOB's Name, in his own Country, is HYUBA, BOON SALU-MENA, BOON HIBRAHEMA; *i.e. JOB,* the Son of *Solomon,* the Son of *Abraham.* The Sirname of his Family is *Jallo.*

JOB, who is now about 31 or 32 Years of age, was born at a Town called *Boonda* in the County of *Galumbo* (in our Maps *Catumbo*) in the Kingdom of *Futa* in *Africa;* which lies on both Sides the River *Senegal,* and on the south Side reaches as far as, the River *Gambia*. These two Rivers, JOB assured me, run pretty near parallel to one another, and never meet, contrary to the Position they have in most of our Maps. The Eastern Boundary of the Kingdom of *Futa* or *Senega* is the great Lake, called in our Maps *Lacus Guarde*. The Extent of it, towards the North, is not so certain. The chief City or Town of it is *Tombut*; over against which, on the other side of the River, is *Boonda*, the Place of JOB's Nativity.

About fifty Years ago *Hibrahim*, the Grandfather of JOB, founded the Town of *Boonda*, in the Reign of *Bubaker*, then King of *Futa*, and was, by his Permission, sole Lord Proprietor and Governor of it, and at the same Time High Priest, or *Alpha*; so that he had a Power to make what Laws and Regulations he thought proper for the Increase and good Government of his new City. Among other Institutions, one was, that no Person who flies thither for Protection shall be made a Slave. This Privilege is in force there to this Day, and is extended to all in general, that can read and know God, as they express it; and it has contributed much to the Peopling of the Place, which is now very large and flourishing. Some time after the Settlement of this Town *Hibrahim* died; and, as the Priesthood is hereditary there, *Salumen* his Son, the Father of JOB, became High Priest. About the same Time *Bubaker* the King dying, his Brother *Gelazi*, who was next Heir, succeeded him. *Gelazi* had a Son, named *Sambo*, whom he put under the Care of Salumen, JOB's Father, to learn the *Koran* and *Arabick* Language. JOB was at this Time also with his Father, was Companion to *Sambo*, and studied along with him. *Sambo*, upon the Death of *Gelazi*, was made King of *Futa*, and reigns there at present. When JOB was fifteen Years old, he assisted his Father as *Emaum*, or Sub-priest. About this Age he married the Daughter of the Alpha of *Tombut*, who was then only eleven Years old. By her he had a Son (when she was thirteen Years old) called *Abdolah*; and after that two more Sons, called *Hibrahim* and *Sambo*. About two Years before his Captivity he married a second Wife, Daughter of the Alpha of *Tomga*; by whom he has a Daughter named *Fatima*, after the Daughter of their Prophet *Mahommed*. Both these Wives, with their Children, were alive when he came from Home.

SECT. II.

Of the Manner of his being taken Captive; and what followed upon it, till his Return.

IN *February*, 1730. JOB's Father hearing of an *English* Ship at *Gambia* River, sent him, with two Servants to attend him, to sell two Negroes and to buy Paper, and some other Necessaries; but desired him not to venture over the River, because the Country of the *Mandingoes*, who are Enemies to the People of *Futa*, lies on the other side. JOB not agreeing with Captain *Pike* (who commanded the Ship, lying then at *Gambia*, in the Service of Captain *Henry Hunt*, Brother to Mr. *William Hunt*, Merchant, in *Little Tower-Street*, *London*) sent back the two Servants to acquaint his Father with it, and to let him know that he intended to go farther. Accordingly, having agreed with another Man, named *Loumein Yoas*, who understood the *Mandingoe* Language, to go with him as his Inter-

preter, he crossed the River *Gambia*, and disposed of his Negroes for some Cows. As he was returning Home, he stopp'd for some Refreshment at the House of an old Acquaintance; and the Weather being hot, he hung up his Arms in the House, while he refresh'd himself. Those Arms were very valuable; consisting of a Gold-hilted Sword, a Gold Knife, which they wear by their Side, and a rich Quiver of Arrows, which King *Sambo* had made him a Present of. It happened that a Company of the *Mandingoes*, who live upon Plunder, passing by at that Time, and observing him unarmed, rush'd in, to the Number of seven or eight at once, at a back Door, and pinioned JOB, before he could get to his Arms, together with his Interpreter, who is a Slave in *Maryland* still. They then shaved their Heads and Beards, which JOB and his Man resented as the highest Indignity; tho' the *Mandingoes* meant no more by it, than to make them appear like Slaves taken in War. On the 27th of *February*, 1730. they carried them to Captain *Pike* at *Gambia*, who purchased them; and on the first of *March* they were put on Board. Soon after JOB found means to acquaint Captain *Pike* that he was the same Person that came to trade with him a few Days before, and after what Manner he had been taken. Upon this Captain *Pike* gave him leave to redeem himself and his Man; and JOB sent to an Acquaintance of his Father's, near *Gambia*, who promised to send to JOB's Father, to inform him of what had happened, that he might take some Course to have him set at Liberty. But it being a Fortnight's journey between that Friend's House and his Father's, and the Ship failing in about a Week after, JOB was brought with the rest of the Slaves to *Annapolis* in *Maryland*, and delivered to Mr. *Vachell Denton*, Factor to Mr. *Hunt*, before mentioned. JOB heard since, by Vessels that came from *Gambia*, that his Father sent down several Slaves, a little after Captain *Pike* failed, in order to procure his Redemption; and that *Sambo*, King of *Futa*, had made War upon the *Mandingoes*, and cut off great Numbers of them, upon account of the Injury they had done to his Schoolfellow.

Mr. *Vachell Denton* sold JOB to one Mr. *Tolsey* in *Kent* Island in *Maryland*, who put him to work in making Tobacco; but he was soon convinced that JOB had never been used to such Labour. He every Day shewed more and more Uneasiness under this Exercise, and at last grew sick, being no way able to bear it; so that his Master was obliged to find easier Work for him, and therefore put him to tend the Cattle. JOB would often leave the Cattle, and withdraw into the Woods to pray; but a white Boy frequently watched him, and whilst he was at his Devotion would mock him, and throw Dirt in his Face. This very much disturbed JOB, and added to his other Misfortunes; all which were increased by his Ignorance of the *English* Language, which prevented his complaining, or telling his Case to any Person about him. Grown in some measure desperate, by reason of his present Hardships, he resolved to travel at a Venture; thinking he might possibly be taken up by some Master, who would use him better, or otherwise meet with some lucky Accident, to divert or abate his Grief. Accordingly, he travelled thro' the Woods, till he came to the County of *Kent*, upon *Delaware Bay*, now esteemed Part of *Pensilvania*; altho' it is properly a Part of *Maryland*, and belongs to my

Lord *Baltimore.* There is a Law in force, throughout the Colonies of *Virginia, Maryland, Pensilvania,* &c. as far as *Boston* in *New England,* viz. That any Negroe, or white Servant who is not known in the County, or has no Pass, may be secured by any Person, and kept in the common Goal, till the Master of such Servant shall fetch him. Therefore JOB being able to give no Account of himself, was put in Prison there.

This happened about the Beginning of *June,* 1731. when I, who was attending the Courts there, and had heard of JOB, went with several Gentlemen to the Goaler's House, being a Tavern, and desired to see him. He was brought into the Tavern to us, but could not speak one Word of *English.* Upon our Talking and making Signs to him, he wrote a Line or two before us, and when he read it, pronounced the Words *Allah* and *Mahommed*; by which, and his refusing a Glass of Wine we offered him, we perceived he was a *Mahometan,* but could not imagine of what Country he was, or how he got thither; for by his affable Carriage, and the easy Composure of his Countenance, we could perceive he was no common Slave.

When JOB had been some time confined, an old Negroe Man, who lived in that Neighbourhood, and could speak the *Jalloff* Language, which JOB also understood, went to him, and conversed with him. By this Negroe the Keeper was informed to whom JOB belonged, and what was the Cause of his leaving his Master. The Keeper thereupon wrote to his Master, who soon after fetch'd him home, and was much kinder to him than before; allowing him a Place to pray in, and some other Conveniencies, in order to make his Slavery as easy as possible. Yet Slavery and Confinement was by no means agreeable to JOB, who had never been used to it; he therefore wrote a Letter in *Arabick* to his Father, acquainting him with his Misfortunes, hoping he might yet find Means to redeem him. This Letter he sent to Mr. *Vachell Denton,* desiring it might be sent to *Africa* by Captain *Pike*; but he being gone to *England,* Mr. *Denton* sent the Letter inclosed to Mr. *Hunt,* in order to be sent to *Africa* by Captain *Pike* from *England*; but Captain *Pike* had sailed for *Africa* before the Letter came to Mr. *Hunt,* who therefore kept it in his own Hands, till he should have a proper Opportunity of sending it. It happened that this Letter was seen by *James Oglethorpe,* Esq; who, according to his usual Goodness and Generosity, took Compassion on JOB, and gave his Bond to Mr. *Hunt* for the Payment of a certain Sum, upon the Delivery of JOB here in *England.* Mr. *Hunt* upon this sent to Mr. *Denton,* who purchas'd him again of his Master for the same Money which Mr. *Denton* had formerly received for him; his Master being very willing to part with him, as finding him no ways fit for his Business. . . .

CONCLUSION;

Containing Some REFLECTIONS upon the whole.

One can't but take Notice of a very remarkable Series of Providence, from the Beginning of JOB's Captivity, till his Return to his own Country. When we reflect upon the Occasion and Manner of his being taken at first, and the Variety of Incidents during his Slavery, which, from slight and unlikely Beginnings, gradually brought about his Redemption, together with the singular Kindness he met with in this Country after he was ransomed, and the valuable Presents which he carried over with him; I say, when all these Things are duly considered, if we believe that the wise Providence of the great Author of Nature governs the World, 'tis natural for us to conclude that this Process, in the divine Oeconomy of Things, is not for nought, but that there is some important End to be served by it.

Our own imperfect Observations have discovered to us innumerable Instances of Design and Contrivance in the natural World; and tho' we cannot assign the immediate Causes and Ends of all the Phenomena of Nature, yet we know enough of them to convince us that the same uniform Design, the same wife and beautiful Order is carried on and maintained throughout the whole. And as there is a manifest Analogy between the Methods of Government in the natural and moral Worlds, so that they seem to be but as different Acts of the same grand Drama; and since the Providence of God is no less certain than his Existence, Chance being as unable to govern a World as to make one; we may safely, and on good Grounds infer, that the various Occurrences in human Life, however inconsiderable or perplex'd they may appear to us, are neither beneath the Care, nor inextricable to the Wisdom of him who rules the Universe: No; they have all their proper Places in the great Scheme; and all conspire in a regular Gradation, to bring about their several Ends, in Subserviency to the whole.

'Tis true, neither the Extent of our Lives nor Capacities will permit us to view any very great Part of the Works of God; and what we do see, we are too apt to put a wrong Construction upon, being unacquainted in a great measure with the secret Springs of Nature, and altogether unable to take in the vast Projects of infinite Wisdom: But the particular Scenes that we are sometime presented with, appear so full of deep Design, and are executed with such divine Art, that they cannot but strike the sober Part of Mankind with Impressions of the highest Wonder, and loudly call for the Attention of a reasonable Being.

History, and our own Experience, furnish us with several amazing Instances of the Conduct of Providence, as well as Nature; which, tho' they cannot be fully or equally accounted for by us, yet may be improved by a well-disposed Mind to very good Purposes; as they serve to increase the high Veneration which we all ought to have for the supreme Lord and Governor of the World, and naturally suggest to us our Dependance upon him; as they tend to confirm our Belief of a Providence, and encourage us to trust our selves intirely in the Hands of our Maker, which is the great Support of every good Man amidst the Calamities of this present Life. In short, as it is very happy for us that the Direction of all Events belongs to God; so we ought to take all Opportunities to excite and strengthen in our selves, and others, a due Sense of his Government, a becoming Regard to his Works, and just Sentiments of the Relation which we bear to him.

With some such Reflections as these JOB used to comfort himself in his Captivity; and upon proper Occasions, in Conversation, would speak very justly and devoutly of the Care of God over his Creatures, and particularly of the remarkable Changes of his own Circumstances; all which he piously ascribed to an unseen Hand. He frequently compared himself to *Joseph*; and when he was informed that the King of *Futa* had killed a great many of the *Mandingoes* upon his Account, he said, with a good deal of Concern, if he had been there he would have prevented it; for it was not the *Mandingoes*, but God, who brought him into a strange Land.

It would be Presumption in us to affirm positively what God is about to do at any Time; but may we not be allowed humbly to hope that one End of JOB's Captivity, and happy Deliverance, was the Benefit and Improvement of himself and his People? His Knowledge is now extended to a Degree which he could never have arrived at in his own Country; and the Instruments which he carried over, are well adjusted to the Exigencies of his Countrymen. Who can tell, but that thro' him a whole Nation may be made happy? The Figure which he makes in those Parts, as Presumptive High-priest, and the Interest which he has with the King of the Country, considering the singular Obligations he is under to the *English*, may possibly, in good time, be of considerable Service to us also; and we have reason to hope this, from the repeated Assurances we had from JOB, that he would, upon all Occasions, use his best Endeavours to promote the *English* Trade before any other. But whatever be the Consequences, we cannot but please our selves with the Thoughts of having acted so good and generous a Part to a distressed Stranger. And as this gives me occasion to recommend Hospitality, I cannot conclude, without saying something in favour of it.

Among the various Branches of Friendship and Beneficence, there is none of a more noble and disinterested Nature, or that tends more directly to the Union, and consequently the Subsistence of the human Species, than that of Hospitality and Kindness to Strangers. In many Instances of private Friendship, we are apt to be guided by our own private Inter-

est; and very often the Exchange of good Offices among Friends, is little better than mere Barter, where an Equivalent is expected on both Sides. In most Acts of Charity and Compassion too, we may be, and very often are wrought upon by the undue Influence of some selfish View, and thereby we destroy in good measure the Merit of them: But in shewing Pity to Strangers, as such, and kindly relieving them in their Distress, there is not such Danger of being influenced by private Regards; nor is it likely that we are so. Here we act for God's sake, and for the sake of human Nature; and we seem to have no Inducement superior to the Will of Heaven, and the Pleasure that results from the Consciousness of a generous Respect for our common Humanity.

There is something singularly sublime, and even Godlike, in this benevolent Disposition towards Strangers. The common Parent of the Universe pours out his Blessings daily upon all Mankind, in all Places of the Earth; the Just and the Unjust, the Rich and the Poor, all the Classes, all the Families of human Creatures, subsist by his Bounty, and have their Share of his universal Favours. The good hospitable Man, in his low Sphere, imitates his Maker, and deals about him to his Fellow Mortals with great Chearfulness. He considers his Species in one complex View, and wishes that his Abilities were as extensive as his Inclinations. He does not confine his Benevolence to his Relations, or any particular Party of Men; his Affections are too warm, too general to be thus circumscribed; they must range round the whole Globe, and exert themselves in all Places, where an Opportunity offers.

Such a happy Temper of Mind appeared eminently in those worthy Gentlemen that promoted and encouraged a Subscription for the Relief of JOB; and we hope there are many such Instances of Hospitality among us, which is one very honourable Part of the Character of the *English*.

Questions

1. What does this narrative tell us about the process of enslavement?

2. Some historians have seen the Middle Passage as producing a sharp break between the former lives of slaves and their new life in the New World. On the evidence of this narrative, how traumatic was the break between Africa and Maryland? Support your answer with details from the document.

3. At the end of this narrative, Diallo's English transcriber suggests that a moral lesson is to be learned from this story. Is it the moral lesson that comes to *your* mind? How might the transcriber's own understanding of the world affect the character of this narrative?

3-7   The Secret Diary of William Byrd II (1709–1711)

William Byrd II   William Byrd II (1674–1744) inherited a fortune and assumed a place among the Virginia elite after his father's death in 1704. Educated abroad, Byrd is perhaps best known for his *History of the Dividing Line*, which was based on his experiences as the leader of a surveying expedition that established the boundary between Virginia and North Carolina in 1728. Byrd's importance to historians also rests in the diaries he kept, which provide insight into the life of the slaveholding gentry in colonial Virginia. The following excerpts focus on Byrd's role as a slave owner. In his descriptions of his "large family," Byrd nearly always included his slaves, and indeed he routinely took a lively interest in their well-being. But, like many slave owners, he used violence to maintain order; his terse reports of his cruelty demonstrate that his behavior was both acceptable and commonplace in Chesapeake society.

Source: Excerpt from Louis B. Wright and Marion Tinling, eds., *The Secret Diary of William Byrd of Westover, 1709–1712* (Richmond, VA: Dietz Press, 1941), 1–2, 22, 46, 78, 112–113, 192, 306–307. Reprinted by permission of the Estate of Marion Rose Tinling.

[February 8, 1709] I rose at 5 o'clock this morning and read a chapter in Hebrew and 200 verses in Homer's *Odyssey*. I ate milk for breakfast. I said my prayers. Jenny and Eugene were whipped. I danced my dance. I read law in the morning and Italian in the afternoon. I ate tough chicken for dinner. . . . In the evening I walked about the plantation. I said my prayers. I had good thoughts, good health, and good humor this day, thanks be to God Almighty.

[April 17, 1709] I rose at 5 o'clock and read a chapter in Hebrew and 150 verses in Homer. I said my prayers, and ate milk for breakfast. I danced my dance. . . . Anaka was whipped yesterday for stealing the rum and filling the bottle up with water. I went to church, where were abundance of people, whom was Mrs. H-m-l-n, a very handsome woman.

[June 9, 1709] . . . My Eugene ran away this morning for no reason but because he had not done anything yesterday. I sent my people after him but in vain. . . . I neglected to say my prayers, for which God forgive me. I had good health, good thoughts, and good humor, thanks be to God Almighty. I danced my dance.

[June 10, 1709] I rose at 5 o'clock this morning but could not read anything because of Captain Keeling, but I played at billiards with him and won half a crown of him and the Doctor. George B-th brought home my boy Eugene. I ate milk for breakfast, but neglected to say my prayers, for which God forgive me. . . . In the evening I took a walk about the plantation. Eugene was whipped for running away and had the [bit] put on him. I said my prayers and had good health, good thoughts, and good humor, thanks be to God Almighty.

[September 3, 1709] I rose at 5 o'clock and was hindered from reading Hebrew by the company; however, I read some Greek in Josephus. I said my prayers and ate chocolate with Mr. Taylor for breakfast. Then he want away. I read some geometry. We had no court this day. My wife was indisposed again but not to much purpose. I ate roast chicken for dinner. In the afternoon I beat Jenny for throwing water on the couch. . . .

[November 30, 1709] I rose at 3 o'clock and read two chapters in Hebrew and some Greek in Cassius. I went to bed again and lay till 7. I said my prayers, danced my dance, and ate milk for breakfast. Eugene was whipped for pissing in bed and Jenny for concealing it. I settled several accounts. I ate boiled beef for dinner. . . .

[December 1, 1709] I rose at 4 o'clock and read two chapters in Hebrew and some Greek in Cassius. I said my prayers and ate milk for breakfast. I danced my dance. Eugene was whipped again for pissing in bed and Jenny for concealing it. About 11 o'clock came Captain Stith and his wife, not on a visit but Mrs. Stith came to desire me justify her to Mrs. Harrison that she had not told me that Mrs. Harrison was delivered of two children before her time. I wrote to Mrs. Harrison to assure her that Mrs. Stith had never told me any such thing. But my wife could not deny but she had told that Mrs. Stith told her so. . . .

[December 3, 1709] I rose at 5 o'clock and read two chapters in Hebrew and some Greek in Cassius. I said my prayers and ate milk for breakfast. I danced my dance. Eugene pissed abed again for which I made him drink a pint of piss. I settled some accounts and read some news. . . .

[June 17, 1710] . . . I ate tongue and chicken for dinner. In the afternoon I caused L-s-n to be whipped for beating his wife and Jenny was whipped for being his whore. In the evening the sloop came from Appomattox with tobacco. I took a walk about the plantation. I said my prayers and drank some new milk from the cow. I had good health, good thoughts, and good humor, thanks be to God Almighty.

[February 25, 1711] . . . I ate roast beef for dinner. In the afternoon I took a walk about the plantation and met negro P-t-s-n who had been off the plantation and brought some bacon with him, for which I threatened to whip him. Then I found also that John was riding out with the stallion without leave, for which I threatened him likewise. . . .

[February 27, 1711] I rose at 6 o'clock and read two chapters in Hebrew and some Greek in Lucian. I said my prayers and ate boiled milk for breakfast. I danced my dance and then went to the brick house to see my people pile the planks and found them all idle for which I threatened them soundly but did not whip them. . . . In the evening my wife and little Jenny had a great quarrel in which my wife got the worst but at last by the help of the family Jenny was overcome and soundly whipped. At night I ate some bread and cheese. I said my prayers and had good health, good thoughts, and good humor, thank God Almighty.

Questions

1. Why did Byrd include his slaves Eugene, Jenny, and Anaka in his descriptions of his plantation "family"? What might be his definition of "family"?

2. There is an unmistakable repetitiveness to Byrd's diary entries: "I rose at 5 o'clock," "I read verses," "I ate milk for breakfast," "I said my prayers," and so forth. What is the significance of these sorts of routine entries? Is it surprising to see his daily routine interrupted by acts of cruelty? Why or why not?

3. Byrd wrote his diary entries in a secret code. Does this make his diary more or less believable? Is a person more likely to tell the truth if he is certain no one else will read his diary, or is he more likely to be truthful if he is certain someone else will read it? Explain.

3-8   Plantation Life in the Eighteenth Century

Benjamin Latrobe and Anonymous

Between 1680 and 1750 the colonies of Virginia, Maryland, and South Carolina were transformed from societies with slaves to slave societies. The quarter-million slaves living in these colonies accounted for three-fourths of all slaves in British North America. The English-born architect Benjamin Latrobe emigrated to Virginia in 1796 and began to record his observations in the journals and sketchbooks he maintained for over two years. In March of 1798 he came upon a scene common in the late-eighteenth-century Chesapeake and sketched "An Overseer doing his duty." At about the same time, another artist painted a scene, purportedly near Charleston, South Carolina, of an entirely different sort. Instead of capturing labor in the fields, the anonymous painting "The Old Plantation" commemorated life in the slave quarters.

Sources: Benjamin Latrobe, "An Overseer doing his duty. Sketched from life near Fredericksburg," 13 March 1798, Latrobe Sketchbooks, courtesy of the Maryland Historical Society. Anonymous, "The Old Plantation," c. 1777–1794, courtesy of the Abby Aldrich Rockefeller Folk Art Collection, Colonial Williamsburg Foundation.

(A)   *Benjamin Latrobe, "An Overseer doing his duty"*

(B)   *Anonymous, "The Old Plantation"*

Questions

1. How is the social divide between free whites and enslaved blacks presented in both of these images?

2. How does Latrobe's sketch depict the overseer? How does it depict the slave women? Does it depict one more favorably than the other?

3. In order to justify exploiting them and treating them cruelly, whites often maintained that slaves were no better than animals. How does the artist's depiction of the slaves in "The Old Plantation" humanize them? Is this image more humanizing than Latrobe's? Explain.

Questions for Further Thought

1. Why did the English begin importing slaves into Virginia in 1619? By the end of the seventeenth century, why had race-based chattel slavery become the labor system of choice, especially in the southern colonies and West Indies?

2. What other types of unfree labor existed in the British North American colonies? Compare and contrast these with chattel slavery.

3. Compare the actions of Symon Overzee and William Byrd II. What do they reveal about the limits of the law?

The New Politics of Empire, 1713–1750

Before 1689 the English government ruled most colonies with authoritarian statutes and in accordance with authoritarian principles. After the Glorious Revolution and Queen Anne's War, however, colonial assemblies gained greater autonomy from governors and royal placemen. In addition, there was a growing colonial interest in defining political liberties, some of which were perceived by colonists as different from the deference and patronage of "the English system" of rule (Document 3-9). European rivalries also affected the politics of empire in the colonies. The proximity of the Spanish in Florida in particular posed a threat to southerners and the institution of slavery on which they depended (Document 3-10).

3-9   A Plantation Parliament (1739)

Martin Bladen

By the middle of the eighteenth century, king and Parliament had long recognized the need to reform the imperial system and to bring the North American colonies under tighter control. To be sure, the Dominion of New England had been a miserable failure, but proposals for improvement through consolidation did not end with its demise. Among the several plans offered for official consideration after 1689, none was more informed than Martin Bladen's 1739 submission to First Minister Robert Walpole. Bladen, a member of Parliament since 1715, had served on the Board of Trade from 1717 to 1720 and fancied himself to be something of a colonial expert. Given the fact that Bladen's proposal came about two months after the start of the War of Jenkins's Ear against Spain, it is not surprising that the British ministry ignored his recommendations and continued its policy of "salutary neglect" toward the colonies.

Source: From "Martin Bladen's Blueprint for a Colonial Union," in *The William and Mary Quarterly,* 3rd series, 17:4 (1960), 521–529. Reprinted with permission of the Omohundro Institute of Early American History and Culture.

Since the Common Judgement of Mankind has determined that America shall be the Theatre of the present War, as the only Place where Spain is vulnerable; and since it is generally expected, that our Colonys should give Us some Assistance upon this Occasion. I have been induced to consider their present State, and to propose such Methods, as may tend to Their Security, and render them more usefull to Us, than they have hitherto been. . . .

But whatever Our Concern may have been for the Colonys, to do them Justice, they have seldom been wanting to themselves, and have too frequently advanced their own Interest at our Expence. Their Trade, their Produce, their Fisherys, their Manufactures and their Navigation, are exceedingly enlarged; their Lands cultivated; and the Number of their People encreased to such a Degree, as might not only be sufficient to defend themselves, but likewise (under proper Regulations) to Act offensively against the European Settlements in their Neighbourhood. . . .

But so long as they shall continue in the State they are in, divided into so many different Provinces, spread over so immense a Tract of Land, as that from Cape Canso to the River of Saint Mattheo; no less than Fifteen hundred Miles in length, in perpetual Contest with each other, upon the Subject of their Trade and Boundarys; Ruled by so many various Forms of Government; so little concerned for each others Prosperity, and as devoid of all Care for the Welfare of the whole, as if they were not the Subjects of the same Prince; a

much less force, than their own, might be able to destroy them; A Force that would not dare to meet them, once United in the Field.

For this Reason it is, as well as for many others, that all those, who have had apportunitys of considering the true State, the Interest of our Plantations, have always wished, that they might be put under one Uniform Direction, and that the Crown would appoint a Captain General for the Government of all the British Colonies on the Continent of North America.

But it must also be confessed, that notwithstanding the Self Evident Utility of this Proposition, two Obstacles have hitherto retarded the Execution of it; the want of a Salary for such an Officer, and the difficulty or rather the Impossibility, of obtaining voluntary Surrenders, or of vacating, by any other Means, Grants made by the Crown to the Proprietary, and Charter Governments. . . .

As to what relates to the Proprietary and Charter Governments, There are so many Absurditys resulting from the Nature of their different Constitutions, that I have often wondered, how they could ever have applyed for them; and much more, how the Crown could ever have established them—What Subordination? What regard to the Trade and Interest of Great Britain? What Obedience to her Laws? could be expected from American Principalitys, and Independent Common Wealths, established at so vast a Distance from their Mother Country? For such in Effect are the

Proprietary and Charter Provinces—Distinct Governments—Various in their Forms—Separate in their Legislatures—Absolute within their respective Dominions—hardly accountable for their Laws or Actions to the Crown—And impatient of Subjection to that Power, from which they draw their Origin, and to whom alone they must be indebted, for their Preservation, in time of danger.

If were therefore much to be desired, that they might all be reduced under his Majesty's immediate Directions, upon the same Plan, with the rest of his Royal Governments; That we might be better secured, of their Dependance, and they, better intitled, to our Protection. But the Justice, the Reason, and the Utility of a Proposition, are not always sufficient to carry it through. Private Combinations are frequently too hard for the Publick Good. . . .

And first it must be considered, that whatever Independency these Colonys may in practice, and Effect, have arrogated to themselves, they are still the Subjects of Great Britain. Our Laws are, or ought to be, obligatory upon them, whenever they are Named in Our Acts of Parliament. On the contrary their Laws, are lyable to be repealed by the Crown, and even in the Charter Governments, least Subject to the Royal Inspection or Authority, Laws Enacted, contrary to those of Great Britain, are in their own Nature Void, and may be declared such, by the King in Council, From whence it is evident, that neither the Crown, nor the Legislature of Great Britain, have in any sort departed from that Sovereignty, which they always had, and ever will retain, over the British Colonys in America. . . .

Thus much being premised with respect to the Nature of these Charters, and to the Authority of the Crown. It is humbly proposed, that His Majesty may be pleased, for the Protection, Advantage, and Defence of his People, to appoint a Captain General and General Governour over all his Colonys in the Continent of America, with full Powers to do all such Acts as may be requisite, for the due Execution of his Commission. And that at the same time his Majesty, may be his Royal Charter, to be issued for that purpose, direct that every British Colony on the Continent, as well those immediately dependant on the Crown, as the Proprietary and Charter Governments, should each of them send a certain Number of Councillors and Assembly Man, Once in the Year, or oftner if requisite, to attend the said Captain General at New York, as a Plantation Parliament; then, and there, to advise and consult, upon such Methods, to raise such Supplys, and such Number of Forces, from time to time, as may be necessary for the Security and Defence of the said Plantations. And also to Enact such Laws as shall be agreed on by Common Consent, according to the Custom of British Parliaments, for their General Welfare and Advantage. And it is humbly conceived that such an Institution, can never be deemed a violation of the Privileges, granted to the Proprietary or Charter Governments; because within their respective Precincts, their Several Patents would still retain their full effect. . . .

There are at present upon the Continent of America Seven Governments, immediately dependant on the Crown. Nova Scotia, New Hampshire, New York, The Jerseys, Virginia, and the two Carolinas. Two Proprietarys, Maryland and Pensilvania. Three Charter Colonys Vizt the Massachusetts Bay, Rhode Island and Connecticut.

Supposing then that all these Colonys, were to send equal Numbers of Councillors and Assembly Men, it is plain the Royal Governments would have a Majority in the Assembly. But as the Majority on that side cannot be too great, it would be advisable to encrease it, as far as can be done without Partiality. And therefore since it is proposed that New York should be the Seat of this New Government, as it lyes in a very healthful Climate, and in the Center of the British Plantations. That Colony, by way of distinction, may reasonably be allowed, a double Number of Councillors and Burgesses; for London as the Seat of Government here, has the same Priviledge. And considering how small a Tract of Land The People of New Hampshire, Rhode Island, and Connecticut, possess, they ought not, in proportion to the Extent of their Territory, to send above half as many Councillors and Burgesses, as the other Governments. Nor can this Reduction be taxed with inequality, inasmuch as the King will in that Case treat one of his own Governments, in the same Manner, with two of the little Charter Colonys.

Agreable to this Scheme, the Plantation Parliament would consist of Twenty three Councillors, and Forty Six Burgesses, wherein the Royal Governments would be sure of a Majority, of near two to one, against the Proprietary and Charter Colonys, as may appear by the following List

New York	4 Councillors and 8 Burgesses
Nova Scotia	2 4
New Hampshire	1 2
Massachusetts Bay	2 4
Rhode Island	1 2
Connecticut	1 2
The Jerseys	2 4
Virginia	2 4
Maryland	2 4
Pensilvania	2 4
North Carolina	2 4
South Carolina	2 4
In all	23 46

The Utility of this Scheme is so obvious, it would be mispending the time, to enlarge much upon the Advantages that would Result from it. It may be sufficient to observe, that the British Power and Interest in America would be United by it; that Our Colonys would be enabled not only to provide for their own Security, but even to drive all other European Nations out of the North Continent of America, if it should become necessary to attempt it. For the imaginary Empire of France, from the Gulph of St. Lawrence to the Embouchure of the Mississippi, is far from containing so great a Number of People, as the British Colonys do; and as we are superior to them in Number, I hope We are at least equal to them in Courage. But it must be allowed they have the advantage of Us in their Dispositions; They have very prudently taken care to fortifye themselves, as the two Extreme parts of their Territorys; And being under One Uniform Government, can direct their Force to the Point, where it may be most needfull—Let Us then imitate them in so laudable, so necessary a Conduct.

Questions

1. As a member of Parliament, Bladen must have been aware of the ministry's preoccupation with matters related to the war with Spain in 1739; and as a former member of the Board of Trade, he must have been contemplating the colonial system for some time prior to 1739. Why would he have offered his plan at this moment? What were his possible motives?

2. Bladen wanted to ensure that a majority of the members of the "Plantation Parliament" would be from the royal colonies. How did he propose to accomplish this? He claimed that the allocation of seats in that body would be done "without partiality." Is there any truth to his claim? What is the significance of including Nova Scotia in this scheme?

3. Given what happened to the Dominion of New England a half century earlier, what were the chances of Bladen's plan being accepted by the colonists? Would any plan of consolidation and stricter imperial control have been accepted by them? If so, what sort of an arrangement was possible? If not, were the colonists already latently revolutionary?

3-10   Stono Rebellion in South Carolina (1739)

Early in the morning on September 9, 1739, a group of slaves gathered at the Stono River outside Charleston, South Carolina, broke into a local store to arm themselves, murdered two storekeepers, and headed south. Their goal ultimately was to reach the city of St. Augustine, where the governor of Spanish Florida, under a royal proclamation issued by Philip V of Spain, had freed a group of runaway slaves a few years earlier. By the time the uprising was crushed later that evening, twenty white colonists and about forty slaves were dead. In the wake of the rebellion, legislators enacted a comprehensive Negro Act, which served as the core of South Carolina's slave code for the next century and attempted to reduce the number of slaves in the colony by heavily taxing all slave imports from Africa and the West Indies. At the time of the Stono Rebellion, South Carolina was the only one among the mainland British colonies to have a black majority, and nervous legislators were convinced that this was the source of the colony's problems. South Carolina's effort to limit its dependence on slave labor was short-lived, however, and by 1750 slave imports were back to their pre-1739 levels. Apprehensions notwithstanding, white Carolinians discovered that they could not prosper without their slaves. The following excerpt is taken from an anonymous account enclosed in a letter from James Oglethorpe, founder of Georgia, to the colony's trustees, October 9, 1739.

Source: From *The Colonial Records of the State of Georgia*, vol. 22, ed. Allen D. Chandler (Atlanta: Charles P. Byrd, 1913).

On the 9th day of September last being Sunday which is the day the Planters allow them to work for themselves, Some Angola Negroes assembled, to the number of Twenty; and one who was called Jemmy was their Captain, they suprized a Warehouse belonging to Mr. Hutchenson at a place called Stonehow [*sic*]; they there killed Mr. Robert Bathurst, and Mr. Gibbs, plundered the House and took a pretty many small Arms and Powder, which were there for Sale. Next they plundered and burnt Mr. Godfrey's house, and killed him, his Daughter and Son. They then turned back and marched Southward along Pons Pons, which is the Road through Georgia to Augustine, they passed M^r. Wallace's Tavern towards day break, and said they would not hurt him, for he was a good Man and kind to his Slaves, but they broke open and plundered M^r. Lemy's House, and killed him, his wife and Child. They marched on towards M^r. Rose's resolving to kill him; but he was saved by a Negroe, who having hid him went out and pacified the others. Several Negroes joyned them, they calling out Liberty, marched on with Colours displayed, and two Drums beating, pursuing all the white people they met with, and killing Man Woman and Child when they could come up to them. Collonel Bull Lieutenant Governour of South Carolina, who was then riding along the Road, discovered them, was pursued, and with much difficulty escaped & raised the Countrey. They burnt Colonel Hext's house and killed his Overseer and his Wife. They then burnt M^r. Sprye's house, then M^r. Sacheverell's, and then M^r. Nash's house, all lying upon the Pons Pons Road, and killed all the white People they found in them. M^r. Bullock got off, but they burnt his House, by this time many of them were drunk with the Rum they had taken in the Houses. They increased every minute by new Negroes coming to them, so that they were above Sixty, some say a hundred, on which they halted in a field, and set to dancing, Singing and beating Drums, to draw more Negroes to them, thinking they were now victorious over the whole Province, having marched ten miles & burnt all before them without Opposition, but the Militia being raised, the Planters with great briskness pursued them and when they came up, dismounting; charged them on foot. The Negroes were soon routed, though they behaved boldly several being killed on the Spot, many ran back to their Plantations thinking they had not been missed, but they were there taken and [sic] Shot, Such as were taken in the field also, were after being examined, shot on the Spot, And this is to be said to the honour of the Carolina Planters, that notwithstanding the Provocation they had received from so many Murders, they did not torture one Negroe, but only put them to an easy death. . . . And this sudden Courage in the field, & the Humanity afterwards hath had so good an Effect that there hath been no farther Attempt, and the very Spirit of Revolt seems over. About 30 escaped from the fight, of which ten marched about 30 miles Southward, and being overtaken by the Planters on horseback, fought stoutly for some time and were all killed on the Spot. The rest are yet untaken. In the whole action about 40 Negroes and 20 whites were killed. The Lieutenant Governour sent an account of this to General Oglethorpe, who met the advices on his return from the Indian Nation He immediately ordered a Troop of Rangers to be ranged, to patrole through Georgia, placed some Men in the Garrison at Palichocolas, which was before abandoned, and near which the Negroes formerly passed, being the only place where Horses can come to swim over the River Savannah for near 100 miles, ordered out the Indians in pursuit, and a Detachment of the Garrison at Port Royal to assist the Planters on any Occasion, and published a Proclamation ordering all the Constables &c. of Georgia to pursue and seize all Negroes, with a Reward for any that should be taken. It is hoped these measures will prevent any Negroes from getting down to the Spaniards. —

Questions

1. The size of the rebel force grew and shrank as some slaves joined and later left the group during its march south. Why is this significant? What impact did this have on South Carolina slave owners?

2. The author of this account claimed that the courage and humanity of the Carolina planters had crushed the very spirit of revolt among their slaves. How credible was this claim? What evidence, if any, in this account suggests the contrary was true?

3. Slaves constituted more than 60 percent of the total population of South Carolina by 1739. How might this demographic characteristic have affected the slave rebels? How might it have affected the behavior of white Carolinians?

Questions for Further Thought

1. By the early eighteenth century, what social, economic, and political developments in colonial American society might have led some colonists to question their place in the British empire? In what ways might the colonial view of the empire have become different from that of the royal authorities in Britain? Why?

2. Why might imperial officials justifiably conclude that the colonists required the supervision and protection of England? Base your answer on Documents 3-9 and 3-10.

3. After 1740, would South Carolinians be more or less likely to demand the liberties due to them as English citizens? Explain.

CHAPTER FOUR

Growth and Crisis in Colonial Society

1720–1765

Freehold Society in New England

After 1720 the population and economies of the mainland British colonies grew dramatically, and those colonies developed distinctively American characteristics. In New England that distinctiveness was characterized by the existence of communities of independent property owners. In Great Britain, 75 percent of the land was owned by the gentry and nobility; in New England, 70 percent was owned by freeholding families. Strategies for maintaining this system varied (Document 4-1).

Although the pattern of land ownership was distinctive, the place of women in rural New England was similar to that in Britain. Women were socialized to accept a subordinate role; their marriage portions were smaller than those of their brothers and they received no land. Women also had few property rights. Although a woman had the right to use a third of the family estate after her husband died, legally it belonged to her children. A woman was expected to be deferential toward her father and then her husband and to work hard to help them. Her work usually included a broad spectrum of household tasks, as well as the bearing and raising of children (Document 4-2).

The stability of the system depended on parents' ability to provide land for their children, but its very success created a crisis. A population of 100,000 in 1700 had grown to 400,000 by 1750, and even though the average birthrate of five to seven children declined to four after 1750, many parents could no longer provide land for their children. Farm communities responded to this crisis in ways that preserved a freehold society: many towns created new communities in frontier areas, and the people who remained increased productivity by introducing new crops and helping one another.

4-1 A New Hampshire Will (1763)

Nicholas Dudley

This document is illustrative of the New England system of inheritance (see text pp. 105–106). The colonial woman's most important legal right was her dower right: under common law a man had to leave his wife at least a life interest in one-third of his real estate, which after her death or remarriage would go to his heirs. At the same time the husband's will was intended to perpetuate the pattern of independent property holding.

Source: "The Will of Nicholas Dudley, 1763," in Dean Dudley, *The History of the Dudley Family* (Montrose, MA, 1894), 1:242–247.

I Nicholas Dudley give and bequeath to my well-beloved wife Elizabeth Dudley the use and improvement of all my lands in Brentwood called my home place, with the buildings thereon, and also the use and improvement of all my stock of cattle, sheep, swine, and horses, and my quarter part of Deer Hill saw mill, so long as she remains my widow. . . .

I give and bequeath to my son Nicholas Dudley all my right in Deer Hill mill pond during his natural life, and also the improvements of the same to Abigail Dudley, his wife, if she should survive him, so long as she remains his widow. And then the said right in the said mill pond I give, devise, and bequeath to my grandson Nicholas Dudley, son of Trueworthy Dudley, deceased, to be at his disposal forever.

I give to my son John Dudley twenty shillings . . . he having received his portion of my estate.

I give to my son Byley Dudley twenty shillings . . . he having received his portion of my estate.

I give to my son Joseph Dudley and to his four sons . . . all my land in the parish of Epping, called my common right, excepting the fifty acres I sold to Nicholas Gilman.

I give, devise, and bequeath to my daughters Sarah Robinson and Betty Hill, and to my grandson John Dudley, son of Trueworthy Dudley, deceased, their heirs and assigns, forever, after the decease or second marriage of my wife aforesaid all my lands in Brentwood, called my home place, except the mill pond aforesaid, with the buildings thereon, my stock of cattle, sheep, swine, and horses, excepting one cow and also all my out-door moveables after the decease or second marriage of my wife aforesaid.

Questions

1. What actions did Nicholas Dudley take to protect the livelihood of his widow? Why do you think he took those actions?

2. Does Dudley treat his male heirs equally? If your answer is no, why do you think he treats them differently?

3. Does he treat his daughters as beneficiaries? Explain.

4-2   The Obligations of a Wife (1712)

Benjamin Wadsworth

This selection comes from a Puritan marriage manual in which the author is attempting to define the duties and obligations of each member of the family, particularly the husband and the wife. It is a good example of what was expected of a deferential wife (see text pp. 104–106).

Source: Benjamin Wadsworth, *The Well-Ordered Family, or Relative Duties* (Boston, 1712), 22–47.

Wives are part of the House and Family, and ought to be under the Husband's Government: they should Obey their own Husbands. Though the Husband is to rule his Family and his Wife yet his Government of his Wife should not be with rigour, haughtiness, harshness, severity; but with the greatest love, gentleness, kindness, tenderness that may be. Though he governs her, he must not treat her as a Servant, but as his own flesh: he must love her as himself. He should make his government of her, as easie and gentle as possible; and strive more to be lov'd than fear'd; though neither is to be excluded. On the other hand, Wives ought readily and cheerfully to obey their Husbands. Wives submit your selves to your own Husbands, be in subjection to them.

Those Husbands are much to blame, who dont carry it [behave] lovingly and kindly to their Wives. O man, if thy Wife be not so young, beautiful, healthy, well temper'd and qualify'd as thou couldst wish; if she brought not so much Estate to thee, or cannot do so much for thee, as some other women brought to or have done for their Husbands; nay, if she does not carry it so well to thee as she should yet she is thy Wife, and the Great God Commands thee to love her, not to be bitter, but kind to her. What can be more plain and express than that? Let every one of you in particular, so love his Wife even as himself. . . . Those Wives are much to blame who dont carry it lovingly and obediently to their own Husbands. O Woman, if thy Husband be not so young, beautiful, healthy, so well temper'd and qualified as thee couldst wish; if he has not such abilities, riches, honours, as some others have; if he does not carry it so well as he should; yet he's thy Husband, and the Great God Commands thee to love, honour and obey him. Yea, though possibly thou hast greater abilities of mind than he has, wast of some high birth, and he of a more mean Extract, or didst bring more Estate at Marriage than he did; yet since he is thy Husband, God has made him thy Head, and set him above thee, and made it thy duty to love and reverence him.

Questions

1. How is a husband expected to behave toward his wife?

2. How is a wife expected to behave toward her husband?

3. Does higher birth, intelligence, or estate alter a wife's obligation to her husband? Why or why not?

Questions for Further Thought

1. What do Nicholas Dudley's will (Document 4-1) and the selection from the Puritan marriage manual (Document 4-2) tell us about the structure of the colonial New England family?

2. What obligations and responsibilities do the different family members have to each other (be sure to consider gender and age)? How does the colonial New England family compare with the American family of today?

3. Based on the readings and your general knowledge of the period, how and in what circumstances was property transferred from father to son? At what point in his life did a father usually pass his property on to his son? How might a son force his father's hand and obtain his inheritance early?

The Middle Atlantic: Toward a New Society, 1720–1765

Unlike New England, the middle colonies of New York, New Jersey, and Pennsylvania had a mixture of peoples with diverse religious and ethnic backgrounds (Document 4-6). Quakers were the dominant group in Pennsylvania and also were highly influential in New Jersey. In the eighteenth century they were followed by three waves of Germans and large numbers of Scots-Irish (Document 4-5).

The middle colonies prospered because of a growing demand for wheat in Western Europe; however, by midcentury this prosperity had turned a system offering early equality into one with increasing social divisions. Tensions continued and could sometimes be traumatic, but many ethnic and religious groups developed self-governing churches and created an increasingly open and competitive political system. This religious, ethnic, and political pluralism was a distinctively American phenomenon (Document 4-3).

4-3   What Is an American? (1782)

J. Hector St. John de Crèvecoeur

Michel-Guillaume Jean de Crèvecoeur was born on January 31, 1735, in Caen, Normandy, and migrated to Canada around 1755. As an officer in the French colonial militia, he was wounded at Quebec. Hoping for a fresh start, he resigned his commission and moved to New York in 1759. There he fashioned a new identify for himself by adopting a new name, J. Hector St. John de Crèvecoeur; a new national allegiance, naturalized subject of New York; a new occupation, farming; and a new language, English. During the imperial crisis leading to American independence, this new "American farmer" found it impossible to "say this side is right, that side is wrong." In 1779, toting a manuscript he had been working on for the past decade, Crèvecoeur began his trek back to Normandy. His *Letters from an American Farmer*, published in 1782, became an international best seller. The book established Crèvecoeur's reputation as an authority on America, and in 1783 Louis XVI appointed him as the French consul in New York. Shortly after the outbreak of the French Revolution, Crèvecoeur returned to France but remained as inconspicuous as possible during the Reign of Terror. Although he continued to write, he never approached the success of the *Letters*.

Source: Excerpts from Letter III, "What Is an American," in *Letters from an American Farmer*, by J. Hector St. John de Crèvecoeur (New York: E. P. Dutton, 1957), 35–40.

I wish I could be acquainted with the feelings and thoughts which must agitate the heart and present themselves to the mind of an enlightened Englishman, when he first lands on this continent. . . . He is arrived on a new continent; a modern society offers itself to his contemplation, different from what he had hitherto seen. It is not composed, as in Europe, of great lords who possess everything, and of a herd of people who have nothing. Here are no aristocratical families, no courts, no kings, no bishops, no ecclesiastical domination, no invisible power giving to a few a very visible one; no great manufacturers employing thousands, no great refinements of luxury. The rich and the poor are not so far removed from each other as they are in Europe. Some few towns excepted, we are all tillers of the earth, from Nova Scotia to West Florida. We are a people of cultivators, scattered over an immense territory, communicating with each other by means of good roads and navigable rivers, united by the silken bands of mild government, all respecting the laws, without dreading their power, because they are equitable. We are all animated with the spirit of an industry which is unfettered and unrestrained, because each person works for himself. If he travels through our rural districts he views not the hostile castle, and the haughty mansion, contrasted with the clay-built hut and miserable cabin, where cattle and men help to keep each other warm, and dwell in meanness, smoke, and indigence. A pleasing uniformity of decent competence appears throughout our habitations. . . .

In this great American asylum, the poor of Europe have by some means met together, and in consequence of various causes; to what purpose should they ask one another what countrymen they are? Alas, two thirds of them had no country. Can a wretch who wanders about, who works and starves, whose life is a continual scene of sore affliction or pinching penury; can that man call England or any other kingdom his country? A country that had no bread for him, whose fields procured him no harvest, who met with nothing but the frowns of the rich, the severity of the laws, with jails and punishments; who owned not a single foot of the extensive surface of this planet? No! urged by a variety of motives, here they came. Every thing has tended to regenerate them; new laws, and new mode of living, a new social system; here they are become men: in Europe they were as so many useless plants, wanting vegetative mould, and refreshing showers; they withered, and were mowed down by want, hunger, and war; but now by the power of transplantation, like all other plants they have taken root and flourished! Formerly they were not numbered in any civil lists of their country, except in those of the poor; here they rank as citizens. . . . What then is the American, this new man? He is either an European, or the descendant of an European, hence that strange mixture of blood, which you will find in no other country. I could point out to you a family whose grandfather was an Englishman, whose wife was Dutch, whose son married a French woman, and whose present four sons have now four wives of different nations. *He* is an American, who, leaving behind him all his ancient prejudices and manners, receives new ones from the new mode of life he has embraced, the new government he obeys, and the new rank he holds. He becomes an American by being received in the broad lap of our great *Alma Mater*. Here individuals of all nations are melted into a new race of men, whose labours and posterity will one day cause great changes in the world. Americans are the western pilgrims, who are carrying along with them that great mass of arts, sciences, vigour, and industry which began long since in the east; they will finish the great circle. The Americans were once scattered all over Europe; here they are incorporated into one of the finest systems of population which has ever appeared, and which will hereafter become distinct by the power of the different climates they inhabit. The American ought therefore to love this country much better than that wherein either he or his forefathers were born. Here the rewards of his industry follow with equal steps the progress of his labour; his labour is founded on the basis of nature, *self-interest*; can it want a stronger allurement? Wives and children, who before in vain demanded of him a morsel of bread, now, fat and frolicsome, gladly help their father to clear those fields whence exuberant crops are to arise to feed and to clothe them all; without any part being claimed, either by a despotic prince, a rich abbot, or a mighty lord. Here religion demands but little of him; a small voluntary salary to the minister, and gratitude to God; can he refuse these? The American is a new man, who acts upon new principles; he must therefore entertain new ideas, and form new opinions. From involuntary idleness, servile dependence, penury, and useless labour, he has passed to toils of a very different nature, rewarded by ample subsistence.—This is an American.

Questions

1. What are the major characteristics of Crèvecoeur's "American"? Are his observations in the main accurate or inaccurate? Explain.

2. Was Crèvecoeur's own life experience reflected in his description of an American? What is the significance of his assuming the title "American Farmer"? What myths about America and Americans was he repeating?

3. Was Crèvecoeur's American a product of a distinctive American environment? Does he place more importance on the physical environment or the cultural? Explain.

4-4   A Description of Philadelphia (1748)

Peter Kalm

Probably the most striking features of the British middle colonies of North America were their prosperity, diverse ethnic makeup, and multiplicity of religious forms. The following selection consists of the observations of Peter Kalm, a Swedish naturalist who toured the colonies from 1748 to 1751. During his visit to Philadelphia in 1748, Kalm noted the town's prosperity and its religious and ethnic diversity.

Source: Peter Kalm, *Travels in North America*, trans. John Reinhold Forester (London, 1770), 1:36–43, 58–60.

The town is now quite filled with inhabitants, which in regard to their country, religion, and trade, are very different from each other. You meet with excellent masters in all trades, and many things are made here full as well as in England. Yet no manufactures, especially for making fine cloth, are established. Perhaps the reason is, that it can be got with so little difficulty from England, and that the breed of sheep which is brought over, degenerates in process of time, and affords but a coarse wool.

Here is great plenty of provisions, and their prices are very moderate. There are no examples of an extraordinary dearth. Every one who acknowledges God to be the Creator, preserver, and ruler of all things, and teaches or undertakes nothing against the state, or against the common peace, is at liberty to settle, stay, and carry on his trade here, be his religious principles ever so strange. No one is here molested on account of the erroneous principles of the doctrine which he follows, if he does not exceed the above-mentioned bounds. And he is so well secured by the laws in his person and property, and enjoys such liberties, that a citizen of Philadelphia may in a manner be said to live in his house like a king.

On a careful consideration of what I have already said, it will be easy to conceive how this city should rise so suddenly from nothing, into such grandeur and perfection, without supposing any powerful monarch's contributing to it, either by punishing the wicked, or by giving great supplies in money. And yet its fine appearance, good regulations, agreeable situation, natural advantages, trade, riches and power, are by no means inferior to any, even of the most ancient towns in Europe. It has not been necessary to force people to come and settle here; on the contrary, foreigners of different languages have left their country, houses, property, and relations, and ventured over wide and stormy seas, in order to come hither. Other countries, which have been peopled for a long space of time, complain of the small number of their inhabitants. But Pennsylvania, which was no better than a desert in the year 1681, and hardly contained five hundred people, now vies with several kingdoms in Europe in number of inhabitants. It has received numbers of people, which other countries, to their infinite loss, have either neglected or expelled.

Questions

1. What factors does Kalm believe were the most significant in accounting for Philadelphia's rapid rise to prominence?

2. What is Kalm's perception of the religious environment in Philadelphia?

3. In Kalm's view, has the immigration to Philadelphia of people neglected in or expelled from other colonies and countries had a positive effect? Why or why not?

4-5   Letter from a Scots-Irish Immigrant (1767)

Job Johnson

In the eighteenth century the character of colonial immigration shifted. As New England became increasingly crowded, and as slave plantations came to dominate the southern colonies, the relatively open middle colonies became the destination of choice for European newcomers to America. Furthermore, a large proportion of the new migrants were non-English. Germans fled from increased crowding and religious persecution, but the greatest immigrant stream now came from the "Celtic fringe" of the British Isles, especially the Presbyterian inhabitants of Scotland and Ulster (Northern Ireland). The latter group, the Scots-Irish, had been recruited to colonize Ulster in the seventeenth century. By the eighteenth century, however, that land was overpopulated, English landlords were raising rents, taxes were rising, and Ulster manufactures were being shut out of English markets. Accordingly, the Scots-Irish began a massive exodus to the New World. Settling at first in Pennsylvania, they soon came to dominate that colony's western frontier and from there spread southward into the backcountry of the southern colonies.

The letter excerpted below was written by Job Johnson, an Ulster immigrant, who arrived in the 1760s and settled near the Susquehanna River to the west of Philadelphia.

Source: From "As Good a Country as Any Man Needs to Dwell In: Letters from a Scotch-Irish Immigrant in Pennsylvania, 1766–1767, and 1785," in *Pennsylvania History* 50 (October 1983), 318–321. Reprinted with the permission of the Pennsylvania Historical Society.

Oxford Township, November 27th 1767.
My Very dear Brethern,
Not being willing to neglect any opportunity that I have in my power to writ unto you, I have thought proper to address myself to you all in a few lines hopeing that they may find you all in good Health, as thanks be to God they Leave Me. . . . I wrote seven letters home last year . . . but I do not know whether or not you have Got them, and I have Got No answer therefore I have nothing further to writ; only knowing that it is common [ ] at home to expect something Concerning this Country its property and Quality, there-fore this is Really my Judgement of it, that it is as Good as Country as any Man needs to Dwell in; and it is Much better than I expected it to be in every way I assure you, and I really likes it so well and it is so pleasant to me that it would be a good Estate in Ireland that would Make Me Stay there, and indeed many times when I have been by myself and think of the Lord's Good Dealings unto Me, I cannot but admire him for his Mercies that ever he turned My face hitherward; and Give Me strength and Confidence in himself and boldness by faith, to oppose all Gainsayers, though never so strong, although I cannot say that then, it seemed

so Clear for Me to leave the land of My Nativity. Yet Now to Me it is a Certainty that My Removal was right and in what I Did I had peace, and in all My exercises by sea and Land, I never felt the Least in Me, as to Desire I had not come forward, but rather rejoiced (Turn over) in the Midst of them all. My Brother was not so clear in these things untill he had Been a year in the Country, Which indeed is Mostly the Case, with all the first year after they Come here: but Blessed be God all is well to our content. And if one heard every objection that lay in the way of Coming here, it would be work enough. But My resolutions were, and my sayings to several opposers, that I would come, if God hindered me not no Man should. And I do not know one that has come here that Desires to be in Ireland again, for to Live there and I have often wondered at our Countryfolk that was hard of belief in regard of what was said of their Country, and would rather live in Slavery, and work all the year round, and not be threepence the better at the years end than stir out of the Chimney Corner and transport themselves to a place where with the like pains, in two or three years, they might know better things. The only encouragement that I had to Come away was because Many Go to America worth nothing yet some of them servants and to hear or see them Come back again, in two or three years worth more than they would have been by staying at home while they lived and yet they would Not Content themselves at home, but went back again which was sufficient to Convince any one that the Country was Good. But there are Many in Ireland that Desire to hear ill of this place, because they would keep their friends there with them, in Bondage and Slavery, rather than let them come here, and they think we never writ enough of the Bad properties of this Country and the Vermin in it. Now this I must say in report that there are Bears, Wolves & Foxes, Rattles snakes, and several other such creatures, but Not in this part as ever I seen, as I have Travelled Many Miles to & fro. But I suppose the fear of those Creatures in Ireland is far worse to Some there, than the hurt of them is here. But I believe that this Province of Pennsylvania by all I have see and heard of it, is a Good a one as any in America. I have seen in all places I have travelled, Orchards Laden with fruit to admiration, their very Limbs torn to pieces with the weight, and Most Delicious to the Taste I have seen a Barrel of Curious Cyder from an apple tree; and peaches in Great plenty. I could Not but at first smile at the Conceit of them, they are a very Delicate fruit, and hang almost like our onions that are tied on a rope. . . . And indeed this is a Brave Country, although no place will please all. And some may be ready to say I writ of Conveniences; but not of Inconveniences; My answer to those I honestly Declare there is some barren Land; as, I suppose there is in Most places of the World; and Land in this part is very high, selling Commonly at six and seven pounds per acre. Neither will such land Produce Corn without something to buy them. Not Bread will not be got with Idleness else it would be a Brave Country indeed, and I Question not, but all them would give it a Good word. For my part I never would had the Least thought of returning home only through regard of seeing you all again.

Questions

1. According to Job Johnson, what are the attractions of Pennsylvania? What did Pennsylvania have to offer the Scots-Irish immigrant that was worth his breaking his ties to the land of his birth?

2. What special concerns does Johnson feel the need to address? What rumors about America does he attempt to dispel?

3. How do you think Johnson's letter was received back home in Ulster?

4-6   An Abolitionist in Pennsylvania in the 1730s

Almost from its inception Pennsylvania acquired a reputation, not undeserved, for being the "best poor man's country in the world." Thousands of Western European immigrants were drawn to the colony on the promise of toleration and an unimpeded pursuit of prosperity. What is less well known is that Pennsylvania was also a slave-owning colony. Even some Quakers, despite their egalitarian principles, owned slaves and condoned the practice of slave owning until the 1750s. A few dissenters, among them the uncompromising Benjamin Lay, challenged slavery in Pennsylvania in the 1730s. Lay, an immigrant from England who arrived in Philadelphia in 1731, believed that slavery contradicted the principles of Christianity and condemned it as a "notorious sin." He took to living in a cave and making his own clothes in order to avoid materials grown by slaves. He even once kidnapped a Quaker child to make a point about the suffering African parents had to endure. Such extreme measures alienated the Society of Friends, and they disowned Lay in 1738.

Source: Courtesy of the Pennsylvania Historical Society.

Anonymous, "Benjamin Lay"

Questions

1. In the 1730s his fellow Quakers viewed Lay as an eccentric whose sanity was questionable. How is this conveyed in this depiction of him? Why might it have been important to depict Lay as slightly insane?

2. Given Lay's fate among the Quakers, what can be said about slavery in Pennsylvania before the American Revolution?

The Enlightenment and the Great Awakening, 1740–1765

As the societies of British North America were transformed from relatively simple frontier communities to complex but distinctive extensions of Europe, they began to participate in the religious and intellectual movements of the larger European world. Two powerful continental movements in particular transformed the cultural and intellectual life of the colonies. The Enlightenment emphasized the power of human reason and had its roots in the scientific revolution of the seventeenth century. If any single individual epitomized the American Enlightenment, it was Benjamin Franklin (Document 4-7); if any single place was its center, it was Franklin's Philadelphia.

The second movement was more spiritual. As some Americans were abandoning, or at least revising, an older religious worldview, many more were embracing a new one. Pietism, which came to America from Europe with German immigrants in the 1720s, led to religious revivals throughout the colonies. Little concerned with formal theology, it emphasized moral behavior and a mystical union with God. Charismatic preachers such as Theodore Jacob Freylinghuysen, William and Gilbert Tennant, and Jonathan Edwards played key roles in the revivals. From 1739 to 1741, the powerful British evangelist George Whitefield preached to huge audiences throughout the colonies, knitting local revivals together into a single movement subsequently known as the Great Awakening.

The Great Awakening was a social upheaval that created controversy and divided churches, leading to the creation of new congregations. It also inspired its adherents to question the need for religious taxes, the idea of an established church, the authority of ministers, and the morality of economic competition (Documents 4-8 and 4-9).

4-7   On Education During the American Enlightenment (1749)

Benjamin Franklin

Benjamin Franklin was one of colonial America's outstanding examples of the influence of Enlightenment ideas (see text pp. 116–117). In the document that follows, Franklin proposes methods for the education of colonial youth that departed dramatically from the founding generations' more modest attention to training in the "domestic arts" or a trade. Franklin's proposal resulted in the creation of an academy in Philadelphia in 1751.

Source: Benjamin Franklin, *Proposals Relating to the Education of Youth in Pensilvania, Philadelphia* (1749; facsimile reprint, edited by William Pepper, Philadelphia: University of Pennsylvania, 1931).

"Proposals Relating to the Education of Youth in Pensilvania, Philadelphia," 1749.

It has long been regretted as a Misfortune to the Youth of this Province, that we have no Academy, in which they might receive the Accomplishments of a regular Education . . . the Sentiments and Advice of Men of Learning, Understanding, and Experience. . . .

The good Education of Youth has been esteemed by wise Men in all Ages, as the surest Foundation of the Happiness both of private Families and of Commonwealths. Almost all Governments have therefore made it a principal Object of their Attention, to establish and endow with proper Revenues, such Seminaries of Learning, as might supply the succeeding Age with Men qualified to serve the Publick with Honour to themselves, and to their Country. . . .

It is propos'd

That some Persons of Leisure and publick Spirit apply for a Charter, by which they may be incorporated, with Power to erect an Academy for the Education of Youth, to govern the same, provide Masters, make Rules, receive Donations, purchase Lands, etc., and to add to their Number, from Time to Time such other Persons as they shall judge suitable.

That the Members of the Corporation make it their Pleasure and in some Degree their Business, to visit the Academy often, . . . advance the Usefulness and Reputation of the Design; that they look on the Students as in some Sort their Children, treat them with Familiarity and Affection. . . .

That a House be provided for the Academy, if not in the Town, not many Miles from it . . . having a Garden, Orchard, Meadow, and a Field or two.

That the House be furnished with a Library . . . with Maps of all Countries, Globes, some mathematical Instruments, an Apparatus for experiments in Natural Philosophy, and for Mechanics; Prints, of all Kinds, Prospects, Buildings, Machines, etc.

That the Rector be a Man of good Understanding, good Morals, diligent and patient, learn'd in the Languages and Sciences, and a correct Speaker and Writer of the English Tongue; to have such Tutors under him as shall be necessary. . . .

As to their Studies, it would be well if they could be taught every Thing that is useful, and every Thing that is ornamental: But Art is long, and their Time is short. It is therefore propos'd that they learn those Things that are likely to be most useful and most ornamental. . . . All should be taught to write a fair Hand, and swift . . . Drawing . . . Arithmetick, Accounts . . . Geometry and Astronomy.

The English Language might be taught by Grammar; in which some of our best Writers, as Tillotson, Addison, Pope, Algernoon Sidney, Cato's Letters, etc. should be Classicks. . . .

Antient Customs, religious and civil . . . Morality, be descanting and making continual Observations on the Causes of the Rise or Fall of any Man's Character, Fortune, Power etc. . . . the Advantages of Temperance, Order, Frugality, Industry, Perseverance etc. . . .

While they are reading Natural History, might not a little Gardening, Planting, Grafting, inoculating, etc., be taught and practised; and now and then Excursions made to the neighbouring Plantations of the best Farmers. . . . The History of Commerce, of the Invention of Arts, Rise of Manufactures, Progress of Trade, Change of its Seats . . . will be useful to all. And this, with the Accounts in other History of . . . Engines and Machines used in War, will naturally introduce a Desire to be instructed in Mechanicks, and to be inform'd of the Principles of that Art by which weak Men perform such Wonders, Labour is sav'd, Manufactures expedited, etc. . . .

With the whole should be constantly inculcated and cultivated, that Benignity of Mind, which shows itself in . . . Good Breeding; highly useful to the Possessor, and most agreeable to all.

Questions

1. According to Franklin, why should young colonial men attend school when there are many practical reasons not to?

2. What are the things young Pennsylvanians should be learning?

3. How does Franklin reconcile public service, the benefits of classical learning, and the necessity of practical training for young people in the colony?

4-8   An Evangelical Preacher's Trials (1760s)

The Reverend James Ireland

Of all the preachers who introduced the evangelical gospel into the southern colonies, James Ireland (1748–1806) has left perhaps the fullest account of his conversion, labors, and trials. Born in Edinburgh, he was raised as a Presbyterian and educated as a lawyer, but he came to Virginia as a young man to serve as a schoolmaster. At first Ireland cut a fine figure in local gentry society, joining the Masonic order and becoming well known for his dancing skill. However, on encountering the Baptists and their message, he underwent an emotional conversion and abandoned his former way of life. The sharpness of the break is shown in the confrontation that opens this document.

After becoming a Baptist minister, Ireland preached extensively throughout the Virginia Piedmont, stirring opposition from both the clergy of the established Church of England and the local gentry. In 1769 the latter briefly jailed him at Culpeper Court House, a place where he had engaged in an earlier controversy with the local parson. The persecution he suffered from "the politest part of the people," though, he contrasted with the piety, tolerance, and religious diversity of the newer settlements of the Shenandoah Valley. Predominantly composed of Scots-Irish and Germans moving southwestward from Pennsylvania, these backcountry settlers were introducing a new sensibility into the southern colonies, and a new source of social division as well.

Source: The Life of the Rev. James Ireland (Winchester, VA: J. Foster, 1819), 82–86, 130–135, 157–160, 181–185.

It comes now into my way to make some remarks about a man whom I referred to some pages back, and from whom I expected to receive some information relative to my parents and relations. Although a friendship existed between his father's family and my father's family, yet he never was an associate and companion of mine, by reason of the disparity of years between us; yet upon the remembrance of past family acquaintance from the instant of seeing each other, we conceived and preserved a singular affection for each other. He was a member of that fraternity [Freemasonry] to which I hinted before, I had joined; and was very instrumental in persuading me thereunto; he at the same time possessing the highest place in that society. The news of my awakening impressions, had diffused itself through every part of the settlement and its vicinity. It became the topic in all companies that "James Ireland was going to be mighty good now, for he is going to get converted." My acquaintance had not seen me for some short period, previous to my soul's distresses. There was a dance appointed to be held the Monday following, at a wealthy neighbour's house. My countryman in company with others, hearing the remarks they were making about me, and being tolerably dissipated in language at times, swore they need not believe any thing about it, for there could not be a dance in the settlement without my being there, and if they would leave it to him, he would convert me, and that to the dance, on Monday; and they would see me lead the ball that day. The deep impressions upon my soul had a very considerable influence upon my exterior appearance of body; that wild vivacity that flashed in my eyes, and natural cheerfulness that appeared in my countenance, was entirely gone; my eyes appeared solemn and heavy, my flesh began to pine away, my ruddy cheeks and countenance had vanished, and all that remained was a solemn gloomy paleness, whilst my head was often hanging down like a bulrush, under the internal pressure of my guilty state. This my friend, who had bound himself under an oath that he would convert me to the ball, had never yet seen. Determined however to prosecute his purpose, which I had also been informed of, disposed me to expect a visit from him, in which he did not deceive me. He came to my school house; being there myself, I heard the noise of a creature's feet some little distance from me, which disposed me to look about, and soon I descryed the rider to be my friend, coming to see me. Being fully persuaded he would use all the influence he was master of, to persuade me to his wishes, I was seized with a momentary panic, which disposed me to lift up my heart to the Lord, and implore him not to suffer any reasonings he could use to have the least influence upon my mind, as also that the Lord would direct some word or other, that might be for his benefit. When I viewed him riding up, I never beheld such a display of pride in any man, before or since, as I beheld in him at that juncture, arising from his deportment, attitude and jesture, he rode a lofty elegant horse, and exhibited all the affectation possible, whilst his countenance appeared to me as bold and daring as satan himself, and with a commanding authority called upon me, if I were there to come out, which I accordingly did, with a fearful and timo-

rous heart. But O! how quickly can God level pride to the ground, if he does but once touch the heart, as was soon manifested in him. In a few minutes did the person, who, no doubt, made sure, as he came to visit me, of making an easy conquest of me, find, that the race is not to the swift nor the battle to the strong. For no sooner did he behold my disconsolate looks, emaciated countenance and solemn aspect, than he instantly appeared, as if he was riveted to the beast he rode on; his passions were so powerfully impressed, that I conceived he would have fainted and dropped from his horse.

For some short space of time, he was past utterance, and did nothing but stare at me with wild amazement. As soon as he could articulate a little his eyes fixed upon me, and his first address was this; "In the name of the Lord, what is the matter with you?" To which I replied if he would light, from his horse, and come into the house, I would tell him. I stepped into the house before him, begging of the Lord to direct my speech unto him; his surprise and consternation still attending him, he repeated his former expression; "In the name of the Lord what is the matter with you?" I instantly took him by the hand, and with a tender heart, and tears streaming from my eyes, spoke to him as follows. "My dear friend I possess a soul that will be either happy or miserable in the world to come; and God has been pleased to give me a view of the worth of my soul, as also of the guilty and condemned state it lies in by reason of sin; and I plainly see that if my soul is not converted, regenerated and born again, I will be damned." Holding my hand fast in his, and looking at me, with all the eagerness of desire, he burst out into the following words—"O! you will not leave me nor forsake me now." To which I answered that "I would not, upon condition he would renounce his former wicked ways, as I had done, and seek God through Jesus Christ, for pardon and salvation to our poor souls." To which he replied, with streaming eyes, "from that moment forward, through the strength of the Lord Jesus Christ, he would." His convictions were formed that very instant; and from my knowledge of him, meeting often by appointment to pray together to God for the salvation of our souls, I am satisfied that his impressions never subsided until he came to a well grounded hope of an interest in the salvation of God, through the merits of the precious Redeemer. . . .

. . . At that time the Church of England Parsons were exalted in domination over all dissenters in the colony, as it was then called, of Virginia. The dissenters had to pay their proportion for the building of Churches, and sixteen thousand weight of tobacco annually for the support of those Clergymen, exclusive of building their own houses for worship, supporting their own Ministers, and being precluded the benefit of marrying the members of their own society, except they procured and paid to the Church Parson of their Parish a full marriage fee for each couple. And this galling yoke continued on the necks of the dissenters until some time after our glorious revolution took place.

The Church Parson in Culpepper County had made it a practice, where any of those Baptist Preachers would have an appointment for preaching, to go in person to those meetings, taking some aids with him, who were as much prejudiced against that sect as he was. Being a man of rapid flow of misrepresentation and persecution, upon religious subjects, would by his dogmatical manner, appear frequently to an audience he would address, to gain his point and acquire the mastery over his opponents.

This personage attended at Capt. McClanagan's in order to detect the falsity of Mr. Pickett's doctrines before his parishioners. Being acquainted with Mr. Pickett's disposition and turn of mind, I felt very uneasy that day, when I saw the position the Parson took. The place Mr. Pickett was to preach in, was pretty capacious for the congregation; the parson had a chair brought for himself, which he placed three or four yards in front of Mr. Pickett, on which he seated himself, taking out his pen, ink and paper, to take down notes of what he conceived to be false doctrine. By the countenance of Parson Meldrum's Parishioners, they appeared to be highly elated, under an assured expectation of his baffling the new light, as they called him. I discovered it was some embarrassment to Mr. Pickett, and impeded his delivery, but I possessed a confidence that he preached the truth, and nothing but the truth, which could be supported and defended against its enemies.

As soon as Mr. Pickett had finished his discourse, the Parson called him a schismatick, a broacher of false doctrines, and that he held up damnable errors that day. Mr. Pickett answered him with a great deal of candour, and supported the doctrines he had advanced, to the satisfaction of all those who were impartial judges of doctrine. He was a man slow in argument, and when contradicted it would in a measure confuse him, which I soon observed, by some points he advanced, in which, in my judgment, he was perfectly right. The Parson at the same time, I observed, was taking notes of what the other said, which made me careful to retain it on my memory, standing close by Mr. Pickett when he spoke. The notes the Parson took, were absolutely the reverse of what Mr. Pickett delivered, and the Parson asserting them with dogmatical precision, and his parishioners exulting in the same, I could not forbear immediately interfering. . . .

Understanding he had been raised a Presbyterian, before he commenced Episcopalian, I formed the plan of entering into a discourse with him. First, upon the doctrines of religion, and secondly, upon the practice of it. This was with a view to endeavour to gain his consent that what he called damnable errors were consistant with gospel principles and practices. . . .

However, I discovered that pursuing the argument was and would be at the risque of incurring the displeasure of both gentlemen and ladies of his society, and perhaps the greater bulk of them. They would look at me with the utmost contempt and disdain, supposing it no doubt, presumption in such a youth as I, to enter into an argument with the teacher of the county. In the course of our argument, they would repeatedly help him to scripture, in order to support his arguments, which made me observe to them that they did not treat me with common justice, that I had

none that helped me, whilst they were supplying their Pastor with every help they could afford. . . .

I immediately got up and addressed one of the gentlemen who had been so officious in helping his teacher; he was a magistrate at that time, and one of those who afterwards committed me to prison. I addressed him in this manner, "Sir, as the dispute between the Parson and myself is ended, if you are disposed to argue the subject over again, I am willing to enter upon it with you." He stretched out his arm straight before him, at that instant, and declared I should not come nigher than that length. I concluded what the consequence would be, therefore made a peaceable retreat.

Mr. Pickett's next meeting was to be contiguous to Col. Easom's, in an old field under some comfortable shades. It being on the Lord's day, the Parson had to attend his parish church, so that we met with no opposition from that quarter, but we it from another; as the congregation was very large, amongst them there were abundance of negroes the patrolers were let loose upon them, being urged thereto by the enemies and opposers of religion. Never having seen such a circumstance before, I was equally struck with astonishment and surprise, to see the poor negroes flying in every direction, the patrolers seizing and whipping them, whilst others were carrying them off prisoners, in order, perhaps, to subject them to a more severe punishment. Meeting being concluded, Mr. Pickett, with myself and a number of others from our parts, that had come over to this day's meeting, took our leave of each other that evening, and returned to our respective settlements. . . .

. . . I went on that evening to Capt. Thomas McClanahan's, a worthy gentleman at whose house I had the dispute with the church parson: there I was informed that if I preached next day at Mr. Manifa's, I should be taken by squire Strother and squire Slaughter. I sat down and counted the cost, freedom or confinement, liberty or a prison; it admitted of no dispute. Having ventured all upon Christ, I determined to suffer all for him. Next morning I set off for Mr. Manifa's, at whose house I was to preach, accompanied with the capt. and his whole family. When I arrived at the place of preaching, Mr. Manifa addressed me thus, "Sir, you may expect to be taken up to day, if you preach, a certain fine (I am told) will be imposed upon you, and so much upon each individual that will attend your preaching, as well as a fine of twenty pounds on me for granting you my house to preach in. This the justices have made me acquainted with, and have advised me for my own advantage, not to suffer the meeting."

Mr. Manifa being a man under awakening impressions, told me not to flinch from my duty, if I thought it a duty, to go on. I requested him to show me the line of his land, ordered a table to be taken out and placed with its feet on each side of the line; whether it might have answered any purpose or not, I cannot tell. However I told him, that when I stood on the table I would not preach on his land no more than on anothers.

Preaching being over, and I concluding with prayer, heard a rustling noise in the woods, and before I opened my eyes to see who it was, I was seized by the collar by two men whilst standing on the table. Stepping down off the table, and beholding a number of others walking up, it produced a momentary confusion in me. The magistrates instantaneously demanded of me, what I was doing there with such a conventicle of people? I replied that I was preaching the Gospel of Christ to them. They asked who gave me authority so to do? I answered, he that was the author of the Gospel, had a right to send forth whom he had qualified to dispense it. They retorted upon me with abusive epithets, and then enquired of me if I had any authority from man to preach? I produced my credentials, but these would avail nothing, not being sactioned and commissioned by the Bishop. They told me that I must give security not to teach, preach or exhort, for twelve months and a day, or go to jail. I choose the last alternative. The magistrates then addressed their neighbours and informed them that they were open to law, but there the preacher stands on one side, and here we stand on the other; and as we believe you have been deceived by him, if you will confess it by coming over from the side where he is, to our side, we will take that act as your concession, and the law will not be put in force against you. The people were much incensed against the magistrates, and told them that they had heard nothing preached but the Gospel of Christ, and that if they had not money to pay their fines, they were willing to go to jail also. The magistrates were much mortified at seeing the ill will they had got from their neighbours, and their ignorance being by me, at the same time exposed before the congregation.

I gave security to attend court in a few days, which I accordingly did. By the complexion of the courts I saw there was no liberty for me. There were eleven magistrates sat as a quorum. They brow-beat me, mall treated me, and throwed out the most approbrious appellations against me—would admit of no defence I could make, but ordered me to hold my tongue, and let them hear no more of my vile, pernicious, abhorrible, detestable, abominable, diabolical doctrines, for they were naucious to the whole court. I found it of no consequence to defend myself any further, since imprisonment was inevitable, and they were determined to make an example of me.

I delivered up my riding horse to a friend to take care of him that night, and apply to me next day for further instructions. The sheriffs were ordered to attend me to my little limbo, with a considerable parade of people, with such vollies of oaths and abuse as if I were a being unfit to exist on the earth. A very uncomfortable night I passed, in consequence of the oaths &c. that continued through the same. Sticks and stones they were throwing during the whole night upon me. . . .

From what has been said, you cannot help taking notice of the awful darkness which overspread Virginia at that time; although in speaking of it more particularly I shall divide it into three districts of country, and touch upon the general character of the inhabitants of each, so far as I was then, and shortly afterwards, acquainted with them.

The first, from the blue ridge of mountains down towards the bay, they were considered as the politest part of the people, prior to any spread of the Gospel therein. Religion was a subject that did not concern their minds, unless it was in their opposition against those who felt the earliest impressions of it; they resigned and gave up their spiritual concerns to the guidance and direction of their spiritual guides: like *priest* like *people*, they appeared all to be in the ditch, put their trust in men, and made flesh their arm. Scarcely a persecution took place, in that quarter, but had a Priest at the head of it, and received the hearty concurrence of their parishoners.

In early stages of my ministry, I made a visit almost down to the Bay; in that course of preaching, I travelled a considerable distance, and met with exceeding few that had any desire for the conversion of their souls.

From reasons heretofore assigned in my narration, I shall not discuss the circumstances attending my journey any further than mentioning a few particulars which I shall blend together.

Opposition attended me every where; in the time of preaching, one body of the congregation would be calling out to the other to whip the fellow off the ground; half a dozen of fists would be drawn at a time, when I expected to be knocked down every minute; sailors were brought on shore from their vessels, through the influence of the people, in order to take me out into the stream, hoist me up to the yards arm and so to give me a ducking. At other places public teachers would, after sermon, introduce controversies, principally on the ordinance of baptism, which I would undertake accordingly to the mortification of those who introduced them; by which their congregations were convinced of the propriety of believing baptism by immersion.

Without any more animadversion, there was always a party in favour of the cause I had espoused; often soliciting me to visit them again: and when ever the Lord was pleased to form any opening upon their minds, it was surprising to see how docile and tractable they were to receive instruction. They were a people possessing good parts naturally; all that they wanted for religious advancement, and divine improvement, was the quickening, awakening, convincing and divine teaching of the holy spirit, attended with the heart changing and efficacious grace of God upon their souls, which was opening upon them at that period, and many of them soon manifested divine progress, in the ways of Jesus.

The prisons, in divers places, were honoured with the poor despised preachers: however their situations were much more comfortable than mine; because none were precluded from visiting them; none of those punishments inflicted on me attended them; whilst several of them at a time would be in company together, by which means, they proved a mutual comfort and establishment to each other. By comparing their situation with mine already given, the reader may easily draw inferences from the premises.

Being two hundred miles from my residence, I longed to be back among those called my own people; that being the *second* division, which lays between the Blue Ridge and Alleghany mountains. The people inhabiting these valleys, were better informed, arising from the following considerations: they were a divided people as to religious persuasions, consisting of Baptists, Presbyterians, Methodists, Quakers, Menonists, Tunkers and Churchmen, with a variety of others. As persecution was not a reigning principle among them, and they lived in a common state of sociability, it gave them an opportunity of being acquainted with each other's principles and practices, by which their *ideas* became more enlarged, and their *judgments* more generally informed than those of the first division.

With regard to the *third* division, who lived beyond the Alleghany mountains, in our western settlements, it would be hard for one to give a proper description of them, until time and opportunity of action, would enable such to form a correct opinion. But as kind providence had allotted, under the Blue Ridge, through all the courses and windings of this valley, (between the Ridge and Alleghany) and from the other side of the Alleghany down upon the Ohio, to be the sphere of my ministerial labours, and public services put in my power, were it necessary, I could give a full detail respecting them. When I went among them, I found them to be an uncultivated people; the farther I went back the more rude and illiterate they were: I often thought they constituted a compound of the barbarian and the indian; although I found among them, a number of respectable and well behaved people. . . .

Questions

1. Why did the Baptists and other evangelical sects pose such a threat to the established religious order in colonial Virginia? How might the threat have been social as well as religious?

2. How are Ireland's attitudes toward slaves shaped by his religious beliefs?

3. To what does Ireland attribute what he describes as the greater tolerance of peoples living in the western valleys of Virginia? How might this illuminate for you the origins of the religion clause of the First Amendment to the U.S. Constitution?

4-9 Fighting Revivalism in the Carolina Backcountry (1768)

Charles Woodmason

Religious revivalism in the southern colonies was often accompanied by social conflict (see text pp. 118–123), and nowhere is this better illustrated than in the accounts of Charles Woodmason. Born into the gentry class in England about 1720, Woodmason arrived in South Carolina in 1752 and established himself as a planter, merchant, and public official. In the early 1760s, however, he grew increasingly worried over the inroads that revivalists, especially New Light Baptists, had made into the Carolina backcountry, and he soon determined to "disperse these Wretches." Woodmason traveled to England to be ordained as an Anglican minister—there were no Anglican bishops in the colonies to perform ordination—and returned to South Carolina in 1766. He spent the next six years in the backcountry, working for the "advancement of religion" and fighting against what he perceived to be the "idleness, beggary, prophaneness, lewdness, and villany" of the revivalists. The following excerpt is taken from an undated sermon, delivered around 1768, in which Woodmason attacks the New Lights.

Source: From Richard J. Hooker, ed., *The Carolina Backcountry on the Eve of the Revolution: The Journal and Other Writings of Charles Woodmason, Anglican Itinerant.* Copyright 1953 by the University of North Carolina Press, renewed 1981 by Richard J. Hooker. Published for the Omohundro Institute of Early American History and Culture. Used by permission of the publisher.

In Singing of Hymns and Spiritual Songs—whereby their Hearts are greatly inflam'd with Divine Love and Heav'nly Joy, and makes the H[oly] G[host] be shed abroad in their Hearts. This is very fine *Talking*: I could wish that all the *Doings* too, were equally Innocent. . . .

But let us go on, and examine if in the General Corruption of Manners these New Lights have made any Reform in the Vice of Drunkenness? . . . There is not one Hogshead of Liquor less consum'd since their visiting us, or any Tavern shut up—So far from it, that there has been

Great Increase of Both. Go to any Common Muster or Vendue, Will you not see the same Fighting, Brawling Gouging, Quarreling as ever? And this too among the Holy ones of our New Israel? Are Riots, Frolics, Races, Games, Cards, Dice, Dances, less frequent now than formerly? Are fewer persons to be seen in Taverns? or reeling or drunk on the Roads? And have any of the Godly Storekeepers given up their Licences, or refus'd to retail Poison? If this can be made appear, I will yield the Point. But if [it] can be made apparent that a much greater Quantity of Rum is now expended in private families than heretofore — That the greater Part of these religious Assemblies are calculated for private Entertainments, where each brings his Quota and which often terminates in Intemperance and Intoxication of both Sexes, Young and Old: That one half of those who resort to these Assemblies Go more for sake of Liquor, than Instruction, or Devotion. That if it be proven that Liquor has been top'd about even in their very Meeting Houses, and the Preachers refreshed with Good Things, and after the Farce ended Stuff'd and Cramm'd almost to bursting, then it must be granted that little or no Reform has been made among the Vulgar in Point of Intemperance save only among some few Persons in some Places where the Mode only is chang'd, and drinking in Public wav'd for the Indulgence of double the Consumption in Private.

The horrid Vice of Swearing has long been a reproach to the Back Inhabitants, and very justly — for few Countries on Earth can equal these Parts as to this grievous Sin. But has it ceas'd since the Admission of rambling Fanatics among us? I grant that it has with and among many, whom they have gain'd to their Sect. Yet still it too much prevails. But the Enormity of this Vice, when at the Highest, produc'd no Evils, Jarrs, disturbances Strifes, Contentions, Variance, Dissimulations, Envyings, Slanders, Backbitings and a thousand other Evils that now disturb both the Public Places and repose of Individuals. So that where they have cast out one Devil, Seven, and twice Seven others have enter'd In and possess the Man. For never was so much Lying, Calumny, Defamation, and all hellish Evils and vexations of this Sort that can spring from the Devil and his Angels, so brief so prevalent, so abounding as since the Arrival of these villanous Teachers, Who blast, blacken, Ruin, and destroy the Characters, Reputations, Credit and Fame of all Persons not linked with them to the Ruin of Society, the Peace of families, and the Settlement of the Country.

We will further enquire, if Lascivousness, or Wantoness, Adultery or Fornication [are] less common than formerly, before the Arrival of these *Holy* Persons? Are there fewer Bastards born? Are more Girls with their Virginity about them, Married, than were heretofore? The Parish Register will prove the Contrary: There are rather more Bastards, more Mullatoes born than before. Nor out of 100 Young Women that I marry in a Year have I seen, or is there seen, Six but what are with Child? . . . And as for Adulteries, the present State of most Persons around 9/10 of whom now labour under a filthy Distemper (as is well known to all) puts that Matter out of all Dispute and shews that the Saints however outwardly Precise and Reserved are not one Whit more Chaste than formerly, and possibly are more privately Vicious.

And nothing more leads to this Than what they call their Love Feasts and Kiss of Charity. To which Feasts, celebrated at Night, much Liquor is privately carried, and deposited on the Roads, and in Bye Paths and Places. . . .

But certainly these Reformers have put some Stop to the many Thefts and Depradations so openly committed of late Years? — To answer this Question recourse must be had to the Magistrates and Courts of Justice, who are ready to declare, that since the Appearance of these New Lights, more Enormities of all Kinds have been committed — More Robberies Thefts, Murders, Plunderings, Burglaries and Villanies of ev'ry Kind, than ever before. And the Reason hereof, Is, That most of these Preaching fellows were most notorious Theives, Jockeys, Gamblers, and what not in the Northern Provinces, and since their Reception and Success here have drawn Crowds of their old Acquaintances after them; So that the Country never was so full as at present of Gamesters Prostitutes, Filchers, Racers, Fidlers and all the refuse of Mankind. All which follow these Teachers, and under the Mask of Religion carry on many detestable Practises. In short, they have filled the Country with Idle and Vagrant Persons, who live by their Criminalities. For it is a Maxim with these Vermin of Religion, That a Person must first be a Sinner e're He can be a Saint. . . .

For only draw a Comparison between them and Us, and let an Imparitial Judge determine where *Offence* may cheifly be taken, At our Solemn, Grave, and Serious Sett Forms, or their Wild Extempore Jargon, nauseaus to any Chaste or refin'd Ear. There are so many Absurdities committed by them, as wou'd shock one of our *Cherokee* Savages; And was a Sensible Turk or Indian to view some of their Extravagancies it would quickly determine them against Christianity. Had any such been in their Assembly as last Sunday when they communicated, the Honest Heathens would have imagin'd themselves rather amidst a Gang of frantic Lunatics broke out of Bedlam, rather than among a Society of religious Christians, met to celebrate the most sacred and Solemn Ordinance of their Religion. Here, one Fellow mounted on a Bench . . . One on his knees in a Posture of Prayer — Others singing — some howling — These Ranting — Those Crying — Others dancing, Skipping, Laughing and rejoycing. Here two or 3 Women falling on their Backs, kicking up their Heels, exposing their Nakedness to all Bystanders and others sitting Pensive, in deep Melancholy lost in Abstraction, like Statues, quite insensible — and when rous'd by the Spectators from their pretended Reveries Transports, and indecent Postures and Actions declaring they knew nought of the Matter. That their Souls had taken flight to Heav'n, and they knew nothing of what they said or did. Spect[at]ors were highly shocked at such vile Abuse of sacred Ordinances! And indeed such a Scene was sufficient to make the vilest Sinner shudder.

Questions

1. What evidence is there in this account to suggest that social conflict was at the root of Woodmason's complaints about the inhabitants of the backcountry? Why might Woodmason, a member of the social elite, feel particularly threatened by the New Lights?

2. What was the primary difference "between them and Us," according to Woodmason? What does this reveal about the nature of the contest between the established churches and the revivalists?

3. What vices did Woodmason single out? What is the significance of his catalogue of sins? Did he suggest any remedies for the ills of the backcountry?

Questions for Further Thought

1. In what ways did the ideas of the Enlightenment and the Great Awakening challenge the authority of the established social and cultural order of colonial American society?

2. Was the conflict between the revivalists and the established clergy rooted in cultural differences? Explain.

3. Why did Americans in the eighteenth century embrace both religion and science with equal fervor? What was it about pietistic religion and Enlightenment rationalism that Americans found so attractive, and why?

The Midcentury Challenge: War, Trade, and Social Conflict, 1750–1765

In the years 1740–1765, the British empire in North America was redefined by three sets of events: the French and Indian War, an expansion of transatlantic trade that increased prosperity but raised colonial debt, and a great westward movement.

In the late 1740s, a shortage of land and the influx of immigrants into the middle and southern colonies brought pressure for expansion, leading to a clash between Britain and France for the interior of North America (Document 4-10). When William Pitt the Elder became first minister in 1757, he devised a strategy that turned the conflict into a great war for empire. The turning point in North America was the British capture of Quebec in 1759; the war ended with the reduction of the French empire in North America to a handful of islands.

As the colonial population continued to expand, serious land shortages led to conflicts over land rights, Indian policy, law and order, and political representation. For example, Connecticut fought with Pennsylvania over settlement in the Wyoming Valley. In Pennsylvania, conflicts between Scots-Irish immigrants along the frontier and the Quaker political establishment stirred violence and nearly led to civil war (Document 4-11).

4-10   Negotiating Peace with the Ohio Indians (1758)

Christian Frederick Post

The French and Indian War began in the Ohio Valley in 1754. As France and Great Britain battled for control of North America, Indian tribes made a series of shifting alliances with both sides to protect their interests and resist European encroachment.

By the summer of 1758, after waging four years of war on the Pennsylvania frontier, both Indians and colonists had grown weary of the fighting. British general John Forbes, charged with taking Fort Duquesne (near present-day Pittsburgh), was eager to negotiate with the Ohio tribes, hoping to persuade them to abandon their alliance with the French. When Forbes learned that the Ohio Indians would reconsider their alliance if Pennsylvania authorities promised to end further encroachments on native lands, Forbes asked Governor William Denny to make the necessary overtures toward peace. Denny obliged by appointing Christian Frederick Post (1710–1785) to meet with the Ohio sachems and to convey the governor's goodwill. A Moravian missionary who had lived among the Delaware tribes for about a decade, learned their language, and had twice been married to Delaware women, Post was uniquely qualified to serve as the colony's negotiator. In late August, after traversing three hundred difficult miles from Philadelphia, Post arrived at the Indian town of Kuskuskies on Beaver Creek, a tributary of the Ohio River. The following excerpt is from Post's account of his meeting with Indians on September 1, 1758.

Source: Reuben Gold Thwaites, ed., *Early Western Travels, 1748–1846* (Cleveland, OH: Arthur H. Clark Co., 1904), 1:213–216.

Shingas, King *Beaver, Delaware George,* and *Pisquetumen,* with several other captains said to me,

"Brother, We have thought a great deal since God has brought you to us; and this is a matter of great consequence, which we cannot readily answer; we think on it, and will answer you as soon as we can. Our feast hinders us; all our young men, women and children are glad to see you; before you came, they all agreed together to go and join the *French*; but since they have seen you, they all draw back; though we have great reason to believe you intend to drive us away, and settle the country; or else, why do you come to fight in the land that God has given us?"

I said, we did not intend to take the land from them; but only to drive the *French* away. They said, they knew better; for that they were informed so by our greatest traders; and some Justices of the Peace had told them the same, and the *French,* said they, tell us much the same thing, — "that the *English* intend to destroy us, and take our lands;" but the land is ours, and not theirs; therefore, we say, if you will be at peace with us, we will send the *French* home. It is you that have begun the war, and it is necessary that you hold fast, and be not discouraged, in the work of peace. We love you more than you love us; for when we take any prisoners from you, we treat them as our own children. We are poor, and yet we clothe them as well as we can, though you see our children are as naked as at the first. By this you may see that our hearts are better than yours. It is plain that you white people are the cause of this war; why do not you and the *French* fight in the old country, and on the sea? Why do you come to fight on our land? This makes every body believe, you want to take the land from us by force, and settle it.

I told them, "Brothers, as for my part, I have not one foot of land, nor do I desire to have any; and if I had any land, I had rather give it to you, than take any from you. Yes, brothers, if I die, you will get a little more land from me; for I shall then no longer walk on that ground, which God has

made. We told you that you should keep nothing in your heart, but bring it before the council fire, and before the Governor, and his council; they will readily hear you; and I promise you, what they answer they will stand to. I further read to you what agreements they made about *Wioming,* and they stand to them."

They said, "Brother, your heart is good, you speak always sincerely; but we know there are always a great number of people that want to get rich; they never have enough; look, we do not want to be rich, and take away that which others have. God has given you the tame creatures; we do not want to take them from you. God has given to us the deer, and other wild creatures, which we must feed on; and we rejoice in that which springs out of the ground, and thank God for it. Look now, my brother, the white people think we have no brains in our heads; but that they are great and big, and that makes them make war with us: we are but a little handful to what you are; but remember, when you look for a wild turkey you cannot always find it, it is so little it hides itself under the bushes: and when you hunt for a rattlesnake, you cannot find it; and perhaps it will bite you before you see it. However, since you are so great and big, and we so little, do you use your greatness and strength in compleating this work of peace. This is the first time that we saw or heard of you, since the war begun, and we have great reason to think about it, since such a great body of you comes into our lands. It is told us, that you and the *French* contrived the war, to waste the *Indians* between you; and that you and the *French* intended to divide the land between you: this was told us by the chief of the *Indian* traders; and they said further, brothers, this is the last time we shall come among you; for the *French* and the *English* intend to kill all the *Indians,* and then divide the land among themselves.

Then they addressed themselves to me, and said, "Brother, I suppose you know something about it; or has the Governor stopped your mouth, that you cannot tell us?"

Then I said, "Brothers, I am very sorry to see you so jealous. I am your own flesh and blood, and sooner than I would tell you any story that would be of hurt to you, or your children, I would suffer death: and if I did not know that it was the desire of the Governor, that we should renew our old brotherly love and friendship, that subsisted between our grandfathers, I would not have undertaken this journey. I do assure you of mine and the people's honesty. If the *French* had not been here, the *English* would not have come; and consider, brothers, whether, in such a case, we can always sit still."

Then they said, "It is a thousand pities we did not know this sooner; if we had, it would have been peace long before now."

Questions

1. According to the Ohio Indians, who or what caused the war between France and England in the 1750s? To what degree were the Indians correct in their views?

2. Given what you know of events in colonial America since the arrival of the first Europeans, did the Indians have good cause to fear the motives of the English? Why might they have accepted the disclaimers of Post with regard to designs upon their land?

3. What might Post have meant when he told the Ohio Indians, "I am your own flesh and blood"?

4-11   Protests on the Frontier: The Paxton Riots (1764)

Thomas Barton

In December 1763 a group of frontiersmen from Paxton Township, Pennsylvania, fell upon a small, peaceful group of Conestoga Indians, killing six. When the magistrates of nearby Lancaster sheltered the Native American survivors in the workhouse, a mob invaded the town, broke into the workhouse, and murdered fourteen more Indians. Soon after, two hundred of the "Paxton Boys" marched on Philadelphia in pursuit of Indian refugees there; civil war was averted only by the diplomacy of Benjamin Franklin and others, who promised a hearing for the Paxton grievances if the men would return home.

The Paxton incident brought to a focus numerous tensions resulting from frontier expansion, the increasingly multiethnic character of Pennsylvania, and continued tight control of the colony by the Penn family and the Quaker elite of Philadelphia. All of these tensions are displayed vividly in this early manifesto, circulated along the frontier and reproduced in a pamphlet written by one of their defenders.

Source: Excerpt from Thomas Barton, "The Conduct of the Paxton-Men, Impartially Represented . . . ," in *The Paxton Papers*, ed. John R. Dunbar (The Hague: Martinus Nijhoff, 1957), 269–275. (Footnotes are from the original document.) Reprinted with kind permission from Springer Science and Business Media.

For my Part, I am no Adept in Politicks, and have but seldom troubled my Head about that Science, beyond the reading of a common News-Paper. — It has long been my unhappy Lot to be a Spectator of the Distresses and Sufferings of my Fellow Subjects; my Heart has often bled for them; — and I should still have continued a secret Mourner for what I had not Power to redress, had not the unaccoutable [*sic*] Conduct of your City Quakers provoked me to speak my Sentiments, and unburthen myself to my Friend. — By my Principles as well as Situation in Life, you know, my dear Sir, that I have no political Ends to serve; that I have nothing to hope or fear from Party Connections; and that I can have no other View in troubling you with this Letter than to rescue the miserable Frontier People, who lately rose in Arms, from the Infamy and Odium thrown upon them, by *those* whose unfeeling Hearts have never suffered them to look beyond their own private Interest and Party.[1]

The INSURGENTS themselves hand about a Kind of *Manifesto*, which contains the following Declaration, Grievances, Complaints, &c. — viz.

---

[1] The Author of this Letter, hopes he will not be understood as approving of these People's having taken up Arms. Such violent Steps can never possibly be productive of anything, but WILD UPROAR and CONFUSION. Whatever therefore can have a Tendency to promote this; or that offers the *least Insult* to the LAWS and GOVERNMENT of this Country, he will ever think it his Duty to bear his Testimony against, and to discountenance by every Means in his Power. [*Barton's note.*]

"That a trifling Dispute, between a few English and French Traders upon the *Ohio*, was neglected; the profer'd Mediation and Assistance of the Indians to end the Quarrel, and the Proprietary-Offer of £. 400, for erecting a small Fortification there, together with £.100 yearly, towards the Support of it, were contemptuously rejected, till it kindled the Flames of War, which at last spread and raged over half the Globe.—That from the Neglect of the *Legislative Part* of this Province, and the horrid Doctrines of *Non-Resistance* at that Times so strenuously maintain'd, such Calamities ensued, that near *one Hundred Miles* of as thriving a Settlement as any in Pennsylvania has been reduced to Desolation; many of the Inhabitants murdered or carried into Captivity, and the Rest often drove from their Habitations in the utmost Distress and Want.—And besides these particular Effects of this War, some of the best Blood in Christendom has been spilt in it—whole Kingdoms have been almost depopulated; and Misery and Ruin entail'd upon Millions of their Fellow Creatures.

"That even in the Midst of this Desolation and Carnage, every publick Measure was clogg'd—the King's Demands for Men and Money procrastinated—unnecessary, or at least ill-timed Disputes, about *Proprietary Instructions and Taxes*, were brought upon the Carpet, in Order to divert the Reproach and Dishonour which the Province, thro' Quakers Measures, had incurr'd, and throw the whole Blame of the War at the Proprietary Doors. And that this villainous Scheme might carry with it a better Face, the late infamous TEDYUSCUNG[2] was treated with, and employed to charge the Proprietaries with having defrauded the Indians of some Lands, and to declare that this was the Occasion of all their Uneasiness and Enmity to the *English*.—But infamous as TEDYUSCUNG was, he own'd at lastt [*sic*] that his Complaints were unjust; publickly renounc'd his Claim, and declared in open Treaty that he was urged to act this base Part, and that he was only the *Mouth of some Persons* in Philadelphia, whom he did not chuse to name.

"That they have always manifested, and are still upon every occasion ready to manifest their Allegiance and Loyalty to their most gracious Sovereign King GEORGE, whom they have ever esteemed as the kind and careful Father of his People.

"That tho' born to Liberty, and all the glorious Rights and Privileges of BRITISH SUBJECTS, they were denied Protection, at a Time when the Cries of Murder and Distress might have made the very Stones relent; and tho' roused to Vengeance and eager to maintain and defend their Lives and sacred Rights, their Hands were basely tied up!

"They could obtain no proper Law to collect their Strength; nor any Sanction or Encouragement to pursue the Enemies of their Country!

"That they have suffered and bled in the Cause of their Country, and have done more to protect it from the Violence of a rapacious Enemy than any others in the Province.

"That agreeable to the Command of the Prophet, they have 'fought for their Brethren, their Sons, and their Daughters, their Wives and their Houses.'—That in this Context, many of them have lost their dearest Relatives; their Houses, their Lands, their all; and from a plentifull independent People have been reduced to Misery and Want.

"That they have been treated as *Aliens* of the Common-Wealth, and denied a just and *proportionable Share in Legislation*: For that out of 36 Members which the eight Counties in the Province send to Assembly, the three Counties of *Philadelphia*, *Chester* and *Bucks*, where the Quakers are chiefly settled, return 26 of that Number; while the 5 remaining Counties, where these LORDLY RULERS could have no Chance of getting elected, are suffered to send but the other Ten.

"That by this iniquitous Policy, the Inhabitants of these five Frontier Counties, altho' a great Majority, have been rendered unable to act in Defense of their Lives and Properties; and therefore have lain for above eight Years at the Mercy of a cruel Savage Enemy and an unrelenting Quaker Faction: Whereas had they been justy [*sic*] represented in Legislation, instead of presenting PACIFICK ADDRESSES to the Assembly, telling them that 'the raising large Sums of Money, and putting them into Hands of COMMITTEES, who might apply them to Purposes inconsistent with their PEACEABLE TESTIMONY, was in its Consequences destructive of RELIGIOUS LIBERTY.' Instead of doing this, I say,—the first great Law of Nature, that of SELF-DEFENCE, would have been administred to the People upon the first Alarm of Danger, and the Hands of the HARDY and the BRAVE would have been set at Liberty, till they had taken ample Vengeance of their MURDERERS.

"That they have often, in the most suppliant Manner, laid their Grievances before the Assembly; and instead of being redress'd, have been abused, insulted, and even by some Members of that *venerable House*, deem'd as unworthy of Protection, as 'A Pack of insignificant SCOTCH-IRISH, who, if they were all *killed* could well enough be spared.'[3]

"That whilst they were thus abused, and thus stript of their Birth-Rights,—ISRAEL and JOSEPH,[4] two petty Fellows, who ought to have no higher Claims than themselves, were permitted to lord it over the Land; and in Contempt of the Government, and the express Orders of the Crown, forbiding them to hold private Treaties with the Indians, exchange Belts of Wampum with them—make them Presents—all this they have done, and in their own Name,

---

[2] *Tedyuscung:* 1700?–1763. Delaware chief. After Braddock's defeat he assembled the Delawares and Shawnees in Wyoming Valley to fight the whites. He was pacified by treaties at Easton in 1756 and 1757. [*Dunbar's note.*]

[3] This unchristian and ungenerous Speech was made by N——L G——B, a Quaker, Member of Assembly for *Chester* County, and some others. [*Barton's note.*]

[4] *Israel Pemberton and Joseph Fox:* This refers to their work as leaders in The Friendly Association. [*Dunbar's note.*]

without so much as including the simple MENONISTS, from whom they had extorted large sums of Money to Support this Expence.——Nay, even with the most matchless Impudence, insinuated to the Indians that they were Rulers and Governors; as plainly appear'd at the late Treaty at LANCASTER, where the Principal CHEIF [sic] and SPEAKER told Mr. H————N,[5] then Governor, 'That as he understood there were two GOVERNORS in the Province, he would be glad to know which of them he was to treat with.'[6]

"That the Indians were induced to look upon ISRAEL as the *first* Man, or CHEIF [sic] SACHEM of the Province, from seeing the Haughtiness and Contempt with which he treated his Fellow Subjects, and his insolent and arrogant Behaviour to Sir W————M J————N[7] at *Easton*; and to Governor H————N, at *Lancaster*: And that this, among other Things, has been productive of manifold Evils, by weakening our Credit with Indians, frustrating the good Intention of holding Treaties with them, and encouraging them, after they return'd from us loaded with Money, Cloaths, Arms and Ammunition, to look with Contempt upon us as a pusillanimous Pack of *old Women*, divided among ourselves, without SPIRIT or RESOLUTION to call them to an Account, let them commit what Outrages they pleased upon us.——

"That they have been made Tributaries to support the immense Expence of Indian Treaties; to which they chearfully submitted, in Hopes that their dear Relations and Fellow Subjects, who have been long detained in barbarous Captivity, would have been restored; But that instead of insisting upon the Promises and Engagements made by the Indians to this End, an extensive and valuable Trade was opened with these faithless and perfidious Villains; and their poor unhappy Friends left to spend perhaps the Remainder of their days, in all the Sorrow and Miseries of Heathenism and Barbarity, and to bow their Necks to the cruel Slavery of Savages.

"That at a Time when their ungenerous and merciless Enemies, had again, without the least provocation, invaded

the Province, with the very Arms and Ammunition which they received at the late Treaties; and when the Frontiers were yet reeking with the Blood of their slaughter'd Inhabitants; and the murdered Ghosts of their Friends and Relatives cry'd aloud for Vengeance, a Number of Indians (many of which were concerned in this horrid Butchery) were escorted to the *Metropolis*, and there protected, cherished, and maintained in Luxury and Idleness, whilst they, the poor Sufferers, were abandoned to Misery, and left to starve, or beg their Bread.

"That upon seeing themselves thus abused and thus neglected, and considering that the Influence of a *Quaker Faction* was the Source from whence all these Evils flow'd; and that *pretended* Scruples against War and Fighting were the Root from whence all their Calamities and heavy Sufferings sprang, and if yet permitted, might produce worse and more heavy, they were determined to bear no longer.

"That *Pennsylvania* appear'd to them to be really in a dangerous CACHEXY;[8] and that at such a Crisis they look'd upon it as their Duty to administer such Remedies (however severe they might be look'd upon by some) as might raise her drooping Head, and restore her to Health and Vigour.—— And should their first Trial fail of Success, that in the Case they are determined to *double the Potion*,[9] which they hope will intirely purge off the peccant Humours, restore the Solids, and secure her hereafter from the Infection of *Quaker Non-Resistance.*"

Such is the Declaration, and such the Complaints of these People.——And indeed nine Tenths of the Inhabitants of the Back-Counties either tacitly, or openly, approve and support them—Every cool and well thinking Man, as well as Men among themselves, are sensibly concern'd that they were reduced to the Necessity of having Recourse to such Methods as might be deem'd an Insult to the Government and Laws of their King and Country.

The Names of RIOTERS, REBELS, MURDERERS, WHITE SAVAGES, &c. have been liberally and indiscriminately bestowed upon them: But all this they look upon only as the Effects of disappointed Malice, and the Resentment of a destructive FACTION, who see their *darling Power* in Danger.——The *Merciful* and the *Good* however, they trust, will rather pity than condemn them.—And they are pleased with the Thoughts that they have been able at last to lay bare the PHARASAICAL BOSOM OF QUAKERISM, by obliging the NONRESISTING QUALITY to take up Arms, and to become Proselytes to *the first great Law of Nature.*

---

[5] James Hamilton. [*Dunbar's note.*]

[6] That you may be convinced that such was the Opinion of the *Indians*, I must observe to you, that one PATRICK AGNEW, of the Borough of *Lancaster*, White-Smith, having been duly sworn upon the HOLY EVANGELISTS, before the CHIEF BURGESS of that Town, hath deposed and said, That he, the said Deponent, being a Constable at the last Indian Treaty at Lancaster, was commanded by the *Governor*, to proclaim, that no Person should sell or give any Kind of spirituous Liquors to the Indians, on any Pretence whatever; that he proclaim'd this Order thro' the Town accordingly, and that upon his making Proclamation, and saying, *by Order of the Governor*, an Indian named TEDYUSCUNG, cry'd out 'D—n your G————r, D—n your G————r; P—m—t-n is my Governor, P—m—t-n is our Governor, he allows RUM enough;' and offer'd Violence to this Deponent; who also, upon his Oath, declares that, notwithstanding the Proclamation, the Indians were privately entertain'd at a certain Tavern in the Town. [*Barton's note.*]

[7] Sir William Johnson. [*Dunbar's note.*]

[8] Depraved condition of the body politic. [*Dunbar's note.*]

[9] By this Expression, I am told, these People mean, that they will renew their Application and ADDRESSES, with DOUBLE the NUMBER of Signers; and it is said, they are likely to get TEN to ONE, that they had before, to remonstrate with them. [*Barton's note.*]

Questions

1.   What do we learn about mid-eighteenth-century Pennsylvania politics from the Paxton manifesto? What sorts of social, economic, political, and religious issues divided the colony?

2.   What grievances does the author of the manifesto articulate? Where does he lay the blame for the conflict, and why?

3.   Why do you think the author of the manifesto feels the need to state explicitly the loyalty of the Paxton Boys to King George?

4-12   Middle Passage (c. 1754)

Olaudah Equiano

Olaudah Equiano's life story is nothing if not extraordinary. According to his autobiographical *Interesting Narrative*, he was born in Isseke, Nigeria, in 1745, and kidnapped and sold to English slave traders at age eleven. Transported first to Barbados and then to a Virginia plantation in 1756, he was subsequently sold to a captain in the Royal Navy and saw action at sea during the Seven Years' War. Expecting to be freed at the end of the war, he was sold instead to a Quaker merchant and slave trader on the West Indian island of Montserrat in 1762. Fortunately for Equiano, his new master included him in the shipping business, and by 1766 he had accumulated enough money to purchase his freedom. Ironically, Equiano worked briefly in the slave trade himself before joining the fledgling antislavery movement in the 1780s. The publication of his *Narrative* in 1789 gained him fame and some wealth before his death in London in 1797. Equiano's description of his tortuous journey from Africa to the New World is the most famous account extant of the Middle Passage.

Source: Excerpts from *The Interesting Narrative of the Life of Olaudah Equiano*, ed. Robert J. Allison, 2nd ed. (Boston: Bedford/St. Martin's, 2007), 1: 64–68.

The first object which saluted my eyes when I arrived on the coast was the sea, and a slave ship, which was then riding at anchor, and waiting for its cargo. These filled me with astonishment, which was soon converted into terror when I was carried on board. I was immediately handled and tossed up to see if I were sound by some of the crew; and I was now persuaded that I had gotten into a world of bad spirits, and that they were going to kill me. Their complexions too differing so much from ours, their long hair, and the language they spoke, (which was very different from any I had ever heard) united to confirm me in this belief. Indeed such were the horrors of my views and fears at the moment, that, if ten thousand worlds had been my own, I would have freely parted with them all to have exchanged my condition with that of the meanest slave in my own country. When I looked round the ship too and saw a large furnace or copper boiling, and a multitude of black people of every description chained together, every one of their countenances expressing dejection and sorrow, I no longer doubted of my fate; and, quite overpowered with horror and anguish, I fell motionless on the deck and fainted. When I recovered a little I found some black people about me, who I believed were some of those who brought me on board, and had been receiving their pay; they talked to me in order to cheer me, but all in vain. I asked them if we were not to be eaten by those white men with horrible looks, red faces, and loose hair. They told me I was not; and one of the crew brought me a small portion of spirituous liquor in a wine glass; but, being afraid of him, I would not take it out of his hand. One of the blacks therefore took it from him and gave it to me, and I took a little down my palate, which, instead of reviving me, as they thought it would, threw me into the greatest consternation at the strange feeling it produced, having never tasted any such liquor before. Soon after this the blacks who brought me on board went off, and left me abandoned to despair. I now saw myself deprived of all chance of returning to my native country, or even the least glimpse of hope of gaining the shore, which I now considered as friendly; and I even wished for my former slavery in preference to my present situation, which was filled with horrors of every kind, still heightened by my ignorance of what I was to undergo. I was not long suffered to indulge my grief; I was soon put down under the decks, and there I received such a salutation in my nostrils as I had never experienced in my life; so that, with the loathsomeness of the stench, and crying together, I became so sick and low that I was not able to eat, nor had I the least desire to taste any thing. I now wished for the last friend, death, to relieve me; but soon, to my grief, two of the white men offered me eatables; and, on my refusing to eat, one of them held me fast by the hands, and laid me across I think the windlass, and tied my feet, while the other flogged me severely. I had never experienced any thing of this kind before; and although, not being used to the water, I naturally feared that element the first time I saw it, yet nevertheless could I have got over the nettings, I would have jumped over the side but I could not, and, besides, the crew used to watch us very closely who were not chained down to the decks, lest we should leap into the water: and I have seen some of these poor African prisoners most severely cut for attempting to do so, and hourly whipped for not eating. This indeed was often the case with myself. In a little time after amongst the poor chained men, I found some of my own nation, which in a small degree gave ease to my mind. I inquired of these what was to be done with us; they gave me to understand we were to be carried to these white people's country to work for them. I then was a little revived, and thought, if it were no worse than working, my situation was not so desperate: but still I feared I should be put to death, the white people looked and acted, as I thought, in so savage a manner; for I had never seen among any people such instances of brutal cruelty; and this not only shewn towards us blacks, but also to some of the whites themselves. One white man in particular I saw, when we were permitted to be on deck, flogged so unmercifully with a large rope near the foremast, that he died in consequence of it; and they tossed him over the side as they would have done a brute. This made me fear these people the more; and I expected nothing less than to be treated in the same manner. . . . The stench of the hold while we were on the coast was so intolerably loathsome, that it was dangerous to remain there for any time, and some of us had been permitted to stay on the deck for the fresh air; but now that the whole ship's cargo were confined together, it became absolutely pestilential. The closeness of the place, and the heat of the climate, added to the number in the ship, which was so crowded that each had scarcely room to turn himself, almost suffocated us. This produced copious perspirations, so that the air soon became unfit for respiration, from a variety of loathsome smells, and brought on a sickness among the slaves, of which many died, thus falling victims to the improvident avarice, as I may call it, of their purchasers. This wretched situation was again aggravated by the galling of the chains, now become insupportable; and the filth of the necessary tubs, into which the children often fell, and were almost suffocated. The shrieks of the women, and the groans of the dying, rendered the whole a scene of horror almost inconceivable. Happily perhaps for myself I was soon reduced so low here that it was thought necessary to keep me almost always on deck; and from my extreme youth I was not put in fetters. In this situation I expected every hour to share the fate of my companions, some of whom were almost daily brought upon deck at the point of death, which I began to hope would soon put an end to my miseries. Often did I think many of the inhabitants of the deep much more happy than myself. I envied them the freedom they enjoyed, and as often wished I could change my condition for theirs. Every circumstance I met with served only to render my state more painful, and heighten my apprehensions, and my opinion of the cruelty of the whites. . . . One day, when we had a smooth sea and moderate wind, two of my wearied countrymen who were chained together (I was near them at the time), preferring death to such a life of misery, somehow made through the nettings and jumped into the sea: immediately another quite dejected fellow, who, on one account of his illness, was suffered to be out of irons, also followed their example; and I believe many more would very soon have done the same if they had not been prevented by the ship's crew, who were instantly alarmed. Those of us that were the most active were in a moment put down under the deck, and here was such a noise and confusion amongst the people of the ship as I never heard before, to stop her, and get the boat out to go after the slaves. However two of the wretches were drowned, but they got the other, and afterwards flogged him unmercifully for thus attempting to prefer death to slavery. In this manner we continued to undergo more hardships than I can now relate, hardships which are inseparable from this accursed trade. Many a time we were near suffocation from the want of fresh air, which we were often without for whole days together. This, and the stench of the necessary tubs, carried off many. . . . At last we came in sight of the island of Barbadoes, at which the whites on board gave a great shout, and made many signs of joy to us. We did not know what to think of this; but as the vessel drew nearer we plainly saw the harbour, and other ships of different kinds and sizes; and we soon anchored amongst them off Bridge Town.

Questions

1. What are the major themes of Equiano's narrative? How might they be incorporated into a general antislavery appeal? Who was Equiano's intended audience?

2. Equiano was an adult when he wrote this account, remembering his experiences as a child some thirty-five years earlier. Is this important? Why or why not?

3. Some recently discovered evidence suggests that Equiano may have been born in South Carolina and not in Africa. If this proves to be true, would his account of the Middle Passage be rendered useless?

Questions for Further Thought

1. What do these documents suggest about the social composition of the colonies in the mid-eighteenth century?

2. What do these documents suggest about tensions arising from differences of race and class in eighteenth-century America?

3. Based on the documents contained in this chapter, how might you modify Crèvecoeur's answer to the question, "What then is the American, this new man?"

CHAPTER FIVE

Toward Independence: Years of Decision

1763–1776

Imperial Reform, 1763–1765

In 1763 all British subjects, including the American colonists, celebrated their victory over the French in the Great War for Empire (see text pp. 125–127), but the celebrations were short-lived. The British national debt had increased by more than 75 percent, and while demanding more in taxes from subjects at home, imperial officials also expected the colonists to bear more of the cost of administering the newly enlarged empire in North America. That these same colonists had a history of evading trade laws and resisting parliamentary control convinced the crown of the need to reform the imperial system to ensure stricter enforcement of any prospective revenue measure. Thus, although the Sugar Act of 1764 cut by one-half the tax imposed by the 1733 Molasses Act, it strengthened the means of collection. Colonial merchants would not be able to avoid this new tax as easily as they had its earlier counterpart, and accused violators could be tried in vice-admiralty courts, that is, in maritime courts without the benefit of juries and likely outside of the jurisdiction where the alleged violations had occurred.

James Otis Jr. wrote the most influential colonial response to the Sugar Act (Document 5-1). Even as the debate over the propriety of the 1764 act was commencing, however, Parliament was already contemplating a more far-reaching stamp bill (Document 5-2). Because the colonists insisted that they could be taxed only with their consent, given directly or through their representatives, Thomas Whately attempted to convince them that they were represented in Parliament in the same way that "nine-tenths of the people of Britain" were—"virtually" (Document 5-3). Daniel Dulany rejected Whately's arguments (Document 5-4), as did the Stamp Act Congress (Document 5-5). Rather abruptly after 1765, the issue of whether the colonists were represented in Parliament disappeared from the public discourse.

5-1   Rights of the Colonies Asserted and Proved (1764)

James Otis Jr.
The French and Indian War, or as it was known in Europe, the Seven Years' War, left Britain in command of over half a continent; however, it also saddled the empire with a huge financial burden. The British national debt had increased by over 75 percent as a result of the

war, and interest charges on that debt alone consumed 60 percent of the annual budget (see text, pp. 138–140). In 1763 Parliament and the ministry saw not only the need for new sources of revenue but also an opportunity to implement imperial reforms that had been left in abeyance for more than a dozen years. The Sugar Act of 1764 was supposed to meet both of these ends. It superseded the widely evaded Molasses Act of 1733 and reduced the duty collected on imported molasses from six pence per gallon to three, but it bolstered the administrative machinery associated with the collection of these taxes. The colonial reaction was first to voice economic concerns regarding the potentially negative impact of the tax, and second to raise constitutional objections to its legitimacy. James Otis Jr., a Harvard-educated lawyer who had already begun to establish a reputation for himself as a champion of colonial rights, wrote the best-known response to the Sugar Act.

Source: Excerpts from *Colonies to Nation: 1763–1789*, ed. Jack P. Greene (New York: Norton, 1975), 28–33. Copyright © 1975 W. W. Norton & Company.

Let no Man think I am about to commence advocate for *despotism*, because I affirm that government is founded on the necessity of our natures; and that an original supreme Sovereign, absolute, and uncontroulable, *earthly* power *must* exist in and preside over every society; from whose final decisions there can be no appeal but directly to Heaven. It is therefore *originally* and *ultimately* in the people. I say this supreme absolute power is *originally* and *ultimately* in the people; and they never did in fact *freely*, nor can they *rightfully* make an absolute, unlimited renunciation of this divine right. It is ever in the nature of the thing given in *trust*, and on a condition, the performance of which no mortal can dispence with; namely, that the person or persons on whom the sovereignty is confered by the people, shall *incessantly* consult *their* good. Tyranny of all kinds is to be abhored, whether it be in the hands of one, or of the few, or of the many. . . .

Every British Subject born on the continent of America, or in any other of the British dominions, is by the law of God and nature, by the common law, and by act of parliament, (exclusive of all charters from the crown) entitled to all the natural, essential, inherent and inseparable rights of our fellow subjects in Great-Britain. Among those rights are the following, which it is humbly conceived no man or body of men, not excepting the parliament, justly, equitably and consistently with their own rights and the constitution, can take away.

1st. *That the supreme and subordinate powers of legislation should be free and sacred in the hands where the community have once rightfully placed them.*

2dly. *The supreme national legislative cannot be altered justly till the commonwealth is dissolved, nor a subordinate legislative taken away without forfeiture or other good cause.* Nor then can the subjects in the subordinate government be reduced to a state of slavery, and subject to the despotic rule of others. . . . The colonists will have an equitable right, notwithstanding any such forfeiture of charter, to be represented in parliament, or to have some new subordinate legislature among themselves. It would be best if they had both. Deprived, however, of their common rights as subjects, they cannot lawfully be, while they remain such. A representation in Parliament from the several colonies, since they are be-

come so large and numerous, as to be called on not only to maintain provincial government, civil and military, among themselves, for this they have chearfully done, but to contribute towards the support of a national standing army, by reason of the heavy national debt, when they themselves owe a large one, contracted in the common cause, cannot be thought an unreasonable thing, nor if asked, could it be called an immodest request. . . .

No representation of the colonies in parliament alone, would, however, be equivalent to a subordinate legislative among themselves; nor so well answer the ends of increasing their prosperity and the commerce of Great-Britain. It would be impossible for the parliament to judge so well of their abilities to bear taxes, impositions on trade, and other duties and burthens, or of the local laws that might be really needful, as a legislative here.

3dly. *No legislative, supreme or subordinate, has a right to make itself arbitrary.*

It would be a most manifest contradiction, for a free legislative, like that of Great-Britain, to make itself arbitrary.

4thly. *The supreme legislative cannot justly assume a power of ruling by extempore arbitrary decrees, but is bound to dispense justice by known settled rules, and by duly authorized independent judges.*

5thly. *The supreme power cannot take from any man any part of his property*, without his consent in *person or by representation.*

6thly. *The legislative cannot transfer the power of making laws to any other hands.*

These are their bounds, which by God and nature are fixed, hitherto have they a right to come, and no further.

1. *To govern by stated laws.*

2. *Those laws should have no other end ultimately, but the good of the people.*

3. *Taxes are not to be laid on the people, but by their consent in person, or by deputation.*

4. *Their whole power is not transferable. . . .*

That the colonists, black and white, born here, are free born British subjects, and entitled to all the essential civil rights of such, is a truth not only manifest from the provincial charters, from the principles of the common law, and acts of parliament; but from the British constitution which was re-established at the revolution, with a professed design to secure the liberties of all the subjects to all generations. . . .

Now can there be any liberty, where property is taken away without consent? Can it with any colour of truth, justice or equity, be affirmed, that the northern colonies are represented in parliament? Has this whole continent, of near three thousand miles in length, and in which, and his other American dominions, his Majesty has, or very soon will have, some millions of as good, loyal and useful subjects, white and black, as any in the three kingdoms, the election of one member of the house of commons?

Is there the least difference, as to the consent of the Colonists, whether taxes and impositions are laid on their trade, and other property, by the crown alone, or by the parliament? As it is agreed on all hands, the Crown alone cannot impose them, we should be justifiable in refusing to pay them, but must and ought to yield obedience to an act of parliament, though erroneous, till repealed.

I can see no reason to doubt, but that the imposition of taxes, whether on trade, or on land, or houses, or ships, on real or personal, fixed or floating property, in the colonies, is absolutely irreconcileable with the rights of the Colonists, as British subjects, and as men. I say men, for in a state of nature, no man can take my property from me, without my consent: If he does, he deprives me of my liberty, and makes me a slave. If such a proceeding is a breach of the law of nature, no law of society can make it just. — The very act of taxing, exercised over those who are not represented, appears to me to be depriving them of one of their most essential rights, as freemen; and if continued, seems to be in effect an entire disfranchisement of every civil right. For what one civil right is worth a rush, after a man's property is subject to be taken from him at pleasure, without his consent? If a man is not his *own assessor* in person, or by deputy, his liberty is gone, or lays intirely at the mercy of others. . . .

To say the parliament is absolute and arbitrary, is a contradiction. The parliament cannot make 2 and 2, 5: Omnipotency cannot do it. The supreme power in a state, is *jus dicere* only: — *jus dare*, strictly speaking, belongs alone to God. Parliaments are in all cases to *declare* what is for the good of the whole; but it is not the *declaration* of parliament that makes it so: There must be in every instance, a higher authority, *viz.* GOD. Should an act of parliament be against any of *his* natural laws, which are *immutably* true, *their* declaration would be contrary to eternal truth, equity and justice, and consequently void: and so it would be adjudged by the parliament itself, when convinced of their mistake. Upon this great principle, parliaments repeal such act, as soon as they find they have been mistaken, in having declared them to be for the public good, when in fact they were not so. . . .

The sum of my argument is, That civil government is of God: that the administrators of it were originally the whole people: that they might have devolved it on whom they pleased: that this devolution is fiduciary, for the good of the whole: that by the British constitution, this devolution is on the King, lords and commons, the supreme, sacred and uncontroulable legislative power, not only in the realm, but through the dominions: that by the abdication, the original compact was broken to pieces: that by the revolution, it was renewed, and more firmly established, and the rights and liberties of the subject in all parts of the dominions, more fully explained and confirmed: that in consequence of this establishment and the acts of succession and union, his Majesty GEORGE III. is rightful king and sovereign, and with his parliament, the supreme legislative of Great-Britain, France and Ireland, and the dominions thereunto belonging: that this constitution is the most free one, and by far the best, now existing on earth: that by this constitution, every man in the dominions is a free man: that no parts of his Majesty's dominions can be taxed without their consent: that every part has a right to be represented in the supreme or some subordinate legislature: that the refusal of this, would seem to be a contradiction in practice to the theory of the constitution: that the colonies are subordinate dominions, and are now in such a state, as to make it best for the good of the whole, that they should not only be continued in the enjoyment of subordinate legislation, but be also represented in some proportion to their number and estates in the grand legislation of the nation: that this would firmly unite all parts of the British empire, in the greatest peace and prosperity; and render it invulnerable and perpetual.

Questions

1. Otis argued that Parliament's legislative power was "supreme" and "uncontroulable," and therefore that the colonists were obligated patiently to submit regardless of how burdensome it proved to be; however, he also claimed that Parliament could not tax the colonists without their consent. How do you explain this apparent contradiction?

2. "To say the parliament is absolute and arbitrary, is a contradiction," Otis declared. Why? Explain his reasoning.

3. How do you explain the fact that people on both sides of the imperial crisis endorsed Otis's pamphlet?

5-2   Report on the Debates in Parliament (1765)

Jared Ingersoll

Jared Ingersoll, a Connecticut lawyer who was in Great Britain on business, accepted a commission from his home colony to do what he could to oppose the Stamp Act, which it appeared Parliament would soon pass. By communicating with Thomas Whately, who played a central role in the drafting of the bill, Ingersoll obtained a few minor modifications. However, he could not persuade British officials to abandon the idea of passing a Stamp Act for America.

As part of his effort to oppose the Stamp Act, Ingersoll attended the debates on the proposed legislation in Parliament. On February 11, 1765, he sent a lengthy report on those debates to Thomas Fitch, the governor of Connecticut. The sections of that letter reprinted here describe the general British attitude and the attitudes of different segments of Parliament toward the Stamp Act.

Source: New Haven Colonial Historical Society, *Papers* (1918), 9:306–315 passim.

The principal Attention has been to the Stamp bill that has been preparing to Lay before Parliament for taxing America. The Point of the Authority of Parliament to impose such Tax I found on my Arrival here was so fully and Universally yielded, that there was not the least hopes of making any impressions that way. Indeed it has appeared since that the House would not suffer to be brought in, nor would any one Member Undertake to Offer to the House, any Petition from the Colonies that held forth the Contrary of that Doctrine. I own I advised the Agents if possible to get that point Canvassed that so the Americans might at least have the Satisfaction of having the point Decided upon a full Debate, but I found it could not be done, and here before I proceed to acquaint you with the Steps that have been taken, in this Matter, I beg leave to give you a Summary of the Arguments which are made Use of in favour of such Authority.

The House of Commons, say they, is a branch of the supreme legislature of the Nation, and which in its Nature is supposed to represent, or rather to stand in the place of, the Commons, that is, of the great body of the people, who are below the dignity of peers; that this house of Commons Consists of a certain number of Men Chosen by certain people of certain places, which Electors, by the Way, they Insist, are not a tenth part of the people, and that the Laws, rules and Methods by which their number is ascertained have arose by degrees and from various Causes and Occasions, and that this house of Commons, therefore, is now fixt and ascertained and is a part of the Supreme unlimited power of the Nation, as in every State there must be some unlimited Power and Authority; and that when it is said they represent the Commons of England, it cannot mean that they do so because those Commons choose them, for in fact by far the greater part do not, but because by their Constitution they must themselves be Commoners, and not Peers, and so the Equals, or of the same Class of Subjects, with the Commons of the Kingdom. They further urge, that the only reason why America has not been heretofore taxed in the fullest Manner, has been merely on Account of their Infancy and Inability; that there have been, however, not wanting Instances of the Exercise of this Power, in the various regulations of the American trade, the Establishment of the post Office etc., and they deny any Distinction between what is called an internal and external Tax as to the point of the Authority imposing such taxes. And as to the Charters in the few provinces where there are any, they say, in the first place, the King cannot grant any that shall exempt them from the Authority of one of the branches of the great body of Legislation, and in the second place say the King has not done, or attempted to do it. In that of Pensilvania the Authority of Parliament to impose taxes is expressly mentioned and reserved; in ours tis said, our powers are generally such as are *According to the Course of other Corporations in England* (both which Instances by way of Sample were mentioned and referred to by Mr. Grenville in the House); in short they say a Power to tax is a necessary part of every Supreme Legislative Authority, and that if they have not that Power over America, they have none, and then America is at once a Kingdom of itself.

On the other hand those who oppose the bill say, it is true the Parliament have a supreme unlimited Authority over every Part and Branch of the Kings dominions and as well over Ireland as any other place, yet we believe a British parliament will never think it prudent to tax Ireland. Tis true they say, that the Commons of England and of the british Empire are all represented in and by the house of Commons, but this representation is confessedly on all hands by Construction and Virtually only as to those who have no hand in choosing the representatives, and that the Effects of this implied Representation here and in America must be infinitely different in the Article of Taxation. Here in England the Member of Parliament is equally known to the Neighbour who elects and to him who does not; the Friendships, the Connections, the Influences are spread through the whole. If by any Mistake an act of Parliament is made that prove injurious and hard the Member of Parliament here sees with his own Eyes and is moreover very accessible to the people, not only so, but the taxes are laid equally by one Rule and fall as well on the Member himself as on the people. But as to America, from the great distance in point of Situation, from the almost total unacquaintedness, Especially in the more northern Colonies, with the Members of Parliament, and they with them, or with the particular Ability and Circumstances of one another, from the Nature of this very tax laid upon others not Equally and in Common with ourselves, but with express purpose to Ease ourselves, we think, say they, that it will be only to lay a foundation of great Jealousy and Continual Uneasiness, and that to no purpose, as we already by the Regulations upon their trade draw from the Americans all that they can spare, at least they say this Step should not take place untill or unless the Americans are allowed to send Members to Parliament; for *who of you*, said Col. Barre Nobly in his Speech in the house upon this Occasion, *who of you reasoning upon this Subject feels warmly from the Heart* (putting his hand to his own breast) *for the Americans as they would for themselves or as you would for the people of your own native Country?* and to this point Mr. Jackson produced Copies of two Acts of Parliament granting the priviledge of having Members to the County Palitine of Chester and the Bishoprick of Durham upon Petitions preferred for that purpose in the Reign of King Henry the Eighth and Charles the first, the preamble of which Statutes counts upon the Petitions from those places as setting forth that being in their general Civil Jurisdiction Exempted from the Common Law Courts etc., yet being Subject to the general authority of Parliament, were taxed in Common with the rest of the Kingdom, which taxes by reason of their having no Members in Parliament to represent their Affairs, often proved hard and injurious etc. and upon that ground they had the priviledge of sending Members granted them—and if this, say they, could be a reason in the case of Chester and Durham, how much more so in the case of America.

Thus I have given you, I think, the Substance of the Arguments on both sides of that great and important Question of the right and also of the Expediency of taxing America by Authority of Parliament. I cannot, however, Content myself without giving you a Sketch of what the aforementioned Mr. Barre said in Answer to some remarks made by Mr. Ch. Townsend in a Speech of his upon this Subject. I ought here to tell you that the Debate upon the American Stamp bill came on before the house for the first time last Wednesday, when the same was open'd by Mr. Grenville the Chanceller of the Exchequer, in a pretty lengthy Speech, and in a very able and I think in a very candid manner he opened the Nature of the Tax, Urged the Necessity of it, Endeavoured to obviate all Objections to it—and took Occasion to desire the house to give the bill a most Serious and Cool Consideration and not suffer themselves to be influenced by any resentments which might have been kindled from any thing they might have heard out of doors—alluding I suppose to the N. York and Boston Assemblys' Speeches and Votes—that this was a

matter of revenue which was of all things the most interesting to the Subject etc. The Argument was taken up by several who opposed the bill (viz) by Alderman Beckford, who, and who only, seemed to deny the Authority of Parliament, by Col. Barre, Mr. Jackson, Sir William Meredith and some others. Mr. Barre, who by the way I think, and I find I am not alone in my Opinion, is one of the finest Speakers that the House can boast of, having been some time in America as an Officer in the Army, and having while there, as I had known before, contracted many Friendships with American Gentlemen, and I believe Entertained much more favourable Opinions of them than some of his profession have done, Delivered a very handsome and moving Speech upon the bill and against the same, Concluding by saying that he was very sure that Most who Should hold up their hands to the Bill must be under a Necessity of acting very much in the dark, but added, perhaps as well in the Dark as any way.

After him Mr. Charles Townsend spoke in favour of the Bill—took Notice of several things Mr. Barre had said, and concluded with the following or like Words:—And now will these Americans, Children planted by our Care, nourished up by our Indulgence untill they are grown to a Degree of Strength and Opulence, and protected by our Arms, will they grudge to contribute their mite to relieve us from the heavy weight of that burden which we lie under? When he had done, Mr. Barre rose and having explained something which he had before said and which Mr Townsend had been remarking upon, he then took up the beforementioned Concluding words of Mr. Townsend, and in a most spirited and I thought an almost inimitable manner, said—

"They planted by your Care? No! your Oppressions planted em in America. They fled from your Tyranny to a then uncultivated and unhospitable Country—where they exposed themselves to almost all the hardships to which human Nature is liable, and among others to the Cruelties of a Savage foe, the most subtle and I take upon me to say the most formidable of any People upon the face of Gods Earth. And yet, actuated by Principles of true english Lyberty, they met all these hardships with pleasure, compared with those they suffered in their own Country, from the hands of those who should have been their Friends.

"They nourished up by *your* indulgence? they grew by your neglect of Em:—as soon as you began to care about Em, that Care was Excercised in sending persons to rule over Em, in one Department and another, who were perhaps the Deputies of Deputies to some Member of this house—sent to Spy out their Lyberty, to misrepresent their Actions and to prey upon Em; men whose behavior on many Occasions has caused the Blood of those Sons of Liberty to recoil within them; men promoted to the highest Seats of Justice, some, who to my knowledge were glad by going to a foreign Country to Escape being brought to the Bar of a Court of Justice in their own.

"They protected by *your* Arms? they have nobly taken up Arms in your defence, have Exerted a Valour amidst their constant and Laborious industry for the defence of a Country, whose frontier, while drench'd in blood, its interior Parts have yielded all its little Savings to your Emolument. And believe me, remember I this Day told you so, that same Spirit of freedom which actuated that people at first, will accompany them still. — But prudence forbids me to explain myself further. God knows I do not at this Time speak from motives of party Heat, what I deliver are the genuine Sentiments of my heart; however superiour to me in general knowledge and Experience the reputable body of this house may be, yet I claim to know more of America than most of you, having seen and been conversant in that Country. The People I believe are as truly Loyal as any Subjects the King has, but a people Jealous of their Lyberties and who will vindicate them, if ever they should be violated — but the Subject is too delicate and I will say no more."

These Sentiments were thrown out so intirely without premeditation, so forceably and so firmly, and the break-

ing off so beautifully abrupt, that the whole house sat awhile as Amazed, intently Looking and without answering a Word.

I own I felt Emotions that I never felt before and went the next Morning and thank'd Col. Barre in behalf of my Country for his noble and spirited Speech.

However, Sir after all that was said, upon a Division of the house upon the Question, there was about 250 to about 50 in favour of the Bill. . . .

The Merchants in London are alarmed at these things; they have had a meeting with the Agents and are about to petition Parliament upon the Acts that respect the trade of North America.

What the Event of these things will be I dont know. . . .
Your Most Obedient Humble Servant.

J. Ingersoll.

Questions

1. On the basis of Ingersoll's observations, how sympathetic were British politicians and the British people to the colonists' view that Parliament did not have the right to tax them?

2. Did the members of Parliament seem well informed about the situation in the mainland colonies of North America? Why or why not?

3. Did the members of Parliament believe that they rather than the colonists were acting to preserve essential British rights? Why or why not?

5-3   Virtual Representation (1765)

Thomas Whately

Beginning with their opposition to the Sugar Act of 1764, the colonists consistently employed a simple syllogism: They could be taxed only by their own representatives; they were not represented in Parliament; therefore, Parliament could not tax them. They did not, contrary to Benjamin Franklin's comments before the House of Commons in 1766, distinguish between "internal" taxes on items produced and consumed largely within the colonies, and "external" duties aimed at regulating trade within the empire as a whole. Franklin claimed that the colonists were opposed to the former but would accept the latter, when instead they found the distinction inconsequential because they were opposed to all forms of taxes not sanctioned by their own representatives. Thomas Whately, secretary of the treasury under George Grenville and the official primarily responsible for drafting the Stamp Act, agreed that the distinction between internal and external taxes was pointless. In his *Regulations Lately Made Concerning the Colonies*, however, Whately argued that the colonists were in fact represented in Parliament, and therefore that their objections were specious.

Source: Excerpts from "The Sugar Act," in *Prologue to Revolution: Sources and Documents on the Stamp Act Crisis, 1764–1766*, ed. Edmund Sears Morgan (Chapel Hill: Published for the Institute of Early American History and Culture at Williamsburg, Virginia 1959), 19–22. Copyright © 1959 by the University of North Carolina Press, renewed 1987 by Edmund S. Morgan. Used by permission of the publisher.

As to the Quota which each Individual must pay, it will be difficult to persuade the Inhabitants of this Country, where the neediest Cottager pays out of his Pittance, however scanty, and how hardly soever earned, our high Duties of Customs and Excise in the Price of all his Consumption; it will be difficult I say, to persuade those who see, who suffer, or who relieve such Oppression; that the *West Indian* out of his Opulence, and the *North American* out of his Competency, can contribute no more than it is now pretended they can afford towards the Expence of Services, the Benefit of which, as a Part of this Nation they share, and as Colonists they peculiarly enjoy. They have indeed their own civil Governments besides to support; but *Great Britain* has her civil Government too; she has also a large Peace Establishment to maintain; and the national Debt, tho' so great a Part, and that the heaviest Part of it has been incurred by a war undertaken for the Protection of the Colonies, lies solely still upon her.

The Reasonableness, and even the Necessity of requiring an *American* Revenue being admitted, the Right of the Mother Country to impose such a Duty upon her Colonies, if duly considered, cannot be questioned: they claim it is true the Privilege, which is common to all *British* Subjects, of being taxed only with their own Consent, given by their Representatives; and may they ever enjoy the Privilege in all its Extent: May this sacred Pledge of Liberty be preserved inviolate, to the utmost Verge of our Dominions, and to the latest Page of our History! but let us not limit the legislative Rights of the *British* People to Subjects of Taxation only: No new Law whatever can bind us that is made without the Concurrence of our Representatives. The Acts of Trade and Navigation, and all other Acts that relate either to ourselves or to the Colonies, are founded upon no other Authority; they are not obligatory if a Stamp Act is not, and every Argument in support of an Exemption from the Superintendence of the *British* Parliament in the one Case, is equally applicable to the others. The Constitution knows no Distinction; the Colonies have never attempted to make one; but have acquiesced under several parliamentary Taxes. . . .

The Instances that have been mentioned prove, that the Right of the Parliament of *Great Britain* to impose Taxes of every Kind on the Colonies, has been always admitted; but were there no Precedents to support the Claim, it would still be incontestable, being founded on the Principles of our Constitution; for the Fact is, that the Inhabitants of the Colonies are represented in Parliament: they do not indeed chuse the Members of that Assembly; neither are Nine Tenths of the People of *Britain* Electors; for the Right of Election is annexed to certain Species of Property, to peculiar Franchises, and to Inhabitancy in some particular Places; but these Descriptions comprehend only a very small Part of the Land, the Property, and the People of this Island: all Copyhold, all Leasehold Estates, under the Crown, under the Church, or under private Persons, tho' for Terms ever so long; all landed Property in short, that is not Freehold, and all monied Property whatsoever are excluded:

the Possessors of these have no Votes in the Election of Members of Parliament; Women and Persons under Age be their Property ever so large, and all of it Freehold, have none. The Merchants of *London*, a numerous and respectable Body of Men, whose Opulence exceeds all that *America* could collect; the Proprietors of that vast Accumulation of Wealth, the public Funds; the Inhabitants of *Leeds*, of *Halifax*, of *Birmingham*, and of *Manchester*, Towns that are each of them larger than the Largest in the Plantations; many of less Note that are yet incorporated; and that great Corporation the *East India* Company, whose Rights over the Countries they possess, fall little short of Sovereignty, and whose Trade and whose Fleets are sufficient to constitute them a maritime Power, are all in the same Circumstances; none of them chuse their Representatives; and yet are they not represented in Parliament? Is their vast Property subject to Taxes without their Consent? Are they all arbitrarily bound by Laws to which they have not agreed? The Colonies are in exactly the same Situation: All *British* Subjects are really in the same; none are actually, all are virtually represented in Parliament; for every Member of Parliament sits in the House, not as Representative of his own Constituents, but as one of that august Assembly by which all the Commons of *Great Britain* are represented. Their Rights and their Interests, however his own Borough may be affected by general Dispositions, ought to be the great Objects of his Attention, and the only Rules for his Conduct; and to sacrifice these to a partial Advantage in favour of the Place where he was chosen, would be a Departure from his Duty; if it were otherwise, *Old Sarum* would enjoy Privileges essential to Liberty, which are denied to *Birmingham* and to *Manchester*; but as it is, they and the Colonies and all *British* Subjects whatever, have an equal Share in the general Representation of the Commons of *Great Britain*, and are bound by the Consent of the Majority of that House, whether their own particular Representatives consented to or opposed the Measures there taken, or whether they had or had not particular Representatives there.

The Inhabitants of the Colonies however have by some been supposed to be excepted, because they are represented in their respective Assemblies. So are the Citizens of *London* in their Common Council; and yet so far from excluding them from the national Representation, it does not impeach their Right to chuse Members of Parliament: it is true, that the Powers vested in the Common Council of *London*, are not equal to those which the Assemblies in the Plantations enjoy; but still they are legislative Powers, to be exercised within their District, and over their Citizens; yet not exclusively of the general Superintendence of the great Council of the Nation: The Subjects of a By-law and of an Act of Parliament may possibly be the same; yet it never was imagined that the Privileges of *London* were incompatible with the Authority of Parliament; and indeed what Contradiction, what Absurdity, does a double Representation imply? What difficulty is there in allowing both, tho' both should even be vested with equal legislative Powers, if the one is to be exercised for local, and the other for general Purposes? and where is the Necessity that the Subordinate Power must derogate from the superior Authority? It would be a singular Objection to a Man's Vote for a Member of Parliament, that being represented in a provincial, he cannot be represented in a national Assembly; and if this is not sufficient Ground for an Objection, neither is it for an Exemption, or for any Pretence of an Exclusion. . . .

We value the Right of being represented in the national Legislature as the dearest Privilege we enjoy; how justly would the Colonies complain, if they alone were deprived of it? They acknowledge Dependance upon their Mother Country; but that Dependance would be Slavery not Con-

nection, if they bore no Part in the Government of the whole: they would then indeed be in a worse Situation than the Inhabitants of *Britain*, for these are all of them virtually, tho' few of them are actually represented in the *House of Commons*; . . . Happily for them, this is not their Condition. They are on the contrary a Part, and an important Part of the Commons of *Great Britain*: they are represented in Parliament, in the same Manner as those Inhabitants of *Britain* are, who have not Voices in Elections; and they enjoy, with the Rest of their Fellow-subjects, the inestimable Privilege of not being bound by any Laws, or subject to any Taxes, to which the Majority of the Representatives of the Commons have not consented.

Questions

1. What were the essential components of the doctrine of "virtual representation"? The colonists rejected it, but did they employ it within their own colonies?

2. The colonists claimed that their own individual legislatures alone could tax them. How did Whately answer this claim? Is his argument convincing? Why or why not?

3. Whately argued that necessity, precedence, and right were all on the side of those defending the stamp tax. Was he correct? Explain.

5-4   Considerations on the Propriety of Imposing Taxes (1765)

Daniel Dulany

The most influential response to Thomas Whately's claim that the colonists were "virtually" represented in Parliament (Document 5-3) was written by Daniel Dulany, an accomplished Maryland lawyer whose father, also named Daniel, had arrived in the colony as a penniless immigrant but gained a fortune and political prominence through hard work, talent, and the patronage of Lord Baltimore. With all the advantages of wealth, the younger Dulany had been educated in England at Eton, Cambridge, and Middle Temple, and elected to the Maryland House of Delegates in 1751, five years after his return to the colony. In 1757 he was elevated to the upper house of the legislature, the council, which was indicative of the prestige and power he commanded well before the onset of the imperial crisis. *Considerations on the Propriety of Imposing Taxes* went through five printings within three months and was subsequently reprinted five times in London. Members of Parliament referred to Dulany's pamphlet during the debates over the repeal of the Stamp Act.

Source: Excerpts from "The American Press," in *Prologue to Revolution: Sources and Documents on the Stamp Act Crisis, 1764–1766*, ed. Edmund Sears Morgan (Chapel Hill: Published for the Institute of Early American History and Culture at Williamsburg, Virginia, 1959), 78–82. Copyright © 1959 by the University of North Carolina Press, renewed 1987 by Edmund S. Morgan. Used by permission of the publisher.

In the Constitution of *England*, the Three principal Forms of Government, Monarchy, Aristocracy, and Democracy, are blended together in certain Proportions; but each of these Orders, in the Exercise of the legislative Authority, hath its peculiar Department, from which the other are excluded. In this Division, the *Granting of Supplies*, or *Laying Taxes*, is deemed to be the Province of the House of Commons, as the

Representative of the People. — All Supplies are supposed to flow from their Gift; and the other Orders are permitted only to Assent, or Reject generally, not to propose any Modification, Amendment, or partial Alteration of it.

This Observation being considered, it will undeniably appear, that, in framing the late *Stamp Act*, the Commons acted in the Character of Representative of the Colonies.

They assumed it as the Principle of that Measure, and the *Propriety* of it must therefore stand, or fall, as the Principle is true, or false: For the Preamble sets forth, That the Commons of *Great-Britain* had resolved to *Give and Grant* the several Rates and Duties imposed by the Act; but what Right had the Commons of *Great-Britain* to be thus Munificent at the Expence of the Commons of *America*?—To give Property, not belonging to the Giver, and without the Consent of the Owner, is such evident and flagrant Injustice, in *ordinary Cases*, that few are hardy enough to avow it; and therefore, when it really happens, the Fact is disguised and varnished over by the most plausible Pretences the Ingenuity of the Giver can suggest.—But it is alledged that there is a *Virtual*, or *implied Representation* of the Colonies springing out of the Constitution of the *British* Government: And, it must be confessed on all Hands, that, as the Representation is not actual, it is virtual, or it doth not exist at all; for no Third Kind of Representation can be imagined. The Colonies claim the Privilege, which is common to all *British Subjects*, of being Taxed *only* with their own Consent, given by their Representatives, and all the Advocates for the *Stamp-Act* admit this Claim. Whether, therefore, upon the whole Matter, the Imposition of the *Stamp Duties* is a *proper* Exercise of Constitutional Authority, or not, depends upon the single Question, Whether the Commons of *Great-Britain* are *virtually* the Representatives of the Commons of *America*, or not.

The Advocates for the Stamp-Act admit, in express Terms, that "the Colonies do not chuse Members of Parliament," but they assert that "the Colonies are *virtually* represented, in the same Manner with the Non-Electors resident in *Great-Britain*."

How have they proved this Position? Where have they defined, or precisely explained what they mean by the Expression, *Virtual Representation*? . . .

They argue, that "the Right of Election being annexed to certain Species of Property, to Franchises, and Inhabitancy in some particular Places, a very small Part of the Land, the Property, and the People of *England*, is comprehended in those Descriptions. All Landed Property, not Freehold, and all Monied Property, are *excluded*. The Merchants of *London*, the Proprietors of the Public Funds, the Inhabitants of *Leeds*, *Halifax*, *Birmingham*, and *Manchester*, and that great Corporation of the *East-India* Company, *None of Them* chuse their Representatives, and yet are they all represented in Parliament, and the Colonies being *exactly* in *their* Situation, are represented in the *same* Manner."

Now, this Argument, which is all that their Invention hath been able to supply, is totally defective; for, it consists of Facts not true, and of Conclusions inadmissible. . . .

Lessees for Years, Copyholders, Proprietors of the Public Funds, Inhabitants of *Birmingham*, *Leeds*, *Halifax*, and *Manchester*, Merchants of the City of *London*, or Members of the Corporation of the *East-India* Company, are, *as such*, under no personal Incapacity to be Electors; for they may acquire the Right of Election, and there are *actually* not only a considerable Number of Electors in each of the Classes of Lessees for Years, &c. but in many of them, if not all, even Members of Parliament. The Interests therefore of the Non-Electors, the Electors, and the Representatives, are individually the same; to say nothing of the Connection among Neighbours, Friends, and Relations. The Security of the Non-Electors against Oppression, is, that their Oppression will fall also upon the Electros and the Representatives. The one can't be injured, and the other indemnified. . . .

The Situation of the Non-Electors in *England*—their Capacity to become Electors—their inseparable Connection with those who are Electors, and their Representatives—their Security against Oppression resulting from this Connection, and the Necessity of imagining a double or virtual Representation, to avoid Iniquity and Absurdity, have been explained—The Inhabitants of the Colonies are, *as such*, incapable of being Electors, the Privilege of Election being exerciseable only in Person, and therefore if *every* Inhabitant of *America* had the requisite Freehold, not *one* could vote, but upon the Supposition of his ceasing to be an Inhabitant of *America*, and becoming a Resident in *Great-Britain*, a Supposition which would be impertinent, because it shifts the Question—Should the Colonies not be Taxed by *Parliamentary Impositions*, their respective Legislatures have a regular, adequate, and constitutional Authority to Tax them, and therefore there would not necessarily be an iniquitous and absurd Exemption, from their not being represented by *the House of Commons*.

There is not that intimate and inseparable Relation between the *Electors of* Great-Britain and the *Inhabitants of the Colonies*, which must inevitably involve both in the same Taxation; on the contrary, not a single *actual* Elector in *England*, might be immediately affected by a Taxation in *America*, imposed by a Statute which would have a general Operation and Effect, upon the Properties of the Inhabitants of the Colonies. The latter might be oppressed in a Thousand Shapes, without any Sympathy, or exciting any Alarm in the former. Moreover, even Acts, oppressive and injurious to the Colonies in an extreme Degree, might become popular in *England*, from the Promise or Expectation, that the very Measures which depressed the Colonies, would give Ease to the Inhabitants of *Great-Britain*. It is indeed true, that the Interests of *England* and the Colonies are allied, and an Injury to the Colonies produced into all its Consequences, will eventually affect the Mother-Country, yet these Consequences being generally remote, are not at once foreseen; they do not immediately alarm the Fears, and engage the Passions of the *English* Electors, the Connection between a Freeholder of *Great-Britain*, and a *British American* being deducible only through a Train of Reasoning, which few will take the Trouble, or can have an Opportunity, if they have Capacity, to investigate; wherefore the Relation between the *British-Americans*, and the *English Electors*, is a Knot too infirm to be relied on as a competent Security, especially against the Force of a present counteracting, Expectation of Relief.

If it would have been a just Conclusion, that the *Colonies* being exactly in the *same* Situation with the *Non-Electors* of

England, are *therefore* represented in the same Manner, it ought to be allowed, that the Reasoning is solid, which, after having evinced a total *Dissimilarity* of Situation, infers that their Representation is *different*.

If the Commons of *Great-Britain* have no Right by the Constitution, to GIVE AND GRANT Property *not* belonging to themselves, but to others, without their Consent actually or virtually given—If the Claim of the Colonies not to be Taxed *without their Consent*, signified by their Representa-

tives, is well founded, if it appears that the Colonies are not actually represented by the Commons of *Great-Britain*, and that the Notion of a double or virtual Representation, doth not with any Propriety apply to the People of *America*; then the Principle of the *Stamp Act*, must be given up as indefensible on the Point of Representation, and the Validity of it rested upon the *Power* which they who framed it, have to carry it into Execution.

Questions

1. Did Dulany totally reject the doctrine of virtual representation? Under what circumstances might he have accepted it as legitimate? Did any of these circumstances apply in the case of the colonies?

2. What was Dulany's definition of representation? Assuming that his definition was shared by many if not most other colonists, what would this signify with regard to the empire?

3. Would it surprise you to learn that Dulany was opposed to most of the actions taken by the radicals after 1774 and that he was a "passive loyalist" after 1776? Explain.

5-5   Declarations of the Stamp Act Congress (1765)

Boston was the scene of the first major crowd actions against the Stamp Act. Those actions and others effectively blocked the implementation of the act. Also, it was Massachusetts that suggested that each colony send delegates to a special intercolonial congress that would formulate a unified response to the detested British legislation. The colonies of Virginia, North Carolina, and Georgia could not attend because their governors refused to convene their assemblies; New Hampshire chose not to send delegates. However, twenty-seven delegates representing the other colonies met in New York on October 7, 1765. During twelve days of deliberations the members of the Stamp Act Congress prepared a petition to the king, a memorial to the House of Lords, a petition to the House of Commons, and a series of "Declarations . . . respecting the most Essential Rights and Liberties of the Colonists." The "Declarations" of the Stamp Act Congress provide the clearest statement of the pragmatic and philosophical positions of the colonists on the Stamp Act and the efforts of the British government to institute general imperial reform.

Source: Proceedings of the Congress at New-York (1766), 15–16.

The Members of this Congress, sincerely devoted, with the warmest Sentiments of Affection and Duty to his Majesty's Person and Government, inviolably attached to the present happy Establishment of the Protestant Succession, and with Minds deeply impressed by a Sense of the present and impending Misfortunes of the *British* Colonies on this Continent; having considered as maturely as Time will permit, the Circumstances of the said Colonies, esteem it our indispensable Duty, to make the following Declarations of our humble Opinion, respecting the most Essen-

tial Rights and Liberties of the Colonists, and of the Grievances under which they labour, by Reason of several late Acts of Parliament.

I. That his Majesty's Subjects in these Colonies, owe the same Allegiance to the Crown of *Great-Britain*, that is owing from his Subjects born within the Realm, and all due Subordination to that August Body the Parliament of *Great-Britain*.

II. That his Majesty's Liege Subjects in these Colonies, are entitled to all the inherent Rights and Liberties of his

Natural born Subjects, within the Kingdom of *Great-Britain.*

III. That it is inseparably essential to the Freedom of a People, and the undoubted Right of *Englishmen*, that no Taxes be imposed on them, but with their own Consent, given personally, or by their Representatives.

IV. That the People of these Colonies are not, and from their local Circumstances cannot be, Represented in the House of Commons in *Great-Britain.*

V. That the only Representatives of the People of these Colonies, are Persons chosen therein by themselves, and that no Taxes ever have been, or can be Constitutionally imposed on them, but by their respective Legislature.

VI. That all Supplies to the Crown, being free Gifts of the People, it is unreasonable and inconsistent with the Principles and Spirit of the *British* Constitution, for the People of *Great-Britain*, to grant to his Majesty the Property of the Colonists.

VII. That Trial by Jury, is the inherent and invaluable Right of every *British* Subject in these Colonies.

VIII. That the late Act of Parliament, entitled, *An Act for granting and applying certain Stamp Duties, and other Duties, in the* British *Colonies and Plantations* in America, etc. by imposing Taxes on the Inhabitants of these Colonies, and the said Act, and several other Acts, by extending the Jurisdiction of the Courts of Admiralty beyond its ancient Limits, have a manifest Tendency to subvert the Rights and Liberties of the Colonists.

IX. That the Duties imposed by several late Acts of Parliament, from the peculiar Circumstances of these Colonies, will be extremely Burthensome and Grievous; and from the scarcity of Specie, the Payment of them absolutely impracticable.

X. That as the Profits of the Trade of these Colonies ultimately center in *Great-Britain*, to pay for the Manufactures which they are obliged to take from thence, they eventually contribute very largely to all Supplies granted there to the Crown.

XI. That the Restrictions imposed by several late Acts of Parliament, on the Trade of these Colonies, will render them unable to purchase the Manufactures of *Great-Britain*.

XII. That the Increase, Prosperity, and Happiness of these Colonies, depend on the full and free Enjoyment of their Rights and Liberties, and an Intercourse with *Great-Britain* mutually Affectionate and Advantageous.

XIII. That it is the Right of the *British* Subjects in these Colonies, to Petition the King, or either House of Parliament.

Lastly, That it is the indispensable Duty of these Colonies, to the best of Sovereigns, to the Mother Country, and to themselves, to endeavour by a loyal and dutiful Address to his Majesty, and humble Applications to both Houses of Parliament, to procure the Repeal of the Act for granting and applying certain Stamp Duties, of all Clauses of any other Acts of Parliament, whereby the Jurisdiction of the Admiralty is extended as aforesaid, and of the other late Acts for the Restriction of *American* Commerce.

Questions

1. Does it appear that the members of the Stamp Act Congress were determined to demonstrate that they were not rebels but loyal British subjects? Why or why not?

2. According to the Congress, what basic constitutional rights did the colonists have?

3. In what ways did the Congress emphasize pragmatic as well as philosophical arguments against British imperial reforms?

4. Considering the British ideas about the mother country's rights explained in Document 5-2, how convincing was the case the Congress made against the Stamp Act?

Questions for Further Thought

1. Given James Otis's assertion that the colonists could not be taxed without their consent (Document 5-1) and the declaration of the Stamp Act Congress that the colonists "are not, and . . . cannot be, Represented" in Parliament (Document 5-5), what, if any, form of taxation would the colonists have accepted in 1765?

2. Critics of the Revolutionaries claimed that the colonists' constitutional objections against parliamentary taxation were inconsistent because they were merely a smoke screen to cover their determination not to pay taxes. Compare the objections raised by James Otis, Daniel Dulany, and the Stamp Act Congress (Documents 5-1, 5-4, and 5-5). Were the critics correct? Were the colonists' arguments inconsistent?

3. In view of the huge imperial debt and the taxes already being paid by subjects living in Britain, what options were open to Parliament at this stage of the crisis? What could Parliament have done to raise needed revenues among the colonies and still keep the peace?

The Dynamics of Rebellion, 1765–1770

Colonial responses to the Stamp Act were not limited to carefully constructed constitutional arguments or to formal statements pertaining to the rights of Englishmen. Some radicals did not concern themselves primarily with the legitimacy of parliamentary taxation; they challenged Parliament's power to enforce the measure it had passed. Establishing extralegal organizations, the most famous of which emerged in the summer of 1765 as the "Sons of Liberty," they undertook a coordinated program of intimidation. In Massachusetts, they forced Andrew Oliver to resign his commission as a stamp distributor (Document 5-6), and in every other colony, stamp distributors met with essentially the same fate. Not a single distributor was able or willing to put the Stamp Act into effect. The Stamp Act proved to be more trouble than it was worth (see text pp. 142–148), and when Lord Rockingham replaced George Grenville as prime minister in 1766 the Act was repealed.

The ineffectiveness and repeal of the Stamp Act left the empire still heavily in debt and with no apparent solution to the problem of raising revenue among the colonists. Perhaps encouraged by Benjamin Franklin's testimony before the House of Commons in 1766, in which the Pennsylvanian claimed that the American colonists were opposed to "internal" taxes but were willing to pay "external" taxes on imports and exports, Charles Townshend oversaw legislation that placed taxes on such colonial imports as paper, paint, glass, and tea. John Dickinson viewed the Townshend duties as potentially more alarming than the sort of tax represented by the late Stamp Act (Document 5-7). For women, who presided over the household economy, the taxes placed on imports politicized consumption decisions and thereby opened up new opportunities for political involvement (Document 5-8).

Many hard-line imperial officials were soon convinced that the repeal of the Stamp Act had been a mistake. Conciliatory gestures met with no suitable return. As Peter Oliver, Andrew Oliver's brother, complained, Lord Rockingham's ministry had placed "too much confidence in the gratitude of the colonists to the parent state"; as a result, it had enabled the radicals to advance their own selfish motives by "mouthing" praises of "liberty" (Document 5-9). In an effort to slow the descent into what Oliver feared would be mob rule in Massachusetts, the British ministry in 1768 stationed two regiments of troops in Boston. Their presence, however, only increased the tensions felt on both sides and resulted finally in a "massacre" (Document 5-10).

5-6   The Stamp Act Riot, 1765

Francis Bernard

The colonists organized a variety of responses to protest the Stamp Act. Their formal protests culminated in the declarations of the Stamp Act Congress (Document 5-5), which questioned Parliament's authority to impose a tax. They also posed direct challenges through organized, but unpredictable, crowd actions. Radicals throughout the colonies systematically engaged in activities aimed at intimidating royal officials into not performing their assigned duties. The most likely targets were the commissioned stamp distributors in each of the colonies. In Boston, where the action began, the crowd's anger was directed against Andrew Oliver, who was rumored to be the appointed stamp distributor for Massachusetts. Oliver, a member of a family whose wealth and connections had secured him a place among the colony's social and political elite, was forced to resign his position twice: first in November, when in fact he had no commission to surrender, and then in December, after his commission finally arrived. In the excerpt here, Massachusetts governor Francis Bernard describes the actions of the Boston crowd in a letter to Lord Halifax, the royal secretary in charge of colonial affairs.

Source: Francis Bernard, "Stamp Act Riot, 1765," in *Prologue to Revolution: Sources and Documents on the Stamp Act Crisis, 1764–1766*, ed. Edmund Sears Morgan. Copyright © 1959 University of North Carolina Press, renewed 1987 by Edmund S. Morgan. Used by permission of the publisher.

Yesterday Morning at break of day was discovered hanging upon a Tree in a Street of the Town an Effigy, with inscriptions, shewing that it was intended to represent Mr. Oliver, the Secretary, who had lately accepted the Office of Stamp Distributor. Some of the Neighbours offered to take it down, but they were given to know, that would not be permitted. Many Gentlemen, especially some of the Council, treated it as a boyish sport, that did not deserve the Notice of the Governor and Council. But I did not think so however I contented myself with the Lt. Governor, as Chief Justice, directing the Sheriff to order his Officers to take down the Effigy; and I appointed a Council to meet in the Afternoon to consider what should be done, if the Sheriff's Officers were obstructed in removing the Effigy.

Before the Council met, the Sheriff reported, that his Officers had endeavoured to take down the Effigy: but could not do it without imminent danger of their lives. The Council met I represented this Transaction to them as the beginning in my Opinion, of much greater Commotions. I desired their Advice, what I should do upon this Occasion. A Majority of the Council spoke in form against doing anything but upon very different Principles: some said, that it was trifling Business, which, if let alone, would subside of itself, but, if taken notice of would become a serious Affair. Others said, that it was a serious Affair already; that it was a preconcerted Business, in which the greatest Part of the Town was engaged; that we had no force to oppose to it, and making an Opposition to it, without a power to support the Opposition, would only inflame the People; and be a means of extending the mischief to persons not at present the Objects of it. Tho' the Council were allmost unanimous in advising, that nothing should be done, they were averse to having such advice entered upon the Council Book. But I insisted upon their giving me an Answer to my Question, and that it should be entered in the Book; when, after a long altercation, it was avoided by their advising me to order the Sheriff to assemble the Peace Officers and preserve the peace which I immediately ordered, being a matter of form rather than of real Significance.

It now grew dark when the Mob, which had been gathering all the Afternoon, came down to the Town House, bringing the Effigy with them, and knowing we were sitting in the Council Chamber, they gave three Huzzas by way of defiance, and passed on. From thence they went to a new Building, lately erected by Mr Oliver to let out for Shops, and not quite finished: this they called the Stamp Office, and pulled it down to the Ground in five minutes. From thence they went to Mr Oliver's House; before which they beheaded the Effigy; and broke all the Windows next the Street; then they carried the Effigy to Fort hill near Mr Oliver's House, where they burnt the Effigy in a Bonfire made of the Timber they had pulled down from the Building. Mr Oliver had removed his family from his House, and remained himself with a few friends, when the Mob returned to attack the House. Mr Oliver was prevailed upon to retire, and his friends kept Possession of the House. The Mob finding the Doors barricaded, broke down the whole fence of the Garden towards fort hill, and coming on beat in all the doors and Windows of the Garden front, and entered the House, the Gentlemen there retiring. As soon as they had got Possession, they searched about for Mr Oliver, declaring they would kill him; finding that he had left the House, a party set out to search two neighbouring Houses, in one of which Mr Oliver was, but happily they were diverted from this pursuit by a Gentleman telling them, that Mr Oliver was gone with the Governor to the Castle. Otherwise he would certainly have been murdered. After 11 o'clock the Mob seeming to grow quiet, the (Lt. Governor) Chief Justice and the Sheriff ventured to go to Mr Oliver's House to endeavour to perswade them to disperse. As soon as they began to speak, a Ringleader cried out, The Governor and the Sheriff! to your Arms, my boys! Presently after a volley of Stones followed, and the two Gentlemen narrowly escaped thro' favour of the Night, not without some bruises. I should have mentioned before, that I sent a written order to the Colonel of the Regiment of Militia, to beat an Alarm; he answered, that it would signify nothing, for as soon as the drum was heard, the drummer would be knocked down, and the drum broke; he added, that probably all the drummers of the Regiment were in the Mob. Nothing more being to be done, The Mob were left to disperse at their own Time, which they did about 12 o'clock.

Questions

1. What message was Bernard sending to his superiors in London? Was he asking for assistance? If so, what kind of assistance?

2. Why did the crowd single out Andrew Oliver? He was hung in effigy in August, but he was not officially commissioned as a stamp distributor until December. Why is this significant? What does this suggest about the Boston crowd? What does it suggest about Oliver?

3. How might Oliver's treatment described here have affected the history of the "Rebellion" written by his brother, Peter, in the 1780s (Document 5-9)? Why were men like the Olivers targeted by the radicals?

5-7 Letter VII from a Farmer (1768)

John Dickinson

John Dickinson was born in Maryland in 1732, studied law in London and returned to Philadelphia in 1757. He began publishing attacks on British reforms in a 1765 pamphlet, *The Late Regulations Respecting the British Colonies.* In that work Dickinson argued that the Sugar Act and Stamp Act (see text pp. 141–148) would be detrimental to the British mercantile system. Writing anonymously under the pen name "A Farmer," this sophisticated lawyer won fame and popularity with a series of twelve essays attacking the Townshend duties (see text pp. 147–148). These essays appeared in the *Pennsylvania Chronicle* between December 1767 and February 1768 and were then issued in pamphlet form as *Letters from a Farmer in Pennsylvania to the Inhabitants of the British Colonies* (1768). Letter VII was first published on January 11, 1768. The essays were so popular that other authors soon could simply refer to "The Farmer" or "The Farmer's Letters" and expect readers to recognize the reference.

Source: Pennsylvania Chronicle and Universal Advertiser, 11 January 1768.

There are two ways of laying taxes. One is, by imposing a certain sum on particular kinds of property, to be paid by the *user* or *consumer*, or by rating the *person* at a certain sum. The other is, by imposing a certain sum on particular kinds of property, to be paid by the *seller*.

When a man pays the first sort of tax, he *knows with certainty* that he pays so much money *for a tax.* The *consideration* for which he pays it, is remote, and, it may be, does not occur to him. He is sensible too, that he is *commanded and obliged* to pay it *as a tax;* and therefore people are apt to be displeased with this sort of tax.

The other sort of tax is submitted to in a very different manner. The purchaser of an article, very seldom reflects that the seller raises his price, so as to indemnify himself for the tax *he* has paid. He knows that the prices of things are continually fluctuating, and if he thinks about the tax, he thinks at the same time, in all probability, that he *might* have paid as much, if the article he buys had not been taxed. He gets something *visible* and *agreeable* for his money; and tax and price are so confounded together, that he cannot separate, or does not chuse to take the trouble of separating them.

This mode of taxation therefore is the mode suited to arbitrary and oppressive governments. The love of liberty is so natural to the human heart, that unfeeling tyrants think themselves obliged to accommodate their schemes as much as they can to the appearance of justice and reason, and to deceive those whom they resolve to destroy, or oppress, by presenting to them a miserable picture of freedom, when the inestimable original is lost.

I shall now apply these observations to the late act of parliament. Certain duties are thereby imposed on paper and glass, etc. imported into these colonies. By the laws of *Great-Britain* we are prohibited to get these articles from any other part of the world. We cannot at present, nor for many years to come, tho' we should apply ourselves to these manufactures with the utmost industry, make enough ourselves for our own use. That paper and glass are not only convenient, but absolutely necessary for us, I imagine very few will contend. Some perhaps, who think mankind grew wicked and luxurious, as soon as they found out another way of communicating their sentiments than by speech, and another way of dwelling than in caves, may advance so whimsical an opinion. But I presume no body will take the unnecessary trouble of refuting them.

From these remarks I think it evident, that we *must* use paper and glass; that what we use *must* be *British*; and that we *must* pay the duties imposed, unless those who sell these articles, are so generous as to make us presents of the duties they pay.

Some persons may think this act of no consequence, because the duties are so *small*. A fatal error. *That* is the very circumstance most alarming to me. For I am convinced, that the authors of this law would never have obtained an act to raise so trifling a sum as it must do, had they not intended by *it* to establish a *precedent* for future use. To console ourselves with the *smallness* of the duties, is to walk deliberately into the snare that is set for us, praising the *neatness* of the workmanship. Suppose the duties imposed by the late act could be paid by these distressed colonies with the utmost ease, and that the purposes to which they are to be applied, were the most reasonable and equitable that can be conceived, the contrary of which I hope to demonstrate before these letters are concluded; yet even in such a supposed case, these colonies ought to regard the act with abhorrence. For WHO ARE A FREE PEOPLE? Not *those*, over whom government is reasonably and equitably exercised, but *those*, who live under a government *so constitutionally checked* and *controuled*, that proper provision is made against its being otherwise exercised.

The late act is founded on the destruction of this constitutional security. If the parliament have a right to lay a duty of Four Shillings and Eight-pence on a hundred weight of glass, or a ream of paper, they have a right to lay a duty of any other sum on either. They may raise the duty, as the author before quoted says has been done in some countries, till it "exceeds seventeen or eighteen times the value of the commodity." In short, if they have a right *to* levy a tax of *one penny* upon us, they have a right to levy a *million* upon us: For where does their right stop? At any given number of Pence, Shillings or Pounds? To attempt to limit their right, after granting it to exist at all, is as contrary to reason — as granting it to exist at all, is contrary to justice. If *they* have any right to tax *us* — then, whether *our own money* shall continue in *our own pockets* or not, depends no longer on *us*, but on *them*. [As Lord Cambden said,] "There is nothing which" we can call our own; or, to use the words of Mr. *Locke* — "WHAT PROPERTY HAVE WE IN THAT, WHICH ANOTHER MAY, BY RIGHT, TAKE, WHEN HE PLEASES, TO HIMSELF?"

These duties, which will inevitably be levied upon us — which are now levying upon us — are *expressly* laid FOR THE SOLE PURPOSES OF TAKING MONEY. This is the true definition of "*taxes*." They are therefore *taxes*. This money is to be taken from *us*. *We* are therefore taxed. *Those* who are *taxed* without their own consent, given by themselves or their representatives, are slaves. *We are taxed* without our own consent, expressed by ourselves or our representatives. We are therefore — I speak it with grief — I speak it with indignation — We are SLAVES.

A FARMER.

Questions

1. Would Dickinson have agreed with those who stated that British politicians were sincerely concerned about the needs and concerns of the colonists? Why or why not?

2. According to Dickinson, why did colonists have to refuse to pay the small Townshend duties?

3. Would you describe Dickinson's argument as an emotional appeal or a pragmatic appeal? Why?

5-8   The Boycott Agreements of Women in Boston (1770)

Women, who in accordance with the standards of the day were not permitted to vote, were traditionally excluded from participating in the hurly-burly of politics (see text p. 148). However, because of their role in the management of households, unless women actively participated, the boycott against the Townshend duties would fail. While never intending that women be allowed to participate in electoral politics, the men who organized the boycott urged them to support liberty by joining the boycott. As the following reports show, women gave positive demonstrations of their ability to organize in support of the boycott.

Source: Boston Evening-Post, 12 February 1770; *Boston Gazette*, 19 February 1770, as reprinted in *Pennsylvania Gazette*, 8 March 1770.

The following Agreement has lately been come into by upwards of 300 Mistresses of Families in this Town; in which Number the Ladies of the highest Rank and Influence, that could be waited upon in so short a Time, are included.
Boston, January 31, 1770.

["]At a Time when our invaluable Rights and Privileges are attacked in an unconstitutional and most alarming Manner, and as we find we are reproached for not being so ready as could be desired, to lend our Assistance, we think it our Duty perfectly to concur with the true Friends of Liberty, in all the Measures they have taken to save this abused Country from Ruin and Slavery: And particularly, we join with the very respectable Body of Merchants, and other Inhabitants of this Town, who met in Faneuil-Hall the 23d of this Instant, in their Resolutions, *totally* to abstain from the Use of TEA: And as the greatest Part of the Revenue arising by Virtue of the late Acts, is produced from the Duty paid upon Tea, which Revenue is wholly expended to support the American Board of Commissioners, We the Subscribers do strictly engage, that we will *totally* abstain from the Use of that Article (Sickness excepted) not only in our respective Families; but that we will absolutely refuse it, if it should be offered to us upon any Occasion whatsoever. This Agreement we chearfully come into, as we believe the very distressed Situation of our Country requires it, and we do hereby oblige ourselves religiously to observe it, till the late Revenue Acts are repealed."

The following is a Copy of the Agreement of the young Ladies of this Town against drinking foreign TEA.
Boston, February 12, 1770.

["]We the Daughters of those Patriots who have, and now do appear for the public Interest, and in *that* principally for *us* their Posterity; *we*, as such, do with Pleasure engage with them, in denying ourselves the drinking of foreign *Tea*, in Hopes to frustrate a Plan that tends to deprive the whole Community of their *All* that is valuable in Life."

To the above Agreement 126 young Ladies have already signed. In Addition to the List of Mistresses of Families, who signed the Agreement against drinking foreign Tea, 110 have been added the Week past.

Questions

1. Do the women who made these agreements appear to have been leaders of the boycott movement, or do they appear to have been responding to the actions of others?

2. To what extent, if any, did the signers of the agreements spell out the basic rights they believed they were supporting?

3. Does it appear that the specifics of the agreements, including any provisions for their enforcement, helped make the tea boycott effective? Why or why not?

5-9   Origin and Progress of the American Rebellion (1780s)

Peter Oliver

Peter Oliver, who was born in Boston in 1713 and educated at Harvard, detested protests against the reform of British imperial policy. A wealthy member of the legal profession, Oliver was a part of the British system: beginning in 1756, he served as a judge of the superior court of Massachusetts. In addition, the first great Stamp Act crowd action (August 14, 1765, in Boston) was directed against the property of Andrew Oliver, his brother (see text p. 145). Once the Revolution broke out, Oliver went to Britain, fully expecting to return to Massachusetts once the "rebellion" had been put down. However, Oliver never returned; he died in Britain in 1791. He expressed his thoughts about the causes of the Revolution in his "Origin & Progress of the American Rebellion." This work, written in the early 1780s, was not published until the twentieth century.

Source: From Douglas Adair and John A. Schutz, eds., *Peter Oliver's Origin & Progress of the American Rebellion: A Tory View*, rev. ed. (Stanford, CA: Stanford University Press, 1967), 60–65 passim. Copyright © 1967. Reprinted with the permission of the Henry E. Huntington Library.

I am now come to the Year 1767, a Year fraught with Occurrences, as extraordinary as 1765, but of a different Texture. Notwithstanding the Warnings that the Colonies had repeatedly given, of their determined Resolution to throw off the Supremacy of the british Parliament, yet the then Ministry chose to make another Trial of Skill; never adverting to the ill Success of former Attempts. They might have known, that the Contest had reached so great an Heighth, that the Colonists would never descend one Step untill they had first ascended the last Round of the Ladder. . . . It required no great Degree of second Sight to calculate Consequences. But the Ministry confiding in their own good Intentions, and placing too much Confidence in the Gratitude of the Colonists to the parent State (which by the Way they did not possess a Spark of, neither is it to be but seldom Expected to find it inhabit any where but in the private Breast, and too seldom there; to the Disgrace of human Nature), they procured a new Act to be passed, laying Duties upon *Tea, Glass, Paper, and Painters Colours.* This Act was not more unreasonable than many other Acts which had been submitted to for many Years past, and which, even at this Time, they made no Objection to. But the Colonists had succeeded in their first Experiment of Opposition, and their new Allies in Parliament increased their Importance.

As to the *Glass* in particular, the Duty was so trifling, that it would not have enhanced the Price of it to the Purchaser; for there were so many Sellers who aimed at a Market for their Commodities, and the Merchants had so great a Profit upon their Goods, that they could render the Duty of little or no Importance in their Sales; and this was actually the Case. For the Glass, during the Continuance of the Act, was sold at the same Price which it commanded before the Commencement of the Act. The true Reason of Opposition was this. The Inhabitants of the Colonies were a Race of Smugglers. . . .

The Smugglers then, who were the prevailing Part of the Traders in the Capitals of the several Provinces, found it necessary for their Interest, to unite in defeating the Operation of the Act; and *Boston* appeared in the Front of the Battle. Accordingly they beat to Arms, and manœuvred in a new invented Mode. They entred into nonimportation Agreements. A Subscription Paper was handed about, enumerating a great Variety of Articles not to be imported from *England*, which they supposed would muster the Manufacturers in *England* into a national Mob to support their Interests. Among the various prohibited Articles, were *Silks, Velvets, clocks, Watches, Coaches and Chariots*; and it was highly diverting, to see the names and marks, to the Subscription, of Porters and Washing Women. But every mean and dirty Art was used to compass all their bad Designs. One of those who handed about a Subscription Paper being asked, whether it could be imagined that such Tricks would effectuate their Purposes? He replyed "Yes! It would do to scare them in England:" and perhaps there never was a Na-

tion so easy to be affrighted: witness the preceding Repeal of the Stamp Act.

In order to effectuate their Purposes to have this Act repealed also, they formed many Plans of Operation. Associations were convened to prevent the Importation of Goods from *Great Britain*, and to oblige all those who had already sent for them, to reship them after their arrival. This was such an Attack upon the mercantile Interest, that it was necessary to use private evasive Arts to decieve the Vulgar. Accordingly, when the Goods arrived, they were to be in Warehouses, which were to be guarded by a publick Key, at the same Time the Owners of the Stores and Goods had a Key of their Own. This amused the Rabble, whom the Merchants had set to mobbing; and such were the blessed Effects of some of those Merchants Villainy, that Bales and Trunks were disgorged of their Contents and refilled with Shavings, Brickbats, Legs of Bacon and other Things, and shipped for *England*; where some of them were opened on the King's Wharves or Quays, and the Fraud discovered. Many of those Merchants also continued to import the prohibited Goods, in Disguise; of which a bold Printer of *Boston* detected them in his publick Papers; for which they, out of Revenge, in 1768, attempted to murder him; but narrowly escaping with his Life he fled to *England*, as the civil Power of the Country was not sufficient to protect any one who was obnoxious to the Leaders of the Faction. . . .

Mr. [James] *Otis's* black Regiment, the dissenting Clergy, were also set to Work, to preach up Manufactures instead of Gospel. They preached about it and about it; untill the Women and Children, both within Doors and without, set their Spinning Wheels a whirling in Defiance of *Great Britain.* The female Spinners kept on spinning for 6 Days of the Week; and on the seventh, the Parsons took their Turns and spun out their Prayers and Sermons to a long Thread of Politicks, and to much better Profit than the other Spinners; for they generally cloathed the Parson and his Family with the Produce of their Labor. This was a new Species of Enthusiasm, and might be justly termed, the Enthusiasm of the Spinning Wheel.

An *American* is an adept in the Arts of Shrewdness. In these he is *generally* an Overmatch for a *Briton*, although he may sometimes fail in the Execution. As an Instance of each, take the following Anecdote of a Deacon of one [of] the dissenting Congregations in *Boston*, who imported large Quantities of Woolens from *England*. *Hogarth* drew his Line of Beauty for the Leg of a Chair; so this Person had sat so long in a Deacon's Seat, that the Muscles of his Face were so contracted into the Line of Sanctity, that he passed himself upon the World as a Man of great Reputation for Honesty. He was also a great Stickler for the Manufactures of *America*; and in the Heighth of his pious Zeal for the good old Cause, wrote to his Correspondent in *London* about american Grievances; and informed him, that unless they were redressed, they not only could, but they would redress them their selves by making Cloths from their own Produce. As a

Proof that they could do it, he sent Patterns of fine broad Cloths, which he said were manufactured in *America*. His Correspondent was surprized on seeing the Patterns, and shewed them to the Manufacturer of whom he had bought them. He also was surprized; but, on examination, told the Merchant that those were the very Cloths he had sold him to ship to *America*—such are the blessed Effects of Cant and Hypocrisy. . . .

All this Struggle and Uproar arose from the selfish Designs of the Merchants. They disguised their Private Views by mouthing it for Liberty. The Magick of this Sound echoed through the interior Parts of the Country, and the deluded Vulgar were charmed with it—like the poor harmless *Squirrel* that runs into the Mouth of the *Rattlesnake*, the Fascination in the Word *Liberty* threw the People into the harpy Claws of their Destroyers; and for what? But to gratifie the artfull Smugglers in carrying on their contraband Tea Trade with the Dutch, to make their deluded Consumers purchase at their Prices who were the Venders; for the act of Parliament had reduced the Duties upon it from 12 d p [Pence per] Pound to three Pence, with a View to prevent Smugling; which would effectually have prevented it, had the Act been

in Force a few Years, and would have broke up the Nests of those worse than Highway Men; who, for many Years, had kept the Province in a Ferment, and created Uneasiness in the parent State.

As for the People in general, they were like the Mobility of all Countries, perfect Machines, wound up by any Hand who might first take the Winch; they were like the poor Negro Boy, who, in the Time of the late Stamp Act, was bid by his Master, in the Evening, to fetch something from his Barn; but did not move at the command. His Master spoke to him with Severity, and asked him why he did not go as he was bid? The poor Wretch replied, with Tears in his Eyes, "me fraid Massah Tamp Act he catch me." Thus the common People had had that Act, and all the Acts of Parliament since, dressed up by their seditious Leaders, either with raw Head and bloody Bones, or with Horns, Tails, and cloven Feet, which were sufficient to affright their weak Followers. And as for Men of Sense, who could see through the Delusion, it would have been imprudent for them to have interposed; for the Government was in the Hands of the Mob, both in Form and Substance, and it was in vain to combat a Whirlwind or a Hurricane.

Questions

1.   What, if any, significance can you discern in the fact that Oliver referred to his study as the "Origin & Progress of the American Rebellion" rather than the "Origin & Progress of the American Revolution"?

2.   Judging from this excerpt, is it accurate to say that Oliver was a philosophical conservative? Why or why not?

3.   On the basis of this excerpt, is it accurate to say that Oliver respected ordinary people? Why or why not?

5-10   An Account of the Boston Massacre (1770)

Captain Thomas Preston

When the British escalated the growing confrontation by placing troops in Boston as a kind of police force to enforce imperial reform measures (see text pp. 149–150), many colonists considered this another step on the road to political slavery. Bostonians' horror at being "occupied" by a standing army in peacetime was only part of the problem. Because off-duty soldiers were allowed to take civilian employment, they competed, often successfully, for jobs that were essential to many in Boston's lower classes. Tensions mounted, and many claimed that Boston would face more dramatic events. The infamous "Boston Massacre" of March 5, 1770, proved them right. The following description of the event was written by Captain Thomas Preston, who was in command of the British troops directly involved in the massacre. Preston was tried for murder and acquitted.

Source: "Historical Chronicle," *Gentlemen's Magazine* 40 (April 1770), 189.

Saturday, 28 April, 1770. The Representation of the Affairs at Boston ["the Massacre," March 5] by the Town Committee, having been inserted in the beginning of the Magazine, the case of Capt. Preston here epitomized, will serve to show the other side of the question.

It is a matter of too great notoriety to need proofs, that the arrival of his majesty's troops in Boston was extremely obnoxious to its inhabitants. They have ever used all means in their power to weaken the regiments, and to bring them into contempt, by promoting desertions, and by grossly and falsely propagating untruths concerning them. On the arrival of the 64th and 65th, their ardour seemingly began to abate; it being too expensive to buy off so many. But the same spirit revived immediately on its being known that those regiments were ordered for Halifax. After their embarkation, one of their justices, from the seat of justice, declared, "that the soldiers must now take care of themselves, nor trust too much to their arms, for they were but a handful." This was an alarming circumstance to the soldiery, since which several disputes have happened between the towns-people and the soldiers of both regiments. In general such disputes have been kept too secret from the officers. On the 2d instant, two of the 29th going through one Gray's Rope Walk,[1] the rope-makers insultingly asked them if they would empty a vault. This unfortunately had the desired effect by provoking the soldiers, and from words they went to blows. Both parties suffered in this affray, and finally, the soldiers retired to their quarters. The insolence, as well as utter hatred of the inhabitants to the troops increased daily; insomuch, that Monday and Tuesday, the 5th and 6th instant, were privately agreed on for a general engagement; in consequence of which, several of the militia came from the country, armed, to join their friends, menacing to destroy any who should oppose them. This plan has since been discovered.

On Monday night about eight o'clock, two soldiers were attacked and beat. About nine some of the guard informed me, the town inhabitants were assembling to attack the troops, and that the bells were ringing as a signal, and not for fire, and the Beacon intended to be fired to bring in the distant people of the country. Being captain of the day, I re-

paired immediately to the main guard. In my way, I saw the people in great commotion. In a few minutes about 100 people passed and went toward the custom-house, where the King's money is lodged. They immediately surrounded the sentinel posted there, and with clubs and other weapons threatened to execute their vengeance on him. A Townsman assured me he heard the mob declare they would murder him. I fearing their plundering the King's chest, immediately sent a non-commissioned officer and 12 men to protect both the sentinel and the King's money, and very soon followed myself, to prevent disorder. The troops rushed thro' the people, and, by charging their bayonets in half circle, kept them at a distance. So far was I from intending death, that the troops went to the spot where the unhappy affair took place, without loading their pieces.

The mob still increased, and were more outrageous, striking bludgeons one against another, and calling out, "Come on, you Rascals, you bloody backs, you lobster scoundrels; fire if you dare; G—d damn you, fire and be damned; we know you dare not;" and much more such language was used. They advanced to the points of the bayonets, stuck some of them, and even the muzzles of the pieces, and seemed to be endeavouring to close with the soldiers. Some well-behaved persons asked me if their guns were charged? I replied, yes. If I intended to order the men to fire? I answered no. While I was speaking, a soldier having received a severe blow with a stick, instantly fired. On reprimanding him, I was struck with a club on my arm, so violent a blow, that had it fallen on my head, probably it would have destroyed me. A general attack was then made on the men by heaving clubs, and snow balls, by which all our lives were in imminent danger; some persons from behind called out, "Damn your bloods, why don't you fire?" Instantly three or four of the soldiers fired, one after another, and directly after, three more in the same confusion and hurry.

The mob then ran away, except three unhappy men who instantly expired. . . . The whole of this melancholy affair was transacted in almost 20 minutes. . . .

On examination before the justices they have sworn, that I used the word fire, and so bitter and inveterate are the malcontents against the officers and troops, that I am, though perfectly innocent, under most unhappy circumstances, having nothing in reason to expect but the loss of life in a very ignominious manner, without the interposition of his majesty's royal goodness.

---

[1] *Rope walk:* A long, narrow building used for the twisting of rope, especially for ships. Rope walks were common in port cities such as Boston.

Questions

1. According to Captain Preston, did the Bostonians have legitimate reasons for being unhappy about the fact that British troops were stationed in their city?

2. Judging from Preston's account, does the term *Boston Massacre* seem accurate? Why or why not?

3. Since Preston would naturally be inclined to present his actions and the actions of his men in the best light, how believable is his account of what happened?

Questions for Further Thought

1. In view of the actions taken by the colonists after 1765, were the hard-line imperial officials correct in their assertion that the repeal of the Stamp Act was a mistake? Explain.

2. Compare Governor Francis Bernard's letter (Document 5-6), Peter Oliver's history (Document 5-9), and Captain Thomas Preston's account (Document 5-10). What common themes are voiced in these documents? Are there any differences in tone or urgency?

3. Peter Oliver wrote that by 1767 the colonists had rejected the sovereignty of Parliament. Was he correct? Did John Dickinson (Document 5-7) and the women of Boston (Document 5-8) accept parliamentary sovereignty? According to these colonial protesters, what authority did Parliament possess over the colonies?

The Road to Independence, 1771–1776

At the time of the Boston Massacre, the colonists did not know that the British government, beset by troubles at home, was again ready to succumb to an economic boycott (see text p. 150). Ironically, Parliament debated repeal on the very day of the massacre and formally rescinded all the Townshend duties except that on tea in April 1770. In response to the massacre itself, the British pulled their troops out of Boston proper. As the relatively quiet period that developed after the traumatic events of 1770 revealed, the British government seemed willing, at least temporarily, to stop escalating the confrontation with the colonists. But when Parliament passed the Tea Act of 1773 (see text pp. 153–154), it raised a new threat of economic monopoly. Colonists looked again to the tactics they had used against the Stamp Act; they also tried newer techniques, such as the threat of tar-and-feathering. Once again Boston became the scene of vigorous action. Document 5-11, a participant's account of the Boston Tea Party of 1773, illustrates the degree of organization and the effectiveness of that crowd operation. Not surprisingly, the Patriots turned again to an economic boycott. The agreement was signed by fifty-one women of Edenton, North Carolina (Document 5-13).

When news of the Boston Tea Party reached Parliament, the members expressed outrage over the destruction of private property (Document 5-12). Determined to punish Boston—which had become known as "the Metropolis of Sedition"—the British government passed the infamous Coercive Acts (see text pp. 154–156). As they had done in response to the Stamp Act, the colonists called an intercolonial congress (Documents 5-14 and 5-16). This Continental Congress, which opened in Philadelphia on September 5, 1774, deliberated until late October. As the textbook authors note, "men of 'loyal principles'" at the Continental Congress supported a plan to create a new structure of empire (see text p. 154). That plan was not adopted, and the Continental Congress became a milestone in the ongoing and organized opposition to Britain's renewed efforts to exert control over the colonies. The Congress's Plan of Association (Document 5-16) shows the detailed program advanced by the Congress to counter the Coercive Acts and the British imperial reform effort; Document 5-17 is Joseph Galloway's proposal for ending the imperial crisis.

5-11   An Account of the Boston Tea Party of 1773

George R. T. Hewes

Boston was the site of many crowd actions that marked the growing confrontation and the march toward the War of Independence. On the night of December 16, 1773, Bostonians staged the Boston Tea Party to show their opposition to the Tea Act of 1773.

George R. T. Hewes, a Boston shoemaker, was one of the participants. Late in his long life, Hewes provided the following description of what occurred in Boston's harbor that December night in 1773.

Source: James Hawkes, *A Retrospect of the Boston Tea-Party, with a Memoir of George R. T. Hewes, a Survivor of the Little Band of Patriots Who Drowned the Tea in Boston Harbour in 1773* (1834), 37–41.

The tea destroyed was contained in three ships, laying near each other, at what was called at that time Griffin's wharf, and were surrounded by armed ships of war; the commanders of which had publicly declared, that if the rebels, as they were pleased to style the Bostonians, should not withdraw their opposition to the landing of the tea before a certain day, the 17th day of December, 1773, they should on that day force it on shore, under the cover of their cannon's mouth. On the day preceding the seventeenth, there was a meeting of the citizens of the county of Suffolk, convened at one of the churches in Boston, for the purpose of consulting on what measures might be considered expedient to prevent the landing of the tea, or secure the people from the collection of the duty. At that meeting a committee was appointed to wait on Governor Hutchinson, and request him to inform them whether he would take any measures to satisfy the people on the object of the meeting. To the first application of this committee, the governor told them he would give them a definite answer by five o'clock in the afternoon. At the hour appointed, the committee again repaired to the governor's house, and on inquiry found he had gone to his country seat at Milton, a distance of about six miles. When the committee returned and informed the meeting of the absence of the governor, there was a confused murmur among the members, and the meeting was immediately dissolved, many of them crying out, Let every man do his duty, and be true to his country; and there was a general huzza for Griffin's wharf. It was now evening, and I immediately dressed myself in the costume of an Indian, equipped with a small hatchet, which I and my associates denominated the tomahawk, with which, and a club, after having painted my face and hands with coal dust in the shop of a blacksmith, I repaired to Griffin's wharf, where the ships lay that contained the tea. When I first appeared in the street, after being thus disguised, I fell in with many who were dressed, equipped and painted as I was, and who fell in with me, and marched in order to the place of our destination. When we arrived at the wharf, there were three of our number who assumed the authority to direct our operations, to which we readily submitted. They divided us into three parties, for the purpose of boarding the three ships which contained the tea at the same time. The name of him who commanded the division to which I was assigned, was Leonard Pitt. The names of the other commanders I never knew. We were immediately ordered by the respective commanders to board all the ships at the same time, which we promptly obeyed. The commander of the division to which I belonged, as soon as we were on board the ship, appointed me boatswain, and ordered me to go to the captain and demand of him the keys to the hatches and a dozen candles. I made the demand accordingly, and the captain promptly replied, and delivered the articles; but requested me at the same time to do no damage to the ship or rigging. We then were ordered by our commander to open the hatches, and take out all the chests of tea and throw them overboard, and we immediately proceeded to execute his orders; first cutting and splitting the chests with our tomahawks, so as thoroughly to expose them to the effects of the water. In about three hours from the time we went on board, we had thus broken and thrown overboard every tea chest to be found in the ship; while those in the other ships were disposing of the tea in the same way, at the same time. We were surrounded by British armed ships, but no attempt was made to resist us. We then quietly retired to our several places of residence, without having any conversation with each other, or taking any measures to discover who were our associates; nor do I recollect of our having had the knowledge of the name of a single individual concerned in the affair, except that of Leonard Pitt, the commander of my division, who I have mentioned. There appeared to be an understanding that each individual should volunteer his services, keep his own secret, and risk the consequences for himself. No disorder took place during the transaction, and it was observed at that time, that the stillest night ensued that Boston had enjoyed for many months.

During the time we were throwing the tea overboard, there were several attempts made by some of the citizens of Boston and its vicinity, to carry off small quantities of it for their family use. To effect that object, they would watch their opportunity to snatch up a handful from the deck, where it became plentifully scattered, and put it into their pockets. One Captain O'Conner, whom I well knew, came on board for that purpose, and when he supposed he was not noticed, filled his pockets, and also the lining of his coat. But I had detected him, and gave information to the captain of what he was doing. We were ordered to take him into custody, and just as he was stepping from the vessel, I seized him by the skirt of his coat, and in attempting to pull him back, I tore it off; but springing forward, by a rapid effort, he made his escape. He had however to run the gauntlet through the crowd upon the wharf; each one, as he passed, giving him a kick or a stroke.

The next day we nailed the skirt of his coat, which I had pulled off, to the whipping post in Charlestown, the place of his residence, with a label upon it, commemorative of the occasion which had thus subjected the proprietor to the popular indignation.

Another attempt was made to save a little tea from the ruins of the cargo, by a tall aged man, who wore a large cocked hat and white wig, which was fashionable at that time. He had slightly slipped a little into his pocket, but being detected, they seized him, and taking his hat and wig from his head, threw them, together with the tea, of which they had emptied his pockets, into the water. In consideration of his advanced age, he was permitted to escape, with now and then a slight kick.

The next morning, after we had cleared the ships of the tea, it was discovered that very considerable quantities of it was floating upon the surface of the water; and to prevent the possibility of any of its being saved for use, a number of small boats were manned by sailors and citizens, who rowed them into those parts of the harbour wherever the tea was visible, and by beating it with oars and paddles, so thoroughly drenched it, as to render its entire destruction inevitable.

Questions

1. How thorough was the planning for the Boston Tea Party?

2. Were the participants eager to have their names known? Why or why not?

3. What, if any, specific rights does Hewes claim that he was trying to support by participating in the Boston Tea Party?

5-12   A British View of Rebellion in Boston (1774)

Philip Dawe

In response to the Boston Tea Party, Parliament closed Boston Harbor until the British East India Company received payment for the tea the "Indians" had destroyed. Closing the harbor, along with other punitive acts, further escalated the animosity between the colonies and the crown. British artist Philip Dawe's satirical cartoon "The Bostonians Paying the Excise-Man" depicts several Bostonians forcefully "reimbursing" a British officer with tea, tar, and feathers, while rebels in the background continue to dump more tea into the harbor. The victim in the cartoon is John Malcolm, the much-despised commissioner of customs. According to the account in the *Massachusetts Gazette*, a crowd dragged Malcolm from his house, gave him a "modern jacket" of tar and feathers, threatened to "cut his ears off," and finally carted him to the gallows "as if they intended to hang him." This violent retaliation strengthened England's resolve to punish the colonists. Dawe's cartoon "The Bostonians in Distress" derides the haughty radicals by depicting them as begging for food while suspended from their own "Liberty Tree." British troops marching in the background are a thinly veiled threat.

Thousands of ordinary people in Massachusetts and other colonies rallied around the Bostonians and began sending them food and supplies while the port was closed. Thus, rather than subduing the radicals in Boston, the Port Act spread their cause to the surrounding colonies.

Sources: Philip Dawe, "The Bostonians Paying the Excise-Man, or Tarring and Feathering," 1774, courtesy of the John Carter Brown Library at Brown University. Philip Dawe, "The Bostonians in Distress," 1774, courtesy of the National Archives and Records Administration.

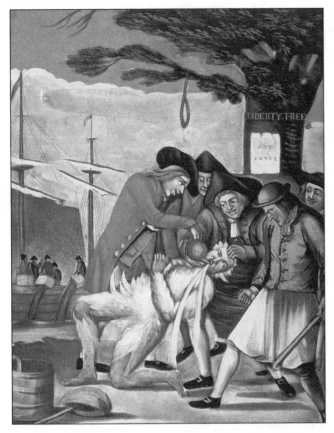

(A)   *Philip Dawe, "Bostonians Paying the Excise-Man"*

(B)   *Philip Dawe, "Bostonians in Distress"*

Questions

1. How do the actions depicted in the background of each print indicate the escalation of the crisis? What is the significance of depicting Malcolm as being forced to drink tea?

2. What is the significance of the "Liberty Tree" in these prints? How is it being mocked? What role did the so-called Liberty Tree play during the Stamp Act crisis?

3. How might British and American audiences interpret these images differently? What opposing lessons might they have drawn from them?

5-13   The Edenton, North Carolina, Boycott Agreement (1774)

When colonists decided to attack the Tea Act of 1773 by boycotting British goods, they were using a tried and heretofore effective means of countering British legislation. Therefore, it was logical for the convention called in New Bern, North Carolina, in August 1774 to protest the Port of Boston Act to call for nonimportation of any British East India Company goods, British manufactures, slaves, and tea, and for a ban on all consumption of tea in the province. Furthermore, as Document 5-8 shows, women had signed such agreements before, at least in Boston in 1770. But the agreement that the women of Edenton, North Carolina, signed on October 25, 1774, shortly after the adjournment of the New Bern convention struck contemporaries as particularly unusual. Indeed, the women's action was judged so extraordinary that a British print, reproduced in the textbook (p. 161), was issued to ridicule it.

Source: Peter Force, ed., *American Archives*, 4th ser. (1837), 1:891–892.

ASSOCIATION SIGNED BY LADIES OF EDENTON, NORTH CAROLINA, OCTOBER 25, 1774

As we cannot be indifferent on any occasion that appears to affect the peace and happiness of our country; and as it has been thought necessary for the publick good to enter into several particular Resolves by a meeting of Members of Deputies from the whole Province, it is a duty that we owe not only to our near and dear relations and connexions, but to ourselves, who are essentially interested in their welfare, to do every thing as far as lies in our power to testify our sincere adherence to the same; and we do therefore accordingly subscribe this paper as a witness of our fixed intention and solemn determination to do so.

Signed by fifty-one Ladies

Questions

1. Do the women who entered into this agreement appear to be leaders of the boycott movement, or do they appear to be responding to the actions of others?

2. To what extent, if any, do the signers of the agreement clearly spell out the basic rights they believed they were supporting?

3. Does it appear that the specifics of the agreement, including any provisions for its enforcement, would help make the boycott effective?

4. If you compare this document with the agreements signed by Boston women in 1770 (Document 5-8), would you say that what the Edenton women did was much more radical than what the Boston women had done? Why or why not?

5-14   A Summary View of the Rights of British America (1774)

Thomas Jefferson

In the summer of 1774, Thomas Jefferson was barely thirty-one years old and a relatively obscure member of the House of Burgesses. It surprised no one, therefore, that he was not among the seven delegates chosen to represent Virginia at the Continental Congress in Philadelphia. Nevertheless, Jefferson's ideas on the proper relationship between the colonies and England became widely known in Williamsburg, Philadelphia, and London through the resolutions he prepared for the Virginia delegation to present. Without his consent these resolutions were published as a pamphlet under the title *A Summary View of the Rights of British America.* Although the resolutions were not adopted at the Continental Congress, the pamphlet succeeded in establishing Jefferson's reputation as a bold and passionate writer of considerable learning. Furthermore, his uncompromising defense of colonial rights and corresponding assault on parliamentary sovereignty placed him in the front ranks of the radicals almost immediately and foreshadowed the sentiments he later expressed in the Declaration of Independence.

Source: Paul Leicester Ford, ed., *The Works of Thomas Jefferson*, Federal Edition, vol. 2 (New York: G. P. Putnam's Sons, 1904), 63–66, 73, 87.

Resolved, that it be an instruction to the said deputies, when assembled in general congress with the deputies from the other states of British America, to propose to the said congress that an humble and dutiful address be presented to his Majesty. . . . To represent to his Majesty that these his states have often individually made humble application to his imperial throne to obtain, through its intervention, some redress of their injured rights, to none of which was ever even an answer condescended; humbly to hope that this their joint address, penned in the language of truth, and divested of those expressions of servility which would persuade his Majesty that we were asking favours, and not rights, shall obtain from his Majesty a more respectful acceptance. And this his Majesty will think we have reason to expect when he reflects that he is no more than the chief officer of the people, appointed by the laws, and circumscribed with definite powers, to assist in working the great machine of government, erected for their use, and consequently subject to their superintendance. And in order that these our rights, as well as the invasions of them, may be laid more fully before his Majesty, to take a view of them from the origin and first settlement of these countries.

To remind him that our ancestors, before their emigration to America, were the free inhabitants of the British dominions in Europe, and possessed a right which nature has given to all men, of departing from the country in which chance, not choice, has placed them, of going in quest of new habitations, and of there establishing new societies, under such laws and regulations as to them shall seem most likely to promote public happiness. . . .

America was conquered, and her settlement made, and firmly established, at the expense of individuals, and not of the British public. Their own blood was spilt in acquiring lands for their settlements, their own fortunes expended in making that settlement effectual; for themselves they fought, for themselves they conquered, and for themselves alone they have right to hold. Not a shilling was ever issued from the public treasures of his Majesty, or his ancestors, for their assistance, till, of very late times, after the colonies had become established on a firm and permanent footing. . . . We do not, however, mean to under-rate those aids, which to us were doubtless valuable, on whatever principles granted; but we would shew that they cannot give a title to that authority which the British Parliament would arrogate over us. . . . That settlements having been thus effected in the wilds of America, the emigrants thought proper to adopt that system of laws under which they had hitherto lived in the mother country, and to continue their union with her by submitting themselves to the same common Sovereign, who was thereby made the central link connecting the several parts of the empire thus newly multiplied.

. . . Not only the principles of common sense, but the common feelings of human nature, must be surrendered up before his majesty's subjects here can be persuaded to believe that they hold their political existence at the will of a British parliament. Shall these governments be dissolved, their property annihilated, and their people reduced to a state of nature, at the imperious breath of a body of men, whom they never saw, in whom they never confided, and over whom they have no powers of punishment or removal, let their crimes against the American public be ever so great? Can any one reason be assigned why 160,000 electors in the island of Great Britain should give law to four millions in the states of America, every individual of whom is equal to every individual of them, in virtue, in understanding, and in bodily strength? Were this to be admitted, instead of being a free people, as we have hitherto supposed, and mean to continue ourselves, we should suddenly be found the slaves not of one but of 160,000 tyrants. . . .

That these are our grievances which we have thus laid before his majesty, with that freedom of language and sentiment which becomes a free people claiming their rights, as derived from the laws of nature, and not as the gift of their chief magistrate: Let those flatter who fear, it is not an American art. To give praise which is not due might be well from the venal, but would ill beseem those who are asserting the rights of human nature. They know, and will therefore say, that kings are the servants, not the proprietors of the people. Open your breast, sire, to liberal and expanded thought. Let not the name of George the third be a blot in the page of history.

Questions

1. According to Jefferson, what was Parliament's position within the British empire? How did Parliament's authority compare to the authority possessed by the colonial legislatures?

2. In 1774 many of Jefferson's contemporaries found the language he used to address the king unacceptable. Why?

3. What was the basis for Jefferson's reasoning on the rights of British America? In his view, what held the various constituent parts of the empire together?

5-15   The Nature and Extent of the Authority of Parliament (1774)

James Wilson

The Coercive Acts of 1774, which Parliament enacted in response to the Boston Tea Party, fundamentally altered the nature of the imperial crisis. Whereas earlier confrontations involved questions pertaining to representation, the issue now became sovereignty itself. Could Parliament legislate on matters unrelated to taxes and representation, such as the administration of justice, or the quartering of soldiers, or the operation of the town governments in Massachusetts? If not, and colonial actions indicated as much, then what powers did it have? Most imperial political theorists asserted that *imperium in imperio*, that is, the operation of two sovereign authorities within a single body politic, was an absurdity. Sovereignty was by definition absolute and indivisible. Either Parliament was sovereign or it was not. If the American colonists refused to recognize Parliamentary sovereignty, then what was their situation within the empire? James Wilson, a Scottish immigrant who had arrived in the colonies during the Stamp Act crisis of 1765 and studied law with John Dickinson (Document 5-7), offered perhaps the clearest statement of the constitutional position of the colonies by differentiating between obedience to Parliament and allegiance to the king.

Source: Excerpts from "James Wilson on Parliament," in *Sources and Documents Illustrating the American Revolution, 1764–1788; and the Formation of the Federal Constitution*, ed. Samuel Eliot Morison, 104–114. Copyright © 1951 by Samuel Eliot Morison. Used by permission of Clarendon Press, an imprint of Oxford University Press.

Many will, perhaps, be surprised to see the legislative authority of the British Parliament over the colonies denied in every instance. Those the writer informs, that, when he began this piece, he would probably have been surprised at such an opinion himself; for that it was the *result*, and not the *occasion*, of his disquisitions. He entered upon them with a view and expectation of being able to trace some constitutional line between those cases in which we ought, and those in which we ought not, to acknowledge the power of Parliament over us. In the prosecution of his inquires, he became fully convinced that such a line does not exist; and that there can be no medium between acknowledging and denying that power in *all* cases. Which of these two alternatives is most consistent with law, with the principles of liberty, and with the happiness of the colonies, let the public determine. . . .

But from what source does this mighty, this uncontrolled authority of the House of Commons flow? From the collective body of the commons of Great Britain. This authority must, therefore, originally reside in them; for whatever they convey to their representatives must ultimately be in themselves. And have those, whom we have hitherto been accustomed to consider as our fellow-subjects, an absolute and unlimited power over us? Have they a natural right to make laws, by which we may be deprived of our properties, of our liberties, of our lives? By what title do they claim to be our masters? What act of ours has rendered us subject to those, to whom we were formerly equal? Is British freedom denominated from the soil, or from the people of Britain? If from the latter, do they lose it by quitting the soil? Do those, who embark freemen in Great Britain, disembark slaves in America? Are those who fled from the oppression of regal and ministerial tyranny, now reduced to a state of vassalage to those who then equally felt the same oppression? Whence proceeds this fatal change? Is this the return made us for leaving our friends and our country—for braving the danger of the deep—for planting a wilderness inhabited only by savage men and savage beasts—for extending the dominions of the British Crown—for increasing the trade of the British merchants—for augmenting the rents of the British landlords—for heightening the wages of the British artificers? Britons should blush to make such a claim: Americans would blush to own it.

It is not, however, the ignominy only, but the danger also, with which we are threatened, that affects us. The many and careful provisions which are made by the British Constitution, that the electors of Members of Parliament may be prevented from choosing representatives who would betray them; and that the representatives may be prevented from betraying their constituents with impunity, sufficiently evince that such precautions have been deemed absolutely necessary for securing and maintaining the system of British liberty. . . .

The Members of Parliament, their families, their friends, their posterity, must be subject as well as others to the laws. Their interest, and that of their families, friends, and posterity, cannot be different from the interest of the rest of the nation. A regard to the former will therefore direct to such measures as must promote the latter. But is this the case with respect to America? Are the legislators of Great Britain subject to the laws which are made for the colonies? Is their interest the same with that of the colonies? If we consider it in a large and comprehensive view we shall discern it to be undoubtedly the same, but few will take the trouble to consider it in that view; and of those who do, few will be influenced by the consideration. Mankind are usually more affected with a near though inferior interest than with one that is superior, but placed at a greater distance. As the conduct is regulated by the passions it is not to be wondered at if they secure the former, by measures which will forfeit the latter. Nay, the latter will frequently be regarded in the same manner as if it were prejudicial to them. It is with regret that I produce some late regulations of Parliament as proofs of what I have advanced. We have experienced what an easy matter it is for a minister with an ordinary share of art to persuade the Parliament and the people that taxes laid on the colonies will ease the burthens of the mother country. . . .

I am sufficiently aware of an objection that will be made to what I have said concerning the legislative authority of the British Parliament. It will be alleged that I throw off all dependence on Great Britain. This objection will be held forth in its most specious colors, by those who, from servility of soul or from mercenary considerations would meanly bow their necks to every exertion of arbitrary power: it may likewise alarm some who entertain the most favorable opinion of the connection between Great Britain and her colonies, but who are not sufficiently acquainted with the nature of that connection which is so dear to them. Those of the first class, I hope, are few; I am sure they are contemptible, and deserve to have very little regard paid to them: but for the sake of those of the second class, who may be more numerous, and whose laudable principles atone for their mistakes, I shall take some pains to obviate the objection, and to show that a denial of the legislative authority of the British Parliament over America is by no means inconsistent with that connection which ought to subsist between the mother country and her colonies, and which, at the first settlement of those colonies, it was intended to maintain between them; but that, on the contrary, that connection would be entirely destroyed by the extension of the power of Parliament over the American plantations. . . .

The original and true ground of the superiority of Great Britain over the American colonies is not shown in any book of the law, unless, as I have already observed, it be derived from the right of conquest. But I have proved, and I hope satisfactorily, that this right is altogether inapplicable to the colonists. The original of the superiority of Great Britain over the colonies is, then, unaccounted for; and when we consider the ingenuity and pains which have lately been employed at home on this subject, we may justly conclude that the only reason why it is not accounted for is that it cannot be accounted for. The superiority of Great Britain over the colonies ought therefore to be rejected; and the dependence of the colonies upon her, if it is to be construed into "an obligation to conform to the will or law of the superior state," ought, in *this* sense, to be rejected also.

My sentiments concerning this matter are not singular. They coincide with the declarations and remonstrances of the colonies against the statutes imposing taxes on them. It was their unanimous opinion that the Parliament have no right to exact obedience to those statutes; and consequently,

that the colonies are under no obligation to obey them. The dependence of the colonies on Great Britain was denied in those instances; but a denial of it in those instances is, in effect, a denial of it in all other instances. For, if dependence is an obligation to conform to the will or law of the superior state, any exceptions to that obligation must destroy the dependence. If, therefore, by a dependence of the colonies on Great Britain, it is meant that they are obliged to obey the laws of Great Britain, reason, as well as the unanimous voice of the Americans, teaches us to disown it. Such a dependence was never thought of by those who left Britain in order to settle in America, nor by their sovereigns who gave them commissions for that purpose. Such an obligation has no correspondent right: for the Commons of Great Britain have no dominion over their equals and fellow-subjects in America; they can confer no right to their delegates to bind those equals and fellow-subjects by laws.

There is another, and a much more reasonable meaning, which may be intended by the dependence of the colonies on Great Britain. The phrase may be used to denote the obedience and loyalty which the colonists owe to the kings of Great Britain. . . .

Those who launched into the unknown deep, in quest of new countries and habitations, still considered themselves as subjects of the English monarchs, and behaved suitably to that character; but it nowhere appears that they still considered themselves as represented in an English Parliament, or that they thought the authority of the English Parliament extended over them. They took possession of the country in the *king's* name: they treated, or made war with the Indians by *his* authority: they held the lands under *his* grants, and paid *him* the rents reserved upon them: they established governments under the sanction of *his* prerogative, or by virtue of *his* charters:—no application for those purposes was made to the Parliament: no ratification of the charters or letters patent was solicited from that assembly, as is usual in England with regard to grants and franchises of much less importance. . . .

This is a dependence which they have acknowledged hitherto; which they acknowledge now; and which, if it is reasonable to judge of the future by the past and the present, they will continue to acknowledge hereafter. It is not a dependence like that contended for on Parliament, slavish and unaccountable, or accounted for only by principles that are false and inapplicable: it is a dependence founded upon the principles of reason, of liberty and of law. Let us investigate its sources.

The colonists ought to be dependent on the King, because they have hitherto enjoyed, and still continue to enjoy, his protection. Allegiance is the faith and obedience which every subject owes to his prince. This obedience is founded on the protection derived from government: for protection and allegiance are the reciprocal bonds which connect the prince and his subjects. Every subject, so soon as he is born, is under the royal protection, and is entitled to all the advantages arising from it. He therefore owes obedience to that royal power, from which the protection which he enjoys is derived. But while he continues in infancy and nonage he cannot perform the duties which his allegiance requires. The performance of them must be respited till he arrive at the years of discretion and maturity. When he arrives at those years, he owes obedience not only for the protection which he now enjoys, but also for that which from his birth he has enjoyed; and to which his tender age has hitherto prevented him from making a suitable return. Allegiance now becomes a duty founded upon principles of gratitude, as well as on principles of interest: it becomes a debt, which nothing but the loyalty of a whole life will discharge. As neither climate, nor soil, nor time entitle a person to the benefits of a subject, so an alteration of climate, of soil, or of time cannot release him from the duties of one. An Englishman who removes to foreign countries, however distant from England, owes the same allegiance to his King there which he owed him at home; and will owe it twenty years hence as much as he owes it now. Wherever he is, he is still liable to the punishment annexed by law to crimes against his allegiance; and still enti-

tled to the advantages promised by law to the duties of it: it is not cancelled, and it is not forfeited. "Hence all children born in any part of the world, if they be of English parents continuing at that time as liege subjects to the King, and having done no act to forfeit the benefit of their allegiance, are *ipso facto* naturalized: and if they have issue, and their descendants intermarry among themselves, such descendants are naturalized to all generations." [Francis Bacon] . . .

Now we have explained the dependence of the Americans. They are the subjects of the King of Great Britain. They owe him allegiance. They have a right to the benefits which arise from preserving that allegiance inviolate. They are liable to the punishments which await those who break it. This is a dependence which they have always boasted of. The principles of loyalty are deeply rooted in their hearts; and there they will grow and bring forth fruit while a drop of vital blood remains to nourish them. Their history is not stained with rebellious and treasonable machinations: an inviolable attachment to their sovereign and the warmest zeal for his glory shine in every page.

Questions

1. What was the basis of Wilson's claim that the colonists were the equals of their "fellow-subjects" within the empire? Why would this be viewed as a radical claim by imperial officials?

2. On what basis did Wilson differentiate between the obligations owed to king and to Parliament? How did he define obedience; dependence; and allegiance?

3. What sort of an empire did Wilson envision? Is it conceivable that his version of an empire would have been acceptable to any eighteenth-century imperial power?

5-16 The Continental Congress Creates the Association (1774)

As described in the textbook (pp. 153–156), the harsh British response to the Boston Tea Party spurred the colonists to create a Continental Congress to coordinate opposition to British imperial reform measures, especially the Coercive Acts. The Congress began deliberations in Philadelphia on September 5, 1774, and adjourned on October 26, 1774. As part of its general effort to defend colonial rights, the Congress created a Plan of Association. The Association, as it was called, outlined actions that the Congress and the people would take to try to force Britain into rescinding the measures that the colonists believed threatened their basic rights. The Association was passed on October 18; the formal copy was signed two days later.

Source: W. C. Ford, ed., *Journals of the Continental Congress, 1774–1789* (1904), 1:75–80.

We, his majesty's most loyal subjects, the delegates of the several colonies of New-Hampshire, Massachusetts-Bay, Rhode-Island, Connecticut, New-York, New-Jersey, Pennsylvania, the three lower counties of New-Castle, Kent and Sussex, on Delaware, Maryland, Virginia, North-Carolina,

and South-Carolina, deputed to represent them in a continental Congress, held in the city of Philadelphia, on the 5th day of September, 1774, avowing our allegiance to his majesty, our affection and regard for our fellow-subjects in Great-Britain and elsewhere, affected with the deepest anxiety, and most alarming apprehensions, at those grievances and distresses, with which his Majesty's American subjects are oppressed; and having taken under our most serious deliberation, the state of the whole continent, find, that the present unhappy situation of our affairs is occasioned by a ruinous system of colony administration, adopted by the British ministry about the year 1763, evidently calculated for inslaving these colonies, and, with them, the British empire. In prosecution of which system, various acts of parliament have been passed, for raising a revenue in America, for depriving the American subjects, in many instances, of the constitutional trial by jury, exposing their lives to danger, by directing a new and illegal trial beyond the seas, for crimes alleged to have been committed in America: and in prosecution of the same system, several late, cruel, and oppressive acts have been passed, respecting the town of Boston and the Massachusetts-Bay, and also an act for extending the province of Quebec, so as to border on the western frontiers of these colonies, establishing an arbitrary government therein, and discouraging the settlement of British subjects in that wide extended country; thus, by the influence of civil principles and ancient prejudices, to dispose the inhabitants to act with hostility against the free Protestant colonies, whenever a wicked ministry shall chuse so to direct them.

To obtain redress of these grievances, which threaten destruction to the lives, liberty, and property of his majesty's subjects, in North America, we are of opinion, that a non-importation, non-consumption, and non-exportation agreement, faithfully adhered to, will prove the most speedy, effectual, and peaceable measure: and, therefore, we do, for ourselves, and the inhabitants of the several colonies, whom we represent, firmly agree and associate, under the sacred ties of virtue, honour and love of our country, as follows:

1. That from and after the first day of December next, we will not import, into British America, from Great-Britain or Ireland, any goods, wares, or merchandise whatsoever, or from any other place, any such goods, wares, or merchandise, as shall have been exported from Great-Britain or Ireland; nor will we, after that day, import any East-India tea from any part of the world; nor any molasses, syrups, paneles, coffee, or pimento, from the British plantations or from Dominica; nor wines from Madeira, or the Western Islands; nor foreign indigo.

2. We will neither import nor purchase, any slave imported after the first day of December next; after which time, we will wholly discontinue the slave trade, and will neither be concerned in it ourselves, nor will we hire our vessels, nor sell our commodities or manufactures to those who are concerned in it.

3. As a non-consumption agreement, strictly adhered to, will be an effectual security for the observation of the non-importation, we, as above, solemnly agree and associate, that, from this day, we will not purchase or use any tea, imported on account of the East-India company,

or any on which a duty hath been or shall be paid; and from and after the first day of March next, we will not purchase or use any East-India tea whatever; nor will we, nor shall any person for or under us, purchase or use any of those goods, wares, or merchandise, we have agreed not to import, which we shall know, or have cause to suspect, were imported after the first day of December, except such as come under the rules and directions of the tenth article hereafter mentioned.

4. The earnest desire we have, not to injure our fellow-subjects in Great-Britain, Ireland, or the West-Indies, induces us to suspend a non-exportation, until the tenth day of September, 1775; at which time, if the said acts and parts of acts of the British parliament herein after mentioned are not repealed, we will not, directly or indirectly, export any merchandise or commodity whatsoever to Great-Britain, Ireland, or the West-Indies, except rice to Europe.

5. Such as are merchants, and use the British and Irish trade, will give orders, as soon as possible, to their factors, agents and correspondents, in Great-Britain and Ireland, not to ship any goods to them, on any pretence whatsoever, as they cannot be received in America; and if any merchant, residing in Great-Britain or Ireland, shall directly or indirectly ship any goods, wares or merchandise, for America, in order to break the said non-importation agreement, or in any manner contravene the same, on such unworthy conduct being well attested, it ought to be made public; and on the same being so done, we will not, from thenceforth, have any commercial connexion with such merchant.

6. That such as are owners of vessels will give positive orders to their captains, or masters, not to receive on board their vessels any goods prohibited by the said non-importation agreement, on pain of immediate dismission from their service.

7. We will use our utmost endeavours to improve the breed of sheep, and increase their number to the greatest extent; and to that end, we will kill them as seldom as may be, especially those of the most profitable kind; nor will we export any to the West-Indies or elsewhere; and those of us, who are or may become overstocked with, or can conveniently spare any sheep, will dispose of them to our neighbours, especially to the poorer sort, on moderate terms.

8. We will, in our several stations, encourage frugality, economy, and industry, and promote agriculture, arts and the manufactures of this country, especially that of wool; and will discountenance and discourage every species of extravagance and dissipation, especially all horse-racing, and all kinds of gaming, cock-fighting, exhibitions of shews, plays, and other expensive diversions and entertainments; and on the death of any relation or friend, none of us, or any of our families, will go into any further mourning-dress, than a black crape or ribbon on the arm or hat, for gentlemen, and a black ribbon and necklace for ladies, and we will discontinue the giving of gloves and scarves at funerals.

9. Such as are venders of goods or merchandise will not take advantage of the scarcity of goods, that may be occasioned by this association, but will sell the same at the rates we have been respectively accustomed to do, for twelve months last past. — And if any vender of goods or merchandise shall sell any such goods on higher terms, or shall, in any manner, or by any device whatsoever violate or depart from this agreement, no person ought, nor will any of us deal with any such person, or his or her factor or agent, at any time thereafter, for any commodity whatever.

10. In case any merchant, trader, or other person, shall import any goods or merchandise, after the first day of December, and before the first day of February next, the same ought forthwith, at the election of the owner, to be either re-shipped or delivered up to the committee of the county or town, wherein they shall be imported, to be stored at the risque of the importer, until the non-importation agreement shall cease, or be sold under the direction of the committee aforesaid; and in the last-mentioned case, the owner or owners of such goods shall be reimbursed out of the sales, the first cost and charges, the profit, if any, to be applied towards relieving and employing such poor inhabitants of the town of Boston, as are immediate sufferers by the Boston port-bill; and a particular account of all goods so returned, stored, or sold, to be inserted in the public papers; and if any goods or merchandises shall be imported after the said first day of February, the same ought forthwith to be sent back again, without breaking any of the packages thereof.

11. That a committee be chosen in every county, city, and town, by those who are qualified to vote for representatives in the legislature, whose business it shall be attentively to observe the conduct of all persons touching this association; and when it shall be made to appear, to the satisfaction of a majority of any such committee, that any person within the limits of their appointment has violated this association, that such majority do forthwith cause the truth of the case to be published in the gazette; to the end, that all such foes to the rights of British-America may be publicly known, and universally contemned as the enemies of American liberty; and thenceforth we respectively will break off all dealings with him or her.

12. That the committee of correspondence, in the respective colonies, do frequently inspect the entries of their custom-houses, and inform each other, from time to time, of the true state thereof, and of every other material circumstance that may occur relative to this association.

13. That all manufactures of this country be sold at reasonable prices, so that no undue advantage be taken of a future scarcity of goods.

14. And we do further agree and resolve, that we will have no trade, commerce, dealings or intercourse whatsoever, with any colony or province, in North-America, which shall not accede to, or which shall hereafter violate this association, but will hold them as unworthy of the rights of freemen, and as inimical to the liberties of their country.

And we do solemnly bind ourselves and our constituents, under the ties aforesaid, to adhere to this association, until such parts of the several acts of parliament passed since the close of the last war, as impose or continue duties on tea, wine, molasses, syrups, paneles, coffee, sugar, pimento, indigo, foreign paper, glass, and painters' colours, imported into America, and extend the powers of the admiralty courts beyond their ancient limits, deprive the American subject of trial by jury, authorize the judge's certificate to indemnify the prosecutor from damages, that he might otherwise be liable to from a trial by his peers, require oppressive security from a claimant of ships or goods seized, before he shall be allowed to defend his property, are repealed. — And until that part of the act of the 12 G. 3. ch. 24, entitled "An act for the better securing his majesty's dock-yards, magazines, ships, ammunition, and stores," by which any persons charged with committing any of the offences therein described, in America, may be tried in any shire or county within the realm, is repealed — and until the four acts, passed the last session of parliament, viz. that for stopping the port and blocking up the harbour of Boston — that for altering the charter and government of the Massachusetts-Bay — and that which is entitled "An act for the better administration of justice, &c." — and that "for extending the limits of Quebec, &c." are repealed. And we recommend it to the provincial conventions, and to the committees in the respective colonies, to establish such farther regulations as they may think proper, for carrying into execution this association.

The foregoing association being determined upon by the Congress, was ordered to be subscribed by the several members thereof; and thereupon, we have hereunto set our respective names accordingly.

IN CONGRESS, PHILADELPHIA, *October 20, 1774*

Questions

1. What essential tool did the Congress hope to use to get Britain to rescind its imperial reforms? Does it appear that the Congress was well versed in the use of that tool?

2. How fully and forcefully, if at all, does the Association state what the Congress considered to be the essential basic rights of the colonists?

3. What measures did the Congress propose to ensure that its dictates were followed? Would you expect those measures to be effective? Why or why not?

4. Judging from the Association, what kind of imperial policies did the Continental Congress want the British government to follow? What would the British government have to do to restore harmony?

5. What insights does the document give you into the principal economic activities of the American colonies at that time?

5-17   A Plan of Union (1774)

Joseph Galloway

Joseph Galloway was a prominent Philadelphia lawyer and Speaker of the Pennsylvania Assembly in 1774 when he was elected as a delegate to the First Continental Congress (September 5—October 26). Convinced that most colonists did not "wish to become aliens to the mother state" but that a few radicals, led by Samuel Adams, whom he described as a man not known for his brilliance but who "eats little, drinks little, sleeps little, thinks much, and is most decisive and indefatigable in the pursuit of his objects," were leading them in precisely that direction, Galloway anxiously sought some middle ground that might put an end to the imperial crisis. Congress's endorsement of the radical Suffolk Resolves on September 17, which declared the Coercive Acts to be null and void, only increased his sense of urgency. On September 28, Galloway presented his compromise plan of union, hoping it might prove effectual in keeping "extremists" on both sides in check.

Source: Excerpts from "Joseph Galloway's Plan of Union," in *Sources and Documents Illustrating the American Revolution, 1764–1788; and the Formation of the Federal Constitution,* ed. Samuel Eliot Morison, 116–118. Copyright © 1951 by Samuel Eliot Morison. Used by permission of Clarendon Press, an imprint of Oxford University Press.

Resolved, That this Congress will apply to His Majesty for a redress of grievances, under which his faithful subjects in America labour, and assure him that the colonies hold in abhorrence the idea of being considered independent communities on the British Government, and most ardently desire the establishment of a political union, not only among themselves, but with the mother state, upon those principles of safety and freedom which are essential in the constitution of all free governments, and particularly that of the British Legislature. And as the colonies from their local circumstances cannot be represented in the Parliament of Great Britain, they will humbly propose to His Majesty, and his two Houses of Parliament, the following plan, under which the strength of the whole Empire may be drawn together on any emergency; the interests of both countries advanced; and the rights and liberties of America secured.

A Plan of a proposed Union between Great Britain and the Colonies of . . .

That a British and American Legislature, for regulating the administration of the general affairs of America, be proposed and established in America, including all the said colonies; within and under which government, each colony shall retain its present constitution and powers of regulating and governing its own internal police in all cases whatsoever.

That the said government be administered by a President-General to be appointed by the King, and a Grand Council to be chosen by the representatives of the people of the several colonies in their respective Assemblies, once in every three years.

That the several Assemblies shall choose members for the Grand Council in the following proportions, viz. : . . . who shall meet at the city of   for the first time, being called by the President-General as soon as conveniently may be after his appointment. That there shall be a new election of members for the Grand Council every three years; and on the death, removal, or resignation of any member, his place shall be supplied by a new choice at the next sitting of Assembly of the colony he represented.

That the Grand Council shall meet once in every year if they shall think it necessary, and oftener if occasions shall require, at such time and place as they shall adjourn to at the last preceding meeting, or as they shall be called to meet at, by the President-General on any emergency.

That the Grand Council shall have power to choose their Speaker, and shall hold and exercise all the like rights, liberties, and privileges as are held and exercised by and in the House of Commons of Great Britain.

That the President-General shall hold his office during the pleasure of the King, and his assent shall be requisite to all Acts of the Grand Council, and it shall be his office and duty to cause them to be carried into execution.

That the President-General, by and with the advice and consent of the Grand Council, hold and exercise all the legislative rights, powers, and authorities, necessary for regulating and administering all the general police and affairs of the colonies, in which Great Britain and the colonies, or any of them, the colonies in general, or more than one colony, are in any manner concerned, as well civil and criminal as commercial.

That the said President-General and Grand Council be an inferior and distinct branch of the British Legisla-ture, united and incorporated with it for the aforesaid general purposes; and that any of the said general regulations may originate, and be formed and digested, either in the Parliament of Great Britain or in the said Grand Council; and being prepared, transmitted to the other for their approbation or dissent; and that the assent of both shall be requisite to the validity of all such general Acts and Statutes.

That in time of war, all bills for granting aids to the Crown, prepared by the Grand Council and approved by the President-General, shall be valid and passed into a law, without the assent of the British Parliament.

Questions

1. How were the issues in dispute since 1763 reflected in Galloway's plan? What was his solution to the problem of taxation and representation? Did he have an answer to the *imperium in imperio* conundrum (Document 5-15)?

2. Which elements of Galloway's plan were aimed at accommodating the colonists? Which were aimed at pleasing king and Parliament? Were the bulk of his specific proposals more favorable to one side? Explain.

3. The delegates in Philadelphia not only rejected Galloway's plan of union, they expunged it from the minutes of the First Continental Congress. Why? Even if Congress had endorsed the plan, would Parliament have approved of it as well?

Questions for Further Thought

1. In what ways were the constitutional arguments offered by Thomas Jefferson (Document 5-14) and James Wilson (Document 5-15) similar? In what ways were they dissimilar?

2. George R. T. Hewes responded to the call for "every man [to] do his duty, and be true to his country" (Document 5-11). Did this Boston shoemaker understand the arguments voiced by Jefferson, Wilson, and the other elite members of the colonial ruling class? What was his motive for participating in the Tea Party?

3. Was the American Revolution inevitable?

CHAPTER SIX

Making War and Republican Governments

1776–1789

The Trials of War, 1776–1778

Many troubles beset the American colonists when they went to war against Great Britain, the greatest imperial power in the world. One problem was that the movement toward war and the opening of hostilities produced a sharpening of the social divisions among Americans. The coming of war brought with it the possibility that artisans and people even lower on the socioeconomic ladder would gain more power. As Gouverneur Morris's observations (Document 6-1) show, some upper-class Patriots were bothered that less politically influential lower-class Patriots would use the Revolutionary War to increase their power.

The Revolution's opponents exploited the contradictions between Revolutionary appeals to "liberty" and Revolutionary leaders' own continuing devotion to race inequality. Lord Dunmore, the last royal governor of Virginia, sought to strike at the slave system on which rested the power of that colony's revolutionaries (Document 6-2), while the London Tory Samuel Johnson openly derided the contradictions of the Patriots' claims (Document 6-3).

As the imperial crisis escalated, moderates were increasingly marginalized, as Document 6-4 illustrates. The rebels also faced opposition from Loyalists and Native Americans as well as the British (Document 6-5). Even before the publication of Thomas Paine's best-selling *Common Sense* in early 1776, the middle ground had disappeared; Document 6-6, from "The American Crisis" essay series, illustrates some of the many difficulties faced by the Patriots. When the Continental Congress finally declared independence on July 2, 1776, and then explained its reasons for doing so in the Declaration of Independence approved two days later, it simply crystallized the thinking of large numbers of its constituents.

6-1 The Poor Reptiles (1774)

Gouverneur Morris

Gouverneur Morris, who came from an established and wealthy New York family, was not a leading revolutionary Patriot in 1774 as many of his contemporaries were (see text p. 194). He graduated from King's College at the age of sixteen in 1768; six years later he was on the verge of starting his career as one of the leaders of the Revolution. Morris's service culminated in his appointment as a delegate to the U.S. Constitutional Convention. In a letter he wrote to Thomas Penn on May 20, 1774, Morris offered his judgment on how the movement toward independence might transform America's political society. In doing so, he illustrates that social divisions were sharpened during the era of the War of Independence.

Source: Peter Force, ed., *American Archives*, 4th ser. (1837) 1:342–343.

DEAR SIR:

You have heard, and you will hear a great deal about politics, and in the heap of chaff you may find some grains of good sense. Believe me, sir, freedom and religion are only watchwords. We have appointed a committee, or rather we have nominated one. Let me give you the history of it. It is needless to premise that the lower orders of mankind are more easily led by specious appearances than those of a more exalted station. This, and many similar propositions, you know better than your humble servant.

The troubles in America during Grenville's administration put our gentry upon this finesse. They stimulated some daring coxcombs to rouse the mob into an attack upon the bounds of order and decency. These fellows became the Jack Cades of the day, the leaders in all the riots, the bell-wethers of the flock. The reason of the manœuvre in those who wished to keep fair with the government, and at the same time to receive the incense of popular applause, you will readily perceive. On the whole, the shepherds were not much to blame in a politic point of view. The bell-wethers jingled merrily and roared out liberty and property, and religion, and a multitude of cant terms which everyone thought he understood, and was egregiously mistaken. For you must know the shepherds kept the dictionary of the day, and like the mysteries of the ancient mythology, it was not for profane eyes or ears. This answered many purposes; the simple flock put themselves entirely under the protection of these most excellent shepherds. By and by, behold a great metamorphosis without the help of Ovid or his divinities, but entirely effectuated by two modern Genii, the god of Ambition and the goddess of Faction. The first of these prompted the shepherds to shear some of their flock, and then in conjunction with the other, converted the bell-wethers into shepherds. That we have been in hot water with the British Parliament ever since everybody knows. Consequently these new shepherds had their hands full of employment. The old ones kept themselves least in sight, and a want of confidence in each other was not the least evil which followed. The port of Boston has been shut up. These sheep, simple as they are, cannot be gulled as heretofore. In short, there is no ruling them, and now, to leave the metaphor, the heads of the mobility grow dangerous to the gentry, and how to keep them down is the question. While they correspond with the other colonies, call and dismiss popular assemblies, make resolves to bind the consciences of the rest of mankind, bully poor printers, and exert with full force all their other tribunitial powers, it is impossible to curb them.

But art sometimes goes farther than force, and therefore, to trick them handsomely a committee of patricians was to be nominated, and into their hands was to be committed the majesty of the people, and the highest trust was to be reposed in them by a mandate that they should take care, that the republic should not suffer injury. The tribunes, through the want of good legerdemain in the senatorial order, perceived the finesse; and yesterday I was present at a grand division of the city, and there I beheld my fellow-citizens very accurately counting all their chickens, not only before any of them were hatched, but before above one half of the eggs were laid. In short, they fairly contended about the future forms of our government, whether it should be founded upon aristocratic or democratic principles.

I stood in the balcony, and on my right hand were ranged all the people of property, with some few poor dependents, and on the other all the tradesmen, etc., who thought it worth their while to leave daily labour for the good of the country. The spirit of the English constitution has yet a little influence left, and but a little. The remains of it, however, will give the wealthy people a superiority this time, but would they secure it they must banish all schoolmasters and confine all knowledge to themselves. This cannot be. The mob begin to think and to reason. Poor reptiles! It is with them a vernal morning; they are struggling to cast off their winter's slough, they bask in the sunshine, and ere noon they will bite, depend upon it. The gentry begin to fear this. Their committee will be appointed, they will deceive the people and again forfeit a share of their confidence. And if these instances of what with one side is policy, with the other perfidy, shall continue to increase and become more frequent, farewell aristocracy. I see, and I see it with fear and trembling, that if the disputes with Great Britain continue, we shall be under the worst of all possible dominions; we shall be under the domination of a riotous mob.

It is the interest of all men, therefore, to seek for reunion with the parent state.

Questions

1. What vital change in the American political system did Morris think was occurring?
2. Did he approve of that change? Why or why not?

3. When Morris talked of the "bell-wethers of the flock," he was talking about the leaders (the bellwethers) of sheep (the flock). What does this image tell you about his view of the average person?

4. In what ways, if any, do Morris's judgments remind you of the Loyalist Peter Oliver's pronouncements (Document 5-9)?

6-2   A Proclamation (1775)

Lord Dunmore

John Murray, earl of Dunmore (1732–1809) and the last royal governor of Virginia, was a beleaguered man in 1775. Lacking a standing army to enforce the king's will, he had effectively lost control of the colony to the Patriot gentry. Nonetheless, he thought he could recover by striking at the colonists' Achilles' heel: slavery. Thanks to a 1772 English court ruling, rumors abounded among Virginia slaves that they would be free if they got to English soil. Shortly after the Battles of Lexington and Concord, a group of slaves had offered Dunmore their services in exchange for their freedom. In November, after a unit of Dunmore's troops that included slaves had defeated the colonial militia, Dunmore issued this famous proclamation. Dunmore's promise was effective in attracting increasing numbers of runaway slaves to the Tory cause, and by December 1775 some three hundred African Americans were members of "Lord Dunmore's Ethiopian Regiment," wearing uniforms inscribed with the slogan "Liberty to Slaves." Shortly afterward, though, Dunmore was forced to abandon the mainland, and over the winter his waterborne troops were decimated by disease. But the episode sufficed to frighten Virginia slaveholders, including Thomas Jefferson.

Source: American Antiquarian Society, *Early American Imprints,* 1st ser., no. 14592.

By his Excellency the Right Honourable JOHN Earl of Dunmore, his Majesty's Lieutenant and Governour-General of the Colony and Dominion of Virginia, and Vice-Admiral of the same:

A PROCLAMATION.

As I have ever entertained Hopes that an Accommodation might have taken Place between *Great Britain* and this Colony, without being compelled, by my Duty, to this most disagreeable, but now absolutely necessary Step, rendered so by a Body of armed Men, unlawfully assembled, firing on his Majesty's Tenders, and the Formation of an Army, and that Army now on their March to attack his Majesty's Troops, and destroy the well-disposed Subjects of this Colony: To defeat such treasonable Purposes, and that all such Traitors, and their Abetters, may be brought to Justice, and that the Peace and good Order of this Colony may be again restored, which the ordinary Course of the civil Law is unable to effect, I have thought fit to issue this my Proclamation, hereby declaring, that until the aforesaid good Purposes can be obtained, I do, in Virtue of the Power and Authority to me given, by his Majesty, determine to execute martial Law, and cause the same to be executed throughout this Colony; and to the End

that Peace and good Order may the sooner be restored, I do require every Person capable of bearing Arms to resort to his Majesty's STANDARD, or be looked upon as Traitors to his Majesty's Crown and Government, and thereby become liable to the Penalty the Law inflicts upon such Offences, such as Forfeiture of Life, Confiscation of Lands, &c. &c. And I do hereby farther declare all indented Servants, Negroes, or others (appertaining to Rebels) free, that are able and willing to bear Arms, they joining his Majesty's Troops, as soon as may be, for the more speedily reducing this Colony to a proper Sense of their Duty, to his Majesty's Crown and Dignity. I do farther order, and require, all his Majesty's liege Subjects to retain their Quitrents, or any other Taxes due, or that may become due, in their own Custody, till such Time as Peace may be again restored to this at present most unhappy Country, or demanded of them for their former salutary Purposes, by Officers properly authorised to receive the same.

GIVEN under my Hand, on Board the Ship William, *off* Norfolk, *the 7th of* November, *in the 16th Year of his Majesty's Reign.*

DUNMORE.

GOD SAVE THE KING.

Questions

1. How did Lord Dunmore instruct the crown's loyal subjects to behave? What did he request that they do?

2. Do you think that Lord Dunmore's move to free the slaves of the "Rebels" convinced many of Virginia's rebellious gentry to switch sides and support the crown? How do you think that Virginia's gentry reacted to Dunmore's edict on the status of their slaves?

3. Looking at this document, do you see any reason why a slave might have found Dunmore's offer suspect?

6-3   On Liberty and Slavery (1775)

Samuel Johnson

At the time of its first meeting in September and October of 1774, the First Continental Congress issued a number of declarations setting forth the position of the colonists against the mother country, declarations that circulated widely in Britain and stirred considerable sympathy for the American cause. In an effort to respond, the government of Lord North recruited the eminent man of letters (and doughty Tory) Samuel Johnson to make its case. Dr. Johnson's product, the pamphlet *Taxation No Tyranny*, had to be toned down by the government before it was issued. Even then, Johnson's derisive tone and blunt conservatism guaranteed his pamphlet a hostile reception. Johnson had a keen eye for the contradictions built into the American case, especially regarding the colonies' claims of a legal right to disobey the government. He also found much merriment in their warnings that the mother country sought to impose "slavery" on a free land, as the following excerpts show.

Source: Donald J. Greene, ed., *Political Writings, The Yale Edition of the Works of Samuel Johnson* (New Haven, CT: Yale University Press, 1977), 411–412, 428–429, 436–437, 441–443, 448–451, 453–454. (Note: Footnotes are from the Yale University Press edition.) Used by Yale University Press.

TAXATION NO TYRANNY; AN ANSWER TO THE RESOLUTIONS AND ADDRESS OF THE AMERICAN CONGRESS

In all the parts of human knowledge, whether terminating in science merely speculative, or operating upon life private or civil, are admitted some fundamental principles, or common axioms, which being generally received are little doubted, and being little doubted have been rarely proved. . . .

Of this kind is the position that "the supreme power of every community has the right of requiring from all its subjects such contributions as are necessary to the public safety or public prosperity,"[1] which was considered by all mankind as comprising the primary and essential condition of all political society, till it became disputed by those zealots of anarchy, who have denied to the Parliament of Britain the right of taxing the American colonies. . . .

But hear, ye sons and daughters of liberty, the sounds which the winds are wafting from the western continent. The Americans are telling one another, what, if we may judge from their noisy triumph, they have but lately discovered, and what yet is a very important truth. "That they are entitled to life, liberty, and property, and that they have never ceded to any sovereign power whatever a right to dispose of either without their consent."

While this resolution stands alone, the Americans are free from singularity of opinion; their wit has not yet betrayed them to heresy. While they speak as the naked sons of Nature, they claim but what is claimed by other men, and have withheld nothing but what all withhold. They are here upon firm ground, behind entrenchments which never can be forced.

Humanity is very uniform. The Americans have this resemblance to Europeans, that they do not always know when they are well. They soon quit the fortress that could neither have been mined by sophistry, nor battered by declamation. Their next resolution declares, that "their ancestors, who

---

[1] If this is a quotation, its source has not been traced. But it may be SJ's own formulation (of a position common enough in earlier works on government). . . . The *Monthly Review* (Mar. 1775, p. 253), which devotes considerable space to examining the proposition, seems to treat the phraseology as SJ's own; so does Sir John Hawkins (*Life*, ed. B. H. Davis, 1961, p. 218). [*Greene's note.*]

first settled the colonies, were, at the time of their emigration from the mother-country, entitled to all the rights, liberties, and immunities of free and natural-born subjects within the realm of England."

This likewise is true; but when this is granted, their boast of original rights is at an end; they are no longer in a state of nature. These lords of themselves, these kings of *Me*, these demigods of independence, sink down to colonists, governed by a charter. If their ancestors were subjects, they acknowledged a sovereign; if they had a right to English privileges, they were accountable to English laws, and what must grieve the lover of liberty to discover, had ceded to the King and Parliament, whether the right or not, at least the power, of disposing, "without their consent, of their lives, liberties, and properties." It therefore is required of them to prove, that the Parliament ever ceded to them a dispensation from that obedience, which they owe as natural-born subjects, or any degree of independence or immunity not enjoyed by other Englishmen.

They say, that by such emigration they by no means forfeited, surrendered, or lost any of those rights; but that "they were, and their descendents now are, entitled to the exercise and enjoyment of all such of them as their local and other circumstances enable them to exercise and enjoy."

That they who form a settlement by a lawful charter, having committed no crime, forfeit no privileges, will be readily confessed; but what they do not forfeit by any judicial sentence, they may lose by natural effects. As man can be but in one place at once, he cannot have the advantages of multiplied residence. He that will enjoy the brightness of sunshine, must quit the coolness of the shade. He who goes voluntarily to America, cannot complain of losing what he leaves in Europe. . . .

It must always be remembered that they are represented by the same virtual representation as the greater part of Englishmen; and that if by change of place they have less share in the legislature than is proportionate to their opulence, they by their removal gained that opulence, and had originally and have now their choice of a vote at home, or riches at a distance. . . .

The friends of the Americans indeed ask for them what they do not ask for themselves. This inestimable right of representation they have never solicited. They mean not to exchange solid money for such airy honour. They say, and say willingly, that they cannot conveniently be represented; because their inference is, that they cannot be taxed. They are too remote to share the general government, and therefore claim the privilege of governing themselves. . . .

One mode of persuasion their ingenuity has suggested, which it may perhaps be less easy to resist. That we may not look with indifference on the American contest, or imagine that the struggle is for a claim, which, however decided, is of small importance and remote consequence, the Philadelphian Congress has taken care to inform us, that they are resisting the demands of Parliament, as well for our sakes as their own.

Their keenness of perspicacity has enabled them to pursue consequences to a great distance; to see through clouds impervious to the dimness of European sight; and to find, I know not how, that when they are taxed, we shall be enslaved.

That slavery is a miserable state we have been often told, and doubtless many a Briton will tremble to find it so near as in America; but how it will be brought hither, the Congress must inform us. The question might distress a common understanding; but the statesmen of the other hemisphere can easily resolve it. Our ministers, they say, are our enemies, and "if they should carry the point of taxation, may with the same army enslave us. It may be said, we will not pay them; but remember," say the western sages, "the taxes from America, and we may add the men, and particularly the Roman Catholics of this vast continent will then be in the power of your enemies. Nor have you any reason to expect, that after making slaves of us, many of us will refuse to assist in reducing you to the same abject state."

Thus formidable are their menaces; but suspecting that they have not much the sound of probability, the Congress proceeds: "Do not treat this as chimerical. Know that in less than half a century the quitrents reserved to the crown from the numberless grants of this vast continent will pour large streams of wealth into the royal coffers. If to this be added the power of taxing America at pleasure, the crown will possess more treasure than may be necessary to purchase *the remains* of liberty in your island."

All this is very dreadful; but amidst the terror that shakes my frame, I cannot forbear to wish that some sluice were opened for these floods of treasure. I should gladly see America return half of what England has expended in her defence; and of the "stream" that will "flow so largely in less than half a century," I hope a small rill at least may be found to quench the thirst of the present generation, which seems to think itself in more danger of wanting money than of losing liberty.

It is difficult to judge with what intention such airy bursts of malevolence are vented: if such writers hope to deceive, let us rather repel them with scorn, than refute them by disputation.

In this last terrifick paragraph are two positions that, if our fears do not overpower our reflection, may enable us to support life a little longer. We are told by these croakers of calamity, not only that our present ministers design to enslave us, but that the same malignity of purpose is to descend through all their successors, and that the wealth to be poured into England by the Pactolus[2] of America will, whenever it comes, be employed to purchase "the remains of liberty."[3] . . .

It has been of late a very general practice to talk of slavery among those who are setting at defiance every power that keeps the world in order. If the learned author of the *Reflections on Learning* has rightly observed, that no man ever

---

[2] The river in which Midas bathed, and which thus became gold-bearing.
[3] Quoted from *Votes and Proceedings*, p. 40.

could give law to language, it will be vain to prohibit the use of the word "slavery"; but I could wish it more discreetly uttered; it is driven at one time too hard into our ears by the loud hurricane of Pennsylvanian eloquence, and at another glides too cold into our hearts by the soft conveyance of a female patriot bewailing the miseries of her "friends and fellow-citizens."[4]

Such has been the progress of sedition, that those who a few years ago disputed only our right of laying taxes, now question the validity of every act of legislation. They consider themselves as emancipated from obedience, and as being no longer the subjects of the British Crown. They leave us no choice but of yielding or conquering, of resigning our dominion, or maintaining it by force.

From force many endeavours have been used, either to dissuade, or to deter us. Sometimes the merit of the Americans is exalted, and sometimes their sufferings are aggravated. We are told of their contributions to the last war, a war incited by their outcries, and continued for their protection, a war by which none but themselves were gainers. All that they can boast is, that they did something for themselves, and did not wholly stand inactive, while the sons of Britain were fighting in their cause.

If we cannot admire, we are called to pity them; to pity those that shew no regard to their mother country; have obeyed no law which they could violate; have imparted no good which they could withold; have entered into associations of fraud to rob their creditors; and into combinations to distress all who depended on their commerce. We are reproached with the cruelty of shutting one port, where every port is shut against us. We are censured as tyrannical for hindering those from fishing, who have condemned our merchants to bankruptcy and our manufacturers to hunger.

Others persuade us to give them more liberty, to take off restraints, and relax authority; and tell us what happy consequences will arise from forbearance: How their affections will be conciliated, and into what diffusions of beneficence their gratitude will luxuriate. They will love their friends, they will reverence their protectors. They will throw themselves into our arms, and lay their property at our feet. They will buy from no other what we can sell them; they will sell to no other what we wish to buy.

That any obligations should overpower their attention to profit, we have known them long enough not to expect. It is not to be expected from a more liberal people. With what kindness they repay benefits, they are now shewing us, who, as soon as we have delivered them from France, are defying and proscribing us.

But if we will permit them to tax themselves, they will give us more than we require. If we proclaim them independent, they will during pleasure pay us a subsidy. The contest is not now for money, but for power. The question is not how much we shall collect, but by what authority the collection shall be made. . . .

The Dean of Gloucester has proposed, and seems to propose it seriously, that we should at once release our claims, declare them masters of themselves, and whistle them down the wind. His opinion is, that our gain from them will be the same, and our expence less. What they can have most cheaply from Britain, they will still buy, what they can sell to us at the highest price they will still sell.

It is, however, a little hard, that having so lately fought and conquered for their safety, we should govern them no longer. By letting them loose before the war, how many millions might have been saved. One wild proposal is best answered by another. Let us restore to the French what we have taken from them. We shall see our colonists at our feet, when they have an enemy so near them. Let us give the Indians arms, and teach them discipline, and encourage them now and then to plunder a plantation. Security and leisure are the parents of sedition.

While these different opinions are agitated, it seems to be determined by the legislature, that force shall be tried. Men of the pen have seldom any great skill in conquering kingdoms but they have strong inclination to give advice. I cannot forbear to wish, that this commotion may end without bloodshed, and that the rebels may be subdued by terrour rather than by violence; and therefore recommend such a force as may take away, not only the power, but the hope of resistance, and by conquering without a battle, save many from the sword.

If their obstinacy continues without actual hostilities, it may perhaps be mollified by turning out the soldiers to free quarters, forbidding any personal cruelty or hurt. It has been proposed, that the slaves should be set free, an act which surely the lovers of liberty cannot but commend. If they are furnished with fire arms for defence, and utensils for husbandry, and settled in some simple form of government within the country, they may be more grateful and honest than their masters. . . .

Since the Americans have made it necessary to subdue them, may they be subdued with the least injury possible to their persons and their possessions. When they are reduced to obedience, may that obedience be secured by stricter laws and stronger obligations.

Nothing can be more noxious to society than that erroneous clemency, which, when a rebellion is suppressed, exacts no forfeiture and establishes no securities, but leaves the rebels in their former state. Who would not try the experiment which promises advantage without expence? If rebels once obtain a victory, their wishes are accomplished; if they are defeated, they suffer little, perhaps less than their conquerors; however often they play the game, the chance is always in their favour. In the mean time, they are growing rich by victualing the troops that we have sent against them, and perhaps gain more by the

---

[4]Catharine Sawbridge Macaulay, *An Address to the People of England, Scotland and Ireland, on the Present Important Crisis of Affairs* (1775), p. 5: "It can be no secret to you, my friends and fellow-citizens. . . ." She continues to use the phrase *ad nauseam.* Mrs. Macaulay's pamphlet was in part a direct attack on SJ's *The Patriot.*

residence of the army than they lose by the obstruction of their port.[5]

Their charters being now, I suppose, legally forfeited, may be modelled as shall appear most commodious to the mother-country. Thus the privileges, which are found by experience liable to misuse, will be taken away, and those who now bellow as patriots, bluster as soldiers, and domineer as legislators, will sink into sober merchants and silent planters, peaceably diligent, and securely rich.

But there is one writer, and perhaps many who do not write, to whom the contraction of these pernicious privileges appears very dangerous, and who startle at the thoughts of "England free and America in chains."[6] Children fly from their own shadow, and rhetoricians are frighted by their own voices. "Chains" is undoubtedly a dreadful word; but perhaps the masters of civil wisdom may discover some gradations between chains and anarchy. Chains need not be put upon those who will be restrained without them. This contest may end in the softer phrase of English superiority and American obedience.

We are told, that the subjection of Americans may tend to the diminution of our own liberties: an event, which none but very perspicacious politicians are able to foresee. If slavery be thus fatally contagious, how is it that we hear the loudest yelps for liberty among the drivers of negroes?[7]

[5] In May 1774 General Gage, the new governor of Massachusetts, arrived in Boston with four regiments, to enforce the Boston Port Act.

[6] Perhaps a reference to the opening of the Continental Congress's Address to the People of Great Britain (in *Votes and Proceedings*): "When a nation, led to greatness by the hand of Liberty, and possessed by all the glory that heroism, munificence, and humanity can bestow, descends to the ungrateful task of forging chains for her Friends and Children, and instead of giving support to Freedom, turns advocate for Slavery and Oppression...." The author may have been John Jay (cf. Edmund Cody Burnett, *The Continental Congress*, 1941, p. 52).

[7] Southern slave owners, notably Patrick Henry and Thomas Jefferson, were among the most voluble propagandists for American "freedom." It may be to this memorable comment that SJ referred four years later in his "Life of Milton": "It has been observed that they who most loudly clamour for liberty do not most liberally grant it" (*Lives*, 1.157, par. 170).

Questions

1. On what grounds did Johnson make the British case against the American position on independence? Where did he believe that the American Patriots exhibited faulty reasoning? What was his overall argument?

2. In Johnson's view, taxes and money were not the real issues at stake. What did he believe that the colonists really wanted? How negotiable was the crown's position?

3. British and Americans alike used words like *freedom*, *liberty*, and *slavery* to define their positions. In the excerpt from Johnson's pamphlet, is it fair to say that to the British and Americans, these words meant very different things to each side? Explain.

6-4   Rule for My Own Conduct (1776)

William Smith Jr.

"Every Tory is a coward," Tom Paine declared in 1776, and subsequent generations of Americans have too often entertained similar sentiments. Those who remained loyal to the empire were labeled "Tories," an epithet suggesting that they were the "king's men," and portrayed by the Revolutionaries as traitors. And because the Revolutionaries were victorious, their version of their opponents became conventional wisdom. From 1776 to the 1950s, chroniclers of the American Revolution either ignored the opponents of independence or generally treated them with disdain. Since the 1960s historians have tried more seriously to understand the logic of loyalism. The fate of William Smith Jr. illustrates well the plight of those who chose to remain loyal to Britain. The last royal chief justice of the colony of New York and a member of the governor's Council, Smith nevertheless had opposed all efforts to tax the colonies against their consent. Like Joseph Galloway (Document 5-17), he longed for reconciliation between Parliament and the colonies. But events after 1774 left little room for moderation or accommodation. Unable to choose sides because he found fault with both, choices were forced upon him. Smith was detained by the Revolutionaries temporarily and forced into exile when the British evacuated New York City in 1783.

Source: Excerpts from *Colonies to Nation: 1763–1789*, ed. Jack P. Greene (New York: Norton, 1975), 286–291. Copyright © 1975 W. W. Norton & Company.

I now set down—My Thoughts as a Rule for my own Conduct, at this melancholy Hour of approaching Distress.—...

(1) That the present Animosities are imputable to the Pride & Avarice of Great Britain, in assuming an Authority, inconsistent with the Compact by which the Empire has been so long prosperously united. The Colonies have the Merit of returning to their Submission, the instant she disharmed them of the Stamp Duties, notwithstanding her irritating Avowal of a Right to unlimited Sovereignty. They remained quiet, till Mr Townsend revived the Imposition, by the Duties upon Paper Paint and Glass in 1767, for raising a Revenue, subversive of the Colony Legislatures and the Old Customs of the Empire.

(2) That the Colonies were justifiable, in resisting the new Law devised to execute the Tea Duty Act; for that aiming to inforce the Claim of absolute Supremacy, they were driven to the alternative of open Violence, or an unconditional Submission. The Mother Country had contemned all their Petitions and Remonstrances, & Force was inevitable agt. the Dutied Article, since a meer Disswasion from the Purchase of Tea, might expose to Prosecution, ruinous to the patriotic Diswader, unless his Countrymen would make Exertions agt. The Government for his Redemption—And it was therefore more eligible immediately to destroy the Commodity, than afterwards to break Jails, and overturn the Colony Government, to defeat the regular Course of Law.

(3) That the Resentment of Great Britain on the Destruction & Expulsion of the Tea, manifested in the hostile Measures of 1774, by altering the Charter of the Massachusetts Bay, extinguishing the Commerce of Boston, collecting an Army there, rendring the Soldiery dispunishable even for Blood wasted, and by Modelling the Province of Quebec, favorable to the Designs of Compulsion & Violence, was utterly unjustifiable & an Infraction of the League; which obliged Great Britain to protect the Colonies. And these Severities were the more inexcusable, since to that Moment her Sovereignty in all Cases (the Matter of Taxation excepted) had not been denied by the Colonies, but was supported by all our Courts and Judicatures. *Jam domiti ut paveant,* as Tacitus said of our British ancestors, *nondum ut serviant*—Subjects not Slaves.

(4) That the Continental Congress now formed in September 1774, might with Justice have resorted to Arms, in Defence of the Massachusetts Bay, agt. the little Army collected there, for the avowed Design of inforcing a Principle destructive of the common Safety of the Provinces.

(5) That it was the Duty of the American Assemblies, and of that Congress, as acting for the whole Continent, to render a Plan to the Mother Country for restoring Peace, consistant with the Compact, by which the Parliament of Great Britain, was to injoy a Supremacy not incompatible with the Common Felicity of the Empire—And consequently that the Declaration they then made, of the Right of the Colonies to an *exclusive* Legislation, not only in all laws of Taxation, but of *internal Polity*, subject only to the negative of their Sovereign, was a Departure in Terms, from the Original Covenant; since it left no Authority to the Parliament of Great Britain, over the Plantations, except for the Regulation of external Commerce, and countenanced a Jealousy, excited by the Mis-Representations of their Enemies, of a Design to maintain a Union only with the Kings, and not with the Legislature of Great Britain—And that the Intimation of that Congress, of the Willingness of the Colonies, to acquiesce in their Condition prior to the Year 1763, gave Great Britain no sufficient Ground, to expect their Submission to the antient, acknowledged Claims of her Parliament; since her Repeal of the offending Statutes, unless we retracted our Denial of her Legislative Authority in Matters of internal Polity, would establish by fair Implication, the Congress's Declaration as the Basis of Peace, and that thenceforth America was to be considered as the Ally of Great Britain, & not a Member of the Empire—...

(6) That it would not have been inconsistent with the Dignity of Great Britain, instead of declaring War against the Colonies, as she did by the joint Address of the Lords & Commons to the King in Jany 1775 to have animadverted upon the Denial of her Authority in all Cases respecting their internal Polity, *as an Error*; And to have specified, in what Particulars America should be restored to a *uti possedetis* [a situation in which each party retains what he possesses.], relative to their Charters, Patents, Assemblies, Elections and Modes of Government, on Condition of her contributing to the Necessities of the Empire—...

(7) That Great Britain is justly blamable, for issuing that Proposal, in Terms countenancing a haughty Attachment to the Principles of unlimited Submission, and accompanying it with Acts for Augmenting her Force at Boston, and restraining the Fishery and Commerce of the Colonies; and for neglecting to command a Cessation of Arms, until the Colonies, had an opportunity to deliberate with Composure of Mind, upon her Proposal; and more especially for her irritating Sally to Concord & Lexington on the 19t April, when no Governor but Mr. Gage was then

possessed of the Parliamentary Resolve, & he had concealed it even from the People committed to his Care.

(8) That as that Vote under those Circumstances, and the partial Direction of her Wrath against the New England Colonies, countenanced the Opinion of its being contrived to deceive and divide the Colonies, the Congress of 1775 had some Pretext for flying to Arms, to repel the further Incursions of the British Troops, till the Government gave them an opportunity, in a Condition less alarming, to explain their Declaration of Sept 1774, into a Consistancy with the antient, acknowledged Supremacy of Parliament, and to state the Limitations requisite for their Safety, in Answer to the February Resolve.

(9) That the total Rejection of the Parliamentary Proposal of 1775, and the neglect of the Congress to recal or explain the Declaration of 1774, tended to exasperate the British Nation; especially as the Successes of the Continental Operations in Canada, and the inefficacious Condition of the British Army at Boston, did leave America in a Condition for a more deliberate Consideration of the Controversy, than could be expected immediately after the bloody Scenes at Lexington Concord and Charles Town—And that both Countries ought then to have tendered conciliatory Propositions to each other, and sent Agents to explain and inculcate their mutual Requisitions.

(10) That the sanguinary Orders to the Navy of Great Britain in June 1775, to sack every Town in America, which should prepare for Defence; and her Neglect to stay Hostilities after the Petition of the Congress preferred in August by Mr. Richd. Penn, to his Majesty, submitting it to his Wisdom to point to some Plan, for the Restoration of Harmony, greatly inhances the Guilt, with which she stands chargeable, for commencing an unnecessary War to maintain an illiberal Dominion.

(11) That every partial View, whether of Great Britain to aggrandize herself, by extortionate Exactions from the Plantations, regardless of their Felicity; or of America to figure among the Nations, as an independent Power, on the Ruins of Great Britain, Ireland, and the other Colonies, is unrighteous in the Sight of God; and upon the Supposition of the Manifestation of his Justice in the Government of Nations, will expose to the Correction & Chastisement of his irresistible and unerring Hand.

(12) That both Countries continue still chargeable, with a guilty Neglect of the Obligations they were under to pursue the Measures requisite to a Reconciliation—Great Britain having begun the War for an unconditional Submission; . . .—Whilst America on the other Hand, instead of tendering a Plan of Peace, consistant with the Union, rejected the British Offers, without proposing any qualifying Clauses or Emendations tending to a friendly Negotiation upon the Subject of their Differences; and has to this Moment adhered to her Denial in 1774 of the whole Authority of Parliament, respecting the internal Polity of the Provinces— . . .

(13) That when Terms are proposed, consistant with the original Compact, neither Party can reject them and be innocent; . . .

(14) That the Approval being made by the Sword to the omniscient Judge of Heaven, who will decide between the contending Parties with unerring Rectitude, and the War daily wasting the Blood and Treasure of both Countries, and tending to a separation, ruinous to millions who have taken no Part in the Quarrel, it concerns those who have excited, or contributed to it, by the Calls and Ties of Justice, Humanity, Patriotism, Benevolence, Honor, Religion, and Interest, to cultivate Concord, and a Return to their antient Union, according to that Compact, which so eminently advanced the Prosperity of the Empire, antecedent to the year 1764.

Questions

1. According to Smith, what were the merits and demerits of each side in the crisis? Was his assessment fair and balanced? Explain.

2. In order to satisfy Smith's desire for reconciliation, what should each side have done after 1774? What "terms consistent with the original compact" did he construe to be binding on each side?

3. Does Smith's dilemma suggest anything about the fate of a moderate in revolutionary times? Why or why not?

6-5   Continental Congress to the Iroquois Confederacy (1775)

In the wake of the battle of Bunker Hill, with the prospect of war with Britain looming, the colonists grew increasingly worried that the British were pursuing an alliance with Native Americans, especially the formidable Six Nations of the Iroquois Confederacy. To counter this possibility, the Continental Congress sought, at the very least, a guarantee of neutrality from the Iroquois. It organized the Committee on Indian Affairs, which received instruction in Iroquois diplomacy from Samuel Kirkland, a longtime missionary among the Oneidas and Tuscaroras, and prepared an address to the Six Nations. In this speech, the Congress described how the "covenant chain" between England and the colonies was being threatened. This phrase was originally used to describe the cooperative relationship between the English colonies and the Iroquois from the late seventeenth century to the mid-1750s. It was invoked in this speech to convince the Iroquois that the Americans were the legitimate descendents of those who helped forge the covenant chain and that the Iroquois should uphold it by not taking up arms against them.

Source: Worthington Chauncey Ford, ed., *Journals of the Continental Congress 1774–1779*, vol. 2 (Washington, DC: U.S. Government Printing Office, 1905), 177–183.

A Speech to the Six Confederate Nations, Mohawks, Oneidas, Tuscaroras, Onondagas, Cayugas, Senecas, *from the Twelve United Colonies, convened in Council at* Philadelphia.

Brothers, Sachems, and Warriors! We, the Delegates from the twelve United Provinces . . . now sitting in General Congress at *Philadelphia*, send this talk to you our Brothers. . . .

. . . When our fathers crossed the great water and came over to this land, the King of *England* gave them a talk, assuring them that they and their children should be his children, and that if they would leave their native country and make settlements, and live here, and buy and sell, and trade with their brethren beyond the water, they should still keep hold of the same covenant chain and enjoy peace; and it was covenanted, that the fields, houses, goods and possessions which our fathers should acquire, should remain to them as their own, and be their children's forever, and at their sole disposal.

. . . *Brothers and Friends of the* Six Nations, *attend!* We upon this island have often spoke and entreated the King and his servants the Counsellors, that peace and harmony might still continue between us; that we cannot part with or lose our hold of the old covenant chain which united our fathers and theirs; that we want to brighten this chain, and keep the way open as our fathers did; that we want to live with them as brothers, labour, trade, travel abroad, eat and drink in peace. We have often asked them to love us, and live in such friendship with us as their fathers did with ours.

We told them again that we judged we were exceedingly injured, that they might as well kill us, as take away our property and the necessaries of life. We have asked why they treat us thus? What has become of our repeated addresses and supplications to them? Who hath shut the ears of the King to the cries of his children in *America*? No soft answer, no pleasant voice from beyond the water has yet sounded in our ears.

Brothers, thus stands the matter betwixt old *England* and *America.* You *Indians* know how things are proportioned in a family—between the father and the son—the child carries a little pack. *England* we regard as the father; this island may be compared to the son.

The father has a numerous family—both at home and upon this island. He appoints a great number of servants to assist him in the government of his family. In process of time, some of his servants grow proud and ill-natured; they were displeased to see the boy so alert and walk so nimbly with his pack. They tell the father, and advise him to enlarge the child's pack; they prevail; the pack is increased; the child takes it up again—as he thought it might be the father's pleasure—speaks but few words—those very small—for he was loth to offend the father. Those proud and wicked servants, finding they had prevailed, laughed to see the boy sweat and stagger under his increased load. By and by, they apply to the father to double the boy's pack, because they heard him complain; and without any reason, said they, he is a cross child; correct him if he complains any more. The boy entreats the father; addresses the great servants in a decent manner, that the pack might be lightened; he could not go any farther; humbly asks, if the old fathers, in any of their records, had described such a pack for the child; after all the tears and entreaties of the child, the pack is redoubled; the child stands a little while staggering under the weight, ready to fall every moment. However, he entreats the father once more, though so faint he could only lisp out his last humble supplication; waits a while; no voice returns. The child concludes the father could not hear; those proud servants had intercepted his supplications, or stopped the ears of the father. He therefore gives one struggle and throws off the pack, and says he cannot take it up again; such a weight would crush him down and kill him, and he can but die if he refuses.

Upon this, those servants are very wroth; and tell the father many false stories respecting the child; they bring a great cudgel to the father, asking him to take it in his hand and strike the child. . . .

Brothers, listen! Notwithstanding all our entreaties, we have but little hope the King will send us any more good Talks, by reason of his evil Counsellors; they have persuaded him to send an army of soldiers and many ships-of-war, to rob and destroy us. They have shut up many of our harbours, seized and taken into possession many of our vessels; the soldiers have struck the blow; killed some of our people; the blood now runs of the *American* children. They have also burned our houses and Towns, and taken much of our goods.

Brothers! We are now necessitated to rise, and forced to fight, or give up our Civil Constitution, run away, and leave our farms and houses behind us. This must not be. Since the King's wicked Counsellors will not open their ears, and consider our just complaints, and the cause of our weeping, and hath given the blow, we are determined to drive away the King's Soldiers, and to kill and destroy all those wicked men we find in arms against the peace of the twelve United Colonies upon this island. . . .

Brothers and Friends! We desire you will hear and receive what we have now told you, and that you will open a good ear and listen to what we are now going to say. This is a family quarrel between us and *Old England.* You *Indians* are not concerned in it. We don't wish you to take up the hatchet against the King's Troops. We desire you to remain at home, and not join on either side, but keep the hatchet buried deep. In the name and behalf of all our people, we ask and desire you to love peace and maintain it, and to love and sympathize with us in our troubles; that the path may be kept open with all our people and yours, to pass and repass, without molestation.

Brothers! We live upon the same ground with you. The same island is our common birthplace. We desire to sit down under the same tree of peace with you; let us water its roots and cherish its growth, till the large leaves and flourishing branches shall extend to the setting sun, and reach the skies.

Brothers, observe well! What is it we have asked of you? Nothing but peace, notwithstanding our present disturbed situation; and if application should be made to you by any of the King's unwise and wicked Ministers to join on their side, we only advise you to deliberate with great caution, and in your wisdom look forward to the consequences of a compliance. For, if the King's Troops take away our property, and destroy us, who are of the same blood with themselves, what can you, who are *Indians,* expect from them afterwards?

Therefore, we say, Brothers, take care; hold fast to your covenant chain. You now know our disposition towards you, the *Six Nations* of *Indians,* and your allies. Let this our good Talk remain at *Onondaga,* your central Council-House. We depend upon you to send and acquaint your allies to the northward, the seven Tribes on the River *St. Lawrence,* that you have this Talk of ours at the Great Council Fire of the *Six Nations.* And when they return, we invite your great men to come and converse farther with us at *Albany,* where we intend to rekindle the Council Fire, which your and our ancestors sat round in great friendship.

Brothers and Friends! We greet you all farewell.

Questions

1. How did Congress describe the imperial crisis to the Iroquois? What is the significance of the metaphors used?

2. According to Congress, who was to be blamed for the crisis? Why is this significant? Was there still hope in the summer of 1775 that the crisis might be resolved without going to war?

3. Why should the Iroquois remain neutral or side with the colonists? What, according to Congress, would have been the result if the colonists were defeated?

6-6   The American Crisis, Number I (December 1776)

Thomas Paine

Thomas Paine's literary contributions to the cause of American independence did not end with the publication of the many editions of *Common Sense.* In the bleak days of December 1776 Paine, who was then serving in the army, published an essay in the *Pennsylvania Journal* (December 19, 1776) that echoed the sense of travail that permeated rebel thought. This was the first essay in a series Paine called "The American Crisis"; he wrote a dozen more essays in the series by April 19, 1783. On December 9, 1783, he published what an editor of his papers called "A Supernumerary Crisis." In that work Paine discussed the question of American trade with the British. The essays that form what is commonly referred to as "The Crisis" reveal Paine's ability to put words together in powerful and memorable ways. That is especially true of the first installment of "The American Crisis," sections of which are reprinted here.

Source: Pennsylvania Journal, 19 December 1776.

THESE are the times that try men's souls. The summer soldier and the sunshine patriot will, in this crisis, shrink from the service of their country; but he that stands it *now*, deserves the love and thanks of man and woman. Tyranny, like hell, is not easily conquered; yet we have this consolation with us, that the harder the conflict, the more glorious the triumph. What we obtain too cheap, we esteem too lightly: it is dearness only that gives every thing its value. Heaven knows how to put a proper price upon its goods; and it would be strange indeed if so celestial an article as FREEDOM should not be highly rated. Britain, with an army to enforce her tyranny, has declared that she has a right (*not only to* TAX) but "to BIND us in ALL CASES WHATSOEVER," and if being *bound in that manner*, is not slavery, then is there not such a thing as slavery upon earth. Even the expression is impious; for so unlimited a power can belong only to God. . . .

I have as little superstition in me as any man living, but my secret opinion has ever been, and still is, that God Almighty will not give up a people to military destruction, or leave them unsupportedly to perish, who have so earnestly and so repeatedly sought to avoid the calamities of war, by every decent method which wisdom could invent. Neither have I so much of the infidel in me, as to suppose that He has relinquished the government of the world, and given us up to the care of devils; and as I do not, I cannot see on what grounds the king of Britain can look up to heaven for help against us: a common murderer, a highwayman, or a housebreaker, has as good a pretence as he.

'Tis surprising to see how rapidly a panic will sometimes run through a country. All nations and ages have been subject to them: Britain has trembled like an ague at the report of a French fleet of flat bottomed boats; and in the fourteenth [fifteenth] century the whole English army, after ravaging the kingdom of France, was driven back like men petrified with fear; and this brave exploit was performed by a few broken forces collected and headed by a woman, Joan of Arc. Would that heaven might inspire some Jersey maid to spirit up her countrymen, and save her fair fellow sufferers from ravage and ravishment! Yet panics, in some cases, have their uses; they produce as much good as hurt. Their duration is always short; the mind soon grows through them, and acquires a firmer habit than before. But their peculiar advantage is, that they are the touchstones of sincerity and hypocrisy, and bring things and men to light, which might otherwise have lain forever undiscovered. In fact, they have the same effect on secret traitors, which an imaginary apparition would have upon a private murderer. They sift out the hidden thoughts of man, and hold them up in public to the world. . . .

I shall conclude this paper with some miscellaneous remarks on the state of our affairs; and shall begin with asking the following question, Why is it that the enemy have left the New-England provinces, and made these middle ones the seat of war? The answer is easy: New-England is not infested with tories, and we are. I have been tender in raising the cry against these men, and used numberless arguments to show

them their danger, but it will not do to sacrifice a world either to their folly or their baseness. The period is now arrived, in which either they or we must change our sentiments, or one or both must fall. And what is a tory? Good God! what is he? I should not be afraid to go with a hundred whigs against a thousand tories, were they to attempt to get into arms. Every tory is a coward; for servile, slavish, self-interested fear is the foundation of toryism; and a man under such influence, though he may be cruel, never can be brave.

But, before the line of irrecoverable separation be drawn between us, let us reason the matter together: Your conduct is an invitation to the enemy, yet not one in a thousand of you has heart enough to join him. Howe is as much deceived by you as the American cause is injured by you. He expects you will all take up arms, and flock to his standard, with muskets on your shoulders. Your opinions are of no use to him, unless you support him personally, for 'tis soldiers, and not tories, that he wants.

I once felt all that kind of anger, which a man ought to feel, against the mean principles that are held by the tories: a noted one, who kept a tavern at Amboy, was standing at his door, with as pretty a child in his hand, about eight or nine years old, as I ever saw, and after speaking his mind as freely as he thought was prudent, finished with this unfatherly expression, "*Well! give me peace in my day.*" Not a man lives on the continent but fully believes that a separation must some time or other finally take place, and a generous parent should have said, "*If there must be trouble, let it be in my day, that my child may have peace;*" and this single reflection, well applied, is sufficient to awaken every man to duty. Not a place upon earth might be so happy as America. Her situation is remote from all the wrangling world, and she has nothing to do but to trade with them. A man can distinguish himself between temper and principle, and I am as confident, as I am that Good governs the world, that America will never be happy till she gets clear of foreign dominion. Wars, without ceasing, will break out till that period arrives, and the continent must in the end be conqueror; for though the flame of liberty may sometimes cease to shine, the coal can never expire.

Quitting this class of men, I turn with the warm ardor of a friend to those who have nobly stood, and are yet determined to stand the matter out: I call not upon a few, but upon all: not on *this* state or *that* state, but on *every* state: up and help us; lay your shoulders to the wheel; better have too much force than too little, when so great an object is at stake. Let it be told to the future world, that in the depth of winter, when nothing but hope and virtue could survive, that the city and the country, alarmed at one common danger, came forth to meet and to repulse it. Say not that thousands are gone, turn out your tens of thousands; throw not the burden of the day upon Providence, but "*show your faith by your works,*" that God may bless you. It matters not where you live, or what rank of life you hold, the evil or the blessing will reach you all. The far and the near, the home counties and the back, the rich and the poor, will suffer or rejoice alike. The heart that feels not now, is dead: the blood of his children will curse his cowardice, who shrinks back at a time when a little might have saved the whole, and made *them* happy. I love the man that can smile in trouble, that can gather strength from distress, and grow brave by reflection. 'Tis the business of little minds to shrink; but he whose heart is firm, and whose conscience approves his conduct, will pursue his principles unto death. . . .

I thank God, that I fear not. I see no real cause for fear. I know our situation well, and can see the way out of it. While our army was collected, Howe dared not risk a battle; and it is no credit to him that he decamped from the White Plains, and waited a mean opportunity to ravage the defenceless Jerseys; but it is great credit to us, that, with a handful of men, we sustained an orderly retreat for near an hundred miles, brought off our ammunition, all our field pieces, the greatest part of our stores, and had four rivers to pass. None can say that our retreat was precipitate, for we were near three weeks in performing it, that the country might have time to come in. Twice we marched back to meet the enemy, and remained out till dark. The sign of fear was not seen in our camp, and had not some of the cowardly and disaffected inhabitants spread false alarms through the country, the Jerseys had never been ravaged. Once more we are again collected and collecting; our new army at both ends of the continent is recruiting fast, and we shall be able to open the next campaign with sixty thousand men, well armed and clothed. This is our situation, and who will may know it. By perseverance and fortitude we have the prospect of a glorious issue; by cowardice and submission, the sad choice of a variety of evils—a ravaged country—a depopulated city—habitations without safety, and slavery without hope—our homes turned into barracks and bawdy-houses for Hessians, and a future race to provide for, whose fathers we shall doubt of. Look on this picture and weep over it! and if there yet remains one thoughtless wretch who believes it not, let him suffer it unlamented.

COMMON SENSE.

Questions

1. According to Paine, what problems did the Patriots face?

2. In what ways did Paine suggest that the war was an *internal* struggle as well as one against an external enemy?

3. In December 1776 the Patriot cause looked "objectively" hopeless. What hope did Paine hold out?

Questions for Further Thought

1. What does Gouverneur Morris's use of words such as "mob," "sheep," and "reptiles" suggest about class conflict in Revolutionary America?

2. In the early twentieth century, historian Carl Becker argued that there was an "internal" dimension to the Revolution, that is, it was not only a movement for independence ("home rule") but also a struggle between classes of individuals ("who should rule at home"). Was Becker correct?

3. Were the Revolutionaries hypocrites? How could they argue for "liberty" while owning slaves? How might they have responded to such critics as Samuel Johnson?

The Path to Victory, 1778–1783

Despite some heroic achievements, the rebel forces fared poorly in the military conflict during 1775–1776 (Document 6-11). Documents 6-7 and 6-8 demonstrate how the Revolutionary effort attracted a broad range of participants, including those from the less powerful segments of society, such as women. Despite the efforts of Lord Dunmore (Document 6-2), and the response of many slaves to British offers of freedom for support of the Loyalist cause, even African Americans fought to win independence for America. Winning independence proved to be a long and difficult task. As a group, Documents 6-7 through 6-10 illustrate the nature of the military conflict that ranged broadly across and even beyond the area of settlement. They reveal that the fighting could be especially vicious when Patriots opposed Loyalists or Native Americans. In a very real sense the American War for Independence was a civil war, and in the end the losers included not only the British but many colonists and Native Americans as well.

An end finally came, however, thanks in large part to the success of American diplomats, notably Benjamin Franklin, in expanding the scope of the conflict by concluding an alliance with the French in 1778. Beset on the high seas by the French and later by the Spanish, and defeated in their efforts to subdue the northern colonies at Saratoga in 1777, British forces devised a "southern strategy" of occupying the wealthy southern colonies while taking advantage of backcountry-Tidewater divisions to recruit Loyalist supporters (see Document 6-10). Southern Patriot militia, however, devised a "partisan war" that effectively neutralized the occupation forces of Lord Cornwallis. In 1781 a coordinated American-French operation finally trapped Cornwallis on the peninsula between the York and James Rivers in Virginia; with his surrender, independence was assured.

6-7 An Account of Life with the Army (1780–1783)

Sarah Osborn

In colonial America women had been almost totally excluded from a role in public politics. However, as Documents 5-8 and 5-13 demonstrate, women were drawn into some of the political conflicts that marked the movement toward independence. Also, as the textbook emphasizes (pp. 174–175), during the war women actively participated in the Patriots' efforts at a number of levels. Sarah Osborn was one of the women who traveled with the army. We know about her activities because in 1832 Congress passed what the historian John C. Dann describes as the first comprehensive pension act for veterans and the widows of veterans of the American Revolution. Under that and subsequent legislation, the applicant had to provide a statement to prove his or her right to a pension. Osborn prepared her account in 1837. It was given in the legal deposition form, which is why Osborn is referred to as "deponent." Osborn was eighty-one in 1837, but her powerful memory had not dimmed; her account, as far as it can be verified, is accurate. The section reprinted here describes her activities as the spouse of Aaron Osborn, a soldier she married in January 1780. Professor Dann, whose work with the pension records led him to edit the insightful collection of accounts entitled *The Revolution Remembered* (Chicago: University of Chicago Press, 1980), notes that Sarah Osborn's deposition may be the only extant autobiographical account of a woman who traveled with the army (*The Revolution Remembered*, 240).

Source: Sarah Osborn's application for a pension, Record Group 15 of the Records of the Veterans Administration, National Archives, in *The Revolution Remembered: Eyewitness Accounts of the War for Independence*, ed. John C. Dann (Chicago: University of Chicago Press, 1980), 242–250 passim. Used by permission of the University of Chicago Press.

After deponent had married said [Aaron] Osborn, he informed her that he was returned during the war, and that he desired deponent to go with him. Deponent declined until she was informed by Captain Gregg that her husband should be put on the commissary guard, and that she should have the means of conveyance either in a wagon or on horseback. That deponent then in the same winter season in sleighs accompanied her husband and the forces under command of Captain Gregg on the east side of the Hudson river to Fishkill, then crossed the river and went down to West Point. There remained till the river opened in the spring, when they returned to Albany. Captain Gregg's company was along, and she thinks Captain Parsons, Lieutenant Forman, and Colonel Van Schaick, but is not positive.

Deponent, accompanied by her said husband and the same forces, returned during the same season to West Point. Deponent recollects no other females in company but the wife of Lieutenant Forman and of Sergeant Lamberson. . . .

Deponent further says that she and her husband remained at West Point till the departure of the army for the South, a term of perhaps one year and a half, but she cannot be positive as to the length of time. While at West

Point, deponent lived at Lieutenant Foot's, who kept a boardinghouse. Deponent was employed in washing and sewing for the soldiers. Her said husband was employed about the camp. . . .

When the army were about to leave West Point and go south, they crossed over the river to Robinson's Farms and remained there for a length of time to induce the belief, as deponent understood, that they were going to take up quarters there, whereas they recrossed the river in the nighttime into the Jerseys and traveled all night in a direct course for Philadelphia. Deponent was part of the time on horseback and part of the time in a wagon. Deponent's said husband was still serving as one of the commissary's guard. . . . They continued their march to Philadelphia, deponent on horseback through the streets, and arrived at a place towards the Schuylkill where the British had burnt some houses, where they encamped for the afternoon and night. Being out of bread, deponent was employed in baking the afternoon and evening. Deponent recollects no females but Sergeant Lamberson's and Lieutenant Forman's wives and a colored woman by the name of Letta. The Quaker ladies who came round urged deponent to stay, but her said husband said, "No, he could not leave her behind." Accordingly, next day they continued their march from day to day till they arrived at Baltimore, where deponent and her said husband and the forces under command of General Clinton, Captain Gregg, and several other officers, all of whom she does not recollect, embarked on board a vessel and sailed down the Chesapeake. . . . They continued sail until they had got up the St. James River as far as the tide would carry them, about twelve miles from the mouth, and then landed, and the tide being spent, they had a fine time catching sea lobsters, which they ate.

They, however, marched immediately for a place called Williamsburg, as she thinks, deponent alternately on horseback and on foot. There arrived, they remained two days till the army all came in by land and then marched for Yorktown, or Little York as it was then called. The York troops were posted at the right, the Connecticut troops next, and the French to the left. In about one day or less than a day, they reached the place of encampment about one mile from Yorktown. Deponent was on foot and the other females above named and her said husband still on the commissary's guard. . . . Deponent took her stand just back of the American tents, say about a mile from the town, and busied herself washing, mending, and cooking for the soldiers, in which she was assisted by the other females; some men washed their own clothing. She heard the roar of the artillery for a number of days, and the last night the Americans threw up entrenchments, it was a misty, foggy night, rather wet but not rainy. Every soldier threw up for himself, as she understood, and she afterwards saw and went into the entrenchments. Deponent's said husband was there throwing up entrenchments, and deponent cooked and carried in beef, and bread, and coffee (in a gallon pot) to the soldiers in the entrenchment.

On one occasion when deponent was thus employed carrying in provisions, she met General Washington, who asked her if she "was not afraid of the cannonballs?"

She replied, "No, the bullets would not cheat the gallows," that "It would not do for the men to fight and starve too."

They dug entrenchments nearer and nearer to Yorktown every night or two till the last. While digging that, the enemy fired very heavy till about nine o'clock next morning, then stopped, and the drums from the enemy beat excessively. Deponent was a little way off in Colonel Van Schaick's or the officers' marquee and a number of officers were present, among whom was Captain Gregg, who, on account of infirmities, did not go out much to do duty.

The drums continued beating, and all at once the officers hurrahed and swung their hats, and deponent asked them, "What is the matter now?"

One of them replied, "Are not you soldier enough to know what it means?"

Deponent replied, "No."

They then replied, "The British have surrendered."

Deponent, having provisions ready, carried the same down to the entrenchments that morning, and four of the soldiers whom she was in the habit of cooking for ate their breakfasts.

Deponent stood on one side of the road and the American officers upon the other side when the British officers came out of the town and rode up to the American officers and delivered up [their swords, which the deponent] thinks were returned again, and the British officers rode right on before the army, who marched out beating and playing a melancholy tune, their drums covered with black handkerchiefs and their fifes with black ribbands tied around them, into an old field and there grounded their arms and then returned into town again to await their destiny. Deponent recollects seeing a great many American officers, some on horseback and some on foot, but cannot call them all by name. Washington, Lafayette, and Clinton were among the number. The British general at the head of the army was a large, portly man, full face, and the tears rolled down his cheeks as he passed along. She does not recollect his name, but it was not Cornwallis. She saw the latter afterwards and noticed his being a man of diminutive appearance and having cross eyes. . . .

After two or three days, deponent and her husband, Captain Gregg, and others who were sick or complaining embarked on board a vessel from Yorktown, not the same they came down in, and set sail up the Chesapeake Bay and continued to the Head of Elk, where they landed. The main body of the army remained behind but came on soon afterwards. Deponent and her husband proceeded with the commissary's teams from the Head of Elk, leaving Philadelphia to the right, and continued day after day till they arrived at Pompton Plains in New Jersey. Deponent does not recollect the county. They were joined by the main body of the army under General Clinton's command, and they set down for winter quarters. Deponent and her husband lived a part of the time in a tent made of logs but covered with cloth, and a part of the time at a Mr. Manuel's near Pompton Meeting-house. She busied herself during the winter in cooking and sewing as usual. Her said husband was on duty among the rest of the army and held the station of corporal from the time he left West Point.

In the opening of spring, they marched to West Point and remained there during the summer, her said husband still with her. In the fall they came up a little back of New-burgh to a place called New Windsor and put up huts on Ellis's lands and again sat down for winter quarters, her said husband still along and on duty. The York troops and Connecticut troops were there. In the following spring or autumn they were all discharged. Deponent and her said husband remained in New Windsor in a log house built by the army until the spring following. Some of the soldiers boarded at their house and worked round among the farmers, as did her said husband also.

Deponent and her said husband spent certainly more than three years in the service, for she recollects a part of one winter at West Point and the whole of another winter there, another winter at Pompton Plains, and another at New Windsor. And her husband was the whole time under the command of Captain Gregg as an enlisted soldier holding the station of corporal to the best of her knowledge.

In the winter before the army were disbanded at New Windsor, on the twentieth of February, deponent had a child by the name of Phebe Osborn, of whom the said Aaron Osborn was the father. A year and five months afterwards, on the ninth day of August at the same place, she had another child by the name of Aaron Osborn, Jr., of whom the said husband was the father. . . .

About three months after the birth of her last child, Aaron Osborn, Jr., she last saw her said husband, who then left her at New Windsor and never returned. He had been absent at intervals before this from deponent, and at one time deponent understood he was married again to a girl by the name of Polly Sloat above Newburgh about fifteen or sixteen miles. Deponent got a horse and rode up to inquire into the truth of the story. She arrived at the girl's father's and there found her said husband, and Polly Sloat, and her parents. Deponent was kindly treated by the inmates of the house but ascertained for a truth that her husband was married to said girl. After remaining overnight, deponent determined to return home and abandon her said husband forever, as she found he had conducted in such a way as to leave no hope of reclaiming him. About two weeks afterwards, her said husband came to see deponent in New Windsor and offered to take deponent and her children to the northward, but deponent declined going, under a firm belief that he would conduct no better, and her said husband the same night absconded with two others, crossed the river at Newburgh, and she never saw him afterwards. This was about a year and a half after his discharge. . . .

After deponent was thus left by Osborn, she removed from New Windsor to Blooming Grove, Orange County, New York, about fifty years ago, where she had been born and brought up, and, having married Mr. [John] Benjamin . . . she continued to reside there perhaps thirty-five years, when she and her husband Benjamin removed to Pleasant Mount, Wayne County, Pennsylvania, and there she has resided to this day. Her said husband, John Benjamin, died there ten years ago last April, from which time she has continued to be and is now a widow.

Questions

1. What motivated Sarah Osborn to serve in what was at least a quasi-military capacity?

2. Does it appear that the officers and men understood the value of Osborn's support of the war effort? Why or why not?

3. Does her account strike you as believable? Why or why not?

6-8   An African American Recounts His War Service (1775–1777)

Jacob Francis

The evidence suggests that for the reasons illustrated in Document 6-2, African Americans were more likely to join the British than join the rebels. However, African Americans fought on both sides in the Revolution. As in the case of Sarah Osborn, we know about the actions of the African American Jacob Francis because he applied for a federal pension. Francis was born to a slave woman in New Jersey in 1754 but apparently was treated as an indentured servant rather than a slave. That interpretation is supported by the fact that he gained his freedom in January 1775, when he turned twenty-one. At that time twenty-one was the standard age at which men who had been bound to service as youngsters achieved their freedom. Francis completed a number of tours of duty and fought in several engagements. The sections of his 1836 deposition reprinted here recount his service in the war in the North in 1776.

Source: Jacob Francis's application for a pension, Record Group 15 of the Records of the Veterans Administration, National Archives, in *The Revolution Remembered: Eyewitness Accounts of the War for Independence,* ed. John C. Dann (Chicago: University of Chicago Press, 1980), 391–396 passim. Used by permission of the University of Chicago Press.

[I arrived in Salem, Massachusetts, about November 1769.] I lived and served in Salem until my time was out, which was in January 1775. I lived in Salem and worked for different persons till the fall of 1775. In the spring of that year the war had commenced, and the battles of Bunker Hill and Lexington had taken place. About the last of October, I enlisted as a soldier in the United States service for one year. I was told they were enlisting men to serve one year from the first of January, 1776, but I should receive pay from the time I enlisted, and I enlisted and entered the service about the last of October and received two months' pay for my service up to 1 January 1776. I enlisted at Cambridge . . . in Col. Paul Dudley Sergeant's regiment. . . . At the time I was enlisted, the British army lay in Boston. After that, I remained with the regiment at Cambridge and in the neighborhood of Boston until the British were driven out of Boston. . . .

In 1776, after the British left Boston, the army, with our regiment and myself along with them, marched by way of Roxbury (that way we could go by land) over a causeway into Boston and lay over two or three days, then were ordered out to Bunker Hill. We marched out and encamped there and lay there some time. Then our regiment was ordered to an island at that time called Castle William. . . . Then we left the island and was ordered to New York from the island. . . . [At] a place called Hell Gate, on the north side of the East River, . . . we threw up breastworks, and the British threw up breastworks on Long Island on the opposite side of the East River and used to fire across. We lay there some time.

While we lay there, the Battle of Long Island took place. There was a number of men detailed from our regiment, so many from each company, to go over and join the American army, perhaps two hundred men. I was one. We crossed the river at Hell Gate and marched on to the island in the direction we was ordered, but did not get to join the army till the battle had commenced and our army was on the retreat. We had to cross a creek to get to our army, who had engaged the enemy on the other side, but before we got to that creek our army was repulsed and retreating, and many of them were driven into the creek and some drowned. The British came in sight, and the balls flew round us, and our officers, finding we could do no good, ordered us to retreat, which we did under the fire of the enemy. We retreated back to Hell Gate and recrossed to our fortifications. Soon after that, we had orders to leave that place and marched to Westchester by way of Kingsbridge. We lay there some time, and every night we had a guard stationed out two or three miles from where the reg-

iment lay at a place called Morrisania. I mounted guard there every time it came to my turn. There was an island near there. The tide made up round it. The British had a station on the island, and a British ship lay there. In an attack on the island one night, Colonel Jackson was wounded. After some time, we were ordered to march to the White Plains. We marched there and there joined General Washington's army.

We lay some time at the White Plains. While we lay there, the British landed and attacked some of our troops and had a brush there. Our regiment and I with them marched by General Washington's orders toward a hill where the engagement was, but the British got possession of the hill, and we retreated back to the camp. The British established a garrison on that hill. I stood sentinel that night in a thicket between the American camp and the hill, so near the British lines that I could hear the Hessians in the garrison, which was between one-quarter and one-half mile from me. The British lay there awhile and then left that place, and our regiments marched after them about three or four miles farther east. Then we received orders and marched to Peekskill on the North River. We halted a day and night a little distance from the river and there crossed at Peekskill to the west side of the river. From thence we marched on, and I do not recollect the names of places we passed through till we got to Morristown, New Jersey. We lay there one night, then marched down near to Baskingridge and lay there the next night. That night General Lee was taken in or about Baskingridge. I heard the guns firing. The next morning we continued our march across Jersey to the Delaware and crossed over to Easton. From thence we marched down the Pennsylvania side into Bucks County.

It was then cold weather, and we were billeted about in houses. Our company lay off from the river a few miles below Coryell's Ferry and above Howell's Ferry. We lay there a week or two; then we received orders to march and, Christmas night, crossed the river and marched down to Trenton early in the morning. . . . We marched down the street from the River Road into the town to the corner where it crosses the street running up towards the Scotch Road and turned up that street. General Washington was at the head of that street coming down towards us and some of the Hessians between us and them. We had the fight. . . . After about half an hour the firing ceased, and some officers, among whom I recollect was General Lord Stirling, rode up to Colonel Sergeant and conversed with him. Then we were ordered to follow them, and with these officers and Colonel Sergeant at our head, we marched down through the town toward Assanpink and up the Assanpink on the north side of it and to the east of the town, where we were formed in line and in view of the Hessians, who were paraded on the south side of the Assanpink and grounded their arms and left them there and marched down to the old ferry below the Assanpink, between Trenton and Lamberton.

Soon after that, a number of men from our regiment were detailed to go down and ferry the Hessians across to Pennsylvania. I went as one, and about noon it began to rain and rained very hard. We were engaged all the afternoon ferrying them across till it was quite dark, when we quit. I slept that night in an old millhouse above the ferry on Pennsylvania side. The next morning I joined my regiment where I had left them the day before up the Assanpink, east of Trenton. We lay there a day or two, and then the time of the year's men was out, and our regiment received part of their pay and were permitted to return home. I did not get a

discharge. At that time I had seven and a half months' pay due to me, and I believe others had the same. I received three months' pay, and all the rest of the regiment received the same, and we were ordered after a certain time to come to Peekskill on the North River, and then we should receive our pay and get our discharges. I was with the regiment and in service from the time of enlistment till that time about fourteen months and never left it until I had received the three months' pay and had permission to return to the place of my nativity in Amwell, about fifteen miles from Trenton. I immediately returned to Amwell and found my mother living, but in ill health. I remained with her, and when the time came to go to Peekskill for my pay and discharge, I gave up going and never received either my pay or a discharge in writing. That pay, four and one-half months at forty shillings a month (nine pounds proclamation money equal to twenty-four dollars), is yet due to me from the United States.

Questions

1. On the basis of his account, what do you believe motivated Francis to serve in the military?

2. Does his account strike you as believable? Why or why not?

3. Does Francis's account support or challenge the views of Peter Oliver (Document 5-9) about the ordinary people of America? Why or why not?

6-9   An Account of War on the Frontier (1777–1782)

John Struthers

As the textbook authors indicate (pp. 178–179), the long-running battle between British colonists and Native Americans for control of the land carried over into the War of Independence. John Struthers, who was born in Maryland in 1759 and moved to Pennsylvania in 1775, was one of the many frontier colonists who became involved in that ongoing conflict. In 1841 Struthers, as many others had, applied for a federal pension for his service (see Documents 6-7 and 6-8). However, as was the case with most of those who asked for pensions on the basis of service on the frontier, his request was denied. The sections of his application reprinted here reveal the nature of the conflict between Native Americans and colonists.

Source: John Struthers's application for a pension, Record Group 15 of the Records of the Veterans Administration, National Archives, in *The Revolution Remembered: Eyewitness Accounts of the War for Independence*, ed. John C. Dann (Chicago: University of Chicago Press, 1980), 253–258 passim. Used by permission of the University of Chicago Press.

The summer of 1777 was a season of great alarm, and the whole settlement from Fort Pitt to Kentucky was broken up. A number of families assembled at the house of my father in order to erect a fort, but, hearing that families had collected at Hoagland's and Beelor's, eight or ten miles nearer to the Ohio, for the same purpose, they only repaired the cabins as

well as they could to resist an attack and remained in them during the summer. The others went on and built forts.

It was early resolved to raise a small company of volunteers to act as spies and wood rangers. Capt. James Scott, a brave and experienced officer, offered his services and appointed a place of rendezvous, and in a few days had upwards of twenty, of whom I was one, enrolled and ready to march with as much provision as we could conveniently carry. We started about the first of May, as nearly as I can now state, and I state it accordingly to be on that day. The country traversed was from a few miles below Fort Pitt, down the Ohio, crossing Raccoon Creek, Traver's and Tomlinson's Runs, Cross Creek, King's and Heoman's creeks, near their junction with the Ohio, passing on our way down Reardon's and Holliday's stations, where we occasionally drew provisions. From Holliday's Cove, we traversed the country backward and forward, carefully watching the Indian warpaths until we arrived at some one of the forts or stations on the headwaters of some of the streams above mentioned, in the vicinity of which most of our company resided, where we remained a day or two to get washing and mending done and a recruit of provisions, and at every station would spend an hour or two in the exercise of the tomahawk and rifle, not only for our own improvement in the use of these weapons of warfare but also to alarm the savages if they should be lurking in the neighborhood.

In the latter part of the season, the alarm was still kept up and increased by the attack (as was reported at the time) of two or three hundred Indians on Wheeling Fort, and in this stage of alarm many others volunteered to protect the frontier, and so effectually was the country scoured from Holliday's Cove to Fort Pitt, that, though we had no triumphs in battle to record nor defeats to lament, yet not an individual was massacred by the savages in that region during this year.

In the spring of 1778 the Indians broke out earlier than usual and committed several murders on Ten Mile Creek, which was then considered an interior settlement and, although not within the range of my excursions the preceding year, was within ten or twelve miles of my father's dwelling. I believe it was in March, and the whole settlement, from Wheeling upwards, was broken up and retired into forts, of which there was now perhaps too many, as from the paucity of males in each they could spare none to act as spies or wood rangers and scarce enough to defend the forts if they should be attacked. On my return from an ineffectual scout in pursuit of the savages who had committed these barbarities, though we passed two men whom they had murdered and scalped and who were not yet cold, yet they escaped punishment. On my return from this scout, which lasted but three or four days, a request was sent me from Hoagland's Fort to turn out with as many volunteers as I could collect. I did so and, referring to my previous acquaintance with the woods and Indian warpaths, was (though among the youngest) elected to head about fifteen or sixteen active and brave men and continued during the greater part of the season, that is, from March to November with short intervals to obtain ammunition, clothing, etc., on the same route as in the preceding year but not quite so extensive. The result, however, was that no Indian depredations were committed in that settlement during the whole season. . . .

In March 1779 I entered a volunteer in Capt. David Vance's company of mounted men, in General McIntosh's campaign to Fort Laurens on Tuscarawas. . . . I returned home in April and spent the remainder of the Indian season on the same route and in the same manner as during the two preceding summers. And during this season, according to the best of my knowledge and belief, I served at least six months.

Early in the spring of 1780 intelligence was received, I do not remember how, that a large body of Indians were on their march to devastate the whole country from Wheeling to Fort Pitt. This news was either not believed or at least not heeded until a party of them, crossing below Wheeling, had penetrated nearly halfway from the Ohio to Catfish Camp, now the seat of justice for Washington County, Pennsylvania. They had taken a number of prisoners but, becoming alarmed, speedily retraced their steps to the Ohio and murdered all their male prisoners on the way. The main body of those who were expected to have ravaged Raccoon Settlement, it was supposed, never crossed the Ohio, but sent two of their warriors to reconnoiter, who, approaching Dillow's Fort late in the evening, spied two boys at play and tomahawked and scalped them within two hundred yards of the fort and escaped. And it was supposed that their report was rather unfavorable, and that they immediately commenced their retrograde march, as no other mischief was done by them this season. Colonel Broadhead commanded at Fort Pitt, and this was the summer of his campaigns to the Muncee towns up the Allegheny River and to Coshocton at the forks of Muskingum, at which two places he was supposed to have destroyed five hundred acres of corn. . . .

Early in the year 1781 the Indians made an incursion into the upper settlements of Buffalo Creek and, notwithstanding the vigilance and bravery of Col. David William son and his party, cruelly murdered several persons in his immediate neighborhood and took others prisoners. This caused a general alarm through all the settlements, and the people crowded into the forts, but still their great dependence for safety was on the volunteer spies and wood rangers; so I spent from April till November, at least five months, in scouting the frontier and watching the Indian crossing places and warpaths.

In the fall of this year too was the first expedition of Colonel Williamson to the Moravian Towns on the Tuscarawas, in which I (at the risk of my popularity as a soldier) declined taking a part. In the latter part of February 1782, the Indians invaded the settlement of Raccoon and murdered the family of a Mr. Wallace and took John Carpenter prisoner and took his two horses. He, however, soon made his escape and brought his horses with him.

In March, another expedition under Colonel Williamson started to the Moravian Towns and destroyed them with the inhabitants, amounting to nearly a hundred of all ages and sexes. In this, also, I refused to be concerned. These occurrences were considered by the settlers as harbingers of great distress and suffering during the summer. Yet such was the vigilance of the settlers and spies that no other mischief was done, save in one instance, and they paid dearly for their temerity. Six Indians had crawled up ten or twelve miles into the settlement and captured an old lone man of the name of William Jackson and plundered his cabin and retreated; but, so instant was the pursuit, they were overtaken at the river before they had time to embark, and a skirmish ensued wherein five Indians were killed and the other wounded in the abdomen. . . . This was the only skirmish that I recollect took place in that region during the Revolutionary War.

In the spring of this year I was elected to the command of a militia company, and my attention to the duties of that office caused necessarily a relaxation of my excursions on the frontiers; yet I spent at least two months in that service during the season, which, added to the services heretofore listed, will amount to two years and seven months. Although from the lapse of so many years and the absence of other data than memory it is impossible to specify correctly the weeks and months spent as a volunteer on the frontier during the Revolutionary War, yet I believe the statement several months less than the services really performed. I am the more confirmed in this opinion by this, that in frequent conversations with several young men, my neighbors, who had listed for three years and returned at the close of the war, it was admitted by all that I and my companions had actually served longer and endured more fatigue and hard-

ship than they had. These conversations it is probable would not now be thought of, but that they were sometimes carried on with a considerable degree of acrimony, the regulars affecting to consider the volunteers as an inferior class, and these retorting on those as a worthless set, not daring to set heads outside the gates but under the protection of volunteers and so on.

The regular soldier performs only during the summer and then retires to winter quarters, receiving pay and clothing and rations for the whole year. The volunteers, to whom I belonged, performed at least an equal amount of service and retired home during the winter, not receiving either pay or rations and not even clothing for any part of the time, with the trifling exception of a little flour obtained now and then at the posts, or stations, and furnishing their own ammunition. Justice therefore requires that these volunteers, on applying for pensions, should have their time calculated in the same rule as the regulars. The few regulars stationed along the Ohio, from Pitt to Wheeling, and I here speak of them only, the only reliance placed on them was to defend the forts should they be attacked. Indeed, it was admitted by everyone at the time that the only security of the people along the river and adjacent settlements was the vigilance of the volunteers in watching their crossing places and warpaths and ferreting them out of their lurking places near the stations, and that by their means, principally, was the settlement saved from savage vengeances.

Questions

1. On the basis of his account, what do you believe motivated Struthers to serve in the military?

2. Does his account strike you as believable? Why or why not?

3. Does Struthers's account support or challenge the views of Peter Oliver (Document 5-9) about the ordinary people of America? Why or why not?

4. To what extent does Struthers's account explain why the fighting between Americans on the frontier and Native Americans was so vicious?

6-10   Civil War in the Southern Backcountry (1781)

The Revolutionary War was by no means simply a war fought by "Americans" against foreign invaders. It also exposed and exacerbated serious divisions among the Americans themselves, adding the dimension of civil war to the conflict. Nowhere was this more true than in the backcountry of North Carolina; there, bitterness over the outcome of the Regulator crisis (see text pp. 129–131), and a diverse population including Scottish Highlanders, Scots-Irish, and German Moravians as well as English, made it difficult for the eastern-based Revolutionary leadership to mobilize full support. What resulted was a crazy quilt of shifting allegiances. Tory guerrilla leaders such as David Fanning committed numerous atrocities, answered in kind by Whigs. The following letters, from the Revolutionary general Herndon Ramsey to Governor Thomas Burke, from Major James H. Craig

(British commander at Wilmington) to Governor Abner Nash, and from Burke to Craig, illustrate the brutality to which the conflict had descended by 1781.

Source: Walter Clark, ed., *The State Records of North Carolina*, 26 vols. (Goldsboro, NC: Nash Brothers, 1886–1907), 22:550–551, 1023–1025, 1026–1029.

(a) Gen. Ramsey and Others to Gov. Burke

CAMP AT MCFALL'S MILL, RAFT SWAMP,
22ND OF JULY, 1781.

Sir:—On Tuesday last we were captured at Chatham Court House by a party under the Command of Col. David Fanning, which party we found consisted of persons who complained of the greatest cruelties, either to their persons or property. Some had been unlawfully Drafted, Others had been whipped and ill-treated, without tryal; Others had their houses burned, and all their property plundered, and Barbarous and cruel Murders had been committed in their Neighborhoods. The Officers they complain of are Maj. Neal, Capt. Robertson, of Bladen, Capt. Crump, Col. Wade and Phil Alston, the latter a day or two ago a few miles in our rear took a man on the road and put him to instant Death, which has much incensed the Highlanders in this part of the County. A Scotch Gentleman the same day was taken at one MacAfee's Mill and ill treated. He is said to be a peaceable and inoffensive man, in name we do not know. He lives in the Raft Swamp. Should be happy if he could be liberated. Notwithstanding the Cruel treatment these people have received, We have been treated with the greatest Civility and with the utmost respect and politeness by our Commanding Officer, Col. Fanning, to whom we are under the greatest Obligations, and we beg leave to inform your Excellency that unless an immediate stop is put to such inhuman practices we plainly discover the whole country will be deluged in Blood, and the innocent will suffer for the guilty. We well know your abhorrence of such inhuman conduct, and your steady intention to prevent it. All we mean is information. We expect to be delivered to Major Craig at Wilmington in two or three days, entirely destitute of Money or Cloathes. How long we shall remain so, God only Knows. All we have to ask is that the perpetrators of such horrid Deeds may be brought to tryall, that prisoners may be well treated in future, and we are

Your Excellency's most obedient Servts.,
GEN'L HERNDON RAMSEY,
JOSEPH HINE,
MATT. RAMSEY,
W. KINCHIN,
JOHN BIRDSONG,
JAMES WILLIAMS,
MATTHEW JONES,
THOS. SURLOCK,
JAMES HERNDON,
M. GREGORY.

P. S. Simon Terril is paroled to carry this Letter and return to Wilmington.

(b) Major Craig of British Troops to Governor Nash

WILMINGTON, 20TH JUNE, 1781.

SIR:

I cannot let pass this opportunity of addressing myself to you on a subject which I expect will meet with more attention than I suppose would be paid to it by the perpetrator of the actions I am forced to complain of—the inhuman treatment imposed on the King's friends on every occasion and by every party of militia now in arms, obliges me to adopt some serious resolution to put, if possible, an end to it—the deliberate and wanton murders daily committed on them call, I should imagine, as much for your attention as they do for vengeance on my part. It is now my business to assure you, sir, that the former alone can prevent the latter.

Had I listened only to the first emotions excited by the account of Mr. Caswell's conduct in *Murdering* five men at Kingstown who were carried to him from New River; Mr. Saml. Ashe and his comrades who were put in irons for the purpose would have become the immediate victims to his unwarrantable cruelty—fortunately for them I am a Soldier and have been taught to look on the deliberate & unnecessary shedding of blood to be repugnant to my principles as such, as the sparing the Enemies of my King in the field. I therefore determined to adopt every method I could think of to prevent the necessity which could alone justify to my own mind that extremity, to the world I am sure I should have been fully justified by the cause alone—several instances which have happened since both in that quarter and in Duplin county, have very nearly forced me to have recourse to the expedient I wish to avoid, even without previous representation, which I was at a loss how to make, as I knew not where to address you, and was determined never to have any communication with people capable of ordering such actions, & whose inhumanity gave me every reason to suppose, their answer would be the immediate occasion of the extremity I wished to avoid.

I now, Sir, call on you to use your efforts to put a stop to a proceeding which promises such additional misery to the people over whom you now preside. I fully discharge my duty in this address and shall think myself perfectly unanswerable for the consequences of its being disregarded. After allowing a reasonable time for the interposition of your authority I shall think myself called on by Justice, Duty, & I may add ultimately by every consideration of humanity, to give the people who from the most laudable principles of loyalty take arms in the King's favour, ample revenge & satisfaction for every instance of *murder* committed by any party of Militia on one of them, and for this purpose I shall not hesitate to deliver over to them those Prisoners who from character or situation are most likely to gratify them in those sentiments, and produce the effect I ardently wish for, of preventing a repition of those barbarities, however I persuade myself there will be no necessity for having recourse to these means as it will be with the utmost regret I shall aggravate the miseries to which all countries are liable when the seat of war. My wish ever is to soften them as much as is consistent with my duty & in this I know my own wishes to coincide with the intentions of my superiors.

I am, Sir,

Your most Obed. Servant,

J. H. CRAIG,
Major 82d Regmt., Commandg. at Wilmington.

(c) Governor Burke to Major Craig

STATE OF NORTH CAROLINA, JUNE 27TH, 1781.

SIR:

Your letter of the 20th instant to my predecessor in office, came to my hands and I am now to return you an Answer.

Being entirely uninformed of the executions you allude to I am unable to say whether they ought to be denominated Murders or not, but I will venture to affirm that if they were and wanton and unnecessary, or contrary to the Laws and Rights of War they were not tollerated by the Government of this State, nor shall such ever be approved by me.

In several parts of the country, the war has, unhappily kindled the most fierce and vindictive animosity between the People who adhere to the Government of Great Britain and those who resolved at all hazards to oppose what they deemed an unconstitutional exercise of power, very lamentable effects have always been apprehended from this disposition and as the best means for preventing them, a resolution was very early taken to remove out of the State those People together with their property who could not reconcile themselves to the Established Government and this resolution was in part executed but the Legislature was afterwards prevailed on by the Entreaties of those very people to dispense in a great measure with the further Execution. The Animosity still continues and on some Occasions when the people have been obliged to take arms has produced reciprocal violences and bloodshed which are entirely unauthorized by the Magistrates of the State, and as much reprobated by them as they can be by his Brittanic Majesty's Officers.

To this cause may probably be attributed the acts of which you complain and whether it has produced more violence on the one side than the other might probably prove a very unpleasant and unsatisfactory Enquiry, but it is certain that many people have been killed by those whom you are pleased to call the King's friends where nothing could be assigned as provocation or excuse.

Duty and Inclination conspire in determining me to use my utmost Efforts for checking and, if possible, entirely preventing those practices which, tho occasioned by the war, are no way necessary for, nor in my opinion conducive to its happy termination. To this restitution your letter could not contribute, for the evil was already perceived and threats have no influence on my Conduct.

With respect to the particular behaviour of General Caswell I shall only say that the Laws reach every officer of this State and so far as it may depend on me they shall be enforced on all for the prevention of offenses against the Law of nations as well as the municipal Law.

I cannot see the Justice of your present Treatment of Mr. Samuel Ashe and his comrades nor of the future measures which you threaten them with. I believe they do not live in the parts of the Country which are infected with the animosity above mentioned nor can I learn that they themselves or any of their Connections have even countenanced such pratices as you complain of and which are unauthorized and unapproved by this Government so far as they come within the description above mentioned, &c. Should you therefore continue your treatment of those citizens or listen to any Emotions which may dictate any measures against them on the ground of retaliation which you refer to, I shall find myself under the unhappy necessity of taking Similar measures against British Prisoners, tho all such measures are utterly repugnant to my disposition.

The delivering over of such Prisoners as from Character or Situation are most likely to gratify the Vengeance of those enraged People to whom you allude which you are pleased to say you will not hesitate to do so is conformable to no pratice that know of among *Civilized* Nations, and should you in any instance put this Threat in execution, the Effect will be very different from what you expect, for altho we should Abhor the following of the Example of our Indian Savage Neighbors in delivering over Prisoners to be tortured at the pleasure of a fierce and vengeful kindred, yet the example of a nation so polite and celebrated as Great Britain would meet with more respect, and we should probably imitate it with peculiar advantages should our humanity be obliged to give way to public utility.

I wish to be favored with your ultimate resolution on this subject because there are at present some Prisoners in my Power to whom I am much disposed to grant some Indulgences which are requested, but which must be delayed until I know the result of your determination.

I concur, Sir, in your wish to mitigate as much as possible the Miseries Incident to War, and am of opinion that clemency and humanity should in every Instance prevail most liberally except where incompatible with Indispensable public utility.

I perceive the letters to my Predecessor are not directed to him in his Official Character tho on an Official Subject, as I can hold no Correspondence with the Subjects of his Brittanic Majesty or other Enemies of the United States except in my Official Character none will be opened but such as those addressed to me as Governor. This, Sir, it will be necessary to observe should I be favored with any future address.

I have the honor to be,

Your Obd. Ser.

THOS. BURKE.

Questions

1. What was the substance of General Ramsey's request? What was the situation that he described, and what did he ask for?

2. Describe the war in the American backcountry. How was the character of the war different there than in the major colonial cities?

3. What was Governor Burke's response to Major Craig? How did the governor define his position, and what did he instruct Craig to do?

6-11   British Perceptions of the War of Independence (1776, 1778)

At the outset of the War of Independence, the Revolutionary forces appeared to be no match for the British. The ragtag Continental army, untrained and ill-equipped, seemed more deserving of ridicule than respect. The drawing "Yankie Doodles Intrenchments near Boston, 1776" reflected the prevailing attitude of most imperial officers and perhaps the bulk of the British populace at the time. By early 1778, however, much had changed. General John Burgoyne had been defeated at Saratoga in October 1777 by a combined

(A)   *"Yankie Doodles Intrenchments near Boston, 1776"*

(B)   *"A Picturesque View of the State of the Nation for February 1778"*

force of Continental army troops and militiamen from New England and New York (see text p. 173). The American victory sealed an alliance with France, which American diplomats in Paris had been seeking since 1776. "A Picturesque View of the State of the Nation for February 1778" was one of the most popular English depictions of the increasingly dismal situation of the empire. In this satirical print, the British lion sleeps while an Englishman wrings his hands and England's commerce, symbolized by the cow, is despoiled by figures representing America and various European rivals.

Sources: "Yankie Doodles Intrenchments near Boston, 1776," published as the Act Directs and "A Picturesque View of the State of the Nation for February 1778" by unknown artists. Licensed by the Trustees of the British Museum. Copyright © the British Museum.

Questions

1. In what specific ways does the first print disparage American troops and the American cause? What is the significance of these insults?

2. How does "A Picturesque View" depict the city of Philadelphia in 1778? What realities does this reflect?

3. Judging from these prints, how did the British public's perceptions of the war change from 1776 to 1778?

Questions for Further Thought

1. Documents 6-7, 6-8, and 6-9 are derived from federal pension records. How reliable is this source of information? Can you think of any reasons why these accounts might be biased? What other sources of information might provide additional and unique perspectives on the Revolutionary War?

2. We commonly think of the colonial War of Independence as a revolutionary war. Is it fair to characterize it as a civil war as well? Explain your answer.

3. The documents in this section illuminate different aspects of warfare in the late eighteenth century. What do we learn about the savagery of warfare? How does this compare with Governor Burke's (Document 6-10) understanding of "civilized warfare"?

4. Assess the different reasons for fighting given by Paine and by the authors of the other accounts in this section. Was the colonial motivation for war simple or complex? How do issues of race, gender, and geography figure in how one experienced the war?

Creating Republican Institutions, 1776–1787

The American Revolutionaries never tired of insisting that their cause was not limited merely to securing independence from Great Britain; they expected to inaugurate a "new order for the ages," *novus ordo seclorum*, by demonstrating that a republic, in which the people were sovereign and governed themselves without the benefit of king or lords, could be a stable and permanent form of government. The Virginia Declaration of Rights (Document 6-12) and Statute of Religious Freedom (Document 6-13) capture some of the optimism of these Revolutionary republicans as they announced their commitment to equality and the "natural rights of mankind." Of course, bold proclamations alone were not enough, as the women who participated in the "mobility" described by Abigail Adams (Document 6-14) discovered as men "stood amazed" by their actions. Similarly, the plight of the Delaware nation illustrates the limits of Revolutionary republicanism, and Pachgantschihilas's statement reminds us that the War of Independence involved more than the contest between the British and Americans (Document 6-15). Finally, proslavery petitioners argued that the Virginia Declaration of Rights notwithstanding, slavery and the principles of the Revolution were not necessarily incompatible (Document 6-16).

6-12   The Virginia Declaration of Rights (1776)

The people of Great Britain and its colonies could look back to the Magna Carta of 1215 as an example of a written guarantee of basic political rights. Moreover, England adopted a Bill of Rights in 1689, and many of the colonies passed laws that amounted to bills of rights. Thus, it was logical that a number of the new Patriot-led governments would formulate statements of what they considered basic rights. The fifth Virginia revolutionary convention was the first to act. Its Declaration of Rights, which was written principally by George Mason and was issued on June 12, 1776, offered a bold vision of how Virginia's—and America's—political system should be built and what that system should do. The democratically inclined men among those who drafted new state constitutions often copied sections of this declaration verbatim.

Source: Francis N. Thorpe, ed., *The Federal and State Constitutions . . . of the United States* (Washington, DC: U.S. Government Printing Office, 1909), 7:3812–3814.

A declaration of rights made by the representatives of the good people of Virginia, assembled in full and free convention; which rights do pertain to them and their posterity, as the basis and foundation of government.

SECTION 1. That all men are by nature equally free and independent, and have certain inherent rights, of which, when they enter into a state of society, they cannot, by any compact, deprive or divest their posterity; namely, the enjoyment of life and liberty, with the means of acquiring and possessing property, and pursuing and obtaining happiness and safety.

SEC. 2. That all power is vested in, and consequently derived from, the people; that magistrates are their trustees and servants, and at all times amenable to them.

SEC. 3. That government is, or ought to be, instituted for the common benefit, protection, and security of the people, nation, or community; of all the various modes and forms of government, that is best which is capable of producing the greatest degree of happiness and safety, and is most effectually secured against the danger of maladministration; and that, when any government shall be found inadequate or contrary to these purposes, a majority of the community hath an indubitable, inalienable, and indefeasible right to reform, alter, or abolish it, in such manner as shall be judged most conducive to the public weal.

SEC. 4. That no man, or set of men, are entitled to exclusive or separate emoluments or privileges from the community, but in consideration of public services; which, not being descendible, neither ought the offices of magistrate, legislator, or judge to be hereditary.

SEC. 5. That the legislative and executive powers of the State should be separate and distinct from the judiciary; and that the members of the two first may be restrained from oppression, by feeling and participating the burdens of the people, they should, at fixed periods, be reduced to a private station, return into that body from which they were originally taken, and the vacancies be supplied by frequent, certain, and regular elections, in which all, or any part of the former members, to be again eligible, or ineligible, as the laws shall direct.

SEC. 6. That elections of members to serve as representatives of the people, in assembly, ought to be free; and that all men, having sufficient evidence of permanent common interest with, and attachment to, the community, have the right of suffrage, and cannot be taxed or deprived of their property for public uses, without their own consent, or that of their representatives so elected, nor bound by any law to which they have not, in like manner, assembled, for the public good.

SEC. 7. That all power of suspending laws, or the execution of laws, by any authority, without consent of the representatives of the people, is injurious to their rights, and ought not to be exercised.

SEC. 8. That in all capital or criminal prosecutions a man hath a right to demand the cause and nature of his accusation, to be confronted with the accusers and witnesses, to call for evidence in his favor, and to a speedy trial by an impartial jury of twelve men of his vicinage, without whose unanimous consent he cannot be found guilty; nor can he be compelled to give evidence against himself; that no man be deprived of his liberty, except by the law of the land or the judgment of his peers.

SEC. 9. That excessive bail ought not to be required, nor excessive fines imposed, nor cruel and unusual punishments inflicted.

SEC. 10. That general warrants, whereby an officer or messenger may be commanded to search suspected places without evidence of a fact committed, or to seize any person or persons not named, or whose offence is not particularly described and supported by evidence, are grievous and oppressive, and ought not to be granted.

SEC. 11. That in controversies respecting property, and in suits between man and man, the ancient trial by jury is preferable to any other, and ought to be held sacred.

SEC. 12. That the freedom of the press is one of the great bulwarks of liberty, and can never be restrained but by despotic governments.

SEC. 13. That a well-regulated militia, composed of the body of the people, trained to arms, is the proper, natural, and safe defence of a free State; that standing armies, in time of peace, should be avoided, as dangerous to liberty; and that in all cases the military should be under strict subordination to, and governed by, the civil power.

SEC. 14. That the people have a right to uniform government; and, therefore, that no government separate from, or independent of the government of Virginia, ought to be erected or established within the limits thereof.

SEC. 15. That no free government, or the blessings of liberty, can be preserved to any people, but by a firm adherence to justice, moderation, temperance, frugality, and virtue, and by frequent recurrence to fundamental principles.

SEC. 16. That religion, or the duty which we owe to our Creator, and the manner of discharging it, can be directed only by reason and conviction, not by force or violence; and therefore all men are equally entitled to the free exercise of religion, according to the dictates of conscience; and that it is the mutual duty of all to practice Christian forbearance, love, and charity towards each other.

Questions

1. According to the Virginia Declaration of Rights, where does legitimate power come from?

2. According to this declaration, what responsibilities does government have?

3. Compare the Virginia Declaration of Rights with the American Declaration of Independence (see text p. 165). To what extent did Thomas Jefferson draw upon the Virginia Declaration as he framed the American Declaration?

6-13   Virginia Statute of Religious Freedom (1786)

As the Patriots waged war against Britain to attain political freedom as a nation, they had, as many of the documents in this set illustrate, to deal with the fact that some Patriots wanted greater freedom at home. This quest for greater freedom could be seen clearly where religion was concerned. One of the landmarks on the road to true religious freedom in the republic was the Virginia statute of religious liberty, which is reprinted in full here. Thomas Jefferson, who authored the law, considered its enactment one of the three principal achievements of his life.

Source: William W. Hening, ed., *The Statutes at Large of Virginia*, 12:84–86.

I. WHEREAS Almighty God hath created the mind free; that all attempts to influence it by temporal punishments or burthens, or by civil incapacitations, tend only to beget habits of hypocrisy and meanness, and are a departure from the plan of the Holy author of our religion, who being Lord both of body and mind, yet chose not to propagate it by coercions on either, as was in his Almighty power to do; that the impious presumption of legislators and rulers, civil as well as ecclesiastical, who being themselves but fallible and uninspired men, have assumed dominion over the faith of others, setting up their own opinions and modes of thinking as the only true and infallible, and as such endeavouring to impose them on others, hath established and maintained false religions over the greatest part of the world, and through all time; that to compel a man to furnish contributions of money for the propagation of opinions which he disbelieves, is sinful and tyrannical; that even the forcing him to support this or that teacher of his own religious persuasion, is depriving him of the comfortable liberty of giving his contributions to the particular pastor, whose morals he would make his pattern, and whose powers he feels most persuasive to righteousness, and is withdrawing from the ministry those temporary rewards, which proceeding from an approbation of their personal conduct, are all additional incitement to earnest and unremitting labours for the instruction of mankind; that our civil rights have no dependence on our religious opinions, any more than our opinions in physics or geometry; that therefore the proscribing any citizen as unworthy the public confidence by laying upon him an incapacity of being called to offices of trust and emolument, unless he profess or renounce this or that religious

opinion, is depriving him injuriously of those privileges and advantages to which in common with his fellow-citizens he has a natural right; that it tends only to corrupt the principles of that religion it is meant to encourage, by bribing with a monopoly of worldly honours and emoluments, those who will externally profess and conform to it; that though indeed these are criminal who do not withstand such temptation, yet neither are those innocent who lay the bait in their way; that to suffer the civil magistrate to intrude his powers into the field of opinion, and to restrain the profession or propagation of principles on supposition of their ill tendency, is a dangerous fallacy, which at once destroys all religious liberty, because he being of course judge of that tendency will make his opinions the rule of judgment, and approve or condemn the sentiments of others only as they shall square with or differ from his own; that it is time enough for the rightful purposes of civil government, for its officers to interfere when principles break out into overt acts against peace and good order; and finally, that truth is great and will prevail if left to herself, that she is the proper and sufficient antagonist to error, and has nothing to fear from the conflict, unless by human interposition disarmed of her natural weapons, free argument and debate, errors ceasing to be dangerous when it is permitted freely to contradict them:

II. *Be it enacted by the General Assembly*, That no man shall be compelled to frequent or support any religious worship, place, or ministry whatsoever, nor shall be enforced, restrained, molested, or burthened in his body or goods, nor shall otherwise suffer on account of his religious opinions or belief; but that all men shall be free to profess, and by argument to maintain, their opinion in matters of religion, and that the same shall in no wise diminish, enlarge, or affect their civil capacities.

III. And though we well know that this assembly elected by the people for the ordinary purposes of legislation only, have no power to restrain the acts of succeeding assemblies, constituted with powers equal to our own, and that therefore to declare this act to be irrevocable would be of no effect in law; yet we are free to declare, and do declare, that the rights hereby asserted are of the natural rights of mankind, and that if any act shall be hereafter passed to repeal the present, or to narrow its operation, such act will be an infringement on natural right.

Questions

1. Does the wording of this statute truly guarantee absolute religious freedom? Why or why not?

2. Does this statute echo the Declaration of Independence in any important ways? If so, how?

3. Why did Thomas Jefferson, as well as many other Americans at the time, believe that an "established church" undermined civil society and obstructed good government? Do you agree with Jefferson's argument?

6-14   Boston Women Support Price Control (1777)

Abigail Adams

Financing the Patriots' war effort produced a range of problems, including disagreements over how to control prices and thus prevent greedy self-interest from overwhelming public virtue (see text pp. 174–176). Given the active role women had played in earlier economic boycotts (Documents 5-8 and 5-13) and were taking in the war effort (Document 6-7 and text p. 174), it seems logical that women would have participated in any program to regulate prices. Such an effort occurred in Massachusetts in 1777. As the following letter of July 31, 1777, from Abigail Adams to her husband, John, shows, what some Boston women did to achieve price regulation proved most intriguing.

Source: Charles F. Adams, ed., *Letters of Mrs. Adams, the Wife of John Adams,* 4th ed. (Boston, 1848), 84–85.

31 July, 1777

I have nothing new to entertain you with, unless it is an account of a new set of mobility, which has lately taken the lead in Boston. You must know that there is a great scarcity of sugar and coffee, articles which the female part of the state is very loth to give up, especially whilst they consider the scarcity occasioned by the merchants having secreted a large quantity. There had been much rout and noise in the town for several weeks. Some stores had been opened by a number of people, and the coffee and sugar carried into the market, and dealt out by pounds. It was rumored that an eminent, wealthy, stingy merchant (who is a bachelor) had a hogshead of coffee in his store, which he refused to sell to the committee under six shillings per pound. A number of females, some say a hundred, some say more, assembled with a cart and trucks, marched down to the warehouse, and demanded the keys, which he refused to deliver. Upon which, one of them seized him by his neck, and tossed him into the cart. Upon his finding no quarter, he delivered the keys, when they tipped up the cart and discharged him; then opened the warehouse, hoisted out the coffee themselves, put it into the truck, and drove off.

It was reported, that he had personal chastisement among them; but this, I believe was not true. A large concourse of men stood amazed, silent spectators of the whole transaction.

Questions

1. What exactly did these women do? Did they do it on their own?

2. Would Gouverneur Morris (Document 6-1) have been surprised by what happened in Boston? Why or why not?

3. Compare the actions these Boston women took with the actions described in Documents 5-8, 5-13, and 6-7. Does it appear that as the Patriot movement progressed into war, women acted more independently? Why or why not?

6-15   Pachgantschihilas Warns About the Long Knives (1781)

John Heckewelder

John Heckewelder, a Moravian, was born in England in 1743 and moved with his parents to Pennsylvania when he was eleven. As an adult he became a missionary among the Native Americans. In 1818, a year after his death, his *An Account of the History, Manners, and Customs of the Indian Nations* was published. In it he recounted and quoted the close of a 1781 speech delivered by Pachgantschihilas, a noted war chief of the Delaware. Pachgantschihilas was addressing a group of Native Americans living in western Pennsylvania who had embraced Christianity and were called Moravian Indians.

When Pachgantschihilas spoke of the *long knives,* he used the term to refer to white people because some white soldiers used swords—literally, long knives. Heckewelder's account of Pachgantschihilas's thoughts and of subsequent events is reprinted here and should be compared with the ideals for western development described in the text.

Source: Memoirs of the Historical Society of Pennsylvania (1876), 12:80–81.

I have given here only a brief specimen of the charges which they exhibit against the white people. There are men among them, who have by heart the whole history of what took place between the whites and the Indians, since the former first came into their country; and relate the whole with ease and with an eloquence not to be imitated. On the tablets of their memories they preserve this record for posterity. I, at one time, in April, 1781, was astonished when I heard one of their orators, a great chief of the Delaware nation, go over this ground, recapitulating the most extraordinary events which had before happened, and concluding in these words: "I admit that there are good white men, but they bear no proportion to the bad; the bad must be the strongest, for they rule. They do what they please. They enslave those who are not of their colour, although created by the same Great Spirit who created us. They would make slaves of us if they could, but as they cannot do it, they kill us! There is no faith to be placed in their words. They are not like the Indians, who are only enemies, while at war, and are friends in peace. They will say to an Indian, 'my friend! my brother!' They will take him by the hand, and at the same moment destroy him. And so you (addressing himself to the Christian Indians) will also be treated by them before long. Remember! that this day I have warned you to beware of such friends as these. I know the *long knives;* they are not to be trusted."

Eleven months after this speech was delivered by this prophetic chief, ninety-six of the same Christian Indians, about sixty of them women and children, were murdered at the place where these very words had been spoken, by the same men he had alluded to, and in the same manner that he had described.

Questions

1. Does Heckewelder seem interested in ensuring that the Native Americans receive justice? Why or why not?

2. Would Pachgantschihilas say that the Americans believe that the ideals expressed in the Virginia Declaration of Rights (Document 6-12) apply to Native Americans? Why or why not?

3. Would Pachgantschihilas say that the Americans believe that the ideals expressed in the Declaration of Independence about the people's equality and "unalienable rights" (see text p. 165) apply to Native Americans? Why or why not?

4. Given Pachgantschihilas's analysis, in what ways, if at all, were Native Americans involved in what Carl Becker has called the conflict over "who should rule at home"?

6-16   Proslavery Petitions in Virginia (1785)

The contradiction apparent in the Revolutionary cause—fighting for liberty while condoning slavery—was too obvious to ignore. By the mid-1780s Massachusetts, Pennsylvania, Connecticut, and Rhode Island had either outlawed slavery or adopted measures for gradual emancipation. Even New York and New Jersey, which had higher concentrations of slaves than any of their northern neighbors, had begun to consider seriously the prospect of abolition. In the South, however, antislavery sentiment was short-lived and ineffectual. Slaves constituted between 30 and 60 percent of the southern population, were the most valuable portion of slave owners' estates, and accounted for much of the prosperity in the plantation economy. But proslavery southerners went beyond a "necessary evil" defense of the institution, especially in Virginia. In 1785 when Methodist reformers began to circulate a general emancipation petition, proslavery Virginians were quick to respond. More than twelve hundred of them signed petitions, like the one included here, reminding their legislators that the principles for which they had risked their lives were completely compatible with slavery. In the end, the legislators unanimously rejected the general emancipation petition.

Source: Library of Virginia.

To the Honorable the General Assembly of Viriginia, The Remonstrance and Petition of the free Inhabitants of the County of Lunenberg,

Gentlemen,

When the british Parliament usurp'd a right to Dispose of our Property, it was not the Matter, but the Manner adopted for that purpose, that alarm'd us; as it tended to establish a principle which might one day prove fatal to our rights of Property: In order therefore to fix a Tenure in our property on a Basis of Security not to be shaken in future, we dissolved our union with our parent Country, and by a self-erected power bravely and wisely establish'd a Constitution and form of Government, grounded on a full and clear Declaration of such rights as naturally pertain to Men born free and determined to be respectfully and absolutely so as human Institutions can make them: This we effected by our representatives, to whom we delegated our power, in General Convention; Whose Wisdom, Integrity, Fortitude, and patriotic Zeal will ever reflect Glory on them and honor on their Constituents. In support of this happy Establishment, with its attendant Blessings we have chearfully sacrificed our Ease, Lives and fortunes, and waded thro' Deluges of civil Blood to that unequivocal Liberty, which alone characterises the free independent Citizen, and distinguishes him from the subjugated Vassal of despotic Rule.

. . . We have seald with our Blood, a Title to the full, free, and absolute Enjoyment of every species of our Property, whensoever, or howsoever legally acquired; a Purchase of too great Value to be sacrificed to the Caprice, or Interest of any rank or Description of Men, however dignified, or distinguished, either by the confidential Suffrages of their fellow-Citizens, or otherwise.

To this free, and we trust, inoffensive, as well as necessary Communication of our Sentiments, on the most important Subject that ever arrested the attention of a free People, we are enforced by a daring attempt now on foot in several Counties in this State by Petitions warmly advocated by some Men of considerable weight to wreste from us, by an Act of the Legislature, the most valuable and indispensable Article of our Property, our Slaves, by a general Emancipation of them: An Attempt that involves in it not only a flagrant Contempt of the constituent Powers of the Commonwealth, in which its Majesty resides and which we are sorry to have occasion to observe seem to be forgotten by too many, and a daring attack on that sacred Constitution thereby establishd; but also, Want, Poverty, Distress and ruin to the free Citizen; the Horrors of all the rapes, Robberies, Murders, and Outrages, which an innumerable Host of unprincipled, unpropertied, vindictive, and remorseless Banditti are capable of perpetrating; Neglect, famine and Death to the abandoned black Infant, and superannuated Parent; inevitable Bankruptcy to the revenue; Desparation and revolt to the disappointed, oppressed Citizen; and sure and final ruin to this once happy, free, and flourishing Country: And all this [*illeg.*] to answer no one civil, religious, or national Purpose, whatever. . . . It therefore cannot be admitted that any Man has a right, to petition or otherwise press the Legislature to divest us of our known rights of Property, which are so clearly defined; so fully acknowledged; and so solemnly ratified and confirmd, by our Bill of rights, as not to admit of an equivocal Construction, nor of the smallest Alteration or Diminution, by any Power, but that which originally authorised its Establishment. To an unequivocal Construction therefore of this Bill of rights we now appeal, and claim the utmost Benefits of it; not doubting the hearty

Concurrence of our faithful representatives in what ever may tend to promote our mutual Interests; preserve our rights inviolate; secure to us all the Blessings of a free, undisturbd, independent Government; and So, an indiscriminate Diffusion of Peace, Wealth, and happiness among the free Citizens of this Commonwealth. And as the lasting Welfare of our Country, and the happiness of its Citizens depend [*illeg.*] invariable Adherence to our Constitution, we most solemnly adjure, and humbly pray, that you, Gentlemen, to whom we have committed the Guardianship of our rights of Property, will in no Instance, permit them to be calld in Question; Particularly, that you will discountenance, and utterly reject every Motion and Proposal for emancipating our Slaves; That you will immediately, and totally repeal the Act for permitting Owners of Slaves to emancipate them; That you will provide effectually for the good Government, and due restraint of those already set free, whose disorderly Conduct, and thefts and outrages, are so generally the just Subject of Complaint; but particularly whose Insolences, and Violences so freequently of late committed to and on our respectable Maids and Matrons, which are a Disgrace to Government.

[Lunenberg County, November 29, 1785, with 161 signatures.]

Questions

1. What arguments did the petitioners use to defend slavery? Were these arguments identical to those used by the Revolutionaries during the imperial crisis?

2. Did the Revolutionary generation differentiate between property rights and human rights? Does the Lockean idea of contractual government make such a distinction?

3. What do the arguments of the Virginia petitioners reveal about the limits of Revolutionary republicanism? How might these petitioners have interpreted the "all men are created equal" doctrine?

Questions for Further Thought

1. Was the American Revolution truly revolutionary? What are we to make of the plight of moderates and Loyalists in Revolutionary America?

2. How were Native Americans affected by the American Revolution? Why did most Native Americans fight on the side of the British during the Revolutionary War? The Treaty of Paris did not end the war for many Native American groups. Why not?

3. How important was the Revolution in the democratization of America? Would improvements in the conditions of women and slaves have been possible without it? Explain.

The Constitution of 1787

Despite its success in dealing with the issues arising from western lands, the weak confederate government was hamstrung by the states' continuing insistence on retaining their own sovereignty. Moreover, the turmoil within the states, illustrated not only by Shays's Rebellion but also by attempts to use state governments in the interests of debtors against creditors, increasingly convinced many analysts that the states themselves were unable to preserve either domestic order or the rights of property (Document 6-18). A number of Revolutionary political leaders were convinced that something needed to be done, both to bolster the power of the Confederation and to rein in the more radical elements in the states. At Virginia's invitation, nine states agreed to meet in Annapolis, Maryland, in September 1786. However, only five states were formally represented when the convention began, and rather than continuing with their business the delegates issued a call for a new convention to meet in Philadelphia in May of 1787. James Madison, who was disappointed by the failure of the Annapolis convention, proceeded to consider what needed to be done to save the federal union (Document 6-17).

The 1787 meeting to discuss revisions to the Articles of Confederation instead produced an entirely new constitution. The proposed new national charter was immediately controversial. Many people feared that imposing a powerful federal government on top of the existing state governments would result in a new tyranny like that of the hated British. Arguing that republics needed to be small in order to stay in touch with the people, "Antifederalists" such as George Clinton of New York vehemently opposed ratification (Document 6-19). In response, James Madison, Alexander Hamilton, and John Jay wrote a series of essays known as *The Federalist*. In *The Federalist* No. 10, Madison argued that the very size of the new federal government would protect the people from the tyranny of special interests (Document 6-20). In *The Federalist* No. 54 (Document 6-21), Madison tackled another potentially explosive issue: slavery and the three-fifths clause of the Constitution. Clearly, sectional interests were becoming more pronounced despite the compromises reached at the federal convention in 1787.

6-17 Vices of the Political System of the United States (1787)

James Madison

James Madison was determined to be the best prepared and perhaps most knowledgeable delegate to the Constitutional Convention. In the winter and spring of 1787, he kept himself busy analyzing the histories of past republics and diagnosing the defects of the current American republic. Having served in the Virginia legislature and the Confederation Congress in the 1780s, he had witnessed firsthand the interrelated failings of each. Under the Articles of Confederation, Congress had been ineffectual in responding to the discriminatory trade policies of Britain and the closing of the Mississippi to American traffic by Spain. It also lacked the means to force the states to comply with its revenue requisitions, even in the face of armed insurrections, as Shays's Rebellion had demonstrated. And the states, each of which retained its sovereignty under Article II, for their part proved unreliable because most state legislators were irresponsible. Rather than committing themselves to disinterested service for the good of the whole, as republican rule required, they responded first and foremost to the advancement of selfish interests. Madison's "Vices of the Political System" was both a summary of his findings and a prescription for the ills he had diagnosed.

Source: Excerpts from Chapter 9, "Diagnosis of the American Confederacy: A Critical Case," in *The Mind of the Founder: Sources of the Political Thought of James Madison*, ed. Marvin Meyers, 83–91. Copyright © 1981 by Trustees of Brandeis University. Reprinted with the permission of University Press of New England.

1. FAILURE OF THE STATES TO COMPLY WITH THE CONSTITUTIONAL REQUISITIONS. This evil has been so fully experienced both during the war and since the peace, results so naturally from the number and independent authority of the States and has been so uniformly exemplified in every similar Confederacy, that it may be considered as not less radically and permanently inherent in than it is fatal to the object of the present system.

2. ENCROACHMENTS BY THE STATES ON THE FEDERAL AUTHORITY. Examples of this are numerous and repetitions may be foreseen in almost every case where any favorite object of a State shall present a temptation. Among these examples are the wars and treaties of Georgia with the Indians. The unlicensed compacts between Virginia and Maryland, and between Pennsylvania & New Jersey—the troops raised and to be kept up by Massachusetts.

3. VIOLATIONS OF THE LAW OF NATIONS AND THE TREATIES. From the number of legislatures, the sphere of life from which most of their members are taken, and the circumstances under which their legislative business is carried on, irregularities of this kind must frequently happen. Accordingly not a year has passed without instances of them in some one or other of the States. The Treaty of Peace—the treaty with France—the treaty with Holland have each been violated. . . . The causes of these irregularities must necessarily produce frequent violations of the law of nations in other respects. . . .

4. TRESPASSES OF THE STATES ON THE RIGHTS OF EACH OTHER. These are alarming symptoms, and may be daily

apprehended as we are admonished by daily experience. See the law of Virginia restricting foreign vessels to certain ports—of Maryland in favor of vessels belonging to her *own citizens*—of New York in favor of the same—...

The practice of many States in restricting the commercial intercourse with other States, and putting their productions and manufacturers on the same footing with those of foreign nations, though not contrary to the federal articles, is certainly adverse to the spirit of the Union, and tends to beget retaliating regulations, not less expensive and vexatious in themselves than they are destructive of the general harmony.

5. WANT OF CONCERT IN MATTERS WHERE COMMON INTEREST REQUIRES IT. This defect is strongly illustrated in the state of our commercial affairs. How much has the national dignity, interest, and revenue, suffered from this cause? Instances of inferior moment are the want of uniformity in the laws concerning naturalization & literary property; of provision for national seminaries, for grants of incorporation for national purposes, for canals and other works of general utility, which may at present be defeated by the perverseness of particular States whose concurrence is necessary.

6. WANT OF GUARANTY TO THE STATES OF THEIR CONSTITUTIONS & LAWS AGAINST INTERNAL VIOLENCE. The confederation is silent on this point and therefore by the second article the hands of the federal authority are tied. . . .

7. WANT OF SANCTION TO THE LAWS, AND OF COERCION IN THE GOVERNMENT OF THE CONFEDERACY. A sanction is essential to the idea of law, as coercion is to that of Government. The federal system being destitute of both, wants the great vital principles of a Political Constitution. Under the form of such a constitution, it is in fact nothing more than a treaty of amity of commerce and of alliance, between independent and Sovereign States. From what cause could so fatal an omission have happened in the articles of Confederation? from a mistaken confidence that the justice, the good faith, the honor, the sound policy, of the several legislative assemblies would render superfluous any appeal to the ordinary motives by which the laws secure the obedience of individuals: a confidence which does honor to the enthusiastic virtue of the compilers, as much as the inexperience of the crisis apologizes for their errors. . . . Even during the war, when external danger supplied in some degree the defect of legal & coercive sanctions, how imperfectly did the States fulfill their obligations to the Union? In time of peace, we see already what is to be expected. How indeed could it be otherwise? . . . If the laws of the States were merely recommendatory to their citizens, or if they were to be rejudged by County authorities, what security, what probability would exist, that they would be carried into execution? Is the security or probability greater in favor of the acts of Congress which depending for their execution on the will of the State legislatures, which are tho' nominally authoritative, in fact recommendatory only?

8. WANT OF RATIFICATION BY THE PEOPLE OF THE ARTICLES OF CONFEDERATION. In some of the States the Confederation is recognized by, and forms a part of the Constitution. In others however it has received no other sanction than that of the legislative authority. . . .

9. MULTIPLICITY OF LAWS IN THE SEVERAL STATES. In developing the evils which viciate the political system of the U.S., it is proper to include those which are found within the States individually, as well as those which directly affect the States collectively, since the former class have an indirect influence on the general malady and must not be overlooked in forming a compleat remedy. Among the evils then of our situation may well be ranked the multiplicity of laws from which no States is exempt. As far as laws are necessary to mark with precision the duties of those who are to obey them, and to take from those who are to administer them a discretion which might be abused, their number is the price of liberty. As far as laws exceed this limit, they are a nuisance; a nuisance of the most pestilent kind. Try the Codes of the several States by this test, and what a luxuriancy of legislation do they present. The short period of independency has filled as many pages as the century which preceded it. Every year, almost every session, adds a new volume. . . .

10. MUTABILITY OF THE LAWS OF THE STATES. This evil is intimately connected with the former yet deserves a distinct notice, as it emphatically denotes a vicious legislation. We daily see laws repealed or superseded, before any trial can have been made of their merits, and even before a knowledge of them can have reached the remoter districts within which they were to operate. In the regulations of trade this instability becomes a snare not only to our citizens, but to foreigners also.

11. INJUSTICE OF THE LAWS OF THE STATES. If the multiplicity and mutability of laws prove a want of wisdom, their injustice betrays a defect still more alarming: more alarming not merely because it is a greater evil in itself; but because it brings more into questions the fundamental principle of republican Government, that the majority who rule in such governments are the safest Guardians both of public Good and private rights. To what causes is this evil to be ascribed?

These causes lie 1. in the Representative bodies. 2. in the people themselves.

1. Representative appointments are sought from 3 motives. 1. ambition. 2. personal interest. 3. public good. Unhappily the two first are proved by experience to be most prevalent. Hence the candidates who feel them, particularly, the second, are most industrious, and most successful in pursing their object: and forming often a majority in the legislative Councils, with interested views, contrary to the interest and views of their constituents, join in a perfidious sacrifice of the latter to the former. A succeeding election it might be supposed, would displace the offenders, and repair the mischief. But how easily are based and selfish measures, masked by pretexts of public good and apparent expediency? How frequently will a repetition of the same arts and industry which succeeded in the first instance, again prevail on the unwary to misplace their confidence?

How frequently too will the honest but unenlightened representative be the dupe of a favorite leader, veiling his selfish views under the professions of public good, and varnishing his sophistical arguments with the glowing colours of popular eloquence?

2. A still more fatal if not more frequent cause, lies among the people themselves. All civilized societies are divided into different interests and factions, as they happen to be creditors or debtors—rich or poor—husbandmen, merchants or manufacturers—members of different religious sects—followers of different political leaders—inhabitants of different districts—owners of different kinds of property &c &c. In republican Government the majority however composed, ultimately give the law. Whenever therefore an apparent interest or common passion unites a majority what is to restrain them from unjust violations of the rights and interests of the minority, or of individuals? Three motives only 1. a prudent regard to their own good as involved in the general and permanent good of the community. This consideration although of decisive weight in itself, is found by experience to be too often unheeded. It is often forgotten, by nations as well as by individuals, that honesty is the best policy. 2dly. respect for character. However strong this motive may be in individuals, it is considered as very insufficient to restrain them from injustice. In a multitude its efficacy is diminished in proportion to the number which is to share the praise or the blame. Besides, as it has reference to public opinion, which within a particular Society, is the opinion of the majority, the standard is fixed by those whose conduct is to be measured by it. The public opinion without the Society will be little respected by the people at large of any Country. Individuals of extended views, and of national pride, may bring the public proceedings to this standard, but the example will never be followed by the multitude. . . . 3dly. Will Religion the only remaining motive be a sufficient restraint? It is not pretended to be such on men individually considered. Will its effect be greater on them considered in an aggregate view? quite the reverse. The conduct of every popular assembly acting on oath, the strongest of religious ties, proves that individuals join without remorse in acts, against which their consciences would revolt if proposed to them under the like sanction, separately in their closets. When indeed Religion is kindled into enthusiasm, its force like that of other passions, is increased by the sympathy of a multitude. But enthusiasm is only a temporary state of religion, and while it lasts will hardly be seen with pleasure at the helm of Government. Besides as religion in is coolest state is not infallible, it may become a motive to oppression as well as a restraint from injustice. Place three individuals in a situation wherein the interest of each depends on the voice of the others; and give to two of them an interest opposed to the rights of the third. Will the latter be secure? The prudence of every man would shun the danger. The rules & forms of justice suppose & guard against it. Will two thousand in a like situation be less likely to encroach on the rights of one thousand? The contrary is witnessed by the notorious factions & oppression which take place in corporate towns limited as the opportunities are, and in little republics when uncontrouled by apprehensions of external danger. If an enlargement of the sphere is found to lessen the insecurity of private rights, it is not because the impulse of a common interest or passion is less predominant in this case with the majority; but because a common interest or passion is less apt to be felt and the requisite combinations less easy to be formed by a great than by a small number. The Society becomes broken into a greater variety of interests, of pursuits of passions, which check each other, whilst those who may feel a common sentiment have less opportunity of communication and concert. It may be inferred that the inconveniences of popular States, contrary to the prevailing Theory, are in proportion not to the extent, but to the narrowness of their limits.

The great desideratum in Government is such a modification of the sovereignty as will render it sufficiently neutral between the different interests and factions, to controul one part of the society from invading the rights of another, and at the same time sufficiently controuled itself, from setting up an interest adverse to that of the whole Society. In absolute Monarchies the prince is sufficiently neutral towards his subjects, but frequently sacrifices their happiness to his ambition or his avarice. In small Republics, the sovereign will is sufficiently controuled from such a sacrifice of the entire Society, but is not sufficiently neutral towards the parts composing it. As a limited monarchy tempers the evils of an absolute one; so an extensive Republic meliorates the administration of a small Republic.

Questions

1. According to the conventional wisdom of the eighteenth century, the fate of a republic was dependent on the "virtue" of its people. Did Madison share this belief? Explain.

2. Did the Constitutional Convention adopt any portion of the program described by Madison? If so, in what ways did it follow Madison's advice?

3. What was Madison's remedy for the vices of the Confederation? How does his proposal here compare with his observations in *Federalist* No. 10 (Document 6-20)?

6-18   A Warning to the Delegates About Leveling (1787)

Elbridge Gerry

Shays's Rebellion (see text pp. 190–192) horrified most Americans. It seemed to demonstrate how impotent the federal government was and how easily the Union might slip into chaos. However, for many Americans Shays's Rebellion also signaled the need to reassess the nature of the American experiment with democracy. That certainly was the case for Elbridge Gerry, a delegate from Massachusetts to the Constitutional Convention. Gerry, a prominent Massachusetts Patriot, had signed the Declaration of Independence and served in the Confederation Congress. On May 31, 1787, during the Constitutional Convention's deliberations about allowing the people to elect members of the U.S. Senate directly, Gerry told his fellow delegates what Shays's Rebellion meant to him.

Source: Max Farrand, ed., *The Records of the Federal Convention of 1787*, rev. ed., 1:48, 50. Copyright © 1911 by Yale University Press. Reprinted by permission.

Mr Gerry. The evils we experience flow from the excess of democracy. The people do not want virtue; but are the dupes of pretended patriots. In Massts. it has been fully confirmed by experience that they are daily misled into the most baneful measures and opinions by the false reports circulated by designing men, and which no one on the spot can refute. One principal evil arises from the want of due provision for those employed in the administration of Governnt. It would seem to be a maxim of democracy to starve the public servants. He mentioned the popular clamour in Massts. for the reduction of salaries and the attack made on that of the Govr. though secured by the spirit of the Constitution itself. He had he said been too republican heretofore: he was still

however republican, but had been taught by experience the danger of the levilling spirit. . . .

Mr Gerry [said he] did not like the election by the people. The maxims taken from the British constitution were often fallacious when applied to our situation which was extremely different. Experience he said had shewn that the State Legislatures drawn immediately from the people did not always possess their confidence. He had no objection however to an election by the people if it were so qualified that men of honor and character might not be unwilling to be joined in the appointments. He seemed to think the people might nominate a certain number out of which the State legislatures should be bound to choose.

Questions

1. According to Gerry, what kind of problems produced the dissatisfaction that burst forth in Shays's Rebellion?

2. According to Gerry, who caused Shays's Rebellion?

3. If democracy is defined as allowing the average person to exercise real political power, would you describe Gerry as a supporter of democracy? Why or why not?

6-19   An Attack on the Proposed Federal Constitution (1787)

George Clinton

The adoption of the proposed new constitution of the Philadelphia Convention was by no means a foregone conclusion. Having repudiated the authority of a remote government a little more than a decade earlier, many delegates were strongly opposed to accepting subordination to a new one. Many, too, feared that the new national charter would fundamentally alter the political balance of power to their disadvantage. Among the leading Antifederalists (as they were unfairly dubbed) was Governor George Clinton of New York, who wrote several letters under the pseudonym Cato attacking the proposal as dangerous to the liberties of the people. In the following letter he set forth one of the strongest arguments against the proposed new federal government, one that James Madison felt necessary to address in his famous essay *Federalist* No. 10 (Document 6-20).

Source: From Morton Borden, ed., *The Antifederalist Papers* (East Lansing: Michigan State University Press, 1965), 36–39. Copyright © 1965 by Morten Borden. Used with permission of Michigan State University Press.

. . . The recital, or premises on which the new form of government is erected, declares a consolidation or union of all the thirteen parts, or states, into one great whole, under the form of the United States, for all the various and important purposes therein set forth. But whoever seriously considers the immense extent of territory comprehended within the limits of the United States, together with the variety of its climates, productions, and commerce, the difference of extent, and number of inhabitants in all; the dissimilitude of interest, morals, and politics, in almost every one, will receive it as an intuitive truth, that a consolidated republican form of government therein, can never *form a perfect union, establish justice, insure domestic tranquility, promote the general welfare, and secure the blessings of liberty to you and your posterity,* for to these objects it must be directed. This unkindred legislature therefore, composed of interests opposite and dissimilar in their nature, will in its exercise, emphatically be like a house divided against itself.

The governments of Europe have taken their limits and form from adventitious circumstances, and nothing can be argued on the motive of agreement from them; but these adventitious political principles have nevertheless produced effects that have attracted the attention of philosophy, which have established axioms in the science of politics therefrom, as irrefragable as any in Euclid. It is natural, says Montesquieu, *to a republic to have only a small territory, otherwise it cannot long subsist: in a large one, there are men of large fortunes, and consequently of less moderation; there are too great deposits to trust in the hands of a single subject; an ambitious person soon becomes sensible that he may be happy, great, and glorious by oppressing his fellow citizens, and that he might raise himself to grandeur, on the ruins of his country. In large republics, the public good is sacrificed to a thousand views; in a small one, the interest of the public is easily perceived, better understood, and more within the reach of every citizen; abuses have a less extent, and of course are less protected.* He also shows you, that the duration of the republic of Sparta was owing to its having continued with the same extent of territory after all its wars; and that the ambition of Athens and Lacedemon to command and direct the union, lost them their liberties, and gave them a monarchy.

From this picture, what can you promise yourselves, on the score of consolidation of the United States into one government? Impracticability in the just exercise of it, your freedom insecure, even this form of government limited in its continuance, the employments of your country disposed of to the opulent, to whose contumely you will continually be

an object. You must risk much, by indispensably placing trusts of the greatest magnitude, into the hands of individuals whose ambition for power, and aggrandizement, will oppress and grind you. Where, from the vast extent of your territory, and the complication of interests, the science of government will become intricate and perplexed, and too mysterious for you to understand and observe; and by which you are to be conducted into a monarchy, either limited or despotic; the latter, Mr. Locke remarks, *is a government derived from neither nature nor compact.*

Political liberty, the great Montesquieu again observes, *consists in security, or at least in the opinion we have of security*; and this *security*, therefore, or the *opinion*, is best obtained in moderate governments, where the mildness of the laws, and the equality of the manners, beget a confidence in the people, which produces this security, or the opinion. This moderation in governments depends in a great measure on their limits, connected with their political distribution.

The extent of many of the states of the Union, is at this time almost too great for the superintendence of a republican form of government, and must one day or other revolve into more vigorous ones, or by separation be reduced into smaller and more useful, as well as moderate ones. You have already observed the feeble efforts of Massachusetts against their insurgents; with what difficulty did they quell that insurrection; and is not the province of Maine at this moment on the eve of separation from her? The reason of these things is, that for the security of the *property* of the community—in which expressive term Mr. Locke makes life, liberty, and estate, to consist—the wheels of a republic are necessarily slow in their operation. Hence, in large free republics, the evil sometimes is not only begun, but almost completed, before they are in a situation to turn the current into a contrary progression. The extremes are also too remote from the usual seat of government, and the laws, therefore, too feeble to afford protection to all its parts, and insure *domestic tranquility* without the aid of another principle. If, therefore, this state [New York], and that of North Carolina, had an army under their control, they never would have lost Vermont, and Frankland, nor the state of Massachusetts suffered an insurrection, or the dismemberment of her fairest district; but the exercise of a principle which would have prevented these things, if we may believe the experience of ages, would have ended in the destruction of their liberties.

Will this consolidated republic, if established, in its exercise beget such confidence and compliance, among the citizens of these states, as to do without the aid of a standing army? I deny that it will. The malcontents in each state, who will not be a few, nor the least important, will be exciting factions against it. The fear of a dismemberment of some of its parts, and the necessity to enforce the execution of revenue laws (a fruitful source of oppression) on the extremes and in the other districts of the government, will incidentally and necessarily require a permanent force, to be kept on foot. Will not political security, and even the opinion of it, be extinguished? Can mildness and moderation exist in a government where the primary incident in its exercise must be force? Will not violence destroy confidence, and can equality subsist where the extent, policy, and practice of it will naturally lead to make odious distinctions among citizens?

The people who may compose this national legislature from the southern states, in which, from the mildness of the climate, the fertility of the soil, and the value of its productions, wealth is rapidly acquired, and where the same causes naturally lead to luxury, dissipation, and a passion for aristocratic distinction; where slavery is encouraged, and liberty of course less respected and protected; who know not what it is to acquire property by their own toil, nor to economize with the savings of industry—will these men, therefore, be as tenacious of the liberties and interests of the more northern states, where freedom, independence, industry, equality and frugality are natural to the climate and soil, as men who are your own citizens, legislating in your own state, under your inspection, and whose manners and fortunes bear a more equal resemblance to your own?

It may be suggested, in answer to this, that whoever is a citizen of one state is a citizen of each, and that therefore he will be as interested in the happiness and interest of all, as the one he is delegated from. But the argument is fallacious, and, whoever has attended to the history of mankind, and the principles which bind them together as parents, citizens, or men, will readily perceive it. These principles are, in their exercise, like a pebble cast on the calm surface of a river—the circles begin in the center, and are small, active and forcible, but as they depart from that point, they lose their force, and vanish into calmness.

The strongest principle of union resides within our domestic walls. The ties of the parent exceed that of any other. As we depart from home, the next general principle of union is amongst citizens of the same state, where acquaintance, habits, and fortunes, nourish affection, and attachment. Enlarge the circle still further, and, as citizens of different states, though we acknowledge the same national denomination, we lose in the ties of acquaintance, habits, and fortunes, and thus by degrees we lessen in our attachments, till, at length, we no more than acknowledge a sameness of species. Is it, therefore, from certainty like this, reasonable to believe, that inhabitants of Georgia, or New Hampshire, will have the same obligations towards you as your own, and preside over your lives, liberties, and property, with the same care and attachment? Intuitive reason answers in the negative. . . .

CATO

Questions

1. Why did George Clinton believe that the new federal Constitution was unworkable and that it would be unable to secure its stated ends?

2. Politicians of this era sought to legitimize their positions by citing the authority of eminent political philosophers. Which authorities does Clinton use to this end?

3. What is Clinton's greatest fear about the course of the American experiment in self-government? What is the primary lesson he draws from Shays's Rebellion? What lessons does he draw from history in general?

4. How does Clinton believe that regional differences will impede the ability of the federal government to function? Based on your general knowledge of U.S. history, how accurate was Clinton in his predictions?

6-20 *The Federalist*, No. 10 (1787)

James Madison

As Document 6-19 demonstrates, advocates of the proposed federal Constitution faced a difficult task, especially in obtaining the ratification of the crucial state of New York. In an effort to respond to Antifederalists such as George Clinton, three Federalists—James Madison, Alexander Hamilton, and John Jay—wrote a series of essays in late 1787 and early 1788 explaining the reasoning behind the charter. While most historians generally agree that these essays, now collectively known as *The Federalist*, probably did not play a major role in convincing New Yorkers to accept the Constitution, scholars and jurists generally consider them indispensable to understanding the thinking of the men who framed it. The most famous of these essays, No. 10, was written by Madison in response to Clinton's argument and is widely regarded as the most insightful analysis of the nature of the American political system ever written. The essay is reprinted here in its entirety.

Source: New-York Daily Advertiser, 22 November 1787.

TO THE PEOPLE OF THE STATE OF NEW-YORK.

Among the numerous advantages promised by a well constructed Union, none deserves to be more accurately developed than its tendency to break and control the violence of faction. The friend of popular governments, never finds himself so much alarmed for their character and fate, as when he contemplates their propensity to this dangerous vice. He will not fail therefore to set a due value on any plan which, without violating the principles to which he is attached, provides a proper cure for it. The instability, injustice and confusion introduced into the public councils, have in truth been the mortal diseases under which popular governments have every where perished; as they continue to be the favorite and fruitful topics from which the adversaries to liberty derive their most specious declamations. The valuable improvements made by the American Constitutions on the popular models, both ancient and modern, cannot certainly be too much admired; but it would be an unwarrantable partiality, to contend that they have as effectually obviated the danger on this side as was wished and expected. Complaints are every where heard from our most considerate and virtuous citizens, equally the friends of public and private faith, and of public and personal liberty; that our governments are too unstable; that the public good is disregarded in the conflicts of rival parties; and that measures are too often decided, not according to the rules of justice, and the rights of the minor party; but by the superior force of an interested and over-bearing majority. However anxiously we may wish that these complaints had no foundation, the evidence of known facts will not permit us to deny that they are in some degree true. It will be found indeed, on a candid review of our situation, that some of the distresses under which we labor, have been erroneously charged on the operation of our governments; but it will be found, at the same time, that other causes will not alone account for many of our heaviest misfortunes; and particularly, for that prevailing and increasing distrust of public engagements, and alarm for private rights, which are echoed from one end of the continent to the other. These must be chiefly, if not wholly, effects of the unsteadiness and injustice, with which a factious spirit has tainted our public administration.

By a faction I understand a number of citizens, whether amounting to a majority or minority of the whole, who are united and actuated by some common impulse of passion, or of interest, adverse to the rights of other citizens, or to the permanent and aggregate interests of the community.

There are two methods of curing the mischiefs of faction: the one, by removing its causes; the other, by controling its effects.

There are again two methods of removing the causes of faction: the one by destroying the liberty which is essential to its existence; the other, by giving to every citizen the same opinions, the same passions, and the same interests.

It could never be more truly said than of the first remedy, that it is worse than the disease. Liberty is to faction, what air is to fire, an aliment without which it instantly expires. But it could not be a less folly to abolish liberty, which is essential to political life, because it nourishes faction, than it would be to wish the annihilation of air, which is essential to animal life, because it imparts to fire its destructive agency.

The second expedient is as impracticable, as the first would be unwise. As long as the reason of man continues fallible, and he is at liberty to exercise it, different opinions will be formed. As long as the connection subsists between his reason and his self-love, his opinions and his passions will have a reciprocal influence on each other; and the former will be objects to which the latter will attach themselves. The diversity in the faculties of men from which the rights of property originate, is not less an insuperable obstacle to a uniformity of interests. The protection of these faculties is the first object of Government. From the protection of different and unequal faculties of acquiring property, the possession of different degrees and kinds of property immediately results: and from the influence of these on the sentiments and views of the respective proprietors, ensues a division of the society into different interests and parties.

The latent causes of faction are thus sown in the nature of man; and we see them every where brought into different degrees of activity, according to the different circumstances of civil society. A zeal for different opinions concerning religion, concerning Government, and many other points, as well of speculation as of practice; an attachment to different leaders ambitiously contending for pre-eminence and power; or to persons of other descriptions whose fortunes have been interesting to the human passions, have in turn divided mankind into parties, inflamed them with mutual animosity, and rendered them much more disposed to vex and oppress each other, than to co-operate for their common good. So strong is this propensity of mankind to fall into mutual animosities, that where no substantial occasion presents itself, the most frivolous and fanciful distinctions have been sufficient to kindle their unfriendly passions, and excite their most violent conflicts. But the most common and durable source of factions, has been the various and unequal distribution of property. Those who hold, and those who are without property, have ever formed distinct interests in society. Those who are creditors, and those who are debtors, fall under a like discrimination. A landed interest, a manufacturing interest, a mercantile interest, a monied interest, with many lesser interests, grow up of necessity in civilized nations, and divide them into different classes, actuated by different sentiments and views. The regulation of these various and interfering interests forms the principal task of modern Legislation, and involves the spirit of party and faction in the necessary and ordinary operations of Government.

No man is allowed to be a judge in his own cause; because his interest would certainly bias his judgment, and, not improbably, corrupt his integrity. With equal, nay with greater reason, a body of men, are unfit to be both judges and parties, at the same time; yet, what are many of the most important acts of legislation, but so many judicial determinations, not indeed concerning the rights of single persons, but concerning the rights of large bodies of citizens; and what are the different classes of legislators, but advocates and parties to the causes which they determine? Is a law proposed concerning private debts? It is a question to which the creditors are parties on one side, and the debtors on the other. Justice ought to hold the balance between them. Yet the parties are and must be themselves the judges; and the most numerous party, or, in other words, the most powerful faction must be expected to prevail. Shall domestic manufactures be encouraged, and in what degree, by restrictions on foreign manufactures? are questions which would be differently decided by the landed and the manufacturing classes; and probably by neither, with a sole regard to justice and the public good. The apportionment of taxes on the various descriptions of property, is an act which seems to require the most exact impartiality; yet there is perhaps no legislative act in which greater opportunity and temptation are given to a predominant party, to trample on the rules of justice. Every shilling with which they overburden the inferior number, is a shilling saved to their own pockets.

It is in vain to say, that enlightened statesmen will be able to adjust these clashing interests, and render them all subservient to the public good. Enlightened statesmen will not always be at the helm: Nor, in many cases, can such an adjustment be made at all, without taking into view indirect and remote considerations, which will rarely prevail over the immediate interest which one party may find in disregarding the rights of another, or the good of the whole.

The inference to which we are brought, is, that the *causes* of faction cannot be removed; and that relief is only to be sought in the means of controling its *effects*.

If a faction consists of less than a majority, relief is supplied by the republican principle, which enables the majority to defeat its sinister views by regular vote: It may clog the administration, it may convulse the society; but it will be unable to execute and mask its violence under the forms of the Constitution. When a majority is included in a faction, the form of popular government on the other hand enables it to sacrifice to its ruling passion or interest, both the public good and the rights of other citizens. To secure the public good, and private rights, against the danger of such a faction, and at the same time to preserve the spirit and the form of popular government, is then the great object to which our enquiries are directed: Let me add that it is the great desideratum, by which alone this form of government can be rescued from the opprobrium under which it has so long labored, and be recommended to the esteem and adoption of mankind.

By what means is this object attainable? Evidently by one of two only. Either the existence of the same passion or interest in a majority at the same time, must be prevented; or the majority, having such co-existent passion or interest, must be rendered, by their number and local situation, unable to concert and carry into effect schemes of oppression. If the impulse and the opportunity be suffered to coincide, we well know that neither moral nor religious motives can be relied on as an adequate control. They are not found to be such on the injustice and violence of individuals, and lose their efficacy in proportion to the number combined together; that is, in proportion as their efficacy becomes needful.

From this view of the subject, it may be concluded, that a pure Democracy, by which I mean, a Society, consisting of a small number of citizens, who assemble and administer the Government in person, can admit of no cure for the mischiefs of faction. A common passion or interest will, in almost every case, be felt by a majority of the whole; a communication and concert results from the form of Government itself; and there is nothing to check the inducements to sacrifice the weaker party, or an obnoxious individual. Hence it is, that such Democracies have ever been spectacles of turbulence and contention; have ever been found incompatible with personal security, or the rights of property; and have in general been as short in their lives, as they have been violent in their deaths. Theoretic politicians, who have patronized this species of Government, have erroneously supposed, that by reducing mankind to a perfect equality in their political rights, they would, at the same time, be perfectly equalized and as similated in their possessions, their opinions, and their passions.

A Republic, by which I mean a Government in which the scheme of representation takes place, opens a different prospect, and promises the cure for which we are seeking. Let us examine the points in which it varies from pure Democracy, and we shall comprehend both the nature of the cure, and the efficacy which it must derive from the Union.

The two great points of difference between a Democracy and a Republic are, first, the delegation of the Government, in the latter, to a small number of citizens elected by the rest: secondly, the greater number of citizens, and greater sphere of country, over which the latter may be extended.

The effect of the first difference is, on the one hand to refine and enlarge the public views, by passing them through the medium of a chosen body of citizens, whose wisdom may best discern the true interest of their country, and whose patriotism and love of justice, will be least likely to sacrifice it to temporary or partial considerations. Under such a regulation, it may well happen that the public voice pronounced by the representatives of the people, will be more consonant to the public good, than if pronounced by the people themselves convened for the purpose. On the other hand, the effect may be inverted. Men of factious tempers, of local prejudices, or of sinister designs, may by intrigue, by corruption or by other means, first obtain the suffrages, and then betray the interests of the people. The question resulting is, whether small or extensive Republics are most favorable to the election of proper guardians of the public weal; and it is clearly decided in favor of the latter by two obvious considerations.

In the first place it is to be remarked that however small the Republic may be, the Representatives must be raised to a certain number, in order to guard against the cabals of a few; and that however large it may be, they must be limited to a certain number, in order to guard against the confusion of a multitude. Hence the number of Representatives in the two cases, not being in proportion to that of the Constituents, and being proportionally greatest in the small Republic, it follows, that if the proportion of fit characters, be not less, in the large than in the small Republic, the former will present a greater option, and consequently a greater probability of a fit choice.

In the next place, as each Representative will be chosen by a greater number of citizens in the large than in the small Republic, it will be more difficult for unworthy candidates to practise with success the vicious arts, by which elections are too often carried; and the suffrages of the people being more free, will be more likely to centre on men who possess the most attractive merit, and the most diffusive and established characters.

It must be confessed, that in this, as in most other cases, there is a mean, on both sides of which inconveniencies will be found to lie. By enlarging too much the number of electors, you render the representative too little acquainted with all their local circumstances and lesser interests; as by reducing it too much, you render him unduly attached to these, and too little fit to comprehend and pursue great and national objects. The Federal Constitution forms a happy combination in this respect; the great and aggregate interests being referred to the national, the local and particular, to the state legislatures.

The other point of difference is, the greater number of citizens and extent of territory which may be brought within the compass of Republican, than of Democratic Government; and it is this circumstance principally which renders factious combinations less to be dreaded in the former, than in the latter. The smaller the society, the fewer probably will be the distinct parties and interests composing it; the fewer the distinct parties and interests, the more frequently will a majority be found of the same party; and the smaller the number of individuals composing a majority, and the smaller the compass within which they are placed, the more easily will they concert and execute their plans of oppression. Extend the sphere, and you take in a greater variety of parties and interests; you make it less probable that a majority of the whole will have a common motive to invade the rights of other citizens; or if such a common motive exists, it will be more difficult for all who feel it to discover their own strength, and to act in unison with each other. Besides other impediments, it may be remarked, that where there is a consciousness of unjust or dishonorable purposes, communication is always checked by distrust, in proportion to the number whose concurrence is necessary.

Hence it clearly appears, that the same advantage, which a Republic has over a Democracy, in controling the effects of faction, is enjoyed by a large over a small Republic—is enjoyed by the Union over the States composing it. Does this advantage consist in the substitution of Representatives, whose enlightened views and virtuous sentiments render them superior to local prejudices, and to schemes of injustice? It will not be denied, that the Representation of the Union will be most likely to possess these requisite endowments. Does it consist in the greater security afforded by a greater variety of parties, against the event of any one party being able to outnumber and oppress the rest? In an equal degree does the encreased variety of parties, comprised within the Union, encrease this security. Does it, in fine, consist in the greater obstacles opposed to the concert and accomplishment of the secret wishes of an unjust and interested majority? Here, again, the extent of the Union gives it the most palpable advantage.

The influence of factious leaders may kindle a flame within their particular States, but will be unable to spread a general conflagration through the other States: a religious sect, may degenerate into a political faction in a part of the Confederacy; but the variety of sects dispersed over the entire face of it, must secure the national Councils against any danger from that source: a rage for paper money, for an abolition of debts, for an equal division of property, or for any other improper or wicked project, will be less apt to pervade the whole body of the Union, than a particular member of it; in the same proportion as such a malady is more likely to taint a particular county or district, than an entire State.

In the extent and proper structure of the Union, therefore, we behold a Republican remedy for the diseases most incident to Republican Government. And according to the degree of pleasure and pride, we feel in being Republicans, ought to be our zeal in cherishing the spirit, and supporting the character of Federalists.

Questions

1. According to Madison, what causes factions to develop?

2. According to Madison, why are factions dangerous?

3. Given his assessment of how factions develop, can Madison be called an economic determinist? Why or why not?

4. If one believes in a democratic-style republic, why, according to Madison, is it logical to want to have a physically large nation? Do you agree or disagree? Why?

5. On the basis of *Federalist* No. 10, would you describe Madison as a democrat? Why or why not?

6-21 *The Federalist*, No. 54 (1787)

James Madison

The Great Compromise (see text p. 194), which called for equal representation in the Senate and proportional representation in the House of Representatives, necessitated a second compromise. Would slaves be counted in apportioning seats in the House? Northern delegates in the Constitutional Convention argued that slaves should not be counted, as Elbridge Gerry of Massachusetts stated, any "more than the cattle & horses of the North." But southerners contended, as Pierce Butler and Charles Pinckney of South Carolina insisted, that "blacks be included in the rule of representation equally with whites." The delegates ultimately accepted the three-fifths compromise for the sake of allowing the business of the Convention to continue, but the issues they raised in Philadelphia did not disappear. During the ratification debates, Antifederalists, especially in the North, pointed to the three-fifths compromise as still another reason for rejecting the Constitution. In *Federalist* No. 54, James Madison attempted to answer their objections.

Source: Alexander Hamilton, James Madison, and John Jay, *The Federalist*, ed. Benjamin Fletcher Wright, 370–373. Copyright © 1961 by the President and Fellows of Harvard College. Reprinted with permission of the publisher.

"We subscribe to the doctrine," might one of our Southern brethren observe, "that representation relates more immediately to persons, and taxation more immediately to property, and we join in the application of this distinction to the case of our slaves. But we must deny the fact, that slaves are considered merely as property, and in no respect whatever as persons. The true state of the case is, that they partake of both these qualities: being considered by our laws, in some respects, as persons, and in other respects as property. In being compelled to labor, not for himself, but for a master; in being vendible by one master to another master; and in being subject at all times to be restrained in his liberty and chastised in his body, by the capricious will of another,—the slave may appear to be degraded from the human rank, and classed with those irrational animals which fall under the legal denomination of property. In being protected, on the other hand, in his life and in his limbs, against the violence of all others, even the master of his labor and his liberty; and in being punishable himself for all violence committed against others,—the slave is no less evidently regarded by the law as a member of the society, not as a part of the irrational creation; as a moral person, not as a mere article of property. The federal Constitution, therefore, decides with great propriety on the case of our slaves, when it views them in the mixed character of persons and of property. This is in fact their true character. It is the character bestowed on them by the laws under which they live; and it will not be denied, that these are the proper criterion; because it is only under the pretext that the laws have transformed the negroes into subjects of property, that a place is disputed them in the computation of numbers; and it is admitted, that if the laws were to restore the rights which have been taken away, the negroes could no longer be refused an equal share of representation with the other inhabitants.

"This question may be placed in another light. It is agreed on all sides, that numbers are the best scale of wealth and taxation, as they are the only proper scale of representation. Would the convention have been impartial or consistent, if they had rejected the slaves from the list of inhabitants, when the shares of representation were to be calculated, and inserted them on the lists when the tariff of contributions was to be adjusted? Could it be reasonably expected, that the Southern States would concur in a system, which considered their slaves in some degree as men, when burdens were to be imposed, but refused to consider them in the same light, when advantages were to be conferred? Might not some surprise also be expressed, that those who reproach the Southern States with the barbarous policy of considering as property a part of their human brethren, should themselves contend, that the government to which all the States are to be parties, ought to consider this unfortunate race more completely in the unnatural light of property, than the very laws of which they complain?

"It may be replied, perhaps, that slaves are not included in the estimate of representatives in any of the States possessing them. They neither vote themselves nor increase the votes of their masters. Upon what principle, then, ought they to be taken into the federal estimate of representation? In rejecting them altogether, the Constitution would, in this respect, have followed the very laws which have been appealed to as the proper guide.

"This objection is repelled by a single observation. It is a fundamental principle of the proposed Constitution, that as the aggregate number of representatives allotted to the several States is to be determined by a federal rule, founded on the aggregate number of inhabitants, so the right of choosing this allotted number in each State is to be exercised by such part of the inhabitants as the State itself may designate. The qualifications on which the right of suffrage depend are not, perhaps, the same in any two States. In some of the States the difference is very material. In every State, a certain proportion of inhabitants are deprived of this right by the constitution of the State, who will be included in the census by which the federal Constitution apportions the representatives. In this point of view the Southern States might retort the complaint, by insisting that the principle laid down by the convention required that no regard should be had to the policy of particular States towards their own inhabitants; and consequently that the slaves, as inhabitants, should have been admitted into the census according to their full number, in like manner with other inhabitants, who, by the policy of other States, are not admitted to all the rights of citizens. A rigorous adherence, however, to this principle, is waived by those who would be gainers by it. All that they ask is that equal moderation be shown on the other side. Let the case of the slaves be considered, as it is in truth, a peculiar one. Let the compromising expedient of the Constitution be mutually adopted, which regards them as inhabitants, but as debased by servitude below the equal level of free inhabitants; which regards the *slave* as divested of two fifths of the *man*.

"After all, may not another ground be taken on which this article of the Constitution will admit of a still more ready defence? We have hitherto proceeded on the idea that representation related to persons only, and not at all to property. But is it a just idea? Government is instituted no less for protection of the property, than of the persons, of individu-

als. The one as well as the other therefore, may be considered as represented by those who are charged with the government. Upon this principle it is, that in several of the States, and particularly in the State of New York, one branch of the government is intended more especially to be the guardian of property, and is accordingly elected by that part of the society which is most interested in this object of government. In the federal Constitution, this policy does not prevail. The rights of property are committed into the same hands with the personal rights. Some attention ought, therefore, to be paid to property in the choice of those hands.

"For another reason, the votes allowed in the federal legislature to the people of each State, ought to bear some proportion to the comparative wealth of the States. States have not, like individuals, an influence over each other, arising from superior advantages of fortune. If the law allows an opulent citizen but a single vote in the choice of his representative, the respect and consequence which he derives from his fortunate situation very frequently guide the votes of others to the objects of his choice; and through this imperceptible channel the rights of property are conveyed into the public representation. A State possesses no such influence over other States. It is not probable that the richest State in the Confederacy will ever influence the choice of a single representative in any other State. Nor will the representatives of the larger and richer States possess any other advantage in the federal legislature, over the representatives of other States, than what may result from their superior number alone. As far, therefore, as their superior wealth and weight may justly entitle them to any advantage, it ought to be secured to them by a superior share of representation. The new Constitution is, in this respect, materially different from the existing Confederation, as well as from that of the United Netherlands, and other similar confederacies. In each of the latter, the efficacy of the federal resolutions depends on the subsequent and voluntary resolutions of the states composing the union. Hence the states, though possessing an equal vote in the public councils, have an unequal influence, corresponding with the unequal importance of these subsequent and voluntary resolutions. Under the proposed Constitution, the federal acts will take effect without the necessary intervention of the individual States. They will depend merely on the majority of votes in the federal legislature, and consequently each vote, whether proceeding from a large or smaller State, or a State more or less wealthy or powerful, will have an equal weight and efficacy: in the same manner as the votes individually given in a State legislature, by the representatives of unequal counties or other districts, have each a precise equality of value and effect; or if there be any difference in the case, it proceeds from the difference in the personal character of the individual representative, rather than from any regard to the extent of the district from which he comes."

Such is the reasoning which an advocate for the Southern interests might employ on this subject; and although it may appear to be a little strained in some points, yet, on the whole, I must confess that it fully reconciles me to the scale of representation which the convention have established.

Questions

1. Did the fictional "Southern brethren" speak for Madison? In no other number of *The Federalist* did Madison resort to this method of argumentation; what might explain his use of it here?

2. How did Madison's "advocate for Southern interests" counter the objection that other forms of "property" were not being counted for purposes of representation? How did he justify the three-fifths ratio?

3. What was this fictional southerner's response to the charge of inconsistency, that is, that no slaveholding state counted slaves when apportioning seats in its own legislature? Was this a states' rights argument?

Questions for Further Thought

1. Can you identify points of consensus between the Federalist (Document 6-20) and Antifederalist (Document 6-19) positions? What did men like James Madison and George Clinton understand the ends of government to be, and what arguments did they put forth?

2. After the ratification of the Constitution and the quick passage of the Bill of Rights, public opposition to the new government of the United States virtually disappeared. Given the heated nature of the ratification debates, how can we explain this sudden show of unanimity? Did both the Federalists and Antifederalists get everything that they wanted? Did the Bill of Rights ameliorate all Antifederalist fears?

3. Given that the U.S. Constitution is still in effect, were Madison's assumptions in *Federalist* No. 10, correct (Document 6-20)? Do you think that the U.S. government has endured because of—or in spite of—the political science of James Madison?

CHAPTER SEVEN

Politics and Society in the New Republic
1787–1820

The Political Crisis of the 1790s

With the adoption of the Constitution and the addition of the Bill of Rights, America's political problems changed but did not disappear. The financial difficulties that had bedeviled the confederation government still existed. Alexander Hamilton—talented, ambitious, and aristocratically inclined—was determined to confront these problems boldly. First, Hamilton successfully worked to restore the public credit in a way that would ally the interests of the states and "monied men" with those of the federal government—but at the expense of small taxpayers (Document 7-1). Having gotten his way on public credit, Hamilton next strove to create a national financial institution, the Bank of the United States. In so doing, he argued for a loose interpretation of the Constitution that would greatly increase the federal government's power. Thomas Jefferson and James Madison, however, fought the bank proposal, presenting as a counterargument a strict interpretation of the Constitution that forbade the Congress to do anything not explicitly authorized by the charter. These positions reflected fundamentally different visions of what America was and should become.

As the fight over the course the government should follow became more heated, it extended into foreign policy and deepened political divisions. The eruption of the French Revolution in 1789 was enthusiastically received by Jefferson's supporters, who increasingly took the name Republican; but the revolution's excesses and radical assaults on religion horrified Hamilton's faction; these men, who retained the name Federalist, saw the new nation's economic future as dependent on good relations with Great Britain, France's enemy. While George Washington (Document 7-2) counseled a policy of aloofness from the contentions of Europe, British and especially French interests increasingly sought influence, adding hysteria over foreign "subversion" to domestic strife. The Federalists, in control of the government, went to great lengths to stifle their opponents, passing the Alien and Sedition Acts in 1798 (Document 7-4). In response, Madison and Jefferson briefly sought, in the Kentucky and Virginia Resolutions, to reassert state sovereignty against what they saw as a tyrannical federal government (Document 7-5).

In the end, though, the contest between Federalists and Jeffersonian Republicans was decided in the electoral arena; in the presidential contest of 1800, Jefferson emerged triumphant. His victory was notable in that it proved that power in the new nation could be transferred peacefully and without serious reprisals against the losers; indeed, in his 1801 inaugural address (Document 7-6), Jefferson stressed the common interest of all parties in preserving and advancing the American experiment in republican government.

7-1   Report on Public Credit (1790)

Alexander Hamilton

As early as 1781, Alexander Hamilton, demonstrating his admiration for British institutions and economic policies, said that "a national debt if it is not excessive will be to us a national blessing, it will be [a] powerfull cement of our union." When he became the nation's first secretary of the treasury in 1789, he tried to implement his ideals by devising innovative financial policies to overcome the fiscal problems that had helped undermine the confederation government. The intricacies of those policies are clearly analyzed in the textbook (pp. 204–207). The sections of Hamilton's "Report on Public Credit" (1790) presented here explain his view on public credit, including his position concerning a national debt.

Source: From Harold C. Syrett, ed., *The Papers of Alexander Hamilton* (New York: Columbia University Press, 1962), 6:65–71, 106. Copyright © 1962 by Harold C. Syrett. Used with permission of Columbia University Press.

Treasury Department, January 9, 1790.
[Communicated on January 14, 1790]
[To the Speaker of the House of Representatives]
The Secretary of the Treasury, in obedience to the resolution of the House of Representatives . . . has . . . applied himself to the consideration of a proper plan for the support of the Public Credit, with all the attention which was due to the authority of the House, and to the magnitude of the object.

In the discharge of this duty, he has felt . . . a deep and solemn conviction of the momentous nature of the truth contained in the resolution under which his investigations have been conducted, "That an *adequate* provision for the support of the Public Credit, is a matter of high importance to the honor and prosperity of the United States."

With an ardent desire that his well-meant endeavors may be conducive to the real advantage of the nation, and with the utmost deference to the superior judgment of the House, he now respectfully submits the result of his enquiries and reflections, to their indulgent construction.

In the opinion of the Secretary, the wisdom of the House, in giving their explicit sanction to the proposition which has been stated, cannot but be applauded by all, who will seriously consider, and trace through their obvious consequences, these plain and undeniable truths.

That exigencies are to be expected to occur, in the affairs of nations, in which there will be a necessity for borrowing.

That loans in times of public danger, especially from foreign war, are found an indispensable resource, even to the wealthiest of them.

And that in a country, which, like this, is possessed of little active wealth, or in other words, little monied capital,

the necessity for that resource, must, in such emergencies, be proportionably urgent.

And as on the one hand, the necessity for borrowing in particular emergencies cannot be doubted, so on the other, it is equally evident, that to be able to borrow upon *good terms*, it is essential that the credit of a nation should be well established.

For when the credit of a country is in any degree questionable, it never fails to give an extravagant premium, in one shape or another, upon all the loans it has occasion to make. Nor does the evil end here; the same disadvantage must be sustained upon whatever is to be bought on terms of future payment.

From this constant necessity of *borrowing* and *buying dear*, it is easy to conceive how immensely the expences of a nation, in a course of time, will be augmented by an unsound state of the public credit.

To attempt to enumerate the complicated variety of mischiefs in the whole system of the social œconomy, which proceed from a neglect of the maxims that uphold public credit, and justify the solicitude manifested by the House on this point, would be an improper intrusion on their time and patience.

In so strong a light nevertheless do they appear to the Secretary, that on their due observance at the present critical juncture, materially depends, in his judgment, the individual and aggregate prosperity of the citizens of the United States; their relief from the embarrassments they now experience; their character as a People; the cause of good government.

If the maintenance of public credit, then, be truly so important, the next enquiry which suggests itself is, by what means it is to be effected? The ready answer to which question is, by good faith, by a punctual performance of contracts. States, like individuals, who observe their engagements, are respected and trusted: while the reverse is the fate of those, who pursue an opposite conduct. . . .

While the observance of that good faith, which is the basis of public credit, is recommended by the strongest inducements of political expediency, it is enforced by considerations of still greater authority. There are arguments for it, which rest on the immutable principles of moral obligation. And in proportion as the mind is disposed to contemplate, in the order of Providence, an intimate connection between public virtue and public happiness, will be its repugnancy to a violation of those principles.

This reflection derives additional strength from the nature of the debt of the United States. It was the price of liberty. The faith of America has been repeatedly pledged for it, and with solemnities, that give peculiar force to the obligation. There is indeed reason to regret that it has not hitherto been kept; that the necessities of the war, conspiring with inexperience in the subjects of finance, produced direct infractions; and that the subsequent period has been a continued scene of negative violation, or non-compliance. But a diminution of this regret arises from the reflection, that the last seven years have exhibited an earnest and uniform effort, on the part of the government of the union, to retrieve the national credit, by doing justice to the creditors of the nation; and that the embarrassments of a defective constitution, which defeated this laudable effort, have ceased.

From this evidence of a favorable disposition, given by the former government, the institution of a new one, cloathed with powers competent to calling forth the resources of the community, has excited correspondent expectations. A general belief, accordingly, prevails, that the credit of the United States will quickly be established on the firm foundation of an effectual provision for the existing debt. . . .

It cannot but merit particular attention, that among ourselves the most enlightened friends of good government are those, whose expectations are the highest.

To justify and preserve their confidence; to promote the encreasing respectability of the American name; to answer the calls of justice; to restore landed property to its due value; to furnish new resources both to agriculture and commerce; to cement more closely the union of the states; to add to their security against foreign attack; to establish public order on the basis of an upright and liberal policy. These are the great and invaluable ends to be secured, by a proper and adequate provision, at the present period, for the support of public credit.

To this provision we are invited, not only by the general considerations, which have been noticed, but by others of a more particular nature. It will procure to every class of the community some important advantages, and remove some no less important disadvantages. . . .

But these good effects of a public debt are only to be looked for, when, by being well funded, it has acquired an *adequate* and *stable* value. Till then, it has rather a contrary tendency. The fluctuation and insecurity incident to it in an unfunded state, render it a mere commodity, and a precarious one. As such, being only an object of occasional and particular speculation, all the money applied to it is so much diverted from the more useful channels of circulation, for which the thing itself affords no substitute: So that, in fact, one serious inconvenience of an unfunded debt is, that it contributes to the scarcity of money.

This distinction which has been little if at all attended to, is of the greatest moment. It involves a question immediately interesting to every part of the community; which is no other than this—Whether the public debt, by a provision for it on true principles, shall be rendered a *substitute* for money; or whether, by being left as it is, or by being provided for in such a manner as will wound those principles, and destroy confidence, it shall be suffered to continue, as it is, a pernicious drain of our cash from the channels of productive industry. . . .

Persuaded as the Secretary is, that the proper funding of the present debt, will render it a national blessing: Yet he is so far from acceding to the position, in the latitude in which it is sometimes laid down, that "public debts are public benefits," a position inviting to prodigality, and liable to dangerous abuse,—that he ardently wishes to see it incorporated, as a fundamental maxim, in the system of public credit of the United States, that the creation of debt should always be accompanied with the means of extinguishment. This he regards as the true secret for rendering public credit immortal. And he presumes, that it is difficult to conceive a situation, in which there may not be an adherence to the maxim. At least he feels an unfeigned solicitude, that this may be attempted by the United States, and that they may commence their measures for the establishment of credit, with the observance of it.

Questions

1. According to Hamilton, why is it essential for a nation to have good public credit?

2. According to Hamilton, what has to be done to ensure that the United States will have sound public credit?

3. Hamilton makes an open appeal to patriotism. Do you find it effective? Why or why not?

7-2   Farewell Address (1796)

George Washington

Foreign aid, especially the direct military aid that resulted from the French Alliance, proved essential to winning American independence. That alliance, however, was made when France was still a monarchy. When the French Revolution transformed France into a republic and then plunged that nation into war, the U.S. government faced a dilemma. Should the United States, a weak nation, honor its alliance with a France that was fundamentally different from the country that had entered into the Alliance of 1778? As the textbook authors indicate (pp. 208–209), the country split over the issue, and President Washington and the Federalist-dominated Congress chose to embrace neutrality. In taking that position, President Washington revealed his Federalist party leanings. Still, his emphasis on keeping America out of harm's way also reflected his view on the foreign policy guidelines that the young, still militarily weak nation should follow. In his 1796 farewell address, which also included extensive comments on "the baneful effects of the spirit of [political] parties," President Washington clearly spelled out his views on foreign policy.

Source: From James D. Richardson, ed., *A Compilation of the Messages and Papers of the Presidents* (Washington, DC: U.S. Government Printing Office, 1896–1899), 1:205–216 passim.

Observe good faith and justice toward all nations. Cultivate peace and harmony with all. Religion and morality enjoin this conduct. And can it be that good policy does not equally enjoin it? It will be worthy of a free, enlightened, and at no distant period a great nation to give to mankind the magnanimous and too novel example of a people always guided by an exalted justice and benevolence. Who can doubt that in the course of time and things the fruits of such a plan would richly repay any temporary advantages which might be lost by a steady adherence to it? . . .

In the execution of such a plan nothing is more essential than that permanent, inveterate antipathies against particular nations and passionate attachments for others should be excluded, and that in place of them just and amicable feelings toward all should be cultivated. The nation which indulges toward another an habitual hatred or an habitual fondness is in some degree a slave. It is a slave to its animosity or to its affection, either of which is sufficient to lead it astray from its duty and its interest. . . .

As avenues to foreign influence in innumerable ways, such attachments are particularly alarming to the truly enlightened and independent patriot. How many opportunities do they afford to tamper with domestic factions, to practice the arts of seduction, to mislead public opinion, to influence or awe the public councils! Such an attachment of a small or weak toward a great and powerful nation dooms the former to be the satellite of the latter. Against the insidious wiles of foreign influence (I conjure you to believe me, fellow-citizens) the jealousy of a free people ought to be *constantly* awake, since history and experience prove that foreign influence is one of the most baneful foes of republican government. But that jealousy, to be useful, must be impartial, else it becomes the instrument of the very influence to be avoided, instead of a defense against it. Excessive partiality for one foreign nation and excessive dislike of another

cause those whom they actuate to see danger only on one side, and serve to veil and even second the arts of influence on the other. Real patriots who may resist the intrigues of the favorite are liable to become suspected and odious, while its tools and dupes usurp the applause and confidence of the people to surrender their interests.

The great rule of conduct for us in regard to foreign nations is, in extending our commercial relations to have with them as little *political* connection as possible. So far as we have already formed engagements let them be fulfilled with perfect good faith. Here let us stop.

Europe has a set of primary interests which to us have none or a very remote relation. Hence she must be engaged in frequent controversies, the causes of which are essentially foreign to our concerns. Hence, therefore, it must be unwise in us to implicate ourselves by artificial ties in the ordinary vicissitudes of her politics or the ordinary combinations and collisions of her friendships or enmities.

Our detached and distant situation invites and enables us to pursue a different course. If we remain one people, under an efficient government, the period is not far off when we may defy material injury from external annoyance; when we may take such an attitude as will cause the neutrality we may at any time resolve upon to be scrupulously respected; when belligerent nations, under the impossibility of making acquisitions upon us, will not lightly hazard the giving us provocation; when we may choose peace or war, as our interest, guided by justice, shall counsel.

Why forego the advantages of so peculiar a situation? Why quit our own to stand upon foreign ground? Why, by interweaving our destiny with that of any part of Europe, entangle our peace and prosperity in the toils of European ambition, rivalship, interest, humor, or caprice?

It is our true policy to steer clear of permanent alliances with any portion of the foreign world, so far, I mean, as we are now at liberty to do it; for let me not be understood as capable of patronizing infidelity to existing engagements. I hold the maxim no less applicable to public than to private affairs that honesty is always the best policy. I repeat, therefore, let those engagements be observed in their genuine sense. But in my opinion it is unnecessary and would be unwise to extend them.

Taking care always to keep ourselves by suitable establishments on a respectable defensive posture, we may safely trust to temporary alliances for extraordinary emergencies.

Harmony, liberal intercourse with all nations are recommended by policy, humanity, and interest. But even our commercial policy should hold an equal and impartial hand, neither seeking nor granting exclusive favors or preferences; consulting the natural course of things; diffusing and diversifying by gentle means the streams of commerce, but forcing nothing; establishing with powers so disposed, in order to give trade a stable course, to define the rights of our merchants, and to enable the Government to support them, conventional rules of intercourse, the best that present circumstances and mutual opinion will permit, but temporary and liable to be from time to time abandoned or varied as experience and circumstances shall dictate; constantly keeping in view that it is folly in one nation to look for disinterested favors from another; that it must pay with a portion of its independence for whatever it may accept under that character; that by such acceptance it may place itself in the condition of having given equivalents for nominal favors, and yet of being reproached with ingratitude for not giving more. There can be no greater error than to expect or calculate upon real favors from nation to nation. It is an illusion which experience must cure, which a just pride ought to discard.

In offering to you, my countrymen, these counsels of an old and affectionate friend I dare not hope they will make the strong and lasting impression I could wish—that they will control the usual current of the passions or prevent our nation from running the course which has hitherto marked the destiny of nations. But if I may even flatter myself that they may be productive of some partial benefit, some occasional good—that they may now and then recur to moderate the fury of party spirit, to warn against the mischiefs of foreign intrigue, to guard against the impostures of pretended patriotism—this hope will be a full recompense for the solicitude for your welfare by which they have been dictated.

How far in the discharge of my official duties I have been guided by the principles which have been delineated the public records and other evidences of my conduct must witness to you and to the world. To myself, the assurance of my own conscience is that I have at least believed myself to be guided by them.

In relation to the still subsisting war in Europe my proclamation of the 22d of April, 1793, is the index to my plan. Sanctioned by your approving voice and by that of your representatives in both Houses of Congress, the spirit of that measure has continually governed me, uninfluenced by any attempts to deter or divert me from it.

After deliberate examination, with the aid of the best lights I could obtain, I was well satisfied that our country, under all the circumstances of the case, had a right to take, and was bound in duty and interest to take, a neutral position. Having taken it, I determined as far as should depend upon me to maintain it with moderation, perseverance, and firmness....

The inducements of interest for observing that conduct will best be referred to your own reflections and experience. With me a predominant motive has been to endeavor to gain time to our country to settle and mature its yet recent institutions, and to progress without interruption to that degree of strength and consistency which is necessary to give it, humanly speaking, the command of its own fortunes.

Questions

1. What foreign policy guidelines did President Washington recommend for the United States?

2. Were Washington's reasons for following those guidelines convincing? Why or why not?

3. What did Washington mean when he said that "a free people ought to be *constantly* awake"? Do you agree or disagree with his assertion? If your answer is yes, is his advice on this point as applicable today as it was in 1796? Why or why not?

7-3   George Washington as a Symbol for America (1799, 1800)

**Alexander Lawson,
David Edwin**

George Washington was larger than life while he was still alive. In that constellation of leaders who came of age in Revolutionary America, no one outshined Washington; indeed, with the possible exception of Benjamin Franklin no one even came close. And the

(A)   *Alexander Lawson, "General Washington's Resignation"*

(B)   *David Edwin, "Apotheosis of Washington"*

single most important event in establishing Washington's fame occurred in 1783, at the end of the War of Independence, when he resigned as commander in chief of the Continental Army and returned to private life. At the peak of his power, the victorious general surrendered that power. When the prospect of Washington's voluntary resignation caught the attention of George III, the incredulous monarch reportedly blurted out, "If he does that, he will be the greatest man in the world." Washington's gesture was celebrated to such an extent that in 1799, sixteen years after the event, John James Barralet chose to commemorate it, rather than the more recent decision by Washington to step down from the presidency.

Washington died barely four months after the first publication of Barralet's etching. Along with the hundreds of sermons and quasi-biographical tributes that flooded the presses, including that of Mason Locke Weems, who famously invented the cherry tree story, dozens of memorial prints began to appear. The "Apotheosis of Washington" by David Edwin was advertised in New York as elegantly capturing "all that can be said of the

Soldier, the Statesman, the Husband and the Friend." Washington is shown rising from Mount Vernon and being greeted by his Revolutionary War comrades Joseph Warren, who died at the Battle of Bunker Hill, and Richard Montgomery, who was killed during the assault on Quebec.

Sources: Alexander Lawson after John Barralet, "General Washington's Resignation (1799)," originally from *Philadelphia Magazine and Review,* January 1799, Library of Congress. David Edwin after Rembrandt Peale, "The Apotheosis of Washington," 1800. Courtesy of the National Portrait Gallery, Smithsonian Institution.

Questions

1. In "General Washington's Resignation," Washington gestures toward an idyllic countryside in the background and an eagle guarding a cornucopia in the foreground. What do these symbolize?

2. Why would Americans find Washington's resignation so extraordinary? According to the documents in this chapter, why did they distrust men in power?

3. In "Apotheosis of Washington," Washington is dressed plainly in his ascent toward heaven. Why? How is this supposed to be a reflection of the situation of the United States?

4. How are Washington's achievements commemorated by Edwin? Why are Warren and Montgomery greeting him?

7-4   The Sedition Act (1798)

As the analysis in the textbook makes clear (pp. 209–212), President Washington was in some measure undoubtedly correct when he spoke of "the baneful effects of the spirit of [political] parties." One baneful effect was the way in which the Federalist Party responded to its declining popularity in the late 1790s, when it was faced with the prospect of becoming a minority party. In an effort to retain power, leading Federalists trampled on the rights of their political opponents and precipitated a major political crisis. This crisis was evidenced and symbolized by the passage of the Alien and Sedition Acts of 1798. The Sedition Act, which is reprinted here, was seen as a direct assault on the Bill of Rights and thus provoked a sharp response.

Source: United States, *Statutes at Large,* 1:596–597.

An Act in addition to the act, entitled "An act for the punishment of certain crimes against the United States."
SEC. 1. *Be it enacted* . . . , That if any persons shall unlawfully combine or conspire together, with intent to oppose any measure or measures of the government of the United States, which are or shall be directed by proper authority, or to impede the operation of any law of the United States, or to intimidate or prevent any person holding a place or office in or under the government of the United States, from undertaking, performing or executing his trust or duty; and if any person or persons, with intent as aforesaid, shall counsel, advise or attempt to procure any insurrection, riot, unlawful assembly, or combination, whether such conspiracy, threatening, counsel, advice, or attempt shall have the proposed effect or not, he or they shall be deemed guilty of a high misdemeanor, and on conviction, before any court of the United States having jurisdiction thereof, shall be punished by a fine not exceeding five thousand dollars, and by imprisonment during a term not less than six months nor exceeding five years; and further, at the discretion of the court may be holden to find sureties for his good behaviour in such sum, and for such time, as the said court may direct.

SEC. 2. That if any person shall write, print, utter, or publish, or shall cause or procure to be written, printed, uttered or published, or shall knowingly and willingly assist or aid in writing, printing, uttering or publishing any false, scandalous and malicious writing or writings against the government of the United States, or either house of the Congress of the United States, or the President of the United States, with intent to defame the said government, or either house of the said Congress, or the said President or to bring them, or either of them, into contempt or disrepute; or to excite against them, or either or any of them, the hatred of the good people of the United States, or to stir up sedition within the United States, or to excite any unlawful combinations therein, for opposing or resisting any law of the United States, or any act of the President of the United States, done in pursuance of any such law, or of the powers in him vested by the constitution of the United States, or to resist, oppose, or defeat any such law or act, or to aid, encourage or abet any hostile designs of any foreign nation against the United States, their people or government, then such person, being thereof convicted before any court of the United States having jurisdiction thereof, shall be punished by a fine not exceeding two thousand dollars, and by imprisonment not exceeding two years.

SEC. 3. That if any person shall be prosecuted under this act, for the writing or publishing any libel aforesaid, it shall be lawful for the defendant, upon the trial of the cause, to give in evidence in his defence, the truth of the matter contained in the publication charged as a libel. And the jury who shall try the cause, shall have a right to determine the law and the fact, under the direction of the court, as in other cases.

SEC. 4. That this act shall continue to be in force until March 3, 1801, and no longer.

Questions

1. Compare the Sedition Act with the First Amendment to the Constitution. Did the Sedition Act violate the First Amendment? Why or why not?

2. Did Section 3 of the Sedition Act offer special protection for those who commented on politics? Why or why not?

3. What is the significance of the fact that the Sedition Act, passed by a Federalist-dominated Congress, would expire on March 3, 1801? (*Hint:* Read the headnote to Document 7-6.) What does this tell you about the Federalists who championed the Sedition Act?

7-5   The Kentucky Resolutions (1798)

Thomas Jefferson

In the spring of 1798, partisan conflict reached new heights when the Federalist-dominated Congress passed the Alien and Sedition Acts (see text pp. 211–212) in order to silence Republican critics of John Adams's administration. Republicans were outraged by these repressive laws and sought to address their grievances in the state legislatures. In the ensuing months, Thomas Jefferson and James Madison coordinated their public responses to the offending pieces of legislation. The Virginia Resolutions, penned by Madison, and the Kentucky Resolutions, written by Jefferson and excerpted here, called on the states to declare the Alien and Sedition Acts unconstitutional and thus collectively to check the abuse of power on the part of the federal government. Jefferson's resolutions and the debate over the Alien and Sedition Acts set the stage for the upcoming presidential election in 1800.

Source: From Paul Leicester Ford, ed., *The Federalist: A Commentary on the Constitution of the United States* (New York: Henry Holt, 1898), 679–683.

Resolved, That the several states composing the United States of America, are not united on the principle of unlimited submission to their general government; but that by compact, under the style and title of a Constitution for the United States, and of amendments thereto, they constituted a general government for special purposes, delegated to that government certain definite powers, reserving, each state to itself, the residuary mass of right to their own self-government; and that whensoever the general government assumes undelegated powers, its acts are unauthoritative, void, and of no force: That to this compact each state acceded as a state, and in an integral party, its co-states forming as to itself, the other party: That the government created by this compact was not made the exclusive or final *judge* of the extent of the powers delegated to itself; since that would have made its discretion, and not the Constitution, the measure of its powers; but that, as in all other cases of compact among parties having no common judge, each party has an equal right to judge for itself, as well of infractions, as of the mode and measure of redress.

Resolved, That it is true as a general principle, and is also expressly declared by one of the amendments to the Constitution, that "the powers not delegated to the United States by the Constitution, nor prohibited by it to the States, are reserved to the states respectively, or to the people"; and that no power over the freedom of religion, freedom of speech, or freedom of the press, being delegated to the United States by the Constitution, nor prohibited by it to the states, all lawful powers respecting the same did of right remain, and were reserved to the states, or to the people; that thus was manifested their determination to retain to themselves the right of judging how far the licentiousness of speech and of the press may be abridged without lessening their useful freedom, and how far those abuses which cannot be separated from their use, should be tolerated rather than the use be destroyed; and thus also they guarded against all abridgment by the United States of the freedom of religious opinions and exercises, and retained to themselves the right of protecting the same, as this state by a law passed on the general demand of its citizens, had already protected them from all human restraint or interference: and that in addition to this general principle and express declaration, another and more special provision has been made by one of the amendments to the Constitution, which expressly declares, that "Congress shall make no law respecting an establishment of religion, or prohibiting the free exercise thereof, or abridging the freedom of speech, or of the press," thereby guarding in the same sentence, and under the same words, the freedom of religion, of speech, and the press, insomuch, that whatever violates either, throws down the sanctuary which covers the others, and that libels, falsehoods, and defamations, equally with heresy and false religion, are withheld from the cognizance of federal tribunals: that therefore the act of the Congress of the United States, passed on the 14th day of July, 1798, entitled, "an act in addition to the act for the punishment of certain crimes against the United States," which does abridge the freedom of the press, is not law, but is altogether void and of no effect.

Resolved, That alien-friends are under the jurisdiction and protection of the laws of the state wherein they are; that no power over them has been delegated to the United States, nor prohibited to the individual states distinct from their power over citizens; and it being true as a general principle, and one of the amendments to the Constitution having also declared, that "the powers not delegated to the United States by the Constitution, nor prohibited by it to the states, are re-

served to the states respectively, or to the people," the act of the Congress of the United States, passed on the 22d day of June, 1798, entitled "an act concerning aliens," which assumes power over alien-friends not delegated by the Constitution, is not law, but is altogether void and of no force.

Resolved, That in addition to the general principle as well as the express declaration, that powers not delegated are reserved, another and more special provision inserted in the Constitution, from abundant caution, has declared, "that the *migration* or importation of such persons as any of the states now existing shall think proper to admit, shall not be prohibited by the Congress prior to the year 1808": that this commonwealth does admit the migration of alien-friends described as the subject of the said act concerning aliens; that a provision against prohibiting their migration, is a provision against all acts equivalent thereto, or it would be nugatory; that to remove them when migrated, is equivalent to a prohibition of their migration, and is therefore contrary to the said provision of the Constitution, and void.

Resolved, That the imprisonment of a person under the protection of the laws of this commonwealth, on his failure to obey the simple *order* of the President, to depart out of the United States, as is undertaken by the said act, entitled "an act concerning aliens," is contrary to the Constitution, one amendment to which has provided, that "no person shall be deprived of liberty without the due process of law," and that another having provided, "that in all criminal prosecutions, the accused shall enjoy the right to a public trial by an impartial jury, to be informed of the nature and cause of the accusation, to be confronted with the witnesses against him, to have compulsory process for obtaining witnesses in his favor, and to have the assistance of counsel for his defense," the same act undertaking to authorize the President to remove a person out of the United States, who is under the protection of the law, on his own suspicion, without accusation, without jury, without public trial, without confrontation of the witnesses against him, without having witnesses in his favor, without defense, without counsel, is contrary to these provisions, also, of the Constitution, is therefore not law, but utterly void and of no force.

Resolved, That the preceding resolutions be transmitted to the senators and representatives in Congress from this commonwealth, who are hereby enjoined to present the same to their respective houses, and to use their best endeavors to procure, at the next session of Congress, a repeal of the aforesaid unconstitutional and obnoxious acts.

Resolved, lastly, . . . that the friendless alien has indeed been selected as the safest subject of a first experiment; but the citizen will soon follow, or rather has already followed; for, already has a sedition-act marked him as its prey: that these and successive acts of the same character, unless arrested on the threshold, may tend to drive these states into revolution and blood, and will furnish new calumnies against republican governments, and new pretexts for those who wish it to be believed, that man cannot be governed but by a rod of iron: that it would be a dangerous delusion, were a confidence in the men of our choice, to silence our fears for the safety of our rights: that confidence is everywhere the parent of despotism; free government is founded in jealousy, and not in confidence; it is jealousy and not confidence which prescribes limited constitutions to bind down those whom we are obliged to trust with power: that our Constitu- tion has accordingly fixed the limits to which and no further our confidence may go; and let the honest advocate of confi- dence read the alien and sedition acts, and say if the Consti- tution has not been wise in fixing limits to the government it created, and whether we should be wise in destroying those limits?

Questions

1. According to Jefferson, who or what agency of government was authorized to rule on the constitutionality of federal actions? How were federal laws to be declared "void and of no force"?

2. What did Jefferson mean by the declaration, "free government is founded in jeal- ousy, and not in confidence"?

3. What remedy did Jefferson propose? What did he propose be done with the voided laws? Why is this important?

7-6   First Inaugural Address (1801)

Thomas Jefferson

The 1800 presidential election was the first one marked by especially vicious mudslinging (see text p. 211). However, by that time it was clear that the vision associated with the Re- publican Party headed by Thomas Jefferson had gained ascendancy. The Federalist Party was in fact disintegrating. Ironically, when a mix-up among the Republicans unexpectedly threw the election into the House of Representatives, Alexander Hamilton championed Thomas Jefferson, his longtime rival, rather than let Aaron Burr become president. Hamilton opposed Burr in part because he considered Burr a scoundrel. However, Hamilton also supported Jefferson because he believed that Jefferson as president would follow a more moderate course than would Jefferson as Republican Party leader. The first proof of how perceptive Hamilton was became clear on March 4, 1801, when Jefferson de- livered his stunning first inaugural address, which is reprinted here in full. In 1801, as in the Declaration of Independence of 1776, Jefferson defined the American republic as a government based on both majority rule and minority rights, with laws that treated citi- zens equally and respected their liberty.

Source: From James D. Richardson, ed., *A Compilation of the Messages and Papers of the Presidents* (Washington, DC: U.S. Government Printing Office, 1913), 1:309–312.

Friends and Fellow-Citizens.

Called upon to undertake the duties of the first executive of- fice of our country, I avail myself of the presence of that por- tion of my fellow-citizens which is here assembled to express my grateful thanks for the favor with which they have been pleased to look toward me, to declare a sincere consciousness that the task is above my talents, and that I approach it with those anxious and awful presentiments which the greatness of the charge and the weakness of my powers so justly in- spire. A rising nation, spread over a wide and fruitful land, traversing all the seas with the rich productions of their in- dustry, engaged in commerce with nations who feel power and forget right, advancing rapidly to destinies beyond the reach of mortal eye—when I contemplate these transcen- dent objects, and see the honor, the happiness, and the hopes of this beloved country committed to the issue and the aus- pices of this day, I shrink from the contemplation, and humble myself before the magnitude of the undertaking. Ut- terly, indeed, should I despair did not the presence of many whom I here see remind me that in the other high authori- ties provided by our Constitution I shall find resources of wisdom, of virtue, and of zeal on which to rely under all dif- ficulties. To you, then, gentlemen, who are charged with the sovereign functions of legislation, and to those associated with you, I look with encouragement for that guidance and support which may enable us to steer with safety the vessel in which we are all embarked amidst the conflicting elements of a troubled world.

During the contest of opinion through which we have passed the animation of discussions and of exertions has sometimes worn an aspect which might impose on strangers unused to think freely and to speak and to write what they think; but this being now decided by the voice of the nation, announced according to the rules of the Constitution, all will, of course, arrange themselves under the will of the law, and unite in common efforts for the common good. All, too, will bear in mind this sacred principle, that though the will of the majority is in all cases to prevail, that will to be rightful must be reasonable; that the minority possess their equal rights, which equal law must protect, and to violate would be oppression. Let us, then, fellow-citizens, unite with one heart and one mind. Let us restore to social intercourse that harmony and affection without which liberty and even life itself are but dreary things. And let us reflect that, having banished from our land that religious intolerance under which mankind so long bled and suffered, we have yet gained little if we countenance a political intolerance as despotic, as wicked, and capable of as bitter and bloody persecutions. During the throes and convulsions of the ancient world, during the agonizing spasms of infuriated man, seeking through blood and slaughter his long-lost liberty, it was not wonderful that the agitation of the billows should reach even this distant and peaceful shore; that this should be more felt and feared by some and less by others, and should divide opinions as to measures of safety. But every difference of opinion is not a difference of principle. We have called by different names brethren of the same principle. We are all Republicans, we are all Federalists. If there be any among us who would wish to dissolve this Union or to change its republican form, let them stand undisturbed as monuments of the safety with which error of opinion may be tolerated where reason is left free to combat it. I know, indeed, that some honest men fear that a republican government can not be strong, that this Government is not strong enough; but would the honest patriot, in the full tide of successful experiment, abandon a government which has so far kept us free and firm on the theoretic and visionary fear that this Government, the world's best hope, may by possibility want energy to preserve itself? I trust not. I believe this, on the contrary, the strongest Government on earth. I believe it the only one where every man, at the call of the law, would fly to the standard of the law, and would meet invasions of the public order as his own personal concern. Sometimes it is said that man can not be trusted with the government of himself. Can he, then, be trusted with the government of others? Or have we found angels in the forms of kings to govern him? Let history answer this question.

Let us, then, with courage and confidence pursue our own Federal and Republican principles, our attachment to union and representative government. Kindly separated by nature and a wide ocean from the exterminating havoc of one quarter of the globe; too high-minded to endure the degrada-

tions of the others; possessing a chosen country, with room enough for our descendants to the thousandth and thousandth generation; entertaining a due sense of our equal right to the use of our own faculties, to the acquisitions of our own industry, to honor and confidence from our fellow-citizens, resulting not from birth, but from our actions and their sense of them; enlightened by a benign religion, professed, indeed, and practiced in various forms, yet all of them inculcating honesty, truth, temperance, gratitude, and the love of man; acknowledging and adoring an overruling Providence, which by all its dispensations proves that it delights in the happiness of man here and his greater happiness hereafter—with all these blessings, what more is necessary to make us a happy and a prosperous people? Still one thing more, fellow-citizens—a wise and frugal Government, which shall restrain men from injuring one another, shall leave them otherwise free to regulate their own pursuits of industry and improvement, and shall not take from the mouth of labor the bread it has earned. This is the sum of good government, and this is necessary to close the circle of our felicities.

About to enter, fellow-citizens, on the exercise of duties which comprehend everything dear and valuable to you, it is proper you should understand what I deem the essential principles of our Government, and consequently those which ought to shape its Administration. I will compress them within the narrowest compass they will bear, stating the general principle, but not all its limitations. Equal and exact justice to all men, of whatever state or persuasion, religious or political; peace, commerce, and honest friendship with all nations, entangling alliances with none; the support of the State governments in all their rights, as the most competent administrations for our domestic concerns and the surest bulwarks against antirepublican tendencies; the preservation of the General Government in its whole constitutional vigor, as the sheet anchor of our peace at home and safety abroad; a jealous care of the right of election by the people—a mild and safe corrective of abuses which are lopped by the sword of revolution where peaceable remedies are unprovided; absolute acquiescence in the decisions of the majority, the vital principle of republics, from which is no appeal but to force, the vital principle and immediate parent of despotism; a well-disciplined militia, our best reliance in peace and for the first moments of war, till regulars may relieve them; the supremacy of the civil over the military authority; economy in the public expense, that labor may be lightly burthened; the honest payment of our debts and sacred preservation of the public faith; encouragement of agriculture, and of commerce as its handmaid; the diffusion of information and arraignment of all abuses at the bar of the public reason; freedom of religion; freedom of the press, and freedom of person under the protection of the habeas corpus, and trial by juries impartially selected. These principles form the bright constellation which has gone before us and guided our steps through an age of revolution and reformation. The wisdom of our sages and blood of our heroes have been devoted to their attainment. They should be the creed of our political faith, the text of civic instruction, the touchstone by which to try the services of those we trust; and should we wander from them in moments of error or of alarm, let us hasten to retrace our steps and to regain the road which alone leads to peace, liberty, and safety.

I repair, then, fellow-citizens, to the post you have assigned me. With experience enough in subordinate offices to have seen the difficulties of this the greatest of all, I have learnt to expect that it will rarely fall to the lot of imperfect man to retire from this station with the reputation and the favor which bring him into it. Without pretensions to that high confidence you reposed in our first and greatest revolutionary character, whose preeminent services had entitled him to the first place in his country's love and destined for him the fairest page in the volume of faithful history, I ask so much confidence only as may give firmness and effect to the legal administration of your affairs. I shall often go wrong through defect of judgment. When right, I shall often be thought wrong by those whose positions will not command a view of the whole ground. I ask your indulgence for my own errors, which will never be intentional, and your support against the errors of others, who may condemn what they would not if seen in all its parts. The approbation implied by your suffrage is a great consolation to me for the past, and my future solicitude will be to retain the good opinion of those who have bestowed it in advance, to conciliate that of others by doing them all the good in my power, and to be instrumental to the happiness and freedom of all.

Relying, then, on the patronage of your good will, I advance with obedience to the work, ready to retire from it whenever you become sensible how much better choice it is in your power to make. And may that Infinite Power which rules the destinies of the universe lead our councils to what is best, and give them a favorable issue for your peace and prosperity.

Questions

1. According to Jefferson, why might some observers have misread the presidential election of 1800? Do you agree with his observations? Why or why not?

2. According to Jefferson, what is the "sacred principle" of American constitutional government?

3. Did the members of the Federalist Party have good reason to applaud Jefferson for his proclamation of that sacred principle? Why or why not?

4. According to Jefferson, what are "the essential principles of our Government"? Would Alexander Hamilton (Document 7-1) generally agree or disagree with Jefferson's assertions? Why or why not?

Questions for Further Thought

1. Do these documents support or challenge the analysis offered by James Madison in *The Federalist* No. 10 (Document 6-20)? Why or why not?

2. On the basis of the documents produced by Hamilton (7-1), Jefferson (7-5 and 7-6), and Washington (7-2), what term — *political ideologue* or *political pragmatist* — would you apply to each of these men? Why did you assign those terms?

3. On the basis of the documents produced by Hamilton (7-1), Jefferson (7-5 and 7-6), and Washington (7-2), would you call any of those men a political idealist? Why or why not?

The Westward Movement and the Jeffersonian Revolution

From its inception, the United States controlled vast territories stretching westward to the Mississippi River. By 1790 farming settlements extended into the western parts of New York, Pennsylvania, and Georgia, crossing or skirting the Appalachian Mountains into parts of Tennessee and Kentucky. The lure of the West was strong among land speculators and farmer-settlers (Document 7-7), but Indian nations west of the Appalachians—the Miami, Shawnee, Creek, Cherokee, Chickasaw, and Choctaw, among others—remained strong and resisted American encroachment. Under Presidents George Washington and Thomas Jefferson, a more orderly, sophisticated policy to promote Indian removal was developed (Documents 7-8 and 7-9); but warfare east of the Mississippi, notably with the Creek and the Shawnee leader Tecumseh, continued through the War of 1812.

The character of western settlement varied considerably by latitude. The earliest western lands to be settled were in Kentucky and Tennessee, where yeomen farmers from the Chesapeake and the southern backcountry began extending settlements even before the Revolution (Document 7-10). To the south, in the future states of Alabama, Mississippi, and Louisiana, a very different sort of westward expansion took hold as southern planters, eager to profit from a lucrative new crop, cotton, snapped up the most suitable lands and settled them with slaves, many of whom were imported directly from Africa before Congress closed American ports to the transatlantic slave trade in 1808. To the north, New Englanders pressed westward from their overcrowded towns and stony farms into western New York and northern Ohio, carrying their distinctive culture along with them.

Life in the West was rude and isolated (Document 7-10). The barrier formed by the Appalachians made trade and communication with the settled East difficult and costly. The Mississippi River and its tributaries, notably the Ohio, afforded the best outlets, and the major early western trading towns—Cincinnati, Louisville, Pittsburgh, Saint Louis, and New Orleans—hugged their banks. However, downstream river traffic flowed away from major markets, and upstream traffic was difficult before the advent of the river steamboat in 1817. Accordingly, early western settlers were forced to live largely from their own produce and local exchange. The expansion of commerce in the West would await the "transportation revolution" of the years following 1820 (see Chapter 9).

7-7   Congressional Resolution on Western Lands (1800)

Wealthy speculators and poor farmer-settlers competed for control of western lands. Because speculators tended to be comfortable with the political processes through which land sales took place, they held the upper hand in this competition (see text pp. 220–221). But the demands of yeomen farmers for access to western lands created political pressure that could not be ignored by eastern politicians. As a groundswell of popular support built for Thomas Jefferson and his Democratic Republican Party, Congress passed the Land Act of 1800, which sharply reduced the minimum acreage offered for sale and provided liberal credit terms for the purchase of land (see text p. 220). In a series of resolutions Congress authorized the drafting of a new land act.

Source: From *Annals of the Congress of the United States, 1789–1824* (Washington, DC: U.S. Government Printing Office, 1799–1800), 6th Cong., 1st sess., 537–538.

The House resolved itself into a Committee of the Whole . . . to inquire whether any, and, if any, what, alterations are necessary in the laws providing for the sale of the lands of the United States Northwest of the Ohio; and, after some time spent therein, the Committee rose and reported several resolutions . . . as follows:

Resolved, That all the townships directed to be sold, either in quarter townships or in tracts of one mile square, by the act "providing for the sale of the lands of the United States, in the Territory Northwest of the river Ohio, and above the mouth of Kentucky river," shall be subdivided into half sections, containing, as nearly as may be, three hundred and twenty acres each: the additional expense of surveying to be paid by the purchasers, at the rate of three dollars per tract.

Resolved, That all the said lands shall be offered for sale at public sale, in tracts of three hun[d]red and twenty acres as above directed: *Provided,* That the same shall not be sold under the price of two dollars per acre, and that the sale shall be at the following places, to wit:

All the lands contained in the seven first ranges of townships, and north of the same, shall be offered for sale at Pittsburg[h].

All the lands contained in the eight next ranges of townships, shall be offered for sale at Marietta.

All the lands lying west of the fifteen first ranges of townships, and east of the Sciota river, shall be offered for sale at Chilicothe.

All the lands lying below the Great Miami shall be offered for sale at Cincinnati.

Resolved, That one or more land offices shall be opened in the Northwestern Territory, and that every person be permitted to locate and purchase at the rate of two dollars per acre, one or more of the half sections that shall not have been sold at public sale.

Resolved, That the payments for lands purchased either at public or private sale . . . shall be made in the following manner, and under the following conditions, viz:

1st. At the time of purchase, every purchaser shall deposit one-twentieth part of the amount of purchase money; to be forfeited, if, within three months, one-fourth of the purchase-money, including the said twentieth part, is not paid.

2d. One-fourth of the purchase-money to be paid as aforesaid, within three months, and the other three-fourths in three equal payments, within two, three, and four years, respectively, after the date of purchase.

3d. No interest to be charged in case of punctual payment; but interest at the rate of six per cent, a year, to be charged from the date of purchase, on any part of the purchase-money which shall not have been paid at the times, respectively, when the same shall have become due.

4th. A discount at the rate of eight per cent. a year, to be allowed on any of the three last payments, which shall be paid before the same shall have become due.

5th. If any tract shall not be completely paid [for] within one year after the date of the last payment, the tract to be sold in such manner as shall be provided by law; and after paying the balance due to the United States, including interest, the surplus, if any, to be returned to the original purchaser.

Ordered, That a bill or bills be brought in pursuant to the said resolutions. . . .

Questions

1. How much money did a farmer need to buy a farm under the terms of this proposed legislation?

2. Did some parts of the proposed legislation clearly favor speculators? Explain.

3. Why did Congress specify the locations for all land sales? Whose interest did this provision serve?

7-8   Proposed Indian Policy for the New Republic (1789)

Henry Knox

The period of the confederation saw increasing tension between American settlers and the native peoples living between the Appalachian Mountains and the Mississippi River. Americans insisted that the Treaty of 1783 with Great Britain gave the American states property rights to western lands under the right of conquest. European settlers and land speculators were eager to exploit these lands but faced mounting Indian resistance. While the states ceded control of the Northwest Territory to the confederation government, state governments continued to control western lands in the South, allowing whites to run roughshod over the indigenous inhabitants.

Worried about frontier instability and fearful of the financial, human, and moral cost of warfare with the Indians, George Washington and his secretary of war, Henry Knox (1750–1806), sought to develop a more orderly and, they thought, more humane approach to Indian affairs. Knox set forth his view of the general principles to be followed by the United States in the following 1789 message.

Source: Henry Knox to George Washington, July 7, 1789, in *American State Papers, Class II: Indian Affairs* (Washington, DC: Gales and Seaton, 1832), 1:52–54.

GEN. KNOX, SECRETARY OF WAR, TO THE PRESIDENT OF THE UNITED STATES, IN CONTINUATION.

The report of the 23d of May, 1789, on the treaties at fort Harmar, by the Governor of the Western Territory, and the paper Number 1, of the Indian Department, contain such a general statement of the circumstances relative to the Indian tribes, within the limits of the United States, northwest of the Ohio, as will probably render their situation sufficiently understood.

The numbers two, three, and four, comprehend a general view of the nations south of the Ohio.

But the critical situation of affairs between the State of Georgia and the Creek nation, requires a more particular consideration. In discussing this subject, it will appear that the interest of all the Indian nations south of the Ohio, as far as the same may relate to the whites, is so blended together as to render the circumstance highly probable, that, in case of a war, they may make it one common cause.

Although each nation or tribe may have latent causes of hatred to each other, on account of disputes of boundaries and game, yet when they shall be impressed with the idea that their lives and lands are at hazard, all inferior disputes will be accommodated, and an union as firm as the six Northern nations may be formed by the Southern tribes.

Their situation, entirely surrounded on all sides, leads naturally to such an union, and the present difficulties of the Creeks and Cherokees may accelerate and complete it. Already the Cherokees have taken refuge from the violence of the frontier people of North Carolina within the limits of the Creeks, and it may not be difficult for a man of Mr. [Creek leader Alexander] McGillivray's abilities to convince the Choctaws and Chickasaws that their remote situation is their only present protection; that the time must shortly arrive when their troubles will commence.

In addition to these causes, impelling to a general confederacy, there is another, of considerable importance—the policy of the Spaniards. The jealousy that Power entertains of the extension of the United States, would lead them into considerable expense to build up, if possible, an impassable barrier. They will, therefore, endeavor to form and cement such an union of the Southern Indians.

Mr. McGillivray has stated that Spain is bound by treaty to protect the Creeks in their hunting grounds. Although it may be prudent to doubt this assertion for the present, yet it is certain that Spain actually claims a considerable part of the territory ceded by Great Britain to the United States.

These circumstances require due weight in deliberating on measures to be adopted respecting the Creeks.

Although the case of the Creeks will be subject of legislative discussion and decisions, it may be supposed that, after due consideration, they will, in substance, adopt one or the other of the following alternatives, to wit:

1. That the national dignity and justice require that the arms of the Union should be called forth in order to chastise the Creek nation of Indians, for refusing to treat with the United States on reasonable terms, and for their hostile invasion of the State of Georgia; or,

2. That it appears to the Congress of the United States that it would be highly expedient to attempt to quiet the hostilities between the State of Georgia and the Creek Nation of Indians, by an amicable negotiation, and for that purpose there be a bill brought in to authorize the President of the United States to appoint three commissioners to repair to the State of Georgia, in order to conclude a peace with the said Creek nation and other nations of Indians to the southward of the Ohio, within the limits of the United States.

Supposing that any measure similar to either of the said alternatives should be adopted, it may be proper to examine into the manner which they are to be executed.

The most effectual mode of reducing the Creeks to submit to the will of the United States, and to acknowledge the validity of the treaties stated to have been made by the nation with Georgia, would be by an adequate army, to be raised and continued until the objects of the war should be accomplished.

When the force of the Creeks is estimated, and the probable combinations they might make with the other Indian nations, the army ought not to be calculated at less than 5,000 men. . . .

The following observations, resulting from a general view of the Indian department, are suggested with the hope, that some of them might be considered as proper principles to be interwoven in a general system, for the government of Indian affairs.

It would reflect honor on the new Government, and be attended with happy effects, were a declarative law to be passed, that the Indian tribes possess the right of the soil of all lands within their limits, respectively, and that they are not to be divested thereof, but in consequence of fair and bona fide purchases, made under the authority, or with the express approbation, of the United States.

As the great source of all Indian wars are disputes about their boundaries, and as the United States are, from the nature of the government, liable to be involved in every war that shall happen on this or any other account, it is highly proper that their authority and consent should be considered as essentially necessary to all measures for the consequences of which they are responsible.

No individual State could, with propriety, complain of invasion of its territorial rights. The independent nations and tribes of Indians ought to be considered as foreign nations, not as the subjects of any particular State. Each individual State, indeed, will retain the right of pre-emption of all lands within its limits, which will not be abridged; but the general sovereignty must possess the right of making all treaties, on the execution or violation of which depend peace or war.

Whatever may have been the conduct of some of the late British colonies, in their separate capacities toward the Indians, yet the same cannot be charged against the national character of the United States.

It is only since they possess the powers of sovereignty, that they are responsible for their conduct.

But, in future, the obligations of policy, humanity, and justice, together with that respect which every nation sacredly owes to its own reputation, unite in requiring a noble, liberal, and disinterested administration of Indian affairs.

Although the disposition of the people of the States, to emigrate into the Indian country, cannot be effectually prevented, it may be restrained and regulated.

It may be restrained, by postponing new purchases of Indian territory, and by prohibiting the citizens from intruding on the Indian lands.

It may be regulated, by forming colonies, under the direction of Government, and by posting a body of troops to execute their orders.

As population shall increase, and approach the Indian boundaries, game will be diminished, and new purchases may be made for small considerations. This has been, and probably will be, the inevitable consequence of cultivation.

It is, however, painful to consider, that all the Indian tribes, once existing in those States now the best cultivated and most populous, have become extinct. If the same causes continue, the same effects will happen; and, in a short period, the idea of an Indian on this side of the Mississippi will only be found in the page of the historian.

How different would be the sensation of a philosophic mind to reflect, that, instead of exterminating a part of the human race by our modes of population, we had persevered, through all difficulties, and at last had imparted our knowledge of cultivation and the arts of the aboriginals of the country, by which the source of future life and happiness had been preserved and extended. But it has been conceived to be impracticable to civilize the Indians of North America. This opinion is probably more convenient than just.

That the civilization of the Indians would be an operation of complicated difficulty; that it would require the highest knowledge of the human character, and a steady perseverance in a wise system for a series of years; cannot be doubted. But to deny that, under a course of favorable circumstances, it could not be accomplished, is to suppose the human character under the influence of such stubborn habits as to be incapable of melioration or change—a supposition entirely contradicted by the progress of society, from the barbarous ages to its present degree of perfection.

While it is contended that the object is practicable, under a proper system, it is admitted, in the fullest force, to be impracticable, according to the ordinary course of things, and that it could be effected in a short period.

Were it possible to introduce among the Indian tribes a love for exclusive property, it would be a happy commencement of the business.

This might be brought about by making presents, from time to time, to the chiefs or their wives, of sheep and other domestic animals; and if, in the first instance, persons were appointed to take charge, and teach the use of them, a considerable part of the difficulty would be surmounted.

In the administration of the Indians, every proper expedient that can be devised to gain their affections, and attach them to the interest of the Union, should be adopted. The British Government had the practice of making the Indians presents of silver medals and gorgets, uniform clothing, and a sort of military commission. The possessors retained an exclusive property to these articles; and the Southern Indians are exceedingly desirous of receiving similar gifts from the United States, for which they would willingly resign those received from the British officers. The policy of gratifying them cannot be doubted.

Missionaries, of excellent moral character, should be appointed to reside in their nation, who should be well supplied with all the implements of husbandry, and the necessary stock for a farm.

These men should be made the instruments to work on the Indians; presents should commonly pass through their hands, or by their recommendations. They should, in no degree, be concerned in trade, or the purchase of lands, to rouse the jealousy of the Indians. They should be their friends and fathers.

Such a plan, although it might not fully effect the civilization of the Indians, would most probably be attended with the salutary effect of attaching them to the interest of the United States.

It is particularly important that something of this nature should be attempted with the Southern nations of Indians, whose confined situation might render them proper subjects for the experiment.

The expense of such a conciliatory system may be considered as a sufficient reason for rejecting it; . . .

All which is humbly submitted to the President of the United States.

H. KNOX

WAR OFFICE, *July 7*, 1789.

Questions

1. Whom did Secretary of War Knox blame for the conflicts on the frontier—settlers or natives?

2. What was Knox's plan to reduce the Creek and other eastern tribes to "the will of the United States"? Would you classify his proposals as "humane"?

3. What, according to Knox, was the major stumbling block to the Indians' peaceful incorporation into U.S. society?

7-9   Message to Congress (January 18, 1803)

Thomas Jefferson   Thomas Jefferson (1743–1826), the third president of the United States, was one of the leading intellectual figures in the early republic. Jefferson's republican belief in the United States as a nation of independent yeomen farmers called for new lands for settlement. He shared the prevailing view that the barrier represented by Native Americans had to be removed one way or another. In the following message to Congress, Jefferson described the peaceful means by which he hoped to induce the Indians to sell their lands to the United States.

Source: From James D. Richardson, ed., *A Compilation of the Messages and Papers of the Presidents* (Washington, DC: U.S. Government Printing Office, 1908), 1:352–353.

The Indian tribes residing within the limits of the United States have for a considerable time been growing more and more uneasy at the constant diminution of the territory they occupy . . . and the policy has long been gaining strength with them of refusing absolutely all further sale on any condition. . . . In order peaceably to counteract this policy of theirs and to provide an extension of territory which the rapid increase of our numbers will call for, two measures are deemed expedient. First. To encourage them to abandon hunting, to apply [themselves] to the raising [of] stock, to agriculture, and domestic manufacture, and thereby prove to themselves that less land and labor will maintain them . . . better than in their former mode of living. The extensive forests necessary in the hunting life will then become useless, and they will see advantage in exchanging them for the means of improving their farms and of increasing their domestic comforts. Secondly. To multiply trading houses among them, and place within their reach those things which will contribute more to their domestic comfort than the possession of extensive but uncultivated wilds. . . . In leading them thus to agriculture, to manufactures, and civilization; in bringing together their and our sentiments, and

in preparing them ultimately to participate in the benefits of our Government, I trust and believe we are acting for their greatest good. . . . In one quarter this is particularly interesting . . . on the Mississippi . . . it is [desirable] to possess a respectable breadth of country . . . so that we may present as firm a front on that as on our eastern border. We possess what is below the Yazoo, and can probably acquire a certain breadth from the Illinois and Wabash to the Ohio; but between the Ohio and Yazoo the country all belongs to the Chickasaws, the most friendly tribe within our limits, but the most decided against the alienation of lands. The portion of their country most important for us is exactly that which they do not inhabit. Their settlements are not on the Mississippi, but in the interior country. They have lately shown a desire to become agricultural, and this leads to the desire of buying implements and comforts. In the strengthening and gratifying of these wants I see the only prospect of planting on the Mississippi itself the means of its own safety. Duty has required me to submit these views to the judgment of the Legislature, but as their disclosure might embarrass and defeat their effect, they are committed to the special confidence of the two Houses.

Questions

1. The United States claimed sovereignty over the Native American nations but recognized the Indians' ownership of the lands they traditionally occupied. How did Jefferson propose to overcome this difficulty?

2. Why did Jefferson believe that Native Americans would be better off with less land?

3. Why did Jefferson want his plans for the Indians—plans he said were "for their greatest good"—kept secret?

7-10   A Pioneer Woman in Post-Revolutionary Kentucky (1840s)

Jane Stevenson

In the 1840s and 1850s, a young Presbyterian minister, John D. Shane (1812–1864), began conducting interviews with the by-then-elderly generation of pioneer European settlers in the Ohio Valley. Among the oldest of his interviewees was a woman, Jane Stevenson, who had been born in 1750; she was past ninety when he recorded her story sometime in the early 1840s. After Shane died in 1864 his notebooks were acquired by Lyman Draper (1815–1891), a major collector and disseminator of lore about the early American West. The following interview, with editorial additions by Shane and Draper (in brackets), follows Stevenson's travels from her birthplace in the Shenandoah Valley, first to the Greenbriar Valley of what is now West Virginia and then over the Wilderness Road into

Kentucky. Stevenson's account is striking for its depiction of the rudeness and violence of life on the frontier, especially in the confrontation between settlers and Indians; the difficulty of travel; and the effort to build familiar institutions in a new country.

Source: From Elizabeth A. Perkins, *Border Life: Experience and Memory in the Revolutionary Ohio Valley* (Chapel Hill: University of North Carolina Press, 1998), 196–200. First published in *The Black Abolitionist Papers: Volume V: The United States, 1859–1865*, ed. C. Peter Ripley. Copyright © 1992 by the University of North Carolina Press. Used by permission of the publisher.

Jane Stevenson, wife of Samuel Stevenson, was born Nov. 15 — 1750, in Augusta County, Virginia.

The first fort I ever was in, a little girl was taken out of it, but from July to November older than me. She was but 7 years old. And was 7 years gone; untill [*sic*] Brocade's campaign [Draper: Bouquet's Campaign]. We walked out and got some haws. They, some of the company, pulled down the limbs, and handed us some of the haws. I wouldn't go any farther. And when I came, went into another cabin, wouldn't go into Mammy's, she would know I had been out. Presently the alarm came. They had gone about 200 yards further, and the Indians took them.

Where we lived was about 35 miles from Staunton. No Lexington then. The country was newly settled. Where Crawford was killed, was some 15 miles from Providence Meeting-house, down towards Staunton. Old Mr. John Brown preached there then. The men carried their guns to meeting, as regular as the congregation met. At Providence Meeting-house. The woman was told, bonie Alex.? Crawford was killed. Well said she, and indeed [Shane: Mr. C? or M? the lady or man who told her?] M [blank] he must take better care next time. This was a year or two after my mother was killed. I was only 9 or 10 then.

I was forted from the time I was 7 years old, 1757, and was never rid of the Indians till I moved to this place.

Carr's Creek was in about 7 miles of us. We were on the Calf-pasture. Mother was killed when I was about 8 years old. Mr. Crawford lived higher up towards Staunton than the Calf-pasture.

The settlement on Carr's Creek was taken twice [Draper: Carr's Creek Massacres]. The first time it was taken, Aunt escaped in the woods. Had but 2 children then, and while she escaped that way, the rout of the Indians was down the river.

The second time it was taken, I had an uncle and a cousin killed. This Aunt and her 3 children, were taken prisoners and carried to the towns. Two of the children died there. The remaining child was brought in at the treaty following Brocade's Campaign [Draper: Bouquet's]. Aunt wasn't brought in, and Uncle went out that same fall and brought her, but didn't get home till next March.

In less than 3 hours, in 2 hours, they killed and took 63 [Draper: Carr's Creek Massacre, 1763]. They no doubt had the ground all spied out. What they would do they knew. And then they came in like race horses. One Jim Milligan, who got away from them at the Ghanty [Draper: Gantey] Mountains, said the Indians there had 450 prisoners; that he

had counted as they passed along. These, besides what they had killed, and a parcel, who at the time were before, in a hunting company.

Two little boys, Jimmy Woods & Jimmy McClung were taken — they went to Staunton when they got back, and had their ears recorded.

The year the Indians took Carr's Creek settlement [Draper: 1763] a second time, they were greatly bad. Almost seemed as if they thought they would make their way to Williamsburgh that year. Shot the cows mightily with bows and arrows.

Simon Girty was from Virginia. He and old John Craig were schoolmates together in Virginia.

We moved to Greenbriar in 1775. The year after the battle of the Point. [Two sentences are struck out here.] There were but one or two families that were not dutch and half-dutch, in that whole settlement. [Shane: what settlement?] But never was a settlement of kinder people. They were great for dancing and singing. 1. William Hamilton. 2. Samuel McClung.

The hard winter was such in Virginia, as well as here.

When I started to Kentucky, I was 100 miles back from Daddy's. My father came from Ireland, when he was a boy. But then he lived on the frontier long before he was married.

John McKinney, the schoolmaster, came out with us. He was nearly killed at the Battle of the Point. We brought him out. We waited on the road a week or so, after we had left Greenbriar, for another family. Were about 2 weeks? getting to Blackamore's station.

We never travelled a Sunday, but one in Powell's Valley, about 5 miles till we came to a beautiful clear spring of water. It must have been 70 miles we travelled in Powell's valley, for we kept all that way down till we crossed at Cumberland ford.

The morning before we came to the ford of Clinch, (Blackamore's station was 10 miles beyond that,) these murders were committed. A mother and 4 children; in sight of the fort too. The husband was in the field, but escaped. A girl about half-grown, and 3 little boys tomahawked and scalped, who were talking while their brains were boiling out. The grandmother asked them if they saw their little brother? What had become of him? Said they didn't know. These were dutch people. We staid there good part of a day. Their Aunt sat on a stump, in sight of the fort, and cried all day.

Went by Blackamore's Station next day, and didn't see the smoke of a chimney after that we go to Boonesborough.

The pretty springs of water, and the woods, rendered Powell's Valley so exceedingly beautiful, I could have stopped very freely in it. A rock road all the way down, and mountains to one side of us.

Just before we got to the foot of the Cumberland Mountain, the company three-quarters of a mile ahead of us, had all their horses stolen. They could do nothing better than just turn their feather beds loose. They could do nothing with them. About their cattle? We never saw any Indians, and were not interrupted.

I was almost afraid coming down Cumberland Mountain. The place was narrow and rocky. Stood up on either side, not broader than a house. Woods more beautiful in Cumberland Valley than any other place.

We come to Lexington in October. [Draper: 1779?] It had been settled the previous April. There were every sort of people there, and that was what took us away. We had no notion of raising our children among that sort of people. Frances McConnell was the first man I knew when I got to Lexington. I had known the McConnells in Pennsylvania.

We went down to McConnell's station second April 1780. It was not settled till the day we went there. It took its name from Frances McConnell, and lay between Frances and William McConnell's places, & about between 1 & 1¼ miles from Lexington. Right where Royall's mill now is — on the rail-road. There was a grave yard there. James, Frances, and William McConnell, were cousins to Alexander and John McConnell.

Robert Edmiston, from Pennsylvania. Daniel Campbell, from Pennsylvania. William Hadden. John Brookey. All Presbyterians I think. All at the station were presbyterians, except two Mooneys, and they were raised presbyterians. John Nutt, Matthew Harper, John Stevenson, killed or taken at the Blue Licks from McConnell's station. [Shane: These 3.]

First summer we came out, Daddy stood sentry, while we milked. Things came on sooner that spring than ever I knew them. In the winter we were crowded. It was the continental war going on. (Safe for to be among Indians.) But as soon as warm weather came on, they put back.

Mr. Brookey didn't come out till the winter following. 1780–81. The first of March 1781, John Brookey went out to cut the first log to build his house. The Indians thought to take him. In the spring they would rather have a prisoner than a scalp. They shot him through the shoulder, and it came out in the hollow of his back. He was a very round shouldered man, and the bullet holes were 15 inches between the places. There was no doctor at the station. But he was taken care of and fed and nursed, on just what we had, and in 4 weeks was able to pick up an axe and hew. I was out, bringing in a pail of water, when I saw the Indians after Brookey. A parcel of children were out at the time; some here, some there. Some got in, and some hid in hollow logs. One so near the passing Indian, who didn't see him, that the boy could see his gun was empty. (lock down.)

The company from Lexington went out in a few minutes, (they heard the gun) and set their dogs on them. They had stripped, and left their clothes behind, in coming up to catch Brookey. Their things were all gotten; and one indian was wounded. The Indians had gotten within 60 yards of the

fort. When Brookey's tree had fallen, he heard a stick crack, and looking around, saw that the Indians had almost gotten between him and the fort.

After the first campaign to Ohio had gone out, John Haggin was in it, (this after Brookey's affair I think,) — one David Hunter determined to go the other side of the river, as a place of more secure safety. Before getting off however he had a dream — that either the women & children, or that he himself would be killed. Henderson. He came down to bid us goodbye, and seemed to stay and stay. He started, and was shot, just in the hollow, about half way between McConnell's station and Lexington.

One Mitchell, was the first that I knew killed by the Indians on the Wilderness road. That was in 1776. When they got back to the first stations on Powell's valley, in June? 1776, they found the place all deserted, and every thing standing, even to the milk-pails on the stumps, as if they had been abruptly forsaken. Mitchell was killed just on this side of the Cumberland Mountain.

[Jane Stevenson's husband, Samuel, apparently speaks up now] Benjamin Blackburn, William Elliott, and Samuel Stevenson, (my father) came out in April, and got back I think in June. Took Billy Campbell with them, whom they got at one Jimmy Gilmore's, over the Kentucky river. Campbell was a wheelwright by trade. He took a parcel of buffalo horns in a bag, to make spoons of. Daddy and Billy Elliott spelled him so as to enable him to get his bag in, by walking & letting him ride some. Blackburn was so stiff with fear, we could hardly get him along. Had to light his pipe for him two or three times a day.

Moses McElwaine, (so says Samuel Stevenson) was never taken but the once, (He has a son now living over in Ohio, back of Urbana) that was in 1779. Cartwright the surveyor was with him. This was in Clarke. One McCormick, that had known him when a boy in Ireland, was a trader among the Indians, and sent McIlvaine back. McCormick afterwards came with the company to the attack on Riddle's station, to avoid the imputation that he favored the Americans, and had sent away McElwaine. But said he never unloaded his gun.

Cartwright told McElwaine he had better not speak so loud, the Indians might be about. He thought there was no danger, untill his horse was shot under him. The horse fell on his leg. One of the Indians was going to kill him, but the other prevented, and showed the horse was holding his foot. He paid the Indian. McCormick afterwards came in, and he paid him.

Daniel Barton was taken over on North Elkhorn, a little beyond Georgetown, at the same time that Samuel Hodge was killed. That day, 12 months, to the very day, from the time he was taken, he returned.

White was killed at Todd's station, down on South Elkhorn, the day we left Lexington to go to McConnell's station. The boy, his son, that was with him, went to go home to his friends in Virginia, through the Wilderness, but took sick and died somewhere on the way, perhaps at Augusta, Virginia. Mrs. Blanchard, a daughter of that Mr. White.

Robert or Charles Knox, started to go on foot up to Lexington, and was killed before he got there. He lived at the upper, we at the lower end of the station, so I didn't see him when he started. He was shot in the thigh. The Indians took him off a piece, but found he could not travel, and shot him. We had moved down to McConnell's station but about a week.

Alexander McConnell had been out to kill a deer, and had skinned and swung it up. He then came in and borrowed a chestnut dun horse, having a white main and tail, of William McConnell, and went out to bring it in. Five Indians were on the look out. This horse was shot from under him, but fell on his leg, the one indian wanted to kill him but the other indian showed that only the horse was on his leg.—This was Thursday to Tuesday he was gone.—McConnell couldn't kill the indian that had saved his life twice. He was the other side of the log.—He got the indians cappo, blue, (in the night, & he wanted to be dark) and set his gun, and pipe, and tomahawk down.—I heard him tell the story many times, and he never varied a word of it.—Tuesday evening, about sundown, he came in. His wife ran out to meet him, but they had to carry her in, she fainted away, overjoyed.

They had killed the horse, and cut off the main and tail to dye for moccasin purposes, &c. They could make it any color, almost, they pleased.—He shot the two guns first. Then shot the others alternately, and both indians fell into the fire, and flared up the ashes and light.—It is said the place where this happened, was never improved, till some 4 or 5 years ago, and that then they discovered the guns. This somewhere a little below Limestone.

We raised 4 crops, and then moved out. That was in 1784. 80–81–82–83.

The first meeting house was built in 1785. Mr. Rankin gave us time about with Lexington. He preached at first out here in private houses. At Capt. William McConnell's. (No kin to the McConnell's at McConnell's station. This William McConnell moved to St. Louis a great while ago.) Here. McElvain's, & Samuel Kelly's. He came in the fall, and the next spring we raised the house. Elders—This Capt. McConnell, Samuel Kelly, Hugh Campbell, (moved afterwards to Missouri) and another.

Was 17 days in the harvest, and every day in the river. When a young woman. Swam the Cowpasture, 300 yards wide, many a time on my back.

[Shane:] Mr. Trabue of Scott Co., Ky., obtained of "Aunt Jane," information, such as was necessary in order to obtain a pension.

Questions

1. Jane Stevenson's childhood and young womanhood coincided with the French and Indian War and the American Revolution. How did those wars shape her experience on the frontier?

2. What characteristics of her fellow settlers did Stevenson typically find worthy of remark?

3. In reading this interview, what do you think Stevenson took the most pride in having achieved in her life?

Questions for Further Thought

1. What assumptions were shared by Congress (Document 7-7), Henry Knox (Document 7-8), and Thomas Jefferson (Document 7-9) with regard to the development of the western territories and the treatment of Native Americans?

2. How might Knox and Jefferson have responded to Jane Stevenson's story of frontier confrontations? What would they have found most commendable about the Stevensons and the other settlers?

3. Henry Knox proposed a policy aimed at "civilizing" the Indians. What was his definition of "civilization"? Did Jefferson employ the same definition?

The War of 1812 and the Transformation of Politics

During the presidential campaign of 1800, Federalists and Republicans alike argued that the very survival of the republic itself was at issue. Federalists charged that the Jeffersonians were "demagogues" intent on transporting the excesses of the French Revolution to

America, while Republicans countered that their opponents were "monarchists" and avowed enemies of popular sovereignty. Given the ideological context of the times, the political crises of the 1790s (see text pp. 208–212), the newness of the American experiment in republicanism, and the absence of the idea of a "loyal opposition," protagonists on each side were not simply mouthing political propaganda; they earnestly believed what they said. Hence, Jefferson insisted that his electoral victory was "as real a revolution in the principles of our government as that of 1776 was in its form." Federalists, however, were alarmed, and John Adams tried to salvage the situation through a series of lame-duck judicial appointments. Jefferson, stung by these "midnight" appointments and determined to undo the "harm" caused by Adams, ordered a halt to the delivery of the commissions to these judges. The result was a landmark Supreme Court case (Document 7-11).

In his inaugural address, Jefferson spoke of an American empire "with room enough for our descendants to the thousandth and thousandth generation" (see Document 7-6). Clearly, he was not alluding to the United States as it stood in 1801; the "chosen country" he envisioned encompassed "all America, North and South." The Louisiana Purchase in 1803 fell squarely in line with this expansive vision of an "empire of liberty," and Jefferson, eager to assert American control over the territory, commissioned Meriwether Lewis and William Clark to explore the new domain, collect ethnographic information, and establish commercial and political relations with its Indian populations (Document 7-12).

While the Louisiana Purchase removed an immediate threat to Jeffersonian policy, the resumption of hostilities between Great Britain and France in 1803 posed even greater problems. Both belligerents refused to honor the neutrality of the United States and began to seize American vessels entering "hostile" waters. Jefferson, who believed in the power of commercial diplomacy, that is, in using American commerce as a weapon in settling international affairs, imposed a trade embargo in 1807. Rather than gaining the ends Jefferson sought, however, the embargo resulted only in economic dislocation and the rejuvenation of the moribund Federalist party (Document 7-13). In addition to coping with the effects of the failed embargo, James Madison, Jefferson's successor, had to deal with the increasingly hostile Creeks in the Southeast and the Western Confederacy led by the Shawnee Tecumseh and his brother Tenskwatawa (Document 7-14). These tensions—with the British on the high seas and with the Indians in the West—culminated in the War of 1812.

In general, the war went poorly for the United States, and New England Federalists, who had opposed the war from the outset, were determined to be heard. Meeting in Hartford, Connecticut, twenty-six delegates from Massachusetts, Connecticut, Rhode Island, and four counties in New Hampshire and Vermont drafted a set of resolutions to present in Washington (Document 7-15). Unfortunately for the Hartford delegation, the timing of their arrival in the nation's capital could not have been worse. News of the Treaty of Ghent ending the war and reports of a stunning American victory in the Battle of New Orleans preceded them. Although the treaty addressed none of the substantive issues that had led to war in the first place, and although the action at New Orleans came two weeks after the Ghent treaty and therefore played no role whatsoever in ending the war, the Federalists never recovered from charges of sedition and treason that came to be associated with the Hartford Convention. In the 1816 elections, the Federalist Party was in disarray; by 1820, it had disappeared.

7-11   Decision in *Marbury v. Madison* (1803)

John Marshall

In February 1801, the outgoing Federalist-controlled Congress passed the Judiciary Act, which increased the number of circuit judges and justices of the peace in the federal judiciary. President John Adams named staunch Federalists to the host of newly created positions just before leaving office. These so-called midnight appointments stung the incoming president, Thomas Jefferson. John Marshall, Adams's secretary of state but also himself a midnight appointment to the Supreme Court, failed to deliver all of the judicial commissions before he left office, and Jefferson promptly ordered James Madison, the new secretary of state, to halt any further deliveries. One of those affected by the president's order was William Marbury, whose signed and sealed appointment as justice of the peace for the District of Columbia was effectively tabled. Marbury petitioned the Supreme Court, claiming that he had been deprived of his rightful property (his job) and asking the Court to issue a writ of mandamus to compel Madison to deliver the commission in question. Marbury's suit placed Marshall, now the chief justice, in a bind. If the Supreme Court issued a writ of mandamus and the executive branch ignored it, Marshall would have no way of enforcing the writ. On the other hand, if the Court rejected Marbury's petition, it would in effect be vindicating Jefferson's position. In February 1803, Marshall issued the unanimous decision, excerpted here, which established the precedent of the Court's judicial review.

Source: Marbury v. Madison, 5 U.S. 137 (1803).

. . . Marshall, C. J. . . . The peculiar delicacy of this case, the novelty of some of its circumstances, and the real difficulty attending the points which occur in it, require a complete exposition of the principles on which the opinion to be given by the court is founded. . . .

In the order in which the court has viewed this subject, the following questions have been considered and decided:

1st. Has the applicant a right to the commission he demands?

2dly. If he has a right, and that right has been violated, do the laws of his country afford him a remedy?

3rdly. If they do afford him a remedy, is it a mandamus issuing from this court?

. . . The first object of enquiry is,

Has the applicant a right to the commission he demands? . . .

It is therefore decidedly the opinion of the court, that when a commission has been signed by the President, the appointment is made; and that the commission is complete, when the seal of the United States has been affixed to it by the secretary of state. . . .

Mr. Marbury, then, since his commission was signed by the President, and sealed by the secretary of state, was appointed; and as the law creating the office, gave the officer a right to hold for five years, independent of the executive, the appointment was not revocable; but vested in the officer legal rights, which are protected by the laws of his country.

To withhold his commission, therefore, is an act deemed by the court not warranted by law, but violative of a vested legal right.

This brings us to the second enquiry; which is,

If he has a right, and that right has been violated, do the laws of his country afford him a remedy? . . .

The government of the United States has been emphatically termed a government of laws, and not of men. It will certainly cease to deserve this high appellation, if the laws furnish no remedy for the violation of a vested legal right.

. . . It is, then, the opinion of the Court,

1st. That by signing the commission of Mr. Marbury, the president of the United States appointed him a justice of peace for the county of Washington in the District of Columbia; and that the seal of the United States, affixed thereto by the secretary of state, is conclusive testimony of the verity of the signature, and of the completion of the appointment; and that the appointment conferred on him a legal right to the office for the space of five years.

2ndly. That, having this legal title to the office, he has a consequent right to the commission; a refusal to deliver which, is a plain violation of that right, for which the laws of his country afford him a remedy.

It remains to be enquired whether,

3rdly. He is entitled to the remedy for which he applies. This depends on

1st. The nature of the writ applied for, and

2dly. The power of this court. . . .

This, then, is a plain case for a mandamus, either to deliver the commission, or a copy of it from the record; and it only remains to be enquired,

Whether it can issue from this court.

The act to establish the judicial courts of the United States [Judiciary Act of 1789] authorizes the supreme court "to issue writs of mandamus, in cases warranted by the principles and usages of law, to any courts appointed, or persons holding office, under the authority of the United States."

The secretary of state, being a person holding an office under the authority of the United States is precisely within the letter of the description; and if this court is not authorized to issue a writ of mandamus to such an officer, it must be because the law is unconstitutional, and therefore absolutely incapable of conferring the authority and assigning the duties which its words purport to confer and assign.

The authority . . . given to the supreme court, by the act establishing the judicial courts of the United States, to issue writs of mandamus to public officers, appears not to be warranted by the constitution; and it becomes necessary to inquire whether a jurisdiction so conferred can be exercised.

The question whether an act repugnant to the constitution can become the law of the land, is a question deeply interesting to the United States; but, happily not of an intricacy porportioned to its interest. It seems only necessary to recognize certain principles supposed to have been long and well established, to decide it. . . .

Certainly all those who have framed written constitutions contemplate them as forming the fundamental and paramount law of the nation, and consequently the theory of every such government must be that an act of the legislature repugnant to the Constitution is void. . . .

It is emphatically the province and duty of the judicial department to say what the law is. Those who apply the rule to particular cases must of necessity expound and interpret that rule. If two laws conflict with each other, the courts must decide on the operation of each. . . .

The judicial power of the United States is extended to all cases arising under the constitution.

Questions

1. How did the Supreme Court decide on the facts of the case? According to Marshall, did Marbury have a right to the commission?

2. The Court did not issue a writ of mandamus, but it also rejected Jefferson's position. How could it do both? How was Marshall able to enhance the power of the Supreme Court while refusing to issue a writ in this case?

3. Given the fact that Marshall was himself a midnight appointment and that his failure to deliver all of the judicial commissions was the basis of Marbury's suit in the first place, was he caught in a conflict of interest? Explain.

7-12   The Journals of the Lewis and Clark Expedition (1804–1806)

Meriwether Lewis

Shortly after completing the Louisiana Purchase, President Jefferson commissioned two army captains, William Clark (the younger brother of the Revolutionary War hero George Rogers Clark) and Meriwether Lewis (Jefferson's personal secretary), to explore the new American territory. In the spring of 1804, Lewis and Clark led an expedition of twenty-five men up the Missouri River to present-day central North Dakota; in the spring of 1805, they followed the Missouri and Columbia Rivers west to the Pacific. The following spring they returned to their point of departure at St. Louis. In their journals the two men recorded a journey of discoveries as they encountered new flora and fauna as well as a rich variety of Native American cultures. In the following passages Lewis relates his encounter with the Shoshone in what is now Idaho, all the while recording careful observations on the strategic situation of the United States in the region.

Source: From Gary E. Moulton and Thomas W. Dunlay, eds., *The Journals of the Lewis and Clark Expedition*, 5:87–89, 91–92, 102–103. Copyright © 1988 by Gary E. Moulton and Thomas W. Dunlay. Used by permission of the University of Nebraska Press.

Wednesday, August 14th

. . . [T]he game which they principally hunt is the Antelope which they pursue on horseback and shoot with their arrows. this animal is so extremely fleet and dureable that a single horse has no possible chance to overtake them or run them down. the Indians are therefore obliged to have recorce to stratagem when they discover a herd of the Antelope they seperate and scatter themselves to the distance of five or six miles in different directions around them generally selecting some commanding eminence for a stand; some one or two now pursue the herd at full speed over the hills valleys gullies and the sides of precipices that are tremendious to view. thus after runing them from five to six or seven miles the fresh horses that were in the waiting head them and drive them back persuing them as far or perhaps further quite to the other extreem of the hunters who now in turn pursue on their fresh horses thus (finally) worrying the poor animal down and finally killing them with their arrows. forty or fifty hunters will be engaged for half a day in this manner and perhaps not kill more than two or three Antelopes. they have but few Elk or black tailed deer, and the common red deer they cannot take as they secrete themselves in the brush when pursued, and they have only the bow and arrow wich is a very slender dependence for killing any game except such as they can run down with their horses. I was very much entertained with a view of this indian chase; it was after a herd of about 10 Antelope and about 20 hunters. it lasted about 2 hours and considerable part of the chase in view from my tent. about 1 A.M. the hunters returned had not killed a single Antelope, and their horses foaming with sweat. my hunters returned soon after and had been equally unsuccessfull. I now directed McNeal to make me a little paist with the flour and added some berries to it which I found very pallateable.

The means I had of communicating with these people was by way of Drewyer who understood perfectly the common language of jesticulation or signs which seems to be universally understood by all the Nations we have yet seen. it is true that this language is imperfect and liable to error but is much less so than would be expected. the strong parts of the ideas are seldom mistaken.

I now prevailed on the Chief to instruct me with rispect to the geography of his country. this he undertook very cheerfully, by delienating the rivers on the ground. but I soon found that his information fell far short of my expectation or wishes. he drew the river on which we now are to which he placed two branches just above us, which he shewed me from the openings of the mountains were in view; he next made it discharge itself into a large river which flowed from the S. W. about ten miles below us, then continued this joint stream in the same direction of this valley or N. W. for one days march and then enclined it to the West for 2 more days march, here he placed a number of heeps of sand on each side which he informed me represented the vast mountains of rock eternally covered by snow through which the river passed. that the perpendicular and even juting rocks so closely hemned in the river that there was no possibilyte of passing along the shore; that the bed of the river was obstructed by sharp pointed rocks and the rapidity of the stream such that the whole surface of the river was beat into perfect foam as far as the eye could reach. that the mountains were also inaccessible to man or horse. he said that this being the state of the country in that direction that himself nor none of his nation had ever been further down the river than these mountains. I then enquired the state of the country on either side of the river but he could not inform me. he said there was an old man of his nation a days march below who could probably give me some information of the country to the N. W. and refered me to an old man then present for that to the S. W. — the Chief further informed me that he had understood from the persed nosed Indians who inhabit this river below the rocky mountains that it ran a great way toward the seting sun and finally lost itself in a great lake of water which was illy taisted, and where the white men lived. . . . I can discover that these people are by no means friendly to the Spaniard their complaint is, that the Spaniards will not let them have fire arms and amunition, that they put them off by telling them that if they suffer them to have guns they will kill each other, thus leaving them defenceless and an easy prey to their blood-thirsty neighbours to the East of them, who being in possession of fire arms hunt them up and murder them without rispect to sex or age and plunder them of their horses on all occasions. they told me that to avoid their enemies who were eternally harrassing them that they were obliged to remain in the interior of these mountains at least two thirds of the year where the[y] suffered as we then saw great heardships for the want of food sometimes living for weeks without meat and only a little fish roots and berries. but this added Cameahwait, with his ferce eyes and lank jaws grown meager for the want of food, would not be the case if we had guns, we could then live in the country of buffaloe and eat as our enimies do and not be compelled to hide ourselves in these mountains and live on roots and berries as the bear do. we do not fear our enimies when placed on an equal footing with them. I told them that the Minnetares Mandans & Recares of the Missouri had promised us to desist from making war on them & that we would indeavou to find the means of making the Minnetares of fort d Prarie or as they call them Pahkees desist from waging war against them also. that after our finally returning to our homes towards the rising sun whitemen would come to them with an abundance of guns and every other article necessary to their defence and comfort, and that they would be enabled to supply themselves with these articles on reasonable terms in exchange for the skins of the beaver Otter and Ermin so abundant in their country. they expressed great pleasure at this information and said they had been long anxious to see the whitemen that traded guns; and that we might rest assured of their friendship and that they would do whatever we wished them. . . .

. . . Drewyer who had had a good view of their horses estimated them at 400. most of them are fine horses. indeed many of them would make a figure of the South side of James River or the land of fine horses. — I saw several with spanish brands on them, and some mules which they informed me that they had also obtained from the Spaniards. I also saw a bridle bit of spanish manufactary, and sundry other articles which I have no doubt were obtained from the same source. notwithstanding the extreem poverty of those poor people they are very merry they danced again this evening untill midnight. each warrior keep one ore more horses tyed by a cord to a stake near his lodge both day and night and are always prepared for action at a moments warning. they fight on horseback altogether. I observe that the large flies are extreemly troublesome to the horses as well as ourselves. . . .

Friday, August 16th 1805.
I sent Drewyer and Shields before this morning in order to kill some meat as neither the Indians nor ourselves had any thing to eat. . . . after the hunters had been gone about an hour we set out. we had just passed through the narrows

when we saw one of the spies comeing up the level plain under whip, the chief pawsed a little and seemed somewhat concerned. I felt a good deel so myself and began to suspect that by some unfortunate accedent that perhaps some of there enimies had straggled hither at this unlucky moment; but we were all agreeably disappointed on the arrival of the young man to learn that he had come to inform us that one of the whitemen had killed a deer. in an instant they all gave their horses the whip and I was taken nearly a mile before I could learn what were the tidings; as I was without [s]tirrups and an Indian behind me the jostling was disagreeable. I therefore reigned up my horse and forbid the indian to whip him who had given him the lash at every jum for a mile fearing he should loose a part of the feast. the fellow was so uneasy that he left me the horse dismounted and ran on foot at full speed, I am confident a mile. when they arrived where the deer was which was in view of me they dismounted and ran in tumbling over each other like a parcel of famished dogs each seizing and tearing away a part of the intestens which had been previously thrown out by Drewyer who killed it; the seen was such when I arrived that had I not have had a pretty keen appetite myself I am confident I should not have taisted any part of the venison shortly. each one had a piece of some discription and all eating most ravenously. some were eating the kidneys the melt and liver and the blood running from the corners of their mouths, others were in a similar situation with the paunch and guts but the exuding substance in this case from their lips was of a different discription. one of the last who attracted my attention particularly had been fortunate in his allotment or reather active in the division, he had provided himself with about nine feet of the small guts one end of which he was chewing on while with his hands he was squezzing the contents out at the other. I really did not untill now think that human nature ever presented itself in a shape so nearly allyed to the brute creation. I viewed these poor starved divils with pity and compassion I directed McNeal to skin the deer and reserved a quarter, the ballance I gave the Chief to be divided among his people; they devoured the whole of it nearly without cooking.

Questions

1. Is the daily life of the western Indians as depicted in Lewis's journal entries what you expected? What challenges did both the Indians and the explorers face on the Plains?

2. What were the goals of the Lewis and Clark expedition? What information from the journals do you think that Thomas Jefferson was particularly interested in?

3. What do we learn about the balance of power in the West from the journals?

7-13 Jefferson and the Embargo (1808, 1809)

George Cruikshank, Peter Pencil

As Great Britain and France waged war in Europe, the United States found it increasingly difficult to remain neutral (see text pp. 222–224). In 1807 Thomas Jefferson devised the Embargo Act of 1807, which prohibited American ships from leaving port until both belligerents lifted their trade restrictions. While this approach provided a creative diplomatic solution, it was an economic disaster. Jefferson had overestimated France and Britain's reliance on American imports and underestimated the potential backlash from American farmers and merchants. Moreover, the issue fueled Federalist opposition as demands to repeal the embargo mounted.

The cartoons presented here satirize Jefferson's widely unpopular embargo. George Cruikshank's "The Happy Effects of that Grand System of Shutting Ports against the English!!" depicts Jefferson justifying his "Grand Philosophical Idea" to a group of disgruntled merchants, while Napoleon whispers to him, "You shall be King hereafter." Peter Pencil's "Intercourse or Impartial Dealings" shows Jefferson being taken advantage of by George III, who is bullying him into submission, and by Napoleon, who is picking his pocket.

Sources: George Cruikshank, "The Happy Effects of that Grand System of Shutting Ports against the English!!," 1808. Courtesy of the Monticello/Thomas Jefferson Foundation, Inc. Peter Pencil (pseud.), "Intercourse or Impartial Dealings," 1809. By permission of the Houghton Library, Harvard University.

(A) George Cruikshank, "The Happy Effects of that Grand System of Shutting Ports against the English!!"

196

(B) *Peter Pencil, "Intercourse or Impartial Dealings"*

Questions

1. What overall point about Jefferson, the man and the president, is being conveyed in these caricatures?

2. What is the significance of the depiction of Napoleon in these prints? What roles is he playing?

3. What is the relationship between Jefferson and Napoleon supposed to signify? In what ways is it a critique of the ongoing relationship between the Jeffersonian Republicans and France?

7-14   Speech to Tecumseh and the Prophet (1811) and Report to the Secretary of War (1814)

William Henry Harrison

William Henry Harrison would be elected president of the United States in 1840 largely because of his reputation as an Indian fighter. His nickname, "Tippecanoe," celebrated his victory over the followers of chief Tecumseh and his brother Tenskwatawa (the Prophet) at the Battle of Tippecanoe on November 7, 1811 (see text p. 224). As governor of the Indiana Territory, Harrison carried out the Democratic Republican policy of divesting Native Americans of their land (see Document 7-9). Tecumseh and Tenskwatawa formed a coalition to resist this policy of piecemeal dispossession. As Harrison warned in his speech to Tecumseh and the Prophet, he had assembled an army of seasoned Indian fighters. He soon moved them to Tippecanoe Creek near the hostile Indian encampment called Prophetstown. Convinced by the Prophet that they were invincible, the Indians swept into the American camp in the predawn darkness. But Harrison's men held their ground, formed a defensive line, and soon turned the Indians back with heavy losses.

Tecumseh's people abandoned Prophetstown (which Harrison subsequently burned) and, fighting in small bands, made war on settlers across the Northwest. During the War of 1812, Tecumseh joined forces with the British. At the Battle of the Thames on October 5, 1813 (see text p. 224), Harrison's forces decisively defeated the Indians and their British allies and killed Tecumseh. In his letter to the secretary of war, Harrison summarized the Democratic Republican Indian policy and his successes in implementing it.

Source: From Benjamin Drake, *Life of Tecumseh* (Cincinnati: E. Morgan & Co., 1841; facsimile reprint, New York: Arno Press and New York Times, 1969).

(a) Harrison to Tecumseh and the Prophet, June 24, 1811

Brothers,—Listen to me. I speak to you about matters of importance, both to the white people and yourselves; open your ears, therefore, and attend to what I shall say.

Brothers, this is the third year that all the white people in this country have been alarmed at your proceedings; you threaten us with war, you invite all the tribes in the north and west of you to join against us. . . .

Brothers, our citizens are alarmed, and my warriors are preparing themselves; not to strike you, but to defend themselves and their women and children. You shall not surprise us as you expect to do; you are about to undertake a vary rash act; as a friend, I advise you to consider well of it. . . . Do you really think that the handful of men that you have about you, are able to contend with the Seventeen Fires [the seventeen states then composing the United States], or even that the whole of the tribes united, could contend against the Kentucky Fire alone?

Brothers, I am myself of the long knife fire; as soon as they hear my voice, you will see them pouring forth their swarms of hunting shirt men, as numerous as the musquetoes [*sic*] on the shores of the Wabash; brothers, take care of their stings.

(b) Harrison to the Secretary of War, March 22, 1814

I received instruction from President Jefferson, shortly after his first election, to make efforts for extinguishing the Indian claims upon the Ohio, below the mouth of the Kentucky river, and to such other tracts as were necessary to connect and consolidate our settlements. It was at once determined, that the community of interests in the lands among the Indian tribes, which seemed to be recognized by the treaty of Greenville, should be objected to. . . . Care was taken . . . to place the title to such tracts as might be desireable to purchase . . . upon a footing that would facilitate the procuring of them, by getting the tribes who had no claim themselves, and who might probably interfere, to recognize the titles of those who were ascertained to posses [*sic*] them.

This was particularly the case with regard to the lands watered by the Wabash, which were declared to be the property of the Miamis, with the exception of the tract occupied by the Delawares on White river, which was to be considered the joint property of them and the Miamis. This arrangement was very much disliked by Tecumseh, and the banditti that he had assembled at Tippecanoe. He complained loudly, as well of the sales that had been made, as of the principle of considering a particular tribe as the exclusive proprietors of any part of the country, which he said the Great Spirit had given to all his red children. . . .

The question of the title to the lands south of the Wabash, has been thoroughly examined; every opportunity was afforded to Tecumseh and his party to exhibit their pretensions [land claims], and they were found to rest upon no other basis than that of their being the common property of all the Indians.

Questions

1. Why did Harrison expect his image of "swarms of hunting shirt men" to intimidate Tecumseh and the Prophet?

2. By what means did Harrison intend to extinguish Native American land claims along the Ohio River?

3. Why did Tecumseh protest against these methods and organize resistance to them?

7-15   Hartford Convention Resolutions (1814)

In 1814 the Federalist minority in Congress and the nation had good cause to complain about "Mr. Madison's war." Few of them had supported going to war against Britain in the first place; indeed, all forty Federalists in Congress in 1812 had opposed the war declaration, and subsequent disasters only confirmed their reservations. Proud claims of the United States' military prowess proved to be empty boasts once the fighting began. The British occupation of Washington, D.C., in August 1814, and the burning of the Capitol and the White House shocked the American public. Buoyed by the rising tide of discontent, the more radical elements of the Federalist Party in Massachusetts called for a general conference of New England states. Connecticut and Rhode Island joined Massachusetts in electing delegates to the proposed convention, but in New Hampshire and Vermont only selected counties chose to send representatives. In all, twenty-six men met at Hartford, Connecticut, from December 15, 1814, to January 5, 1815, and agreed to the following resolutions.

Source: From Paul Leicester Ford, ed., *The Federalist: A Commentary on the Constitution of the United States* (New York: Henry Holt, 1898), 687–689.

Therefore resolved.—That it be and hereby is recommended to the Legislatures of the several States represented in this Convention, to adopt all such measures as may be necessary effectually to protect the citizens of said States from the operation and effects of all acts which have been or may be passed by the Congress of the United States, which shall contain provisions, subjecting the militia or other citizens to forcible drafts, conscriptions, or impressments, not authorized by the Constitution of the United States.

Resolved.—That it be and hereby is recommended to the said Legislatures, to authorize an immediate and earnest application to be made to the Government of the United States, requesting their consent to some arrangement, whereby the said States may separately or in concert, be empowered to assume upon themselves the defense of their territory against the enemy; and a reasonable portion of the taxes, collected within said States, may be paid into the respective treasuries thereof, and appropriated to the payment of the balance due said States, and to the future defense of the same. The amount so paid into the said treasuries to be credited, and the disbursements made as aforesaid to be charged to the United States.

Resolved.—That it be, and it hereby is, recommended to the Legislatures of the aforesaid States, to pass laws (where it has not already been done) authorizing the Governors or Commanders in Chief of their militia to make detachments from the same, or to form voluntary corps, as shall be most convenient and conformable to their Constitutions, and to cause the same to be well armed, equipped and disciplined, and held in readiness for service; and upon the request of the Governor of either of the other States, to employ the whole of such detachment or corps, as well as the regular forces of the State, or such part thereof as may be required and can be spared consistently with the safety of the State, in assisting the State, making such request to repel any invasion thereof which shall be made or attempted by the public enemy.

Resolved.—That the following amendments of the Constitution of the United States, be recommended to the States as aforesaid, to be proposed by them for adoption by the State Legislatures, and, in such cases as may be deemed expedient, by a Convention chosen by the people of each State.

And it is further recommended, that the said States shall persevere in their efforts to obtain such amendments, until the same shall be effected.

First.—Representatives and direct taxes shall be apportioned among the several States which may be included within this union, according to their respective numbers of free persons, including those bound to serve for a term of years, and excluding Indians not taxed, and all other persons.

Second.—No new State shall be admitted into the union by Congress in virtue of the power granted by the Constitution, without the concurrence of two-thirds of both Houses.

Third.—Congress shall not have power to lay any embargo on the ships or vessels of the citizens of the United States, in the ports or harbors thereof, for more than sixty days.

Fourth.—Congress shall not have power, without the concurrence of two-thirds of both Houses, to interdict the commercial intercourse between the United States and any foreign nation or the dependencies thereof.

Fifth.—Congress shall not make or declare war, or authorize acts of hostility against any foreign nation, without the concurrence of two-thirds of both Houses, except such acts of hostility be in defense of the territories of the United States when actually invaded.

Sixth.—No person who shall hereafter be naturalized, shall be eligible as a member of the Senate or House of Representatives of the United States, nor capable of holding any civil office under the authority of the United States.

Seventh.—The same person shall not be elected President of the United States a second time; nor shall the President be elected from the same State two terms in succession.

Resolved.—That if the application of these States to the government of the United States, recommended in a foregoing Resolution, should be unsuccessful, and peace should not be concluded, and the defense of these States should be neglected, as it has been since the commencement of the war, it will in the opinion of this Convention be expedient for the Legislatures of the several States to appoint Delegates to another Convention, to meet at Boston, in the State of Massachusetts, on the third Thursday of June next, with such powers and instructions as the exigency of a crisis so momentous may require.

Questions

1. What was the reason for the resolution that would allow the New England states to defend themselves militarily? Were they inadequately protected during the War of 1812?

2. What were some of the problems targeted by the proposed amendments? For example, what provision of the Constitution was targeted by the first proposal? What would have happened in Congress had the Constitution been amended in the manner proposed? Similarly, what past problem was the seventh proposal intended to remedy?

3. Were these resolutions radical? Explain.

Questions for Further Thought

1. As president, did Jefferson abandon the strict constructionist principles he had championed in the 1790s? Explain.

2. James Madison was an ardent nationalist in the 1780s (Document 7-5), a states' rights advocate in the 1790s (see text pp. 192–195), and a nationalist again as president. How do you explain these apparent inconsistencies?

3. What might be said in defense of the Federalist position before and during the War of 1812? After 1800, the Federalist Party's base was increasingly confined to the New England states. Why?

CHAPTER EIGHT

Creating a Republican Culture
1790–1820

The Capitalist Commonwealth

Between 1790 and 1820 increasing numbers of Americans sought to enlarge the scope of domestic manufacturing in the new republic. The Jeffersonian Republicans, who after 1800 were in control of the executive branch and Congress, were generally hostile to the use of federal power to encourage economic growth, especially in the nonagricultural sector of the economy. Therefore, these entrepreneurial-minded merchants, artisans, and farmers looked to political leaders at the state and local level for assistance (see text pp. 238–243)—and many received it. After the Jeffersonians allowed the first Bank of the United States to expire by refusing to renew its charter in 1811, state legislatures responded to the appeals of the mercantile community by chartering more than 240 state banks in five years. Additionally, state governments conferred special privileges to manufacturing and transportation companies—limiting the liability of shareholders, allowing monopolistic practices, and using the power of eminent domain to force the sale of private property for public purposes.

Although these developments proceeded without the support of the president or Congress, they were aided by the Supreme Court. Led by Chief Justice John Marshall, the Court issued several landmark decisions that laid the groundwork for the creation of a truly national economy. In *Fletcher v. Peck*, the Marshall Court upheld the inviolability of contractual obligations, in this case involving the claimants of the so-called Yazoo land fraud in Georgia, even when the circumstances under which such contracts were drawn up might be "much reprobated" (Document 8-1). In the *Dartmouth College* case, the Court endorsed the argument offered by Daniel Webster, who relied on the earlier *Fletcher* decision to conclude that a "grant is a contract," whether to private individuals or corporations, and therefore protected under the contract clause of the Constitution (Document 8-2). Finally, in *McCulloch v. Maryland*, Marshall ruled that the second Bank of the United States, chartered by Congress in 1816, was "necessary and proper" and therefore constitutional, and that the Maryland law placing a tax on it was unconstitutional and void because it entailed the "power to destroy" a legitimate federal institution (Document 8-3). Capitalists could now move freely throughout the nation in search of opportunities, secure in the knowledge that their vested interests would be protected by the Supreme Court.

8-1   Decision in *Fletcher v. Peck* (1810)

John Marshall

In January 1801, in one of his last acts as president, John Adams appointed the staunchly Federalist John Marshall of Virginia chief justice of the U.S. Supreme Court. Marshall presided over the Court for the next thirty-four years until his death in 1835. Marshall's significance is difficult to overemphasize (see text pp. 228–231): he shaped the direction of the Supreme Court as the guarantor of national capitalism. The fact that he did so in the era of the democratic republican "Virginia Dynasty" — that is, during the presidencies of Thomas Jefferson, James Madison, and James Monroe — makes this achievement truly remarkable. During most of his tenure, Marshall presided over a Court majority that had been appointed by Jefferson, Madison, and Monroe. Eventually Marshall was the only remaining Federalist appointee. Nevertheless, Marshall shaped the direction of the Court, repeatedly carrying a majority of the justices with him in a series of landmark decisions, including *Fletcher v. Peck* (1810). In his decision, Marshall acknowledged the corruption that tainted a Georgia land grant, but he relied on a strict construction of Article 1, Section 10, of the Constitution (protecting "obligation of Contracts") to strike down a law passed by the state of Georgia.

Source: Fletcher v. Peck, 6 Cranch 87 (1810), in Joseph P. Cotton, Jr., ed., *The Constitutional Decisions of John Marshall* (New York: P. D. Commanger, 1905; facsimile reprint, New York: Da Capo Press, 1969), 1:243–250.

In this case the [Georgia] legislature may have had ample proof that the original grant was obtained by practices which can never be too much reprobated, and which would have justified its abrogation so far as respected those to whom crime was imputable. But the grant, when issued, conveyed an estate in fee-simple to the grantee, clothed with all the solemnities which law can bestow. This estate was transferable; and those who purchased parts of it were not stained by that guilt which infected the original transaction.... Their situation was the same, their title was the same, with that of every other member of the community who holds land by regular conveyances from the original patentee....

The validity of this rescinding act [by the Georgia legislature] ... might well be doubted, were Georgia a single sovereign power. But Georgia cannot be viewed as a single unconnected, sovereign power, on whose legislature no other restrictions are imposed than may be found in its own constitution. She is a part of a large empire; she is a member of the American Union; and that Union has a constitution the supremacy of which all acknowledge, and which imposes limits to the legislatures of the several states, which none claim a right to pass. The constitution of the United States declares that no state shall pass any bill of attainder, *ex post facto* law, or law impairing the obligation of contracts.

Does the case now under consideration come within this prohibitory section of the constitution? ...

Since ... in fact, a grant is a contract executed, the obligation of which still continues, and since the constitution uses the general term contract ... it must be construed to comprehend the latter as well as the former....

Whatever respect might have been felt for the state sovereignties, it is not to be disguised that the framers of the constitution viewed, with some apprehension, the violent acts which might grow out of the feelings of the moment; and that the people of the United States, in adopting that instrument, have manifested a determination to shield themselves and their property from the effects of those sudden and strong passions to which men are exposed. The restrictions on the legislative power of the states are obviously founded in this sentiment; and the constitution of the United States contains what may be deemed a bill of rights for the people of each state....

It is, then, the unanimous opinion of the court, that, in this case, the estate having passed into the hands of a purchaser for a valuable consideration, without notice, the state of Georgia was restrained, either by general principles, which are common to our free institutions, or by the particular provisions of the constitution of the United States, from passing a law whereby the estate of the plaintiff in the premises so purchased could be constitutionally and legally impaired and rendered null and void.

Questions

1. In Marshall's view, why did the framers of the Constitution place restrictions on state legislatures?

2. The passage of the Constitution cited by Marshall appears in Article 1, Section 10. Locate that passage in the Constitution (see text p. D-9). Do you agree with Marshall's interpretation of its meaning?

3. How did Marshall's decision help lay the foundation for national capitalism?

8-2   Argument for the Plaintiff in *Dartmouth College v. Woodward* (1818)

Daniel Webster

In addition to his distinguished political career, Daniel Webster (1782–1852) established himself as an influential and financially successful constitutional lawyer. When the New Hampshire legislature circumvented a colonial charter establishing Dartmouth College by attempting to make the college a state institution, Webster defended his alma mater (and the inviolability of contracts) before the Supreme Court (see text p. 231). The Court agreed with Webster, endorsing a static view of property that protected established property rights for the next two decades. In this case, Dartmouth College was the plaintiff and William Woodward (the college's treasurer, who had been directed by state law to report to a new board of trustees) was the defendant.

Source: Rev. B. F. Tefft, ed., *The Speeches of Daniel Webster* (New York: Lincoln Centenary Association, n.d. [186?]), 11–59 passim.

The charter of 1769 created and established a corporation, to consist of twelve persons, and no more; to be called the "Trustees of Dartmouth College." . . . The charter, or letters patent, then proceed to create such a corporation . . . to have perpetual existence, as such corporation, and with power to hold and dispose of lands and goods, for the use of the college with all the ordinary powers of corporations. They are in their discretion to apply the funds and property of the college to the support of the president, tutors, ministers, and other officers of the college. . . .

No funds are given to the college by this charter. A corporate existence and capacity are given to the trustees, with the privileges and immunities which have been mentioned, to enable the founder and his associates the better to manage the funds which they themselves had contributed, and such others as they might afterwards obtain.

After the institution thus created and constituted had existed, uninterruptedly and usefully, nearly fifty years, the legislature of New Hampshire passed the acts in question.

The first act makes the twelve trustees under the charter, and nine other individuals, to be appointed by the governor and council, a corporation, by a new name; and to this new corporation transfers all the *property, rights, powers, liberties, and privileges* of the old corporation; with further power to establish new colleges and an institute, and to apply all or any part of the funds to these purposes; subject to the power and control of a board of twenty-five overseers, to be appointed by the governor and council.

The second act makes further provisions for executing the objects of the first, and the last act authorizes the defendant, the treasurer of the plaintiffs, to retain and hold their property, against their will.

If these acts are valid, the old corporation is abolished, and a new one created. . . . It will be contended by the plaintiffs, that these acts are not valid . . . because they are repugnant . . . to the tenth section of the first article of the constitution of the United States. The material words of that section are: "No state shall pass any bill of attainder, *ex post facto* law, or law impairing the obligation of contracts."

The object of these most important provisions in the national constitution has often been discussed. . . . It has already been decided in this court, that a *grant* is a contract, within the meaning of this provision; and that a grant by a state is also a contract, as much as the grant of an individual. In Fletcher *v.* Peck, this court says: ". . . A grant, in its own nature, amounts to an extinguishment of the right of the grantor, and implies a contract not to reassert that right. . . . The restrictions on the legislative power of the states are obviously founded in this sentiment; and the constitution of the United States contains what may be deemed a bill of rights for the people of each state."

It has also been decided that a grant by a state before the revolution is as much to be protected as a grant since. . . . This court, then, does not admit the doctrine that a legislature can repeal statutes creating private corporations. . . . And because charters of incorporation are of the nature of contracts, they cannot be altered or varied but by consent of the original parties. . . .

The case before the court is not of ordinary importance, or of every-day occurrence. It affects not this college only, but every college. . . . They have all a common principle of existence, the inviolability of their charters. It will be a dangerous, a most dangerous experiment, to hold these institutions subject to the rise and fall of popular parties, and the fluctuations of political opinions. If the franchise may be at any time taken away, or impaired, the property, also, may be taken away, or its use perverted. . . . Party and faction will be cherished in the places consecrated to piety and learning. These consequences are neither remote nor possible only. They are certain and immediate.

Questions

1. In what ways did the New Hampshire legislature change Dartmouth College's charter?

2. What constitutional argument did Webster employ to defend the original charter?

3. In Webster's view, why should colleges such as Dartmouth be privately controlled and therefore beyond the reach of "party and faction"?

8-3   Decision in *McCulloch v. Maryland* (1819)

John Marshall

In 1791 Alexander Hamilton, as secretary of the treasury, called for the creation of a bank of the United States. Thomas Jefferson and James Madison led the opposition, arguing that such an institution would be unconstitutional. Employing the doctrine of strict constructionism, they contended that the Constitution granted only specifically enumerated powers to Congress, and the establishment of a bank was not one of them. Hamilton disagreed. He argued that a national bank would be constitutional under the "necessary and proper" clause of Article I, section 8, because it was directly related to powers delegated to Congress, such as borrowing money on the credit of the United States or collecting taxes. Although President Washington was not completely taken by Hamilton's explanation, he signed the bill chartering the bank of the United States for twenty years. In 1811, with Madison as president and Republicans in control of Congress, the original charter was not renewed and the bank expired. The ensuing financial distress and the clumsy efforts of private banks to secure loans during the nearly disastrous War of 1812 changed more than a few Republican minds. Madison himself championed the chartering of the Second Bank of the United States in 1816. But the opposition continued, and in Maryland it took the form of a state law that imposed a $15,000 tax on the operations of the Baltimore branch of the national bank. When that branch refused to comply, James McCulloch, an officer of the bank, was indicted for violating the terms of the Maryland law. Acting for the bank, he appealed to the Supreme Court. The Marshall Court's unanimous decision revisited some of the fundamental questions raised by Hamilton and Jefferson in 1791.

Source: Excerpts from "The Establishment of Federal Judicial Review," in *Major Problems in American Constitutional History*, ed. Kermit L. Hall (Boston: Houghton Mifflin Company, 1992), 1:292–298.

This government is acknowledged by all to be one of enumerated powers. The principle, that it can exercise only the powers granted to it, would seem too apparent to have required to be enforced by all those arguments which its enlightened friends, while it was depending before the people, found it necessary to urge. That principle is now universally admitted. But the question respecting the extent of the powers actually granted, is perpetually arising, and will probably continue to arise, as long as our system shall exist. In discussing these questions, the conflicting powers of the State and general governments must be brought into view, and the supremacy of their respective laws, when they are in opposition, must be settled.

If any one proposition could command the universal assent of mankind, we might expect it would be this: that the government of the Union, though limited in its powers, is supreme within its sphere of action. This would seem to result necessarily from its nature. It is the government of all; its powers are delegated by all; it represents all, and acts for all. Though any one State may be willing to control its operations, no State is willing to allow others to control them. The nation, on those subjects on which it can act, must necessarily bind its component parts. But this question is not left to mere reason: the people have, in express terms, decided it, by saying, "this constitution, and the laws of the United States, which shall be made in pursuance thereof," "shall be the supreme law of the land," and by requiring that the members of the State legislatures, and the officers of the executive and judicial departments of the States, shall take the oath of fidelity to it.

The government of the United States, then, though limited in its powers, is supreme; and its laws, when made in pursuance of the constitution, form the supreme law of the land, "anything in the constitution or laws of any State, to the contrary, notwithstanding."

Among the enumerated powers, we do not find that of establishing a bank or creating a corporation. But there is no phrase in the instrument which, like the articles of confederation, excludes incidental or implied powers; and which requires that everything granted shall be expressly and minutely described. Even the 10th amendment, which was framed for the purpose of quieting the excessive jealousies which had been excited, omits the word "expressly," and declares only that the powers "not delegated to the United States, nor prohibited to the States, are reserved to the States or to the people"; thus leaving the question, whether the particular power which may become the subject of contest, has been delegated to the one government, or prohibited to the other, to depend on a fair construction of the whole instrument. The men who drew and adopted this amendment, had experienced the embarrassments resulting from the insertion of this word in the articles of confederation, and probably omitted it to avoid those embarrassments. A constitution, to contain an accurate detail of all the subdivisions of which its great powers will admit, and of all the means by which they may be carried into execution, would partake of the prolixity of a legal code, and could scarcely be embraced by the human mind. It would probably never be understood by the public. Its nature, therefore, requires that only its great outlines should be marked, its important objects designated, and the minor ingredients which compose those objects be deduced from the nature of the objects themselves. That this idea was entertained by the framers of the American constitution, is not only to be inferred from the nature of the instrument, but from the language. Why else were some of the limitations, found in the 9th section of the first article, introduced? It is also, in some degree, warranted by their having omitted to use any restrictive term which might prevent its receiving a fair and just interpretation. In considering this question, then, we must never forget, that it is a *constitution* we are expounding.

Although, among the enumerated powers of government, we do not find the word "bank," or "incorporation," we find the great powers to lay and collect taxes; to borrow money; to regulate commerce; to declare and conduct a war; and to raise and support armies and navies. The sword and the purse, all the external relations, and no inconsiderable portion of the industry of the nation, are intrusted to its government. It can never be pretended that these vast powers draw after them others of inferior importance, merely because they are inferior. Such an idea can never be advanced. But it may, with great reason, be contended, that a government, intrusted with such ample powers, on the due execution of which the happiness and prosperity of the nation so vitally depends, must also be instructed with ample means for their execution. The power being given, it is the interest of the nation to facilitate its execution. It can never be their interest, and cannot be presumed to have been their intention, to clog and embarrass its execution by withholding the most appropriate means. . . .

It is not denied that the powers given to the government imply the ordinary means of execution. That, for example, of raising revenue and applying it to national purposes, is admitted to imply the power of conveying money from place to place, as the exigencies of the nation may require, and of employing the usual means of conveyance. But it is denied that the government has its choice of means, or that it may employ the most convenient means, if to employ them it be necessary to erect a corporation. . . .

The government which has the right to do an act, and has imposed on it the duty of performing that act, must, according to the dictates of reason, be allowed to select the means; and those who contend that it may not select any appropriate means, that one particular mode of effecting the object is excepted, take upon themselves the burden of establishing that exception. . . .

But the constitution of the United States has not left the right of Congress to employ the necessary means, for the execution of the powers conferred on the government, to general reasoning. To its enumeration of powers is added that of making "all laws which shall be necessary and proper, for carrying into execution the foregoing powers, and all other powers vested by this constitution, in the government of the United States, or in any department thereof."

The counsel for the State of Maryland have urged various arguments, to prove that this clause, though in terms a grant of power, is not so in effect; but is really restrictive of the general right, which might otherwise be implied, of selecting means of executing the enumerated powers. . . .

But the argument on which most reliance is placed, is drawn from the peculiar language of this clause. Congress is not empowered by it to make all laws, which may have relation to the powers conferred on the government, but such only as may be "*necessary and proper*" for carrying them into execution. The word "*necessary*" is considered as controlling the whole sentence, and as limiting the right to pass laws for the execution of the granted powers, to such as are indispensable, and without which the power would be nugatory. That it excludes the choice of means, and leaves to Congress, in each case, that only which is most direct and simple.

Is it true, that this is the sense in which the word "necessary" is always used? Does it always import an absolute physical necessity, so strong, that one thing, to which another may be termed necessary cannot exist without that other? We think it does not. If reference be had to its use, in the common affairs of the world, or in approved authors, we find that it frequently imports no more than that one thing is convenient, or useful, or essential to another. To employ the means necessary to an end, is generally understood as employing any means calculated to produce the end, and not as being confined to those single means, without which the end would be entirely unattainable. Such is the character of human language, that no word conveys to the mind, in all situations one single definite idea; and nothing is more common than to use words in a figurative sense. Almost all compositions contain words, which, taken in their rigorous sense, would convey a meaning different from that which is obviously intended. It is essential to just construction, that many words which import something excessive, should be understood in a more mitigated sense — in that sense which common usage justifies. The word "necessary" is of this description. It has not a fixed character peculiar to itself. It admits of all degrees of comparison; and is often connected with other words, which increase or diminish the impression the mind receives of the urgency it imports. A thing may be necessary, very necessary, absolutely or indispensably necessary. To no mind would the same idea be conveyed, by these several phrases. . . . This word, then, like others, is used in various senses; and, in its construction, the subject, the context, the intention of the person using them, are all to be taken into view. . . .

This clause, as construed by the State of Maryland, would abridge and almost annihilate this useful and necessary right of the legislature to select its means. That this could not be intended is, we should think, had it not been already controverted, too apparent for controversy. . . .

It being the opinion of the Court, that the act incorporating the bank is constitutional; and that the power of establishing a branch in the State of Maryland might be properly exercised by the bank itself, we proceed to inquire —

2. Whether the State of Maryland may, without violating the constitution, tax that branch?

That the power of taxation is one of vital importance; that it is retained by the States; that it is not abridged by the grant of a similar power to the government of the Union; that it is to be concurrently exercised by the two governments: are truths which have never been denied. But, such is the paramount character of the constitution, that its capacity to withdraw any subject from the action of even this power, is admitted. The States are expressly forbidden to lay any duties on imports or exports, except what may be

absolutely necessary for executing their inspection laws. If the obligation of this prohibition must be conceded — if it may restrain a state from the exercise of its taxing power on imports and exports, the same paramount character would seem to restrain, as it certainly may restrain, a state from such other exercise of this power, as is in its nature incompatible with, and repugnant to, the constitutional laws of the Union. A law, absolutely repugnant to another, as entirely repeals that other as if express terms of repeal were used.

On this ground the counsel for the bank place its claim to be exempted from the power of a State to tax its operations. There is no express provision for the case, but the claim has been sustained on a principle which so entirely pervades the constitution, is so intermixed with the materials which compose it, so interwoven with its web, so blended with its texture, as to be incapable of being separated from it, without rending it into shreds.

This great principle is, that the constitution and the laws made in pursuance thereof are supreme; that they control the constitution and laws of the respective States, and cannot be controlled by them. From this, which may be almost termed an axiom, other propositions are deduced as corollaries, on the truth or error of which, and on their application to this case, the cause has been supposed to depend. These are, 1. That a power to create implies a power to preserve. 2. That a power to destroy, if wielded by a different hand, is hostile to, and imcompatible with, these powers to create and preserve. 3. That where this repugnancy exists, that authority which is supreme must control, not yield to that over which it is supreme. . . .

The power of Congress to create, and of course to continue, the bank, was the subject of the preceding part of this opinion; and is no longer to be considered as questionable.

That the power of taxing it by the States may be exercised so as to destroy it, is too obvious to be denied. But taxation is said to be an absolute power, which acknowledges no other limits than those expressly prescribed in the constitution, and like sovereign power of every other description, is trusted to the discretion of those who use it. . . .

The argument on the part of the State of Maryland, is, not that the states may directly resist a law of Congress, but that they may exercise their acknowledged powers upon it, and that the Constitution leaves them this right in the confidence that they will not abuse it. . . .

. . . That the power to tax involves the power to destroy; that the power to destroy may defeat and render useless the power to create, that there is a plain repugnance, in conferring on one government a power to control the constitutional measures of another, which other, with respect to those very measures, is declared to be supreme over that which exerts the control, are propositions not to be denied. . . .

If we apply the principle for which the State of Maryland contends, to the constitution generally, we shall find it capable of changing totally the character of that instrument. We shall find it capable of arresting all the measures of the government, and of prostrating it at the foot of the states. The American people have declared their constitution, and the laws made in pursuance thereof, to be supreme; but this principle would transfer the supremacy, in fact to the States.

If the States may tax one instrument, employed by the government in the execution of its powers, they may tax any and every other instrument. They may tax the mail; they may tax the mint; they may tax patent rights; they may tax the papers of the custom-house; they may tax judicial process; they may tax all the means employed by the government, to an excess which would defeat all the ends of government. This was not intended by the American people. They did not design to make their government dependent on the States. . . .

The question is, in truth, a question of supremacy; and if the right of the States to tax the means employed by the general government be conceded, the declaration that the constitution, and the laws made in pursuance thereof, shall be the supreme law of the land, is empty and unmeaning declamation. . . .

The Court has bestowed on this subject its most deliberate consideration. The result is a conviction that the States have no power, by taxation or otherwise, to retard, impede, burden, or in any manner control, the operations of the constitutional laws enacted by Congress to carry into execution the powers vested in the general government. This is, we think, the unavoidable consequence of that supremacy which the constitution has declared. We are unanimously of opinion, that the law passed by the legislature of Maryland, imposing a tax on the Bank of the United States, is unconstitutional and void. . . .

Questions

1. What were the main points raised by the Marshall Court in declaring the Bank of the United States to be constitutional? Did they differ from Hamilton's 1791 arguments?

2. How did the Court interpret the "necessary and proper" clause of the Constitution? What are the strengths and weaknesses of the Court's definition of "necessary"?

3. The McCulloch decision ranks among the most important issued by the Marshall Court. How did it define federal and state powers? How did it define the Tenth Amendment? How might states' rights advocates have responded to the McCulloch decision?

Questions for Further Thought

1. The documents in this section and in the previous chapter deal with the powers of the federal and state governments. How instrumental was the Marshall Court in defining these powers? What limits did the Court place on state power?

2. Compare the views of Marshall and Webster with those of Thomas Jefferson and Alexander Hamilton. Whose vision of America ultimately prevailed?

3. The emerging capitalist economic order was supposedly still influenced by republican ideology, which placed public good over private gain. Which documents in this section support this view? Which do not? Explain.

Toward a Democratic Republican Culture

During the first half century of American independence, the citizens of the United States struggled with the implications of the experiment in self-government they had launched in 1776. Many, especially James Madison, were troubled by what they perceived to be the selfish and shortsighted policies of the states under the Articles of Confederation, and the drafting and ratification of the Constitution provided them with some reassurance that good, disinterested government would finally prevail (see Document 6-17). The plans for the new capital city embodied this hopeful vision of a well-ordered republic, in which a separation of powers coupled with a carefully constructed balance among the branches of government might advance the good of the whole despite the defects of human nature (Document 8-4).

In a republic, as Thomas Jefferson explained, because the people were the "ultimate guardians of their own liberty," it was crucial that they be rendered "safe" through education. Thus he proposed a broadly based educational system in Virginia aimed at raising the "mass of the people to the high ground of moral respectability necessary to their own safety, and to orderly government." Benjamin Rush, the Philadelphia physician and Jefferson's friend, agreed that a "suitable education" was essential to the health of the republic, but he believed that no system would be complete without a provision for educating females; mothers, after all, would be the first teachers responsible for "instructing their sons in the principles of liberty and government" (Document 8-7).

Unfortunately, for those who yearned after "liberty" and "orderly" government, the people often behaved in ways that seemed incompatible with such ends. Hugh Henry Brackenridge's alter ego, Captain Farrago, was dumbfounded to discover that the sovereign masses were intent on exercising their newfound constituent power so foolishly (Document 8-5). And while plans for a respectable federal city were being implemented, some of its potential occupants were anything but respectable. Madison was mortified by the "affair of Lyon and Griswold" (Document 8-6), but even more disturbed that it had become a "topic of tedious and disgraceful debates in Congress." To Abigail Adams, the "dirty affair of Lyons" was symptomatic of the decline of American politics.

8-4   The Plan of the City of Washington (1791)

Pierre Charles L'Enfant

In 1791 Pierre Charles L'Enfant, a French engineer and friend of George Washington, created an impressive design for the new capital city, Washington, D.C. The proposed site on the banks of the Potomac was largely undeveloped, giving L'Enfant full license to create something entirely new. His subsequent plan for the city embodied the principles of the new federal government and symbolized Americans' effort to translate the ideas of the Revolution into concrete and lasting institutions.

L'Enfant's plan consists of a grid system, with long radial avenues named after the states superimposed over it. The two main focal points of the city are the Capitol building, which houses the legislature, and the president's house.

Source: Pierre Charles L'Enfant, "Plan of the City of Washington," in Issac Weld's *Travels Through the States of North America*, 1807. Courtesy of the New York Public Library.

Questions

1. The president's house and the Capitol are connected by a main avenue but separated by a distance of about one and a half miles. What does this signify about the new government?

2. Note that the broad avenues named for the states radiate from the seats of the legislative and executive branches, and that prominent squares are drawn at their points of intersection. L'Enfant intended for these squares to be filled with monuments to state citizens who had become national heroes. How does this plan reflect the balance between state and federal power?

3. There are no spaces set aside for extensive agricultural or commercial development. Therefore, the capital city was not envisioned to be self-sufficient. Why is this significant? How might it be related to Article 1, Section 8, Clause 17 of the Constitution, which gave Congress the power to create a federal city? (See text p. D-3.)

4. L'Enfant's plan includes no walls or protective barriers of any sort around the capital city. What message does this convey?

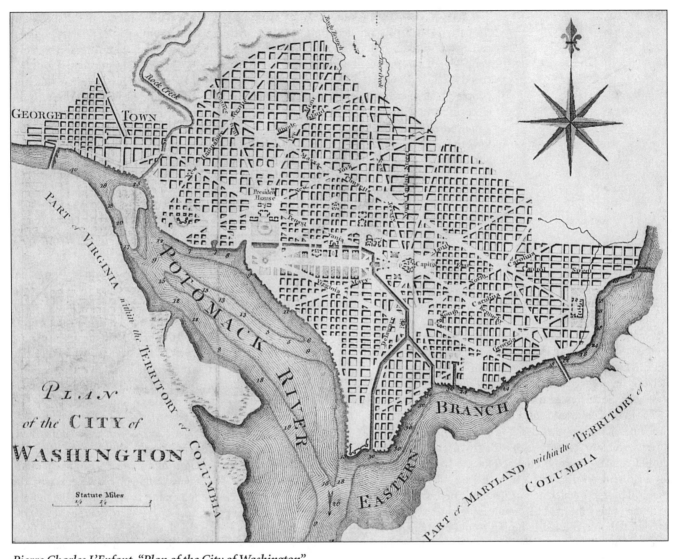

Pierre Charles L'Enfant, "Plan of the City of Washington"

8-5   *Modern Chivalry* (1792)

Hugh Henry Brackenridge

One measure of the radicalism of the American Revolution was the increased participation of ordinary adult white males in the political life of the republic. The "people" began to elect men much like themselves to look after their interests, especially in the powerful state legislatures. Many of these new legislators were men who prior to 1776 could not qualify to vote, let alone hold office. Not surprisingly, those accustomed to the "ordered liberty" fostered by traditional elites (see text, p. 243) were alarmed by the emergence of these "upstarts." To be sure, republicanism meant that the people were sovereign and ruled without the benefit of king or lords, but not all men were capable of understanding the sometimes abstruse affairs of state. Thus only "natural aristocrats," those few whom nature had blessed with superior merit and genius, were actually supposed to govern; the duty of the vast majority of the people was to identify these natural aristocrats, elect them to public office, and defer to their superior judgment. No one expressed these ideas, and the frustrations that accompanied them, better than Hugh Henry Brackenridge (1748–1816). The son of a poor Scottish immigrant, Brackenridge managed through hard work and no small amount of talent to graduate from Princeton in 1771, establish himself as a man of letters by the late 1770s, become a lawyer of local prominence in Pittsburgh in the early 1780s, and gain election to the Pennsylvania state assembly in 1786. His political career was cut short, however, after he opposed a bill, popular among farmers in western Pennsylvania, to permit the use of state certificates of indebtedness to purchase land. Accused of abandoning the interests of his constituents, Brackenridge suggested that the people-at-large were not the best judges of public policy. He was defeated in his bid for re-election in 1787 by an ex-weaver.

Modern Chivalry, which Brackenridge wrote piecemeal between 1792 and 1815, follows the adventures of Captain John Farrago, a man of "good natural sense and considerable reading," and Teague O'Regan, his illiterate servant.

Source: Excerpts from Chapter III, in *Modern Chivalry*, by Hugh Henry Brackenridge, ed. Claude M. Newlin (New York: American Book Co., 1937), 13–17. Reprinted by permission.

The Captain rising early next morning, and setting out on his way, had now arrived at a place where a number of people were convened, for the purpose of electing persons to represent them in the legislature of the state. There was a weaver who was a candidate for this appointment, and seemed to have a good deal of interest among the people. But another, who was a man of education, was his competitor. Relying on some talent of speaking which he thought he possessed, he addressed the multitude.

Said he, Fellow citizens, I pretend not to any great abilities; but am conscious to myself that I have the best good will to serve you. But it is very astonishing to me, that this weaver should conceive himself qualified for the trust. For though my acquirements are not great, yet his are still less. The mechanical business which he pursues, must necessarily take up so much of his time, that he cannot apply himself to political studies. I should therefore think it would be more answerable to your dignity, and conducive to your interest, to be represented by a man at least of some letters, than by an illiterate handicraftsman like this. It will be more honourable for himself, to remain at his loom and knot threads, than to come forward in a legislative capacity: because, in the one case, he is in the sphere where God and nature has placed him; in the other, he is like a fish out of water, and must struggle for breath in a new element. . . .

The Captain hearing these observations, and looking at the weaver, could not help advancing, and undertaking to subjoin something in support of what had been just said. Said he, I have no prejudice against a weaver more than another man. . . .

But to rise from the cellar to the senate house, would be an unnatural hoist. To come from counting threads, and adjusting them to the splits of a reed, to regulate the finances of a government, would be preposterous; there being no congruity in the case. There is no analogy between knoting threads and framing laws. It would be a reversion of the order of things. Not that a manufacturer of linen or woolen, or other stuff, is an inferior character, but a different one, from that which ought to be employed in affairs of state. It is unnecessary to enlarge on this subject; for you must all be convinced of the truth and propriety of what I say. But if you will give me leave to take the manufacturer aside a little, I think I can explain to him my ideas on the subject; and very probably prevail with him to withdraw his pretensions. The people seeming to acquiesce, and beckoning to the weaver, they drew aside, and the Captain addressed him in the following words:

Mr. Traddle, said he, for that was the name of the manufacturer, I have not the smallest idea of wounding your sensibility; but it would seem to me, it would be more your interest to pursue your occupation, than to launch out into that of which you have no knowledge. When you go to the senate house, the application to you will not be to warp a web; but to make laws for the commonwealth. Now, suppose that the making these laws, requires a knowledge of commerce, or of the interests of agriculture, or those principles upon which the different manufactures depend, what service could you render. It is possible you might think justly enough; but could you speak? You are not in the habit of public speaking. You are not furnished with those common place ideas, with which even very ignorant men can pass for knowing something. There is nothing makes a man so ridiculous as to attempt what is above his sphere. . . . It is a disagreeable thing for a man to be laughed at, and there is no way of keeping ones self from it but by avoiding all affectation.

While they were thus discoursing, a bustle had taken place among the croud. Teague hearing so much about elections, and serving the government, took it into his head, that he could be a legislator himself. The thing was not displeasing to the people, who seemed to favour his pretensions; owing, in some degree, to there being several of his countrymen among the croud; but more especially to the fluctuation of the popular mind, and a disposition to what is new and ignoble. For though the weaver was not the most elevated object of choice, yet he was still preferable to this tatterdemalion, who was but a menial servant, and had so much of what is called the brogue on his tongue, as to fall far short of an elegant speaker.

The Captain coming up, and finding what was on the carpet, was greatly chagrined at not having been able to give the multitude a better idea of the importance of a legislative trust; alarmed also, from an apprehension of the loss of his servant. Under these impressions he resumed his address to the multitude. Said he, This is making the matter still worse, gentlemen: this servant of mine is but a bog-trotter; who can scarcely speak the dialect in which your laws ought to be written; but certainly has never read a single treatise on any political subject; for the truth is, he cannot read at all. . . . This young man, whose family name is Oregan, has been my servant for several years. And, except a too great fondness for women, which now and then brings him into scrapes, he has demeaned himself in a manner tolerable enough. But he is totally ignorant of the great principles of legislation; and more especially, the particular interests of the government. A free government is a noble possession to a people: and this freedom consists in an equal right to make laws, and to have the benefit of the laws when made. Though doubtless, in such a government, the lowest citizen may become chief magistrate; yet it is sufficient to possess the right; not absolutely necessary to exercise it. . . . You are surely carrying the matter too far, in thinking to make a senator of this hostler; to take him away from an employment to which he has been bred, and put him to another, to which he has served no apprenticeship: to set those hands which have been lately employed in currying my horse, to the draughting bills, and preparing business for the house.

The people were tenacious of their choice, and insisted on giving Teague their suffrages; and by the frown upon their brows, seemed to indicate resentment at what has been said; as indirectly charging them with want of judgment; or calling in question their privilege to do what they thought proper. It is a very strange thing, said one of them, who was a speaker for the rest, that after having conquered Burgoyne and Cornwallis, and got a government of our own, we cannot put in it whom we please. This young man may be your servant, or another man's servant; but if we chuse to make him a delegate, what is that to you. He may not be yet skilled in the matter, but there is a good day a-coming. We will impower him; and it is better to trust a plain man like him, than one of your high flyers, that will make laws to suit their own purposes.

Said the Captain, I had much rather you would send the weaver, though I thought that improper, than to invade my household, and thus detract from me the very person that I have about me to brush my boots, and clean my spurs. The prolocutor of the people gave him to understand that his surmises were useless, for the people had determined on the choice, and Teague they would have, for a representative.

Finding it answered no end to expostulate with the multitude, he requested to speak a word with Teague by himself. Stepping aside, he said to him, composing his voice, and addressing him in a soft manner; Teague, you are quite wrong in this matter they have put into your head. Do you know what it is to be a member of a deliberate body? What qualifications are necessary? Do you understand any thing of geography? If a question should be, to make a law to dig a canal in some part of the state, can you describe the bearing of the mountains, and the course of the rivers? Or if commerce is to be pushed to some new quarter, by the force of regulations, are you competent to decide in such a case? There will be questions of law, and astronomy on the carpet. How you must gape and stare like a fool, when you come to be asked your opinion on these subjects? Are you acquainted with the abstract principles of finance; with the funding public securities; the ways and means of raising the revenue; providing for the discharge of the public debts, and all over things which respect the economy of the government? Even if you had knowledge, have you a facility of speaking. I would suppose you would have too much pride to go to the house just to say, Ay, or No. This is not the fault of your nature, but of your education; having been accustomed to dig turf in your early years, rather than instructing yourself in the classics, or common school books. . . .

. . . You have nothing but your character, Teague, in a new country to depend upon. Let it never be said, that you quitted an honest livelihood, the taking care of my horse, to follow the new fangled whims of the times, and to be a statesman.

Teague was moved chiefly with the last part of the address, and consented to give up the object.

The Captain, glad of this, took him back to the people, and announced his disposition to decline the honour which they had intended him.

Teague acknowledged that he had changed his mind, and was willing to remain in a private station.

The people did not seem well pleased with the Captain; but as nothing more could be said about the matter, they turned their attention to the weaver, and gave him their suffrages.

Questions

1. Was Brackenridge optimistic or pessimistic about the future of the American republic? What did he mean by the proper "order of things"? How did he propose to restore this proper order?

2. What did Teague O'Regan represent? What, if anything, was the significance of casting an Irish immigrant as the ridiculous foil to Captain Farrago?

3. The course of Brackenridge's own life would suggest that he must have been an advocate of upward social mobility. What then was so objectionable, even absurd, about the aspirations of Teague and the weaver? Who or what was principally to blame for their pretensions?

8-6   Congressional Pugilists (1798)

Unidentified Artist

On January 30, 1798, Matthew Lyon, a Republican congressman from Vermont, was ranting about the duplicity and hypocrisy of his Federalist colleagues, when Representative Roger Griswold of Connecticut, tiring of the insults, responded with a disparaging reference to Lyon's dismissal from service in the Continental Army in 1776. Thus provoked, Lyon spat in Griswold's face. House Federalists immediately sought to have the "spitting Lyon" expelled for behavior of the "very grossest and most indecent nature," but could not gain the necessary two-thirds majority prescribed by the Constitution. Two weeks later, Griswold attempted a redress of grievances on his own. Confronting his rival on the floor of the House, he beat the sitting Lyon with a hickory walking stick. Lyon eventually freed himself from his desk and managed to grab a pair of fireplace tongs. The brawl lasted for some time, as some representatives wanted to separate the combatants, while others, including the Speaker of the House, Jonathan Dayton, preferred leaving them alone.

Source: Etching, *Congressional Pugilists* (Philadelphia, 1798). Library of Congress. Prints and Photographs Division, LC-USZ62-9242.

Congressional Pugilists

Questions

1.   What does this brawl suggest about the nature of national politics in the 1790s? What does it suggest about the sense of honor of these early congressmen?

2.   Speaker Dayton, seated on the left, and others seemed to be more than mildly amused by the fracas. Was this simply because they found it entertaining? Explain.

3. Alexander Hamilton and Aaron Burr famously ended their dispute in 1804 by engaging in a duel. Instead of caning him, why didn't Griswold seek satisfaction by challenging Lyon to a duel?

8-7 The Education of Republican Women (1798)

Benjamin Rush

Benjamin Rush (1745–1813) studied medicine in Philadelphia and the University of Edinburgh. He returned to Philadelphia in 1769 to practice medicine and advance American republican values. For Rush, republicanism implied a host of social and moral reforms as Americans distinguished their society from that of monarchical Great Britain. Here he advocates improved education for young women to prepare them to be republican mothers (see text pp. 248–249). Rush addressed his remarks on female education to "The Visitors of the Young Ladies' Academy in Philadelphia, 28th July, 1787." The essay was first published in 1798.

Source: Benjamin Rush, *Essays Literary, Moral, and Philosophical* (Philadelphia, 1798; reprint, Schenectady, NY: Union College Press, 1988), 44–54.

The first remark that I shall make upon this subject, is, that female education should be accommodated to the state of society, manners, and government of the country, in which it is conducted.

This remark leads me at once to add, that the education of young ladies, in this country, should be conducted upon principles very different from what it is in Great Britain, and in some respects, different from what it was when we were part of a monarchical empire.

There are several circumstances in the situation, employments, and duties of women in America, which require a peculiar mode of education. . . .

The equal share that every citizen has in the liberty, and the possible share he may have in the government of our country, make it necessary that our ladies should be qualified to a certain degree by a peculiar and suitable education, to concur in instructing their sons in the principles of liberty and government. . . .

Vocal music should never be neglected, in the education of a young lady, in this country. Besides preparing her to join in that part of public worship which consists in psalmody, it will enable her to soothe the cares of domestic life. The distress and vexation of a husband—the noise of a nursery, and, even, the sorrows that will sometimes intrude into her own bosom, may all be relieved by a song, where sound and sentiment unite to act upon the mind. . . .

The attention of our young ladies should be directed, as soon as they are prepared for it, to the reading of history—travels—poetry—and moral essays. These studies are accommodated, in a peculiar manner, to the present state of society in America, and when a relish is excited for them, in early life, they subdue that passion for reading novels, which so generally prevails among the fair sex. . . . As yet the intrigues of a British novel, are . . . foreign to our manners. . . . Let it not be said, that the tales of distress, which fill modern novels, have a tendency to soften the female heart into acts of humanity. The fact is the reverse of this. The abortive sympathy which is excited by the recital of imaginary distress, blunts the heart to that which is real; and, hence, we sometimes see instances of young ladies, who weep away a whole forenoon over the criminal sorrows of a fictitious Charlotte . . . turning with disdain at three o'clock from the sight of a beggar, who solicits in feeble accents or signs, a small portion only of the crumbs which fall from their fathers' tables. . . .

It should not surprize us that British customs, with respect to female education have been transplanted into our American schools and families. . . . It is high time to awake from this servility—to study our own character—to examine the age of our country—and to adopt manners in every thing, that shall be accommodated to our state of society, and to the forms of our government. In particular it is incumbent upon us to make ornamental accomplishments yield to principles and knowledge, in the education of our women. . . . The influence of female education would be still more extensive and useful in domestic life. The obligations of gentlemen to qualify themselves by knowledge and industry to discharge the duties of benevolence, would be encreased [*sic*] by marriage; and the patriot—the hero—and the legislator, would find the sweetest regard of their toils, in the approbation and applause of their wives. Children would discover the marks of maternal prudence and wisdom in every station of life; for it has been remarked that there have been few great or good men who have not been blessed with wise and prudent mothers. . . . I know that the elevation of the female mind, by means of moral, physical and religious truth, is considered by some men as unfriendly to the domestic character of a woman. But this is a prejudice of little minds, and springs from the same spirit which opposes the general diffusion of knowledge among the citizens of our republic. If men believe that ignorance is favourable to the government of the female sex, they are certainly deceived; for a weak and ignorant woman will always be governed with the greatest difficulty. . . . It will be in our power, LADIES, to correct the mistakes and practice of our sex upon these subjects, by demonstrating, that the female temper can only be governed by reason, and that the cultivation of reason in women, is alike friendly to the order of nature, and to private as well as public happiness.

Questions

1. Why did Rush want to discourage young American women from reading novels?

2. What did he mean when he insisted that "ornamental accomplishments" must "yield to principles and knowledge"?

3. In what ways would the proper education of women promote republican virtue?

Questions for Further Thought

1. How "democratic" was the new nation? What are the characteristics of a democratic government?

2. Where does the notion of equality fit into the larger constellation of republican ideals—particularly in regard to race, class, and gender differences?

3. How were the requirements of a republican citizen different from those of a monarch's subject? Why?

Aristocratic Republicanism and Slavery

The impact of the Revolutionary commitment to republicanism was felt in all regions of the nation; however, in the South it was tempered by the dominance of plantation slavery. Driven by the demands of British and American textile factories for cotton, southern planters surged halfway across the continent in pursuit of their own version of American opportunity. By 1819 the slaveholders' understanding of republican expansion was starting to clash with that of northern whites. In particular, those opposed to the "peculiar institution" were determined to keep slavery out of the western territories. The Missouri controversy brought into sharp relief the issues separating the opposing sides. Robert Walsh Jr. thought the Constitution empowered Congress to curtail the "migration" of slaves into the new territories, and he sought confirmation of his position from James Madison, the father of the Constitution (Document 8-8). Daniel Raymond was fearful lest the profits generated by the domestic traffic in slaves should transform the old South into a "second Africa," from which the "pestilence, misery, and desolation" of slavery would overspread the "western country" and eventually the "world" (Document 8-9). But even Raymond, who described slavery as a "curse" and found the prospect of its expanding into new territories "appalling," focused almost exclusively on its negative impact on whites rather than on the slaves themselves. Not surprisingly, the goal of the American Colonization Society, the most prominent "antislavery" organization prior to the 1830s, was to send free blacks to Africa (Document 8-10). The "unalterable prejudices" of most white Americans, Madison reasoned, required of free blacks that they be "permanently removed beyond the region occupied by or allotted to a White population."

8-8   Original Intent and Slavery (1819)

James Madison

When Missouri's application for admission into the union as a slave state came before Congress in 1819, James Tallmadge of New York proposed an amendment that would have prohibited any further migration of slaves into the state. Southerners objected to the proposed amendment, contending that any interference with the domestic slave trade was unconstitutional. To be sure, Congress had outlawed the importation of slaves from abroad after January 1, 1808, they argued, but that prohibition was permissible under the Constitution because Article I, Section 9, only prevented Congress from interfering with the "migration or importation of such persons as any of the States now existing shall think proper to admit" *before* 1808. There was no corresponding authority to restrict the domestic movement of slaves. Northerners, however, were not convinced, and Robert Walsh Jr., a young Philadelphia writer and longtime acquaintance of James Madison's, wrote to the retired president seeking clarification of the framers' intent with regard to the movement of slaves within the United States. In particular, he wished to know whether he was correct in assuming that the phrase "migration or importation" referred to two different phenomena—"migration," to the domestic movement of slaves; and "importation," to the international slave trade—in which case the Tallmadge amendment was constitutionally sound. Portions of Madison's reply are included here.

Source: Gaillard Hunt, ed., *The Writings of James Madison*, vol. 9 (New York: G. P. Putnam's Sons, 1910), 1–6.

TO ROBERT WALSH

. . . As to the intention of the framers of the Constitution in the clause relating to "the migration and importation of persons, &c" the best key may perhaps be found in the case which produced it. The African trade in slaves had long been odious to most of the States, and the importation of slaves into them had been prohibited. Particular States however continued the importation, and were extremely averse to any restriction on their power to do so. In the convention the former States were anxious, in framing a new constitution, to insert a provision for an immediate and absolute stop to the trade. The latter were not only averse to any interference on the subject; but solemnly declared that their constituents would never accede to a Constitution containing such an article. Out of this conflict grew the middle measure providing that Congress should not interfere until the year 1808; with an implication, that after that date, they might prohibit the importation of slaves into the States then existing, & previous thereto, into the States not then existing.

. . . But some of the States were not only anxious for a Constitutional provision against the introduction of slaves. They had scruples against admitting the term "slaves" into the Instrument. Hence the descriptive phrase, "migration or importation of persons;" the term migration allowing those who were scrupulous of acknowledging expressly a property in human beings, to view *imported* persons as a species of emigrants, while others might apply the term to foreign malefactors sent or coming into the country. It is possible tho' not recollected, that some might have had an eye to the case of freed blacks, as well as malefactors.

But whatever may have been intended by the term "migration" or the term "persons," it is most certain, that they referred exclusively to a migration or importation from other countries into the U. States; and not to a removal, voluntary or involuntary, of slaves or freemen, from one to another part of the U. States. Nothing appears or is recollected that warrants this latter intention. Nothing in the proceedings of the State conventions indicates such a construction there.

. . . Neither is there any indication that Congress have heretofore considered themselves as deriving from this Clause a power over the migration of removal of individuals, whether freemen or slaves, from one State to another, whether new or old: For it must be kept in view that if the power was given at all, it has been in force eleven years over all the States existing in 1808, and at all times over the States not then existing. Every indication is against such a construction by Congress of their constitutional powers. Their alacrity in exercising their powers relating to slaves, is a proof that they did not claim what they did not exercise. They punctually and unanimously put in force the power accruing in 1808 against the further importation of slaves from abroad. They had previously directed their power over American vessels on the high seas, against the African trade. They lost no time in applying the prohibitory power to Louisiana, which having maritime ports, might be an inlet for slaves from abroad. But they forebore to extend the prohibition to the introduction of slaves from other parts of the Union.

Questions

1. According to Madison, what moved the framers of the Constitution to adopt the phrase "migration or importation of persons"? What was the intent of the framers?

2. Assuming that Madison's recollection of the events of 1787 was accurate, would his response have pleased Walsh and his cohorts?

3. Even before he received Madison's answer to his query, Walsh finished a pamphlet in which he argued that the "migration or importation" clause of the Constitution gave Congress the power to restrict the movement of slaves within the United States. What does this suggest about the nature of Walsh's motives in writing to Madison? How valid is any appeal to the "original intent" of the founders?

8-9   The Blight of Slavery (1819)

Daniel Raymond

Daniel Raymond (1786–1849) was born in New Haven, Connecticut, but at the time of the Missouri controversy was a member of the Baltimore bar. A former Federalist, Raymond was much enamored of the economic ideas of Alexander Hamilton and, like his older contemporary Mathew Carey, believed that the government should take a hand in developing the economic capacities of the people. Raymond's ideas, like Carey's, helped provide the theoretical underpinnings for the later Whig Party. It was Raymond's insistence on the links between broad-based economic prosperity and republican liberty that led him to join the Missouri controversy on the antislavery side. To Raymond, slavery was not simply an affront to humanity; it was also an impediment to the development of a prosperous and truly egalitarian republic—and he saw evidence for this position in the relative stagnation of the slaveholding South. Unlike Richard Mentor Johnson, Raymond was beginning to see slavery—and the South—not as bulwarks of the republic but as threats to it. In the following treatise, he gave voice to many of the deeper fears for the future of American (white) liberty that underlay the exalted moral and constitutional arguments of the antislavery side.

Source: Daniel Raymond, *The Missouri Question* (Baltimore: Schaeffer and Maund, 1819), 3–5, 8–9, 18–21, 23, 30–34.

THERE is no subject so interesting and important to the real lovers of their country, as that of slavery, because there is none which involves the happiness, prosperity and glory of our country in so great a degree—none attended with so many difficulties in remidying. It is admitted by all parties, slave-holders or not, that slavery is the greatest curse our country is afflicted with—it is a foul stain upon our national escutcheon—A canker which is corroding the moral and political vitals of our country. There is but one voice on this subject, and that is the voice of condemnation, as an enormous, and an alarming evil.

But although there is such an union of sentiment, as to the existence and nature of the evil, there is a vast diversity of opinion as to the remedy to be applied, for its correction or its cure.

The true policy of every wise legislator is to consider his country immortal, and to legislate for it as if it were to exist forever; but unfortunately, most legislators act as though they thought their country as short lived as themselves, and instead of adopting a policy, which is to look prospectively to future generations and centuries; they adopt a policy which looks only to themselves and to the present race. Unless the fruits of a policy are to be gathered by themselves, they think it unworthy their attention. This is eminently the case in the Southern States, in regard to their policy towards their slaves. They reprobate slavery as the eldest and greatest curse, and *at the same time* adopt measures *calculated* to increase and perpetuate it to the latest generations. They affect to despise the traitor, but they *love* the treason. This may appear to be a bold charge, but I trust, I shall be able to make it good; which, if I do not, I shall be very ready to retract.

A writer in the Federal Gazette of the 23d Nov. under the signature of PHOCION, says, "since the establishment of our independence, every state has engaged in the humane work of freeing our country from this curse, or where this could not be done with safety to the state or advantage to the slaves, in ameliorating their condition." This writer speaks the general sentiment of the southern public on this subject; but I trust I shall show before I conclude, that the southern states, Maryland excepted, not only have not done any thing towards freeing our country from this curse; but that they have on the contrary done and are doing all in their power, both to magnify the *curse* beyond all calculation, and to perpetuate it to the latest ages. That under the policy they are now persuing, the evil will continue to increase in a geometrical ratio, and that there can be no hope of its ever being ameliorated—nay farther, that *the policy* they are now pursuing, and *the policy* they wish the United States to adopt, will not only magnify and perpetuate the evil in the present slave holding states, but will extend it in all its horrors over a vast and boundless tract of country. I allude to the policy of permitting the new states west of the Mississippi, to become slave holding states. And here I will observe, that if the admission of slaves into the western world, would diminish the evil in the old slave states, I would say, *let them be admitted.* But I believe, I shall be able to prove upon the soundest principles of political æconomy, that the admission of slaves into those western states, so far from diminishing the evil in the old states, will have directly the contrary effect—that it will be the very means of preventing the southern states from ever ridding themselves of that *curse.* I shall also endeavour to free myself from the charge which Phocion brings against the eastern writers and eastern presses, of "upbraiding their neighbours, when they can suggest no remedy for the evil for which they upbraid them."

The idea, however, that this curse is to be increased and perpetrated through all succeeding generations, is very appalling, and our southern politicians either refrain from looking at so forbidding a picture, or they cast about for some remedy, which they flatter themselves, may mitigate its horrors. I shall attempt to show that they have not yet devised any plan that can in the smallest perceptible degree, effect their purpose, and that their policy is in fact increasing and perpetuating that evil upon their posterity. Slavery is a poisonous plant of vigorous and rapid growth—plant but a scion in any soil, and it will soon spread forth its pestiferous branches, overshadowing, choaking and finally destroying every thing within the sphere of its influence. . . .

The first proposition which I will lay down, is *That in our country, a free black population does not increase by procreation so fast by nearly 50 per cent. in twenty years, as a white population in a non slave holding state.*

2. *That a free black population does not increase so fast by procreation as a slave population.*

3. *That the white population in a slave state, does not increase so fast by at least 30 or 40 per cent. in twenty years, as the same population does in a state where there are none, or but few slaves.*

4. *That a slave population increases by procreation, faster than the white population in a slave state.*

And 5. (As a corollary from the foregoing propositions) *that in proportion as you restrain the increase of a slave population, you promote the increase of the white population;* and then the question for politicians to decide, arises, to wit: Whether that policy is best which promotes the increase of a free white population, by restraining the increase of a slave population, or that which promotes the increase of a slave population, by restraining the increase of a free white population. And can there be any doubt upon this question? Does that man live and breathe the air of this free country, who would dare to say, that a legislature ought to hesitate for a moment, in adopting that policy which would promote the increase of a white population, rather than of a black slave population? If there be such a man, he is a disgrace to his species. . . .

From all these estimates, it is clear, that the white population in a slave state, does not increase so fast as the white population in a non slave holding state, nor is this difference a small one. It is at a moderate calculation a difference of from 40 to 60 per cent. in 20 years. The difference is 86 per cent. against Maryland, 74 against Virginia, 68 against North Carolina, and 35 per cent. against South Carolina. This is certainly a matter of no trifling consideration. The great end of government in our country, is to promote the increase of our species, especially the free portion of them; and any cause, whatever it be, that prevents their increase, ought to be removed. There can be no doubt that slavery is the primary cause of the white population in the southern states, not increasing so fast as in the northern. I admit there may, and doubtless are at present, other immediate causes to be found in the manners, customs and habits of the people; but this difference in the manners, customs and habits of the people, is traceable to slavery as the primary cause. If the southern people are less industrious, less enterprising, less provident, it is because they are and have been cursed with slavery. It is an old maxim, that idleness is the parent of vice and dissipation, but there is nothing which so much conduces to idleness in a white population as slavery.—May it not then be said that slavery is a poisonous plant which takes deep root in any soil, and shoots forth its vigorous branches in all directions, blasting, withering, and ultimately destroying every goodly plant. Is it not in fact that *bohun upas* which has been supposed to exist only in the imagination of fanciful travellers?

The reasons why the white population does not increase so fast in a slave state, as in a state where there are no slaves, are neither doubtful nor mysterious. They are apparent to the most superficial observer. It is a self-evident axiom, that population or the increase of population must be limited to the means of subsistence. . . . If all the product of the earth be consumed by slaves, a white population cannot subsist; and whatever portion of the product of the earth be consumed by slaves, in the same proportion will the means of subsistence be taken from a white population, and in the same proportion will the increase of the white population be limited or restrained. In other words, every slave in the world, especially in our country occupies the place of a free man. Nay he does much more than this, or I will show hereafter that no country can be the nature of things contain or support so many human beings where slavery exists, as it would do if there was no slavery.

In all countries the great mass of the population is poor and obliged to depend upon manual labour for the subsistence of themselves and families. This is as much the case in the slave states, as in those where there are no slaves—A large portion of the white population in the southern states, are neither slave owners nor land owners, and are as much dependant on the labor of their lands for subsistence as the eastern people. But where slavery abounds they have no market for their labour—they cannot obtain employment. How then are they to raise families? Besides, it is in slave states a disgrace for white people to labour—the labourer is reduced to the level of slaves. . . .

I have said that no country can support as many human beings where slavery exists, as it would do if there was no slavery. We have already seen that population is always restrained and kept down to the means of subsistence. The means of subsistence depends upon the industry of man—the earth yielding more or less abundantly, in proportion to the labour bestowed upon it. It is ordained of God that it shall be so. There certainly needs no argument to prove that slaves are less industrious, and less faithful in their labours, than a free white population who labour for their own benefit, and reap that which they sow, universal experience proves that this is the case. It follows then that slaves will never produce the means of subsistence so abundantly as free whites, and of course so many of them cannot subsist in the same country.

The most important proposition still remains to be examined, which is, *that a slave population increases faster than the white population in a slave state.* A most momentous and alarming proposition this! one which portends more mischief, misery, insurrection, bloodshed and desolation to our country and our race, than any the imagination can conceive, provided the present policy of the southern states in regard to their slaves is still pursued. Who can tell what is to be the issue of this, and where it is to end? If the slave population, increase faster than the white, it will ere long be the most numerous, and not only the most numerous, but vastly the most numerous. And shall ten men be in subjection to one, or will a thousand quietly remain in bondage to an hundred? Such things cannot be—it was not intended by Him who made the black man as well as the white, that such things should be. We may put far off the evil day, but it will surely come upon us or our posterity.—The day of desolation and wrath is sure to overtake us, unless we avert it by a timely reformation of our policy. . . .

The reason then why a slave population increases faster than the white in a slave state, is because their means of subsistence are more abundant. The slaves usually belong to men of wealth, who have the means of supplying them with food, and whose interest it is that the slaves should multiply as fast as possible, at least it is their interest so long as there is a demand for slaves, and the increase of the slaves will always be proportionate to the demand. The greater and more extensive the market, therefore the faster they will increase.

They are raised as an article of traffic, the same as cattle and horses and the market regulates the increase of the one in the same manner that it does the other. If the market would justify it, we should see masters promoting the increase of their slaves, treating their breeding slaves with the same care, and nursing their offspring with the same attention and tenderness, that they now bestow upon their breeding mares and their foals. When this comes to be the case we shall find that the slave population will double at least every fifteen or twenty years, and there is nothing wanting to make this the case but an extensive demand and a high market. . . .

The main question still remains to be discussed. That question is the policy of admitting slavery into the new states hereafter to be formed beyond the Mississippi. A more momentous question has never been agitated in Congress—a more momentous question has never been agitated in this country since the declaration of independence. I am aware of its importance—I am aware of the interest it excites in the southern states—I am aware of its delicacy—of the angry feelings it has already produced, and being aware of all these things, I would wish to treat the subject if possible, in a manner calculated to assuage these feelings, and produce reflection and calculation in the thinking part of the community, rather than abuse or evil thinking of these gentlemen who differ with them in opinion, as being actuated with disposition to do a thing either unjust, unconstitutional, or impolitic.

This question naturally divides itself into two branches, 1st, What effect upon those new states will the introduction of slavery produce? 2d, What effect will it produce upon the old slave holding states? In other words, will either the old states or the new, be benefitted by such introduction, or will both be prejudiced by it? I purposely leave out all consideration of the slaves themselves in the discussion of this question. I am willing to discuss it like a politician, without any regard to the iniquity, morality, or injustice, which it may involve. If I show that the introduction of slavery into these states will not only prejudice the new states but the old ones also, I shall expect the southern gentlemen to join heart and hand with the northern, in preventing so great a curse. I expect to be able to do this.

As it regards the first branch of this question, I believe there is very little difference of opinion between the northern and southern gentlemen. It is generally admitted that slavery is a curse to any state, and of course it would be a curse to these new states. The calculations and observations which have been already made, are, I think, sufficient to satisfy any man whose mind is not impervious to the power of argument, of the truth of this fact. Slavery would restrain the increase of the white population in those states which is of itself sufficient to satisfy any man of its injurious tendency, who does not think a slave a more valuable member of society, than a free white citizen. I shall therefore take it for granted, that the introduction of slavery into those states would be a curse to them, and proceed to examine the second branch of the question, to wit: *what effect would the introduction of slavery into these new states have upon the old slave states.* If I show that it would have no good effect—that it would not in the smallest degree alleviate the evil of slavery in those states—I shall show all that will be necessary to secure the cordial co-operation of every honest man in preventing its introduction. It is true there are men who would have slavery introduced into those states for their own individual profit, even though they knew the ruin of the states, both old and new, in the next generation, would be the consequence.—But I hope and trust there are not many, if any such men in Congress. . . .

. . . Suppose then 50,000 slaves were to be annually exported to the western country, would that number in the smallest degree diminish the number in the old states?—not one whit. If that were the case, we should see the planters then using as great exertion to increase their annual product of slaves, as they now are to increase their annual product of sugar and cotton—and we should find that the slaves would re-produce their number every fifteen years. This would be establishing the slave trade in our country with a vengeance. The old states would become a second Africa, overspreading the world with pestilence, misery, and desolation. It is therefore I think plain reasoning a *priori*, that the old slave states would derive no benefit from introducing slaves into the new.

Questions

1. Raymond accused southern political leaders of failing to do what they *know* to be best for the country. What case did he make? Was he right?

2. Would you say that Raymond would have agreed with those who were already suggesting that the South was falling short of being truly republican?

3. To what extent was Raymond worried about the presence of *slaves* in Missouri, and to what extent was he worried about the presence of *blacks*?

8-10 James Madison and the American Colonization Society (1819)

For the founders of the American Colonization Society, established in 1817, emancipation and the relocation of the freed black population were two sides of the same coin (see textbook pp. 256–257). Slaveowners were unlikely to consider the one without the other, and most white Americans assumed that free blacks and whites could not live together in harmony; indeed, they believed that deep-seated racial hostility would eventually result in race war. In 1819 James Madison, a lifelong member of the Colonization Society, explained to Robert J. Evans, a Philadelphia antislavery writer, his reasons for endorsing the goals of the society and the basis of his hopes for the "extinguishment of slavery in the U.S."

Source: Excerpt from Marvin Meyers, ed., *The Mind of the Founder: Sources of the Political Thought of James Madison* (Hanover, NH: Published for Brandeis University Press by University Press of New England, 1981), 399–402. Copyright © 1981 Trustees of Brandeis University. Reprinted by permission of the University Press of New England.

A general emancipation of slaves ought to be 1. gradual. 2. equitable & satisfactory to the individuals immediately concerned. 3. consistent with the existing & durable prejudices of the nation.

That it ought, like remedies for other deeprooted and widespread evils, to be gradual, is so obvious that there seems to be no difference of opinion on that point.

To be equitable & satisfactory, the consent of both the Master & the slave should be obtained. That of the Master will require a provision in the plan for compensating a loss of what he held as property guarantied by the laws, and recognised by the Constitution. That of the slave, requires that his condition in a state of freedom, be preferable in his own estimation, to his actual one in a state of bondage.

To be consistent with existing and probably unalterable prejudices in the U.S. the freed blacks ought to be permanently removed beyond the region occupied by or allotted to a White population. The objections to a thorough incorporation of the two people are, with most of the Whites insuperable; and are admitted by all of them to be very powerful. If the blacks, strongly marked as they are by Physical & lasting peculiarities, by retained amid the Whites, under the degrading privation of equal rights political or social, they must be always dissatisfied with their condition as a change only from one to another species of oppression; always secretly confederated against the ruling & privileged class; and always uncontroulled by some of the most cogent motives to moral and respectable conduct. The character of the free blacks, even where their legal condition is least affected by their colour, seems to put these truths beyond question. It is material also that the removal of the blacks be to a distance precluding the jealousies & hostilities to be apprehended from a neighboring people stimulated by the contempt known to be entertained for their peculiar features; to say nothing of their vindictive recollections, or the predatory propensities which their State of Society might foster. Nor is it fair, in estimating the danger of Collisions with the Whites, to charge it wholly on the side of the Blacks. There would be reciprocal antipathies doubling the danger.

The colonizing plan on foot, has as far as it extends, a due regard to these requisites; with the additional object of bestowing new blessings civil & religious on the quarter of the Globe most in need of them. The Society proposes to transport to the African Coast all free & freed blacks who may be willing to remove thither; to provide by fair means, &, it is understood with a prospect of success, a suitable territory for their reception; and to initiate them into such an establishment as may gradually and indefinitely expand itself.

The experiment, under this view of it, merits encouragement from all who regard slavery as an evil, who wish to see it diminished and abolished by peaceable & just means; and who have themselves no better mode to propose. Those who have most doubted the success of the experiment must at least have wished to find themselves in an error.

But the views of the Society are limited to the case of blacks already free, or who may be *gratuitously* emancipated. To provide a commensurate remedy for the evil, the plan must be extended to the great Mass of blacks, and must embrace a fund sufficient to enduce the Master as well as the slave to concur in it. Without the concurrence of the Master, the benefit will be very limited as it relates to the Negroes; and essentially defective, as it relates to the United States; and the concurrence of Masters, must, for the most part, be obtained by purchase.

Can it be hoped that voluntary contributions, however adequate to an auspicious commencement, will supply the sums necessary to such an enlargement of the remedy? May not another question be asked? Would it be reasonable to throw so great a burden on the individuals, distinguished by their philanthropy and patriotism?

The object to be obtained, as an object of humanity, appeals alike to all; as a National object, it claims the interposition of the nation. It is the nation which is to reap the benefit. The nation therefore ought to bear the burden.

Must then the enormous sums required to pay for, to transport, and to establish in a foreign land all the slaves in the U.S. as their Masters may be willing to part with them, be taxed on the good people of the U.S. or be obtained by loans swelling the public debt to a size pregnant with evils next in degree to those of slavery itself?

Happily it is not necessary to answer this question by remarking that if slavery as a national evil is to be abolished, and it be just that it be done at the national expence, the amount of the expence is not a paramount consideration. It is the peculiar fortune, or, rather a providential blessing of the U.S. to possess a resource commensurate to this great object, without taxes on the people, or even an increase of the public debt.

I allude to the vacant territory the extent of which is so vast, and the vendible value of which is so well ascertained.

Supposing the number of slaves to be 1,500,000, and their price to average 400 dollars, the cost of the whole would be 600 millions of dollars. These estimates are probably beyond the fact; and from the number of slaves should be deducted 1. those whom their Masters would not part with. 2. those who may be gratuitously set free by their Masters. 3. those acquiring freedom under emancipating regulations of the States. 4. those preferring slavery where they are, to freedom in an African settlement. On the other hand, it is to be noted that the expence of removal & settlement is not included in the estimated sum; and that an increase of the slaves will be going on during the period required for the execution of the plan.

On the whole the aggregate sum needed may be stated at about 600 millions of dollars.

This will require 200 millions of Acres at 3 dollars per Acre; or 300 millions at 2 dollars per Acre a quantity which tho' great in itself, is perhaps not a third part of the disposable territory belonging to the U.S. And to what object so good so great & so glorious, could that peculiar fund of wealth be appropriated? Whilst the sale of territory would, on one hand be planting one desert with a free & civilized people, it would on the other, be giving freedom to another people, and filling with them another desert. And if in any instances, wrong has been done by our forefathers to people of one colour, by dispossessing them of their soil, what better atonement is now in our power than that of making what is rightfully acquired a source of justice & of blessings to a people of another colour?

Questions

1. According to Madison, for a plan of general emancipation to be successful it must satisfy certain conditions. What were they? Which of these conditions were satisfied by the colonization scheme? Which were not?

2. What were Madison's reasons for supporting colonization? How was removal supposed to benefit free blacks? Given your understanding of this period of American history, was Madison correct in his assumptions?

3. Madison addressed what he and many others considered to be the greatest obstacle to colonization: the costs. What was his solution to this problem? Were the costs associated with the colonization scheme the primary reason for its failure? Explain.

Questions for Further Thought

1. Historians have been sharply divided over the character of the nineteenth-century South, with some describing it as aristocratic and others viewing it as essentially similar to the larger American society but with a peculiarly nasty twist. Considering these documents and those in the preceding section, how different would you say the South was from the Northeast at this time?

2. Daniel Raymond called slavery a "poisonous plant . . . overshadowing, choking, and finally destroying every thing within the sphere of its influence." By this he meant far more than its effects on African American slaves. What were the larger effects of slavery on the American landscape, and why did people like Raymond fear its expansion?

3. Prior to the American Revolution, slavery was common in all the colonies. By 1820, those states north of the Ohio River and the Mason-Dixon line had either abolished it or committed themselves to its ultimate extinction. Accordingly, discussions of the relative merits of slavery and free labor increasingly involved comparisons of North and South. What regional stereotypes do you see coming into play in these discussions?

Protestant Christianity as a Social Force

The so-called Great Awakening of the eighteenth century had introduced to America the variant of Protestant Christianity we call *evangelicalism*—a form of Christian faith that stressed emotion over doctrinal correctness, judged people less by their social station or their education than by the genuineness of their "call," and demanded of all believers that they work to share the "good news" with others. In the years following the Revolution, massive social change, most especially the surge of white settlers into the West, brought on a countermovement to bring order to the new societies. A new evangelizing institution, the camp meeting, brought thousands together in massive displays of religious fervor. While many outside observers were appalled or bemused by the reported excesses of these revivals, they introduced a new order to the frontier, recruiting large numbers of souls into local congregations (Document 8-11). While older churches had been organized from the top down, the newer congregations were voluntary societies that joined together into a new kind of church, the *denomination*. Denominations existed less to enforce orthodoxy than to organize missionary efforts to combat what they feared was the rampant infidelity and social chaos accompanying geographic and economic expansion. In time, religious folk began to organize across denominational lines, creating a "benevolent empire" of national organizations. These denominations and agencies printed newspapers, Bibles, books, and tracts; spread them across the nation through the postal system and their networks of local affiliates; and deployed armies of missionaries both at home and abroad. In so doing, they played a major role in tying Americans together into a national community (Document 8-12).

Thanks to both revival enthusiasm and organizational genius, evangelical precepts increasingly pervaded American life; biblical themes and rhetoric shaped the ways in which Americans understood their world and discussed it with each other. Evangelicals were pleased at this development but wished to go much further. While they were happy to live in a land without an established church, they nonetheless believed that public, as well as private, life should be dominated by their own understanding of Christian principles. Theirs was hardly a pluralistic vision of the promise of America, for it shut out not only non-Christians but also Roman Catholics. But it also made the evangelical mission one of saving society as well as individuals. If Americans were in fact a new chosen people of God, their country needed to conform to God's will—a notion that in the hands of a Frederick Douglass, an Abraham Lincoln, or a Martin Luther King Jr. would become a powerful force for change.

8-11   Defending the Revival at Cane Ridge, Kentucky (1802)

Reverend George Baxter

The meeting held at Cane Ridge, Kentucky, in August 1801 was the signature event of the Second Great Awakening (see text p. 260). Originally meant to be an outdoor communion service of the sort that frontier Presbyterians had brought from their homelands in Scotland and Ireland, it drew hosts of settlers from far and wide to camp in the vicinity. Thousands experienced conversion, often accompanied by spectacular emotional and physical displays. Cane Ridge quickly became nationally notorious for the behavior of those attending. More orthodox Calvinist ministers expressed grave concern at the proceedings, especially given the accounts of sensuous singing and dancing and reports of sexual excesses, which suggested that the revival was at best a mass delusion and at worst the product of demonic possession. A distinguished eastern Presbyterian, Reverend George Baxter, the principal of Washington Academy in Virginia (now Washington and Lee University), traveled to the area in the fall of 1801 to assess the aftermath of the revival and to assure his skeptical colleagues that it was in fact the work of the Holy Spirit.

Source: W. W. Woodward, ed., *Increase of Piety, or the Revival of Religion in the United States of America . . .* (Philadelphia: W. W. Woodward, 1802), 57–66.

In the older settlement of Kentucky the revival made its first appearance among the Presbyterians last spring; the whole of that country about a year before was remarkable for vice and dissipation; and I have been credibly informed that a decided majority of the people were professed infidels. During the last winter appearances were favourable among the *Baptists*, and great numbers were added to their churches: early in the spring, the ministrations of the Presbyterian Clergy began to be better attended than they had been for many years before. Their worshipping assemblies became more solemn, and the people after they were dismissed shewed a strange reluctance at leaving the place: they generally continued some time in the meeting-house—in singing or in religious conversation. Perhaps about the last of May or the first of June the awakenings became general in some congregations, and spread through the country in every direction with amazing rapidity. I left that country about the first of November, at which time this revival in connexion with the one on Cumberland had covered the whole state, excepting a small settlement which borders on the waters of Greenriver, in which no Presbyterian ministers are settled; and I believe very few of any denomination. The power with which this revival has spread; and its influence in moralizing the people, are difficult for you to conceive of, and more difficult for me to describe. I had heard many accounts and seen many letters respecting it before I went to that country; but my expectations though greatly raised were much below the reality of the work. The congregations, when engaged in worship, presented scenes of solemnity superior to what I had ever seen before; and in private houses it was no uncommon thing to hear parents relate to strangers the wonderful things which God had done in their neighbourhoods, whilst a large circle of young people would be in tears. On my way to Kentucky I was told by settlers on the road, that the character of Kentucky travellers was entirely changed, and that they were now as distinguished for sobriety as they had formerly been dissoluteness; and indeed I found Kentucky the most moral place I had ever been in; a profane expression was hardly heard; a religious awe seemed to pervade the country; and some Deistical characters had confessed that from whatever cause the revival might originate, it certainly made the people better.—Its influence was not less visible in promoting a friendly temper; nothing could appear more amiable than that undissembled benevolence which governs the subjects of this work: I have often wished that the mere politician or Deist could observe with impartiality their peaceful and amicable spirit. He would certainly see that nothing could equal the religion of JESUS, for promoting even the temporal happiness of society—some neighbourhoods visited by the revival had been formerly notorious for private animosities; and many petty law-suits had commenced on that ground. When the parties in these quarrels were impressed with religion, the first thing was to send for their antagonists; and it was often very affecting to see their meeting. Both had seen their faults, and both contended that they ought to make concessions, till at last they were obliged to request each other to forbear all mention of the past, and to act as friends and brothers for the future. Now sir, let modern philosophists talk of reforming the world by banishing Christianity and introducing their licentious systems. The blessed gospel of our God and Saviour is shewing what it can do.

Some circumstances have concurred to distinguish the Kentucky revival from most others, of which we have had any account, I mean the largeness of the assemblies of sacramental occasions.

The length of the time they continued on the ground in devotional exercises. And the great numbers who have fallen down under religious impressions,—on each of these particulars I shall make some remarks.

With respect to the largeness of the assemblies. It is generally supposed that at many places there were not fewer than 8, 10, or 12 thousand people—at a place called Cane Ridge meeting-house, many are of opinion there were at least 20 thousand, there were 140 waggons which came loaded with people, besides other wheel carriages. Some persons had come 200 miles. The largeness of these assemblies was an inconvenience—they were too numerous to be addressed by one speaker, it therefore became necessary for several ministers to officiate at the same time at different stands: this afforded an opportunity to those who were but slightly impressed with religion to wander to and fro between the different places of worship which created an appearance of confusion, and gave ground to such as were unfriendly to the work to charge it with disorder. Another cause also conduced to the same effect; about this time the people began to fall down in great numbers under serious impressions: this was a new thing among Presbyterians; it excited universal astonishment, and created a curiosity which could not be restrained when people *fell* even during the most solemn parts of divine service; those who stood near were so extremely anxious to see how they were affected, that they often crouded about them so as to disturb the worship.—But these causes of disorder were soon removed; different sacraments were appointed on the same Sabbath, which divided the people; and the falling down became so familiar as to excite no disturbance.

In October I attended three Sacraments, at each there were supposed to be 4 or 5 thousand people, and every thing was conducted with strict propriety; when persons fell, those who were near took care of them, and every thing continued quiet until the worship was concluded.

The length of time that people continue at the places of worship, is another important circumstance of the Kentucky revival; at Cane Ridge they met on Friday and continued till Wednesday evening, night and day without intermission, either in public or private exercises of devotion; and with such earnestness that heavy showers of rain were not sufficient to disperse them. On other Sacramental occasions they generally continued on the ground until Monday or Tuesday evening; and had not the preachers been exhausted and obliged to retire, or had they chosen to prolong the worship they might have kept the people any length of time they pleased, and all this was, or might have been done, in a country where less than twelve months before the Clergy found it difficult to detain the people during the usual exercises of the Sabbath. The practice of camping on the ground was introduced, partly by necessity, and partly by inclination; the assemblies were generally too large to be received by any common neighbourhood; every thing indeed was done which hospitality and brotherly kindness could do, to accommodate the people; public and private houses were opened, and free invitations given to all persons who wished to retire. Farmers gave up their meadows before they were mown to supply the horses; yet notwithstanding all this liberality it would have been impossible in many cases, to have accommodated the whole assemblies with private lodgings: but besides the people were unwilling to suffer any interruption in their devotions; and they formed an attachment to the place where they were continually seeing so many careless sinners receiving their first impressions, and so many Deists constrained to call on the formerly despised name of JESUS; they conceived a sentiment like what Jacob felt in Bethel. "Surely the Lord is in this place," "This is none other than the house of God, and this is the gate of heaven."

The number of persons who have fallen down under serious impressions in this revival, is another matter worthy of attention, and on this I shall be more particular, as it seems to be the principal cause why this work should be more suspected of enthusiasm than some other revivals.

At Cane Ridge Sacrament it is generally supposed not less than 1000 persons fell prostrate to the ground, among whom were many infidels. At one sacrament which I attended, the number that fell was thought to be more than 300. Persons who fall, are generally such as had manifested symptoms of the deepest impressions for some time previous to the event. It is common to see them shed tears plentifully for about an hour.

Immediately before they become totally powerless they are seized with a general tremor and sometimes, though not often, they utter one or two piercing shrieks in the moment of falling; persons in this situation are affected in different degrees; sometimes when unable to stand or sit they have the use of their hands and can converse with perfect composure. In other cases they are unable to speak, the pulse becomes weak, and they draw a difficult breath about once in a minute: in some instances their extremities become cold, and pulsation, breathing, and all the signs of life forsake them for nearly an hour; persons who have been in this situation have uniformly avowed that they felt no bodily pain, that they had the entire use of their reason and reflection, and when recovered, they could relate every thing that had been said or done near them, or which could possibly fall within their observation. From this it appears that their falling is neither common fainting, nor a nervous action. Indeed this strange phenomenon appears to have taken every possible turn to baffle the conjectures of those who are not willing to consider it a supernatural work. Persons have sometimes fallen on their way from public worship; and sometimes after they arrived at home, and in some cases when they were pursuing their common business on their farms, or when retired for secret devotion. It was above observed that persons generally are seriously affected for some time previous to their falling; in many cases however, it is otherwise. Numbers of thoughtless sinners have fallen as suddenly as if struck with lightening. Many professed Infidels, and other vicious characters, have been arrested in this way, and sometimes at the very moment when they were uttering blasphemies against the work.

At the beginning of the revival in Shelby county the appearances, as related to me by eye-witnesses, were very surprising indeed. The revival had before this spread with irresistible power through the adjacent counties: and many of the pious had attended distant sacraments with great benefit. These were much engaged, and felt unusual freedom in their addresses at the throne of grace, for the outpouring of the divine Spirit at the approaching sacrament in Shelby. The Sacrament came on in September. The people, as usual, met on Friday: but all were languid, and the exercises went on heavily. On Saturday and Sunday morning it was no better, at length the communion service commenced, everything was still lifeless; whilst the minister of the place was speaking at one of the tables, without any unusual animation, suddenly there were several shrieks from different parts of the assembly; instantly persons fell in every direction; the feelings of the pious were suddenly revived, and the work progressed with extraordinary power, till the conclusion of the solemnity: this phenomenon of falling is common to all ages, sexes and characters; and when they fall they are differently exercised. Some pious people have fallen under a sense of ingratitude and hardness

of heart, and others under affecting manifestations of the love and goodness of GOD. Many thoughtless persons under legal convictions, have obtained comfort before they arose. But perhaps the most numerous class consists of those who fall under distressing views of their guilt, who arise with the same fearful apprehensions, and continue in that state for some days, perhaps weeks, before they receive comfort. I have conversed with many who fell under the influence of comfortable feelings, and the account they gave of their exercises while they lay entranced was very surprising. I know not how to give you a better idea of them than by saying that in many cases they appeared to surpass the dying exercises of Dr. Finley: their minds appeared wholly swallowed up in contemplating the perfections of Deity, as illustrated in the plan of salvation, and whilst they lay apparently senseless, and almost lifeless, their minds were more vigorous and their memories more retentive and accurate than they had ever been before. I have heard men of respectability assert that their manifestations of gospel truth were so clear as to require some caution when they began to speak, less they should use language which might induce their hearers to suppose they had seen those things with their bodily eyes; but at the same time they had seen no image nor sensible representation, nor indeed any thing besides the old truths contained in the Bible.

Among those whose minds were filled with the most delightful communications of divine love, I but seldom observed any thing ecstatic. Their expressions were just and rational, they conversed with calmness and composure, and on their first recovering the use of speech, they appeared like persons recovering from a violent disease which had left them on the borders of the grave. I have sometimes been present when persons who fell under the influence of convictions obtained relief before they arose; in these cafes it was impossible not to observe how strongly the change in their minds was depicted in their countenances, instead of a face of horror and despair, they assumed one open, luminous, serene and expressive of all the comfortable feelings of religion. As to those who fall down under legal convictions and continue in that state, they are not different from those who receive convictions in other revivals, excepting that their distress is more severe. Indeed extraordinary power is the leading characteristic of this revival; both saints and sinners have more striking discoveries of the realities of another world, than I have ever known on any other occasion.

I trust I have said enough on this subject to enable you to judge how far the charge of enthusiasm is applicable to it. Lord Lyttleton in his letter on the conversion of St. Paul observes, (I think justly) that enthusiasm is a vain self-righteous spirit, swelled with self-sufficiency and disposed to glory in its religious attainments. If this be a good definition there has been perhaps as little enthusiasm in the Kentucky revival as in any other, never have I seen more genuine marks of that humility which disclaims the merit of its own duties, and looks to the Lord Jesus Christ as the only way of acceptance with God, I was indeed highly pleased to find that

Christ was all and all in their religion, as well as in the religion of the gospel. Christians in their highest attainments seemed most sensible of their entire dependance on divine grace, and it was truly affecting to hear with what agonizing anxiety awakened sinners enquired for Christ, as the only physician who could give them any help.—Those who call these things enthusiasm ought to tell us what they understand by the spirit of christianity. In fact, sir, this revival operates as our Saviour promised the Holy Spirit should when sent into the world, it convinces of sin, of righteousness, and of judgment, a strong confirmation to my mind, both that the promise is divine, and that this is a remarkable fulfilment of it. It would be of little avail to object to all this, that probably the professions of many were counterfeited, such as objection would rather establish what it meant to destroy, for where there is no reality, there can be no counterfeit, and besides when the general tenor of a work is such as to dispose the more insincere professors to counterfeit what is right, the work itself must be genuine; but as an eye-witness in the café, I may be permitted to declare that the professions of those under religious convictions were generally marked with such a degree of engagedness and feeling as wilful

hypocrisy could hardly assume—the language of the heart when deeply impressed is very distinguishable from the language of affection. Upon the whole, sir, I think the revival in Kentucky among the most extraordinary that have ever visited the church of Christ, and, all things considered, peculiarly adapted to the circumstances of that country. Infidelity was triumphant, and religion at the point of expiring. Something of an extraordinary nature seemed necessary to arrest the attention of a giddy people, who were ready to conclude that Christianity was a fable, and futurity a dream. This revival has done it; it has confounded infidelity, awed vice into silence, and brought numbers beyond calculation, under serious impressions.

Whilst the Blessed Saviour was calling home his people, and building up his church in this remarkable way, opposition could not be silent—At this I hinted above; but it is proper to observe, that the clamorous opposition which assailed the work at its commencement has been in a great measure borne down before it. A large proportion of those who have fallen, were at first opposers, and their example has taught others to be cautious, if it has not taught them to be wise.

Questions

1. What evidence did Reverend Baxter cite as proof of the good and lasting effects of the Cane Ridge revival? Could the facts he stated be interpreted differently?

2. Reverend Baxter went to great lengths to defend the "devotional exercises" and extreme religious "enthusiasm" that set the Cane Ridge camp meeting apart from other frontier revivals. Why do you think he felt the need to do so? Who might have been skeptical of the goings-on at Cane Ridge, and why?

3. What challenges did the frontier camp meeting pose to its organizers? From a logistical and organizational standpoint, how did a camp meeting work?

8-12   What Makes Religion Powerful in America? (1831)

Alexis de Tocqueville

Without the structure of an established church, Christianity in America came to be characterized by sectarian rivalries that resembled nothing so much as the emerging democratic marketplace. The most successful churches were those that bested their competition by attracting more followers and then holding on to them. Alexis de Tocqueville (1805–1859), a French aristocrat who came to the United States in 1831 and who wrote extensively about the American people and their institutions, was struck by the fact that religion was a more powerful presence in the United States than it was in Europe. In a selection from his two-volume classic *Democracy in America* (1835, 1840), Tocqueville seeks to explain this phenomenon.

Source: From Harvey C. Mansfield and Delba Winthrop, eds., *Democracy in America*. Copyright © 2000 by the University of Chicago Press. Reprinted by permission of the University of Chicago Press.

There is a certain European population whose disbelief is equaled only by their brutishness and ignorance, whereas in America one sees one of the freest and most enlightened peoples in the world eagerly fulfill all the external duties of religion.

On my arrival in the United States it was the religious aspect of the country that first struck my eye. As I prolonged my stay, I perceived the great political consequences that flowed from these new facts.

Among us, I had seen the spirit of religion and the spirit of freedom almost always move in contrary directions. Here I found them united intimately with one another: they reigned together on the same soil.

I felt my desire to know the cause of this phenomenon growing daily.

To learn it, I interrogated the faithful of all communions; above all, I sought the society of priests, who keep the depositories of the different beliefs and who have a personal interest in their duration. The religion that I profess brought me together particularly with the Catholic clergy, and I was not slow to bond in a sort of intimacy with several of its members. To each of them I expressed my astonishment and exposed my doubts: I found that all these men differed among themselves only on details; but all attributed the peaceful dominion that religion exercises in their country principally to the complete separation of church and state. I do not fear to affirm that during my stay in America I did not encounter a single man, priest or layman, who did not come to accord on this point.

. . . I wondered how it could happen that in diminishing the apparent force of a religion one came to increase its real power, and I believed that it was not impossible to discover this.

I know that there are times when religion can add to the influence that is proper to it the artificial power of the laws and the support of the material powers that direct society. One has seen religions intimately united with earthly governments, dominating souls by terror and by faith at the same time; but when a religion contracts an alliance like this, I do not fear to say that it acts as a man would: it sacrifices the future with a view to the present, and in obtaining a power that is not due to it, it risks its legitimate power.

When a religion seeks to found its empire only on the desire for immortality that torments the hearts of all men equally, it can aim at universality; but when it comes to be united with a government, it must adopt maxims that are applicable only to certain peoples. So, therefore, in allying itself with a political power, religion increases its power over some and loses the hope of reigning over all.

As long as a religion is supported only by sentiments that are the consolation of all miseries, it can attract the hearts of the human race to it. Mixed with the bitter passions of this world, it is sometimes constrained to defend allies given it by interest rather than love; and it must repel as adversaries men who often still love it, while they are combating those with whom it has united. Religion, therefore, cannot share the material force of those who govern without being burdened with a part of the hatreds to which they give rise.

In uniting with different political powers, religion can therefore contract only an onerous alliance. It does not need their assistance to live, and in serving them it can die. . . .

Insofar as a nation takes on a democratic social state, the societies are seen to incline toward republics, it becomes more and more dangerous for religion to unite with authority; for the time approaches when power is going to pass from hand to hand, when political theories will succeed one another, when men, laws, and constitutions themselves will disappear or be modified daily—and this lasting not only for a time, but constantly. Agitation and instability are due to the nature of democratic republics, just as immobility and sleep form the law of absolute monarchies.

If the Americans, who change their head of state every four years, who every two years make a choice of new legislators and replace provincial administrators each year; if the Americans, who have delivered the political world to the attempts of innovators, had not placed their religion somewhere outside of that, what could it hold onto in the ebb and flow of human opinions? In the midst of the parties' struggle, where would the respect be that is due it? What would become of its immortality when everything around it was perishing?

In America, religion is perhaps less powerful than it has been in certain times and among certain peoples, but its influence is more lasting. It is reduced to its own strength, which no one can take away from it; it acts in one sphere only, but it covers the whole of it and dominates it without effort.

One encounters among us, therefore, an accidental and particular cause that prevents the human spirit from following its inclination, and pushes it beyond the limits within which it ought naturally to halt.

I am profoundly convinced that this particular and accidental cause is the intimate union of politics and religion.

The unbelievers of Europe hound Christians as political enemies rather than as religious adversaries: they hate faith as the opinion of a party much more than as an erroneous belief; and it is less the representative of God that they repel in the priest than the friend of power.

In Europe, Christianity has permitted itself to be intimately united with the powers of the earth. Today these powers are falling and it is almost buried under their debris. It is a living [thing] that someone wanted to attach to the dead: cut the bonds that hold it back and it will rise again.

Questions

1. According to Tocqueville, how was the spirit of religion linked to the spirit of freedom in America? How do his ideas compare with those espoused by Thomas Jefferson in the Virginia statute of religious freedom (Document 6-13)?

2. Why would religion inevitably lose some of its power by allying itself with political power?

3. Why is it more important in a democracy than in an absolute monarchy that religion and politics be kept separate?

Questions for Further Thought

1. At the same time that Americans set out to create a democratic society, in the first few decades of the nineteenth century, they also transformed the United States into a fundamentally Christian nation. Were these two phenomena related in any way? Explain.

2. Were there any common themes in the "quest for a republican society"?

CHAPTER NINE

Economic Transformation
1820–1860

The American Industrial Revolution

At first it seemed unlikely that the United States would become an industrial nation. Only one nation in the world—Great Britain—had progressed very far toward industrialization at the beginning of the nineteenth century, and its factories owed much of their success to the cheap labor resulting from widespread poverty. Blessed with large amounts of land (once the Indian population was dealt with) and relatively few people, Americans such as Thomas Jefferson expected the nation to remain agricultural; indeed, since they saw factories and industrial cities as teeming with mobs of poor, dependent people, they hoped that such "unrepublican" institutions would remain far from their shores. Others, however, did not share Jefferson's enthusiasm for the virtues of an ideal agrarian economy. In reality, much of the agriculture in America depended on slave labor, and the evils of this system blatantly contradicted the republican ideals of Jefferson's vision.

The emergence of the textile industry depended on several factors: entrepreneurs with access to capital, an abundant source of cheap labor, and a reliable source of energy. In New England, wealthy merchants Francis Cabot Lowell and Nathan Appleton successfully invested in a number of textile factories powered by waterwheels. They obtained their workforce by hiring children (Document 9-1) and large numbers of young women from New England farms to work temporarily at their mills while living in well-supervised boardinghouses. At least initially, these factory jobs were quite attractive to the young women, who found in them a means of escaping the drudgery of the farm, an opportunity to enjoy some freedom between childhood and marriage, and a means of accumulating some money (Documents 9-2 and 9-3). The paternalism of what was called the Waltham plan also seemed to offer a "republican" American alternative to the specter of the pauper labor that haunted industrial Great Britain and Thomas Jefferson alike (Document 9-4).

By the 1840s the impact of the Industrial Revolution in America was becoming increasingly apparent. New machinery and new ways of organizing labor had resulted in unparalleled economic growth. Some observers thus welcomed these innovations as necessary for the United States to join the industrial powers, but others were not certain that their benefits exceeded their costs. Joseph Whitworth and Orestes A. Brownson represent these extremes. While the former celebrated the contributions and independence of the "labouring classes" (Document 9-5), the latter thought their situation was worse than that of southern slaves (Document 9-8).

9-1   Calculating the Value of Children's Labor (1816)

Niles' Weekly Register

Alexander Hamilton's vision of the United States was neatly compressed into three reports he presented, as the first secretary of the treasury, to the House of Representatives in 1790–1791. The first two, dealing with public credit and a national bank, were enacted. The third, in which he outlined a program of protective tariffs and bounties aimed at promoting domestic manufacturing, was ignored. The vast majority of Americans were wedded to the Jeffersonian vision of the United States as an agricultural nation. Nevertheless, domestic industries became an increasingly important part of the American economy in the early nineteenth century (see text pp. 272–278). Textile factories, for the most part concentrated in southern New England, were in the forefront of this industrial revolution, and children formed an essential component of the new industrial workforce. *Niles' Weekly Register* was a popular magazine founded by the printer Hezekiah Niles in 1811.

Source: Excerpt from *Children and Youth in America: A Documentary History*, ed. Robert H. Bremner (Cambridge, MA: Harvard University Press), 1:180–182. Copyright © 1970 by the American Public Health Organization.

By calculations made upon the data furnished by the census of 1810, it appears that the children, under 10 years, averaged, for the middle states, are 35 per cent. of the whole population; and that those of 10 and under 16, in like manner, are about 15 per cent. making together 50 per cent. Or, in other words, that the children under 16 years of age are one half of all the inhabitants of this section of the United States.

A certain town, in one of these states, well situated and healthy, had by that census 4416 inhabitants; and, consequently, the children under 16 years old may be estimated at 2208.

But we have no datum to determine what proportion of these children were under 7 years — we may suppose them at a half, or 1104; which we may also suppose incapable of any employment other than the little services they can render in domestic affairs; — and we have 1104 between the ages of 7 and 16 capable of some sorts of business not immediately connected with the concerns of the families of which they are members. By an actual enumeration of the children at school, in the town alluded to, in 1814, they amounted to 650 — but of these 60 were from other places, and the number of *town* children was only 590, leaving of 1104 a balance of 514. Of which 514 we may suppose 100 were apprenticed — 50 at school in other places, and 100 in the employ of their parents, who prefer keeping them at home to sending them to earn a living in the manufactories adjacent — deducting, then, 250 from the 514, we have 264 in the town unemployed, unless they be engaged in the cotton, woolen or card-making establishments, within it or in its neighborhood. Say 200 — and let us attempt to calculate the difference to the community in employing them and suffering them to remain unemployed.

A cotton manufactory of 5 or 6000 spindles will employ those 200 children, and their wages may be reckoned as follows:

100 at 125 cents per week,	$125 00
50 at 150 do.	75 00
50 at 200 do.	100 00
	300 00
Say for 45 weeks in the year,	$13,500 00

Calculations pretty accurately made show that it will require $25 a year to clothe a child of 7 years old, in an economical way — the clothing of these children would cost 5000 dollars, leaving 8,500 dollars towards their board and education. If we suppose, that, before the establishment of these manufactories, there were 200 children, between 7 and 16 years of age, that contributed nothing towards, their maintenance and that they are now employed, it makes an *immediate* difference of 13,500 dollars a year to the value produced in the town, and may also make a considerable saving by reducing the cost of clothing. Let us see the effects of this employment on agriculture and commerce.

Daily experience teaches, us, that as the means of subsistence are facilitated, the people are disposed to enjoy what is called the comforts of life — to eat better or richer food, and wear better or more costly clothing; and as these 200 children create a value of 13,500 dollars a year, we may fairly suppose that nearly so much more will be expended for these things . . .

If such be the effects of the introduction of manufactures into a small district (I do not wish to be understood as meaning only those of cotton and wool, but of all that give employment to children from 7 to 16 years of age) let us see how the calculation will apply to all the United States.

It is pretty clear that a gross population of 4,416 persons *may* have 200 children wanting employment — the United States contains 7 millions of white inhabitants, and, by the same ratio, may have 317,000 such children, whose annual wage, as above, would amount to $21,397,500. This is more than the average annual revenue of the general and state governments, united, and equal to about half the value of our exports of domestic produce and manufacture.

But it cannot be thought possible to employ all the children in the United States as calculated above: 1st, because they are too widely scattered to be brought into such employment; and 2ndly, because it supposes a progress in manufactures that we may not attain to for a generation to come, if so soon as that—for to employ 317,000 children would require the establishment of nearly 8 millions of cotton spindles, or of something else equivalent thereto—an increase not to be expected or desired: but there are a great variety of businesses yet to be introduced amongst us, necessary to secure to us what we consider the comforts, if not the necessaries of life, and make us independent of all nations . . .

Questions

1. Based on these calculations, at what age might a child have been expected to enter the industrial workforce? Given the fact that children since the colonial period had worked on farms and contributed to household production, was there anything novel here?

2. The word *statisticks* was formally incorporated into American English in the early 1800s, and *Niles' Weekly Register* made statistical reports a regular feature in the 1810s. Does this essay tell us more about the writer or about American society by this time? What might account for this increasing interest in numbers?

3. In 1791 the nation seemed unprepared for Hamilton's proposals, but his program may have appeared modest to some members of the next generation of Americans. What benefits did this writer anticipate would accompany the implementation of his recommendations? Was there any hint of a negative impact?

9-2   A Mill Worker Describes Her Work and Life (1844)

A majority of the workers in the early years of the textile industry were young women from New England farm families (see text pp. 274–277). The women mill hands in Lowell, Massachusetts, published their own poetry and other compositions in *The Lowell Offering*. The following letters, written by a worker identified only as "Susan," were published in 1844.

Source: From *The Lowell Offering* (June and August 1844), 169–172, 237–240, in *Looking for America: The People's History*, ed. Stanley I. Kutler, 2nd ed., 1:260–265. Copyright © 1979 by Stanley I. Kutler. Used with permission of W. W. Norton and Company, Inc.

DEAR MARY:

In my last I told you I would write again, and say more of my life here; and this I will now attempt to do.

I went into the mill to work a few days after I wrote to you. It looked very pleasant at first, the rooms were so light, spacious, and clean, the girls so pretty and neatly dressed, and the machinery so brightly polished or nicely painted. The plants in the windows, or on the overseer's bench or desk, gave a pleasant aspect to things. You will wish to know what work I am doing. I will tell you of the different kinds of work.

There is, first, the carding-room, where the cotton flies most, and the girls get the dirtiest. But this is easy, and the females are allowed time to go out at night before the bell rings—on Saturday night at least, if not on all other nights. Then there is the spinning-room, which is very neat and pretty. In this room are the spinners and doffers. The spinners watch the frames; keep them clean, and the threads mended if they break. The doffers take off the full bobbins, and put on the empty ones. They have nothing to do in the long intervals when the frames are in motion, and can go out to their boarding-houses, or do any thing else that they like. In some of the factories the spinners do their own doffing, and when this is the case they work no harder than the weavers. These last have the hardest time of all—or can have, if they choose to take charge of three or four looms, instead of the one pair which is the allotment. And they are the most constantly confined. The spinners and dressers have but the weavers to keep supplied, and then their work can stop. The dressers never work before breakfast, and they stay out a great deal in the afternoons. The drawers-in, or girls who draw the threads through the harnesses, also work in the dressing-room, and they all have very good wages—better than the weavers who have but the usual work. The dressing-rooms are very neat, and the frames move with a gentle undulating motion which is really graceful. But these rooms are kept very warm, and are disagreeably scented with the "sizing," or starch, which stiffens the "beams," or unwoven webs. There are many plants in these rooms, and it is really a good green-house for them. The dressers are generally quite tall girls, and must have pretty tall minds too, as their work requires much care and attention.

I could have had work in the dressing-room, but chose to be a weaver; and I will tell you why. I disliked the closer air of the dressing-room, though I might have become accustomed to that. I could not learn to dress so quickly as I could to weave, nor have work of my own so soon, and should have had to stay with Mrs. C. two or three weeks before I could go in at all, and I did not like to be "lying upon my oars" so long. And, more than this, when I get well learned I can have extra work, and make double wages, which you know is quite an inducement with some.

Well, I went into the mill, and was put to learn with a very patient girl—a clever old maid. I should be willing to be one myself if I could be as good as she is. You cannot think how odd every thing seemed to me. I wanted to laugh at every thing, but did not know what to make sport of first. They set me to threading shuttles, and tying weaver's knots, and such things, and now I have improved so that I can take care of one loom. I could take care of two if I only had eyes in the back part of my head, but I have not got used to "looking two ways of a Sunday" yet.

At first the hours seemed very long, but I was so interested in learning that I endured it very well; and when I went out at night, the sound of the mill was in my ears, as of crickets, frogs, and jewsharps [small musical instrument; it twangs], all mingled together in strange discord. After that it seemed as though cotton-wool was in my ears, but now I do not mind it at all. You know that people learn to sleep with the thunder of Niagara in their ears, and a cotton mill is no worse, though you wonder that we do not have to hold our breath in such a noise.

It makes my feet ache and swell to stand so much, but I suppose I shall get accustomed to that too. The girls generally wear old shoes about their work, and you know nothing is easier; but they almost all say that when they have worked here a year or two they have to procure shoes a size or two larger than before they came. The right hand, which is the one used in stopping and starting the loom, becomes larger than the left; but in other respects the factory is not detrimental to a young girl's appearance. Here they look delicate, but not sickly; they laugh at those who are much exposed, and get pretty brown; but I, for one, had rather be brown than pure white. I never saw so many pretty looking girls as there are here. Though the number of men is small in proportion there are many marriages here, and a great deal of courting. I will tell you of this last sometime.

You wish to know minutely of our hours of labor. We go in at five o'clock; at seven we come out to breakfast; at half-past seven we return to our work, and stay until half-past twelve. At one, or quarter-past one four months in the year, we return to our work, and stay until seven at night. Then the evening is all our own, which is more than some laboring girls can say, who think nothing is more tedious than a factory life.

When I first came here, which was the last of February, the girls ate their breakfast before they went to their work. The first of March they came out at the present breakfast hour, and the twentieth of March they ceased to "light up" the rooms, and come out between six and seven o'clock.

You ask if the girls are contented here: I ask you, if you know of *any one* who is perfectly contented. Do you remember the old story of the philosopher, who offered a field to the person who was contented with his lot; and when one claimed it, he asked him why, if he was so perfectly satisfied, he wanted his field. The girls here are not contented; and there is no disadvantage in their situation which they do not perceive as quickly, and lament as loudly, as the sternest opponents of the factory system do. They would scorn to say they were contented, if asked the question; for it would compromise their Yankee spirit—their pride, penetration, independence, and love of "freedom and equality" to say that they were *contented* with such a life as this. Yet, withal, they are cheerful. I never saw a happier set of beings. They appear blithe in the mill, and out of it. If you see one of them, with a very long face, you may be sure that it is because she has heard bad news from home, or because her beau has vexed her. But, if it is a Lowell trouble, it is because she has failed in getting off as many "sets" or "pieces" as she intended to have done; or because she had a sad "break-out," or "break-down," in her work, or something of that sort.

You ask if the work is not disagreeable. Not when one is accustomed to it. It tried my patience sadly at first, and does now when it does not run well; but, in general, I like it very much. It is easy to do, and does not require very violent exertion, as much of our farm work does.

You also ask how I get along with the girls here. Very well indeed. . . .

DEAR MARY: . . .

The mill girls are the prettiest in the city. You wonder how they can keep neat. Why not? There are no restrictions as to the number of pieces to be washed in the boarding-house. And, as there is plenty of water in the mill, the girls can wash their laces and muslins and other nice things themselves, and no boarding woman ever refuses the conveniences for starching and ironing. You say too that you do not see how we can have so many conveniences and comforts at the price we pay for board. You must remember that the boarding-houses belong to the companies, and are let to the tenants far below the usual city rent—sometimes the rent is remitted. Then there are large families, so that there are the profits of many individuals. The country farmers are quite in the habit of bringing their produce to the boarding-houses for sale, thus reducing the price by the omission of the market-man's profit. So you see there are many ways by which we get along so well.

You ask me how the girls behave in the mill, and what are the punishments. They behave very well while about their work, and I have never heard of punishments, or scoldings, or anything of that sort. Sometimes an overseer finds fault, and sometimes offends a girl by refusing to let her stay out of the mill, or some deprivation like that; and then, perhaps, there are tears and pouts on her part, but, in general, the tone of intercourse between the girls and overseers is very good—pleasant, yet respectful. When the latter are fatherly sort of men the girls frequently resort to them for advice and assistance about other affairs than their work. Very seldom is this confidence abused; but, among the thousands of overseers who have lived in Lowell, and the tens of thousands of girls who have in time been here, there are legends still told of wrong suffered and committed. "To err is human," and when the frailties of humanity are exhibited by a factory girl it is thought of for worse than are the errors of any other persons.

The only punishment among the girls is dismission from their places. They do not, as many think, withhold their wages; and as for corporal punishment—mercy on me! To strike a female would cost any overseer his place. If the superintendents did not take the affair into consideration the girls would turn out [go on strike], as they did at the Temperance celebration, "Independent day;" and if they didn't look as pretty, I am sure they would produce as deep an impression. . . .

Do you wish to hear anything more about the overseers? Once for all, then, there are many very likely intelligent public-spirited men among them. They are interested in the good movements of the day; teachers in the Sabbath schools; and some have represented the city in the State Legislature. They usually marry among the factory girls, and do not connect themselves with their inferiors either. Indeed, in almost all the matches here the female is superior in education and manner, if not in intellect, to her partner.

The overseers have good salaries, and their families live very prettily. I observe that in almost all cases the mill girls make excellent wives. They are good managers, orderly in their households, and "neat as waxwork." It seems as though they were so delighted to have houses of their own to take care of, that they would never weary of the labor and the care.

Questions

1. What appears to have been the purpose of Susan's letters to Mary?

2. How did Susan describe the work environment?

3. What did she consider the advantages and disadvantages of working in the mill?

9-3   Morals of Manufactures (1837)

Harriet Martineau

Harriet Martineau (1802–1876) joined a steady stream of British and European visitors to the United States in the early nineteenth century. She published her observations about society in America after a two-year stay from 1834 to 1836. Martineau enthusiastically embraced the radical social implications of the Industrial Revolution and saw in the United States a brave social experiment in human equality. An ardent feminist and abolitionist, Martineau noted that the subordination of women and slaves in the United States contradicted the egalitarian principles enunciated in the Declaration of Independence. But she saw signs of future progress emerging in New England's new industrial order. The Waltham plan (see text pp. 274–277) offered young American women of modest means an alternative to domestic service; the factory system also suggested to Martineau the manner in which the United States could protect itself from the ills of poverty that infected industrial society in Britain.

Source: Harriet Martineau, *Society in America* (London: Saunders and Otley, 1837; reprint, New York: AMS Press, 1966), 2:355–358.

The morals of the female factory population may be expected to be good when it is considered of what class it is composed. Many of the girls are in the factories because they have too much pride for domestic service. Girls who are too proud for domestic service as it is in America, can hardly be low enough for any gross immorality; or to need watching; or not to be trusted to avoid the contagion of evil example. To a stranger, their pride seems to take a mistaken direction, and they appear to deprive themselves of a respectable home and station, and many benefits, by their dislike of service: but this is altogether their own affair. They must choose for themselves their way of life. But the reasons of their choice indicate a state of mind superior to the grossest dangers of their position.

I saw a bill fixed up in the Waltham mill which bore a warning that no young lady who attended dancing-school that winter should be employed: and that the corporation had given directions to the overseer to dismiss any one who should be found to dance at the school. I asked the meaning of this; and the overseer's answer was, "Why, we had some trouble last winter about the dancing-school. It must, of course, be held in the evening, as the young folks are in the mill all day. They are very young, many of them; and they forget the time, and everything but the amusement, and dance away till two or three in the morning. They are unfit for their work the next day; or, if they get properly through their work, it is at the expense of their health. So we have forbidden the dancing-school; but, to make up for it, I have promised them that, as soon as the great new room at the hotel is finished, we will have a dance once a-fortnight. We shall meet and break up early; and my wife and I will dance; and we will all dance together."

I was sorry to see one bad and very unnecessary arrangement, in all the manufacturing establishments. In England, the best friends of the poor are accustomed to think it the crowning hardship of their condition that solitude is wholly forbidden to them. It is impossible that any human being should pass his life as well as he might do who is never alone. . . . The silence, freedom and collectedness of solitude are absolutely essential to the health of the mind. . . . In the dwellings of the English poor, parents and children are crowded into one room. . . . All wise parents above the rank of poor, make it a primary consideration so to arrange their families as that each member may, at some hour have some place where he may enter in, and shut his door, and feel himself alone. If possible, the sleeping places are so ordered. In America, where space is of far less consequence . . . these same girls have no private apartments, and sometimes sleep six or eight in a room, and even three in a bed. This is very bad. . . .

Now are the days when these gregarious habits should be broken through. . . . If the change be not soon made, the American factory population, with all its advantages of education and of pecuniary sufficiency, will be found, as its numbers increase, to have been irreparably injured by its subjection to a grievance . . . to which poverty exposes artisans in old countries.

Questions

1. Why did the young women at Waltham prefer factory work to domestic service?

2. Why was Martineau concerned about the "morals" of industrial employment?

3. What social dangers did Martineau think would result from the absence of solitude in the new industrial order?

9-4   The "Factory Girls" (1844, 1845)

The images reproduced here complement the written accounts of factory life given in Documents 9-2 and 9-3. The first is a daguerreotype of mill workers from the Amoskeag Manufacturing Company, Manchester, New Hampshire, c. 1844. The daguerreotype, invented in 1839, was considered a democratic medium because it was the first to produce affordable portraits. Before this new technology was invented, the only way to have one's portrait made was to commission an artist to paint it, an expense that was not within the average person's reach. The second image is the cover of an issue of the *Lowell Offering*. This literary magazine, a collection of poems, letters, and sketches by the factory workers at Lowell, is excerpted in Document 9-2.

Sources: Daguerreotype of Amoskeag Manufacturing Company workers, Manchester, New Hampshire, c. 1844. Courtesy the Manchester (NH) Historic Association. Title page from the *Lowell Offering*, December 1845. Courtesy of the American Textile History Museum, Lowell, MA.

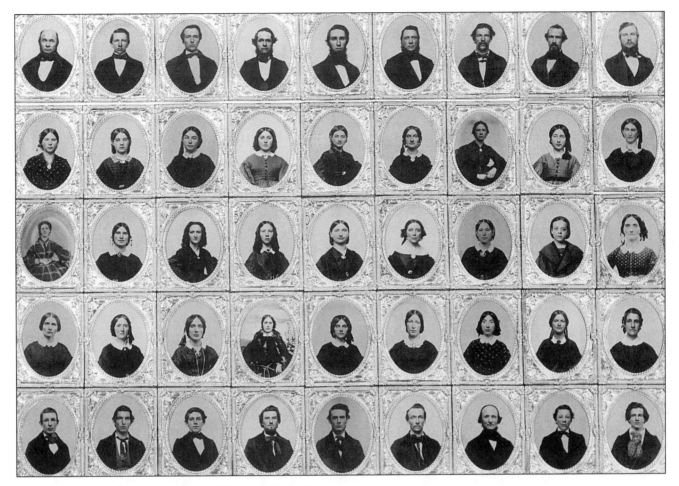

(A)   *Mill Workers from the Amoskeag Manufacturing Company*

Questions

1. When examining visual sources, it is often important to understand why, how, and by whom they were created. Who might have made the daguerreotype images of the mill workers at Amoskeag? Why were they all framed together instead of separately?

2. What do the dress and deportment of the mill workers convey? To what extent does the intended message correspond with what you've read in Documents 9-2 and 9-3?

3. In what way does the image from the *Lowell Offering* idealize the female factory worker? What criticisms might the factory owners have been trying to deflect by projecting this idealized image?

(B) *The Cover of an Issue of the* Lowell Offering

9-5 The American System of Manufactures (1854)

Joseph Whitworth

At London's Great (or "Crystal Palace") Exhibition of 1851, widely regarded as the first world's fair, the British sought to demonstrate their technological supremacy in the world. However, the American exhibit quickly indicated that Britain's cousins across the water were rapidly coming to the fore. Moreover, as the exhibit of Samuel Colt's machine-made revolvers attested, Americans had developed their own distinctive technological style, which was soon dubbed "the American system of manufactures." Several years later, the British government sent investigators to America, including Joseph Whitworth (1803–1887), the world's leading manufacturer of machine tools, to assess the progress made by American manufacturers. The conclusion of Whitworth's 1854 report to Parliament contains the following observations on the environmental characteristics he believed made Americans such an innovative people.

Source: "Special Report of Mr. Joseph Whitworth," in Nathan Rosenberg, ed., *The American System of Manufactures* (Edinburgh: Edinburgh University Press, 1969), 387–389.

NEW YORK INDUSTRIAL EXHIBITION, SPECIAL REPORT OF MR. JOSEPH WHITWORTH. PRESENTED TO THE HOUSE OF COMMONS BY COMMAND OF HER MAJESTY, IN PURSUANCE OF THEIR ADDRESS OF FEBRUARY 6, 1854. LONDON: PRINTED BY HARRISON AND SON.

Conclusions

The parts of the United States which I visited form, geographically, a small portion of their extended territory, but they are the principal seats of manufactures, and afford ample opportunities for arriving at general conclusions. I could not fail to be impressed, from all that I saw there, with the extraordinary energy of the people, and their peculiar aptitude in availing themselves to the utmost of the immense natural resources of the country.

The details which I have collected in this report show, by numerous examples, that they leave no means untried to effect what they think it is possible to accomplish, and they have been signally successful in combining large practical results with great economy in the methods by which these results are secured.

The labouring classes are comparatively few in number, but this is counter-balanced by, and indeed may be regarded as one of the chief causes of, the eagerness with which they call in the aid of machinery in almost every department of industry. Wherever it can be introduced as a substitute for manual labour, it is universally and willingly resorted to; of this the facts stated in my report contain many conclusive proofs, but I may here specially refer, as examples, to plough making, where eight men are able to finish thirty per day; to door making, where twenty men make 100 panelled doors per day; to last making, the process of which is completed in 1½ minutes; to sewing by machinery, where one woman does the work of 20; to net making, where one woman does the work of 100. It is this condition of the labour market, and this eager resort to machinery whenever it can be applied, to which, under the guidance of superior education and intelligence, the remarkable prosperity of the United States is mainly due. That prosperity is frequently attributed to the possession of a soil of great natural fertility, and it is doubtless true that in certain districts the alluvial deposits are rich and the land fruitful to an extraordinary degree; but while traversing many hundred miles of country in the Northern States, I was impressed with the conviction that the general character of the soil there was the reverse of fertile.

It is not for a moment denied that the natural resources of the United States are immense, that the products of the soil seem capable of being multiplied and varied to almost any extent, and that the supplies of minerals appear to be nearly unlimited.

The material welfare of the country, however, is largely dependent upon the means adopted for turning its natural resources to the best account, at the same time that the calls made upon human labour are reduced as far as practicable.

The attention paid to the working of wood, some details connected with which I have included in the report, is a striking illustration of this. The early settlers found in the forests which they had to clear an unlimited supply of material, which necessity compelled them to employ in every possible way, in the construction of their houses, their furniture, and domestic utensils, in their implements of labour, and in their log-paved roads.

Wood thus became with them a universal material, and work-people being scarce, machinery was introduced as far as possible to supply the want of hands. The character thus given to one branch of manufactures has gradually extended to others. Applied to stone-dressing, for example, one man is enabled, as I have shown, to perform as much work as twenty masons by hand. So great again are the improvements effected in spinning machinery, that one man can attend to a mule containing 1,088 spindles, each spinning 3 hanks, or 3,264 hanks in the aggregate per day. In Hindoostan, where they still spin by hand, it would be extravagant to expect a spinner to accomplish one hank per day; so that in the United States we find the same amount of manual labour, by improved machinery, doing more than 3,000 times the work. But a still more striking comparison between hand and machine labour may be made in the case of lace making in England. Lace of an ordinary figured pattern used to be made "on the cushion" by hand, at the rate of about three meshes per minute. At Nottingham, a machine attended by one person will now produce lace of a similar kind at the rate of about 24,000 meshes per minute; so that one person can, by the employment of a machine, produce 8,000 times as much work as one lace maker by hand.

The results which have been obtained in the United States, by the application of machinery wherever it has been practicable to manufactures, are rendered still more remarkable by the fact, that combinations to resist its introduction there are unheard of. The workmen hail with satisfaction all mechanical improvements, the importance and value of which, as releasing them from the drudgery of unskilled labour, they are enabled by education to understand and appreciate. With the comparatively superabundant supply of hands in this country, and therefore a proportionate difficulty in obtaining remunerative employment, the working classes have less sympathy with the progress of invention. Their condition is a less favourable one than that of their American brethren for forming a just and unprejudiced estimate of the influence which the introduction of machinery is calculated to exercise on their state and prospects. I cannot resist the conclusion, however, that the different views taken by our operatives and those of the United States upon this subject are determined by other and powerful causes, besides those dependent on the supply of labour in the two countries. The principles which ought to regulate the relations between the employer and the employed seem to be thoroughly understood and appreciated in the United States, and while the law of limited liability affords the most ample facilities for the investment of capital in business, the intelligent and educated artizan is left equally free to earn all that he can, by making the best use of his hands, without let or hindrance by his fellows.

It may be that the working classes exhibit an unusual independence of manner, but the same feeling insures the due performance of what they consider to be their duty with less supervision than is required where dependence is to be placed upon uneducated hands.

It rarely happens that a workman who possesses peculiar skill in his craft is disqualified to take the responsible position of superintendent, by the want of education and general knowledge, as is frequently the case in this country. In every State in the Union, and particularly in the north, education is, by means of the common schools, placed within the reach of each individual, and all classes avail themselves of the opportunities afforded. The desire of knowledge so early implanted is greatly increased, while the facilities for diffusing it are amply provided through the in-strumentality of an almost universal press. No taxation of any kind has been suffered to interfere with the development of this powerful agent for promoting the intelligence of the people, and the consequence is, that where the humblest labourer can indulge in the luxury of his daily paper, everybody reads, and thought and intelligence penetrate through the lowest grades of society. The benefits which thus result from a liberal system of education and a cheap press to the working classes of the United States can hardly be over-estimated in a national point of view; but it is to the co-operation of both that they must undoubtedly be ascribed. For if, selecting a proof from among the European States, the condition of Prussia be considered, it will be found that the people of that country, as a body, have not made that progress which, from the great attention paid to the education of all classes, might have been anticipated; and this must certainly be ascribed to the restrictions laid upon the press, which have so materially impeded the general advancement of the people. Wherever education and an unrestricted press are allowed full scope to exercise their united influence, progress and improvement are the certain results, and among the many benefits which arise from their joint co-operation may be ranked most prominently the value which they teach men to place upon intelligent contrivance; the readiness with which they cause new improvements to be received, and the impulse which they thus unavoidably give to that inventive spirit which is gradually emancipating man from the rude forms of labour, and making what were regarded as the luxuries of one age to be looked upon in the next as the ordinary and necessary conditions of human existence.

signed   JOSEPH WHITWORTH

Questions

1. How did Joseph Whitworth explain the rapid development of manufacturing in the United States? What factors did he believe were the most important?

2. Whitworth linked the existence of a free press to the accommodation of machinery by American workers. Was his reasoning sound?

3. How, according to Whitworth, did English and American workers compare with each other? Why did Whitworth believe that American laborers perceived machinery as a positive good rather than a threat?

Questions for Further Thought

1. What might have accounted for the mixed responses to the advent of industrialism in the United States?

2. How might industrialization have affected family life in America?

3. How might Susan (Document 9-2) have responded to Harriet Martineau's observations (Document 9-3)?

The Market Revolution

The developing factory system was made possible by an ever-broadening national market, and in turn encouraged its further extension. Trade expanded first within regions and then, more gradually, between regions. The rise in manufacturing and the growth of cities and towns increased the demand for surplus agricultural produce, and farmers responded by abandoning less productive lands in the East for fertile virgin lands in the West. As westward expansion proceeded, though, the burgeoning population of the interior needed better means of transportation to the outside. In response, a "transportation revolution" developed new means of tying producers and consumers together: the turnpike, the steamboat, the canal, and the railroad. Railroads showed special promise; not only were they more flexible and reliable than water transportation, but they offered promoters great and small the opportunity to carve out economic empires that would sprawl across the continent (Document 9-6). The West in particular fired the imaginations of men who dreamed of creating great cities like Chicago on top of swampland and prairie. Many of these schemes failed, and indeed many of them were designed to swindle the gullible (Document 9-7), but the "boosters" of the West, working through both private enterprises and state undertakings such as canals, knitted the continental interior into an emerging national market and laid the groundwork for the mighty cities and industries of the post–Civil War Midwest.

9-6   Western Railroads (1845)

Jesup W. Scott

Jesup W. Scott (1798–1873) was born in Connecticut and spent his early manhood in South Carolina, but in 1830 he moved to Ohio, where he became a journalist and land speculator. Caught up in the great land boom of the 1830s, he made—and lost—a fortune before settling into life as a real estate dealer and editor of the *Toledo Blade*. In his own time, Scott was best known for his grand vision of economic empire in the Midwest. While others still saw the promise of the West as Jeffersonian utopia, Scott envisioned networks of railroads linking together mighty metropolises, including "the future great city of the world," Toledo. While Scott's prophetic talents obviously had their limits, his writings offer us a glimpse into the mind of a typical western booster, a type of American whose imaginings, however extravagant, would ultimately transform the Midwest into an urban-industrial giant.

Source: Jesup W. Scott, "The Western Railroad Movement," *Hunt's Merchants' Magazine* 12 (1845): 323–330.

THE WESTERN RAILROAD MOVEMENT.

. . . For a time, nearly all the railroads in the country were under the ban of public opinion, almost as much as speculations in corner lots. The tide is evidently again turning in favor of these improvements. It is not, however, a blind or headlong impulse, like that which existed in 1836. It looks back calmly on the past, discriminates what has been wisely done, from what has been done in the spirit of wild speculation, and is ready to embark with caution in new enterprises. In selecting routes for these expensive iron ways, there was, of course, at the commencement, a wide field for the exercise of a well-informed judgment. The country, in all its length and breadth, was open for a choice. Some were so strongly pointed out by the finger of nature, that he who ran might read. Such was the route from New York to Philadelphia and Baltimore, and that between Utica and Albany. These completed, it was plain that the great commercial city of Boston should be connected with the lake region. Yankee enterprise said, and it was done. The commercial and manufacturing towns of New England have already access to lake Erie by locomotive engines. Soon the great commercial emporium, New York, will link herself to this chain. Will this stop at Buffalo, or will it pass westward, and become the great road between New England and the Mississippi? No sane man can doubt that it will be continued, some day, to the center of the great western valley. The practical question now to be answered is—can any part of it be made now, with a fair prospect of paying interest?

We believe there is a portion of it which should be constructed without delay; and we will briefly give our reasons for this belief. The location, between Buffalo and the west end of lake Erie, is painfully directed by the commercial towns on its souther shore, and the uniform level of that shore. From Toledo westward, the indications of nature are not less plain. The shortest route across the Michigan peninsula, that will approach lake Michigan, and admit a continuous line to the Mississippi at its great eastern bend, near the mouth of Rock river, is the natural route, against which no competition can be successfully maintained. It should be connected, either in its main line or by branches, with Michigan city and Chicago. From Toledo to Michigan city, 186 miles, and to the west line of Indiana, 220 miles, the line has been surveyed by competent engineers, and found highly favorable. If it were continued to the Mississippi, the whole length of railroad from Toledo to the Mississippi would be less than 370 miles. The portion from Toledo to the west line of Indiana is that which would pay best; and, as we believe, warrant the outlay of money necessary to complete it without delay. It would encounter no successful competition, in winter or summer; whereas that between Buffalo and Toledo would have a large portion of travel and trade diverted by the steamers on the lake, for some five months every year. The counties through which this road would pass are admirably adapted to the growth of wheat; and although they are at present but partially settled, such is the ease with which a large portion (being openings and prairies) could be improved, that the construction of the railroad would itself nearly fill it with settlers, and cause it to produce a large surplus of wheat before the work should be completed. A district of country, equal to 40 miles in breadth, lying on both sides of this road for, say 180 miles, might be safely calculated on to use it for its exports and imports. This district alone has an area of 7,200 square miles—about equal to the state of Massachusetts. With an average population equal to that of Ohio in 1840, it would contain 270,000 inhabitants. We believe it would contain that number by the time the work could be completed, if entered on within one year. This route would take all the travel, summer and winter, between the country eastward of Toledo and a vast extent of country lying westward, northwestward, and southwestward of its western termination. Much of the travel between the southwestern states, Louisiana, Mississippi, Arkansas, and the northeastern states, may be expected to take this route, until a more direct road is made from St. Louis to Toledo. This travel is now large, and no intelligent man need be told that the summer migrations of the people of the lower Mississippi country may be relied on, with a moral certainty of a regular increase. In the winter, a railroad between Toledo and Chicago would take all the travel and trade of the whole Wisconsin and Iowa, and the north half of Illinois, in the intercourse of these extensive regions with the Atlantic states. It would also draw largely from the peninsula of Michigan. In five years, Wisconsin, Iowa, and the north half of Illinois, will have a population of at least 700,000, being nearly equal to that of Massachusetts. Can it be possible that this road, well built and well managed, would not be profitable? Its construction would be cheap. . . . What would be its probable income when brought into operation? By that time it would command the business and travel of not less than 1,000,000 people living westward of Toledo, eight or nine months of the year, in all their intercourse with the east. During the period of navigation on lake Michigan, say three or four months of the year, the number depending on it could scarcely be 500,000. The country on which this population is settled and settling is not excelled in natural resources, and it is undeniably receiving more immigrants than any other great section. In seven years its numbers will be doubled. The road will then have the winter trade and travel of 2,000,000 living westward of Toledo, and the summer business of half that number. . . .

Of the character of the country along the line it may be well to particularize. In Ohio, about one-half the line is through openings, and the other half through timbered land. Both are well adapted to the growth of wheat, and contain an abundant supply of timber for the construction of the road. Through Indiana, the line traverses an almost uninterrupted chain of prairies, along, or near the route, in its whole extent, of sizes convenient for cultivating the entire surface, and of a productiveness to yield a large surplus for exportation. Many of these prairies are already reclaimed, and the whole will soon be under cultivation.

The water power, for durability and ease of management, is excelled nowhere, in proportion to its magnitude, and it is very abundant after the waters of the St. Josephs, of Michigan, are reached. Everywhere in this region, the productive wheat crop may be converted into flour in the neighborhood where it is grown. For 30 miles along the same portion of the line, are extensive beds of iron ore. These are now wrought to some extent, and eventually must add considerable to the resources of the country. It is stated by Joseph Orr, president of the Indiana road, in his address to the stockholders, that during the season of 1837, insurance on goods shipped from Buffalo to the head of lake Michigan, taking the average of a number of receipts which he had compared, cost $12.50 per ton. This would pay the freight on a railroad 416 miles long, at the rate of 3 cents per mile per ton. He truly says: "No thoroughfare now projected, is more rational in its character, or will be more general in its benefit—none uniting more natural advantages, or combining more interest. Nor is there any, in the vast extent of line, more direct. All others, natural or artificial, must be circumscribed in their usefulness by the close of navigation."

The charters given by Ohio and Indiana are of the most liberal character. The first in its operations would be perpetual, the last is to continue seventy-five years, with a right reserved to the state to buy out the stockholders after thirty-five years, by paying the cost with 18 percent interest. Five years were given in Indiana to complete the road in that state. Such an opportunity as these charters hold out for an investment which must be exceedingly profitable, would, in Europe, or the Eastern States, be seized with avidity. As a project, it stands out bold and strong, before any other of the kind in this country. Let the reader place himself before a large map of the United States, and first fixing his eyes on the 40th parallel of latitude, south of lake Michigan, let it then survey all the country north of that parallel, and west of that longitude, and it will take in nearly one-fourth of our entire country. What other route, during the fall, winter, and spring months, can the travel of this great region take to the commercial and manufacturing states eastward, than the railroad under consideration? It has no other: for it would be preposterous to suppose it would go by way of New Orleans, and not at all probable that it would go down to St. Louis, and thence by the national road. But if the prospects of profit from this road were small instead of large on its completion, there are persons enough interested in its construction to make it politic to build it without delay. How deeply the owners of the railroad from Buffalo to Boston and New York are interested, needs buy few words to illustrate. In winter, almost every traveller passing eastward on it, would be a passenger added to the whole line of travel from Buffalo to Boston or New York; and a great portion passing west, will have come over those eastern roads from those great marts of trade. The next Congress will probably make a large appropriation for the Cumberland road.

That road has a strong tendency to draw travel from the broad west to Baltimore and Philadelphia; and the farther it is continued west, the wider is the sweep of country which it will control. New York and Boston have a great stake in securing the winter, spring, and fall travel and trade of the great valley. With a railroad from Buffalo to the Mississippi, above the mouth of Rock river, and a branch of this road from Elkhast county, Indiana, to St. Louis, Boston and New York, would control the trade of the best part of the great valley, during the entire year. They would then have no dull season of winter; but their public houses at all seasons would be full of merchants and business men from the west and south. We say south, for, with these roads completed, the Louisiana, Mississippi, Arkansas, and Texas travel would, to a great extent, come this way. If a railroad were made as straight as practicable from Toledo to St. Louis, its length would not exceed 440 miles. Branching at Elkhast, its length would not be over 465 miles. This will be its best route, because it would pass so far from the Wabash and Erie canal as not to interfere with its business. Indeed, it would be about midway between that canal and the Illinois canal and river, and thus be out of the way of rivalry, and at the same time have its length increased on the whole line but 25 miles. Supposing Alton to be taken in its route, by either course, and the increase of distance over the most direct route will not

exceed 20 miles, and that over a level country, where locomotives may go 25 miles an hour.

This, then, is the great plan to be carried out in the future. But the link between the west end of lake Erie and the navigable waters of the Illinois river, is that which should be first constructed; and the time for it to be commenced with a certainty of success has arrived. . . .

. . . To the feasibility of the route, no serious objection can be urged. The shore is nearly a uniform elevation above the lake—so that the road might be almost perfectly horizontal. The main cost of its superstructure would be the erection of bridges, for which abundant material of timber and stone exist on the spot.

But we feel that enough, and more than enough has been said in favor of this link of the great iron chain that is to grapple the west to the east. We will, therefore, return to the main subject of this article—the railroad across the base of the peninsula of Michigan. The water route from lake Erie to the head of lake Michigan has been regularly opened to the keels of commerce but little more than ten years; yet it has become one of the greatest thoroughfares in the nation. About three large steamers a day, including propellers, besides a great fleet of sailing vessels, have found full employment in plying between lake Erie and Chicago the past season; and every year is adding a large per centage to the business of the preceding year. To the friends of the proposed railroad, it is a question of extreme interest, whether a large portion of this great and increasing business may not be diverted from its circuitous water channel, and be made to roll across the isthmus that separates lake Erie from the head of lake Michigan. The following reasons in favor of this diversion seem to possess no little strength. The railroad connecting Albany and Boston is 200 miles long, although these cities are but 140 miles apart in a straight line. The distance by water between them is 450 miles. Between Toledo and the south end of lake Michigan is 200 miles, and by water between the same points 750 miles. Our railroad will be straight, with trifling exceptions, through its whole length; that of Boston and Albany loses by a deviation from a straight line 60 miles in 200. The Massachusetts road has cost upwards of $40,000 per mile, with grades of 82 feet to the mile. The Toledo road, made as good, would cost but one-third as much with a grade of 32 feet to the mile, and not over two-fifths as much with a grade of 20 feet to the mile. The road connecting Boston and Albany was built with a view of transacting the travel and transportation business between these points, in successful competition with the water route; and also with the expectation that the 200 mile railroad from Albany would, to some extent, divert the western trade from the 145 mile water route to New York. The 200 mile railway has competed successfully with the 450 mile water route from Boston to Albany. Even flour (one of the heaviest articles in proportion to its value) has given the railroad the preference. Of the 244,984 barrels passing, in 1844, from Albany to Boston, 151,721 barrels passed over the railroad. How would it have been, if the distance had been

300 miles greater—the cost of the railroad three-fifths less—and the power of traction required two-thirds less? Unless the object of Massachusetts in extending a railroad to Albany was utterly European, a railroad from Toledo to the west line of Indiana, near the south end of lake Michigan, will control the business now passing around from the head of that lake to lake Erie. The central railroad of Michigan in its business of the last year affords a practical, but faint illustration of the profits to be expected from this. That road extends 100 miles—from Detroit to Marshall. The western section was in operation only after the 10th of August. If we suppose the average length run during the year, to have been 100 miles, and the cost of that 100 miles what such a road could now be built for—say $1,000,000—the clear income (as stated by Governor Barry) of $121,750, would give a dividend for the year of over 12 per cent. The board of internal improvement of Michigan estimate the receipts of the road, for 1845, at $275,000. If the expense bears the same proportion to receipts as in 1844, the clear income will be $158,000 or nearly 16 per cent on a capital of $1,000,000. Now, this central railroad of Michigan does but little more than the business of the country through which it passes; having as yet not been pushed far enough toward lake Michigan to compete, to any great extent in summer, with the Chicago steamers. The country west of Toledo, and near the line of the proposed railway, is not less fertile than that traversed by the central railroad, and the obstruction to an easy grade and cheap construction are much less, and more easily overcome. But its great advantage is the control it will hold of the entire fall and winter business of northern Illinois and the whole of Wisconsin, during the long season of suspended and highly dangerous navigation of lake Michigan. If, in addition to this, it can be made to enter into successful competition with the lake route in summer, in the carriage of passengers and freight—thereby securing the immense business now centering in Michigan city, Chicago, and other ports at the end of lake Michigan, how strong beyond any other road, become its claims on the attention of men who wish to invest in railroad stock. The certainty, that all the goods on lake Erie, moving on their way to the country west and southwest of Chicago, would find the cost of transport on this road smaller than the insurance around the lakes, would seem to render it certain that, besides salt, no up freights would be carried by water; and in consequence that down freights would have to pay the loss and profit on the upward voyage. This would materially enhance the price of down freights by water, and thus give the railroad an additional advantage in the competition. With a heavy T or H rail, and a grade of not over 20 feet to the mile, we believe that competition may be made overwhelmingly successful.

Questions

1. At the opening of his article, Scott refered to the fact that in the mid-1830s, railroad construction across the nation had suddenly ground to a halt. Why had public opinion shifted against railroad projects at this time?

2. In what ways, according to Scott, did the building of railroads spur local development? Is his account accurate, or do you think that he painted too optimistic a picture?

3. From Scott's piece of western boosterism and your reading of the text, what role did government—whether local, state, or national—play in the building of the railroads? What challenges did railroad entrepreneurs encounter, and how did they overcome these difficulties? Why was railroad construction such a risky enterprise?

9-7   A Satire on Western Boosterism (1845)

If hope sprang eternal in the imagination of a Jesup Scott (Document 9-6), the consequences of such imaginings burned many another soul caught up in western speculation. In 1845, in the eastern Whig journal *The American Review*, an anonymous writer penned a satirical first-person account of what he claimed were his own bruising encounters with western boosters such as Scott. But the following essay does more than illustrate the rampant fraud and excess of the time; like Scott's article, it vividly captures the boundless optimism stirring the western entrepreneurs of that era.

Source: "'Commercial Delusions'—Speculations," *The American Review* 2 (October 1845): 347, 349–357.

Down to 1834, the emigration to the West had been steadily increasing, and was of a beneficial and healthy character; for thus far all became actual settlers. From this time forward it was of a mixed character. Actual, bonâ fide settlers still thronged the thoroughfares and crowded the government land-offices: others went to purchase for their own future use, or for the benefit of their children; but a great majority were speculators who expected to make large gains by buying tracts of land at low prices, holding them until the surrounding country should be partially settled and improved, and then selling at advanced rates. . . .

That was the era of imaginary villages. We once saw a party of surveyors in midwinter laying out a village on the ice. The spot of ground, a marsh or swamp, with a small stream creeping lazily through it, was so low and wet that it could only be traversed by boats in summer. The proprietor had failed in business in one of the Eastern States, and found himself with a debt of thousands on his shoulders and no apparent means of paying for it. He was a " 'cute Yankee," and of course turned speculator. He bought two or three hundred acres of this swamp, caused a survey to be made, then a village map showing the usual proportion of streets and squares, all named after presidents and generals of note. His next step was to visit his creditors, and offer them "village property at reduced prices," in payment of their claims. The creditors, not expecting much, were highly delighted of course, and willingly took each a few "lots," and gave him acquittances. Some were even more liberal than this, and paid the proprietor considerable sums in cash for additional lots. Thus he got rid of his debts, and found himself provided with money to commence business on a larger scale. We believe he is still out of the penitentiary.

The mania for speculation in village property at that time is unaccountable; it was so great, so universally prevalent, that one can hardly trust to his own knowledge and recollection on the subject. Common sense was entirely thrown aside in the calculations of village and city-makers, and impossibilities were deemed feasible of execution. On all the rivers village plots were found staked out at intervals of two or three miles; not only every inland county, but every remote township, had its village, and often scores of them, in which land was sold by the foot and inch, at prices varying from one hundred to twenty thousand dollars per acre — the land the while worth barely the government price of one dollar and a quarter. Each of these places were to be *cities*, and had some remarkable advantages that were possessed by none other, which must bring in a large population. So thought the "operators." There is not in all probability coin and bullion enough on this continent, if brought together, to purchase a mile in width on each side of the Maumee river, for twenty miles from its mouth, at the prices demanded for it in 1836; and this is only one point in the "great West" out of thousands equally rich and promising.

The method of operating was simple, and but little money was required to get up a respectable village on paper.

About two hundred acres of land was necessary, which, if purchased of the government, must be paid for in cash, at ten shillings the acre; if bought of second hands, from three to ten dollars per acre was sufficient, and one-half of this would be in most cases secured by mortgage on the whole plot. Then a surveyor would be employed to divide the land into lots of about three rods by ten, leaving streets between every second tier, and others running at right angles, and stakes were then driven into the ground making the divisions. Afterwards came the "map," drawn with precision and care, and the more splendidly executed the better; next the erection of a few buildings, generally of logs or loose boards, except one which must be large and gaudily painted, as it was to be "the Hotel." All this required but little money, and now the operator was ready for business. He would circulate the maps over the country, and write puffs for publication in the newspapers, wherein was duly heralded "great sales of village property" — "flourishing village in the centre of a rich and growing country" — "on the great thoroughfare between the East and the West" — "emigration rapidly pouring in" — and much more, set forth with all the flourish of Western eloquence. . . .

As a pendant to the foregoing remarks, and as illustrative in some measure of the experience of hundreds, we have furnished to our hands by one who it seems has "suffered some," a chapter in his history.

MY FIRST SPECULATION

In the height of the fever for land speculations in the renowned era of 1835, a very verdant young gentleman — since grown a trifle wiser — might have been seen one fair morning preparing for a journey to the "great west," where riches, even mines of wealth, were to be had for the asking, where villages and *eke* cities grew up into perfect being, like Jonah's gourd, in a night. My neighbor Dickens, an honest, plodding carpenter, had emigrated but a few months before, with hardly a sous in his pocket, leaving behind divers mementos in the hands of his friends with his name attached, and which, by a pleasant legal fiction, were made to represent a certain amount in dollars and cents. His anxious friends had now received intelligence that he had founded a city, and that by selling corner and other "city lots," he had become worth at least half a million dollars. Now our quondam neighbor never enjoyed any especial reputation for acuteness or sagacity, and the apparent ease with which he had slipped into a fortune operated with the force and speed of an electrical battery upon his old acquaintance.

But this was not all the evidence we had "bearing upon the case," as gentlemen of the legal school are wont to say. One Timothy Jenkins, a fiddling village tailor, and withal a very great "loafer," having a soul above buttons, had also some twelve months previous left the circle of his numerous admirers, without even the ceremony of an adieu — going off, indeed, between two days — and he too, it was ascertained, had made a fortune. In fact, he had become a nabob, lived like a gentleman, and was in a fair way, ere long, to represent his enlightened fellow-citizens in the National Legislature, if he did not conclude to accept in lieu the more dignified, but less profitable post of Governor of the Northwestern Territory. . . .

Besides these tangible evidences, we had other proofs of Western wealth. The newspapers—and they are always to be credited—were filled with glowing accounts of the construction of railroads and canals without number (as certain Indiana and Illinois bond-holders will no doubt well recollect)—of boundless immigration—of towns suddenly arising full grown, armed with all the civic strength of mayors, aldermen and police—and, most captivating of all, of vast individual wealth suddenly acquired. There was no resisting the temptation; the idea of saving pennies and shillings in the old-fashioned slow-and-sure way, appeared sufficiently ridiculous, after it was once well authenticated that thousands could be made in a single operation any day before dinner. . . .

Embarking on a steamboat, I found its decks crowded with keen-eyed, thin-visaged, anxious-looking gentlemen, all like myself bound to the land of promise. . . . Descending to the spacious cabin, I soon found game more worthy of notice. There the sound of "dollars—dollars," in thousands, again met my ear; all were discussing the flattering prospects of the "great West;" choice locations were spoken of in the most positive terms; great cities and towns were named, of whose existence I had no previous knowledge; banks, railways and canals were discussed, as means of accumulating wealth, and every man seemed to be the owner of one. "What a wonderful country!" was my internal ejaculation; "yes! what a wonderful people!"

A portly good-looking man of middle age was seated at a table listening with apparent unconcern to the conversation around him. His appearance attracted my attention. . . . I resolved to make his acquaintance and obtain his advice as to the best mode of investing my small means. . . . Gradually narrowing down the circle of his encomiastic remarks, he proved, conclusively, that the State of Illinois was the very seat and center of the West, and one spot in particular, he declared, after mature reflection, *must* inevitably become the metropolis of that favored country. The city of Franklin, he continued, was to be [to] the West what New York is to the East, and New Orleans to the South.

Notwithstanding a dubious smile on the faces of a few quiet elderly gentlemen who had been listeners to this harangue, I was convinced by the evident sincerity and candor of the speaker. I ventured to inquire where the city was situated. The surprise he manifested at my ignorance somewhat disconcerted me, but he condescended to inform me that it was near the center of the State, and the geographical center of —— County. Here he unrolled a spacious map representing that city in sections, blocks and lots. It was a beautiful lithograph, the first I had examined, on which streets, squares and public buildings were laid down with the most captivating conspicuousness. Here was

the ground for "St. Paul's Church," evidently an extensive Park; on an opposite corner was "University Square;" here figured the "North American Bank," and there the "market house" and the "town hall." Railroads and canals on this map seemed innumerable and all centered in the city of Franklin. . . .

Such glowing descriptions increased my impatience. The steamer moved quite too slow. The white villages that decked the shore of the Lake seemed beckoning to me to "come and buy." "How could one," said I, "live so long without real estate!" . . .

I inquired if I could not through his assistance get hold of a little property in the city of Franklin, it being my aim to make a permanent investment. . . . In half an hour he had my thousand dollars safe in his pocket; I, a deed—duly "signed, sealed and delivered,"—conveying to me "Lots 500 and 501, on National Avenue in the City of Franklin," bound by what other squares, parks, or streets I do not now recollect. And it was conveyed not only to me, but to my "heirs forever." The phrase added something to my posthumous importance.

I was now a "freeholder," an owner of "Real Estate."— "Blessed be all deeds of conveyance!" said I, gloating over the fair, smooth paper and writing, on and by which the delightful transfer was effected.—"What will my dear mother say, heaven bless her!—yes, and how shall I be envied by all my cousins and kinsfolk at home! Did they not predict that I would lose all my careful earnings? Will I not show them a few things yet?"—All the evening of this auspicious day I paced the deck of the steamer, ruminating upon my present good fortune and future consequence. For I was able to look beyond a few years—a *very* few, as it was not necessary to consider a great many vanished. I saw myself a man of substance and standing. In due time, I was an alderman—in the city of Franklin, finally, a mayor. I was looked up to by all of my name, as the "head of their house." I was the owner of blocks of buildings, stores, warehouses, and offices—had a handsome rent-roll—kept an open hall, feasted my friends, knew the finest carriage in the city as mine, and was conscious of much stock in banks. At last, I died:—"For we must all go," said I—'omnes eodem cogimur'—repeating a solemn line from Flaccus:—

'Omnium
Versatur urna serius, ocius,'—

I added, from the same melancholy poet, 'every one kicks the bucket finally!'" But I went off highly respected, and all the city journals—very numerous then in Franklin—recorded the demise of "a wealthy and munificent Father of the City" gone to glory! . . .

. . . In this idea, among others, I was indulging, when the boat—an old one—put in unexpectedly at Toledo, to caulk up a leak and take in wood.

Here the conversation all turned on the growth of Toledo, and other amazing cities adorning the Maumee.

That river, indeed, was expected to rival the Nile—which, in the matter of mud and bulrushes, it does. Our boat was visited at once by the possessors of city property at various points up the shore. One smooth-faced gentleman—with the exception of a wen on one side of his nose—set forth such advantages of a particular point, where "*he* hadn't much interest, but a *friend of his* something," as to induce several to transfer themselves to another boat—a small "half-pony power" affair, which plied up the Maumee—"in general," the Captain said, "as far as it *could git*, more or less!" I was of that fortunate number. Such a chance to make a purchase, equal, if not superior, to that already achieved, was not to be lost. It was a sultry day. The interest of the shores was exhausted in the first half-mile. Books I had none. Newspapers were unknown in that region. . . .

By means of a rickety skiff, three at a time were deposited on a lubricated log, tilted down from the swampy bank into the water. My confidence in the owner of lots was somewhat diminished. Still, I and one or two others followed him, valise in hand, as with map sticking out from my pocket behind, he made his way through a mile and a-half of marshy grounds,—*very rich*, as he said—till we came to a bend in the river where some twenty acres were just being cleared, half of it lying level with the Maumee. "This is the spot, gentlemen," said he, mounting a log: "a most desirable locality. No great city can ever rise between Toledo and this point (which is undoubtedly true!) it is the head of navigation on the Maumee, as you experienced by your boat being stopped—a *very* little below here—and as to these low lands, a slight draining, gentlemen,"—Here, by a flourish of his lithograph, the eloquent expositor of rising towns, slipping off, slumped standing into a habitation of the "green gentry"—of whom there were a hoarse acre or two on each side—forming, as the speculator next to me said, the finest example of a proprietor "*locum tenens.*" Helping him out, I concluded "not to purchase," and made "the *best* of my way" (and wretched enough it was) back through the woods for Toledo, which I reached the next day about noon—immediately taking a chance steamer for my original landing-place, Detroit. . . .

I visited all those mighty cities on the West shore of Lake Erie; Brest, Havre, and a score of others, whose names have fled from my memory. Tacitus, in describing the destruction by fire of a town in Gaul, used the sententious words: "Between a great city and none, but a single night intervened." I might in another sense make the same observation of these mighty towns. A survey, and the making of a map, and the work was done to your hands. Buildings, streets, and inhabitants, were absolute superfluities. Some of them were without a single house, others were in a morass, made life-like only by the hum of musquitoes, and the evening song of multitudinous frogs; others again were under water, or in a dense forest. A pleasant sight for an innocent purchaser, on his first visit to his landed acquisitions! But my faith in my steamboat-friend was great; I never doubted the value of *my* purchase;—although the specimens I had seen were enough to shatter the nerves of an elephant. Longing to set foot on my own ground, I equipped myself, speculator-fashion, with a Canadian pony—an ugly obstinate, crabbed rascal as ever a man bestrode, a pair of capacious saddlebags, a pocket map, and a Mackinaw blanket, set out for Illinois and the city of Franklin. . . .

I pass over all the incidents of the journey, many of which were amusing to me, but might not be so to the reader. I must not forget, however, to mention one remarkable fact: every river on the route, large enough to bear up a canoe, had a village on either bank, every six or seven miles. Moreover, at each one was the actual head of navigation, beyond which no steamer or other craft could possibly pass. This imparted a peculiar value to each point. Another fact quite as singular I discovered. Every village, taken by itself, was uncommonly healthy; no one ever died *there*—that was certain; but the next village was sickly, and always would be—at least so I was informed again and again by many a poor fellow, upon whom the "fever and ague" had plainly exerted their utmost ingenuity. I also found that village and city property grew more valuable the further it was removed from the business and population of the East. . . .

I passed through Michigan City, then in its infancy, but possessing a mayor and city council—through Chicago, where land was valued at about as high a price per foot as it was in Broadway or Wall Street, "water lots" especially—through Romeo and Juliette, and countless lesser cities. . . .

At last I reached ——— county and in "hot haste" for the aforesaid city. I very naturally looked forward to my arrival with no small degree of interest. In the first place I was in need of rest and repose; my "accommodations" had been none of the best, on the route, and there I imagined I should find a good hotel and an obliging host, and, in virtue of my proprietorship, thought it very likely I should receive some extra attentions. Then again I was anxious to see the character of the town, the mode of building, and to become acquainted with my future neighbors. I had made up my mind to assume an air of dignity, as became a freeholder. I made due inquiries as I entered the limits of the county, cautiously and modestly at first, but at last with agitation and vehemence. I was informed that there was no such city, town or village in the county! My hair fairly rose on end, like "quills upon the fretful porcupine." I perused my deed of conveyance again and again. There it was, plainly, in black and white, "the city of Franklin"—"lots 500 and 501 on National Avenue." I traversed the county in all directions, wearied every traveler with my inquiries, disturbed the inmates of every log hut, and got myself kicked out of one or two for my impetuosity of manner. It was labor lost. In the language of the region, I was "done for"—"diddled." Civic honors!—rent roll!—blocks of buildings! Alas! My dreams had fled—so had my money. My obliging friend of the steamboat was a man of imagination, as well as profound morality; the city existed *on his map.* "The scoundrel!" said I, "let me catch him again!"—But instead of my catching him he had evidently caught me—something of a difference as I found. One thing I did catch—the fever-and-ague. I took it at a log-house, in the vicinity of a "slight swamp"—as the owner of the shantee called a three mile morass—and had it a trifle over nine weeks. The ghost of my father wouldn't have known me!

This was my *first speculation*. It may be imagined in what mood I traveled after this adventure, but it cannot well be imagined why, after this lesson, I continued the pleasing game of getting rich without labor. The result of my gains as a speculator may be expressed by a cipher, or any number of them together, as $0,000, etc. I returned "a sadder, but a wiser man," the owner of eighty acres of wild land, and in debt eleven thousand dollars!

Questions

1. What was the point of the *American Review* satire? What is the moral or lesson that the author was trying to convey?

2. From your reading of the *American Review* satire, what do you learn about the tactics of western land swindlers? How did these con men dupe easterners into purchasing worthless tracts of land? What language did they use, and what ideals and values did they appeal to?

3. How much of the *American Review* satire do you think is myth, and how much is reality? What aspects of the West did the author illuminate?

Questions for Further Thought

1. What do Jesup W. Scott's article (Document 9-6) and the *American Review* satire (Document 9-7) reveal about the American Dream in the first half of the nineteenth century? Many Americans viewed the West as a land of opportunity; how accurate do you think these visions were?

2. What role did the settlement and development of the West play in the larger story of the growth of the United States during the nineteenth century? Why was westward expansion so important to so many? What effects did the development of the West have in the East, and vice versa?

3. Compare the society depicted by Scott and the *American Review* satirist with Thomas Jefferson's vision of the West as an "Empire of Liberty." Would Jefferson have been happy with how his vision turned out?

Changes in the Social Structure

Economic changes brought about by the Industrial Revolution necessarily affected the social structure and social values of most Americans. New machinery and new ways of organizing labor had resulted in unparalleled economic growth and national prosperity, but such advances often came at the expense of personal and communal contentment. To be sure, opportunities for individual advancement were multiplied, but the riches generated by the new economy were not shared equally. Indeed, Orestes A. Brownson contended, the condition of the poor wage laborers of the North was truly lamentable, worse than that of the slaves in the South (Document 9-8). Alexis de Tocqueville agreed that the rise of the industrial economy in the democratic United States had resulted in perhaps unavoidable inequalities between "masters" and "workers" (Document 9-9). Furthermore, in a fluid society with no artificial distinctions, a kind of "restlessness" in the pursuit of wealth had become nearly universal (Document 9-10). For anxious businessmen caught up in this pursuit, Freeman Hunt offered a set of "sound rules" for success (Document 9-11), somewhat reminiscent of Benjamin Franklin's "Advice to a Young Tradesman" (1748).

9-8   The Laboring Classes (1840)

Orestes A. Brownson

The tensions and contradictions associated with the Age of Jackson were reflected in the varied career and writings of Orestes A. Brownson (1803–1876). By the time he had founded the *Boston Quarterly Review* at the age of thirty-four, Brownson had successively been a Presbyterian, an ordained Universalist minister, an agnostic, and a Unitarian minister. He had also worked politically to organize urban artisans and laborers under the direction of Frances Wright and the New York Working Men's Party (see text pp. 321–324) before abandoning politics and becoming a champion of social salvation through "Christian Union" and moral exhortation. In the late 1830s Brownson's seemingly mercurial career accommodated yet another change as he began to despair of the efficacy of a moralistic remedy for the afflictions of industrial America. More radical than before, he was unsparing in his criticism of the existing economic order, which he claimed enabled proprietors to become inordinately wealthy by denying workers a fair share of the fruits of their own labor. In the selection below, which appeared in the *Boston Quarterly Review* in July 1840, Brownson offered his readers a controversial assessment of industrial society in general and the condition of wage laborers in the United States in particular.

Source: Excerpts from *American Philosophic Addresses, 1700–1900,* ed. Joseph L. Blau (New York: Columbia University Press, 1946), 182–185.

In regard to labor two systems obtain; one that of slave labor, the other that of free labor. Of the two, the first is, in our judgment, except so far as the feelings are concerned, decidedly the least oppressive. If the slave has never been a free man, we think, as a general rule, his sufferings are less than those of the free laborer at wages. As to actual freedom one has just about as much as the other. The laborer at wages has all the disadvantages of freedom and none of its blessings, while the slave, if denied the blessings, is freed from the disadvantages. We are no advocates of slavery, we are as heartily opposed to it as any modern abolitionist can be; but we say frankly that, if there must always be a laboring population distinct from proprietors and employers, we regard the slave system as decidedly preferable to the system at wages. It is no pleasant thing to go days without food, to lie idle for weeks, seeking work and finding none, to rise in the morning with a wife and children you love, and know not where to procure them a breakfast, and to see constantly before you no brighter prospect than the almshouse. Yet these are no unfrequent incidents in the lives of our laboring population. Even in seasons of general prosperity, when there was only the ordinary cry of "hard times," we have seen hundreds of people in a not very populous village, in a wealthy portion of our common country, suffering for the want of the necessaries of life, willing to work, and yet finding no work to do. Many and many is the application of a poor man for work, merely for his food, we have seen rejected. These things are little thought of, for the applicants are poor; they fill no conspicuous place in society, and they have no biographers. But their wrongs are chronicled in heaven. It is said there is no want in this country. There may be less than in some other countries. But death by actual starvation in this country is we apprehend no uncommon occurrence. The sufferings of a quiet, unassuming but useful class of females in our cities, in general sempstresses, too proud to beg or to apply to the almshouse, are not easily told. They are industrious; they do all that they can find to do; but yet the little there is for them to do, and the miserable pittance they receive for it, is hardly sufficient to keep soul and body together. And yet there is a man who employs them to make shirts, trousers, &c., and grows rich on their labors. He is one of our respectable citizens, perhaps is praised in the newspapers for his liberal donations to some charitable institution. He passes among us as a pattern of morality, and is honored as a worthy Christian. And why should he not be, since our *Christian* community is made up of such as he, and since our clergy would not dare question his piety, lest they should incur the reproach of infidelity, and lose their standing, and their salaries? Nay, since our clergy are raised up, educated, fashioned, and sustained by such as he? Not a few of our churches rest on Mammon for their foundation. The basement is a trader's shop.

We pass through our manufacturing villages; most of them appear neat and flourishing. The operatives are well dressed, and we are told, well paid. They are said to be healthy, contented, and happy. This is the fair side of the picture; the side exhibited to distinguished visitors. There is a dark side, moral as well as physical. Of the common operatives, few, if any, by their wages, acquire a competence. . . . We stand and look at these hard working men and women hurrying in all directions, and ask ourselves, where go the proceeds of their labors? The man who employs them, and for whom they are toiling as so many slaves, is one of our city nabobs, revelling in luxury; or he is a member of our legislature, enacting laws to put money in his own pocket; or he is a member of Congress, contending for a high Tariff to tax the poor for the benefit of the rich; or in these times he is shedding crocodile tears over the deplorable condition of the poor laborer, while he docks his wages twenty-five per cent.; building miniature log cabins, shouting Harrison and "hard cider." And this man too would fain pass for a Christian and a republican. He shouts for liberty, stickles for equality, and is horrified at a Southern planter who keeps slaves.

One thing is certain; that of the amount actually produced by the operative, he retains a less proportion than it costs the master to feed, clothe, and lodge his slave. Wages is a cunning device of the devil, for the benefit of tender consciences, who would retain all the advantages of the slave system, without the expense, trouble, and odium of being slave-holders.

Messrs. Thome and Kimball, in their account of the emancipation of slavery in the West Indies, establish the fact that the employer may have the same amount of labor done 25 per ct. cheaper than the master. What does this fact prove, if not that wages is a more successful method of taxing labor than slavery? We really believe our Northern system of labor is more oppressive, and even more mischievous to morals, than the Southern. We, however, war against both. We have no toleration for either system. We would see a slave a man, but a free man, not a mere operative at wages. This he would not be were he now emancipated. Could the abolitionists effect all they propose, they would do the slave no service. Should emancipation work as well as they say, still it would do the slave no good. He would be a slave still, although with the title and cares of a freeman. If then we had no constitutional objections to abolitionism, we could not, for the reason here implied, be abolitionists.

The slave system, however, in name and form, is gradually disappearing from Christendom. It will not subsist much longer. But its place is taken by the system of labor at wages, and this system, we hold, is no improvement upon the one it supplants. Nevertheless the system of wages will triumph. It is the system which in name sounds honester than slavery, and in substance is more profitable to the master. It yields the wages of iniquity, without its opprobrium. It will therefore supplant slavery, and be sustained — for a time.

Questions

1. Not long after the publication of this essay, Brownson discarded his egalitarian principles and adopted more authoritarian ones. Does this surprise you? What, besides personal idiosyncrasy, might account for this transformation?

2. "Democracy, as I understand and accept it," Brownson once explained, "requires me to sacrifice myself *for* the masses, not *to* them. Who knows not, that if you would save the people, you must often oppose them?" Was Brownson's understanding of democracy apparent in this essay on the "laboring classes"?

3. Brownson said that he was as opposed to slavery "as any . . . abolitionist can be." Was he? What did he say that might have caused some discomfort for the defenders of slavery?

9-9   The Rise of an Industrial Aristocracy (1831)

Alexis de Tocqueville

Convinced that all of Europe was moving inexorably toward a "great democratic revolution," Alexis de Tocqueville (1805–1859) was drawn to America in search of "lessons" from which Europeans might profit. Among the many peculiarities that captured the young French aristocrat's attention, none fascinated him more than the unanticipated consequences of the social and political equality embodied in the American system. Mindful of the existence of slavery in the midst of "democratic freedom," Tocqueville nevertheless asserted that there were no inherited distinctions of rank in America. Unlike Europe, there were no prescribed professions, no assignments of place, and no permanent rules of behavior. In the absence of such traditional restraints, however, new forms of inequality and oppression had arisen. In the excerpt below, he links democracy directly to the advancement of an industrial aristocracy and describes the growing gap between the rich and the laboring poor.

Source: From Harvey C. Mansfield and Delba Winthrop, eds., from *Democracy in America.* Copyright © 2000 by the University of Chicago Press. Reprinted by permission of the University of Chicago Press.

I have shown how democracy favors developments in industry and multiplies the number of industrialists without measure; we are going to see the path by which industry in its turn could well lead men back to aristocracy.

It has been recognized that when a worker is occupied every day with the same detail, the general production of the work comes more easily, more rapidly, and with more economy.

It has also been recognized that the more an industry is a large-scale undertaking with great capital and great credit, the cheaper are its products.

These truths have been glimpsed for a long time, but in our day they have been demonstrated. They have already been applied to several very important industries, and in turn the least are taking hold of them.

I see nothing in the political world that should preoccupy the legislator more than these two new axioms of industrial science.

When an artisan engages constantly and uniquely in the manufacture of a single object, in the end he performs this work with singular dexterity. But at the same time he loses the general faculty of applying his mind to the direction of the work. Each day he becomes more skillful and less industrious, and one can say that the man in him is degraded as the worker is perfected.

As the principle of the division of labor is more completely applied, the worker becomes weaker, more limited, and more dependent. The art makes progress, the artisan retrogresses. On the other hand, as it is more plainly discovered that the products of an industry are so much more perfect and less dear as manufacture is vaster and capital greater, very wealthy and very enlightened men come forward to exploit industries which, until then, had been left to ignorant or awkward artisans. They are attracted by the greatness of the necessary efforts and the immensity of the results to be obtained.

So, therefore, at the same time that industrial science constantly lowers the class of workers, it elevates that of masters.

While the worker brings his intelligence more and more to the study of a single detail, each day the master casts his eye over a more far-reaching ensemble, and his mind extends as the worker's shrinks. Soon the latter will have to have only physical force without intelligence; the former will need science and almost genius to succeed. The one resembles more and more the administrator of a vast empire, the other a brute.

Master and worker here have nothing alike, and each day they differ more. They are joined only as two links at the extremes of a long chain. Each occupies a place that is made for him and that he cannot leave. The one is in a continual, strict, and necessary dependence on the other, and he seems born to obey as the latter is to command.

What is this if not aristocracy?

With conditions coming to be more and more equalized in the body of the nation, the need for manufactured objects becomes more general and increases in it, and the cheapness that puts these objects within the reach of mediocre fortunes becomes a greater element in success.

Each day, therefore, one finds that more opulent and more enlightened men devote their wealth and their science to industry and seek to satisfy the new desires that are manifest in all parts by opening great workshops and by dividing work strictly.

Thus as the mass of the nation turns to democracy, the particular class occupied with industry becomes more aristocratic. Men show themselves more and more alike in the one, and more and more different in the other, and inequality increases in the small society as it decreases in the great.

Thus, when one goes back to the source, it seems that one sees aristocracy issue by a natural effort from within the very heart of democracy.

But this aristocracy does not resemble those that have preceded it.

One will remark at first that in being applied only to industry and to some of the industrial professions, it is an exception, a monster, in the entirety of the social state.

The small aristocratic societies that certain industries form amid the immense democracy of our day contain, like the great aristocratic societies of former times, some very opulent men and a very miserable multitude.

The poor have few means of leaving their condition and of becoming rich, but the rich constantly become poor or quit trade after they have realized their profits. Thus the elements that form the class of the poor are nearly fixed; but the elements that compose the class of the rich are not. To tell the truth, although there are rich, the class of the rich does not exist; for the rich have neither common spirit nor objects, neither common traditions nor hopes. There are then members, but no corps.

Not only are the rich not solidly united among themselves, but one can say that there is no genuine bond between one who is poor and one who is rich.

They are not fixed in perpetuity, the one next to the other; at each instant interest brings them together and separates them. The worker depends generally on masters, but not on such and such a master. These two men see each other at the factory and do not know each other elsewhere, and while they touch each other at one point they remain very distant at all others. The manufacturer asks of the worker only his work, and the worker expects only a wage from him. The one is not engaged to protect, nor the other to defend, and they are not bound in a permanent manner either by habit or by duty.

The aristocracy founded by trade almost never settles in the midst of the industrial population that it directs; its goals is not to govern the latter, but to make use of it.

An aristocracy thus constituted cannot have a great hold on those it employs; and, should it come to seize them for a moment, they will soon escape it. It does not know what it wants and cannot act.

The territorial aristocracy of past centuries was obliged by law or believed itself to be obliged by mores to come to the aid of its servants and to relieve their miseries. But the manufacturing aristocracy of our day, after having impoverished and brutalized the men whom it uses, leaves them to be nourished by public charity in times of crisis. This results naturally from what precedes. Between worker and master relations are frequent, but there is no genuine association.

I think that all in all, the manufacturing aristocracy that we see rising before our eyes is one of the hardest that has appeared on earth; but it is at the same time one of the most restrained and least dangerous.

Still, the friends of democracy ought constantly to turn their regard with anxiety in this direction; for if ever permanent inequality of conditions and aristocracy are introduced anew into the world, one can predict that they will enter by this door.

Questions

1. How might an aristocracy arise in an industrial economy? What would draw "enlightened men" to industry?

2. What was Tocqueville's view of the worker in industrial America? How was the industrial worker different from his artisan counterpart in the past?

3. In what ways were the new industrial aristocrats different from the hereditary aristocrats of the past? Did Tocqueville consider these differences to be improvements? Explain.

9-10   Influence of the Trading Spirit on Social and Moral Life (1845)

The American Whig Review   The impact of the industrial and transportation revolutions was far-reaching. Sophisticated looms, standardized parts, factories, canals, steam engines, and railroads were essential in transforming the national economy and establishing the United States as a manufacturing power second only to Britain and France by 1860. However, these impressive gains came at a price. Factory work was not only strictly regimented and monotonous but low-paying, and factory workers had little control over the conditions of their employment. The growth of the market economy generated substantial increases in per capita wealth after 1820, but economic inequality also increased in these decades. Ironically, the age of the common man may also have been the age of uncommon disparities in the distribution of wealth in America. Editorials in the *American Whig Review*, a journal of political commentary and literature established in New York in 1844 to compete with the *Democratic Review*, often voiced concern over issues related to the cost of industrial advancement. The writer of the following essay questions whether commercial pursuits have detrimentally affected the moral character of the people.

Source: Excerpts from *Ideology and Power in the Age of Jackson*, ed. Edwin C. Rozwenc (Garden City, NY: Doubleday, 1964), 48–51.

All strangers who come among us remark the excessive anxiety written in the American countenance. The widespread comfort, the facilities for livelihood, the spontaneous and cheap lands, the high price of labor are equally observed, and render it difficult to account for these lines of painful thoughtfulness. It is not poverty, nor tyranny, nor over-competition which produces this anxiety; that is clear. It is the concentration of the faculties upon an object, which in its very nature is unattainable—the perpetual improvement of the outward condition. There are no bounds among us to the restless desire to be better off; and this is the ambition of all classes of society. We are not prepared to allow that wealth is more valued in America than elsewhere, but in other countries the successful pursuit of it is necessarily confined to a few, while here it is open to all. No man in America is contented to be poor, or expects to continue so. There are here no established limits within which the hopes of any class of society must be confined, as in other countries. There is consequently no condition of hopes realized, in other words, of contentment. In other lands, if children can maintain the station and enjoy the means, however moderate, of their father, they are happy. Not so with us. This is not the spirit of our institutions. Nor will it long be otherwise in other countries. That equality, that breaking down of artificial barriers which has produced this universal ambition and restless activity in America, is destined to prevail throughout the earth. But because we are in advance of the world in the great political principle, and are now experiencing some of its first effects, let us not mistake these for the desirable fruits of freedom. Commerce is to become the universal pursuit of men. It is to be the first result of freedom, of popular institutions everywhere. Indeed, every land not steeped in tyranny is now feeling this impulse. But while trade is destined to free and employ the masses, it is also destined to destroy for the time much of the beauty and happiness of every land. This has been the result in our own country. We are free. It is a glorious thing that we have no serfs, with the large and unfortunate exception of our slaves—no artificial distinctions—no acknowledged superiority of blood—no station which merit may not fill—no rounds in the social ladder to which the humblest may not aspire. But the excitement, the commercial activity, the restlessness, to which this state of things has given birth, is far from being a desirable restlessness or a natural condition. It is natural to the circumstances, but not natural to the human soul. It is good and hopeful to the interests of the race, but destructive to the happiness, and dangerous to the virtue of the generation exposed to it.

Those unaccustomed, by reading or travel, to other states of society, are probably not aware how very peculiar our manner of life here is. The laboriousness of Americans is beyond all comparison, should we except the starving operatives of English factories. And when we consider that here, to the labor of the body is added the great additional labor of mental responsibility and ambition, it is not to be wondered at that as a race, the commercial population is dwindling in size, and emaciated in health, so that *palor* is the national complexion. If this devotion to business were indispensable to living, it would demand our pity. It is unavoidable, we know, in one sense. That is, it is customary—it is universal. There is no necessity for the custom; but there is a necessity, weakly constituted as men are, that every individual should conform greatly to the prevailing habits of his fellows, and the expectations of the community in and with which he deals. It is thus that those who deeply feel the essentially demoralizing and wretched influences of this system are yet doomed to be victims of it. Nay, we are all, no matter what our occupations, more or less, and all greatly, sufferers from the excessive stimulus under which every thing is done. We are all worn out with thought that does not develop our thinking faculties in a right direction, and with feeling expended upon poor and low objects. There is no profession that does not feel it. The lawyer must confine himself to his office, without vacation, to adjust a business which never sleeps or relaxes. The physician must labor day and night to repair bodies, never well from over-exertion, over-excitement, and over-indulgence. The minister must stimulate himself to supply the cravings of diseased moral appetites, and to arouse the attention of men deafened by the noise, and dizzy with the whirl in which they constantly live.

We call our country a *happy* country; happy, indeed, in being the home of noble political institutions, the abode of freedom; but very far from being happy in possessing a cheerful, light-hearted, and joyous people. Our agricultural regions even are infected with the same anxious spirit of gain. If ever the curse of labor was upon the race, it is upon us; nor is it simply now "by the sweat of thy brow thou shalt earn thy bread." Labor for a livelihood is dignified. But we labor for bread, and labor for pride, and *labor* for pleasure. A man's life with us *does* consist of the abundance of the things which he possesseth. To get, and to have the reputation of possessing, is the ruling passion. To it are bent all the energies of nine-tenths of our population. Is it that our people are so much more miserly and earth-born than any other? No, not by any constitutional baseness; but circumstances have necessarily given this direction to the American mind. In the hard soil of our common mother, New England—the poverty of our ancestors—their early thrift and industry—the want of other distinctions than those of property—the frown of the Puritans upon all pleasures; these circumstances combined, directed our energies from the first into the single channel of trade. And in that they have run till they have gained a tremendous head, and threaten to convert our whole people into mere money-changers and producers. Honor belongs to our fathers, who in times of great necessity met the demand for a most painful industry with such manly and unflinching hearts. But what was their hard necessity we are perpetuating as our willing servitude!

Questions

1. Compare the sentiments expressed in this editorial with those of Alexis de Tocqueville (Document 9-9). Did they share the same anxieties?

2. Was this writer an opponent of equality? Was he opposed to commercial activity? Was there a remedy for the ills he perceived in American society?

3. How might the readers of this editorial have responded to its complaints? Which groups were most likely to respond favorably?

9-11   Advice for Businessmen (1856)

Freeman Hunt

Freeman Hunt (1804–1858) was born in Quincy, Massachusetts, but was orphaned at an early age. Learning the printer's trade, he worked for a succession of newspapers and advanced rapidly thanks to both his skill and his pen. From 1828 on, he published a succession of newspapers and magazines. In 1839 he established the journal with which he is most closely identified, *Hunt's Merchants' Magazine*, which he edited until his death in 1858. Through his magazine, Hunt became one of the foremost spokespersons for the emerging business culture of the nation. In 1856 he compiled a number of his short pieces, along with some written by others, into a collection of maxims he entitled *Worth and Wealth*. In a society in which success and failure were never far apart, Hunt provided both reassurance and a vision of the businessman as a new kind of hero.

Source: Freeman Hunt, *Worth and Wealth* (New York: Stringer and Townsend, 1856). Also available in Merle Curti et al., eds., *American Issues: The Social Record*, 4th ed. (Philadelphia and New York: Lippincott, 1941), 1:258–259.

A man of business should be able to fix his attention on details, and be ready to give every kind of argument a hearing. This will not encumber him, for he must have been practised before-hand in the exercise of his intellect, and be strong in principles. One man collects materials together, and there they remain, a shapeless heap; another, possessed of method, can arrange what he has collected; but such a man as I would describe, by the aid of principles, goes farther, and builds with his materials.

He should be courageous. The courage, however, required in civil affairs, is that which belongs rather to the able commander than the mere soldier. But any kind of courage is servicable.

Besides a stout heart, he should have a patient temperament, and a vigorous but disciplined imagination; and then he will plan boldly, and with large extent of view, execute calmly, and not be stretching out his hand for things not yet within his grasp. He will let opportunities grow before his eyes until they are ripe to be seized. He will think steadily over possible failure, in order to provide a remedy or a retreat. There will be the strength of repose about him.

He must have a deep sense of responsibility. He must believe in the power and vitality of truth, and in all he does or says, should be anxious to express as much truth as possible.

His feeling of responsibility and love of truth will almost inevitably endow him with diligence, accuracy, and discreetness—those commonplace requisites for a good man of business, without which all the rest may never come to be "translated into action." . . .

Almost every merchant has been rich, or at least prosperous, at some point of his life; and if he is poor now, he can see very well how he might have avoided the disaster which overthrew his hopes. He will probably see that his misfortunes arose from neglecting some of the following rules:—

Be industrious. Everybody knows that industry is the fundamental virtue in the man of business. But it is not every sort of inidustry which tends to wealth. Many men work hard to do a great deal of business, and, after all, make less money than they would if they did less. Industry should be expended in seeing to all the details of business—in the careful finishing up of each separate undertaking, and in the maintainance of such a system will keep everything under control.

Be economical. This rule, also, is familiar to everybody. Economy is a virtue to be practised every hour in a great city. It is to practiced in pence as much as in pounds. A shilling a day saved, amounts to an estate in the course of a life. Economy is especially important in the outset of life, until the foundations of an estate are laid. Many men are poor all their days, because, when their necessary expenses were small, they did not seize the opportunity to save a small capital, which would have changed their fortunes for the whole of their lives.

Stick to the business in which you are regularly employed. Let speculators make their thousands in a year or day; mind your own regular trade, never turning from it to the right hand or the left. If you are a merchant, a professional man, or a mechanic, never buy lots or stocks unless you have surplus money which you wish to invest. Your own business you understand as well as other men; but other people's business you do not understand. Let your business be some one which is useful to the community. All such occupations possess the elements of profits in themselves, while mere speculation has no such element.

Never take great hazards. Such hazards are seldom well balanced by the prospects of profit; and if they were, the habit of mind which is induced is unfavorable, and generally the result is bad. To keep what you have, should be the first rule; to get what you can fairly, the second.

Do not be in a hurry to get rich. Gradual gains are the only natural gains, and they who are in haste to be rich, break over sound rules, fall into temptations and distress of various sorts, and generally fail of their object. There is no use in getting rich suddenly. The man who keeps his business under his control, and saves something from year to year, is always rich. At any rate, he possesses the highest enjoyment which riches are able to afford.

Never do business for the sake of doing it, and being counted a great merchant. There is often more money to be made by a small business than a large one; and that business will in the end be most respectable which is most successful.

Do not get deeply in debt; but so manage as always, if possibly, to have your financial position easy, so that you can turn any way you please.

Do not love money extravagantly. We speak here merely with reference to getting rich. In morals, the inordinate love of money is one of the most degrading vices. But the extravagant desire of accumulation induces an eagerness, many times, which is imprudent, and so misses its object from too much haste to grasp it. . . .

Success in life mainly depends upon perseverance. When a man has determined to follow a certain line of business, he must at the same time learn to persevere until success crowns his efforts. He must never be cast down by the difficulties which may beset his path—for whoever conquers difficulty, conquers a weakness of his own frail nature likewise. How many men have commenced business under the most favorable auspices, and yet when a cloud has momentarily overshadowed their path, have lost all command over themselves and fled before the temporary gloom, instead of persevering on until the cloud has been dispersed, and sunshine once more smiled upon their efforts. Others, more fickle, have thought their business, in some minor departments, unworthy of their perseverance and energy, and forgetting the golden maxim that, "whatever is worth doing is worth doing well," have ceased to persevere in small matters, until sloth has entered deeply into their minds, and their whole business greatly neglected.

We are too apt to attribute success in business to good fortune, instead of great perseverance. This is a great evil, and should be eshewed, as it leads many to suppose that Dame Fortune will do that for them which they are unwilling to do for themselves.

The history of every great success in business is the history of great perseverance. By perseverance the mind is strengthened and invigorated, and the difficulty that once seemed so formidable is a second time surmounted with ease and confidence.

Energy and great perseverance are never thrown away on a good cause, or left unrewarded; and to every man of business, perseverance should be his motto, and then he may look with confidence to fortune as his reward.

Questions

1. According to Hunt, what qualities should a successful businessman possess, and what rules should he follow?

2. What relationship between individual success and the community was suggested?

3. Why did Hunt warn against speculation and the pursuit of sudden wealth?

Questions for Further Thought

1. Would Tocqueville and the editorialist in the *American Whig Review* have agreed with Freeman Hunt's prescription for business success in America? Why or why not?

2. Did these writers share the same assumptions about the impact of "democracy" on the American economy and worker?

3. Were the anxieties (and hopes) expressed by these writers realized? How accurate were they in describing changes in the social life of America?

CHAPTER TEN

A Democratic Revolution

1820–1844

The Rise of Popular Politics, 1820–1829

The American Revolution marked the beginning of a long-term breakdown of classical republicanism, in which the "common folk" recognized their natural "superiors" and deferred to their better judgment. By the end of the 1820s, this traditional pattern of deference to ruling elites had been upset by the advent of universal adult white male suffrage (Document 10-1), the expansion of economic opportunities in commerce and manufacturing (Document 10-2), and social and geographic mobility (see text pp. 302–303). In an egalitarian democracy, quantity rather than quality counted; therefore, majority rule was almost irresistible (Document 10-3). In such a situation, where the "whole mass of a people" are authorized to exercise "unexampled power," the Massachusetts reformer Horace Mann explained, it was essential that they be fortified with "unexampled wisdom and rectitude"; otherwise, "we shall perish by the very instruments prepared for our happiness" (Document 10-4).

In the meantime, the economic expansion of the nation raised a host of new political issues. While many Americans continued to fear special privilege and the use of government to further private interests, others, such as Henry Clay, began to argue that government aid to economic development, such as the use of tariffs to raise the prices of foreign imports in competition with American manufactures, would benefit all Americans. Cultural conflicts growing out of the rise of the evangelicals, and later from increased immigration, likewise spilled over into politics. These new political concerns cut across community lines and could not be contained by the old deferential politics. Instead, a new class of professional politicians, epitomized by Martin Van Buren, began to develop the modern mass political party; operating at first in the states, they mobilized armies of local workers and voters to "campaign" for party control of government policy and patronage jobs. During the administration of President John Quincy Adams, increasing polarization between Adams's National Republican supporters and the democratic republican (soon to be Democratic) supporters of Andrew Jackson allowed Van Buren, a Jackson supporter, to extend his organization to the national level. The result was not only a victory for Jackson in the election of 1828 but also the first great national victory for the new mass electorate.

10-1   An Argument Against Universal Suffrage (1821)

James Kent

Thomas Jefferson's characterization of John Quincy Adams's presidential policies as the "splendid government of an aristocracy" and Adams's criticism of democracy (see text pp. 305–306) illustrate the divergence of political ideology that was central to the age of democratic revolution. In an increasingly commercial society the agricultural simplicity of the early republic faded, and critics of democracy warned that the foundations of republican liberty could be eroded by poor men seeking equality with the wealthy. James Kent (1763–1847), a New York Federalist, was a leading jurist and the author of the most influential treatise on American law in the nineteenth century. Kent expressed the antidemocratic point of view with striking clarity at the New York Constitutional Convention of 1821.

Source: From *Reports of the Proceedings and Debates of the Convention of 1821 Assembled for the Purpose of Amending the Constitution of the State of New York* (Albany: E. and E. Hosford, 1821).

[W]e propose . . . to bow before the idol of universal suffrage. That extreme democratic principle . . . has been regarded with terror by the wise men of every age because, in every European republic, ancient and modern, in which it has been tried, it has terminated disastrously and been productive of corruption, injustice, violence, and tyranny. And dare we flatter ourselves that we are a peculiar people . . . exempted from the passions which have disturbed and corrupted the rest of mankind? . . . I wish those who have an interest in the soil to retain the exclusive possession of a branch in the legislature as a stronghold in which they may find safety through all the vicissitudes which the state may be destined . . . to experience. I wish them to be always enabled to say that their freeholds cannot be taxed without their consent. The men of no property, together with the crowds of dependents connected with great manufacturing and commercial establishments, and the motley and undefinable population of crowded ports, may, perhaps, at some future day, under skillful management, predominate in the assembly, and yet we should be perfectly safe if no laws could pass without the free consent of the owners of the soil. . . .

The apprehended danger from the experiment of universal suffrage applied to the whole legislative department is no dream of the imagination. . . . The tendency of universal suffrage is to jeopardize the rights of property and the principles of liberty. There is a constant tendency . . . in the poor to covet and to share the plunder of the rich; in the debtor to relax or avoid the obligation of contracts; in the majority to tyrannize over the minority and trample down their rights; in the indolent and the profligate to cast the whole burdens of society upon the industrious and the virtuous. . . . We are no longer to remain plain and simple republics of farmers. . . . We are fast becoming a great nation, with great commerce, manufactures, population, wealth, luxuries, and with the vices and miseries that they engender. . . . [W]e have to apprehend the establishment of unequal and, consequently, unjust systems of taxation and all the mischiefs of a crude and mutable legislation.

Questions

1. In Kent's view, how did property qualifications protect America against "corruption, injustice, violence, and tyranny"?

2. What dangers did Kent see as the nation ceased to be composed of "simple republics of farmers"?

3. If Kent's view had prevailed, how might representative government have been structured in New York?

10-2   Speech on the Tariff (March 30–31, 1824)

Henry Clay

A native of Virginia, Henry Clay (1777–1852) migrated to Kentucky, where he established himself as a substantial slaveholding planter and lawyer. A strong nationalist and war hawk, Clay won election to the House of Representatives in 1810 and became Speaker the following year. A candidate for president in 1824, Clay advocated what he called the "American System" (see text pp. 304–305) and later played a leading role in building the Whig opposition to Andrew Jackson.

Clay's American System envisioned an integrated national economy in which a protective tariff would encourage domestic manufacturing while it generated revenues to support federally financed harbors, canals, and other major internal improvements. Clay was largely successful in his immediate aim: the Tariff of 1824, raising rates, passed. But his larger goal of harnessing the federal government to the development of the national economy fell victim to sectional rivalry and to a democratic critique of the special privilege enjoyed by established elites in the mainstream of economic development.

In the following excerpts from Clay's two-day-long speech of March 1824 in the House of Representatives, he explains why he believes it would be in the nation's interest to impose a tariff on imports to protect domestic manufacturing.

Source: From *Annals of the Congress of the United States, 1789–1824* (Washington, DC: U.S. Government Printing Office), 18th Cong., 1st sess. (1824), 1962–2001.

And what is this tariff? It seems to have been regarded as a sort of monster, huge and deformed; a wild beast, endowed with tremendous powers of destruction, about to be let loose among our people, if not to devour them, at least to consume their substance. But let us calm our passions, and deliberately survey this alarming, this terrific being. The sole object of the tariff is to tax the produce of foreign industry, with the view of promoting American industry. The tax is exclusively levelled at foreign industry. . . .

It has been treated as an imposition of burthens upon one part of the community by design for the benefit of another; as if, in fact, money were taken from the pockets of one portion of the people and put into the pockets of another. But, is that a fair representation of it? No man pays the duty assessed on the foreign article by compulsion, but voluntarily; and this voluntary duty, if paid, goes into the common exchequer, for the common benefit of all. . . . According to the opponents of the domestic policy, the proposed system will force capital and labor into new and reluctant employments; we are not prepared, in consequence of the high price of wages, for the successful establishment of manufactures, and we must fail in the experiment. We have seen that the existing occupations of our society, those of agriculture, commerce, navigation, and the learned professions, are overflowing with competitors, and that the want of employment is severely felt. Now what does this bill propose? To open a new and extensive field of business, in which all that choose may enter. There is no compulsion upon any one to engage in it. An option only is given to industry, to continue in the present unprofitable pursuits, or to embark in a new and promising one. The effect will be to lessen the competition in the old branches of business and to multiply our resources for increasing our comforts and augmenting the national wealth. The alleged fact of the high price of wages is not admitted. The truth is, that no class of society suffers more, in the present stagnation of business, than the laboring class. That is a necessary effect of the depression of agriculture, the principal business of the community. The wages of able-bodied men vary from five to eight dollars per month; and such has been the want of employment, in some parts of the Union, that instances have not been unfrequent, of men working merely for the means of present subsistence. . . . We are now, and ever will be, essentially, an agricultural people. Without a material change in the fixed habits of the country, the friends of this measure desire to draw to it, as a powerful auxiliary to its industry, the manufacturing arts. The difference between a nation with, and without the arts, may be conceived, by the difference between a keel-boat and a steam-boat, combatting the rapid torrent of the Mississippi. How slow does the former ascend, hugging the sinuosities of the shore, pushed on by her hardy and exposed crew, now throwing themselves in vigorous concert on their oars, and then seizing the pendant boughs of over-hanging trees: she seems hardly to move; and her scanty cargo is scarcely worth the transportation! With what ease is she not passed by the steam-boat, laden with the riches of all quarters of the world, with a crowd of gay, cheerful, and protected passengers, now dashing into the midst of the current, or gliding through the eddies near the shore. . . . The adoption of the restrictive system, on the part of the United States, by excluding the produce of foreign labor, would extend the consumption of American produce, unable, in the infancy and unprotected state of the arts, to sustain a competition with foreign fabrics. Let our arts breathe under the shade of protection; let them be perfected as they are in England, and we shall then be ready, as England now is said to be, to put aside protection, and to enter upon the freest exchanges. . . .

Other and animating considerations invite us to adopt the policy of this system. Its importance, in connexion with the general defence in time of war, cannot fail to be duly estimated. Need I recal [*sic*] to our painful recollection the sufferings, for the want of an adequate supply of absolute necessaries, to which the defenders of their country's rights and our entire population were subjected during the late war [the War of 1812]? Or to remind the committee of the great advantage of a steady and unfailing source of supply, unaffected alike in war and in peace? Its importance, in reference to the stability of our Union, that paramount and greatest of all our interests, cannot fail warmly to recommend it, or at least to conciliate the forbearance of every patriot bosom. Now our people present the spectacle of a vast assemblage of jealous rivals, all eagerly rushing to the sea-board, jostling each other in their way, to hurry off to glutted foreign markets the perishable produce of their labor. The tendency of that policy, in conformity to which this bill is prepared, is to transform these competitors into friends and mutual customers; and, by the reciprocal exchanges of their respective productions, to place the confederacy upon the most solid of all foundations, the basis of common interest. . . .

Even if the benefits of the policy were limited to certain sections of our country, would it not be satisfactory to behold American industry, wherever situated, active, ani-

mated, and thrifty, rather than persevere in a course which renders us subservient to foreign industry? But these benefits are twofold, direct, and collateral, and in the one shape or the other, they will diffuse themselves throughout the Union. All parts of the Union will participate, more or less, in both. As to the direct benefit, it is probable that the North and the East will enjoy the largest share. But the West and the South will also participate in them. . . . And where the direct benefit does not accrue, that will be enjoyed of supplying the raw material and provisions for the consumption of artisans. . . . I appeal to the South—to the high-minded, generous, and patriotic South—with which I have so often co-operated. . . . Of what does it complain? A possible temporary enhancement [i.e., price increase] in the objects of consumption. Of what do we complain? A total incapacity, produced by the foreign policy, to purchase, at any price, necessary foreign objects of consumption. In such an alternative, inconvenient only to it, ruinous to us, can we expect too much from Southern magnanimity?

Questions

1. How did Clay explain the importance to an agricultural nation of the "manufacturing arts"?

2. According to Clay, how would a protective tariff promote a "common interest" across the nation?

3. How did Clay answer the South's complaint that the benefits of the tariff went primarily to the manufacturing sector in the Northeast?

10-3   The Tyranny of the Majority (1831)

Alexis de Tocqueville

The American Revolution enunciated two principles of free government that became democratic dogma after the mid-1820s: popular sovereignty and majority rule. However, ever since the constitutional debates, Americans have grappled with the potential danger posed by the rule of a majority faction. The so-called tyranny of the majority, the ability of a democratically elected group to impose its collective will on a powerless minority, was at the very core of Madison's *The Federalist*, No. 10 (Document 6-20). Madison assumed, however, that the masses would choose only "fit characters" as their representatives, and that in a large republic the chances of a self-interested majority forming were remote. The advent of political democracy in the 1820s, especially the extension of the franchise, the rise of disciplined political parties, and the elevation of the "common man," seemed to raise anew the specter of popular oppression. In the following excerpt from *Democracy in America*, Alexis de Tocqueville famously describes the links between equality and popular sovereignty on the one hand, and the tyranny of the majority on the other.

Source: From Harvey C. Mansfield and Delba Winthrop, eds., *Democracy in America*. Copyright © 2000 by the University of Chicago Press. Reprinted by permission of the University of Chicago Press.

It is of the very essence of democratic governments that the empire of the majority is absolute; for in democracies, outside the majority there is nothing that resists it.

Several particular circumstances also tend to render the power of the majority in America not only predominant, but irresistible.

The moral empire of the majority is founded in part on the idea that there is more enlightenment and wisdom in many men united than in one alone, in the number of legislators than in their choice. It is the theory of equality applied to intellects. . . .

The majority in the United States therefore has an immense power in fact, and a power in opinion almost as great; and once it has formed on a question, there are so to speak no obstacles that can, I shall not say stop, but even delay its advance, and allow it the time to hear the complaints of those it crushes as it passes.

The consequences of this state of things are dire and dangerous for the future.

. . . Now, if you accept that one man vested with omnipotence can abuse it against his adversaries, why not accept the same thing for a majority? Have men changed in character by being united? Have they become more patient before obstacles by becoming stronger? As for me, I cannot believe it; and I shall never grant to several the power of doing everything that I refuse to a single one of those like me.

Omnipotence seems to me to be an evil and dangerous thing in itself. Its exercise appears to me above the strength of man, whoever he may be, and I see only God who can be omnipotent without danger, because his wisdom and justice are always equal to his power. There is therefore no authority on earth so respectable in itself or vested with a right so sacred that I should wish to allow to act without control and to dominate without obstacles. Therefore, when I see the right and the ability to do everything granted to any power whatsoever, whether it is called people or king, democracy or aristocracy, whether it is exercised in a monarchy or in a republic, I say: there is the seed of tyranny, and I seek to go live under other laws.

What I most reproach in democratic government, as it has been organized in the United States, is not, as many people in Europe claim, its weakness, but on the contrary, its irresistible force. And what is most repugnant to me in America is not the extreme freedom that reigns there, it is the lack of a guarantee against tyranny.

When a man or a party suffers from an injustice in the United States, whom do you want him to address? Public opinion? that is what forms the majority; the legislative body? it represents the majority and obeys it blindly; the executive power? it is named by the majority and serves as its passive instruments; the public forces? the public forces are nothing other than the majority in arms; the jury? the jury is the majority vested with the right to pronounce decrees: in certain states, the judges themselves are elected by the majority. Therefore, however iniquitous or unreasonable is the measure that strikes you, you must submit to it.

. . . When one comes to examine what the exercise of thought is in the United States, then one perceives very clearly to what point the power of the majority surpasses all the powers that we know in Europe.

Thought is an invisible and almost intangible power that makes sport of all tyrannies. In our day the most absolute sovereigns of Europe cannot prevent certain thoughts hostile to their authority from mutely circulating in their states and even in the heart of their courts. It is not the same in America: as long as the majority is doubtful, one speaks; but when it has irrevocably pronounced, everyone becomes silent and friends and enemies alike then seem to hitch themselves together to its wagon. The reason for this is simple: there is no monarch so absolute that he can gather in his hands all the strength of society and defeat resistance, as can a majority vested with the right to make the laws and execute them.

A king, moreover, has only a material power that acts on actions and cannot reach wills; but the majority is vested with a force, at once material and moral, that acts on the will as much as on actions, and which at the same time prevents the deed and the desire to do it.

In America the majority draws a formidable circle around thought. Inside those limits, the writer is free; but unhappiness awaits him if he dares to leave them. It is not that he has to fear an auto-da-fé, but he is the butt of mortifications of all kinds and of persecutions every day. A political career is closed to him: he has offended the only power that has the capacity to open it up. Everything is refused him, even glory. Before publishing his opinions, he believed he had partisans; it seems to him that he no longer has any now that he has uncovered himself to all; for those who blame him express themselves openly, and those who think like him, without having his courage, keep silent and move away. He yields, he finally bends under the effort of each day and returns to silence as if he felt remorse for having spoken the truth.

Chains and executioners are the coarse instruments that tyranny formerly employed; but in our day civilization has perfected even despotism itself, which seemed, indeed, to have nothing more to learn.

Princes had so to speak made violence material; democratic republics in our day have rendered it just as intellectual as the human will that it wants to constrain. Under the absolute government of one alone, despotism struck the body crudely, so as to reach the soul; and the soul, escaping from those blows, rose gloriously above it; but in democratic republics, tyranny does not proceed in this way; it leaves the body and goes straight for the soul. The master no longer says to it: You shall think as I do or you shall die; he says: You are free not to think as I do; your life, your goods, everything remains to you; but from this day on, you are a stranger among us. You shall keep your privileges in the city, but they will become useless to you; for if you crave the vote of your fellow citizens, they will not grant it to you, and if you demand only their esteem, they will still pretend to refuse it to you. You shall remain among men, but you shall lose your rights of humanity. When you approach those like you, they shall flee you as being impure; and those who believe in your innocence, even they shall abandon you, for one would flee them in their turn. Go in peace, I leave you your life, but I leave it to you worse than death.

. . . Governments ordinarily perish by powerlessness or by tyranny. In the first case power escapes them; in the other, it is torn from them.

Many people, on seeing democratic states fall into anarchy, have thought that government in these states was naturally weak and powerless. The truth is that when war among their parties has once been set aflame, government loses its action on society. But I do not think that the nature of democratic power is to lack force and resources; I believe, on the contrary, that almost always the abuse of its strength and the bad use of its resources bring it to perish. Anarchy is almost always born of its tyranny or its lack of skillfulness, but not of its powerlessness.

One must not confuse stability with force, the greatness of the thing and its duration. In democratic republics, the power that directs society is not stable, for it often changes hands and purpose. But everywhere it is brought, its force is almost irresistible.

The government of the American republics appears to me to be as centralized and more energetic than that of absolute monarchies of Europe. I therefore do not think that it will perish from weakness.

If ever freedom is lost in America, one will have to blame the omnipotence of the majority that will have brought minorities to despair and have forced them to make an appeal to material force. One will then see anarchy, but it will have come as a consequence of despotism.

Questions

1. Why was the threat of a tyrannical majority greater in America than elsewhere? What underlying assumptions does Tocqueville make about the power of the majority?

2. Were Tocqueville's fears about the dangers of power unchecked similar to those held by leaders of the American Revolution? If so, in what ways? If not, why not?

3. According to Tocqueville, why was the power of a tyrannical majority greater than the power of an absolute monarch? How would the majority silence all opposition?

10-4   Necessity of Education in a Republic (1837)

Horace Mann

Probably because of his personal background, Horace Mann (1796–1859) was a firm believer in the power of education. Born into a poor family in rural Massachusetts, he managed to escape a life of grinding poverty by making the most of the sporadic formal schooling he received as a child and adolescent. In 1816, after six months of sustained preparation, he gained admission to Brown University. Graduating in 1819, Mann was a tutor at Brown for two years before entering the Litchfield (Connecticut) Law School and passing the Massachusetts bar in 1823. He then commenced a promising career as a lawyer and politician, serving first in the Massachusetts house and then the senate, where he championed all manner of reform but was perhaps most ardent about the cause of public education. In 1837 Mann chose to abandon his career in law and politics, much to the consternation of his friends, to head the newly created state board of education. It was in this position, however, that he made his most lasting contribution to American society and culture. Under Mann's direction, the board rejuvenated public education in Massachusetts and influenced the common school movement in the rest of the United States.

Source: Excerpts from *Ideology and Power in the Age of Jackson*, ed. Edwin C. Rozwenc (Garden City, NY: Doubleday, 1964), 144–148.

It is a truism, that free institutions multiply human energies. A chained body cannot do much harm; a chained mind can do as little. In a despotic government, the human faculties are benumbed and paralyzed; in a Republic, they glow with an intense life, and burst forth with uncontrollable impetuosity. In the former, they are circumscribed and straitened in their range of action; in the latter, they have "ample room and verge enough," and may rise to glory or plunge into ruin. Amidst universal ignorance, there cannot be such wrong notions about right, as there may be in a community partially enlightened; and false conclusions which have been reasoned out are infinitely worse than blind impulses. . . .

Now it is undeniable that, with the possession of certain higher faculties,—common to all mankind,—whose proper cultivation will bear us upward to hitherto undiscovered regions of prosperity and glory, we possess, also, certain lower faculties or propensities;—equally common;—whose improper indulgence leads, inevitably, to tribulation, and anguish, and ruin. The propensities to which I refer seem indispensable to our temporal existence, and, if restricted within proper limits, they are promotive of our enjoyment; but, beyond those limits, they work dishonor and infatuation, madness and despair. As servants, they are indispensable; as masters, they torture as well as tyrannize. Now despotic and arbitrary governments have dwarfed and crippled the powers of doing evil as much as the powers of doing good; but a republican government, from the very fact of its freedom, unreins their speed, and lets loose their strength. It is justly alleged against despotisms, that they fetter, mutilate, almost extinguish the noblest powers of the human soul; but there is a *per contra* to this, for which we have not given them credit;—they circumscribe the ability to do the greatest evil, as well as to do the greatest good.

My proposition, therefore, is simply this:—If republican institutions do wake up unexampled energies in the whole mass of a people, and give them implements of unexampled power wherewith to work out their will, then these same institutions ought also to confer upon that people unexampled wisdom and rectitude. If these institutions give greater scope and impulse to the lower order of faculties belonging to the human mind, then they must also give more authoritative control and more skillful guidance to the higher ones. If they multiply temptations, they must fortify against them. If they quicken the activity and enlarge the sphere of the appetites and passions, they must, as least in an equal ratio, establish the authority and extend the jurisdiction of reason and conscience. In a word, we must not add to the impulsive, without also adding to the regulating forces.

If we maintain institutions, which bring us within the action of new and unheard-of powers, without taking any corresponding measures for the government of those powers, we shall perish by the very instruments prepared for our happiness.

The truth has been so often asserted, that there is no security for a republic but in morality and intelligence, that a repetition of it seems hardly in good taste. But all permanent blessings being founded on permanent truths, a continued observance of the truth is the condition of a continued enjoyment of the blessing. I know we are often admonished that, without intelligence and virtue, as a chart and a compass, to direct us in our untried political voyage, we shall perish in the first storm; but I venture to add that, without these qualities, we shall not wait for a storm,—we cannot weather a calm. If the sea is as smooth as glass we shall founder, for we are in a stone boat. Unless these qualities pervade the general head and the general heart, not only will republican institutions vanish from amongst us, but the words *prosperity* and *happiness* will become obsolete. . . .

. . . Our institutions furnish as great facilities for wicked men, in all departments of wickedness, as phosphorus and lucifer matches furnish to the incendiary. What chemistry has done, in these preparations, over the old art of rubbing two sticks together, for the wretch who would fire your dwelling, our social partnerships have done for flagitious and unprincipled men. Through the right,—almost universal,—of suffrage, we have established a community of power; and no proposition is more plain and self-evident, than that nothing but mere popular inclination lies between a community of power and a community in every thing else. And though, in the long-run, and when other things are equal, a righteous cause always has a decisive advantage over an evil one, yet, in the first onset between right and wrong, bad men posses one advantage over the good. They have double resources,—two armories. The arts of guilt are as welcome to them as the practices of justice. They can use poisoned weapons as well as those approved by the usages of war.

Again; has it been sufficiently considered, that all which has been said,—and truly said,—of the excellence of our institutions, if administered by an upright people, must be reversed and read backwards, if administered by a corrupt one? I am aware that some will be ready to say, "We have been unwise and infatuated to confide all the constituents of our social and political welfare to such irresponsible keeping." But let me ask of such,—of what avail is their lamentation? The irresistible movement in the diffusion of power is still progressive, not retrograde. Every year puts more of social strength into the hands of physical strength. The arithmetic of numbers is more and more excluding all estimate of moral forces, in the administration of government. And this, whether for good or for evil, will continue to be. Human beings cannot be remanded to the dungeons of imbecility, if they are to those of ignorance. The sun can as easily be turned backwards in its course, as one particle of that power, which has been conferred upon the millions, can be again monopolized by the few. To discuss the question, therefore, whether our institutions are not too free, is, for all practical purposes, as vain as it would be to discuss the question whether, on the whole, it was a wise arrangement on the part of Divine Providence, that the American continent should ever have been created, or that Columbus should have discovered it.

Questions

1. Compare Mann's ideas with those expressed by Benjamin Rush on female education (Document 8-7) and by Alexis de Tocqueville on the tyranny of the majority (Document 10-3). What are their similarities and differences?

2. Was Mann optimistic or pessimistic about the state of American society? What did he say were the advantages and disadvantages of American democracy? According to Mann, what were the characteristics of the ideal American citizen?

3. Mann was a leader among Massachusetts Whigs. Why was this a logical commitment for him? Why wouldn't a champion of public schooling be a Jacksonian Democrat?

Questions for Further Thought

1. Compare Henry Clay's statements about American industry with those of Orestes Brownson (Document 9-8) and the writer in the *American Whig Review* (Document 9-10). What are their similarities and dissimilarities?

2. Would Horace Mann's remedy for averting the dangers of democracy have satisfied Tocqueville?

3. Are the views of Tocqueville and Mann regarding democratic politics consistent with those voiced by Hugh Henry Brackenridge (Document 8-5)? Were they equally skeptical about its potential for doing good?

The Jacksonian Presidency, 1829–1837

Andrew Jackson entered the White House in 1829 determined to reverse what he saw as a dangerous alliance of federal government power with the forces of special privilege. An advocate of limited government, he sought to block enactment of Henry Clay's American System and to dismantle those elements of it (protective tariffs, the Bank of the United States) that were already in place. Yet in order to achieve his goals, he had to take a traditionally weak office and expand its power. Jackson used his control of federal patronage to build a strong party organization loyal to him. He pressed for tariff reduction; when South Carolina denied the right of the federal government to collect tariffs within the state (Document 10-8), he firmly asserted the supremacy of the federal government and his right to use military force against a state to enforce federal law. Above all, Jackson went to war with the Second Bank of the United States, which he and his followers regarded as a grant of extensive public powers to a small, well-heeled band of eastern capitalists, who in turn used it for their own self-interest rather than the public good (Document 10-5). Although his goals were similar to those of Jefferson, he pursued them by means that greatly (and, to some, dangerously) extended executive power; he vetoed the proposed rechartering of the Second Bank, and after his triumphant re-election in 1832, withdrew federal deposits from the bank in defiance of Congress.

Jackson also moved to accelerate the removal of the remaining Indian peoples east of the Mississippi to new "Indian Territories" far to the west. In the South, states were seeking to extend their authority over territory held by the so-called Five Civilized Tribes (the Cherokee, Chickasaw, Choctaw, Creek, and Seminole), who insisted instead that they were sovereign peoples. Jackson sided with his white constituents and their insistence on states' rights against even the Cherokee, whose land claims were deemed "unquestionable" by the Supreme Court (Documents 10-6 and 10-7). In 1830 he obtained passage of the Indian Removal Act, and he began to use both cajolery and military force to drive Indian tribes westward—a process that culminated after his administration in the famous Trail of Tears.

10-5   Bank Veto Message (1832)

Andrew Jackson   The first Bank of the United States had been established at the behest of President Washington's treasury secretary, Alexander Hamilton, and was rechartered for a twenty-year period in 1816 during the Era of Good Feeling. The bank had become a political issue after the Panic of 1819, when the question of the country's monetary policy suddenly became associated with financial collapse and economic depression. The bank issue had for some years generated factional political divisions at the state level, and Jackson entered the presidency opposed to the existing structure and policies of the Second Bank of the United States. He also found himself in an intense personal struggle with the bank's president, Nicholas Biddle. When Congress approved an extended charter for Biddle's bank, Jackson vetoed the legislation (see text p. 312). Jackson made his veto message the opening shot in a campaign to destroy the bank, a war that became the defining event of his presidency. In the following extracts from his veto message, Jackson explains why he viewed the Bank as an undemocratic concentration of economic power and a threat to the republic.

Source: James D. Richardson, ed., *A Compilation of the Message and Papers of the Presidents* (Washington, DC: U.S. Government Printing Office, 1896–1899), 2:576–591.

The bill "to modify and continue" the act entitled "An act to incorporate the subscribers to the Bank of the United States" was presented to me on the 4th July instant. Having considered it with that solemn regard to the principles of the Constitution which the day was calculated to inspire, and come to the conclusion that it ought not to become a law, I herewith return it to the Senate, in which it originated, with my objections.

A bank of the United States is in many respects convenient for the Government and useful to the people. Entertaining this opinion, and deeply impressed with the belief that some of the powers and privileges possessed by the existing bank are unauthorized by the Constitution, subversive of the rights of the States, and dangerous to the liberties of the people, I felt it my duty at an early period of my Administration to call the attention of Congress to the practicability of organizing an institution combining all its advantages and obviating these objections. I sincerely regret that in the act before me I can perceive none of these modifications of the bank charter which are necessary, in my opinion, to make it compatible with justice, with sound policy, or with the Constitution of our country. . . .

But this act does not permit competition in the purchase of this monopoly [the bank]. It seems to be predicated on the erroneous idea that the present stockholders have a prescriptive right not only to the favor but to the bounty of Government. It appears that more than a fourth part of the stock is held by foreigners and the residue is held by a few hundred of our own citizens, chiefly of the richest class. For their benefit does this act exclude the whole American people from competition in the purchase of this monopoly and dispose of it for many millions less than it is worth. This seems the less excusable because some of our citizens not now stockholders petitioned that the door of competition might be opened, and offered to take a charter on terms much more favorable to the Government and country. . . .

It is to be regretted that the rich and powerful too often bend the acts of government to their selfish purposes. Distinctions in society will always exist under every just government. Equality of talents, of education, or of wealth can not be produced by human institutions. In the full enjoyment of the gifts of Heaven and the fruits of superior industry, economy, and virtue, every man is equally entitled to protection by law; but when the laws undertake to add to these natural and just advantages artificial distinction, to grant titles, gratuities, and exclusive privileges, to make the rich richer and the potent more powerful, the humble members of society—the farmers, mechanics, and laborers—who have neither the time nor the means of securing like favors to themselves, have a right to complain of the injustice of their Government. There are no necessary evils in government. Its evils exist only in its abuses. If it would confine itself to equal protection, and, as Heaven does its rains, shower its favors alike on the high and the low, the rich and the poor, it would be an unqualified blessing. In the act before me there seems to be a wide and unnecessary departure from these just principles. . . .

Many of our rich men have not been content with equal protection and equal benefits, but have besought us to make them richer by act of Congress. By attempting to gratify their desires we have in the results of our legislation arrayed section against section, interest against interest, and man against man, in a fearful commotion which threatens to shake the foundations of our Union. If we can not at once, in justice to interests vested under improvident legislation, make our Government what it ought to be, we can at least take a stand against all new grants of monopolies and exclusive privileges, against any prostitution of our Government to the advancement of the few at the expense of the many, and in favor of compromise and gradual reform in our code of laws and system of political economy.

Questions

1. In his veto message, Jackson did not question the ability of the bank to regulate currency and credit. What public policy objectives did his message attempt to advance?

2. Despite the Supreme Court's decision in *McCulloch v. Maryland* (1819), Jackson insisted in his veto message that some of the "powers and privileges possessed by the existing bank are unauthorized by the Constitution." What reasons did he give for that judgment?

3. What did the "humbler members of society" rightly complain about, in Jackson's view?

10-6   On Indian Removal (1829)

**Andrew Jackson,
Elias Boudinot**

In 1829, in his first annual message (what we now call the State of the Union Address, but in those days not delivered as a speech), President Jackson, alluding to the conflict between the Cherokee and the states of Georgia and Alabama, used the occasion to present his broader views about the "Indian problem" and its solution. Earlier in 1829, when Jackson and his secretary of war, John Eaton, had announced their position on the issue between the Cherokee and Georgia, Elias Boudinot, editor of the *Cherokee Phoenix*, set forth the Cherokee case.

Source: From Theda Perdue, ed., *Cherokee Editor: The Writings of Elias Boudinot* (Knoxville: University of Tennessee Press, 1983), 108–109. Copyright © 1983. Reprinted by permission of the University of Tennessee Press. Originally published in *A Compilation of the Messages and Papers of the President, 1789–1902* by James D. Richardson, ed. (1904), 2:457–459.

(a) Andrew Jackson, First Annual Message, December 8, 1829

. . . The condition and ulterior destiny of the Indian tribes within the limits of some of our States have become objects of much interest and importance. It has long been the policy of Government to introduce among them the arts of civilization, in the hope of gradually reclaiming them from a wandering life. This policy has, however, been coupled with another wholly incompatible with its success. Professing a desire to civilize and settle them, we have at the same time lost no opportunity to purchase their lands and thrust them farther into the wilderness. By this means they have not only been kept in a wandering state, but been led to look upon us as unjust and indifferent to their fate. Thus, though lavish in its expenditures upon the subject, Government has constantly defeated its own policy, and the Indians in general, receding farther and farther to the west, have retained their savage habits. A portion, however, of the Southern tribes, having mingled much with whites and made some progress in the arts of civilized life, have lately attempted to erect an independent government within the limits of Georgia and Alabama. These States, claiming to be the only sovereigns within their territories, extended their laws over the Indians, which induced the latter to call upon the United States for protection. . . .

. . . I informed the Indians inhabiting parts of Georgia and Alabama that their attempt to establish an independent government would not be countenanced by the Executive of the United States, and advised them to emigrate beyond the Mississippi or submit to the laws of those States.

Our conduct toward these people is deeply interesting to our national character. Their present condition, contrasted with what they once were, makes a most powerful appeal to our sympathies. Our ancestors found them the uncontrolled possessors of these vast regions. By persuasion and force they have been made to retire from river to river and from mountain to mountain, until some of the tribes have become extinct and others have left but remnants to preserve for awhile their once terrible names. Surrounded by the whites with their arts of civilization, which by destroying the resources of the savage doom him to weakness and decay, the fate of the Mohegan, the Narragansett, and the Delaware is fast overtaking the Choctaw, the Cherokee, and the Creek. That this fate surely awaits them if they remain within the limits of the States does not admit of a doubt. Humanity and national honor demand that every effort should be made to avert so great a calamity. It is too late to inquire whether it was just in the United States to include them and their territory within the bounds of new States, whose limits they could control. That step can not be retraced. A State can not be dismembered by Congress or restricted in the exercise of her constitutional power. But the people of those States and every State, actuated by feelings of justice and a regard of our national honor, submit to you the interesting question whether something can not be done, consistently with the rights of the States, to preserve this much-injured race.

As a means of effecting this end I suggest for your consideration the propriety of setting apart an ample district west of the Mississippi, and without the limits of any State or Territory now formed, to be guaranteed to the Indian tribes as long as they shall occupy it, each tribe having a distinct control over the portion designated for its use. There they may be secured in the enjoyment of governments of their own choice, subject to no other control from the United States than such as may be necessary to preserve peace on the frontier and between the several tribes. There the benevolent may endeavor to teach them the arts of civilization, and, by promoting union and harmony among them, to raise up an interesting commonwealth, destined to perpetuate the race and to attest the humanity and justice of this Government.

This emigration should be voluntary, for it would be as cruel as unjust to compel the aborigines to abandon the graves of their fathers and seek a home in a distant land. But they should be distinctly informed that if they remain within the limits of the States they must be subject to their laws. In return for their obedience as individuals they will without doubt be protected in the enjoyment of those possessions which they have improved by their industry. But it seems to me visionary to suppose that in this state of things claims can be allowed on tracts of country on which they have neither dwelt nor made improvements, merely because they have seen them from the mountain or passed them in the chase. Submitting to the laws of the States, and receiving, like other citizens, protection in their persons and property, they will ere long become merged in the mass of our population. . . .

(b) Elias Boudinot, Excerpted from the *Cherokee Phoenix*, June 17, 1829

From the documents which we this day lay before our readers, there is not a doubt of the kind of policy, which the present administration of the General Government intends to pursue relative to the Indians. President Jackson has, as a neighboring editor remarks, "recognized the doctrine contended for by Georgia in its full extent." It is to be regretted that we were not undeceived long ago, while we were hunters and in our savage state. It appears now from the communication of the Secretary of War to the Cherokee Delegation, that the illustrious Washington, Jefferson, Madison and Monroe were only tantalizing us, when they encouraged us in the pursuit of agriculture and Government, and when they afforded us the protection of the United States, by which we have been preserved to this present time as a nation. Why were we not told long ago, that we could not be permitted to establish a government within the limits of any state? Then we could have borne disappointment much easier than now. The pretext of Georgia to extend her jurisdiction over the Cherokees has always existed. The Cherokees have always had a government of their own. Nothing, however, was said when we were governed by savage laws, when the abominable law of retaliation carried death in our midst, when it was a lawful act to shed the blood of a person charged with witchcraft, when a brother could kill a brother with impunity, or an innocent man suffer for an offending relative. At that time it might have been a matter of charity to have extended over us the mantle of Christian laws & regulations. But how happens it now, after being fostered by the U. States, and advised by great and good men to establish a government of regular law; when the aid and protection of the General Government have been pledged to us; when we, as dutiful "children" of the President, have followed his instructions and advice, and have established for ourselves a government of regular law; when everything looks so promising around us, that a storm is raised by the extension of tyrannical and unchristian laws, which threatens to blast all our rising hopes and expectations?

There is, as would naturally be supposed, a great rejoicing in Georgia. It is a time of "important news" — "gratifying intelligence" — "The Cherokee lands are to be obtained speedily." It is even reported that the Cherokees have come to the conclusion to sell, and move off to the west of the Mississippi — not so fast. We are yet at our homes, at our peaceful firesides . . . attending to our farms and useful occupations.

We had concluded to give our readers fully our thoughts on the subject, which we, in the above remarks, have merely introduced, but upon reflection & remembering our promise, that we will be moderate, we have suppressed ourselves, and have withheld what we had intended should occupy our editorial column. We do not wish, by any means, unnecessarily to excite the minds of the Cherokees. To our home readers we submit the subject without any special comment. They will judge for themselves. To our distant readers, who may wish to know how we feel under present circumstances, we recommend the memorial, the leading article in our present number. We believe it justly contains the views of the nation.

Questions

1. Jackson contended that the federal government's Indian policy to date (1829) had been counterproductive to its stated goals. What information did Jackson provide to support his position? Was his reasoning sound?

2. What did Elias Boudinot argue, and how did his position concerning federal Indian policy compare with Jackson's?

3. Do you think Jackson truly believed that he was helping the Indians? Or was Jackson's rhetoric merely a cynical cover for yet another white seizure of Indian lands? Explain.

10-7   Decision in *Cherokee Nation v. Georgia* (1831)

John Marshall

After the War of 1812, rapid population growth and the transportation revolution combined to increase pressure on federal and state authorities to make lands held by Indians east of the Mississippi River available to whites. The state of Georgia, which had ceded its western territorial claims in 1802 in return for a promise of federal assistance in securing its possession of all land within its current borders, was particularly adamant about asserting its dominion over the Cherokees and Creeks. Annoyed by what it perceived to be the slow pace of federal action, Georgia encroached on Creek lands in 1826, eliciting a warning from President John Quincy Adams and nearly precipitating an armed confrontation with federal forces. The Creeks salvaged the situation by reluctantly agreeing to their removal west; most Cherokees, however, refused to move. Bolstered by treaties dating back to the 1790s, in which the United States recognized the Cherokee nation and its laws, they drafted a constitution in 1827 that proclaimed their sovereignty and exclusive jurisdiction over specifically demarcated ancestral lands. Georgia responded by promptly declaring Cherokee laws to be null and void and announcing its intention to seize all remaining Indian lands. Turning to the federal judiciary for relief, the Cherokees sought an injunction in the Supreme Court which would prevent Georgia from carrying out its designs. The case put the Marshall Court in a bind. Marshall thought the Cherokees were on solid legal ground, but judicial intervention in 1831 seemed futile in the face of a hostile state, a hostile public, and a hostile president, Andrew Jackson, who not only endorsed Georgia's assertion of state sovereignty but had also recently pushed through Congress the Indian Removal Act of 1830. The Supreme Court needed to state its opinion on the merits of the case without provoking a conflict with the president.

Source: Cherokee Nation v. The State of Georgia 5 Peters 1 (1831).

This bill is brought by the Cherokee Nation, praying an injunction to restrain the State of Georgia from the execution of certain laws of that State, which as it is alleged, go directly to annihilate the Cherokees as a political society, and to seize, for the use of Georgia, the lands of the nation which have been assured to them by the United States in solemn treaties repeatedly made and still in force.

If the courts were permitted to indulge their sympathies, a case better calculated to excite them can scarcely be imagined. A people once numerous, powerful, and truly independent, found by our ancestors in the quiet and uncontrolled possession of an ample domain, gradually sinking beneath our superior policy, our arts and our arms, have yielded their lands by successive treaties, each of which contains a solemn guarantee of the residue, until they retain no more of their formerly extensive territory than is deemed necessary to their comfortable subsistence. To preserve this remnant the present application is made.

Before we can look into the merits of the case, a preliminary inquiry presents itself. Has this court judisdiction of the cause?

The third article of the Constitution describes the extent of the judicial power. The second section closes an enumeration of the cases to which it is extended, with "controversies" "between the State or the citizens thereof, and foreign states, citizens, or subjects." A subsequent clause of the same section gives the Supreme Court original jurisdiction in all cases in which a state shall be a party. The party defendant may then unquestionably be sued in this court. May the plaintiff sue in it? Is the Cherokee Nation a foreign state in the sense in which that term is used in the Constitution?

The counsel for the plaintiffs have maintained the affirmative of this proposition with great earnestness and ability. So much of the argument as was intended to prove the character of the Cherokees as a State, as a distinct political society separated from others, capable of managing its own affairs and governing itself, has, in the opinion of a majority of the judges, been completely successful. They have been uniformly treated as a State from the settlement of our country. The numerous treaties made with them by the United States recognize them as a people capable of maintaining the relations of peace and war, of being responsible in their political character for any violation of their engagements, or for any aggression committed on the citizens of the United States by any individual of their community. Laws have been enacted in the spirit of these treaties. The acts of our government plainly recognize the Cherokee Nation as a State, and the courts are bound by those acts.

A question of much more difficulty remains. Do the Cherokees constitute a foreign state in the sense of the Constitution?

The counsel have shown conclusively that they are not a State of the Union, and have insisted that individually they are aliens, not owing allegiance to the United States. An aggregate of aliens composing a State must, they say be a foreign state. Each individual being foreign, the whole must be foreign.

This argument is imposing, but we must examine it more closely before we yield to it. The condition of the Indians in relation to the United States is perhaps unlike that of any other two people in existence. In the general, nations not owing a common allegiance are foreign to each other. The term "foreign nation" is, with strict property, applicable by either to the other. But the relation of the Indians to the United States is marked by peculiar and cardinal distinctions which exist nowhere else. . . .

Though the Indians are acknowledged to have an unquestionable, and, heretofore, unquestioned right to the lands they occupy until that right shall be extinguished by a voluntary cession to our government, yet it may well be doubted whether those tribes which reside within the acknowledged boundaries of the United States can, with strict accuracy, be denominated foreign nations. They may, more correctly, perhaps, be denominated domestic dependent nations. They occupy a territory to which we assert a title independent of their will, which must take effect in point of possession when their right of possession ceases. Meanwhile they are in a state of pupilage. Their relation to the United States resembles that of a ward to his guardian.

They look to our government for protection; rely upon its kindness and its power; appeal to it for relief to their wants; and address the President as their great father. They and their country are considered by foreign nations, as well as by ourselves, as being so completely under the sovereignty and dominion of the United States, that any attempt to acquire their lands, or to form a political connection with them, would be considered by all as an invasion of our territory, and an act of hostility.

These considerations go far to support the opinion that the framers of our Constitution had not the Indian tribes in view when they opened the courts of the Union to controversies between a State of the citizens thereof, and foreign states.

In considering this subject, the habits and usages of the Indians in their intercourse with their white neighbors ought not to be entirely disregarded. At the time the Constitution was framed, the idea of appealing to an American court of justice for an assertion of right or a redress of wrong, had perhaps never entered the mind of an Indian or of his tribe. Their appeal was to the tomahawk, or to the government. This was well understood by the statesmen who framed the Constitution of the United States, and might furnish some reason for omitting to enumerate them among the parties who might sue in the courts of the Union. Be this as it may, the peculiar relations between the United States and the Indians occupying our territory are such that we should feel much difficulty in considering them as designated by the term "foreign State," were there no other part of the Constitution which might shed light on the meaning of these words. But we think that in construing them, considerable aid is furnished by that clause in the eighth section of the third article, which empowers Congress to "regulate commerce with foreign nations, and among the several States, and with the Indian tribes."

In this clause they are as clearly contradistinguished by a name appropriate to themselves from foreign nations as from the several States composing the Union. They are designated by a distinct appellation; and as this appellation can be applied to neither of the others, neither can the appellation distinguishing either of the others be in fair construction applied to them. The objects to which the power of regulating commerce might be directed, are divided into three distinct classes—foreign nations, the several States, and Indian tribes. When forming this article, the convention considered them as entirely distinct. We cannot assume that the distinction was lost in framing a subsequent article, unless there be something in its language to authorize the assumption.

The counsel for the plaintiffs contend that the words "Indian tribes" were introduced into the article empowering Congress to regulate commerce for the purpose of removing those doubts in which the management of Indian affairs was involved by the language of the ninth article of the confederation. Intending to give the whole power of managing those affairs to the government about to be instituted, the convention conferred it explicitly; and omitted those qualifications which embarrassed the exercise of it as granted in the confederation. This may be admitted without weakening the construction which has been intimated. Had the Indian tribes been foreign nations, in the view of the convention, this exclusive power of regulating intercourse with them might have been, and most probably would have been, specifically given in language indicating that idea, not in language contradistinguishing them from foreign nations. Congress might have been empowered "to regulate commerce with foreign nations, including the Indian tribes, and among the several States." This language would have suggested itself to statesmen who considered the Indian tribes as foreign nations, and were yet desirous of mentioning them particularly.

It has been also said that the same words have not necessarily the same meaning attached to them when found in different parts of the same instrument: their meaning is controlled by the context. This is undoubtedly true. In common language the same word has various meanings, and the peculiar sense in which it is used in any sentence is to be determined by the context. This may not be equally true with respect to proper names. Foreign nations is a general term, the application of which to Indian tribes, when used in the American Constitution, is at best extremely questionable. In one article in which a power is given to be exercised in regard to foreign nations generally, and to the Indian tribes particularly, they are mentioned as separate in terms clearly contradistinguishing them from each other. We perceive plainly that the Constitution in this article does not comprehend Indian tribes in the general term "foreign nations;" not, we presume, because a tribe may not be a nation, but because it is not foreign to the United States. When, afterwards, the term "foreign State" is introduced, we cannot impute to the convention the intention to desert its former meaning, and to comprehend Indian tribes within it, unless the context force that construction on us. We find nothing in the context, and nothing in the subject of the article, which leads to it.

The court has bestowed its best attention on this question, and, after mature deliberation, the majority is of opinion that an Indian tribe or nation within the United States is not a foreign state in the sense of the Constitution, and cannot maintain an action in the courts of the United States. . . .

If it be true that the Cherokee Nation have rights, this is not the tribunal in which those rights are to be asserted. If it be true that wrongs have been inflicted, and that still greater are to be apprehended, this is not the tribunal which can redress the past or prevent the future.

The motion for an injunction is denied.

Questions

1. On what constitutional grounds were the Cherokees basing their appeal to the Supreme Court? What kinds of cases fall under the jurisdiction of the federal courts?

2. How did Marshall arrive at the conclusion that the Cherokees were not a "foreign state" under the meaning of the Constitution? What was the significance of the "domestic dependent nation" status with regard to constitutional rights of the Cherokee Nation?

3. Andrew Jackson supported Georgia's claims of state sovereignty in this case and in the 1832 *Worcester v. Georgia* case; however, he opposed South Carolina's assertion of state sovereignty during the Nullification Crisis of 1832–1833 (see text pp. 309–310). How do you explain this apparent contradiction?

10-8   South Carolina Ordinance of Nullification (1832)

Protective tariffs became a divisive issue after the War of 1812. Beginning in 1816, Congress enacted a series of measures intended to protect domestic iron and textile manufacturers as well as the producers of such raw materials as wool, hemp, and flax. These import taxes found no favor among southerners, who needed no protection for their cotton and were forced to pay higher prices for the protected goods they consumed. South Carolinians, in particular, also viewed the imposition of tariffs as a dangerous encroachment on states' rights. With an economy and way of life dependent on the presence of slaves, they were fearful that an increasingly powerful federal government might promote a policy of general emancipation contrary to the best interests of the state. Thus when Congress passed yet another tariff in 1832, South Carolina balked. Led by slave owners anxious to contain federal power within narrow limits, the South Carolina legislature called for a state convention to meet in Columbia in November. The following Ordinance of Nullification was passed by the convention on November 24.

Source: Paul Leicester Ford, *The Federalist: A Commentary on the Constitution of the United States* (New York: Henry Holt, 1898), 150–152.

An Ordinance to Nullify certain acts of the Congress of the United States, purporting to be laws laying duties and imposts on the importation of foreign commodities.

Whereas the Congress of the United States, by various acts, purporting to be acts laying duties and imposts on foreign imports, but in reality intended for the protection of domestic manufacturers, and the giving of bounties to classes and individuals engaged in particular employments, at the expense and to the injury and oppression of other classes and individuals, and by wholly exempting from taxation certain foreign commodities, such as are not produced or manufactured in the United States, to afford a pretext for imposing higher and excessive duties on articles similar to those intended to be protected, hath exceeded its just powers under the Constitution, which confers on it no authority to afford such protection, and hath violated the true meaning and intent of the Constitution, which provides for equality in imposing the burthens of taxation upon several States and portions of the Confederacy: *And whereas* the said Congress, exceeding its just power to impose taxes and collect revenue for the purpose of effecting and accomplishing the specific objects and purposes which the Constitution of the United States authorizes it to effect and accomplish, hath raised and collected unnecessary revenue for objects unauthorized by the Constitution:

We, therefore, the people of the State of South Carolina in Convention assembled, do declare and ordain . . . That the several acts and parts of acts of the Congress of the United States, purporting to be laws for the imposing of duties and imposts on the importation of foreign commodities . . . and, more especially . . . [the tariff acts of 1828 and 1832] . . . are unauthorized by the Constitution of the United States, and violate the true meaning and intent thereof, and are null, void, and no law, nor binding upon this State, its officers or citizens; and all promises, contracts, and obligations, made or entered into, or to be made or entered into, with purpose to secure the duties imposed by the said acts, and all judicial proceedings which shall be hereafter had in affirmance thereof, are and shall be held utterly null and void.

And it is further Ordained, That it shall not be lawful for any of the constituted authorities, whether of this State or of the United States, to enforce the payment of duties imposed by the said acts within the limits of this State; but it shall be the duty of the Legislature to adopt such measures and pass such acts as may be necessary to give full effect to this Ordinance, and to prevent the enforcement and arrest the operation of the said acts and parts of acts of the Congress of the United States within the limits of this State, from and after the 1st day of February next. . . .

And it is further Ordained, That in no case of law or equity, decided in the courts of this State, wherein shall be drawn in question the authority of this ordinance, or the validity of such act or acts of the Legislature as may be passed for the purpose of giving effect thereto, or the validity of the aforesaid acts of Congress, imposing duties, shall any appeal be taken or allowed to the Supreme Court of the United States, nor shall any copy of the record be printed or allowed for that purpose; and if any such appeal shall be attempted to be taken, the courts of this State shall proceed to execute and enforce their judgments, according to the laws and usages of the State, without reference to such attempted appeal, and the person or persons attempting to take such appeal may be dealt with as for a contempt of the court.

And it is further Ordained, That all persons now holding any office of honor, profit, or trust, civil or military, under this State (members of the Legislature excepted), shall, within such time, and in such manner as the Legislature shall prescribe, take an oath well and truly to obey, execute, and enforce, this Ordinance, and such act or acts of the Legislature as may be passed in pursuance thereof, according to the true intent and meaning of the same; and on the neglect or omission of any such person or persons so to do, his or their office or offices, shall be forthwith vacated . . . and no person hereafter elected to any office of honor, profit, or trust, civil or military (members of the Legislature excepted), shall, until the Legislature shall otherwise provide and direct, enter on the execution of his office . . . until he shall, in like manner, have taken a similar oath; and no juror shall be empannelled in any of the courts of this State, in any cause in which shall be in question this Ordinance, or any act of the Legislature passed in pursuance thereof, unless he shall first, in addition to the usual oath, have taken an oath that he will well and truly obey, execute, and enforce this Ordinance, and such act or acts of the Legislature as may be passed to carry the same into operation and effect, according to the true intent and meaning thereof.

And we, the People of South Carolina, to the end that it may be fully understood by the Government of the United States, and the people of the co-States, that we are determined to maintain this, our Ordinance and Declaration, at every hazard, *Do further Declare* that we will not submit to the application of force, on the part of the Federal Government, to reduce this State to obedience; but that we will consider the passage, by Congress, of any act . . . to coerce the State, shut up her ports, destroy or harass her commerce, or to enforce the acts hereby declare to be null and void, otherwise than through the civil tribunals of the country, as inconsistent with the longer continuance of South Carolina in the Union: and that the people of this State will thenceforth hold themselves absolved from all further obligation to maintain or preserve their political connexion with the people of the other States, and will forthwith proceed to organize a separate Government, and do all other acts and things which sovereign and independent States may of right do.

Questions

1. How did the convention frame its attack on the tariff? According to the Ordinance of Nullification, how was the tariff unconstitutional?

2. South Carolina claimed the Kentucky and Virginia Resolutions as precedents for their action, but James Madison repudiated the claim. What differences can you identify between the Kentucky Resolutions (Document 7-5) and the Ordinance of Nullification?

3. South Carolina was the first state to secede from the Union at the start of the Civil War. How did the Ordinance of Nullification foreshadow this?

Questions for Further Thought

1. From your reading of Documents 10-5 through 10-8 as well as your understanding of the text, is it possible to piece together Jackson's position on the limits of the power of the federal government? On the one hand, Jackson used federal power to act swiftly during the nullification crisis (Document 10-8) and against the Second Bank of the United States (Document 10-5); on the other, Jackson claimed that the federal government could do little to curb the actions of Georgia and Alabama against the Indians (Document 10-6). Is Jackson's constitutional position consistent or contradictory? Explain.

2. Jackson was the last U.S. president to have fought in the Revolution, and the war had a formative and lasting impact on his understanding of both the power of the federal government and the uses of that power. How did Jackson understand the Revolution, and what type of society did he believe America should be? In what ways did Jackson view the bank as undermining the goals of the Revolution as he understood them? Do you agree?

3. Like Thomas Jefferson before him and Ronald Reagan after him, Andrew Jackson ran successfully for president on a platform that promised to get government off the backs of the people (in 1980, Reagan's campaign slogan stated that the government was the problem, not the solution). Once in office Jackson, like Jefferson and Reagan, expanded the power of the government rather than shrinking it — and all three were overwhelmingly elected to a second term of office. How can this be explained?

Class, Culture, and the Second Party System

Jackson's high-handed wielding of the powers of the presidency, as much as his actual policies, horrified many Americans, notably those who advocated Clay's American System. These opponents of "King Andrew" coalesced into an opposition political party, calling themselves Whigs after the eighteenth-century British opponents of royal prerogative. Whigs believed that government could best foster liberty not by attacking special privilege, but by encouraging economic development, which, like the proverbial rising tide, would lift the boats of even the humblest of Americans. They also believed that government had a critical role to play in helping foster virtue; they were among the leading advocates of expanded public education and the use of government institutions such as penitentiaries to "reform" criminals. Whigs especially attracted support from New Englanders and evangelicals who believed that the state needed to foster "Christian" morality (thereby offending Catholics, who flocked to the Democrats).

Meanwhile, by the 1830s, the progress of industrialization and urbanization had begun to generate a large laboring class in the United States. As household production was increasingly replaced by merchant-organized outwork and by factories, more and more Americans found themselves faced with the prospect of being permanent employees. Workers found this development disturbing, for it began to appear that Americans had thrown off rule by an aristocracy of birth only to replace it with an aristocracy of wealth (Document 10-9). In an effort to reverse what they described as their slide into "wage slavery," workers established workingmen's parties to agitate for such reforms as the ten-hour day; by the mid-1830s, many of these parties had allied with the Democrats.

The devastating depression following the financial panic of 1837 sent the early labor movement into reverse. Because it occurred on the Democrats' watch, and because the policies of Jackson and his successor, Martin Van Buren, could be blamed for it, the Whigs were provided a golden opportunity to gain power. Even though the party appealed chiefly to evangelicals and commercial interests, from the outset Whig politicians were eager to participate in the rough-and-tumble of mass politics (Document 10-10), competing with the Democrats for the workingman's vote (Document 10-11). In 1840 the Whigs turned the tables on the Democrats, successfully depicting Van Buren as an "aristocrat" and their own candidate, William Henry Harrison (of Virginia gentry background), as a log-cabin-dwelling, cider-swilling man of the people. With two parties now contending to be the "people's choice," mass party politics had arrived.

10-9   Address to the Working Men of New England (1832)

Seth Luther

Seth Luther (1817?–1846), who probably was born in Providence, Rhode Island, became a strong voice for workingmen in Jacksonian America. A carpenter by trade, Luther had little formal education, but he was an avid reader of newspapers and books and became a leading figure in the fight for the ten-hour day. In the following speech, delivered to a gathering of workingmen, Luther described an American System dedicated not to expanding manufactures (see Document 10-2) but to securing the equality of men.

Source: The Globe (Washington, DC), May 13, 1832.

I would ask if persons not possessing one hundred and thirty four dollars in soil, are permitted to address this meeting. If so, I wish to make a few remarks. This community seems to be divided into two parties. Not Jackson men and Clay men . . . but the Aristocracy and Democracy. The term Aristocracy denotes a privileged class. Although the Constitution of the United States acknowledges no hereditary right, yet there exists among us a class well deserving the name of Aristocrats. I will mention some of their privileges. . . . Sir, this aristocracy of wealth claims the right to shut up in the Cotton Mill the almost infant child for . . . 13 or 14 hours per diem, with only 20 or 30 minutes for each meal . . . thereby depriving them of the best of all earthly good, an education. . . . Sir, we are in favor of an American System that will benefit all interests. But we are not satisfied with *the* System, whatever it may be, which enables a favored few to accumulate mountains of wealth, at the expense of our dearest interests. . . . We hear the philanthropist moaning over the fate of the South-

ern slave, when there are thousands of children in this State as truly slaves as the blacks of the South. . . .

Sir, we find the aristocracy in all countries, using their efforts, either directly or indirectly, to hold the poorer classes in ignorance; that they may rivet the chains of oppression more effectually. Where, Sir, is the difference in the effect between Southern measures, and measures now practiced by the Manufacturer, to accomplish this dreadful object?

Much, Sir, have we heard respecting the happiness of a manufacturing population. The Hon. H.[enry] Clay . . . draws a most beautiful picture. He has seen *one* Cotton Mill in Cincinnati. . . . He exclaims, "'Tis a paradise!"—But . . . one of my friends remarked, if a *Cotton Mill* is paradise, it is "Paradise Lost." . . . [W]e would presume to advise the Hon. Senator from Kentucky to . . . see . . . instead of rosy cheeks, the *pale,* the *sickly,* the *haggard,* countenance of the ragged child from six to twelve years of age. Haggard from the worse than slavish confinement in the cotton mill.

Questions

1. What did Luther mean by the "aristocracy of wealth"?

2. Why was Luther not moved by a philanthropic concern for southern slaves?

3. What was it about the factory system that Luther opposed?

10-10   The Election of 1836

Edward C. Clay

Andrew Jackson's direct appeal to voters in the presidential elections of 1824, 1828, and 1832 ended the reign of "King Caucus" and left a legacy of sharply contested partisan contests for the presidency. In this Whig cartoon, the election of 1836 (see text p. 320) is depicted as a fistfight between Martin Van Buren and one of his Whig opponents, William Henry Harrison of Ohio. Van Buren won in 1836 but would be defeated by Harrison in 1840. Supporting Van Buren in the cartoon are Amos Kendall, the principal author of Jackson's bank veto, and Jackson himself. Backing Harrison are Davy Crockett, onetime Whig congressman immortalized at the Alamo, and a war veteran.

Source: Library of Congress, Washington, D.C.

TEXT OF DIALOGUE FROM "SET-TO BETWEEN THE CHAMPION OLD TIP AND THE SWELL DUTCHMAN"

"Amos" [drinking]:
I begin to tremble for Matty [Martin Van Buren].
There appears to be a Surplus Fund [a surplus of federal revenue from land sales distributed to the states during the 1836 campaign]
in this Bottle, so I'll een [var. of "even"]
take a pull to raise my spirits
Oh dear.

Andrew Jackson character:
By the Eternal! what a severe
counterhit! It's bunged up Matty's
peeper, and if he don't keep his other eye
Open he'll get a Cross buttock [a wrestling move to throw an opponent with the thrust of a hip or buttock] He
begins to be a little queerish already
D——n his *Dutch* courage [bravery induced by drinking]!
Amos
where's the Bottle? after this
Round put some more into him

Martin Van Buren character:
Stand by me Old Hickory
or I'm a gone chicken!

William Henry Harrison character:
Look out for your bread-basket
Matty, I'll remove the deposits
for you

Davy Crockett character:
Whoop! wake snakes! Go it
Old Tip! by the Immortals he
puts it into him as fast as a
streak of greased lightning
through a gooseberry bush
That *Cold Blooded* Kinderhooker [Van Buren's nickname: "Red Fox of Kinderhook" (Kinderhook, New York)]
will be rowed up Salt river or I'm a nigger!

War veteran character:
Thank Heaven
the people have a
Champion at last
who will support the
Constitution and laws
that we fought and bled
to obtain! Huzza for my
old Comrade

Edward C. Clay, *"Set-To Between the Champion Old Tip and the Swell Dutchman of Kinderhook"*

275

Questions

1. This cartoon suggests that Americans had come to view the election of a president as a rough-and-tumble fight. Why would a Whig want to depict the contest in this way?

2. Examine the cartoon for its symbolic meanings. What messages are the characters meant to convey?

3. Evaluate the cartoon from the perspective of the debate over the extension of the voting franchise (see Document 10-1). Did this depiction of electoral politics express the fears of those who opposed the eradication of property qualifications?

10-11   Protecting Domestic Industry (1842)

Francis P. Blair

By the election of 1840, the two new mass political parties—the Democrats and Whigs—had established both their organizations and their platforms. (The platforms would remain stable until the crisis of the 1850s.) At the core of the issues separating the two parties were their differing views about the relationship of government to individual liberty. Democrats generally held to the "old republican" view that government was inherently dangerous to the liberties of the people and needed to be kept well pruned. They also saw government power as intrinsically allied with the forces of private privilege. That had been Jackson's view of the "Monster Bank," and it was also the view Democrats took of Whig proposals for tariffs to "protect domestic industry." In the following passage, Francis P. Blair (1791–1876), a member of Jackson's "Kitchen Cabinet" and editor of Washington's Democratic Party organ, the *Globe*, crafts an appeal to working-class voters by linking their own fear of employer power to the Democrats' fear of government power. While this piece is dated 1842, it is representative of attitudes established years earlier.

Source: The Globe (Washington, DC), 11 January 1842.

In the good old days of the Republic, when every man minded his own business and left others to take care of their own; when dependence was placed on personal exertion alone, and people did not look up to HERCULES Congress to get them out of the slough into which they had plunged by their own folly and improvidence; in those times, domestic industry was a different thing from what it is now. If we are to believe the assertions of members of Congress advocating a protective tariff, there is no other domestic industry than that employed in our great manufactories. According to their definition, tending spinning jennies in a stupendous brick building, six or seven stories high, some ten or twenty miles from home, surrounded by hundreds of strapping "operatives," from all quarters of the world, with tremendous whiskers, is your only domestic industry for the young and blooming daughters of the land.

"DOMESTIC INDUSTRY" is no longer represented by the ruddy matron sitting at her own fireside in her own home, turning the spinning wheel with one foot and rocking a chubby bantling with the other, while singing it to sleep with lullabies. . . .

"DOMESTIC INDUSTRY," according to the tariff definition, is not that of the healthy mechanic or artisan, who works for himself at his own shop, or if he goes abroad, returns home to his meals every day, and sleeps under his own roof every night; whose earnings are regulated by the wants of the community at large, not by the discretion of a penurious master; whose hours of labor depend on universal custom; who, when the sun goes down, is a freeman until he rises again; who can eat his meals in comfort, and sleep as long as nature requires. . . . Domestic industry is nothing but bondage in its most oppressive form, labor in its utmost extremity of degradation.

"DOMESTIC INDUSTRY," according to the protective tariff cant, is that which separates wives, husbands, parents and children; annihilates every domestic tie and association, and renders all domestic duties subservient to the will, not of a husband or parent, but that of an unfeeling taskmaster, to whom the sacrifice of every moment of time, and every comfort of life, is wealth and prosperity.

Questions

1. What was the meaning of "domestic industry" in tariff legislation (see Document 10-2)?

2. What ironic meanings did Blair find in the term *domestic industry*?

3. How did Blair define the "healthy mechanic"? In his view, why was the mechanic's "health" in jeopardy?

10-12   A Whig Discusses How to Appeal to the Workingman (1833)

John Scholefield

If Democrats couched their antitariff message in terms of their fear of privilege, Whigs responded by asserting a "harmony of interests" uniting employers and artisans. Such measures as protective tariffs, the Whigs contended, benefited everyone, not just industrialists. Indeed, they had to make such arguments; the Whig leadership realized that in order to be competitive the party would need to build the same sort of massive, top-to-bottom organization as the Jacksonian Democrats had. Party building required that Whig leaders engage in extensive correspondence with local political figures and learn from them how to express the Whig program in terms that ordinary voters could appreciate. In the following letter, Henry Clay is offered advice by a Philadelphia carpet manufacturer on how to appeal to the numerically powerful workingmen of that city.

Source: John Scholefield, Philadelphia, to Henry Clay, 13 November 1833, in *The Papers of Henry Clay*, ed. Robert Seager II and Melba Porter Hay (Lexington: University Press of Kentucky, 1985?), 8:666–667. Used by permission of the University Press of Kentucky.

From JOHN SCHOLEFIELD

Philadelphia, November 13, 1833

[Asks if a group of Philadelphia "Manufacturers and Merchants" could honor Clay, "the Father of the American System," by greeting him in New York and escorting him to Philadelphia on his return trip to Washington. Continues:]

May I be permitted, Sir to embrace this opportunity for acquainting you with a little piece of history — partly secret — belonging to the present times? — About two weeks ago, Gen. Duff Green — alarmed at the notice you have recently attracted, and, as we understand, at an expression in your favor from the South — left Washington for New York, on a political mission. He commenced his operations at Baltimore: — got up a meeting of "Working Men," so called, at which John McLean was nominated as a candidate for the Presidency. The scheme failed. His next attempt was in our city, where he also tried to operate on the same description of persons. At a very early stage of the business, we became acquainted with his designs, and measures were accordingly taken to frustrate them. We succeeded, and consequently he was defeated: he could not even get a meeting. He then went to Trenton, Newark, and New York, for the same *avowed* purpose; and he was every where unsuccessful. Since that time, we have heard no more of him, except of his return home. — A few days ago, however, the partisans of

Mr. McLean in this City, made another clandestine attempt; in a similar way, and for the same purpose; and again they have been defeated.

Now, Sir, in order to a right understanding of their movements, it is necessary to state, that the "Working Men," when well organised, constitute a considerable portion of the political strength of the city and county of Philadelphia. They have formerly been found quite available for party porpuses [*sic*]. At the present moment they are not very firmly bound together, not having recently moved in unison. It is evident that although many of their most influential men are decidedly of one party, they have among them political characters of every shade.

Such being the materials of which this class of our citizens is composed, a question presents itself as to the best mode of operating upon them, for the advantage of the public. The knowledge of one little secret gives us a ready answer to the question. It is simply to make them of some consequence in the world — to give them an air of importance in the eyes of others. As a body, they are very ambitious to possess some weight in society. Let this feeling be gratified, and they are content. It is for these reasons that we apprehend they may some time or other, be induced to unite for evil as well as good. And in in [*sic*] order to prevent the former, we must endeavour to ensure the latter. As manufacturers and mechanics, in other words, as "working men," they have a deep interest at stake in the support of "the protective system." But, Sir, many of them do not perfectly understand it; nor, in this respect, is there any other way in which a favorable and lasting impression can possibly be made upon their minds, like that which would come from the lips of the *Father* of that system. Greatly therefore should I rejoice if by any means an opportunity co[u]ld consistently be embraced for doing so much go[od]. The benefit thus to be conferred on a great pu[bl]ic cause, would be incalculable—But m[ore] of this when we have the happiness to see you here.

Questions

1. What was John Scholefield's core advice to Henry Clay? What, specifically, was his "one little secret"?

2. Do you think that Scholefield's advice was sincere or cynical—substantive advice or political spin? What do the remarks of Scholefield, a carpet manufacturer, tell us about early-nineteenth-century working-class culture in the United States?

3. From what you already know about Henry Clay, how do you think he received Scholefield's advice? How much political power did working-class Americans have at the time?

Questions for Further Thought

1. In what ways did workers define their interests as different from other social groups, and how did they go about trying to achieve them? How did the American working class compare with the working classes in England and Europe?

2. While many workers articulated their grievances in the language of the Revolution, other members of American society rejected as un-American working-class demands and organizations. Why was this so, and which group—working-class defenders or their detractors—do you think had the better argument?

3. Looking at the Democrats and the Whigs, which party had the better appeal to the working class?

CHAPTER ELEVEN

Religion and Reform
1820–1860

Individualism

The explosion of economic opportunity that manifested itself in the industrial and market revolutions and rapid expansion into the West weakened old social restraints and obligations and encouraged new visions of an ideal social order. To many Americans, especially among the middle-class beneficiaries of what seemed to be limitless economic opportunity, the restraints and obligations of the past seemed artificial and contrived. They searched for society's "natural" foundations, seeking principles that at once would secure the autonomy of the individual and define the individual's social responsibility in terms of his or her highest interests.

Certain themes connected these enthusiastic crusades and suggest the ways in which middle-class radicalism influenced society in industrializing America. One of these themes was individualism. The faith of transcendentalist intellectuals such as Ralph Waldo Emerson and Henry David Thoreau in the power of the individual to tap directly into natural and spiritual wisdom stood in sharp contrast to the forms of deference and coercion that still pervaded American life (Document 11-1). Individualism and self-restraint required self-reliance and a capacity to distinguish what was necessary and good from all that was frivolous and distracting. It also required the absolute freedom of the individual to seek out the truth and to act upon it (Document 11-2). It thus strongly implied—even required—radical assaults on all forms of domination, including those of masters over slaves and of men over women, whether in public or in the most intimate settings.

11-1   Obedience (1831)

Francis Wayland

Relations between parents and children were fundamentally altered by the American Revolution and the corresponding commitment to republicanism. Rearing good republican citizens, it seemed, sometimes required a degree of parental indulgence anathema to earlier generations. The child's mind is "pure" and "always ready to receive" moral instruction which was best conveyed through gentle lessons, Lydia Maria Child opined in *The*

Mother's Book (1831). And yet, such advice was neither universally welcomed nor uniformly practiced. Francis Wayland (1790–1865), Baptist minister, professor of moral philosophy, and president of Brown University, advocated an authoritarian model of parenting perhaps more characteristic of the evangelicals of the Second Great Awakening (see text pp. 259–264). Wayland did not believe that children were born "pure," nor did he share the transcendentalists' faith in the virtues of defiant individualism. Self-restraint began with the self-restrained, and not in communion with nature. The following episode, which Wayland recounted in a letter to the editor of *The American Baptist Magazine* in 1831, illustrated his first "Law of Children": obedience.

Source: Excerpt from William G. McLoughlin, "Evangelical Child-Rearing in the Age of Jackson: Francis Wayland's Views on When and How to Subdue the Willfulness of Children," in *Journal of Social History* 9 (1975): 35–36. Reprinted with permission of the publisher.

My youngest child is an infant about 15 months old, with about the intelligence common to children of that age. It has for some months been evident, that he was more than usually self willed, but the several attempts to subdue him, had been thus far relinquished, from the fear that he did not truly understand what was said to him. It so happened, however, that I had never been brought into collision with him myself, until the incident occurred which I am about to relate. Still I had seen enough to convince me of the necessity of subduing his temper, and resolved to seize upon the first favorable opportunity which presented, for settling the question of authority between us.

On Friday last before breakfast, on my taking him from his nurse, he began to cry violently. I determined to hold him in my arms until he ceased. As he had a piece of bread in his hand, I took it away, intending to give it to him again after he became quiet. In a few minutes he ceased, but when I offered him the bread he threw it away, although he was very hungry. He had, in fact, taken no nourishment except a cup of milk since 5 o'clock on the preceding afternoon. I considered this a fit opportunity for attempting to subdue his temper, and resolved to embrace it. I thought it necessary to change his disposition, so that he would receive the bread *from me,* and also be so reconciled to me that he would *voluntarily* come to me. The task I found more difficult than I had expected.

I put him into a room by himself, and desired that no one should speak to him, or give him any food or drink whatever. This was about 8 o'clock in the morning. I visited him every hour or two during the day, and spoke to him in the kindest tones, offering him the bread and putting out my arms to take him. But throughout the whole day he remained inflexibly obstinate. He did not yield a hair's breadth. I put a cup of water to his mouth, and he drank it greedily, but would not touch it with his hands. If a crumb was dropped on the floor he would eat it, but if *I* offered him the piece of bread, he would push it away from him. When I told him to come to me, he would turn away and cry bitterly.

He went to bed supperless. It was now twenty-four hours since he had eaten any thing.

He woke the next morning in the same state. He would take nothing that I offered him, and shunned all my offers of kindness. He was now truly an object of pity. He had fasted thirty-six hours. His eyes were wan and sunken. His breath hot and feverish, and his voice feeble and wailing. Yet he remained obstinate. He continued thus, till 10 o'clock A.M. when hunger overcame him, and he took from me a piece of bread, to which I added a cup of milk, and hoped that the labor was at last accomplished.

In this however I had not rightly judged. He ate his bread greedily, but when I offered to take him, he still refused as pertinaciously as ever. I therefore ceased feeding him, and recommenced my course of discipline.

He was again left alone in his crib, and I visited him as before, at intervals. About one o'clock Saturday, I found that he began to view his condition in its true light. The tones of his voice in weeping were graver and less passionate, and had more the appearance of one bemoaning himself. Yet when I went to him, he still remained obstinate. You could clearly see in him the abortive efforts of the will. Frequently he would raise his hands an inch or two, and then suddenly put them down again. He would look at me, and then hiding his face in the bedclothes weep most sorrowfully. During all this time I was addressing him, whenever I came into the room, with invariable kindness. But my kindness met with no suitable return. All I required of him was, that he should come to me. This he would not do, and he began now to see that it had become a serious business. Hence his distress increased. He would not submit, and he found that there was no help without it. It was truly surprising to behold how much agony so young a being could inflict upon himself.

About three o'clock I visited him again. He continued in the state I have described. I was going away, and had opened the door, when I thought that he looked somewhat softened, and returning, put out my hands, again requesting him to come to me. To my joy, and I hope gratitude, he rose up and put forth his hands immediately. The agony was over. He was completely subdued. He repeatedly kissed me, and would do so whenever I commanded. He would kiss any one when I directed him, so full of love was he to all the family. Indeed, so entirely and instantaneously were his feelings towards me changed, that he preferred me now to any of the family. As he had never done before, he moaned after me when he saw that I was going away.

Questions

1. Was the Wayland child more than usually self-willed? Why did Wayland view the breaking of his child's will as a first step toward moral instruction?

2. Did Francis Wayland view his child as a rational being? Did he assume that his child had the capacity to reason? Was his regimen of discipline rational or irrational?

3. Was Wayland guilty of child abuse? Under what circumstances would it be appropriate to pose this question about an action taken more than a century and a half ago?

11-2 *Walden* (1854)

Henry David Thoreau

Henry David Thoreau (1817–1862) was born and lived most of his life in Concord, Massachusetts. A graduate of Harvard, he taught for a time in Concord but soon devoted himself to the transcendentalist movement (see text pp. 332–336). His most famous works, an account of his residence at Walden Pond and the essay "On Civil Disobedience," although not widely read in his day, have become an enduring legacy of transcendentalism. In contrast to Emerson (see text pp. 334–335), whose romantic individualism stayed aloof from material conditions, Thoreau offered a subversive twist to a principal tenet of liberal capitalism: the proposition that individuals exchange labor for leisure to promote future pleasure. If the highest sphere of individual pleasure is transcendental contemplation, Thoreau reasoned, an individual should strive to exchange the least labor for the most leisure.

Source: Excerpt from Henry David Thoreau, *Walden or, Life in the Woods* and "On the Duty of Civil Disobedience" (Boston, 1854; reprint, New York: NAL Penguin, 1960).

ECONOMY

When I wrote the following pages, or rather the bulk of them, I lived alone, in the woods, a mile from any neighbor, in a house which I had built myself, on the shore of Walden Pond, in Concord, Massachusetts, and earned my living by the labor of my hands only. I lived there two years and two months. At present I am a sojourner in civilized life again. . . . It would be some advantage to live a primitive and frontier life, though in the midst of an outward civilization, if only to learn what are the gross necessaries of life and what methods have been taken to obtain them. . . . By the words, *necessary of life*, I mean whatever, of all that man obtains by his own exertions, had been from the first, or from long use has become, so important to human life that few, if any, whether from savageness, or poverty, or philosophy, ever attempt to do without it. . . .

Though we are not so degenerate but that we might possibly live in a cave or a wigwam or wear skins to-day, it certainly is better to accept the advantages, though so dearly bought, which the invention and industry of mankind offer. In such a neighborhood as this, boards and shingles, lime and bricks, are cheaper and more easily obtained than suitable caves. . . .

Near the end of March, 1845, I borrowed an axe and went down to the woods by Walden Pond. . . . It is difficult to begin without borrowing, but perhaps it is the most generous course thus to permit your fellow-men to have an interest in your enterprise. . . .

I hewed the main timbers six inches square, most of the studs on two sides only, and the rafters and floor timbers on one side, leaving the rest of the bark on, so that they were just as straight and much stronger than sawed ones. Each stick was carefully mortised or tenoned by its stump, for I had borrowed other tools by this time. . . .

By the middle of April, for I made no haste in my work, but rather made the most of it, my house was framed and ready for raising. . . . At length, in the beginning of May, with the help of some of my acquaintances, rather to improve so good an occasion for neighborliness than from any necessity, I set up the frame of my house. . . . Before winter I built a chimney, and shingled the sides of my house. . . . I have thus a tight shingled and plastered house, ten feet wide by fifteen long, and eight-feet posts, with a garret and a closet, a large window on each side. . . .

One says to me, "I wonder that you do not lay up money; you love to travel." . . . But I am wiser than that. . . . I say to my friend, Suppose we try who will get there first. The distance is thirty miles; the fare ninety cents. That is almost a day's wages. . . . Well, I start now on foot, and get there before night. . . . You will in the meanwhile have earned your fare, and arrive there some time to-morrow, or possibly this evening, if you are lucky enough to get a job in season. . . .

Such is the universal law, which no man can ever outwit, and with regard to the railroad even we may say it is as broad as it is long. To make a railroad round the world available to all mankind is equivalent to grading the whole surface of the planet. Men have an indistinct notion that if they keep up this activity of joint stocks and spades long enough all will at length ride somewhere, in next to no time, and for nothing; but though a crowd rushes to the depot, and the conductor shouts "All aboard!" when the smoke is blown away and the vapor condensed, it will be perceived that a few are riding, but the rest are run over,—and it will be called, and will be, "A melancholy accident." . . .

For more than five years I maintained myself thus solely by the labor of my hands, and I found that, by working about six weeks in a year, I could meet all the expenses of living. The whole of my winters, as well as most of my summers, I had free and clear for study. . . .

As I preferred some things to others, and especially valued my freedom. . . . I did not wish to spend my time in earning rich carpets or other fine furniture, or delicate cookery, or a house in the Grecian or the Gothic style just yet. . . . In short, I am convinced, both by faith and experience that to maintain one's self on this earth is not a hardship but a pastime, if we live simply and wisely.

Questions

1. Thoreau lived alone at Walden Pond, but was he isolated from society?

2. What was the purpose of Thoreau's exercise in self-sufficiency?

3. What did Thoreau mean when he wrote that railroads would produce "a melancholy accident"? Analyze this passage as a critique of industrialization.

Questions for Further Thought

1. For Thoreau (Document 11-2), an ideal social order consisted of free and mutually beneficial interaction among autonomous, self-restrained individuals. Would Francis Wayland have agreed with this definition of the ideal social order? Would Thoreau have been alarmed by Wayland's method of child rearing?

2. How might the advent of industrialization have affected Thoreau's and Wayland's assumptions about individualism? Did they share the same concerns? What were the sources of Wayland's concerns? Were they the same as Thoreau's?

3. Is being "individualistic" the same as being "self-willed"? Explain.

Rural Communalism and Urban Popular Culture

The period from the 1820s through the 1850s constituted a great age of reform. Unsettled by the economic and demographic changes that characterized these decades but inspired by a belief in the capacity of human beings to shape their own destinies, thousands of Americans engaged in a wide array of reform activities. Some, like Ralph Waldo Emerson and Henry David Thoreau, emphasized individual freedom and self-realization (see text pp. 332–335); others hoped that carefully constructed institutions, such as asylums and penitentiaries, might help cure society's ills; still others sought to improve their condition by creating utopian communities. The first of these, formed in 1784 by the so-called Shakers after the death of their founder, Mother Ann Lee, proscribed sexual intercourse and therefore relied on conversions and orphans for their increase (Document 11-3). In the Oneida community of upstate New York, John Humphrey Noyes sought to free the pleasures of sexuality from the dangers of pregnancy and childbirth (Document 11-4).

While utopian reformers challenged the social norms of the emerging capitalist society, many more Americans were affected by a "strange unrest" in pursuit of opportunities to better their material lives, as Alexis de Tocqueville observed in the 1830s. One manifestation of this quest, aided by the transportation revolution, was the migration westward (see text pp. 280–287). In 1810 only one-seventh of the American population lived west of the Appalachians; by 1840 more than one-third did. But the movement of rural people and immigrants to America's cities was equally impressive. In 1800 New York City and Philadelphia had populations of 60,000 and 41,000 respectively; by 1840 New York had more than 310,000 inhabitants, and Philadelphia some 150,000. Unfortunately, racism and nativism increased along with the population. Minstrel shows, in which white actors in blackface entertained their audiences by promoting crude racial stereotypes, became perhaps the most popular form of theater (see text pp. 345–347). Edward C. Clay's popularity as a cartoonist was built on the same racist foundation, as his caricatures of "Life in Philadelphia" indicate (Document 11-5).

11-3   The Shakers (1850)

Rebecca Cox Jackson

Rebecca Cox Jackson (1795–1871) was a free African American woman who renounced a relatively secure life with her husband in Philadelphia to become an itinerant Methodist preacher. During the 1830s she traveled throughout the countryside, accompanied by a younger disciple, Rebecca Perot. In 1843 the "two Rebeccas" became committed Shakers, eventually settling in the community of Watervliet, near Albany, New York (see text pp. 336–339). They remained ambivalent about Shaker isolation, however, and in 1851 they resumed their ministry in the free black community. In 1858 Jackson founded her own Shaker family in Philadelphia. In the 1840s, Jackson began to write a memoir of her religious experiences, including powerful dreams and visions.

In these passages Jackson expressed three key elements of the Shaker faith: that they received the direct guidance of the Holy Ghost; that Mother Ann Lee (the movement's founder) represented the female embodiment of a God comprising both male and female attributes; and that the millennium (the end of human time) was near at hand.

Source: From Jean McMahon Humez, ed., *Gifts of Power: The Writings of Rebecca Jackson, Black Visionary, Shaker Eldress* (Amherst: University of Massachusetts Press, 1981), 220–221. Copyright © 1981 by the University of Massachusetts Press. Reprinted by permission.

Monday evening, February 18, 1850. I was instructed concerning the atmosphere and its bounds. I saw its form — it is like the sea, which has her bounds.... It covered land and sea, so far above all moving things, and yet so far beneath the starry heavens. Its face is like the face of the sea, smooth and gentle when undisturbed by the wind. So is the atmosphere, when undisturbed by the power of the sun and moon. When agitated by these, it rages like the sea and sends forth its storms upon the earth. Nothing can live above it. A bird could no more live or fly above its face, than a fish can live or swim out of the water. It is always calm and serene between its face and the starry heaven. The sight, to me, was beautiful.

March 1, 1850. . . . Prayer given to me by Mother Ann Lee: "Oh God, my Everlasting Father, to Thee do I lift up my soul in prayer and thanksgiving for the gift of Thy dear Son, our Blessed Savior, who has begotten to us a living hope. And to Thee, Holy Mother Wisdom, do I lift up my soul in prayer and thanksgiving, for the gift of Thy Holy Daughter, whose blessed Spirit has led me and instructed me in this, the holy way of God, lo! these many years, and has borne with my infirmities and many shortcomings. And lo! Thou hast comforted me in all my sorrows and Thy blessed Spirit comforts me today."

Then I saw our Heavenly Parents look on me and smile, and Mother Ann gave me sweet counsel. And I was greatly strengthened in the way of God.

March 15, 1850. After I came to Watervliet . . . and saw how the Believers seemed to be gathered to themselves, in pray-ing for themselves and not for the world, which lay in midnight darkness, I wondered how the world was to be saved, if Shakers were the only people of God on earth, and they seemed to be busy in their own concerns, which were mostly temporal. . . .

Then seeing these at ease in Zion, I cried in the name of Christ and Mother that He in mercy would do something for the helpless world. At that time, it seemed as if the whole world rested upon me. I cried to the Lord both day and night, for many months, that God would make a way that the world might hear the Gospel—that God would send spirits and angels to administer to their understanding, that they might be saved in the present tense, for I knew by revelation, that it was God's will that they should be.

Questions

1. What significance do you think Jackson attached to her vision of the atmosphere and the heavens?

2. Examine the prayer given to Jackson by Mother Ann Lee. In what ways does it deviate from the language of patriarchal religion?

3. How did Jackson's millenarianism affect her attitude toward the Shakers at Watervliet?

11-4   *Male Continence* (1872)

John Humphrey Noyes

John Humphrey Noyes (1811–1886) was born in Brattleboro, Vermont. After graduation from Dartmouth College he was drawn to the revivalist ministry. Noyes carried the logic of moral perfectionism (the belief that people, while living, could achieve the perfection of Christ) in a new direction, arguing that Christ had returned to earth in A.D. 70 and had established the one true Christian church. When he announced his own state of moral perfection in 1834, he broke his ties with established religion and society and began a spiritual journey that would lead him to the Christian communist and free-love community he founded at Oneida (see text pp. 338–339). In the treatise *Male Continence*, he explained his theory of controlled propagation and complex marriage.

Source: John Humphrey Noyes, *Male Continence* (Oneida, NY, 1872).

I was married in 1838, and lived in the usual routine of matrimony till 1846. It was during this period of eight years that I studied the subject of sexual intercourse in connection with my matrimonial experience, and discovered the principle of Male Continence. And the discovery was occasioned and even forced upon me by very sorrowful experience. In the course of six years my wife went through the agonies of five births. Four of them were premature. Only one child lived. . . . After our last disappointment, I pledged my word to my wife that I would never again expose her to such fruitless suffering. I made up my mind to live apart from her, rather than break this promise. This was the situation in the summer of 1844. At that time I conceived the idea that the sexual organs have a social function which is distinct from the propagative function; and that these functions may be separated practically. I experimented on this idea, and found that the self-control which it requires is not difficult; also that my enjoyment was increased; also that my wife's experience was very satisfactory, as it had never been before; also that we have escaped the horrors and the fear of involuntary propagation. This was a great deliverance. It made a happy household. . . . In 1848, soon after our removal to Oneida, I published the new theory in a pamphlet. . . .

The pamphlet referred to embraced a general exhibition of the principles of the kingdom of heaven promised in the Bible, and for this reason it was entitled *The Bible Argument*; but the most important chapter of it was that which undertook to show *"How the sexual function is to be redeemed and true relations between the sexes are to be restored."* . . . I will now venture to reprint that notable chapter.

FROM THE BIBLE ARGUMENT, PRINTED IN 1848

The amative and propagative functions of the sexual organs are distinct from each other, and may be separated practically. . . . If amativeness is the first and noblest of the social affections, and if the propagative part of the sexual relation was originally secondary, and became paramount by the subversion of order in the fall [as had previously been shown], we are bound to raise the amative office of the sexual organs into a distinct and paramount function. . . . We insist, then, that the amative function—that which consists in a simple union of persons, making "of twain one flesh," and giving a medium of magnetic and spiritual interchange—is a distinct and independent function, as superior to the reproductive as we have shown amativeness to be to propagation. . . .

The method of controlling propagation which results from our argument is natural, healthy, favorable to amativeness, and effectual.

First, it is *natural.* The useless expenditure of seed certainly is not natural. . . . Our method simply proposes the subordination of the flesh to the spirit, teaching men to seek principally the elevated spiritual pleasures of sexual connection, and to be content with them in their general intercourse with women, restricting the more sensual part to its proper occasions. . . .

The separation of the amative from the propagative, places amative sexual intercourse on the same footing with other ordinary forms of social interchange. . . . In society trained in these principles . . . amative intercourse will have place among the "fine arts" . . . when sexual intercourse becomes an honored method of innocent and useful communion, and each is married to all.

Questions

1. How did Noyes change the "usual routine of matrimony"? How did he separate, "practically," amative from propagative sexual intercourse?

2. Assuming that amative and propagative sexual intercourse can be distinguished, how and why do you think Noyes concluded that amative intercourse would become indistinguishable from "ordinary forms of social interchange"?

3. Does sexuality separated from procreation and marriage promote equality between women and men? Why or why not?

11-5   Satirizing Free Blacks (1829)

Edward C. Clay

Influenced by the abolition movement, a growing number of moderate northern and midwestern whites came to condemn slavery as immoral. However, their disapproval of the institution itself did not alter their racist attitudes toward blacks. While the free black population in the North was very small in the early nineteenth century, a few northern cities such as Philadelphia had begun to witness the rise of a black middle class. Blacks established themselves as shopkeepers, shoemakers, carpenters, tailors, barbers, cooks, and bakers. Unfortunately, their success, combined with the heightened awareness of race consciousness brought on by the abolition movement (see text pp. 351–355) precipitated a form of "Negrophobia," a militant antiblack sentiment that manifested itself in a variety of ways. Edward C. Clay, who became one of the most popular cartoonists of the period, expressed his racism in a particularly vicious series of caricatures entitled "Life in Philadelphia" (1828–1830).

Source: "Miss Chloe" from *Life in Philadelphia* by Edward Clay (1829). Courtesy of the Library Company of Philadelphia.

Edward C. Clay, "Miss Chloe"

Questions

1. What is the connection between the characters' dress and the woman's statement "I aspire too much"? How are these meant to be demeaning to free blacks?

2. Why might this (somewhat) subtle form of racism have developed in conjunction with the success of the free black community in Philadelphia?

3. How did this cartoon play on the fears of northern whites?

Questions for Further Thought

1. The word *utopian* is often used to mean "impractical." Were the communitarian reformers of this period impractical? Are all reformers *utopian*?

2. Is it inconsistent that racism and nativism intensified in this period, even as reform activity increased? Assuming that these were not simply different constituencies acting in separate locales, how might one explain this phenomenon?

3. The period from the 1820s to 1860 was generally one of economic growth, democratic politics, and religious optimism. Is the "spirit of reform" more likely to prevail in such a period? Explain.

Abolitionism

The moral crusade against slavery had its origin in the evangelical reforms of the Second Great Awakening. Given that each human being was understood to be a responsible moral agent in the eyes of God, abolitionists argued that the relationship of master and slave fundamentally violated Christian morality because the slave was deprived of the right to follow his or her conscience, and the master was tempted to assert himself in place of God. Animated by the apocalyptic spirit of the age, abolitionists attacked slavery with a zeal that alarmed many northerners and outraged most white southerners (Document 11-6). Even if they opposed slavery, most whites were so racist that they loathed the idea of elevating the status of blacks. Thus, the abolitionists had their work cut out for them. In their eyes slavery was not a problem confined to exotic corners of the nation; its influence permeated national life, and all Americans had to confront it in order to restore the ideals of the Declaration of Independence (Document 11-7). Southerners, of course, were neither convinced by the abolitionists' attacks nor willing to concede that the free labor system was less oppressive than slavery (Document 11-8).

11-6   Commencement of *The Liberator* (1831)

William Lloyd Garrison

In 1829 William Lloyd Garrison (1805–1879) broke with traditional abolitionist proposals for gradual emancipation to demand the immediate abolition of slavery in the United States (see text pp. 351–354). Later in that year he added his voice to those of African American freedmen in the North who denounced the American Colonization Society as a thinly disguised plot to remove free blacks, not slaves, from America. In 1830 Garrison prepared to launch the Boston *Liberator* to express his new views; the paper's first number appeared on January 1, 1831. The publication of *The Liberator* in January and the bloody slave rebellion led by Nat Turner in Southampton County, Virginia, in August 1831 (see text pp. 350–351) reinforced each other in ways that unsettled northern and southern whites and prompted the supporters of Andrew Jackson to attempt to silence the abolitionist "incendiaries." The following extracts are from Garrison's opening editorial, "Commencement of *The Liberator*," in the first issue.

Source: William Lloyd Garrison, "Commencement of *The Liberator*," *Liberator*, 1 January 1831, in *Selections from the Writings and Speeches of William Lloyd Garrison* (New York: New American Library, 1969), 62–63.

In Park Street Church, on the Fourth of July, 1829, in an address on slavery, I unreflectingly assented to the popular but pernicious doctrine of gradual abolition. I seize this opportunity to make a full and unequivocal recantation, and thus publicly to ask pardon of my God, of my country, and of my brethren, the poor slaves, for having uttered a sentiment so full of timidity, injustice and absurdity. . . .

I am aware, that many object to the severity of my language; but is there not cause for severity? I will be as harsh as truth, and as uncompromising as justice. On this subject, I do not wish to think, or speak, or write, with moderation. No! no! Tell a man, whose house is on fire, to give a moderate alarm; tell him to moderately rescue his wife from the hands of the ravisher; tell the mother to gradually extricate her babe from the fire into which it has fallen; but urge me not to use moderation in a cause like the present! I am in earnest. I will not equivocate—I will not excuse—I will not retreat a single inch, AND I WILL BE HEARD. . . .

It is pretended, that I am retarding the cause of emancipation by the coarseness of my invective, and the precipitancy of my measures. The charge is not true. On this question, my influence, humble as it is, is felt at this moment to a considerable extent, and shall be felt in coming years—not perniciously, but beneficially—not as a curse, but as a blessing; and POSTERITY WILL BEAR TESTIMONY THAT I WAS RIGHT.

Questions

1. Why did Garrison describe the doctrine of gradual abolition as "pernicious"?

2. What reasons did Garrison give for rejecting moderation? Are they convincing?

3. What did Garrison express more effectively—his belief in himself or his belief in his cause? Do you think his tone worked for him or against him?

11-7   What to the Slave Is the Fourth of July? (1852)

Frederick Douglass

Born a slave on a Maryland plantation, Frederick Douglass (1817?–1895) escaped to the North as a young man (see text p. 403). There he became a leading abolitionist speaker; having learned to read and write while a slave, he was also a powerful and eloquent writer, editing the antislavery newspaper *The North Star* in Rochester, New York. An astute reformer and political leader, Douglass became the dominant African American public figure in nineteenth-century America; his literary works, especially his autobiographies, are regarded as classics.

In 1852 the Rochester Ladies' Anti-Slavery Society invited Douglass to deliver the principal address at a Fourth of July celebration. (Because that year the holiday fell on Sunday, the celebration was actually held on July 5.) Douglass began in a conventional fashion, setting forth the case of the colonists against Great Britain and extolling the founding fathers. But then he veered off in a different direction entirely.

Source: From *The Frederick Douglass Papers, Series One: Speeches, Debates, and Interviews*, vol. 2, John W. Blassingame, ed. Copyright © 1982 by Yale University Press. Reprinted by permission of Yale University Press.

I leave, therefore, the great deeds of your fathers to other gentlemen whose claim to have been regularly descended will be less likely to be disputed than mine! . . .

Fellow-citizens, pardon me, allow me to ask, why am I called upon to speak here to-day? What have I, or those I represent, to do with your national independence? Are the great principles of political freedom and of natural justice, embodied in that Declaration of Independence, extended to us? and am I, therefore, called upon to bring our humble offering to the national altar, and to confess the benefits and express devout gratitude for the blessings resulting from your independence to us?

Would to God, both for your sakes and ours, that an affirmative answer could be truthfully returned to these questions! Then would my task be light, and my burden easy and delightful. For *who* is there so cold, that a nation's sympathy could not warm him? Who so obdurate and dead to the claims of gratitude, that would not thankfully acknowledge such priceless benefits? Who so stolid and selfish, that would not give his voice to swell the hallelujahs of a nation's jubilee, when the chains of servitude had been torn from his limbs? I am not that man. In a case like that, the dumb might eloquently speak, and the "lame man leap as an hart." . . .

But, such is not the state of the case. I say it with a sad sense of the disparity between us. I am not included within the pale of this glorious anniversary! Your high independence only reveals the immeasurable distance between us. The blessings in which you, this day, rejoice, are not enjoyed in common. The rich inheritance of justice, liberty, prosperity, and independence, bequeathed by your fathers, is shared by you, not by me. The sunlight that brought life and healing to you, has brought stripes of death to me. This Fourth [of] July is *yours*, not *mine*. *You* may rejoice, *I* must mourn. To drag a man in fetters into the grand illuminated temple of liberty, and call upon him to join in joyous anthems, were inhuman mockery and sacrilegious irony. Do you mean, citizens, to mock me, by asking me to speak to-day? If so, there is a parallel to your conduct. And let me warn you that it is dangerous to copy the example of a nation whose crimes, towering up to heaven, were thrown down by the breath of the Almighty, burying that nation in irrecoverable ruin! I can to-day take up the plaintive lament of a peeled and woesmitten people!

"By the rivers of Babylon, there we sat down. Yea! we wept when we remembered Zion. We hanged our harps upon the willows in the midst thereof. For there, they that carried us away captive, required of us a song: and they who wasted us required of us mirth, saying, Sing us one of the songs of Zion. How can we sing the Lord's song in a strange land? If I forget thee, O Jerusalem, let my right hand forget her cunning. If I do not remember thee, let my tongue cleave to the roof of my mouth."

Fellow-citizens; above your national, tumultuous joy, I hear the mournful wail of millions! whose chains, heavy and grievous yesterday, are, to-day, rendered more intolerable by the jubilee shouts that reach them. If I do forget, If I do not faithfully remember those bleeding children of sorrow this day, "may my right hand forget her cunning, and may my tongue cleave to the roof of my mouth!" To forget them, to pass lightly over their wrongs, and to chime in with the popular theme, would be treason most scandalous and shocking, and would make me a reproach before God and the world. My subject, then fellow-citizens, is AMERICAN SLAVERY. I shall see, this day, and its popular characteristics, from the slave's point of view. Standing, there, identified with the American bondman, making his wrongs mine, I do not hesitate to declare, with all my soul, that the character and conduct of this nation never looked blacker to me than on this 4th of July! Whether we turn to the declarations of the past, or to the professions of the present, the conduct of the nation seems equally hideous and revolting. America is false to the past, false to the present, and solemnly binds herself to be false to the future. Standing with God and the crushed and bleeding slave on this occasion, I will, in the name of humanity which is outraged, in the name of liberty which is fettered, in the name of the constitution and the Bible, which are disregarded and trampled upon, dare to call in question and to denounce, with all the emphasis I can command, everything that serves to perpetuate slavery — the great sin and shame of America! "I will not equivocate; I will not excuse;" — I will use the severest language I can command; and yet not one word shall escape me that any man, whose judgement is not blinded by prejudice, or who is not at heart a slaveholder, shall not confess to be right and just.

But I fancy I hear some one of my audience say, it is just in this circumstance that you and your brother abolitionists fail to make a favorable impression on the public mind. Would you argue more, and denounce less, would you persuade more, and rebuke less, your cause would be much more likely to succeed. But, I submit, where all is plain there is nothing to be argued. . . .

At a time like this, scorching irony, not convincing argument, is needed. O! had I the ability, and could I reach the nation's ear, I would, to-day, pour out a fiery stream of biting ridicule, blasting reproach, withering sarcasm, and stern rebuke. For it is not light that is needed, but fire; it is not the gentle shower, but thunder. We need the storm, the whirlwind, and the earthquake. The feeling of the nation must be quickened; the conscience of the nation must be roused; the propriety of the nation must be startled; the hypocrisy of the nation must be exposed; and its crimes against God and man must be proclaimed and denounced.

What, to the American slave, is your 4th of July? I answer: a day that reveals to him, more than all other days in the year, the gross injustice and cruelty to which he is the constant victim. To him, your celebration is a sham; your boasted liberty, an unholy license; your national greatness, swelling vanity; your sounds of rejoicing are empty and heartless; your denunciations of tyrants, brass fronted impudence; your shouts of liberty and equality, hollow mockery; your prayers and hymns, your sermons and thanksgivings, with all your religious parade, and solemnity, are, to him, mere bombast, fraud, deception, impiety, and hypocrisy — a thin veil to cover up crimes which would disgrace a nation of savages. There is not a nation on the earth guilty of practices, more shocking and bloody, than are the people of these United States, at this very hour.

Go where you may, search where you will, roam through all the monarchies and despotisms of the old world, travel through South America, search out every abuse, and when you have found the last, lay your facts by the side of the everyday practices of this nation, and you will say with me, that, for revolting barbarity and shameless hypocrisy, America reigns without a rival. . . .

Americans! your republican politics, not less than your republican religion, are flagrantly inconsistent. You boast of your love of liberty, your superior civilization, and your pure Christianity, while the whole political power of the nation (as embodied in the two great political parties), is solemnly pledged to support and perpetuate the enslavement of three millions of your countrymen. You hurl your anathemas at the crowned headed tyrants of Russia and Austria, and pride yourselves on your Democratic institutions, while you yourselves consent to be the mere *tools* and *bodyguards* of the tyrants of Virginia and Carolina. You invite to your shores fugitives of oppression from abroad, honor them with banquets, greet them with ovations, cheer them, toast them, salute them, protect them, and pour out your money to them like water; but the fugitives from your own land you advertise, hunt, arrest, shoot and kill. You glory in your refinement and your universal education; yet you maintain a system as barbarous and dreadful as ever stained the character of a nation — a system begun in avarice, supported in pride, and perpetuated in cruelty. You shed tears over fallen Hungary, and make the sad story of her wrongs the theme of your poets, statesmen and orators, till your gallant sons are ready to fly to arms to vindicate her cause against her oppressors; but, in regard to the ten thousand wrongs of the American slave, you would enforce the strictest silence, and would hail him as an enemy of the nation who dares to make those wrongs the subject of public discourse! You are all on fire at the mention of liberty for France or for Ireland; but are as cold as an iceberg at the thought of liberty for the enslaved of America. You discourse eloquently on the dignity of labor; yet, you sustain a system which, in its very essence, casts a stigma upon labor. You can bare your bosom to the storm of British artillery to throw off a threepenny tax on tea; and yet wring the last hard-earned farthing from the grasp of the black laborers of your country. You profess to belief "that, of one blood, God made all nations of men to dwell on the face of all the earth," and hath commanded all men, everywhere, to love one another, yet you notoriously hate, (and glory in your hatred), all men whose skins are not colored like your own. You declare, before the world, and are understood by the world to declare, that you *"hold these truths to be self evident, that all men are created equal; and are endowed by their Creator with certain inalienable rights; and that, among these are, life, liberty, and the pursuit of happiness;"* and yet, you hold securely, in a bondage which, according to your own Thomas Jefferson, *"is worse than ages of that which your fathers rose in rebellion to oppose,"* a seventh part of the inhabitants of your country.

Fellow-citizens! I will not enlarge further on your national inconsistencies. The existence of slavery in this country brands your republicanism as a sham, your humanity as a base pretence, and your Christianity as a lie. It destroys your moral power abroad; it corrupts your politicians at home. It saps the foundation of religion; it makes your name a hissing, and a by-word to a mocking earth. It is the antagonistic force in your government, the only thing that seriously disturbs and endangers your *Union.* It fetters your progress; it is the enemy of improvement, the deadly foe of education; it fosters pride; it breeds insolence; it promotes vice; it shelters crime; it is a curse to the earth that supports it; and yet, you cling to it, as if it were the sheet anchor of all your hopes. Oh! be warned! be warned! a horrible reptile is coiled up in your nation's bosom; the venomous creature is nursing at the tender breast of your youthful republic; *for the love of God, tear away, and fling from you the hideous monster, and let the weight of twenty millions crush and destroy it forever!* . . .

Allow me to say, in conclusion, notwithstanding the dark picture I have this day presented of the state of the nation, I do not despair of this country. There are forces in operation, which must inevitably work the downfall of slavery. *"The arm of the Lord is not shortened,"* and the doom of slavery is certain. I therefore, leave off where I began, with hope. While drawing encouragement from the Declaration of Independence, the great principles it contains, and the genius of American Institutions, my spirit is also cheered by the obvious tendencies of the age. Nations do not now stand in the same relation to each other that they did ages ago. No nation can now shut itself up from the surrounding world, and trot round in the same old path of its fathers without interference. The time *was* when such could be done. Long established customs of hurtful character could formerly fence themselves in, and do their evil work with social impunity. Knowledge was then confined and enjoyed by the privileged few, and the multitude walked on in mental darkness. But a change has now come over the affairs of mankind. Walled cities and empires have become unfashionable. The arm of commerce has borne away the gates of the strong city. Intelligence is penetrating the darkest corners of the globe. It makes its pathway over and under the sea, as well as on the earth. Wind, steam, and lightning are its chartered agents. Oceans no longer divide, but link nations together. From Boston to London is now a holiday excursion. Space is comparatively annihilated. Thoughts expressed on one side of the Atlantic are distinctly heard on the other.

The far off and almost fabulous Pacific rolls in grandeur at our feet. The Celestial Empire, the mystery of ages, is being solved. The fiat of the Almighty, *"Let there be Light,"* has not yet spent its force. No abuse, no outrage whether in taste, sport or avarice, can now hide itself from the all-pervading light. The iron shoe, and crippled foot of China must be seen, in contrast with nature. *Africa must rise and put on her yet unwoven garment. "Ethiopia shall stretch out her hand unto God."* In the fervent aspirations of William Lloyd Garrison, I say, and let every heart join in saying it:

> God speed the year of jubilee
> The wide world o'er!
> When from their galling chains set free,
> Th' oppress'd shall vilely bend the knee,
> And wear the yoke of tyranny
> Like brutes no more.
> That year will come, and freedom's reign,
> To man his plundered rights again
> Restore.
> God speed the day when human blood
> Shall cease to flow!
> In every clime, be understood,
> The claims of human brotherhood,
> And each return for evil, good,
> Not blow for blow;
> That day will come all feuds to end,
> And change into a faithful friend
> Each foe.
>
> God speed the hour, the glorious hour,
> When none on earth
> Shall exercise a lordly power,
> Nor in a tyrant's presence cower;
> But all to manhood's stature tower,
> By equal birth!
> THAT HOUR WILL COME, to each, to all
> And from his prison-house, the thrall
> Go forth.
>
> Until that year, day, hour, arrive,
> With head, and heart, and hand I'll strive,
> To break the rod, and rend the gyve,
> The spoiler of his prey deprive—
> So witness Heaven!
> And never from my chosen post,
> What'er the peril or the cost,
> Be driven.

Questions

1. How did Douglass make effective use of the Declaration of Independence to confront white Americans with their shortcomings? What sort of imagery did Douglass use, and how effective do you think his speech was?

2. In what ways did Douglass indicate that all white Americans, not just white southerners, were implicated in the crime of slavery? Do you agree that slavery was a national, rather than local, sin?

3. How did Douglass use scriptural passages to reinforce his point?

11-8   Slavery as It Exists (1850)

Defenders of slavery not only forged arguments based on Greek and Roman history, the Bible, the property rights of slave owners, and pseudoscientific evidence of black inferiority, they also asserted that the institution of slavery was ultimately more humane than the prevailing system of wage labor (see Document 12-6). Their favorite point of comparison in this regard was England—because England had a highly industrialized economy and because Parliament had abolished slavery throughout the British empire in 1833. The life of the southern slave, they argued, was far superior to that of the ostensibly free English "wage slave." The former received food, housing, clothing, and the personal care of a paternalistic master, whereas the latter was exposed to all manner of abuse by employers who valued them only for their labor. "Slavery as It Exists" comprises two scenes: the first set in America where two northern visitors learn that they have been misled by "false reports" about the evils of slavery; and the second in England, where factory "slaves" bemoan the wretched conditions under which they barely survive.

Source: Print, *Slavery as It Exists in America* (Boston: Joshua P. Haven, 1850), Library of Congress, Prints and Photographs Division LC-USZ62–1285.

TEXT OF DIALOGUE FROM "SLAVERY AS IT EXISTS IN AMERICA"

First Northerner: "Is this the way that slaves are treated at the South?"

Second Northerner: "Is it possible that we of the North have been so deceived by false Reports? Why did we not visit the South before we caused this trouble between the North and the South, and so much hard feelings amongst our friends at home?"

First Southerner: "It is a general thing, some few exceptions, after mine have done a certain amount of Labor which they finish by 4 or 5 P.M. I allow them to enjoy themselves in any reasonable way."

Second Southerner: "I think our Visitors will tell a different Story when they return to the North, the thoughts of this Union being dissolved is to[o] dreadful a thing to be contemplated, but we must stand up for our rights let the consequence be as it may."

TEXT OF DIALOGUE FROM "SLAVERY AS IT EXISTS IN ENGLAND"

Gentleman: "Why my Dear Friend, how is it that you look so old? you know we were playmates when boys."

Stooped Figure: "Ah! Farmer we operatives are 'fast men,' and generally die of old age at Forty."

Mother (in background): "Oh Dear! what wretched Slaves, this Factory life makes me & my children."

First Youth (foreground): "I say, Bill, I am going to run away from the Factory, and go to the Coal Mines where they have to work only 14 hours a Day instead of 17 as you do here."

Second Youth: "Oh! how I would like to have such a comfortable place. . . .'"

Man (sitting on rock): "Thank God my Factory Slavery will soon be over."

At page bottom: [George] Thompson—the English Anti-Slavery Agitator

Quotation: "I am proud to boast that Slavery does not breathe in England"

Attribution: In his speech at the African Church in Belknap St.

Questions

1. Would anyone in 1850 have found this political illustration to be convincing? Who was its intended audience?

2. The second southerner refers to "rights" that had to be defended, even at the expense of the Union. What were these "rights"?

3. Would Orestes A. Brownson (Document 9-8) have approved of the message conveyed by this illustration? Explain.

Questions for Further Thought

1. Do the writings of William Lloyd Garrison (Document 11-6) and Frederick Douglass (Document 11-7) embody the evangelical spirit of the Second Great Awakening? Was religion the basis of Douglass's appeal?

2. What sort of appeal was made by the defenders of slavery (Document 11-8)? Were they influenced by the evangelical Christianity of the Second Great Awakening?

3. The twentieth-century conservative American politician Barry Goldwater once said that "extremism in defense of liberty is no vice." Were the abolitionists extremists? If they were, did their extremism help or hurt their cause? Was Goldwater right?

The Women's Rights Movement

In the female-centered middle-class home, women were indeed insulated from the workplace, but their new roles as moral stewards of their families suggested new responsibilities and authority. The moral reform movements of the early nineteenth century provided these women with a forum for the advancement of their rights as individuals and opportunities to assert equality with men in discussions of public policy. The anti-slavery movement projected a striking analogy between the dominion of master over slave and the dominion of man over woman (Document 11-9). As women reformers noted, all the evils of the former applied to the latter. The participation of women in public discussions of government policy implied that women deserved the full rights of citizenship, most prominently property rights and the right to vote (Document 11-10). Women made significant progress in acquiring property rights, but woman suffrage proved far more elusive. Even in reform circles the agitation for women's rights produced deep divisions. The assertion of female equality in the American Anti-Slavery Society, for example, contributed to a major schism in the ranks of abolitionists in 1840. Many male reformers—and even a number of female reformers—who embraced the equality of the races as a moral principle turned a deaf ear to advocates for women's rights. Nevertheless, perceptions of women's "proper place" began to shift, however haltingly.

11-9   Breaking Out of Women's Separate Sphere (1838)

Angelina E. Grimké

Angelina E. Grimké (1805–1879) was born in Charleston, South Carolina, and raised in a wealthy, aristocratic, conservative family. Deeply influenced by her older sister, Angelina soon rejected Charleston society, converted from Episcopalianism to Quakerism during a visit to Philadelphia, and quickly embraced moral reform (see text pp. 352–354). In 1835 she wrote to William Lloyd Garrison to express her support for abolitionism. When Garrison published the letter in his newspaper, *The Liberator,* her public reform career began. Criticism of Grimké's public opposition to slavery soon led her to advocate women's rights in conjunction with abolitionism. One of Grimké's principal opponents was Catharine Beecher (1800–1878), the daughter of prominent Congregationalist minister Lyman Beecher. Catharine Beecher was an early advocate of education for women but was also a formative figure in defining the female domestic sphere. Defending this sphere from the public activity of abolitionist women, Beecher published *An Essay on Slavery and Abolitionism, with Reference to the Duty of American Females* (1837). The following extracts are taken from Grimké's reply to Beecher.

Source: Angelina E. Grimké, *Letters to Catharine E. Beecher, in Reply to an Essay on Slavery and Abolitionism, Addressed to A. E. Grimké* (Boston, 1838; facsimile reprint, New York: Arno Press, 1969), 103–113.

I come now to that part of thy book, which is, of all others, the most important to the women of this country; thy "general views in relation to the place woman is appointed to fill by the dispensations of heaven." . . .

Thou sayest, "Heaven has appointed to one sex the *superior*, and to the other the *subordinate* station. . . ." This is an assertion without proof. Thou further sayest, that "it was designed that the mode of faining influence and exercising power should be *altogether different and peculiar*." Does the Bible teach this? . . . Did Jesus . . . give a different rule of action to men and women? . . . I read in the Bible, that Miriam, and Deborah, and Huldah, were called to fill *public stations* in Church and State. I find Anna, the prophetess, speaking in the temple "unto all them that looked for redemption in Jerusalem." . . . I see them even standing on Mount Calvary, around his cross . . . but he never *rebuked* them; He never told them it was unbecoming *their sphere of life* to mingle in the crowds which followed his footsteps. . . .

Thou sayest . . . "make no claims, and maintain no rights, but what are the gifts of honor, rectitude and love." From whom does woman receive her *rights*? From God, or from man? . . . I understand . . . her *rights* are an integral part of her moral being; they cannot be withdrawn; they must live with her forever. Her rights lie at the foundation of all her duties; and, so long as the divine commands are binding upon her, so long must her rights continue. . . .

Thou sayest, "In this country, petitions to Congress, in reference to official duties of legislators, seem IN ALL CASES, to fall entirely without the sphere of female duty. Men are the proper persons to make appeals to the rulers whom they appoint," etc. Here I entirely dissent from thee. The fact that women are denied the right of voting for members of Congress, is but a poor reason why they should also be deprived of the right of petition. If their numbers are counted to swell the number of Representatives in our State and National Legislatures, the *very least* that can be done is to give them the right of petition in all cases whatsoever. . . . If not, they are mere slaves, known only through their masters."

Questions

1. What arguments did Grimké use to link moral reform with women's rights and political action?

2. The campaign to collect signatures on antislavery petitions to Congress was an important aspect of the abolitionist movement in the 1830s. How did that campaign raise women's rights issues?

3. How did Grimké differ with Beecher on the issue of women's rights? How did Grimké define the relationship between rights and duties?

11-10   Declaration of Sentiments and Resolutions (1848)

Elizabeth Cady Stanton

Elizabeth Cady Stanton (1815–1902) and Lucretia Mott (1793–1880) met in London at the World's Anti-Slavery Convention in 1840 (see text pp. 358–359). Stanton attended with her husband, the abolitionist Henry B. Stanton. Mott, a Quaker minister, attended as a delegate for the American Anti-Slavery Society. The convention's decision to deny recognition to women consigned Stanton and Mott to the gallery as observers, and they resolved to link the struggle against slavery with a struggle for women's rights. In 1848 they convened the first women's rights convention at Seneca Falls, New York, and Stanton drafted its famous "Declaration of Sentiments and Resolutions," using the Declaration of Independence as a model.

Source: Elizabeth Cady Stanton, Susan B. Anthony, and Matilda Joslyn Gage, *History of Woman Suffrage* (1881–1922; reprint, New York: Arno Press and New York Times, 1969), 1:70–73.

When, in the course of human events, it becomes necessary for one portion of the family of man to assume among the people of the earth a position different from that which they have hitherto occupied, but one to which the laws of nature and nature's God entitle them, a decent respect to the opinions of mankind requires that they should declare the causes that impel them to such a course.

We hold these truths to be self-evident: that all men and women are created equal; that they are endowed by their Creator with certain inalienable rights. . . . Whenever any form of government becomes destructive of these ends, it is the right of those who suffer from it to refuse allegiance to it, and to insist upon the institution of a new government. . . .

The history of mankind is a history of repeated injuries and usurpations on the part of man toward woman, having in direct object the establishment of an absolute tyranny over her. To prove this, let facts be submitted to a candid world.

He has never permitted her to exercise her inalienable right to the elective franchise. . . .

He has withheld from her rights which are given to the most ignorant and degraded men—both natives and foreigners. . . .

He has made her, if married, in the eye of the law, civilly dead.

He has taken from her all right in property, even to the wages she earns. . . .

After depriving her of all rights as a married woman, if single, and the owner of property, he has taxed her to support a government which recognizes her only when her property can be made profitable to it. . . .

He has denied her the facilities for obtaining a thorough education, all colleges being closed against her. . . .

He has created a false public sentiment by giving the world a different code of morals for men and women, by which moral delinquencies which exclude women from society, are not only tolerated, but deemed of little account in man. . . .

He has endeavored, in every way that he could, to destroy her confidence in her own powers, to lessen her self-respect and to make her willing to lead a dependent and abject life. . . .

Resolved, That all laws which prevent woman from occupying such a station in society as her conscience shall dictate, or which place her in a position inferior to that of man, are contrary to the great precept of nature, and therefore of no force or authority.

Resolved, That woman is man's equal—was intended to be so by the Creator, and the highest good of the race demands that she should be recognized as such. . . .

Resolved, That it is the duty of the women of this country to secure to themselves their sacred right to the elective franchise.

Questions

1. Read the Declaration of Independence (see text p. D-1) and consider the structural as well as ideological reasons why Stanton used it as a model.

2. In light of the tone and substance of Stanton's protest, why did so many male abolitionists fail to see these "self-evident" truths?

3. How were Stanton's arguments related to the interests and experiences of middle-class women?

Questions for Further Thought

1. Grimké and Stanton were both concerned with women's rights (Documents 11-9 and 11-10). How did their respective concerns with transcendentalism, moral reform, and political reform shape their arguments?

2. Use Grimké's and Stanton's arguments to describe the world they hoped to transform. By what logic were women traditionally considered subordinate to men?

3. In 1870 the Fifteenth Amendment to the U.S. Constitution prohibited states from denying the vote to black men; in 1920 the Nineteenth Amendment prohibited states from denying the vote to women. In your opinion, why did gender discrimination last fifty years longer in this arena than did racial discrimination?

CHAPTER TWELVE

The South Expands: Slavery and Society
1820–1860

Creating the Cotton South

By the 1820s slavery was rapidly expanding westward as southern planters moved into the lower Mississippi River Valley in search of increased profits. The Chesapeake states of Virginia and Maryland, which had endured repeated cycles of depression throughout much of the eighteenth century due to soil depletion and fluctuations in the price of tobacco, could not compete with the developing cotton and sugar economies of Alabama, Mississippi, and Louisiana. The success of these newer enterprises, however, was dependent on the availability of slaves. Some masters took their slaves with them (Document 12-1), but about 60 percent of the slaves working in the cotton and sugar fields were "sold south" (see text pp. 364–369). Most of these came from the Upper South, especially Virginia and Maryland, victims of the burgeoning domestic slave trade (Document 12-2). A particularly revealing account of a slave auction in Richmond (Document 12-3) captures some of the stark realities of this trade.

Slaves were property, "chattels personal" in the language of the law, but neither the slave owners themselves nor casual outside observers could ignore the fact that they were a peculiar form of property—human. Thus an inventory, such as that done by James Coles Bruce in 1849, was never merely an accounting of net worth (Document 12-5). Frederick Law Olmsted's comments on plantation management suggest that slaves could not be controlled unless certain concessions relating to their basic humanity were made (Document 12-4). Even proslavery apologists felt compelled to justify the peculiar institution by enumerating the advantages visited upon a supposedly inferior people (Document 12-6).

12-1   The Slaveholders' Frontier: Moving to Mississippi (1808–1809)

Leonard Covington

The early-nineteenth-century frontier attracted well-heeled emigrants with commercial concerns. Southern slaveholders in particular were eager to take up lands in the lower Mississippi Valley, where the yields were much higher than in the older, increasingly exhausted tobacco lands of the Chesapeake, and where new and lucrative crops such as sugar and especially cotton were viable. One such slaveholder was Leonard Covington

297

(1768–1813) of Calvert County, Maryland, along Chesapeake Bay south of Annapolis. Covington, a military officer and former member of Congress, was deeply in debt; his traditional crops of tobacco and wheat were losing their profitability, and exports of both were suffering from Jefferson's Embargo Act (see text p. 222). Accordingly, he began to make plans to move to the vicinity of Natchez, Mississippi—a move previously made by his brother Alexander. Covington discussed the move in a series of letters to Alexander and others, extracts from which follow.

Source: From John R. Commons et al., *A Documentary History of American Industrial Society* (Cleveland: The Arthur H. Clark Co., 1910), 2:201–208.

(a) Extract from a Letter from Aquasco, Md., Aug. 17, 1808, to Alexander Covington in Mississippi

I find that I can dispose of my Calvert lands, but for the present forbear to do so until every information and advice is received which I hold to be necessary for enabling me to mature my plans upon a [basis(?)] at once extended and profitable. Let me therefore beg your thoughts and reflections, upon the following points particularly, and in general such other information as you may deem useful to my purpose. You have never been circumstantial as to the manner and terms of hiring your people. It would certainly be material to the owner of slaves, whether their treatment in many respects was such as would be desirable, and in what manner the payments for hirelings were made; if in advance, or punctually at the months end. Whether the slaves were well fed; and only compelled to work from "sun to sun." It is possible that so much labor may be required of hirelings and so little regard may be had for their constitutions as to render them in a few years, not only unprofitable, but expensive. In your case, who pays the doctor, abides the loss from death or running away? Do the negroes in that country generally look as happy and contented as with us, and do they as universally take husbands and wives and as easily rear their young as in Maryland? Would your negroes, think you, willingly return to Maryland? Are they satisfied with the change and with their treatment. Is the culture of cotton much easier, and a more certain crop? than our tobacco? Is there any probability that you will have any better market for your cotton than we shall have for our tobacco should our differences with Europe terminate in a war? Will this not depend upon the progress of manufactures in this country? Is the expense of making a cotton crop, where a man has hands of his own, considerable? What seems to be the current price of horses, cattle, &c., &c. The expense of clothing must be less than in a more northern climate. On lands of the U.S., such as you would like to purchase, what would be the probable expense of rough buildings and clearing for a small crop, say for ten or twelve hands? What time would such a preparation take? Fruit—is it abundant and well flavored, &c., &c? What seems to be the usual fare or allowance for working negroes, where a planter has a good many, from ten to 20, for example? Have you any sudden or great changes from heat to cold, and do you suffer as much from droughts or violent falls of rain as with us? I have a thousand more questions in my head, but pushed for time just now, must hope that you will say everything that I could ask, not forgetting politicks, the state of religion, if there be much amongst you. As to dealings generally, are the folks pretty punctual, or is there much use for lawyers? Have you found the summer sun more intolerable than in this climate? Has the thermometer been at a greater degree of heat than 85 or 86, what we experience about the latter end of June?

(b) Extract from a Letter from Aquasco, Aug. 7, 1808, to Capt. Jas. T. Magruder, Washington, Miss.

I am sorry that the prices and titles of land seem for the present in some measure to obstruct your plans, but it appears to me that your time cannot be illy spent under your existing arrangement, and possibly a purchase of lands, under existing circumstances could not be made to so great advantage as when the public office for the sale of lands shall be established, and as when the political horizon shall have been cleared of its present gloomy bodements. You mention that cash is scarce and cannot be had for produce (Cotton). I should think that this consideration alone would decide the preference in favor of your present plan of hiring your negroes, to that of cultivating the soil at your own expense and risk, if indeed the wages for hirelings are regularly and promptly paid up, (but of this neither of you have given particulars) and if the treatment in all respects to the slaves are such as we ought to wish for. Indeed I am extremely anxious to be informed of all these particular matters, and to have your full opinion and advice as to the propriety of my removing to that country, for I seriously assure (tho' I know you will be started at the assurance) you that I am at this moment earnestly employed in making arrangements to that end. I am now negotiating for the sale of the whole of my Calvert lands, with a full view to an investment and settlement in your country. Our friend Rawlings and myself have certainly got our affairs in such a train that I really think it probable that we shall set out this fall, and winter in the lower part of Kentucky, but possibly we may be delayed until the following spring. I will briefly give you the reasons which have moved me to the desire and resolution above advised you of, and again repeat my request that you will both favor me with your opinion and advice. In the first place, I find it will be extremely difficult, if not impossible, for me to meet all my pecuniary engagements, and to sink the debt incurred for the purchase of my lands. The interest upon 5 or 6 thousand dollars, under our present and apparent future commercial embarrassments, is really of itself not a slight matter, then no other means are to be found for its extinction than the uncertain and fluctuating one of a tobacco crop, which I verily believe has seen very much its best days. Add to this consideration the little chance I should have of adding to my property with my present prospect for a growing and large family, which must necessarily begin to be very expensive, and again, should a war with G. Britain terminate our present political disputes with that nation, I cannot but dread the predatory incursions which their naval superiority could enable them to make, when my little all would be entirely exposed to their merciless depredations, and, lastly, the negroes which I contemplate to take with me (amounting to 25, out of which 19 may be hired or worked to advantage) at the prices you have hired yours at, will be infinitely more productive in my expectations of compassing about $3000, and your advice will bear me out in it, I have it in contemplation to carry out with me some 10 or 15 families who are urgent in their requests for me to enlist them in my service of clearing and cultivating such lands as I may make purchase of. I mean not to defray their expenses; this they can do themselves (such men as Billy Watson, J. Letchworth, H. Watson, etc., etc.) but they want a conductor and some place to settle upon when they shall have reached their place of destination with exhausted pockets and anxious minds. With a view to the permanence of my plans, I have to beg that you will cause your people (several of them at least) to write favorable accounts of their situation, and of the country, etc., etc. Sam is now in the hire of W. B. Ellis, but I still have hopes that some means will be found to forward him to you. At any rate, should I be with you the next Spring, something to your satisfaction shall be done.

(c) Extract of a Letter from Feb. 15, 1809, to Alexander Covington

. . . The times are tough, but in other respects the good folks jog on as usual. The following is a list of my people, [i.e., slaves] such as go and such as stay:

FOR MISSISSIPPI				FOR AQUASCO			
Watt	32	Tom	36	Nick	50	Ned	24
Bess	24	Salisbury	32	Jack	22	Tabs	22
Dick	17	Moses	15	Bob	34	Nancy	46
Phill	12	Major	10	Pegg	20	Betsy	18
Dyche	35	Carolina	19	Isaac	10	Grace	5
Sal	10	Tom	5	Kitty	6	Charles	6
Pool	6	Nick	5	Charles	3	Nell	2
Hanna	1	Rachel	22	Henry	2 mos.	Christy	32
Ben	3	John	1	Flora	5	Nell	30
Jenny	26	Eliza	3	Nick	30	Dine	26
Nat	1	Jim	11	Nancy	5	Sophia	2
Rachel	11	Clem	9	Lucy	34	Joe	1
Tom	7	Cesar	5	Fanny		Moll	
Dasy	3	Cilla	12				
Bessie	11	George	9				
Flora	5						

Questions

1. When discussing a move, what characteristics of the Natchez region most concerned Covington? What characteristics interested him less?

2. What did Covington expect to do when he and his force arrive in Natchez?

3. From the evidence of these letters, would you describe Covington as someone who cared about his slaves? Why or why not?

12-2   Forced Migration to the Cotton South: The Narrative of Charles Ball (1837)

As the cotton boom began to consume the Lower (or Deep) South at the beginning of the nineteenth century, a large and lucrative domestic slave trade sprang up to supply slaves from Virginia and Maryland to the expanding plantations of the cotton belt. Among those caught up in the trade was Charles Ball, a slave in Calvert County, Maryland (Leonard Covington's home county; see Document 12-1), whose master sold him to a trader in the year 1805. Ball was moved, first to central South Carolina, and then to frontier Georgia, before escaping and returning to his family in Maryland. Later recaptured, he escaped again, settling near Philadelphia in the 1830s. There his story was recorded by a sympathetic abolitionist who rendered Ball's narrative in genteel nineteenth-century language and embellished the story with numerous anecdotes about southern society obtained from other sources. For this and other reasons, the veracity of the narrative was sharply attacked at the time by proslavery apologists; however, modern scholars have confirmed that those parts of the narrative dealing with Ball's own experience are consistent with what is known about the times and places he visited. Used with care (as should be done with all the other documents reproduced in this collection), Ball's story provides an extraordinary glimpse at life in the Old South at a critical moment in its development. The excerpts reproduced below recount Ball's sale to the trader in 1805, the conditions of his journey to South Carolina, and his observations of the land and the people along his route.

Source: From Charles Ball, *Slavery in the United States: A Narrative of the Life and Adventures of Charles Ball, a Black Man . . .* (New York: John S. Taylor, 1837), 35–39, 41, 44, 50–51, 67–68, 71–73, 79–83.

My master kept a store at a small village on the bank of the Patuxent river, called B——, although he resided at some distance on a farm. One morning he rose early, and ordered me to take a yoke of oxen and go to the village, to bring home a cart which was there, saying he would follow me. He arrived at the village soon after I did, and took his breakfast with his store-keeper. He then told me to come into the house and get my breakfast. Whilst I was eating in the kitchen, I observed him talking earnestly, but lowly, to a stranger near the kitchen door. I soon after went out, and hitched my oxen to the cart, and was about to drive off, when several men came round about me, and amongst them the stranger whom I had seen speaking with my master. This man came up to me, and, seizing me by the collar, shook me violently, saying I was his property, and must go with him to Georgia. At the sound of these words, the thoughts of my wife and children rushed across my mind, and my heart died away within me. I saw and knew that my case was hopeless, and that resistance was vain, as there were near twenty persons present, all of whom were ready to assist the man by whom I was kidnapped. I felt incapable of weeping or speaking, and in my despair I laughed loudly. My purchaser ordered me to cross my hands behind, which were quickly bound with a strong cord; and he then told me that we must set out that very day for the south. I asked if I could not be allowed to go to see my wife and children, or if this could not be permitted, if they might not have leave to come to see me; but was told that I would be able to get another wife in Georgia.

My new master, whose name I did not hear, took me that same day across the Patuxent, where I joined fifty-one other slaves, whom he had bought in Maryland. Thirty-two of these were men, and nineteen were women. The women were merely tied together with a rope, about the size of a bed cord, which was tied like a halter round the neck of each; but the men, of whom I was the stoutest and strongest, were very differently caparisoned. A strong iron collar was closely fit-

ted by means of a padlock round each of our necks. A chain of iron, about a hundred feet in length, was passed through the hasp of each padlock, except at the two ends, where the hasps of the padlocks passed through a link of the chain. In addition to this, we were handcuffed in pairs, with iron staples and bolts, with a short chain, about a foot long, uniting the handcuffs and their wearers in pairs. In this manner we were chained alternately by the right and left hand; and the poor man, to whom I was thus ironed, wept like all infant when the blacksmith, with his heavy hammer, fastened the ends of the bolts that kept the staples from slipping from our arms. For my own part, I felt indifferent to my fate. It appeared to me that the worst had come, that could come, and that no change of fortune could harm me.

After we were all chained and handcuffed together, we sat down upon the ground; and here reflecting upon the sad reverse of fortune that had so suddenly overtaken me, and the dreadful suffering which awaited me, I became weary of life, and bitterly execrated the day I was born. It seemed that I was destined by fate to drink the cup of sorrow to the very dregs, and that I should find no respite from misery but in the grave. I longed to die, and escape from the hands of my tormentors; but even the wretched privilege of destroying myself was denied me; for I could not shake off my chains, nor move a yard without the consent of my master. Reflecting in silence upon my forlorn condition, I at length concluded that as things could not become worse—and as the life of man is but a continued round of changes, they must, of necessity, take a turn in my favour at some future day. I found relief in this vague and indefinite hope, and when we received orders to go on board the scow, which was to transport us over the Patuxent, I marched down to the water with a firmness of purpose of which I did not believe myself capable, a few minutes before.

We were soon on the south side of the river, and taking up our line of march, we travelled about five miles that evening, and stopped for the night at one of those miserable public houses, so frequent in the lower parts of Maryland and Virginia, called *"ordinaries."*

Our master ordered a pot of mush to be made for our supper; after despatching which, we all lay down on the naked floor to sleep in our handcuffs and chains. The women, my fellow-slaves, lay on one side of the room; and the men who were chained with me, occupied the other. I slept but little this night, which I passed in thinking of my wife and little children, whom I could not hope ever to see again. I also thought of my grandfather, and of the long nights I had passed with him, listening to his narratives of the scenes through which he had passed in Africa. . . .

From this time, to the end of our journey southward, we all slept, promiscuously, men and women, on the floors of such houses as we chanced to stop at. We had no clothes except those we wore, and a few blankets; the larger portion of our gang being in rags at the time we crossed the Potomac. Two of the women were pregnant; the one far advanced— and she already complained of inability to keep pace with our march; but her complaints were disregarded. We crossed the Rappahannock at Port Royal, and afterwards passed through the village of Bowling Green; a place with which I became better acquainted in after times; but which now presented the quiet so common to all the small towns in Virginia, and indeed in all the southern states. . . .

In Virginia, it appeared to me that the slaves were more rigorously treated than they were in my native place. It is easy to tell a man of colour who is poorly fed, from one who is well supplied with food, by his personal appearance. A half-starved negro is a miserable looking creature. His skin becomes dry, and appears to be sprinkled over with whitish husks, or scales; the glossiness of his face vanishes, his hair loses its colour, becomes dry, and when stricken with a rod, the dust flies from it. These signs of bad treatment I perceived to be very common in Virginia; many young girls who would have been beautiful, if they had been allowed enough to eat, had lost all their prettiness through mere starvation; their fine glossy hair had become of a reddish colour, and stood out round their heads like long brown wool. . . .

As I advanced southward, even in Virginia, I perceived that the state of cultivation became progressively worse. Here, as in Maryland, the practice of the best farmers who cultivate grain, of planting the land every alternate year in corn, and sowing it in wheat or rye in the autumn of the same year in which the corn is planted, and whilst the corn is yet standing in the field, so as to get a crop from the same ground every year, without allowing it time to rest or recover, exhausts the finest soil in a few years, and in one or two generations reduces the proprietors to poverty. Some, who are supposed to be very superior farmers, only plant the land in corn once in three years; sowing it in wheat or rye as in the former case; however, without any covering of clover or other grass to protect it from the rays of the sun. The culture of tobacco prevails over a large portion of Vir-

ginia, especially south of James river, to the exclusion of almost every other crop, except corn. This destructive crop ruins the best land in a short time; and in all the lower parts of Maryland and Virginia the traveller will see large old family mansions, of weather-beaten and neglected appearance, standing in the middle of vast fields of many hundred acres, the fences of which have rotted away, and have been replaced by a wattled work in place of a fence, composed of short cedar stakes driven into the ground, about two feet apart, and standing about three feet above the earth, the intervals being filled up by branches cut from the cedar trees, and worked into the stakes horizontally, after the manner of splits in a basket. . . .

As we approached the Yadkin river, the tobacco disappeared from the fields, and the cotton plant took its place, as an article of general culture. We passed the Yadkin by a ferry, on Sunday morning; and on the Wednesday following, in the evening, our master told us we were in the state of South Carolina. We staid this night in a small town called Lancaster; and I shall never forget the sensations which I experienced this evening, on finding myself in chains, in the state of South Carolina. From my earliest recollections, the name of South Carolina had been little less terrible to me than that of the bottomless pit. In Maryland, it had always been the practice of masters and mistresses, who wished to terrify their slaves, to threaten to sell them to South Carolina; where, it was represented, that their condition would be a hundred fold worse than it was in Maryland. I had regarded such a sale of myself, as the greatest of evils that could befall me, and had striven to demean myself in such manner, to my owners, as to preclude them from all excuse for transporting me to so horrid a place. At length I found myself, without having committed any crime, or even the slightest transgression, in the place and condition, of which I had, through life, entertained the greatest dread. I slept but little this night, and for the first time felt weary of life. . . .

. . . Early in the morning, our master called us up; and distributed to each of the party, a cake made of corn meal, and a small piece of bacon. On our journey, we had only eaten twice a day, and had not received breakfast until about nine o'clock; but he said this morning meal was given to welcome us to South Carolina. He then addressed us all, and told us we might now give up all hope of ever returning to the places of our nativity; as it would be impossible for us to pass through the states of North Carolina and Virginia, without being taken up and sent back. He further advised us to make ourselves contented, as he would take us to Georgia, a far better country than any we had seen; and where we would be able to live in the greatest abundance. About sunrise we took up our march on the road to Columbia, as we were told. Hitherto our master had not offered to sell any of us, and had even refused to stop to talk to any one on the subject of our sale, although he had several times been addressed on this point, before we reached Lancaster; but soon after we departed from this village, we were overtaken on the road by a man on horseback, who accosted our driver by asking him if his *niggers* were for sale. The latter replied, that he believed he would not sell any yet, as he was on his way to Georgia, and cotton being now much in demand, he expected to obtain high prices for us from persons who were going to settle in the new purchase. He, however, contrary to his custom, ordered us to stop, and told the stranger he might look at us, and that he would find us as fine a lot of hands, as were ever imported into the country—that we were all prime property, and he had no doubt would command his own prices in Georgia.

The stranger, who was a thin, weather-beaten, sunburned figure, then said, he wanted a couple of breeding-wenches, and would give as much for them as they would bring in Georgia—that he had lately heard from Augusta, and that *niggers* were not higher there than in Columbia and, as he had been in Columbia the week before, he knew what *niggers* were worth. He then walked along our line, as we stood chained together, and looked at the whole of us—then turning to the women, asked the prices of the two pregnant ones. Our master replied, that these were two of the best breeding-wenches in all Maryland—that one was twenty-two, and the other only nineteen—that the first was already the mother of seven children, and the other of four—that he had himself seen the children at the time he bought their mothers—and that such wenches would be cheap at a thousand dollars each; but as they were not able to keep up with the gang, he would take twelve hundred dollars for the two. The purchaser said this was too much, but that he would give nine hundred dollars for the pair. This price was promptly refused; but our master, after some consideration, said he was willing to sell a bargain in these wenches, and would take eleven hundred dollars for them, which was objected to on the other side; and many faults and failings were pointed out in the merchandise. After much bargaining, and many gross jests on the part of the stranger, he offered a thousand dollars for the two; and said he would give no more. He then mounted his horse, and moved off; but after he had gone about one hundred yards, he was called back; and our master said, if he would go with him to the next blacksmith's shop on the road to Columbia, and pay for taking the irons off the rest of us, he might have the two women. . . .

The landlord assured my master that at this time slaves were much in demand, both in Columbia and Augusta; that purchasers were numerous and prices good; and that the best plan of effecting good sales would be to put up each *nigger*, separately, at auction, after giving a few days' notice, by an advertisement, in the neighbouring country. Cotton, he said, had not been higher for many years, and as a great many persons, especially young men, were moving off to the new purchase in Georgia, prime hands were in high demand, for the purpose of clearing the land in the new country—that the boys and girls, under twenty, would bring almost any price at present, in Columbia, for the purpose of picking the growing crop of cotton, which promised to be very heavy; and as most persons had planted more than their hands would be able to pick, young *niggers*, who would soon learn to pick cotton, were prime articles in the market. As to those more advanced in life, he seemed to think the prospect of selling them at an unusual price, not so good, as they could not so readily become expert cotton-pickers—he said further, that from some cause, which he could not comprehend, the price of rice had not been so good this year as usual; and that he had found it cheaper to purchase rice to feed his own *niggers* than to provide them with corn, which had to be brought from the upper country. He therefore, advised my master, not to drive us towards the rice plantation of the low country. My master said he would follow his advice, at least so far as to sell a portion of us in Carolina, but seemed to be of opinion that his prime hands would bring him more money in Georgia, and named me, in particular, as one who would be worth, at least, a thousand dollars, to a man who was about making a settlement, and clearing a plantation in the new purchase. . . . For several days past, I had observed that in the country through which we travelled, little attention was paid to the cultivation of any thing but cotton. Now this plant was almost the sole possessor of the fields. It covered the plantations adjacent to the road, as far as I could see, both before and behind me, and looked not unlike buckwheat before it blossoms. I saw some small fields of corn, and lots of sweet potatoes, amongst which the young vines of the water-melon were frequently visible. The improvements on the plantations were not good. There were no barns, but only stables and sheds, to put the cotton under, as it was brought from the field. Hay seemed to be unknown in the country, for I saw neither hay-stacks nor meadows; and the few fields that were lying fallow, had but small numbers of cattle in them, and these were thin and meagre. We had met with no flocks of sheep of late, and the hogs that we saw on the road-side, were in bad condition. The horses and mules that I saw at work in the cotton-fields, were poor and badly harnessed, and the half-naked condition of the negroes, who drove them, or followed with the hoe, together with their wan complexions, proved to me that they had too much work, or not enough food. We passed a cotton-gin this morning, the first that I ever saw; but they were not at work with it. We also met a party of ladies and gentlemen on a journey of pleasure, riding in two very handsome carriages, drawn by sleek and spirited horses, very different in appearance from the moving skeletons that I had noticed drawing the ploughs in the fields. The black drivers of the coaches were neatly clad in gay-coloured clothes, and contrasted well with their half-naked brethren, a gang of whom were hoeing cotton by the road-side, near them, attended by an overseer in a white linen shirt and pantaloons, with one of the long negro whips in his hand.

I observed that these poor people did not raise their heads, to look either at the fine coaches and horses then passing, or at us; but kept their faces steadily bent towards the cotton-plants, from among which they were removing the weeds. I almost shuddered at the sight, knowing, that I myself was doomed to a state of servitude, equally cruel and debasing, unless, by some unforeseen occurrence, I might fall into the hands of a master of less inhumanity of temper than the one who had possession of the miserable creatures before me.

It was manifest, that I was now in a country, where the life of a black man was no more regarded than that of an ox, except as far as the man was worth the more money in the market. On all the plantations that we passed, there was a want of live stock of every description, except slaves, and they were deplorably abundant.

Questions

1. Compare Ball's experience with what you know about the experience of Leonard Covington's slaves (Document 12-1). All in all, how would you characterize the impact on slaves of this sort of westward movement?

2. Why do you think Ball regarded "the name of South Carolina" as "little less terrible... than that of the bottomless pit"?

3. How would you characterize the whites depicted in these excerpts? To what extent do they fit your prior understandings of the character of southern slaveholders?

12-3 Slave Auction in Richmond, Virginia (1854)

William Chambers

William Chambers (1800–1883) was a Scotsman of considerable reputation as a printer and publisher at the time of his visit to the United States in 1853. Apprenticed to an Edinburgh bookseller at the age of fourteen, he had managed, in partnership with his brother Robert, to establish a highly profitable business in 1832, publishing an inexpensive weekly paper, *Chambers's Edinburgh Journal*, which aimed to instruct and entertain the "humbler orders" of society. The *Journal* was followed by *Chambers's Historical Newspaper* (1833) and *Chambers's Information for the People* (1833–1835). As part of his plan to disseminate "useful knowledge" among the masses, Chambers also wrote travel commentaries, including two books based on his tour of the United States: *Things as They Are in America* (1854) and *American Slavery and Colour* (1857). On his visit to Richmond, which by then was "known as the principal market for the supply of slaves for the [lower] south," Chambers was immediately struck by the presence of blacks "everywhere" and at the sight of an "armed sentinel" in the state capitol. It was a stark reminder, he thought, of the "danger" posed by the "large infusion of slaves" into the city. Curious to learn "by what means and at what prices slaves" were sold, Chambers discovered soon enough that such "research" was easily accomplished, for the "exposure of ordinary goods in a store is not more open to the public than are the sales of slaves in Richmond." In the excerpt reprinted below, he recounts his first experience at a slave auction.

Source: Excerpt from *A Documentary History of Slavery in North America*, ed. Willie Lee Rose (New York: Oxford University Press, 1976), 146–150. Reprinted by permission of Oxford University Press.

On my arrival, and while making these preliminary observations, the lots for sale had not made their appearance. In about five minutes afterwards they were ushered in, one after the other, under the charge of a mulatto, who seemed to act as principal assistant. I saw no whips, chains, or any other engine of force. Nor did such appear to be required. All the lots took their seats on two long forms near the stove; none shewed any sign of resistance; nor did any one utter a word. Their manner was that of perfect humility and resignation.

As soon as all were seated, there was a general examination of their respective merits, by feeling their arms, looking into their mouths, and investigating the quality of their hands and fingers—this last being evidently an important particular. Yet there was no abrupt rudeness in making these examinations—no coarse or domineering language was employed. The three negro men were dressed in the usual manner—in gray woolen clothing. The woman, with three children, excited my peculiar attention. She was neatly attired, with a coloured handkerchief bound round her head, and wore a white apron over her gown. Her children were all girls, one of them a baby at the breast, three months old, and the others two and three years of age respectively, rigged out with clean white pinafores. There was not a tear or an emotion visible in the whole party. Everything seemed to be considered as a matter of course; and the change of owners was possibly looked forward to with as much indifference as ordinary hired servants anticipate a removal from one employer to another.

While intending purchasers were proceeding with personal examinations of the several lots, I took the liberty of putting a few questions to the mother of the children. The following was our conversation:—

"Are you a married woman?"

"How many children have you had?"

"Seven."

"Where is your husband?"

"In Madison county."

"When did you part from him?"

"On Wednesday—two days ago."

"Were you sorry to part from him?"

"Yes, sir," she replied with a deep sigh; "my heart was a'-most broke."

"Why is your master selling you?"

"I don't know—he wants money to buy some land—suppose he sells me for that."

There might not be a word of truth in these answers, for I had no means of testing their correctness; but the woman seemed to speak unreservedly, and I am inclined to think that she said nothing but what, if necessary, could be substantiated. I spoke also, to the young woman who was seated near her. She, like the others, was perfectly black, and appeared stout and healthy, of which some of the persons present assured themselves by feeling her arms and ankles, looking into her mouth, and causing her to stand up. She told me she had several brothers and sisters, but did not know where they were. She said she was a house-servant, and would be glad to be bought by a good master—looking at me, as if I should not be unacceptable.

I have said that there was an entire absence of emotion in the party of men, women, and children, thus seated preparatory to being sold. This does not correspond with the ordinary accounts of slave-sales, which are represented as tearful and harrowing. My belief is, that none of the parties felt deeply on the subject, or at least that any distress they experienced was but momentary—soon passed away, and was forgotten. One of my reasons for this opinion rests on a trifling incident which occurred. While waiting for the commencement of the sale, one of the gentlemen present amused himself with a pointer-dog, which, at command,

stood on its hind-legs, and took pieces of bread from his pocket. These tricks greatly entertained the row of negroes, old and young; and the poor woman, whose heart three minutes before was almost broken, now laughed as heartily as any one.

"Sale is going to commence—this way, gentlemen," cried a man at the door to a number of loungers outside; and all having assembled, the mulatto assistant led the woman and her children to the block, which he helped her to mount. There she stood with her infant at the breast, and one of her girls at each side. The auctioneer, a handsome, gentlemanly personage, took his place, with one foot on an old deal-chair with a broken back, and the other raised on the somewhat more elevated block. It was a striking scene. "Well, gentlemen," began the salesman, "here is a capital woman and her three children, all in good health—what do you say for them? Give me an offer. (Nobody speaks.) I put up the whole lot at 850 dollars—850 dollars—850 dollars (speaking very fast)—850 dollars. Will no one advance upon that? A very extraordinary bargain, gentlemen. A fine healthy baby. Hold it up. (Mulatto goes up the first step of the block; takes the baby from the woman's breast, and holds it aloft with one hand, so as to shew that it was a veritable sucking-baby.) That will do. A woman, still young, and three children, all for 850 dollars. An advance, if you please, gentlemen. (A voice bids 860.) Thank you, sir—860; any one bids more? (A second voice says, 870; and so on the bidding goes as far as 890 dollars, when it stops.) That won't do, gentlemen. I cannot take such a low price. (After a pause, addressing the mulatto): She may go down." Down from the block the woman and her children were therefore conducted by the assistant, and, as if nothing had occurred, they calmly resumed their seats by the stove.

The next lot brought forward was one of the men. The mulatto beckoning to him with his hand, requested him to come behind a canvas screen, of two leaves, which was standing near the back-window. The man placidly rose, and having been placed behind the screen, was ordered to take off his clothes, which he did without a word or look of remonstrance. About a dozen gentlemen crowded to the spot while the poor fellow was stripping himself, and as soon as he stood on the floor, bare from top to toe, a most rigorous scrutiny of his person was instituted. The clear black skin, back and front, was viewed all over for sores from disease; and there was no part of his body left unexamined. The man was told to open and shut his hands, asked if he could pick cotton, and every tooth in his head was scrupulously looked at. The investigation being at an end, he was ordered to dress himself; and having done so, was requested to walk to the block.

The ceremony of offering him for competition was gone through as before, but no one would bid. The other two men, after undergoing similar examinations behind the screen, were also put up, but with the same result. Nobody would bid for them, and they were all sent back to their seats. It seemed as if the company had conspired not to buy anything that day. Probably some imperfections had been detected in the personal qualities of the negroes. Be this as it may, the auctioneer, perhaps a little out of temper from his want of success, walked off to his desk, and the affair was so far at an end. . . .

Such were a forenoon's experiences in the slave-market of Richmond. Everything is described precisely as it occurred, without passion or prejudice. It would not have been difficult to be sentimental on a subject which appeals so strongly to the feelings; but I have preferred telling the simple truth.

Questions

1. Chambers said that he sought to "touch the heart[s]" of the readers of his weekly paper. He also said, however, that in this instance he self-consciously avoided being "sentimental," that he wished to describe the day's events "without passion or prejudice." Which did he accomplish in this description of a slave auction? Explain.

2. Was the fact that Britain had abolished slavery in 1833 reflected in Chambers's account? Explain.

3. How were the slaves portrayed by Chambers? Is the overall impression he conveys of their behavior largely positive or negative? How are the potential buyers and the auctioneer depicted?

12-4 Slave Management on a Mississippi Plantation (1852)

Frederick Law Olmsted

In the years before the Civil War, a number of journalists traveled through the South, reporting their observations on the lives and labors of slaves and their masters. The keenest of these observers was Frederick Law Olmsted, who first journeyed through the South in 1852 on a commission from the *New York Times*. In the following excerpt Olmsted describes an extremely large cotton plantation in Mississippi. The basic principles of its organization, notably the use of labor in highly regimented gangs, were developed in the early nineteenth century, when cotton became, for the first time, the major staple crop of the slave South. While Olmsted made his observations much later, near the close of the slave-plantation era, his comments on the plantation system and its operations were so acute that they bear examination here.

Source: From "Creating Central Park, 1857–1861" in *The Papers of Frederick Law Olmsted*, 3:72–83. Copyright © 1983 The Johns Hopkins University Press. Reproduced with permission of The Johns Hopkins University Press.

SLAVE MANAGEMENT ON THE LARGEST SCALE

The estate I am now about to describe, was situated upon a tributary of the Mississippi, and accessible only by occasional steamboats; even this mode of communication being frequently interrupted at low stages of the rivers. The slaves upon it formed about one twentieth of the whole population of the county, in which the blacks considerably out-number the whites. . . .

The property consisted of four adjoining plantations, each with its own negro-cabins, stables and overseer, and each worked to a great extent independently of the others, but all contributing their crop to one [cotton] gin-house and warehouse, and all under the general superintendence of a bailiff or manager, who constantly resided upon the estate, and in the absence of the owner, had vice-regal power over

the overseers, controlling, so far as he thought fit, the economy of all the plantations. . . .

. . . The overseers were superior to most of their class, and, with one exception, frank, honest, temperate and industrious, but their feelings toward negroes were such as naturally result from their occupation. They were all married, and lived with their families, each in a cabin or cottage, in the hamlet of the slaves of which he had especial charge. Their wages varied from $500 to $1,000 a year each. . . .

. . . Of course, to secure their own personal safety and to efficiently direct the labor of such a large number of ignorant, indolent, and vicious negroes, rules, or rather habits and customs, of discipline, were necessary, which would in particular cases be liable to operate unjustly and cruelly. It is apparent, also, that, as the testimony of negroes against them would not be received as evidence in court, that there was very little probability that any excessive severity would be restrained by fear of the law. A provision of the law intended to secure a certain privilege to slaves, was indeed disregarded under my own observation, and such infraction of the law was confessedly customary with one of the overseers, and was permitted by the manager, for the reason that it seemed to him to be, in a certain degree, justifiable and expedient under the circumstances, and because he did not like to interfere unnecessarily in such matters.

In the main, the negroes appeared to be well taken care of and abundantly supplied with the necessaries of vigorous physical existence. A large part of them lived in commodious and well-built cottages, with broad galleries in front, so that each family of five had two rooms on the lower floor, and a loft. The remainder lived in log-huts, small and mean in appearance, but those of their overseers were little better, and preparations were being made to replace all of these by neat boarded cottages. Each family had a fowl-house and hog-sty (constructed by the negroes themselves), and kept fowls and swine, feeding the latter during the summer on weeds and fattening them in the autumn on corn *stolen* (this was mentioned to me by the overseers as if it were a matter of course) from their master's corn-fields. I several times saw gangs of them eating the dinner which they had brought, each for himself, to the field, and observed that they generally had plenty, often more than they could eat, of bacon, corn-bread, and molasses. The allowance of food is weighed and measured under the eye of the manager by the drivers, and distributed to the head of each family weekly: consisting of— for each person, 3 pounds of pork, 1 peck [8 quarts] of meal; and from January to July, 1 quart of molasses. Monthly, in addition, 1 pound tobacco, and 4 pints salt. No drink is ever served but water, except after unusual exposure, or to ditchers working in water, who get a glass of whisky at night. All hands cook for themselves after work at night, or whenever they please between nightfall and daybreak, each family in its own cabin. Each family had a garden, the products of which, together with eggs, fowls and bacon, they frequently sold, or used in addition to their regular allowance of food. Most of the families bought a barrel of flour every year. The manager endeavored to encourage this practice, and that they might spend their money for flour instead of liquor, he furnished it to them at rather less than what it cost him at wholesale. There were many poor whites within a few miles who would always sell liquor to the negroes, and encourage them to steal, to obtain the means to buy it of them. These poor whites were always spoken of with anger by the overseers, and they each had a standing offer of much more than the intrinsic value of their land, from the manager, to induce them to move away. . . .

Near the first quarters we visited there was a large blacksmith's and wheelwright's shop, in which a number of mechanics were at work. Most of them, as we rode up, were eating their breakfast, which they warmed at their fires. Within and around the shop there were some fifty plows

which they were putting in order. The manager inspected the work, found some of it faulty, sharply reprimanded the workmen for not getting on faster, and threatened one of them with a whipping for not paying closer attention to the directions which had been given him. He told me that he once employed a white man from the North, who professed to be a first-class workman, but he soon found he could not do nearly as good work as the negro mechanics on the estate, and the latter despised him so much, and got such high opinions of themselves in consequence of his inferiority, that he had been obliged to discharge him in the midst of his engagement.

HOURS OF LABOR

Each overseer regulated the hours of work on his own plantation. I saw the negroes at work before sunrise and after sunset. At about eight o'clock they were allowed to stop for breakfast, and again about noon, to dine. The length of these rests was at the discretion of the overseer or drivers, usually, I should say, from half an hour to an hour. There was no rule.

OVERSEERS

The number of hands directed by each overseer was considerably over one hundred. The manager thought it would be better economy to have a white man over every fifty hands, but the difficulty of obtaining trustworthy overseers prevented it. Three of those he then had were the best he had ever known. He described the great majority as being passionate, careless, inefficient men, generally intemperate, and totally unfitted for the duties of the position. The best overseers, ordinarily, are young men, the sons of small planters, who take up the business temporarily, as a means of acquiring a little capital with which to purchase negroes for themselves.

PLOW-GIRLS

The plowing, both with single and double mule teams, was generally performed by women, and very well performed, too. I watched with some interest for any indication that their sex unfitted them for the occupation. Twenty of them were plowing together, with double teams and heavy plows. They were superintended by a male negro driver, who carried a whip, which he frequently cracked at them, permitting no dawdling or delay at the turning; and they twitched their plows around on the head-land, jerking their reins, and yelling to their mules, with apparent ease, energy, and rapidity. Throughout the Southwest the negroes, as a rule, appear to be worked much harder than in the eastern and northern slave States. I do not think they accomplish as much daily, as agricultural laborers at the North usually do, but they certainly labor much harder, and more unremittingly. They are constantly and steadily driven up to their work, and the stupid, plodding, machine-like manner in which they labor, is painful to witness. This was especially the case with the hoe-gangs. One of them numbered nearly two hundred hands (for the force of two plantations was working together), moving across the field in parallel lines, with a considerable degree of precision. I repeatedly rode through the lines at a canter, with other horsemen, often coming upon them suddenly, without producing the smallest change or interruption in the dogged action of the laborers, or causing one of them to lift an eye from the ground. A very tall and powerful negro walked to and fro in the rear of the line, frequently cracking his whip, and calling out, in the surliest manner, to one and another, "Shove your hoe, there! shove your hoe!" But I never saw him strike any one with the whip.

DISCIPLINE

The whip was evidently in constant use, however. There were no rules on the subject, that I learned; the overseers and drivers punished the negroes whenever they deemed it necessary, and in such manner, and with such severity, as they thought fit. "If you do n't work faster," or "If you do n't work better," or "If you do n't recollect what I tell you, I will have you flogged," are threats which I have often heard. I said to one of the overseers, "It must be very disagreeable to have to punish them as much as you do?" "Yes, it would be to those who are not used to it—but it's my business, and I think nothing of it. Why, sir, I would n't mind killing a nigger more than I would a dog." I asked if he had ever killed a negro? "Not quite," he said, but overseers were often obliged to. Some negroes are determined never to let a white man whip them, and will resist you, when you attempt it; of course you must kill them in that case. Once a negro, whom he was about to whip in the field, struck at his head with a hoe. He parried the blow with his whip, and drawing a pistol tried to shoot him, but the pistol missing fire he rushed in and knocked him down with the butt of it. At another time a negro whom he was punishing, insulted and threatened him. He went to the house for his gun, and as he was returning, the negro, thinking he would be afraid of spoiling so valuable a piece of property by firing, broke for the woods. He fired at once, and put six buck-shot into his hips. He always carried a bowie-knife, but not a pistol.

Questions

1. Did the plantation Olmsted described more resemble a great landed estate or a modern factory?

2. Do you think the treatment of slaves on this plantation was typical of cotton plantations in the South? Would it have applied to plantations growing other crops, such as rice, sugar, or tobacco?

3. Olmsted was seeking to be an "objective" reporter here. Can you determine from this passage his own views of slavery?

12-5 Inventory of Slave Property (1849)

James Coles Bruce

In *The Federalist*, No. 54, James Madison's fictional "Southern brethren" defends the three-fifths compromise by denying that slaves in the South were "considered merely as property and in no respect whatever as persons." They were in fact of a "mixed character," possessing the qualities both "of persons and of property" (see Document 6-21). All of the documents in this section and the next are illustrative of this duality, but none presents it more starkly than the slave inventory of James Coles Bruce (1806–1865).

Bruce, a wealthy plantation owner who gained a seat in the Virginia General Assembly after Nat Turner's 1831 slave rebellion (see Document 12-9), was at once a supporter of slavery and an opponent of secession. Nevertheless, elected to the Virginia secession convention in 1861 as a delegate from Halifax County, he sided with his state and ultimately contributed more than $50,000 to the Confederacy. Bruce died in March of 1865, less than two weeks before Robert E. Lee surrendered to Ulysses S. Grant at Appomattox Courthouse.

The following inventory, done in 1849 of the slaves at a Louisiana sugar plantation owned jointly by Bruce and two of his relatives, is indicative of the sort of accounting most slave owners were obliged periodically to complete. Slaves were "chattels personal" whose market value had to be established, but they were persons as well; therefore, their "value," was dependent not only on their age or occupation, but on their "disposition." A "superior hand" was generally worth more than a "good hand," but so was a "well disposed" slave compared to one possessed of a "great temper."

Source: Excerpt from *A Documentary History of Slavery in North America*, ed. Willie Lee Rose (New York: Oxford University Press, 1976), 338–343. Reprinted by permission of Oxford University Press.

List of Negro Men & Boys, also their ages & Value

Names	Ages	Full Hands	Half Hands	Value	Remarks
Perry—Driver	40 [Years]	1″		$900 00	Disposed to medle with women
Old Daniel	70 ″		½	100 00	old and decriped
John Miller	28 ″	Full Hand		600 00	a Runaway
Jim Bassy	25 ″	″		600 00	Sickly
Claiborn West	28 ″	″		800 00	good Negro
Jack Page	35 ″	″		700 00	has Runaway
Claiborn Anderson	35 ″	″		400 00	has runaway
Orange	28 ″	″		800 00	good Hand
Anderson. M	25 ″	″		800 00	good Negro
Bob. Scooner	28 ″	″		700 00	Well disposed but Sloe
Izor M	45 ″	″		500 00	African, good but Sloe
George. M.	25 ″	″		600 00	a cooper, Sickly but good
Jin. Wilbot	45 ″	″		400 00	a Runaway no account
Carter Allen	23 [Years]	″		400 00	a Runaway, verry Sloe
Charles Mena	45 ″	″		500 00	African, very good
Randle	45 ″	″		800 00	Sugar Maker, good hand
Edmond	40 ″	″		600 00	A great drunkard
Sam Williams	25 ″	″		600 00	A good hand
Gallant	45 ″	″		500 00	rather trifling, but will do
Old Mat M.	35 ″		½	300 00	Sickly consumption
Bill Kenty	45 ″	″		700 00	good hand
Fleming	45 ″	″		400 00	a runaway
Jefferson	28 ″	″		800 00	Superior Hand
Simond (Carpenter)	45 ″	″		800 00	the greatest rascal on Plantation
Friday	40 ″		½	350 00	Sickly Subject to fits
Milton	20 ″	″		700 00	good hand
Ezekiel	25 ″	″		800 00	good hand
John Davis	45 ″	″	½	400 00	Sickly, & a runaway
Jackson Tailor	28 ″	″		800 00	good hand
Sam Briggs	23 ″	″		700 00	good hand
David	44 ″	″		700 00	well disposed but sloe

List of Negro Men & Boys, also their ages & Value

Names	Ages		Full Hands	Half Hands	Value	Remarks
John Henderson	20	"	"		700 00	a fine hand
Richmond	23	"	"		800 00	a good hand
Simond Melacha	25	"	"		700 00	good hand but tricky
Ned Duck	35	"	"		500 00	not much account
Granison	26	"	"		600 00	good hand
Ransom	25	"	"		800 00	good hand
Tellemark	50	"		½	200 00	African King, no account
Charles Sims	28	"	"		700 00	good hand
Jack Coopper	30	"	"		1000 00	Jack Cooper, good hand
Bill Pleasant	28	"	"		700 00	good hand
Bill Sprague	30	"	"		600 00	good hand
Wyatt	30	"	"		700 00	good hand
Isaac Pascal	35 [Years]		"		700 00	very Sloe and high tempe[red]
Bill Berry	35	"	"		700 00	Sugar Maker, a great Liar
Squire	50	"		½	200 00	not much account
Ceazor	50	"		½	200 00	well disposed but no account
Little Daniel	40	"	"		600 00	disposed to fein sickness
Patrick	50	"		½	200 00	gardner no account
Ephraim	30	"	"		800 00	excelent hand
Old Champ	50	"		¼	100 00	most Blind, but well disposed
Washington	20	"	"		600 00	a Runaway
Carter M.	35	"	"		600 00	verry deceptive
John Comedy	45	"	"		600 00	a great Rascal & Runaway
Jack Allen	18	"		½	300 00	Sickly (Breast complaint)
Jo Blacksmith	30	"	"		1200 00	Blacksmith good hand
Old Luis	50	"		½	200 00	water hauler no account
Richard	15	"	"	½	500 00	good hand
One Leg Bob	50	"		0	000 00	no earthly use
John Robinson	16	"	"	½	500 00	assistant Black-smith good
Emmanuel	45	"		½	100 00	criple, (in the Doct yard)
Old Charles	60	"		0	5 00	wore out, no account
General	30	"	"		800 00	No 1 hand
Little Mat M.	17	"		½	300 00	reumatic (but well disposed)
Little Jo	15	"		½	500 00	excelent Boy
Israel	20	"	"		600 00	Brick layer fair hand

List of Negro Men & Boys, also their ages & Value

Names	Ages		Full Hands	Half Hands	Value	Remarks
Willson	22	"	"		600 00	Brick layer fair hand
Pleasant	26 [Years]		"		1000 00	Carpenter fine Negro
Moses	27	"	"		1000 00	Engineer good Negro
Phill	10	"		⅓	300 00	wants much watching
Sandy	9	"		⅓	300 00	verry fine Boy
Jo	8	"		⅓	250 00	verry trifling
Anderson M	25	"	"		900 00	good hand
Will Shoemaker	28	"	"		800 00	good hand
Jim Wilkins	27	"	"		700 00	good hand
Little Bob	12	"		½	300 00	a verry good Boy
Julius	12	"		½	300 00	good Boy
One hand Luis	30	"		½	400 00	Bad Negro Runaway
Old Jake	50	"		½	300 00	well disposed
John Wilkins	30	"	"		600 00	verry good
Ballard Doct	12	"		½	300 00	good Boy but Sloe
Little Jack Doct	10	"		½	300 00	verry Smart Boy
William	6	"	0	0	200 00	verry good Boy
Nelson	4	"	0	0	150 00	rather young to Judge
Lunon	3	"	0	0	150 00	" "
Maldry	4	"	0	0	150 00	" "
Mose	4	"	0	0	200 00	" "
Ceazor	4	"	0	0	200 00	" "
George	2	"	0	0	100 00	" "
Pier	5	"	0	0	250 00	" "
Henry Lewis (Louisa child 9 months)	0	"	0	0	100 00	" "
Prince (Araminta child 8 months)	0	"	0	0	100 00	" "
92 Men & Boys & <u>44</u> Women & Children						

A List of Women their ages & value

Names	Ages		Full Hands	Half Hands	Value	Remarks
Letha	20 [Years]		"		500 00	good hand
Elmira	25	"		½	400 00	Sickly
Eliza Ann	18	"	"		500 00	good hand
Nanny	16	"	"		500 00	good hand
Long Mariah	45	"		½	200 00	not much account
Tena	40	"	"		400 00	well disposed fair hand
Eliza	20	"	"		400 00	fair hand
Amy	35	"	"		400 00	fair hand

A List of Women their ages & value

Names	Ages		Full Hands	Half Hands	Value	Remarks
Jennette	35	"	"		400 00	verry good cook
Peggy	30	"	"		500 00	good hand
Fanny	18	"	"		500 00	good hand
Nancy	16	"	"		500 00	good hand
Harriet (Black)	25	"	"		500 00	good hand
Olive	20	"	"		500 00	good hand
Hager	50	"		½	200 00	excells in telling lies
Angelina	30	"	"		400 00	verry good hand
Mariah (Cook)	40		"		300 00	all mouth. plantation cook
Polly	40		"		300 00	verry Bad woman (great temper)
Lucy	20		"		500 00	good hand
Martha	35		"		500 00	good hand
Lydia	25		"		400 00	good hand
Yellow Harriet	18			¼	100 00	verry little account sickly
Cathrine	20		"		400 00	fair hand
Penelopy	60			½	200 00	Plantation Nurse
Mary Jose	55			½	100 00	wash woman, no account
Little Mary	14	"		½	400 00	good Girl
Dina	40	"	"		400 00	Hospital nurse. fair
Julia	20	"	"		400 00	fair hand
Vina	30	"		½	200 00	Sickly
Tamor	30	"	"		400 00	fair hand
Matilda	16	"	"		500 00	good hand
Rose	10 [Years]			0	300 00	a great Liar (but will do)
Mary Creole	20	"	"		500 00	good hand
Hannah	45	"		½	300 00	mischief maker (all talk)
Terese	11	"		½	300 00	will Lie & Steal
Farma	30	"	"		500 00	good hand
Louisa (Doctors)	22	"	"		500 00	good hand
Araminta	22	"	"		500 00	good hand
Micky	5	"	0	0	150 00	well disposed
Eliza	7	"	0	0	250 00	great Liar (but will do)
Rebecca 6 mo	0	"	0	0	100 00	to young to Judge
Nancy (5 months)	0	"	0	0	100 00	" " " "
Rachael (3 months)	0	"	0	0	100 00	" " " "
Delphy 2 months	0	"	0	0	100 00	" " " "

Questions

1. Inventories have proven to be a valuable source of information for social historians. This inventory, for example, provides us with enough information to begin to construct a demographic profile of the slave community on Bruce's plantation. How

many men, women, and children were slaves? What was the percentage of each? What were the average ages of the male and female slaves? Based on your answers to these and other related questions, what tentative conclusions can you offer with regard to the profile of this particular slave community?

2. The inventory states that there were "92 Men & Boys & 44 Women & Children." Is there anything puzzling about this count? What might explain the apparent discrepancy between your count and that of the inventory-taker?

3. What was the average assessed "value" of a male slave? What was it for female slaves? How do you explain the difference? Why might "average" value be misleading? In addition to gender, what categories would you suggest for getting the most information possible out of this inventory?

12-6   Edmund Ruffin Defends Slavery (1853)

The American Revolution was a pivotal moment in the history of slavery. Before the onset of the imperial crisis, the institution existed largely unchallenged in every colony. After the War of Independence, slavery came increasingly under attack for being inconsistent with the professed ideals of the new republic. As the antislavery movement gained momentum in the North, however, proslavery forces mounted a spirited defense in the South. Beginning in the 1780s, these proslavery southerners marshaled a variety of arguments, some of them linked to the principles of the Revolution itself (see Document 6-15), to justify the perpetuation of the slave system. The intensification of sectional strife and the advent of Garrisonian abolitionism (see text pp. 351–354) in the antebellum years led many southerners to forge ever more impassioned defenses of the institution, and none did so with greater conviction than Edmund Ruffin (1794–1865). In the three decades prior to the Civil War, Ruffin emerged as a leader among militant secessionists in Virginia. When his home state did not immediately secede from the union following Abraham Lincoln's election in 1860, Ruffin chose to move to South Carolina. In April 1861, his adopted state gave him the "honor" of firing the first shot at Fort Sumter. In June 1865, barely two months after Robert E. Lee surrendered to Ulysses S. Grant at Appomattox Courthouse, Ruffin committed suicide.

Source: Excerpts from Paul Finkelman, *Defending Slavery: Proslavery Thought in the Old South: A Brief History with Documents* (Boston: Bedford/St. Martin's, 2003), 61–65, 67, 71.

Whether in savage or civilized life, the lower that individuals are degraded by poverty and want, and the fewer are their means for comfort, and the enjoyment of either intellectual or physical pleasures, or of relief from physical sufferings, the lower do they descend in their appreciation of actual and even natural wants; and the more do they magnify and dread the efforts and labors necessary to protect themselves against the occurrence of the privations and sufferings with which they are threatened. When man sinks so low as not to feel artificial wants, or utterly to despair of gratifying any such wants, he becomes brutishly careless and indolent, even in providing for natural and physical wants, upon which provision even life is dependent. All such persons soon learn to regard present and continuous labor as an evil greater than the probable but uncertain future occurrence of extreme privation, or even famine, and consequent death from want. . . . In all such cases—whether in civilized or in savage society, or whether in regard to individuals, families in successive generations, or to more extended communities—a good and proper remedy for this evil, if it could be applied, would be the enslaving of these reckless, wretched drones and cumberers of the earth, and thereby compelling them to habits of labor, and in return satisfying their wants for necessaries, and raising them and their progeny in the scale of humanity, not only physically, but morally and intellectually. Such a measure would be the most beneficial in young or rude communities, where labor is scarce and dear, and the means for subsistence easy to obtain. . . .

But the disposition to indulge indolence (even at great sacrifices of benefit which might be secured by industrious labor) is not peculiar to the lowest and most degraded classes of civilized communities. It is notorious that, whenever the demand for labor is much greater than the supply, or the wages of labor are much higher than the expenses of living, very many, even of the ordinary laboring class, are remarkable for indolence, and work no more than compelled by necessity. The greater the demand, and the higher the rewards, for labor, the less will be performed, as a general rule, by each individual laborer. If the wages of work for one day will support the laborer or mechanic and his family for three, it will be very likely that he will be idle two-thirds of his time.

Slave labor, in each individual case, and for each small measure of time, is more slow and inefficient than the labor of a free man. The latter knows that the more work he performs in a short time, the greater will be his reward in earnings. Hence, he has every inducement to exert himself while at work for himself, even though he may be idle for a longer time afterwards. The slave receives the same support, in food, clothing, and other allowances, whether he works much or little; and hence he has every inducement to spare himself as much as possible, and to do as little work as he can, without drawing on himself punishment, which is the only incentive to slave labor. It is, then, an unquestionable general truth, that the labor of a free man, for any stated time, is more than the labor of a slave, and if at the same cost, would be cheaper to the employer. Hence it has been inferred, and asserted by all who argue against slavery, and is often admitted even by those who would defend its expediency, that, as a general rule, and for whole communities, free labor is cheaper than slave labor. The rule is false, and the exceptions only are true. Suppose it admitted that the labor of slaves, for each hour or day, will amount to but two-thirds of what hired free laborers would perform in the same time. But the slave labor is continuous, and every day at least it returns to the employers and to the community, this two-thirds of full labor. Free laborers, if to be hired for the like duties, would require at least double the amount of wages to perform one-third more labor in each day, and in general, would be idle and earning nothing, more length of time than that spent in labor. Then, on these premises and suppositions, it is manifest that slave labor, with its admitted defect in this respect, will be cheapest and most profitable to the employer, and to the whole community, and will yield more towards the general increase of production and public wealth; and that the free laborer who is idle two days out of three, even if receiving double wages for his days of labor, is less laborious, and less productive for himself, and for the community, and the public wealth, than the slave. . . .

But in every country, when covered by a dense population, and when subsistence to free laborers becomes difficult to be obtained, the competition for employment will tend to depress the price of labor, gradually, to the lowest rate at which a bare subsistence can be purchased. The indolence natural to man, and especially in his lowest and most degraded state, can then no longer be indulged; because to be idle would not be to suffer privation only, and to incur risks of greater suffering, but absolutely and speedily to starve and die of want. If domestic slavery could have continued to exist so long, the slaves then would be in a very much better condition than the free laborers, because possessing assured means for support, and that for much less labor and hardship. For sharp want, hunger and cold, are more effective incentives to labor than the slaveowner's whip, even if its use is not restrained by any feeling of justice or mercy. But under such conditions of free labor, domestic or individual slavery could not exist. For whenever want and competition shall reduce the wages of free labor below the cost of slave labor, then it will be more profitable for the slaveowner and employer to hire free labor (both cheapened and driven by hunger and misery) than to maintain slaves, and compel their labor less effectually and at greater expense. Under such conditions, slaves (if they could not be sold and removed to some other country, where needed) would be readily emancipated by masters to whom they had become burdensome. Soon, under the operating influence of self-interest alone on the master class, domestic slavery would come to an end of itself—give place to the far more stringent and oppressive rule of want, as a compeller of labor, and be substituted by class-slavery, or the absolute subjection of the whole class of laborers to the whole class of employers—or of labor to capital. . . .

So long as domestic slavery in general in any country, and for the most part supplies the labor of the country, there is no possibility of the occurrence of the sufferings of the laboring class, such as were described above. There, the evils which are caused by extreme want and destitution, the competition for sustenance, class slavery of labor to capital, and lastly pauper slavery, are all the incidents and necessary results of free society, and "free labor." Before such evils can visit any laboring class of personal slaves, they must have first been emancipated, and personal slavery abolished. This abolition of slavery is indeed like to occur in every country in the progress of society, and where the increasing population has no sufficient and advantageous outlet. But so long as domestic slavery remains, and is the main supply of labor, among any civilized people, it is a certain indication, and the most unquestionable evidence, that extensive and long continued suffering from want or hunger have as yet had no existence in that country. The first great effect of such distress will be to reduce (by competition) the wages of free labor below the cost of maintaining slaves—and this effect would next cause the extinction of slavery, by the mode of sale and exportation, or otherwise the emancipation of all the slaves. After this step has been made, of course, in due time, the want and suffering, which are the necessary incidents and consequences of free society, are to be expected to follow in after times.

Questions

1. Compare Ruffin's defense of slavery with Orestes A. Brownson's critique of free labor (Document 9-8). Did they share the same assumptions? Would Ruffin have agreed with Brownson's assessment?

2. What are the shortcomings of Ruffin's analysis of strengths and weaknesses of slave and free labor?

3. Ruffin suggested that slavery would end once the wages paid to free laborers fell below the costs of maintaining slaves. What's wrong with his reasoning?

Questions for Further Thought

1. How did the cessation of slave imports in 1808 affect the lives of slaves already in the United States? Comparatively speaking, were their lives improved? If so, in what ways? If not, why not?

2. "I felt indifferent to my fate," Charles Ball said of his sale to a slave trader in 1805. How might his reaction be explained? How did the slaves William Chambers saw for sale in Richmond respond to their situation? How might you explain their responses?

3. What evidence is there in Charles Ball's narrative, Leonard Covington's letters, and Frederick Law Olmsted's observations that slave owners other than James Coles Bruce considered "disposition" when assessing the "value" of individual slaves?

The African American World

Slaves developed a life and culture of their own in the slave quarters away from the purview of their masters and overseers (see text pp. 378–387). An essential component of this way of life was a distinctive brand of worship that combined evangelical Protestantism and African influences (see text pp. 378–380). Equally important were slave marriages, which while not legally sanctioned were almost universally acknowledged to exist. The families resulting from these unions afforded slave parents a semblance of normality in everyday life; however, family units were always in danger of being broken up through sales (Document 12-7). The demands of the plantation labor system also placed some mothers and their children in situations of extreme jeopardy (Document 12-8).

Although the defenders of slavery frequently pointed to its advantages over alternative forms of "wage slavery" (see Document 11-8), they could not afford to be sanguine. Organized slave insurrections of the sort initiated by Nat Turner (Document 12-9) were few in number, but instances of individual resistance were commonplace occurrences. Even masters who routinely ordered the "whipping [of] one or more slaves at least once a day," as John Thompson observed of George Thomas, knew that some slaves, like Ben, were off limits when it came to "meddling" (Document 12-10). And Ben was not alone in refusing to be subdued by cruelty. The circumstances involved in Solomon Northup's resistance were different (Document 12-11), but he and Ben shared a common humanity in the face of inhumane treatment.

12-7   Memories of a Slave Childhood

Despite southern claims that slaves were happy and treated well, the evidence is overwhelming that those in bondage resented their condition and fought back whenever and however they could. Slave owners recognized this, and in order to keep their slaves in line often resorted to harsh disciplinary measures or sold slaves who were difficult to handle to planters west of the Mississippi.

The following excerpt displays not only the anger felt by slaves over their treatment but also the subtle interplay that took place among slaves as well as between slave and master. The source is an oral history interview from the 1930s with an elderly woman who had spent her youth as a slave.

Source: Reprinted with permission of Scribner, an imprint of Simon & Schuster Adult Publishing Group, from Gerda Lerner, ed., *The Female Experience: An American Documentary* (Indianapolis: Bobbs-Merrill, 1977), 11–14. Copyright © 1977 by Gerda Lerner. All rights reserved.

[The] overseer . . . went to my father one morning and said, "Bob, I'm gonna whip you this morning." Daddy said, "I ain't done nothing," and he said, "I know it, I'm gonna whip you to keep you from doing nothing," and he hit him with that cowhide—you know it would cut the blood out of you with every lick if they hit you hard—and daddy was chopping cotton, so he just took up his hoe and chopped right down on that man's head and knocked his brains out. Yes'm, it killed him, but they didn't put colored folks in jail them, so when old Charlie Merrill, the nigger trader, come along they sold my daddy to him, and he carried him way down in Mississippi. Ole Merrill would buy all the time, buy and sell niggers just like hogs. They sold him Aunt Phoebe's little baby that was just toddling long, and Uncle Dick—that was my mammy's brother.

The way they would whip you was like they done my oldest sister. They tied her, and they had a place just like they're gonna barbecue a hog, and they would strip you and tie you and lay you down. . . . Old Aunt Fanny had told marster that my sister wouldn't keep her dress clean, and that's what they was whipping her 'bout. So they had her down in the cellar whipping her, and I was real little. I couldn't say "Big Sis," but I went and told Mammy. "Old Marster's got 'Big Jim' down there in the cellar beating her," and mammy got out of bed and went in there and throwed Aunt Fan out the kitchen door, and they had to stop whipping Big Sis and come and see about Aunt Fan. You see, she would tell things on the others, trying to keep from getting whipped herself. I seed mistress crack her many a time over the head with a broom, and I'd be so scared she was gonna crack me, but she never did hit me, 'cept slap me when I'd turn the babies over. I'd get tired and make like I was sleep, and would ease the cradle over and throw the baby out. I never would throw mammy's out, though. Old Miss would be setting there just knitting and watching the babies; they had a horn and every woman could tell when it was time to come and nurse her baby by the way they would blow the horn. The white folks was crazy 'bout their nigger babies, 'cause that's where they got their profit. . . . When I'd get tired, I would just ease that baby over and Mistress would slap me so hard; I didn't know a hand could hurt so bad, but I'd take the slap and get to go out to play. She would slap me hard and say, "Git on out of here and stay till you wake up," and that was just what I wanted, 'cause I'd play then. . . .

Questions

1. Why do you think Bob wasn't prosecuted for murdering the overseer?

2. Do you think that slaves normally stood up to their masters the way that Bob did? Why or why not?

3. Why would whites take such a great interest in slave babies?

12-8   The Plight of Female Slaves (1839)

Frances Anne Kemble

Frances Anne Kemble (1809–1893), a famous English actress, came to the United States on tour in 1832 and married Pierce Butler, an American, in Philadelphia in 1834. A woman of decidedly antislavery convictions, she was disturbed to find out after her marriage that her husband was the absentee proprietor of two Georgia plantations and a slave owner. In 1838 Butler's plantation overseers resigned, and he was forced to return to Georgia with Kemble and their two daughters. Thrust into the world of planter aristocrats and slaves, Kemble recorded her condemnation of the slave labor system in a journal that took the form of a series of letters, never mailed, to a friend in Massachusetts. In the following excerpt, she describes the havoc that slavery, and the backbreaking work of the plantation, wreaked on slave mothers.

Source: Excerpt from Frances Anne Kemble, "Women in Slavery, 1839" from *Journal of a Residence on a Georgia Plantation in 1838–1839*, John A. Scott, ed. Copyright © 1961 by Alfred A. Knopf, Inc. Used by permission of Alfred A. Knopf, a division of Random House, Inc.

Yesterday evening I had a visit that made me very sorrowful, if anything connected with these poor people can be called more especially sorrowful than their whole condition; but Mr. [Butler]'s declaration, that he will receive no more statements of grievances or petitions for redress through me, makes me as desirous now of shunning the vain appeals of these unfortunates as I used to be of receiving and listening to them. The imploring cry: "Oh missis!" that greets me whichever way I turn, makes me long to stop my ears now; for what can I say or do any more for them? The poor little favors—the rice, the sugar, the flannel—that they beg for with such eagerness, and receive with such exuberant gratitude, I can, it is true, supply, and words and looks of pity, and counsel of patience, and such instruction in womanly habits of decency and cleanliness as may enable them to better, in some degree, their own hard lot; but to the entreaty: "Oh, missis, you speak to massa for us! Oh, missis, you beg massa for us! Oh, missis, you tell massa for we, he sure do as you say!" I cannot now answer as formerly, and I turn away choking and with eyes full of tears from the poor creatures, not even daring to promise any more the faithful transmission of their prayers.

The women who visited me yesterday evening were all in the family way, and came to entreat of me to have the sentence (what else can I call it?) modified which condemns them to resume their labor of hoeing in the fields three weeks after their confinement [meaning three weeks after they give birth]. They knew, of course, that I cannot interfere with their appointed labor, and therefore their sole entreaty was that I would use my influence with Mr. [Butler] to obtain for them a month's respite from labor in the field after childbearing. Their principal spokeswoman, a woman with a bright sweet face, called Mary, and a very sweet voice, which is by no means an uncommon excellence among them, appealed to my own experience; and while she spoke of my babies, and my carefully tended, delicately nursed, and tenderly watched confinement and convalescence, and implored me to have a kind of labor given to them less exhausting during the month after their confinement, I held the table before me so hard in order not to cry that I think my fingers ought to have left a mark on it. At length I told them that Mr. [Butler] had forbidden me to bring him any more complaints from

them, for that he thought the ease with which I received and believed their stories only tended to make them discontented, and that, therefore, I feared I could not promise to take their petitions to him; but that he would be coming down to "the Point" soon, and that they had better come then sometime when I was with him, and say what they had just been saying to me; and with this, and various small bounties, I was forced, with a heavy heart, to dismiss them; and when they were gone, with many exclamations of: "Oh yes, missis, you will, you will speak to massa for we; God bless you, missis, we sure you will!" I had my cry out for them, for myself, for *us.* All these women had had large families, and *all* of them had lost half their children, and several of them had lost more. How I do ponder upon the strange fate which has brought me here, from so far away, from surroundings so curiously different—how my own people in that blessed England of my birth would marvel if they could suddenly have a vision of me as I sit here, and how sorry some of them would be for me! . . .

Before closing this letter, I have a mind to transcribe to you the entries for today recorded in a sort of daybook, where I put down very succinctly the number of people who visit me, their petitions and ailments, and also such special particulars concerning them as seem to me worth recording. You will see how miserable the physical condition of many of these poor creatures is; and their physical condition, it is insisted by those who uphold this evil system, is the only part of it which is prosperous, happy, and compares well with that of Northern laborers. Judge from the details I now send you; and never forget, while reading them, that the people on this plantation are well off, and consider themselves well off, in comparison with the slaves on some of the neighboring estates.

Fanny has had six children; all dead but one. She came to beg to have her work in the field lightened.

Nanny has had three children; two of them are dead. She came to implore that the rule of sending them into the field three weeks after their confinement might be altered.

Leah, Caesar's wife, has had six children; three are dead.

Sophy, Lewis's wife, came to beg for some old linen. She is suffering fearfully; has had ten children; five of them are dead. The principal favor she asked was a piece of meat, which I gave her.

Sally, Scipio's wife, has had two miscarriages and three children born, one of whom is dead. She came complaining of incessant pain and weakness in her back. This woman was a mulatto daughter of a slave called Sophy, by a white man of the name of Walker, who visited the plantation.

Charlotte, Renty's wife, had had two miscarriages, and was with child again. She was almost crippled with rheumatism, and showed me a pair of poor swollen knees that made my heart ache. I have promised her a pair of flannel trousers, which I must forthwith set about making.

Sarah, Stephen's wife; this woman's case and history were alike deplorable. She had had four miscarriages, and brought seven children into the world, five of whom were dead, and was again with child. She complained of dreadful pains in the back, and an internal tumor which swells with the exertion of working in the fields; probably, I think, she is ruptured. She told me she had once been mad and had run into the woods, where she contrived to elude discovery for some time, but was at last tracked and brought back, when she was tied up by the arms, and heavy logs fastened to her feet, and was severely flogged. After this she contrived to escape again, and lived for some time skulking in the woods, and she supposes mad, for when she was taken again she was entirely naked. She subsequently recovered from this derangement, and seems now just like all the other poor creatures who come to me for help and pity. I suppose her constant childbearing and hard labor in the fields at the same time may have produced the temporary insanity.

Sukey, Bush's wife, only came to pay her respects. She had had four miscarriages; had brought eleven children into the world, five of whom are dead.

Molly, Quambo's wife, also only came to see me. Hers was the best account I have yet received; she had had nine children, and six of them were still alive.

This is only the entry for today, in my diary, of the people's complaints and visits. Can you conceive a more wretched picture than that which it exhibits of the conditions under which these women live? . . . Even the poor wretch who told that miserable story of insanity . . . did so in a sort of low, plaintive, monotonous murmur of misery, as if such sufferings were "all in the day's work."

I ask these questions about their children because I think the number they bear as compared with the number they rear a fair gauge of the effect of the system on their own health and that of their offspring. There was hardly one of these women, as you will see by the details I have noted of their ailments, who might not have been a candidate for a bed in a hospital, and they had come to me after working all day in the fields.

Questions

1. Why did Kemble describe the poor physical condition of the slave women in such great detail?

2. Compare the ordeal of the female slaves to the experiences of female factory workers described in Document 9-2. Were the slave women better or worse off than the factory workers?

3. In what ways did the slave labor system, as represented in this selection, contradict the republican ideals of an agrarian society?

12-9   Religion in the Quarters (1832)

Nat Turner

Among the major influences shaping the culture of American slaves in the early nineteenth century was their widespread adoption of evangelical Protestant Christianity. Christianity, as the "masters' religion," had made little headway among slaves before evangelical preachers such as the Reverend James Ireland (Document 4-8) began making special appeals to them. The demonstrative conversion experiences characteristic of camp meetings such as that at Cane Ridge (Document 8-11) resembled in some ways African beliefs in spirit possession. More important, though, evangelicals preached the equality of all human beings before God and declared that social status counted for nothing in the scales of salvation. To be sure, white evangelicals drew back quickly from the more radical implications of this stance, but the slaves took it to heart and created their own distinctive brand of Christianity—a faith that has lain at the core of the African American cultural experience ever since. To some degree it helped slaves accommodate to their situation by counseling patience until the Lord should call his children out of Egypt. But what would happen if God in fact called? In that case, slave religion could take the faithful in unexpected directions—as it did with Nat Turner, who in 1831 led the greatest slave rebellion of the antebellum era (text pp. 350–351). The following is his own account, dictated in his jail cell.

Source: From Kenneth S. Greenberg, ed., *The Confessions of Nat Turner and Related Documents* (Boston: Bedford/St. Martin's, 1996), 44–48.

Agreeable to his own appointment, on the evening he was committed to prison, with permission of the jailer, I visited NAT on Tuesday the 1st November, when, without being questioned at all, he commenced his narrative in the following words:—

Sir,—You have asked me to give a history of the motives which induced me to undertake the late insurrection, as you call it—To do so I must go back to the days of my infancy, and even before I was born. I was thirty-one years of age the 2d of October last, and born the property of Benj. Turner, of this county. In my childhood a circumstance occurred which made an indelible impression on my mind, and laid the ground work of that enthusiasm, which has terminated so fatally to many, both white and black, and for which I am about to atone at the gallows. It is here necessary to relate this circumstance—trifling as it may seem, it was the commencement of that belief which has grown with time, and even now, sir, in this dungeon, helpless and forsaken as I am, I cannot divest myself of. Being at play with other children, when three or four years old, I was telling them something, which my mother overhearing, said it had happened before I was born—I stuck to my story, however, and related somethings which went, in her opinion, to confirm it—others being called on were greatly astonished, knowing that these things had happened, and caused them to say in my hearing, I surely would be a prophet, as the Lord had shewn me things that had happened before my birth. And my father and mother strengthened me in this my first impression, saying in my presence, I was intended for some great purpose, which they had always thought from certain marks on my head and breast—[a parcel of excrescences which I believe are not at all uncommon, particularly among negroes, as I have seen several with the same. In this case he has either cut them off or they have nearly disappeared]—My grandmother, who was very religious, and to whom I was much attached—my master, who belonged to the church, and other religious persons who visited the house, and whom I often saw at prayers, noticing the singularity of my manners, I suppose, and my uncommon intelligence for a child, remarked I had too much sense to be raised, and if I was, I would never be of any service to any one as a slave—To a mind like mine, restless, inquisitive and observant of every thing that was passing, it is easy to suppose that religion was the subject to which it would be directed, and although this subject principally occupied my thoughts—there was nothing that I saw or heard of to which my attention was not directed—The manner in which I learned to read and write, not only had great influence on my own mind, as I acquired it with the most perfect ease, so much so, that I have no recollection whatever of learning the alphabet—but to the astonishment of the family, one day, when a book was shewn me to keep me from crying, I began spelling the names of different objects—this was a source of wonder to all in the neighborhood, particularly the blacks—and this learning was constantly improved at all opportunities—when I got large enough to go to work, while employed, I was reflecting on many things that would present themselves to my imagination, and whenever an opportunity occurred of looking at a book, when the school children were getting their lessons, I would find many things that the fertility of my imagination had depicted to me before; all my time, not devoted to my master's service, was spent either in prayer, or in making experiments in casting different things in moulds made of earth, in attempting to make paper, gunpowder, and many other experiments, that although I could not perfect, yet convinced me of its practicability if I had the means. I was not addicted to stealing in my youth, nor have ever been—Yet such was the confidence of the negroes in the neighborhood, even at this early period of my life, in my superior judgment, that they would often carry me with them when they were going on any roguery, to plan for them. Growing up among them, with this confidence in my superior judgment, and when this, in their opinions, was perfected by Divine inspiration, from the circumstances already alluded to in my infancy, and which belief was ever afterwards zealously inculcated by the austerity of my life and manners, which became the subject of remark by white and black.—Having soon discovered to be great, I must appear so, and therefore studiously avoided mixing in with society, and wrapped myself in mystery, devoting my time to fasting and prayer—By this time, having arrived to man's estate, and hearing the scriptures commented on at meetings, I was struck with that particular passage which says: "Seek ye the kingdom of Heaven and all things shall be added unto you." I reflected much on this passage, and prayed daily for light on this subject—As I was praying one day at my plough, the spirit spoke to me, saying "Seek ye the kingdom of Heaven and all things shall be added unto you.["] *Question*—what do you mean by the Spirit. *Ans.* The Spirit that spoke to that prophets in former days—and I was greatly astonished, and for two years prayed continually, whenever my duty would permit—and then again I had the same revelation, which fully confirmed me in the impression that I was ordained for some great purpose in the hands of the Almighty. Several years rolled round, in which many events occurred to strengthen me in this my belief. At this time I reverted in my mind to the remarks made of me in my childhood, and the things that had been shewn me—and as it had been said of me in my childhood by those by whom I had been taught to pray, both white and black, and in whom I had the greatest confidence, that I had too much sense to be raised, and if I was, I would never be of use to any one as a slave. Now finding I had arrived to man's estate, and was a slave, and these revelations being made known to me, I began to direct my attention to this great object, to fulfil the purpose for which, by this time, I felt assured I was intended. Knowing the influence I had obtained over the minds of my fellow servants, (not by the means of conjuring and such like tricks—for to them I always spoke of such things with contempt) but by the communion of the Spirit whose revelations I often communicated to them, and they believed and said my wisdom came from God. I now began to prepare them for my purpose, by telling them something was about to happen that would terminate in fulfilling the great promise that had been made to me—About this time I was placed under an overseer, from whom I ran away—and after remaining in the woods thirty days, I returned, to the astonishment of the negroes on the plantation, who thought I had made my escape to some other part of the country, as my father had done before. But the reason of my return was, that the Spirit appeared to me and said I had my wishes directed to the things of this world, and not to the kingdom of Heaven, and that I should return to the service of my earthly master—"For he who knoweth his Master's will, and doeth it not, shall be beaten with many stripes, and thus have I chastened you." And the negroes found fault, and murmured against me, saying that if they had my sense they would not serve any master in the world. And about this time I had a vision—and I saw white spirits and black spirits engaged in battle, and the sun was darkened—the thunder rolled in the Heavens, and blood flowed in streams—and I heard a voice saying, "Such is your luck, such you are called to see, and let it come rough or smooth, you must surely bare it." I now withdrew myself as much as my situation would permit, from the intercourse of my fellow servants, for the avowed purpose of serving the Spirit more fully—and it appeared to me, and reminded me of the things it had already shown me, and that it would then reveal to me the knowledge of the elements, the revolution of the planets, the operation of tides, and changes of the seasons. After this revelation in the year 1825, and the knowledge of the elements being made known to me, I sought more than ever to obtain true holiness before the great day of judgment should appear, and then I began to receive the true knowledge of faith. And from the first steps of righteousness until the last, was I made perfect; and the Holy Ghost was with me, and said, "Behold me as I stand in the Heavens"—and I looked and saw the forms of men in different attitudes—and there were lights in the sky to which the children of darkness gave other names than what they really were—for they were the lights of the Saviour's hands, stretched forth from east to west, even as they were extended on the cross on Calvary for the redemption of sinners. And I wondered greatly at these miracles, and prayed to be informed of a certainty of the meaning thereof—and shortly afterwards, while laboring in the field, I discovered drops of blood on the corn as though it were dew from heaven—and I communicated it to many, both white and black, in the neighborhood—and I then found on the leaves in the woods hieroglyphic characters, and numbers, with the forms of men in different attitudes, portrayed in blood, and representing the figures I had seen before in the heavens. And now the Holy Ghost had revealed itself to me, and made plain the miracles it had shown me—For as the blood of Christ had been shed on this earth, and had ascended to heaven for the salvation of sinners, and was now returning to earth again in the form of dew—and as the leaves on the trees bore the impression of the figures I had seen in the heavens, it was plain to me that the Saviour was about to lay down the yoke he had borne for the sins of men, and the great day of judgment was at hand. About this time I told these things to a white man, (Etheldred T. Brantley) on whom it had a wonderful effect—and he ceased from his wickedness, and was attacked immediately with a cutaneous eruption, and blood oozed from the pores of his skin, and after praying and fasting nine days, he was healed, and the Spirit appeared to me again, and said, as the Saviour had been baptized so should we be also—and when the white people would not let us be baptised by the church, we went down into the water together, in the sight of many who reviled us, and were baptised by the Spirit—After this I rejoiced greatly, and gave thanks to God. And on the 12th of May, 1828, I heard a loud noise in the heavens, and the Spirit instantly appeared to me and said the Serpent was loosened, and Christ had laid down the yoke he had borne for the sins of men, and that I should take it on and fight against the Serpent, for the time was fast approaching when the first should be last and the last should be first. *Ques.* Do you not find yourself mistaken now? *Ans.* Was not Christ crucified. And by signs in the heavens that it would make known to me when I should commence the great work—and until the first sign appeared, I should conceal it from the knowledge of men—And on the appearance of the sign, (the eclipse of the sun last February) I should arise and prepare myself, and slay my enemies with their own weapons. And immediately on the sign appearing in the heavens, the seal was removed from my lips, and I communicated the great work laid out for me to do, to four in whom I had the greatest confidence. (Henry, Hark, Nelson, and Sam)—It was intended by us to have begun the work of death on the 4th July last—Many were the plans formed and rejected by us, and it affected my mind to such a degree, that I fell sick, and the time passed without our coming to any determination how to commence—Still forming new schemes and rejecting them, when the sign appeared again, which determined me not to wait longer.

Questions

1. What attracted Nat Turner to the "calling" of a slave preacher?

2. What can you deduce from this passage about the relationship of Turner and his fellow slave Christians to the whites around them?

3. In what ways did Turner compare himself to Jesus Christ?

12-10   A Slave Named Ben (c. 1826)

John Thompson

Most of what is known about John Thompson comes from his autobiographical *Life of John Thompson, A Fugitive Slave*, which was first published in Massachusetts in 1856. Born on a large Maryland plantation around 1808, he endured the barbarities of the slave system for at least twenty years before escaping to freedom sometime prior to 1831. Thompson's narrative is filled with stark descriptions of whippings, slave auctions, forced separations, abandonment, hypocrisy, broken promises and betrayals, and murder. But his was not simply a story of victimization. Thompson and his fellow slaves were never merely passive objects acted upon by cruel masters and oppressive overseers. Some refused to work at the pace set by their overseers, others secretly fed runaways at night, and many attended Methodist revivals against the express wishes of their masters (see text pp. 378–380). Thompson himself surreptitiously learned to read and write, forged travel passes for runaways, and refused to be whipped. His daring escape, which included his joining the crew of a whaling vessel in order to elude his pursuers, was only the final episode of resistance recounted in the *Life*. Ben was the slave of George Thomas, whom Thompson described as "inhuman" and given to the "practice of whipping one or more slaves at least once a day"; the incident related below occurred when Thompson was about eighteen years old.

Source: Excerpt from Chapter 12 in *African American Slave Narratives: An Anthology*, ed. Sterling Lecater Bland Jr. (Westport, CT: Greenwood Press, 2001), 3:634–635. Copyrigth © 2001 by Sterling Lecater Bland Jr. Reproduced with permission of the publisher.

On the plantation was a slave named Ben, who was highly prized by Mr. T., being, as he thought, the best and most faithful servant on the farm. Ben was a resolute and brave man, and did not fear death. Such courage did not suit the overseer, who wanted each slave to temble with fear when he addressed him. Ben was too high-minded for such humiliation before any insignificant overseer. He had philosophically concluded that death is but death any way, and that one might as well die by hanging as whipping; so he resolved not to submit to be whipped by the overseer.

One day in the month of November, when the slaves were in the field gathering corn, which Ben was carting to the barn, the overseer thought he did not drive his oxen fast enough. As soon then as Ben came within hearing of his voice, while returning from the barn, where he had just discharged his load, to the field, the overseer bellowed to him to drive faster. With this order Ben attempted to comply, by urging his beasts to their utmost speed. But all was of no avail. As soon as they met, the overseer struck Ben upon the head with the butt of his whip, felling him to the ground. But before he could repeat the blow, Ben sprang from the ground, seized his antagonist by the throat with one hand, while he felled him to the ground with the other; then jumping upon his breast, he commenced choking and beating him at the same time, until he had nearly killed him. In fact he probably would have killed his enemy, had not two of the slaves hastened to his rescue, which they with difficulty accomplished, so firm and determined was Ben's hold of him. For a while the discomfited man was senseless, his face became of the blackness of his hat, while the blood streamed down his face.

When he had recovered his senses, and was able to walk, he started for the house, to relate this sad circumstance to Mr. Thomas. Ben loaded his cart and followed after. No sooner had he entered the barn, than his master sprang forward to seize him; but Ben eluded his grasp and fled to the woods, where he remained about three weeks, when he returned to his work.

No allusion was made to the circumstance for about five weeks, and Ben supposed all was past and forgotten. At length a rainy time came on, during which the hands could neither labor in the field nor elsewhere out of doors, but were forced to work in the corn-house, shelling the corn.

While all were thus busily employed, the doors closed, there entered five strong white men, besides our master, armed with pistols, swords, and clubs. What a shocking sight! thus to take one poor unarmed negro, these men must be employed, and the county aroused to action.

Ben was soon bound in hemp enough, comparatively speaking, to rig a small vessel. Thus bound, he was led to the place of torture, where he was whipped until his entrails could be seen moving within his body. Poor Ben! his crime, according to the laws of Maryland, was punishable with death; a penalty far more merciful than the one he received.

The manner of whipping on Mr. Thomas's plantation, was to bind the victim fast, hands, body and feet, around a hogshead or cask, so that he was unable to move. After Ben was thus flogged, he said, "I wish I had killed the overseer, then I should have been hung and an end put to my pain. If I have to do the like again, I will kill him and be hung at once!"

Ben was, for five weeks, unable to walk, or sit, or lie down. He could only rest upon his knees and elbows, and his wounds became so offensive, that no person could long remain in his presence. He crawled about upon his hands and knees, gritting his teeth with pain and vengeance, and often exclaiming, "How I wish I had taken his life!"

After this, Mr. Thomas forbade his overseers meddling with Ben, telling them that he would kill them if they did; also, that he was a good hand, and needed no driving. When Ben got well, Mr. Thomas knowing his disposition, was afraid to go near or speak to him; consequently, he was sent to a distant part of the farm to work by himself, nor was he ever again struck by master or overseer.

Ben was a brave fellow, nor did this flogging lessen his bravery in the least. Nor is Ben the only brave slave at the South; there are many there who would rather be shot than whipped by any man.

Questions

1. Historians have argued that force alone could not have sustained the slave system; the interaction between masters and slaves was of necessity a "negotiated" relationship. Was the relationship between Ben and George Thomas "negotiated"?

2. Compare Frederick Law Olmsted's description of discipline on a Mississippi plantation (Document 12-4) with Thompson's account. What are the similarities and dissimilarities? What conclusions might be drawn about the slave system in general?

3. What are the advantages and disadvantages of using autobiographies as a source of historical information?

12-11   The Enslavement of Solomon Northup (1841)

Solomon Northup, a free person of color, lived peacefully with his wife in upstate New York. A musician of local prominence, Northup supported himself in part by playing the violin at dances and parties. In 1841 he took the word of two strangers that they would find work for him in a traveling circus. Lured by the money they offered and undoubtedly by a desire for adventure, Northup accompanied his new friends to New York and then to Washington, D.C., a center of the interstate slave trade. Evidently drugged, Northup awoke to find himself the slave of James H. Birch, Washington's leading slave trader. Birch sold Northup to a New Orleans slave trader, who in turn sold him to a planter in the developing Red River district of Louisiana. For twelve years Northup lived and labored as a slave in Louisiana. Finally, placing his trust in an itinerant white workingman (a native of Canada who had expressed hostility toward slavery), Northup managed to get a letter delivered to his former employers in New York, who secured his freedom in 1853. Following Northup's narrative of his enslavement is an advertisement placed in 1834 in the Washington, D.C., *Globe* by the slave trader Birch.

Source: Solomon Northup, *Twelve Years a Slave, Narrative of Solomon Northup, a Citizen of New-York, Kidnapped in Washington City in 1841, and Rescued in 1853, From a Cotton Plantation Near the Red River, in Louisiana* (Auburn, NY: Derby and Miller, 1853; reprint, edited by Sue Eakin and Joseph Logsdon, Baton Rouge: Louisiana State University Press, 1968), 12–26. Advertisement "Cash for Negroes," appeared in *The Globe* (Washington, DC), June 10, 1834.

One morning, towards the latter part of the month of March, 1841, having at that time no particular business to engage my attention, I was walking about the village of Saratoga Springs.... I was met by two gentlemen of respectable appearance ... introduced to me by some of my acquaintances ... with the remark that I was an expert player on the violin.... [T]hey immediately entered into conversation on that subject, making numerous inquiries touching my proficiency in that respect. My responses being to all appearances satisfactory, they proposed to engage my services for a short period, stating, at the same time, I was just such a person as their business required.... They were connected, as they informed me, with a circus company, then in the city of Washington; that they were on their way thither to rejoin it.... They also remarked that they had found much difficulty in procuring music for their entertainments, and that if I would accompany them as far as New-York, they would give me one dollar for each day's service, and three dollars in addition for every night I played at their performances, besides sufficient to pay the expenses of my return from New-York to Saratoga.

I at once accepted the tempting offer, both for the reward it promised, and from a desire to visit the metropolis. They were anxious to leave immediately.... [I]n due course ... we reached New-York [and] ... I supposed my journey was at an end.... [H]owever [they] began to importune me to continue with them to Washington.... They promised me a situation and high wages if I would accompany them.... I finally concluded to accept the offer.... All the way from New-York, their anxiety to reach the circus seemed to grow more and more intense. We ... proceeded to Washington, at which place we arrived just at nightfall, the evening previous to the funeral of [President] General Harrison....

My friends, several times during the [next] afternoon, entered drinking saloons, and called for liquor ... after serving themselves, they would pour out a glass and hand it to me.... Towards evening, and soon after partaking of one of these potations, I began to experience most unpleasant sensations.... I only remember, with any degree of distinctness that I was told it was necessary to go to a physician and procure medicine.... From that moment I was insensible. How long I remained in that condition—whether only that night, or many days and nights—I do not know; but when consciousness returned, I found myself alone, in utter darkness, and in chains.... A key rattled in the lock—a strong door swung back upon its hinges, admitting a flood of light, two men entered and stood before me. One of them was a large powerful man, forty years of age.... His name was James H.

Burch [Birch], as I learned afterwards—a well-known slave-dealer in Washington....

"Well, my boy, how do you feel now?" said Burch, as he entered through the open door. I replied that I was sick, and inquired the cause of my imprisonment. He answered that I was his slave—that he had bought me, and that he was about to send me to New-Orleans. I asserted, aloud and boldly, that I was a free man—a resident of Saratoga, where I had a wife and children, who were also free, and that my name was Northup.... He denied that I was free, and with an emphatic oath, declared that I came from Georgia. Again and again I asserted I was no man's slave.... With blasphemous oaths, he called me a black liar, a runaway from Georgia, and every other profane and vulgar epithet that the most indecent fancy could conceive.... Burch ordered the paddle and cat-o'-ninetails to be brought in....

As soon as these formidable whips appeared, I was seized by both of them and roughly divested of my clothing.... With the paddle, Burch commenced beating me.... When his unrelenting arm grew tired, he stopped and asked if I still insisted I was a free man, I did insist upon it, and then the blows were renewed.... When again tired, he would repeat the same question, and receiving the same answer, continued his cruel labor.... At length the paddle broke.... Casting madly on the floor the handle of the broken paddle, he seized the rope. This was far more painful than the other. I struggled with all my power, but it was in vain. I prayed for mercy, but my prayer was only answered with imprecations and with stripes. I thought I must die beneath the lashes of the accursed brute. Even now the flesh crawls upon my bones, as I recall the scene....

At last I became silent to his repeated questions. I would make no reply. In fact, I was becoming almost unable to speak. Still he plied the lash without stint upon my poor body, until it seemed that the lacerated flesh was stripped from my bones at every stroke.... He swore that he would either conquer or kill me.... I was left in darkness as before.

CASH FOR NEGROES.

We will pay the highest cash price for any number of likely Negroes, from 12 to 25 years of age. As we are at this time permanently settled in the market, we can at all times be found at Mr. Isaac Beers's Tavern, a few doors below Lloyd's Tavern, opposite to the Centre Market, in Washington, D.C., or at Mr. McCandless's Tavern, corner of Bridge and High Street, Georgetown. Persons having servants to dispose of, will find it to their advantage to give us a call.

June 10—dw&swtf   BIRCH & JONES.

Questions

1. What does the kidnapping of Solomon Northup suggest about the profitability of the interstate slave trade?

2. What does the kidnapping of Northup suggest about the status of free blacks in slave territories? How could Northup have proved he was a free man?

3. Comment on the significance of coercion in the slave system as you consider what purpose Birch had in mind in committing this act of ruthless violence.

Questions for Further Thought

1. Some historians contend that slavery was essentially a "paternalistic" institution; others argue that it was fundamentally "capitalistic." Based on the information contained in documents 12-3, 12-5, 12-6, 12-7, and 12-8, how would you characterize slavery? Was it paternalistic or capitalistic?

2. Slave societies were not homogeneous because the institution of slavery varied with time and over space. What varieties of slave experiences are you able to identify in the documents in this section? What factors shaped the nature of these experiences?

3. Interaction between masters and slaves was never simply one-dimensional. Using documents 12-3, 12-8, 12-9, and 12-10, how would you characterize the master-slave relationship? What other relationships did slaves have? How did these affect their interaction with their masters?

CHAPTER THIRTEEN

The Crisis of the Union
1844–1860

Manifest Destiny: South and North

For a quarter century after the annexation of Florida in 1819, the boundaries of the United States remained the same. Although the extension of slavery into new territories had become a bone of contention between North and South in the Missouri Controversy of 1819–1821, the settlement of that crisis by the Missouri Compromise had been accepted by all. Moreover, with the rise of mass party politics, both major parties courted support from both sections and were therefore eager to keep slavery out of public debate.

But the land hunger of white North Americans continued unabated. To the southwest, American settlers had pressed beyond national borders into the newly independent nation of Mexico, where they came to dominate the northeastern province of Texas. When the Mexican central government attempted to bring the Americans under closer central rule, they rebelled and successfully established their independence. Their request for annexation to the United States, however, was initially rebuffed; Texas was a slave-holding republic, and Martin Van Buren was fearful that his party would split over the issue.

Texas was not the only territory attracting the attention of Americans, however. In the early 1840s large numbers of settlers began traveling overland to the Oregon Territory; to its south, California, with its fertile valleys and great harbors, attracted both settlers and strategic interest. Back East, the heady optimism resulting from explosive economic growth and American pride in the creation of a new society fed an expansionist ideology that took the label "Manifest Destiny" (Documents 13-1 and 13-2).

With sentiment for territorial expansion rising in both North and South, southern Democrats, fearing that an independent Texas might abandon slavery and pose a threat to the security of the institution, began a new push for annexation. Whigs and many northern Democrats were virulently opposed, but the Democratic Party's 1844 convention united the party behind an expansionist candidate, James K. Polk, and a promise to pursue expansion in both Texas and Oregon. Although the antislavery Liberty Party complicated the election, Democrats took their victory as an endorsement of vigorous pursuit of what they deemed America's Manifest Destiny.

13-1 Texas, California, and Manifest Destiny (1845)

John L. O'Sullivan

John L. O'Sullivan (1813–1895) came from a line of Irish-American adventurers, and he carried his family's love of grand gestures into journalism, politics, and diplomacy. In 1837, at the age of twenty-three, O'Sullivan, a lawyer and Democratic Party activist, founded *The United States Magazine and Democratic Review*, which he made into a mouthpiece for Democratic Party propaganda; a vehicle for his own expansive, romantic views on the future of American democracy; and an outlet for such emerging American writers as Emerson, Hawthorne, Thoreau, and Whitman. O'Sullivan was especially obsessed with the notion that the mission of the United States was to spread the gospel of democracy across the continent; it was he who coined the term *Manifest Destiny* (used for the first time in the following article) to justify American expansion (see text p. 396).

O'Sullivan later sought to practice what he preached; he became involved in efforts by private adventurers to seize Cuba and annex it to the United States, a project that ruined him financially and nearly threw him into prison. He later moved back to Europe, where he promoted the Confederate cause during the Civil War. He returned to the United States in the 1870s, broken by years spent promoting grand schemes; but his bumptious, continental vision of his country's promise fundamentally shaped the ways in which Americans understood their relationship to their neighbor countries and, later, the world.

Source: John L. O'Sullivan, "Annexation," *The United States Magazine and Democratic Review* 17 (July and August 1845): 5–10.

Why, were other reasoning wanting, in favor of now elevating this question of the reception of Texas into the Union, out of the lower region of our past party dissensions, up to its proper level of a high and broad nationality, it surely is to be found, found abundantly, in the manner in which other nations have undertaken to intrude themselves into it, between us and the proper parties to the case, in a spirit of hostile interference against us, for the avowed object of thwarting our policy and hampering our power, limiting our greatness and checking the fulfilment of our manifest destiny to overspread the continent allotted by Providence for the free development of our yearly multiplying millions. This we have seen done by England, our old rival and enemy. . . .

It is wholly untrue, and unjust to ourselves, the pretence that the Annexation has been a measure of spoliation, unrightful and unrighteous—of military conquest under forms of peace and law—of territorial aggrandizement at the expense of justice, and justice due by a double sanctity to the weak. . . . If Texas became peopled with an American population, it was by no contrivance of our government, but on the express invitation of that of Mexico herself; accompanied with such guaranties of State independence, and the maintenance of a federal system analogous to our own, as constituted a compact fully justifying the strongest measures of redress on the part of those afterwards deceived in this guaranty, and sought to be enslaved under the yoke imposed by its violation. She was released, rightfully and absolutely released, from all Mexican allegiance, or duty of cohesion to the Mexican political body, by the acts and fault of Mexico herself, and Mexico alone. There never was a clearer case. It was not revolution; it was resistance to revolution; and resistance under such circumstances as left independence the necessary resulting state, caused by the abandonment of those with whom her former federal association had existed. What then can be more preposterous than all this clamor by Mexico and the Mexican interest, against Annexation, as a violation of any rights of hers, any duties of ours? . . .

California will, probably, next fall away from the loose adhesion which, in such a country as Mexico, holds a remote province in a slight equivocal kind of dependence on the metropolis. Imbecile and distracted, Mexico never can exert any real governmental authority over such a country. The impotence of the one and the distance of the other, must make the relation one of virtual independence; unless, by stunting the province of all natural growth, and forbidding that immigration which can alone develope its capabilities and fulfil the purposes of its creation, tyranny may retain a military dominion which is no government in the legitimate sense of the term. In the case of California this is now impossible. The Anglo-Saxon foot is already on its borders. Already the advance guard of the irresistible army of Anglo-Saxon emigration has begun to pour down upon it, armed with the plough and the rifle, and marking its trail with schools and colleges, courts and representative halls, mills and meeting-houses. A population will soon be in actual occupation of California, over which it will be idle for Mexico to dream of dominion. They will necessarily become independent. All this without agency of our government, without responsibility of our people—in the natural flow of events, the spontaneous working of principles, and the adaptation of the tendencies and wants of the human race to the elemental circumstances in the midst of which they find themselves placed. And they will have a right to independence—to self-government—to the possession of the homes conquered from the wilderness by their own labors and dangers, sufferings and sacrifices—a better and a truer right than the artificial title of sovereignty in Mexico a thousand miles distant, inheriting from Spain a title good only against those who have none better. Their right to independence will be the natural right of self-government belonging to any community strong enough to maintain it—distinct in position, origin and character, and free from any mutual obligations of membership of a common political body, binding it to others by the duty of loyalty and compact of public faith. This will be their title to independence; and by this title, there can be no doubt that the population now fast streaming down upon California will both assert and maintain that independence. . . .

Away, then, with all idle French talk of *balances of power* on the American Continent. There is no growth in Spanish America! Whatever progress of population there may be in the British Canadas, is only for their own early severance of their present colonial relation to the little island three thousand miles across the Atlantic; soon to be followed by Annexation, and destined to swell the still accumulating momentum of our progress. And whosoever may hold the balance, though they should cast into the opposite scale all the bayonets and cannon, not only of France and England, but of Europe entire, how would it kick the beam against the simple solid weight of the two hundred and fifty, or three hundred millions—and American millions—destined to gather beneath the flutter of the stripes and stars, in the fast hastening year of the Lord 1945!

Questions

1. Explain what John L. O'Sullivan meant by the phrase "Manifest Destiny." By what right did O'Sullivan believe that the United States must annex Texas? Do you agree with his argument?

2. According to O'Sullivan, who was responsible for Texas's declaration of independence?

3. Why did O'Sullivan believe that California would "fall" next? For what reasons did he argue that California would inevitably declare its independence from Mexico? Why did O'Sullivan consider Mexico's title of sovereignty over California to be "artificial"?

13-2   The Importance of California (1845)

Thomas Oliver Larkin

Born in 1802, Thomas O. Larkin grew up in Lynn, Massachusetts, where his stepfather was a wealthy leather merchant. After failing at several enterprises in the East, Larkin in 1832 followed a relative to Monterey, California, where he became the leading merchant of that town, the capital of Mexico's northwestern state. Remote from central authority, its "Californio" inhabitants restive and sometimes rebellious, the region's natural wealth and strategic importance made it a center of intrigue among major powers as well as an attractive destination for American immigrants. In 1843 Larkin, who had never taken Mexican citizenship, became American consul. Eager to see California shake off Mexican rule, and fearful that it might become prey to British or French ambitions, he became an advocate of peaceful annexation, and in 1845 became a confidential agent of the U.S. government seeking to effect it. In the meantime, Larkin became the leading source of news about California to readers of the eastern press. If John L. O'Sullivan spoke romantically of "destiny," Larkin, the man in the field, spoke roughly and practically, as the following sample shows.

Source: From Thomas Oliver Larkin to *Journal of Commerce*, July 1845, in *The Larkin Papers: Personal, Business, and Official Correspondence of Thomas Oliver Larkin, Merchant and United States Consul in California,* ed. George P. Hammond (Berkeley and Los Angeles: University of California Press, 1952), 3:292–296. (*Note:* Spelling original to the document.) Reprinted with permission of Copyright Clearance Center.

California July 1845

By almost evry newspaper from the united States and many from England we find extracts and surmises respectng the sale of this country. One month England is the purchaser the next month the U. States. In the meantime the prorgress of California is onward, and would still be more so if Mexico would not send eviry few years a band of theivng soldiers and rapacous officers.

Should the supreme Governmet alow the Californias to rule there own Country they would have peace and prosperity. . . . We have now news that Mexico is fitting out an expedition of troops in Acapulco for Californa the expences to be paid by two or three English houses in Mexico who it is said are responsible for the pay for Eighteen months. . . .

The British Govermt have apponted one of her subjects (he formerly resided in N York where he owns property) Vice Consul of Californa with a salarey of 1000$ pr anum. This salay is small but as he can live on his own Rancho he has no expence in entertaining company Etc. nor does he attend to any distresed Eng seamen who may apply to him. In fact as he is much at his Country house they can not visit him unless under a heavy personal expence for horse hire.

The French Consul lives in Mont. with a Salery of over 4000$. There is not one E or French vessel dng business on this Coast nor has been for years. Ther Consul therefore have nothig to do *apparenty*. Why they are in Service there Govt best know and Uncle Sam will know to his cost.

The whole forign trade of C. in the hands of Amricans. There is now Sevn Boston Ships & Barks hire. The Am Consul has a jurisdictin of 1000 miles of Sea Coast, while the nature of the trade is such that he has barely any fees. Governmt allows no salary. The fees of this Consular is under 200$ a year, the Stationry bill about the same which is not allowed by the Dept of State.

There are many owners of large tracts of land in C. who hold them under the idea of the Country chang owners, having no preset use for thm, as the Indians tame & wild steal several thousand head of Horses yearly from the Rancho. Most of these horses are stole for food. The Indins cut up the meat in strips and dry it in the sun. While this continue Grazng of Cattle can not be profitible conducted. There is no expectiation that this Govt. will find a prevntive—nothng but the fear of the Indian for the American Settlers will prevent it. They steal but a few horse from Foreigner as there is to much danger of bng followed. Mexico may fret and treatent as much as she pleases but all her Cal Gov & Gen. give Cal land to all who apply for thm and from the nature of thigs will continue to do so. Foreignrs arring here expect to live & die in the Country, Mexican officers to remain 2 or 3 years & be shipt off by force unless they choose to marry a Native and becone a Californian, Body & Soul. This Ports in C. with the exceptin of Mazalan are the only Mexican Pacific Ports that are flourishng. All othrs are fallig & fallig fast. Here there is much advance in every thng and the Country pres-

ent each year a bolder front to the world. It must change owners. Its of no use to Mexico. To hir its but a eye sore a shame and bone of Contentin. Here are many fine Ports, the land produces wheat over 100 fold. Cotten & hemp will grow here and every kind of fruit there is in New Eng—granes in abundance of the furst qualuty. Wine of many kinds are made, yet there is no faciluty of makng. Much of it will pass for Port. The Bays are full of fish, the Woods of game. Bears, and Whales can be seen from one view. The latter are offen in the way of the Boats near the Beach. Finaly there is San Francisco with its rivers. This Bay will hold all the ship in the U. S. The entranc is verry narrow between two mountains easly defended and prehaps the most magnuficnt Harbour in the World and at present of as much use to the civilized world as if it did not exist. Some day or other this will belong to som Naval power. This every Native is prepared for. . . . Letters nor words can not express the advantag and importance of San F. to a Naval power. There is 500 to 1000 Am Whalers with 20000 Amn Seamn in the Pacific. Half of them will be withen 20 day sail of San F. While the port belogs to Mex. its a safe place for whale ship in a war with England fran or Russian. Should one of these Native own the port and at some future day declare war aganst the U.S. what the results. It require not the discruptin from the writer nor from anyone. If Congres wishes the exention[?] of the Navy, our Naval power or our commerce St F. must be obtaind, or the Origon & Cali must becone a Nation withn themsefs. Time is continualy brngng this into notice, and one of the two must soon be consumated or if the Origon dispute continues let E. take 8 degrees N of the Columbia and purchase 8 Degres S. of 42 of Mex. and exchange.

The Origon will never be a benefit to the U. S. if England owns St. F. Vessels sometimes lay withen the bar of the Columbia 30 to 40 days waiting an opportunitey to go out. When once out they can reach St. F. in 4 days, a Steam Boat in less than two days. The time will soon arrive when by steam a person will go from the Columbia to Mont. & back in less in 4 days. For Navagation of the Columbia is of little use. A few English Vessel could prevent any vessels gong in— even if the wind allowed them. Whalers now from the N. W. pass the place for C.

The Settlers of the Origon anticipate the supplyng of California. Under present curcumstances they may. A California will not work if he can avoid it. The time will come, must come, when this Country is peopled by another race. This is as fully expected here as any other natual course of events. Many children have been sent to the Oahu English School to learn the Eng language to prepare them for the coming events, be the visit from John Bull or Uncle Sam. One of the two will have the Country. When once this is accomplished, the place will team with a busy race. As I before observed all fruits will grow here. Hemp, Cotten every Variuty of grain, timber from the tender Willow to Trees 17 feet in diamater. The Natives now expecting Troops from Acupulco to reconquer the Country are drillng many young men in preparation intended to surround the first port the Mexicans arrive at, drive away the Cattle, prevent all intercours with the Ranchos, and by this mean drive them out of C. If they can not succeed in this manner take to the mountans and worry them out.

There is no doubt but these soldiers are sent by Mexico under the instigatin of the English under the pretext that the Am are settlng in the C too fast and will one day obtain possessin. In the time the C do not believe this story but give land to all that come, be they from what nation they may be.

These letter contans many facts well known to the writer and should be know to his Countrymen. Each paragraph contans matter sufficent for much thought & reflectin and are sent to you because from your paper the writer has read many subjects respectng C. and give you his information in return.

Questions

1. Why did Larkin believe that the British and French were positioning themselves to seize California? What evidence did Larkin give to support his suspicion?

2. How did Larkin view the Indians in California? According to Larkin, what challenges did the Indians pose to the settlement and development of California, and what did he view as their inevitable fate?

3. How did Larkin's assessment of California compare with John L. O'Sullivan's? What economic and political potential did Larkin believe California possessed? Why was San Francisco so important?

13-3 The Great Prize Fight (1844)

In the 1840s, expansionists, emboldened by the idea that American possession of the entire continent had been providentially ordained, "our manifest destiny," were determined to add Texas and California to the Union (see Documents 13-1 and 13-2). Texas had already declared its independence from Mexico and its desire to be annexed into the United States; however, neither Andrew Jackson nor Martin Van Buren chose to act on the matter for fear of inflaming northern opposition to the enlargement of the slave south. In the meantime, southern suspicions that British antislavery advocates were conspiring to keep Texas independent in order to check the growth of the United States only added to the urgency with which annexationists approached the issue. The "Great Prize Fight" depicted the American eagle defending its "natural" offspring, including unhatched Texas and California, against competing challengers: Spain, represented by Don Quixote betting Cuba, and Britain with John Bull risking Canada. The ghost of George Washington encourages America: "Go it, my Boy, you will beat them all!"

Source: Print, *The Great Prize Fight* (1844). New York Historical Society.

Questions

1. What was the significance of Cuba and Canada to the Americans? Had expansionists expressed any interest in these territories?

2. Why was the slave (in the foreground) depicted as essentially uninterested in the outcome of the "prize fight"?

3. The inclusion of Washington's ghost was an attempt to link the expansionists of the 1840s to the Revolutionary generation. Was there some basis for this beyond a simple appeal to authority? Were the Revolutionaries also expansionists? Explain.

Questions for Further Thought

1. Is it fair to say that Manifest Destiny was a fancy way for Americans to rationalize the conquest of the West? Or, do you think that many Americans really believed they had a God-given mission to "civilize" the West? What features of American culture might have contributed to this sense of mission?

2. In your opinion, was it inevitable that the United States would expand its control westward to the Pacific Ocean? Was Manifest Destiny a foregone conclusion? Based on your knowledge of the text, what rights and territories did the British, French, Russians, and Mexicans claim in the West, and why did the United States eventually get its way?

3. From your reading of Documents 13-1 and 13-2 as well as your reading of the text, what was Mexico's internal political situation in the 1830s and 1840s? How did the Americans exploit Mexico's weaknesses to their own advantage? What place did westward expansion have in domestic politics in the United States—specifically, the party rivalry between the Democrats and the Whigs?

War, Expansion, and Slavery, 1846–1850

Following his victory in the election of 1844, President James K. Polk pursued an aggressively expansionist policy. To the northwest, he ended joint American-British control of the Oregon Territory, though he agreed to dividing control along the forty-ninth parallel rather than insisting on seizing the entire territory south of the "Fifty-Four Forty or Fight" line. Polk proved far more aggressive in the southwest against a weaker opponent, Mexico (Document 13-4). Goading the Mexicans into providing him a pretext, Polk got Congress to declare war in May 1846. The war proved both popular (despite significant opposition from "Conscience" Whigs) and successful, resulting not only in the annexation of an enlarged Texas but in the seizure of California and New Mexico.

However, Polk's very success in pursuing the United States' Manifest Destiny immediately sharpened intersectional conflict over slavery. Mexico had abolished slavery, and many northerners were averse to seeing American power used to extend the "peculiar institution" to regions where freedom had been established. Many other white northerners, feeling that western lands should be reserved for white small farmers, not great planters (and blacks), were beginning to adhere to a new form of antislavery, the free-soil movement. If it was morally inferior to humanitarian antislavery, free soil was politically much more potent; one of its leaders, Representative David Wilmot, proposed a popular measure to bar slavery from the Mexican territories.

The 1846 Wilmot Proviso quickly became a flash point for North-South conflict, but it was soon joined by other issues, including a free-state movement in California and increasing northern resistance to enforcement of the constitutional requirement that fugitive slaves be returned to their masters. Antislavery spokesmen warned that to give in to what they saw as southern bullying would extend the sway in federal affairs of what they called the "Slave Power"—a southern interest hostile not simply to abolitionists but to the rights of white northerners as well (Document 13-5). The Southern response was that, short of secession, which remained a right of last resort (Document 13-7), the only remedy for the increasingly polarized situation was constitutional reform (Document 13-6).

13-4   The American Invasion of Mexico (1847)

Carlos Maria de Bustamante

The legendary Battle of the Alamo was effectively used to whip up overwhelming support for war with Mexico (see text pp. 393–394), making it easy for Americans to recast their aggression against the Mexicans as a fight for freedom and liberty. Carlos Maria de Bustamante (1774–1848) reminds us that there was another side to the story. A journalist and prolific writer, Bustamante initially admired the United States, which he viewed as a model republic. However, with the events of the 1830s and 1840s, he became disenchanted with American policy toward Mexico. The following excerpt, which details U.S. transgressions, is taken from Bustamante's last book, *The New Bernal Díaz del Castillo or History of the Anglo-American Invasion of Mexico* (1847). Note that Bernal Díaz del Castillo chronicled the Spanish conquest of Mexico led by Hernán Cortés in the sixteenth century (Document 1-2).

The complaints of Mexico against the United States before the annexation of Texas are the following:

The introduction of troops from the United States army in the course of Mexico's campaign in Texas. A considerable number of cavalry under General Gaines crossed the Sabine. This was protested by our minister in Washington. The public enlistment and military equipping of troops, which has been done on various occasions in the port city of New Orleans, in order to invade Mexico through Texas and other points, despite the fact that the United States maintained diplomatic relations with Mexico and the guarantees of treaties of peace and commerce remained in force. This also has been the subject of altercations between the two governments. Mexico has never had the forthrightness to ask of the United States that it lend its assistance against Texas, but Mexico certainly has had the right to demand of the United States that it maintain absolute neutrality. The above mentioned palpable actions demonstrate that the United States has not done so.

As for the recognition of the independence of Texas by other nations, there is nothing unusual in that. The various powers recognize de facto governments, but that in no way takes away from Mexico the right to recover, if it were possible, the territory which it had lost. The independence of Mexico was equally recognized by the European powers and by the United States itself, but nevertheless Spain did not recognize Mexico until a great deal of time had passed, and it made an attempt in the year 1829 to invade Mexico without opposition from any nation.

Now, if Texas were to be considered strong and capable of backing up its declaration of independence, why did it attach itself to the United States? Why did it seek this method to get the United States to come to its support in Mexico? This is just one more proof that Texas cannot be compared to other nations, including the United States, that have declared their independence and by deed have been able to sustain it and triumph.

As for the annexation, the person who is writing this piece was in the United States when these events were happening and was a witness to the fact that the greater part of the press in the northern states clamored strongly against this step, calling those who belonged to the annexation party thieves and usurpers, and setting forth strong and well-founded reasons, which at this point I will not repeat in order to prevent this exposition from becoming too lengthy. If the wise and honorable Henry Clay had attained the seat of the presidency, would the annexation of Texas have come to pass? Certainly not. . . .

Thus matters have arrived at the state in which they are now, because evil parties and evil men, of which there are as many in this country as in the United States, have operated according to their partisan tendencies and have not attended to the well-being and justice of both republics. Can you deny this, American citizens, if you are not blind? Will you not confess that Mexico has suffered more than any other nation? The act of annexation was the equivalent of taking away from Mexico a considerable part of its territory, which had, rightly or wrongly, carried on a dispute with Mexico, but in no way can a nation be construed as friendly which has mixed itself in this affair to the point that Mexico has been deprived of its rights. Did not our minister in Washington protest against the annexation? Did he not declare that it would be a hostile act which would merit a declaration of war? Who, then, provoked the war—Mexico which only defended itself and protested, or the United States which became aggressors and scorned Mexico, taking advantage of its weakness and of its internecine agitations.

. . . Thus, from the point of view of the Mexican government, the occupying of Corpus Christi by troops of the United States amounted to the same thing as if they had occupied the port of Tampico. In every way it was a violation of all treaties, of friendly relations, and of good faith. I wish now that you would judge these events with a Mexican heart and would ask yourself: Which has been the aggressor country? What would your government have done in the controversy with England over the Maine border if that nation had brought in troops, large or small in number? Without any doubt your government would have declared war and would not have entertained any propositions put forth until the armed force had evacuated the territory.

The war began because there was no other course, and Mexico will always be able to present a serene front before the world and maintain its innocence despite whatever misfortunes might befall it. . . .

It is necessary that in these matters the truth be spoken, because these events which have just happened now belong to history.

Questions

1. Why did Bustamante use Bernal Díaz del Castillo's name in the title of his book? What does this say about how he perceived the United States' war with Mexico?

2. How did Bustamante convey his sense of outrage over American actions? Is his style of writing as important as the substance of his arguments in getting his message across to his readers?

3. Was Bustamante simply an apologist for Mexico? How accurate were his descriptions of the actions of the United States?

13-5 Defining the Constitutional Limits of Slavery (1850)

Salmon P. Chase

Born in New Hampshire and educated at Dartmouth College, Salmon P. Chase (1808–1873) studied law with President John Quincy Adams's attorney general, William Wirt, before moving west to establish himself as a successful young lawyer in Cincinnati, Ohio. Chase voted for William Henry Harrison in 1840 but soon afterward joined the fledgling abolitionist Liberty Party. Chase volunteered to be the defense attorney in a celebrated 1836 fugitive slave case involving a woman named Matilda and James G. Birney (the Liberty Party presidential candidate in 1840 and 1844), who employed her in his home. Chase lost the case, but the state supreme court ordered his argument printed, securing for Chase the title "attorney general of the fugitive slave" in antislavery circles. Chase took a leading role in the formation of the Free-Soil Party in 1848 and forged a Free Soil–Democratic coalition in Ohio that elected him to the U.S. Senate (see text p. 402). In the Senate Chase opposed the compromise measures crafted by Henry Clay, Daniel Webster, and Stephen Douglas. The argument he developed became the central tenet of the Republican Party.

Source: Salmon P. Chase, *Union and Freedom, without Compromise. Speech of Mr. Chase of Ohio, On Mr. Clay's Compromise Resolutions* (Washington, DC: Buell and Blanchard, 1850).

I think, Mr. President, that two facts may now be regarded as established: First that in 1787 the national policy in respect to slavery was one of restriction, limitation, and discouragement. Second that it was generally expected that under the action of the State Governments slavery would gradually disappear from the States.

Such was the state of the country when the Convention met to frame the Constitution of the United States. . . . The framers of the Constitution acted under the influence of the general sentiment of the country. Some of them had contributed in no small measure to form that sentiment. Let us examine the instrument [the Constitution] in its light, and ascertain the original import of its language.

What, then, shall we find in it? The guaranties so much talked of? Recognition of property in men? Stipulated protection for that property in national territories and by national law? No, sir: nothing like it.

We find, on the contrary, extreme care to exclude these ideas from the Constitution. Neither the word "slave" nor "slavery" is to be found in any provision. There is not a single expression which charges the National Government with any responsibility in regard to slavery. No power is conferred on Congress either to establish or sustain it. The framers of the Constitution left it where they found it, exclusively within and under the jurisdiction of the States. Wherever slaves are referred to at all in the Constitution, whether in the clause providing for the apportionment of representation and direct taxation [Article I, section 2], or in that stipulating for the extradition of fugitive from service [the "fugitive slave" clause, Article IV, section 2], or in that restricting Congress as to the prohibition of importation or migration [Article I, section 9], they are spoken of, not as persons held as property, but as persons held to service, or having their condition determined, under State laws. We

learn, indeed from the debates in the Constitutional Convention that the idea of property in men was excluded with special solicitude. . . .

Unhappily . . . the original policy of the Government and the original principles of the Government in respect to slavery did not permanently control its action. A change occurred—almost imperceptible at first but becoming more and more marked and decided until nearly total. . . . It was natural, though it does [not] seem to have been anticipated, that the unity of the slave interest strengthened by this accession of political power, should gradually weaken the public sentiment and modify the national policy against slavery. . . . Mr. President, I have spoken freely of slave State ascendency in the affairs of this Government, but I desire not to be misunderstood. I take no sectional position. The supporters of slavery are the sectionalists. . . . Freedom is national; slavery only is local and sectional. . . .

What have been the results . . . of the subversion of the original policy of slavery restriction and discouragement . . . instead of slavery being regarded as a curse, a reproach, a blight, an evil, a wrong, a sin, we are now told that it is the most stable foundation of our institutions; the happiest relation that labor can sustain to capital; a blessing to both races . . . this is a great change, and a sad change. If it goes on, the spirit of liberty must at length become extinct, and a despotism will be established under the forms of free institutions. . . . There can be no foundation whatever for the doctrine advanced . . . that an equilibrium between the slaveholding and non-slaveholding sections of our country has been, is, and ought to be, an approved feature of our political system. . . . I shall feel myself supported by the precepts of the sages of the Revolutionary era, by the example of the founders of the Republic, by the original policy of the Government, and by the principles of the Constitution.

Questions

1. Why was Chase concerned with the history of the slavery issue? What difference did it make?

2. Locate in the Constitution (see text p. D-3) the passages cited by Chase as referring to slaves. Do you agree with Chase that these passages were part of an original policy of "slavery restriction and discouragement"? Explain why.

3. What are the implications of Chase's conclusion that "Freedom is national; slavery . . . is local"?

13-6 *A Discourse on the Constitution* (1850)

John C. Calhoun

John C. Calhoun (1782–1850) of South Carolina, perhaps the best-known defender of states' rights, began his career as a nationalist. Elected to the U.S. House of Representatives in 1810 as a so-called war hawk, he was stunned by the setbacks the nation suffered in the War of 1812 and became a determined advocate of extending federal power for the sake of bolstering national defense. As such, Calhoun advanced a program that included support for internal improvements and the Second Bank of the United States. Meanwhile, his political fortunes rose as he moved from Congress to the executive branch, first as James Monroe's secretary of war, then as vice president under John Quincy Adams, and finally as vice president under Andrew Jackson. But the events of the 1820s changed all of this. Successive protective tariffs enacted by Congress and the Denmark Vesey slave conspiracy in 1822 convinced most South Carolinians that actions taken by the federal government might jeopardize their lives as well as their livelihoods. By the early 1830s Calhoun had publicly abandoned his earlier nationalist impulses. With little hope of advancing further on the national stage, he resigned the vice presidency during the nullification crisis (Document 10-8) and was elected to the U.S. Senate as an unyielding advocate of South Carolina's interests and southern sectionalism. *A Discourse on the Constitution and Government of the United States* (1850), written in the last few years of his life, was Calhoun's valedictory address on the nature of the "federal" system established by the American Revolutionaries, the "disease" to which it had succumbed, and the "remedy" that might save it.

Source: From Ross M. Lence, ed., *Union and Liberty: The Political Philosophy of John C. Calhoun.* Copyright © 1992 by the Liberty Fund. Used with permission.

What has been done cannot be undone. The equilibrium between the two sections has been permanently destroyed. . . . The northern section, in consequence, will ever concentrate within itself the two majorities of which the government is composed; and should the southern be excluded from all territories, now acquired, or to be hereafter acquired, it will soon have so decided a preponderance in the government and the Union, as to be able to mould the constitution to its pleasure. . . .

The nature of the disease is such, that nothing can reach it, short of some organic change—a change which shall so modify the constitution, as to give to the weaker section, in some form or another, a negative on the action of the government. Nothing short of this can protect the weaker, and restore harmony and tranquillity to the Union, by arresting, effectually, the tendency of the dominant and stronger section to oppress the weaker. When the constitution was formed, the impression was strong, that the tendency to conflict would be between the larger and smaller States; and effectual provisions were, accordingly, made to guard against it. But experience has proved this to have been a mistake; and that, instead of being, as was then supposed, the conflict is between the two great sections, which are so strongly distinguished by their institutions, geographical character, productions and pursuits. . . . It is for us, who see and feel it, to do, what the framers of the constitution would have done, had they possessed the knowledge, in this respect, which experience has given to us—that is—provide against the dangers which the system has practically developed; and which, had they been foreseen at the time, and left without guard, would undoubtedly have prevented the States, forming the southern section of the confederacy, from ever agreeing to the constitution; and which, under like circumstances, were they now out of, would forever prevent them from entering into, the Union.

How the constitution could best be modified, so as to effect the object, can only be authoritatively determined by the amending power. It may be done in various ways. Among others, it might be effected through a reorganization of the executive department; so that its powers, instead of being vested, as they now are, in a single officer, should be vested in two—to be so elected, as that the two should be constituted the special organs and representatives of the respective sections, in the executive department of the government; and requiring each to approve all the acts of Congress before they shall become laws. . . .

Indeed, it may be doubted, whether the framers of the constitution did not commit a great mistake, in constituting a single, instead of a plural executive. Nay, it may even be doubted whether a single chief magistrate—invested with all the powers properly appertaining to the executive department of the government, as is the President—is compatible with the permanence of a popular government; especially in a wealthy and populous community, with a large revenue and a numerous body of officers and employees. Certain it is, that there is no instance of a popular government so constituted, which has long endured. Even ours, thus far, furnishes no evidence in its favor, and not a little against it; for, to it, the present disturbed and dangerous state of things, which threatens the country with monarchy, or disunion, may be justly attributed. . . .

But it is objected that a plural executive necessarily leads to intrigue and discord among its members; and that it is in-consistent with prompt and efficient action. This may be true, when they are all elected by the same constituency; and may be a good reason, where this is the case, for preferring a single executive, with all its objections, to a plural executive. But the case is very different where they are elected by different constituencies—having conflicting and hostile interests; as would be the fact in the case under consideration. Here the two would have to act, concurrently, in approving the acts of Congress—and, separately, in the sphere of their respective departments. The effect, in the latter case, would be, to retain all the advantages of a single executive, as far as the administration of the laws were concerned; and, in the former, to insure harmony and concord between the two sections, and, through them, in the government. For as no act of Congress could become a law without the assent of the chief magistrates representing both sections, each, in the elections, would choose the candidate, who, in addition to being faithful to its interests, would best command the esteem and confidence of the other section. And thus, the presidential election, instead of dividing the Union into hostile geographical parties, the stronger struggling to enlarge its powers, and the weaker to defend its rights—as is now the case—would become the means of restoring harmony and concord to the country and the government. It would make the Union a union in truth—a bond of mutual affection and brotherhood—and not a mere connection used by the stronger as the instrument of dominion and aggrandizement—and submitted to by the weaker only from the lingering remains of former attachment, and the fading hope of being able to restore the government to what it was originally intended to be, a blessing to all.

Such is the disease—and such the character of the only remedy which can reach it. In conclusion, there remains to be considered, the practical question—Shall it be applied? Shall the only power which can apply it be invoked for the purpose?

Questions

1. Compare Calhoun's description of "equilibrium" with Madison's discussion of factions in an extended republic (Document 6-21). What had changed? What major assumption had Madison made that Calhoun explicitly rejected?

2. Why would Calhoun single out the executive department for constitutional reform?

3. Were Calhoun's proposed changes practical? Could they have been implemented? Why or why not? What do they reveal about the state of sectional relations?

13-7 The Right of Secession (1856)

Frederick Grimké

Frederick Grimké (1791–1863) was one of fourteen children born into a prominent South Carolina family, and an older brother of abolitionists Sarah and Angelina Grimké (see text, pp. 352–353 and Document 11-9). Unlike his more famous sisters, however, Frederick never rejected the institution of slavery; indeed, he defended it as a necessary form of "guardianship" over a race of people whose "period of infancy and youth is . . . protracted through the whole of life." But Grimké himself did not remain a slave owner. After the death of his father in 1819, he moved to Ohio, where his Yale education, prior legal practice in Charleston, and reputation as a "man of fine talents" gained him an appointment as presiding judge in the Court of Common Pleas. In 1836 Grimké was elevated to the Supreme Court of Ohio. He wrote *The Nature and Tendency of Free Institutions*, a lengthy meditation on the perils of self-government and a celebration of the constituent power of middle-class Americans, after resigning from state supreme court in 1842.

Source: Excerpt from Frederick Grimké, *The Nature and Tendency of Free Institutions*, ed. John William Ward (Cambridge, MA: The Belknap Press of Harvard University Press, 1968), 510–513, 516. Copyright © 1968 by the President and Fellows of Harvard College. Reprinted with permission of the publisher.

Secession is not the exercise of an act of sovereignty, but the reverse. Between it and the veto of a state there is a clear and broad distinction. Secession is an unequivocal admission that the sovereignty does not reside in the state seceding. An act of sovereignty removes officers, abolishes offices, alters constitutions, extinguishes the powers exercised by the government. In the case of secession, instead of the constitution and laws being removed out of the way of the discontented state, the state itself removes out of the way. This is a plain recognition that it is not vested with sovereignty over the federal government, has no right to assume it, and that it is obliged to succumb to it. It is precisely like the emigration of individuals from a country whose government is a consolidated one, who become discontented with the condition in which they are placed or with the institutions under which they live, and remove to another country. They are aware that as individual members of society they have no right to control the government. Instead of assuming to do so, they quietly withdraw from it. A confederate government being the result of a joint compact between the members and not the act of any one singly, the veto would be the usurpation of a power which cannot belong to a single member. It would transform a joint into a single government. Secession admits the incompetency of the seceding state to do so, and instead of bending the government to its will, it is compelled to bend to the will of the government. Great mistakes have been committed from confounding secession with the veto. They are entirely different from each other, as the preceding observations sufficiently show. . . .

When the federal government depends upon the states for the execution of the laws and they are not executed, the delinquent member may be coerced into obedience by the whole force of the confederacy. But the coercion of a state implies the coercion of the individuals composing it, and thus we are led to the same conclusion, that every form of confederacy is a constitution and government, that the laws are equally obligatory upon the citizens, and that the distinction between them consists in the more or less perfect machinery which is employed to enforce them. In all there is a division of the sovereignty, one portion being retained by the states separately and the residue alienated, not to the central government, but to the states jointly. The distinction, then, so far as it affects the right of secession, is not between the more or less perfect form of federal government, but between a federal and consolidated government. This is the only test in our power in order to determine when the right of secession exists. . . .

A great principle can never depend for proof of its validity upon examples, since these may contradict some other principle of equally high authority. But where the example has been deduced from the principle, and could not have existed without it, it is of wonderful use in testing its value. It is then a direct corollary from the principle and not merely a happy illustration of it. The confederation of 1778 was broken up by secession. The articles on which it was founded provided that no alteration should ever be made unless with the unanimous consent of the states who were parties to it. The states were not unanimous in the change which substituted another ordinance and converted the government into the present confederation. Rhode Island and North Carolina rejected the scheme and may have remained out of the Union to the present day. Eleven states thus seceded from the old confederation. If it should be said that these states did not secede because the new government erected in place of the old was itself a federal union, the answer is that any change of the articles, much more the radical change which led to the formation of a new government, was absolutely prohibited unless the consent of each state was obtained. Indeed the futility of the objection will be manifest on a very little reflection. If two or more states were now to assemble in convention, or if all the states were so to assemble, and by a majority of votes should form a different federal government, it would be absurd to say they had not seceded because the form of polity which they had established had one or more features in common with the former. But if in order to test the bearing of the objection, we should admit it to be well-founded, the difficulty still exists. The states of North Carolina and Rhode Island then seceded. Their right to remain out of the new union was never disputed; it was openly and unequivocally admitted. The Congress under the new government never dreamed of coercing them into an adherence to it, but dealt with them as independent nations; and as I have before observed, they may have continued to this day separate and independent states.

The great risk which will be incurred by the seceding member, the disadvantageous position in which it will be placed, standing alone in the midst of a firm and compact league, will operate as a powerful check upon its conduct and will prevent recourse to such an extreme measure unless it can be justified before the bar of public opinion. At the same time, the open recognition of the right to secede will render it disgraceful to embark in any scheme of concerted resistance to the laws while the state continues a member of the Union. The explicit recognition of the right will also operate as a salutary restraint upon the central government. If one or two states seceded, they would inevitably be the losers; it would be staking everything upon the cast of a die. But if several threatened to do the same, the confederacy would be in danger of being deprived of so much strength and importance that every measure which prudence and calm judgment could suggest would be adopted to avert so great a calamity. The public councils would be marked by more reflection when a moral agency was substituted in the place of brute force. Rhode Island and North Carolina were resolute in their opposition to the present constitution, and for a time refused to enter into the Union. Congress pursued towards them the same course which it did towards the European states: it treated them as independent nations, and applied to them the laws relative to discriminating duties. This contributed greatly to change their resolution. They entered the confederacy, one of them two years after it was formed, and motives still more powerful will deter either from now seceding. The right of secession, then, is a weapon of defense of great efficacy in the hands of the states, but it supposes one still more efficacious in the hands of the federal government. The advantages of union are so manifold, the position of a member when isolated is so insignificant and when united with others so commanding, that nothing but the greatest injustice or the most irreconcilable diversity of interests will occasion the exercise of the right. Instances of secession are accordingly very rare.

Questions

1. Compare Grimké's view of the constitutional union with that of John Calhoun (see Document 13-6). In what ways are they similar and dissimilar?

2. Grimké was an opponent of the idea that a single state had the power to nullify a federal law, and therefore a critic of the position assumed by South Carolina in 1832 (see Document 10-8). What was the basis of his distinction between a state's veto power and a state's right to withdraw from the Union, that is, between nullification and secession?

3. How accurate is Grimké's version of the creation and ratification of the Constitution in 1787–1788? Was the union under the Confederation "broken up by secession"? Explain.

Questions for Further Thought

1. Compare Chase's and Grimké's discussions of the framers' intent (Documents 13-5 and 13-7) with that of Madison (Document 8-8). Do these accounts correspond? Why or why not?

2. How does the emerging Republican Party's position on slavery as articulated by Chase (Document 13-5) differ from the abolitionist position as expressed by William Lloyd Garrison (Document 11-6) and Frederick Douglass (Document 11-7)? Do you think the southerners could see these differences?

3. What assumptions did Chase, Calhoun, and Grimké (Documents 13-5, 13-6, and 13-7) share with regard to the Constitution? What assumptions did they share with regard to the evolution of the political system?

The End of the Second Party System, 1850–1858

While many Americans celebrated the Compromise of 1850 as a "final settlement" of all outstanding sectional issues, its central provisions served only to keep those issues visible. The Fugitive Slave Act of 1850, for instance, made it federal policy not simply to allow slavery in the states where it existed, but to extend the reach of the institution into the heart of the North itself (Document 13-8). In response, antislavery militants increasingly turned to direct action both to free slaves and to protect fugitives from slave catchers and federal marshals (Document 13-10). Northerners saw the Fugitive Slave Act as demonstrating the lengths to which the "Slave Power" would go in attacking the liberties even of Americans in the "free states"; white southerners saw northern resistance as evidence that free-state residents refused to accept their constitutional obligations.

Meanwhile, in 1854 the issue of whether to allow the expansion of slavery in the western territories reasserted itself with the passage of the Kansas-Nebraska Act, which repealed the Missouri Compromise and allowed settlers in the newly organized territories of Kansas and Nebraska to determine the future of slavery there. Alarmed at what they viewed as a fresh triumph of the "Slave Power," a resurgent antislavery movement launched a new political party, the Republican Party, of unprecedentedly broad appeal. As Kansas degenerated into civil war between proslavery and antislavery factions, atrocity stories provided grist for sectional propagandists on both sides, while violence spread to the floor of the U.S. Senate itself (Document 13-11). The Supreme Court finally sought to resolve the issues in its 1857 *Dred Scott* decision (Document 13-12). However, its declaration that Congress had no constitutional right to bar slavery from the territories outraged Republicans and raised northern fears that the Court would ultimately declare slavery a *national* institution. To many northerners, it was becoming increasingly evident that the federal government had to be purged of all "Slave Power" influences—and the vehicle for doing so would be the Republican Party.

13-8   The Fugitive Slave Act of 1850

Under the Constitution (Article 4, Section 2), states were obligated to surrender escaped slaves back to their owners. Growing antislavery sentiment in the North had led most states to ignore that provision, and as tensions rose, the South insisted that the northern states live up to their constitutional obligation. As part of the Compromise of 1850, Congress enacted a tougher fugitive slave statute to satisfy southern demands (see text pp. 404–406).

Source: U.S. Statutes at Large, 9:462ff.

Be it enacted by the Senate and House of Representatives of the United States of America in congress assembled, . . .

SEC. 6. *And be it further enacted,* That when a person held to service or labor in any State or Territory of the United States, has heretofore or shall hereafter escape into another State or Territory of the United States, the person or persons to whom such service or labor may be due, or his, her, or their agent or attorney, duly authorized, by power of attorney, in writing, acknowledged and certified under the seal of some legal officer or court of the State or Territory in which the same may be executed, may pursue and reclaim such fugitive person, either by procuring a warrant from some one of the courts, judges, or commissioners aforesaid, of the proper circuit, district, or county, for the apprehension of such fugitive from service or labor, or by seizing and arresting such fugitive, where the same can be done without process, and by taking, or causing such person to be taken, forthwith before such court, judge, or commissioner, whose duty it shall be to hear and determine the case of such claimant in a summary manner. . . . In no trial or hearing under this act shall the testimony of such alleged fugitive be admitted in evidence; and the certificates in this and the first [fourth] section be mentioned, shall be conclusive of the right of the person or persons in whose favor granted, to remove such fugitive to the State or Territory from which he escaped, and shall prevent all molestation of such person or persons by any process issued by any court, judge, magistrate, or other person whomsoever.

SEC. 7. *And be it further enacted,* That any person who shall knowingly and willingly obstruct, hinder, or prevent such claimant, his agent or attorney, or any person or persons lawfully assisting him, her, or them, from arresting such a fugitive from service or labor, either with or without process as aforesaid, or shall rescue, or attempt to rescue, such fugitive from service or labor, from the custody of such claimant, his or her agent or attorney, or other person or persons lawfully assisting as aforesaid, when so arrested, pursuant to the authority herein given and declared; or shall aid, abet, or assist such person so owing service or labor as aforesaid, directly or indirectly, to escape from such claimant, his agent or attorney, or other person or persons legally authorized as aforesaid; or shall harbor or conceal such fugitive, so as to prevent the discovery and arrest of such person, after notice or knowledge of the fact that such person was a fugitive from service or labor as aforesaid, shall, for either of said offences, be subject to a fine not exceeding one thousand dollars, and imprisonment not exceeding six months . . . and shall moreover forfeit and pay, by way of civil damages to the party injured by such illegal conduct, the sum of one thousand dollars, for each fugitive so lost as aforesaid. . . .

SEC. 9. *And be it further enacted,* That, upon affidavit made by the claimant of such fugitive, his agent or attorney, after such certificate has been issued, that he has reason to apprehend that such fugitive will be rescued by force from his or their possession before he can be taken beyond the limits of the State in which the arrest is made, it shall be the duty of the officer making the arrest to retain such fugitive in his custody, and to remove him to the State whence he fled, and there to deliver him to said claimant, his agent, or attorney. And to this end, the officer aforesaid is hereby authorized and required to employ so many persons as he may deem necessary to overcome such force, and to retain them in his service so long as circumstances may require. The said officer and his assistants, while so employed, to receive the same compensation, and to be allowed the same expenses, as are now allowed by law for transportation of criminals, to be certified by the judge of the district within which the arrest is made, and paid out of the treasury of the United States.

Questions

1. How did the act discourage people from helping fugitive slaves?

2. The Constitution called for the states to surrender runaways. Which people were specifically charged in the act with the enforcement of this law?

3. According to the act, whose responsibility was it to pay the expenses of slave catchers? Why was this provision included?

13-9   Fulfilling a Constitutional Duty with Alacrity (1850)

The Compromise of 1850 included a new Fugitive Slave Act that could conceivably have forced free-state citizens to assist slave catchers in the apprehension and return of runaway slaves to their masters. Not surprisingly, abolitionists were alarmed by the measure and determined to prevent its enforcement. That Daniel Webster had spoken in favor of the Compromise in his famous "Seventh of March" speech before the Senate, indeed going so far as to lambaste northern "fanatics and abolitionists" for their part in the crisis of union, ruined his reputation among his one-time avid admirers. The antislavery poet John Greenleaf Whittier lamented:

> So fallen! so lost! the light withdrawn
>   Which once he wore!
> The glory from his gray hairs gone
>   For evermore!

'CONQUERING PREJUDICE,'
or
"Fulfilling a Constitutional duty with alacrity."

"My God!_ My Child!_ Will no one help!_ Is there no mercy!"

"Any man can perform an agreeable duty_ it is not every one that can perform a disagreeable duty."

"By Heaven! he exceeds my most sanguine expectation_he marks his way so clearly & treads so loyally on the track of the Constitution_It is more than great_it is sublime_ I feel a great sense of relief."

Political cartoonists were less given to lamentation as they assailed the once formidable reputation of the "Godlike Daniel."

Source: Lithograph, *Conquering Prejudice: Fulfilling a Constitutional Duty with Alacrity* (1850). Worcester Art Museum, Worcester, MA. The Charles A. Goodspeed Collection, Museum purchase.

Questions

1. Webster was opposed to slavery. Why did he support the Compromise of 1850? What did his defense of the Compromise, including the Fugitive Slave Act, reveal about his priorities in 1850?

2. What was the significance of the cartoonist's emphasis on "Constitutional duty"? Were competing constitutional rights at issue in the Fugitive Slave Act? What was the basis of Webster's reputation as a lawyer; that is, what were some of his most famous cases?

3. "He exceeds my most sanguine expectation," exclaims the slave catcher, as he and Webster pursue a runaway slave and her child. How might southerners have reacted to this depiction of the consequences of the Fugitive Slave Act?

13-10   Opposing Accounts of the Rescue of a Fugitive (1851)

Although personal liberty laws helped impede the enforcement of the Fugitive Slave Act, their effect was slight at best; the new federal machinery ground on and moreover was supported by large segments of the public, who regarded the law as the price to be paid for sectional peace and continued to see abolitionists as disruptive and potentially treasonous. Feeling increasingly beleaguered, abolitionists and free blacks living in the North sought to protect alleged fugitive slaves through direct action. One of the more famous early examples of such action was the "Jerry Rescue" of October 1851 in Syracuse, New York. The following account, from a sympathetic reporter for the *New York Tribune*, was reprinted in William Lloyd Garrison's newspaper *The Liberator*. Following the account is a hostile editorial from a New York City Whig newspaper. (Note: Earlier that year, Daniel Webster, in a speech in Syracuse, had predicted that the law would be enforced there.)

Sources: The Liberator (Boston), 10 October 1851; *National Intelligencer* (Washington, DC), 7 October 1851.

(a) From the *New York Tribune*: Slave Catching in Syracuse — Intense Excitement.

I.

SYRACUSE, Wednesday, Oct. 1, 1851 — 9 P.M.

Our city is perfectly wild with excitement. A negro man named Jerry was arrested here to-day, claimed by a man named McHenry of Missouri, as a fugitive slave. The United States Marshal, with aids from the neighboring cities congregated here, arrested Jerry and brought him before United States Commissioner Sabine. The news spread over the city, — the bells in the various churches were tolled, — and the people assembled in knots at the corners of the streets, — one general feeling pervaded every breast, that of disgust and abhorrence at the Fugitive Slave Law, and this its first foul offspring in Syracuse. Our County Fair was being held in the city, and the farmers from the surrounding country were all here. In addition, a Liberty Party Convention was called for to-day, and I notice, prominent in our streets, some of the leaders of that party. — The Court of appeals is also in session here, and have had a good opportunity to witness the feeling here to-day.

The examination of Jerry, who is a fine athletic man, commenced at the Commissioner's office about 2 o'clock, P.M. The Court room and every avenue leading to it was densely crowded. The prosecution was conducted by three lawyers, named Anderson, Loomis and Lawrence. The defence was by Hillis, Morgan and Sheldon. The Commissioner adjourned the Court for half an hour, at about half-past 2 o'clock, P.M. The adjournment had no sooner been made, than a band of negroes and others seized the alleged fugitive, rescued him from the custody of the officers, and rushed down Water and Genessee streets, through Market Square, and down Water street to Lock street, over Lock street bridge, where he was caught by the officers and taken back to the police office of Justice House. Jerry was heavily handcuffed, which prevented his successful escape this time.

In the meantime, the crowd and excitement became intense; and the feeling gained upon the people, that the Fugitive Slave Law must not be executed in Syracuse. The military companies were ordered out by the Sheriff of the county, and got under arms, and prepared for action. Only one company, however, would leave their armory, and finally they went back, and the whole military of the city refused to aid and abet in carrying Jerry back into slavery. The Commissioner resumed the examination at 5 P.M., at the police office of Justice House. The crowd outside, unable to gain admittance, became more and more excited, and the noise and confusion frequently prevented the prosecution of the examination on the inside. Stones were thrown through the windows of the room, and the crowd exhibited certain other unmistakable signs that they were decidedly hostile to the Fugitive Slave Law. About 7 P.M., the crowd outside became more and more clamorous, and stones, &c., becoming more and more frequent, the Commissioner decided to adjourn the examination until tomorrow morning, at 8 o'clock.

This was announced to the crowd by Mr. Hillis, counsel for the prisoner, but the excitement could not be allayed. The officers in charge of the fugitive soon found it necessary to board up the windows, and in so doing, they got pretty well pelted. They next tried the effect of a few shots fired over the heads of the people, but it only increased the excitement. About 9 P.M., a desperate onslaught was made, and the doors and windows of the office were broken in, the lights extinguished, and the fugitive taken from the custody of the officers, and carried away to breathe freedom and liberty in the rural districts of our delightful country. So Mr. Webster's prophecy proves false, and the Fugitive Slave Law cannot be executed in Syracuse. The agent of the claimant at the final rescue jumped from the window of the police office, on the heel path of the canal, (or into the canal, I don't know which,) where he was caught by the crowd, but he claimed to be a line-boat passenger, and the crowd believed the story, and let him go. A barrel of tar and feathers had been provided for his accommodation, and were within a convenient distance, but he escaped them by his dexterous subterfuge. I understand the Marshal from Rochester had his arm broken in the melee at the last escape, and rumor is busy reporting other injuries, none, however, of a serious nature, and I have no faith in any of the reports. Some two or three persons fell from an awning into a cellar-way, and were somewhat injured. The appearance of the police office is rather dejected, and looks some as if it had stood pretty hard fire. The general sentiment was and is against the law and its execution; and one general congratulation is passing around the streets, and from mouth to mouth, at this final issue of the attempt to kidnap a human being in the 'Central City' of the Empire State.   G.B.

[October 2, 1851]

The chief movers in the crowd appeared to be negroes, although no one could be recognized in the darkness of the night, and amid the excitement and whirl of the occasion. No one was foremost in the rescue, no one did it, and I have seen no one of our citizens this morning so unfortunate in his opinions as to condemn the act. Indeed, congratulatory remarks and smiles prevail on every countenance. No sooner do two persons meet, than one begins to grin, and the other to say, 'Where's Jerry?' The one strong sentiment in the heart of the whole city is, that the Slave Law is wrong.

(b) from the *New York Express*: Lawlessness in Syracuse

Syracuse, in this State, is a city of salt; and if there be a city in this broad Union which especially lives, thrives, or *exists* on the Federal Government of the thirty-one United States, and upon the laws, it is this Syracuse, this city of salt, salt works, and salt boilers, and that surrounding country of farmers that feed these Syracusans.

In the first place, this Federal Republic—this Government of thirty-one States, fifteen of which are slaveholding—gives this Syracuse a protective duty of twenty per cent. *ad volorem* on every bushel of salt it makes. In 1850 the imports of salt into the United States were 11,224,185 bushels; and on every bushel of that salt, mainly to aid, strengthen, and support Syracuse and such like manufacturing places, the people of these United States, and slaveholding people among them, paid a duty of twenty per cent. *ad valorem.*

In the second place, the more to protect, build up, and make rich Syracuse and her salt-boilers, the State of New York levies a discriminating duty by tolls on her canals against all foreign salt, so that nearly a MONOPOLY of the sale of salt in the western and central parts of this State, and in the Lake States, is thus secured by protective LAW to Syracuse.

Nevertheless, now for some years this Syracuse has been the hot-bed of abolitionism, but especially so since the passage of the compromise bills of 1850; and one leading (so misnamed) Whig paper there, but more especially one (so called) clergyman, a Rev. Mr. May, have deliberately preached what inevitably led to the nullification of law by force. Hence, under such teachings, we have such scenes as are reported at Syracuse.

To rescue a *negro* man *against law*, a *white* man, acting *under the imperative obligations of law*, is maimed, having his right arm broken in two places!

Further comment is unnecessary. Every fact set forth above speaks trumpet-tongued for itself. All we have to add is, that beyond all question there is a very large majority of law-loving, law-abiding people in Syracuse who abhor all such enormous outrages as these. We know, of our own knowledge, at least thirty leading men there who abhor such things, if possible, more heartily than we do. Their only fault is, that they have not met the very beginnings of treason, when it was counselled in theory, with hearty fearless opposition, or that they have taken into their dwellings papers that preach treason, or endured in their pulpits preachers that represented it as of God, and godly.

Questions

1. Judging from the above accounts, who took the lead in rescuing Jerry?

2. Could this rescue have been successfully carried off *anywhere* in the North or was Syracuse special?

3. What accounts for the hostility of the *New York Express* editor toward the rescue? Which do you think was more reflective of public opinion in the North — the rescue itself, or this reaction to it?

13-11 The Crime Against Kansas (1856)

Charles Sumner

Born in Boston and educated at Harvard, Charles Sumner (1811–1874) entered the world of New England social reform in the 1840s and moved quickly into antislavery political activity after the organization of the Free-Soil Party in 1848. A political coalition of Free-Soilers and Democrats in Massachusetts sent Sumner to the U.S. Senate in 1851, replacing Daniel Webster, whose authorship of and support for the Compromise of 1850 and the Fugitive Slave Act outraged the growing antislavery sentiment in Massachusetts. Sumner's purpose in the Senate was first and foremost to fight the Slave Power, which he blamed for the outbreak of violence in Kansas (see text pp. 409–410). Sumner took the floor of the Senate over two days (May 19 and 20, 1856) to defend the free-soil settlers and denounce as barbarians the proslavery forces that were attempting to seize control of the territory. In the course of that speech, "The Crime against Kansas," Sumner made derogatory personal references to South Carolina's elderly senator Andrew Butler, who had recently suffered a stroke. Two days later Senator Butler's nephew, Representative Preston S. Brooks of South Carolina, severely beat Sumner with a cane. Brooks became a hero in South Carolina (see text p. 391). Sumner, revered as a martyr to the cause of freedom, won reelection to the Senate until he died.

Source: Charles Sumner: His Complete Works (Lee and Shepard, 1900; reprint, New York: Negro Universities Press edition, 1969), 5:125–126.

Mr. President, — You are now called to redress a great wrong. Seldom in the history of nations is such a question presented. Tariffs, army bills, navy bills, land bills, are important, and justly occupy your care; but these all belong to the course of ordinary legislation. . . . Far otherwise is it with the eminent question now before you, involving, as it does, Liberty in a broad Territory, and also involving the peace of the whole country, with our good name in history forevermore. . . .

The wickedness which I now begin to expose is immeasurably aggravated by the motive which prompted it. Not in any common lust for power did this uncommon tragedy have its origin. It is the rape of a virgin Territory, compelling it to the hateful embrace of Slavery; and it may be clearly traced to a depraved desire for a new Slave State, hideous offspring of such a crime, in the hope of adding to the power of Slavery in the National Government. Yes, Sir, when the whole world alike . . . is rising up to condemn this wrong . . . here in our Republic, *force* — ay, Sir, FORCE — is openly employed in compelling Kansas to this pollution, and all for the sake of political power. . . .

Before entering upon the argument, I must say something of a general character, particularly in response to what has fallen from Senators who have raised themselves to eminence on this floor in championship of human wrong: I mean the Senator from South Carolina [Mr. Butler]. . . . The Senator from South Carolina had read many books of chivalry, and

believes himself a chivalrous knight, with sentiments of honor and courage. Of course he has chosen a mistress to whom he has made his vows, and who, though ugly to others, is always lovely to him, — though polluted in the sight of the world, is chaste in his sight: I mean the harlot Slavery. For her his tongue is always profuse with words. Let her be impeached in character, or any proposition be made to shut her out from the extension of her wantonness, and no extravagance of manner or hardihood of assertion is then too great for this Senator. . . .

I undertake, in the first place, to expose the CRIME AGAINST KANSAS, in origin and extent. . . . The debate [over the Kansas-Nebraska bill], which convulsed Congress, stirred the whole country. From all sides attention was directed upon Kansas, which at once became the favorite goal of emigration. The bill loudly declares that its object is "to leave the people perfectly free to form and regulate their domestic institutions in their own way"; and its supporters everywhere challenge the determination of the question between Freedom and Slavery by a competition of emigration. . . . The populous North, stung by sense of outrage, and inspired by a noble cause, are pouring into the debatable land, and promise soon to establish a supremacy of Freedom.

Then was conceived the consummation of the Crime against Kansas. What could not be accomplished peaceably was to be accomplished forcibly. . . . The violence, for some time threatened, broke forth on the 29th of November, 1854, at the first election of a Delegate to Congress, when companies from Missouri, amounting to upwards of one thousand, crossed into Kansas, and with force and arms proceeded to vote for . . . the candidate of Slavery. . . . Five . . . times and more have these invaders entered Kansas in armed array, and thus five . . . times and more have they trampled upon the organic law of the Territory. These extraordinary expeditions are simply the extraordinary witnesses to successive, uninterrupted violence. . . . Border incursions, which in barbarous ages or barbarous lands fretted and harried an exposed people, are here renewed, with this peculiarity, that our border robbers do not simply levy blackmail and drive off a few cattle . . . they commit a succession of deeds in which . . . the whole Territory is enslaved.

Private griefs mingle their poignancy with public wrongs. I do not dwell on the anxieties of families exposed to sudden assault, and lying down to rest with the alarms of war ringing in the ears, not knowing that another day may be spared to them. . . . Our souls are wrung by individual instances. . . .

Thus was the Crime consummated. Slavery stands erect, clanking its chains on the Territory of Kansas, surrounded by a code of death, and trampling upon all cherished liberties. . . . Emerging from all the blackness of this Crime . . . I come now to the APOLOGIES which the Crime has found. . . .

With regret I come again upon the Senator from South Carolina [Butler. His speech slurred by a stroke, Butler had interjected critical comments on more than thirty occasions while Sumner spoke] who, omnipresent in this debate, overflows with rage at the simple suggestion that Kansas has applied for admission as a State, and, with incoherent phrase, discharges the loose expectoration of his speech, now upon her representative, and then upon her people. . . . [I]t is against the [free-soil majority in] . . . Kansas that sensibilities of the Senator are particularly aroused. . . .

The contest, which, beginning in Kansas, reaches us will be transferred soon from Congress to that broader stage, where every citizen is not only spectator, but actor; and to their judgment I confidently turn. To the people, about to exercise the electoral franchise, in choosing a Chief Magistrate of the Republic, I appeal, to vindicate the electoral franchise in Kansas. Let the ballot-box of the Union . . . protect the ballot-box in that Territory.

Questions

1. According to Sumner, why did the Slave Power no longer support the "popular sovereignty" solution to the question of the extension of slavery?

2. Read Sumner's comments about Senator Butler from the perspective of Representative Preston Brooks. How had Sumner challenged the honor of his uncle?

3. What was the political intent of Sumner's speech? Whom did he expect to agitate with his heated remarks? To what purpose?

13-12 The *Dred Scott* Decision (1857)

In his inaugural address on March 4, 1857, President James Buchanan announced that the constitutional issues associated with the struggle between proslavery and antislavery forces in Kansas would soon be "speedily and finally settled" by the judicial branch of the federal government. Two days later the Supreme Court announced its decision in the case of *Dred Scott v. Sandford*, which the Court had accepted for review in 1854. Scott had been the slave of Dr. John Emerson, a surgeon in the U.S. Army. While on active duty, Emerson had taken Scott to Illinois in 1834 and to the upper Louisiana Purchase territory in 1836 and then had returned to Missouri. Slavery had been excluded in Illinois by the Northwest Ordinance of 1787 and from the upper Louisiana Purchase territory by the Missouri Compromise of 1820. In his suit Scott claimed to have been freed by reason of his residence in free territory (see text p. 414). The Supreme Court's decision came in nine separate decisions, two in dissent. But it was the wide-ranging opinion of Chief Justice Roger B. Taney that was popularly considered the decision of the Court. Taney had been in correspondence with Buchanan before the president's inaugural address. In his decision Taney endeavored to provide a final settlement to the question of slavery.

Source: Dred Scott v. Sandford, 19 How. 393 (1857).

Chief Justice Taney delivered the opinion of the Court.

The question is simply this: Can a negro, whose ancestors were imported into this country, and sold as slaves, become a member of the political community formed and brought into existence by the constitution of the United States, and as such become entitled to all the rights, and privileges, and immunities, guarantied by that instrument to the citizen? One of which rights is the privilege of suing in a court of the United States in the cases specified in the constitution. . . .

The words "people of the United States" and "citizens" are synonymous terms, and mean the same thing. They both describe the political body who, according to our republican institutions, form the sovereignty, and who hold the power and conduct the government through their representatives. They are what we familiarly call the "sovereign people," and every citizen is one of this people, and a constituent member of this sovereignty. The question before us is, whether the class of persons described in the plea in abatement compose a portion of this people, and are constituent members of this sovereignty? We think they are not, and that they are not included, and were not intended to be included, under the word "citizens" in the constitution, and can therefore claim none of the rights and privileges which that instrument provides for and secures to citizens of the United States. On the contrary, they were at that time considered as a subordinate and inferior class of beings, who had been subjugated by the dominant race, and, whether emancipated or not, yet remained subject to their authority, and had no rights or privileges but such as those who held the power and the government might choose to grant them. . . .

In discussing this question, we must not confound the rights of citizenship which a State may confer within its own limits, and the rights of citizenship as a member of the Union. It does not by any means follow, because he [Scott] has all the rights and privileges of a citizen of a State, that he must be a citizen of the United States. He may have all of the rights and privileges of the citizen of a State, and yet not be entitled to the rights and privileges of a citizen in any other State. For, previous to the adoption of the constitution of the United States, every State had the undoubted right to confer on whomsoever it pleased the character of citizen, and to endow him with all its rights. But this character of course was confined to the boundaries of the State, and gave him no rights or privileges in other States beyond those secured to him by the laws of nations and the comity of States. Nor have the several States surrendered the power of conferring these rights and privileges by adopting the constitution of the United States. . . .

It is very clear, therefore, that no State can, by any act or law of its own, passed since the adoption of the constitution, introduce a new member into the political community created by the constitution of the United States. It cannot make him a member of this community by making him a member of its own. And for the same reason it cannot introduce any person, or description of persons, who were not intended to be embraced in this new political family, which the constitu-

tion brought into existence, but were intended to be excluded from it.

The question then arises, whether the provisions of the constitution, in relation to the personal rights and privileges to which the citizen of a State should be entitled, embraced the negro African race, at that time in this country, or who might afterwards be imported, who had then or should afterwards be made free in any State; and to put it in the power of a single State to make him a citizen of the United States, and endue him with the full rights of citizenship in every other State without their consent? Does the constitution of the United States act upon him whenever he shall be made free under the laws of a State, and raised there to the rank of a citizen, and immediately clothe him with all the privileges of a citizen in every other State, and in its own courts?

In the opinion of the court, the legislation and histories of the times, and the language used in the declaration of independence, show, that neither the class of persons who had been imported as slaves, nor their descendants, whether they had become free or not, were then acknowledged as a part of the people, nor intended to be included in the general words used in that memorable instrument. . . .

It is too clear for dispute, that the enslaved African race were not intended to be included, and formed no part of the people who framed and adopted this declaration; for if the language, as understood in that day, would embrace them, the conduct of the distinguished men who framed the declaration of independence would have been utterly and flagrantly inconsistent with the principles they asserted; and instead of the sympathy of mankind, to which they so confidently appealed, they would have deserved and received universal rebuke and reprobation.

We proceed . . . to inquire whether the facts relied on by the plaintiff entitled him to his freedom. . . .

The act of Congress, upon which the plaintiff relies, declares that slavery and involuntary servitude, except as a punishment for crime, shall be forever prohibited in all that part of the territory ceded by France, under the name of Louisiana, which lies north of thirty-six degrees thirty minutes north latitude and not included within the limits of Missouri. And the difficulty which meets us at the threshold of this part of the inquiry is whether Congress was authorized to pass this law under any of the powers granted to it by the Constitution; for, if the authority is not given by that instrument, it is the duty of this Court to declare it void and inoperative and incapable of conferring freedom upon anyone who is held as a slave under the laws of any one of the states.

The counsel for the plaintiff has laid much stress upon that article in the Constitution which confers on Congress the power "to dispose of and make all needful rules and regulations respecting the territory or other property belonging to the United States"; but, in the judgment of the Court, that provision has no bearing on the present controversy, and the power there given, whatever it may be, is confined, and was intended to be confined, to the territory which at that time belonged to, or was claimed by, the United States and was within their boundaries as settled by the [1783] treaty with Great Britain and can have no influence upon a territory afterward acquired from a foreign government. It was a special provision for a known and particular territory, and to meet a present emergency, and nothing more. . . .

. . . It may be safely assumed that citizens of the United States who migrate to a territory belonging to the people of the United States cannot be ruled as mere colonists, dependent upon the will of the general government, and to be governed by any laws it may think proper to impose. The principle upon which our governments rest, and upon which alone they continue to exist, is the union of states, sovereign and independent within their own limits in their internal and domestic concerns, and bound together as one people by a general government, possessing certain enumerated and restricted powers, delegated to it by the people of the several states, and exercising supreme authority within the scope of the powers granted to it, throughout the dominion of the United States. A power, therefore, in the general government to obtain and hold colonies and dependent territories, over which they might legislate without restriction, would be inconsistent with its own existence in its present form. Whatever it acquires, it acquires for the benefit of the people of the several states who created it. It is their trustee acting for them and charged with the duty of promoting the interests of the whole people of the Union in the exercise of the powers specifically granted. . . .

But the power of Congress over the person or property of a citizen can never be a mere discretionary power under our Constitution and form of government. The powers of the government and the rights and privileges of the citizen are regulated and plainly defined by the Constitution itself. And, when the territory becomes a part of the United States, the federal government enters into possession in the character impressed upon it by those who created it. It enters upon it with its powers over the citizen strictly defined and limited by the Constitution, from which it derives its own existence, and by virtue of which alone it continues to exist and act as a government and sovereignty. . . .

Upon these considerations it is the opinion of the Court that the act of Congress which prohibited a citizen from holding and owning property of this kind in the territory of the United States north of the line therein mentioned is not warranted by the Constitution and is therefore void; and that neither Dred Scott himself, nor any of his family, were made free by being carried into this territory; even if they had been carried there by the owner with the intention of becoming a permanent resident.

Questions

1. What did the Court decide about whether a slave had standing to sue in a federal court?

2. If the Court lacked jurisdiction, why do you think Chief Justice Taney went ahead and dealt with the merits? Why did he not just say: "This Court lacks jurisdiction; case dismissed"?

3. What status did Taney say slaves enjoyed at the time the Constitution was adopted?

Questions for Further Thought

1. The passage of the Fugitive Slave Act in 1850 (Document 13-8) and the Supreme Court's 1857 *Dred Scott* decision (Document 13-12) had disturbing implications for Salmon Chase's argument (Document 13-5) about the relationship of the federal government to slavery. In what ways did antislavery forces respond to these reverses?

2. In the debate over the status of slavery in the territories, all sides appealed to the Constitution as legitimizing the validity of their position. From your reading of Documents 13-8 through 13-12 as well as Documents 13-5 and 13-6, what were the specific constitutional issues in question, and how did the different participants in the debate argue their case?

3. Do you think that by the 1850s, northerners like Chase (Document 13-5) and Sumner (Document 13-11) and southerners like Calhoun (Document 13-6) and Taney (Document 13-12) were able to understand one another's positions concerning slavery? Had the political debate in the United States become so polarized that rational discussion on the topic of slavery was impossible?

Abraham Lincoln and the Republican Triumph, 1858–1860

By 1858 the Republican Party had effectively become the major vehicle of opposition to the still-dominant Democrats, supplanting the Whigs and the short-lived, anti-immigrant American ("Know-Nothing") Party. The Republicans, though, were an exclusively northern party; indeed, by building its appeal around opposition to the Slave Power, the Republican Party was as much antisouthern as antislavery. The Democratic Party, on the other hand, spanned the two sections; while southerners dominated its councils and the administration of President James Buchanan, the party retained considerable northern support. Its foremost figure was Senator Stephen A. Douglas of Illinois, the champion of popular sovereignty in Kansas and Nebraska.

In 1858, though, Douglas was challenged for reelection by a prominent Republican lawyer, Abraham Lincoln. Though born poor and largely self-educated, Lincoln was a brilliant debater, and in his celebrated joint appearances with Douglas demonstrated that popular sovereignty was unworkable (Document 13-13). While he won reelection, Douglas's efforts to straddle the sections only excited suspicion of him in both North and South. Southerners were further inflamed the following year when a notorious antislavery bushwhacker from "Bleeding Kansas," John Brown, hoping to foment a slave revolt, launched a private invasion of Virginia (Document 13-14). Brown's character and even his sanity soon became matters of dispute; however, the action he took was almost universally celebrated among abolitionists (Document 13-15).

Southern disaffection with Douglas, and Douglas's increasing resistance to southern demands, led to a split in the Democratic Party in 1860. In the meantime, the Republican Party built a strong coalition tying its crusade against the Slave Power to a number of positive programs that it argued would benefit ordinary white northerners. Behind Lincoln, their standard-bearer, the Republicans received less than 40 percent of the vote in the 1860 elections. But with the Democrats in disarray, and with strong Republican majorities in the populous free states, they gained a majority of electoral votes. For the first time in the history of the Republic, a presidential election had been won solely with the votes of one section, by a party whose core principle was hostility to the other section. The final conflict was now at hand.

13-13   The Lincoln–Douglas Debates (1858)

Stephen Douglas had tried to finesse the issue of slavery in the territories with his theory of popular sovereignty, by which the people could decide. But the *Dred Scott* decision seemed to cut the ground from under his argument. When Lincoln and Douglas ran for the Senate in 1858, they engaged in a series of debates (see text p. 416). At Freeport, Lincoln put the issue to him squarely, and Douglas attempted to resolve the seeming inconsistencies between the Court's ruling and his own political views.

Source: From Alonzo T. Jones, ed., *Political Speeches and Debates of Abraham Lincoln and Stephen A. Douglas, 1854–1861* (Battle Creek, MI, 1895).

LINCOLN'S OPENING SPEECH

As to the first one, in regard to the fugitive slave law, I have never hesitated to say, and I do not now hesitate to say, that I think, under the Constitution of the United States, the people of the southern states are entitled to a congressional fugitive slave law. Having said that, I have had nothing to say in regard to the existing fugitive slave law further than that I think it should have been framed so as to be free from some of the objections that pertain to it, without lessening its efficiency. And inasmuch as we are not now in an agitation in regard to an alteration or modification of that law, I would not be the man to introduce it as a new subject of agitation upon the general question of slavery.

In regard to the other question of whether I am pledged to the admission of any more slave states into the Union, I state to you very frankly that I would be exceedingly sorry ever to be put in a position of having to pass upon that question. I should be exceedingly glad to know that there would never be another slave state admitted into the Union; . . . but I must add, that if slavery shall be kept out of the territories during the territorial existence of any one given territory, and then the people shall, having a fair chance and a clear field, when they come to adopt the constitution, do such an extraordinary thing as to adopt a slave constitution, uninfluenced by the actual presence of the institution among them, I see no alternative, if we own the country, but to admit them into the Union. . . .

The fourth one is in regard to the abolition of slavery in the District of Columbia. In relation to that, I have my mind very distinctly made up. I should be exceedingly glad to see slavery abolished in the District of Columbia. . . . I believe that Congress possesses the constitutional power to abolish it. Yet as a member of Congress, I should not with my present views, be in favor of *endeavoring* to abolish slavery in the District of Columbia, unless it would be upon these conditions. *First*, that the abolition should be gradual. *Second*, that it should be on a vote of the majority of qualified voters in the District, and *third*, that compensation should be made to unwilling owners. With these three conditions, I confess I would be exceedingly glad to see Congress abolish slavery in the District of Columbia, and, in the language of Henry Clay, "sweep from our Capital that foul blot upon our nation." . . .

My answer as to whether I desire that slavery should be prohibited in all the territories of the United States is full and explicit within itself, and cannot be made clearer by any comments of mine. So I suppose in regard to the question of whether I am opposed to the acquisition of any more territory unless slavery is first prohibited therein, my answer is such that I could add nothing by way of illustration, or making myself better understood, than the answer which I have placed in writing. . . .

I now proceed to propound to the Judge the interrogatories, as far as I have framed them. . . . The first one is—

Question 1. If the people of Kansas shall, by means entirely unobjectionable in all other respects, adopt a state constitution, and ask admission into the Union under it, *before* they have the requisite number of inhabitants according to the English Bill—some ninety-three thousand—will you vote to admit them? . . .

Q. 2. Can the people of a United States territory, in any lawful way, against the wish of any citizen of the United States, exclude slavery from its limits prior to the formation of a state constitution? . . .

Q. 3. If the Supreme Court of the United States shall decide that states can not exclude slavery from their limits, are you in favor of acquiescing in, adopting and following such decision as a rule of political action? . . .

Q. 4. Are you in favor of acquiring additional territory, in disregard of how such acquisition may affect the nation on the slavery question? . . .

DOUGLAS'S REPLY

In a few moments I will proceed to review the answers which he has given to these interrogatories; but in order to relieve his anxiety I will first respond to those which he has presented to me. . . .

First, he desires to know if the people of Kansas shall form a constitution by means entirely proper and unobjectionable and ask admission into the Union as a state, before they have the requisite population for a member of Congress, whether I will vote for that admission. . . . In reference to Kansas; it is my opinion, that as she has population enough to constitute a slave state, she has people enough for a free state. . . . I will not make Kansas an exceptional case to the other states of the Union. ("Sound," and "hear, hear.") I hold it to be a sound rule of universal application to require a territory to contain the requisite population for a member of Congress, before it is admitted as a state into the Union. I made that proposition in the Senate in 1856, and I renewed it during the last session, in a bill providing that no territory of the United States should form a constitution and apply for admission until it had the requisite population. . . .

The next question propounded to me by Mr. Lincoln is, can the people of a territory in any lawful way against the wishes of any citizen of the United States; [*sic*] exclude slavery from their limits prior to the formation of a state constitution? I answer emphatically, as Mr. Lincoln has heard me answer a hundred times from every stump in Illinois, that in my opinion the people of a territory can, by lawful means, exclude slavery from their limits prior to the formation of a state constitution. . . . Mr. Lincoln knew that I had answered that question over and over again. He heard me argue the Nebraska Bill on that principle all over the state in 1854, in 1855 and in 1856, and he has no excuse for pretending to be in doubt as to my position on that question. It matters not what way the Supreme Court may hereafter decide as to the abstract question whether slavery may or may not go into a territory under the Constitution, the people have the lawful means to introduce it or exclude it as they please, for the reason that slavery cannot exist a day or an hour anywhere, unless it is supported by local police regulations. . . . Those police regulations can only be established by the local legislature, and if the people are opposed to slavery they will elect representatives to that body who will by unfriendly legislation effectually prevent the introduction of it into their midst. If, on the contrary, they are for it, their legislation will favor its extension. Hence, no matter what the decision of the Supreme Court may be on that abstract question, still the right of the people to make a slave territory or a free territory is perfect and complete under the Nebraska Bill. I hope Mr. Lincoln deems my answer satisfactory on that point. . . .

The third question which Mr. Lincoln presented is, if the Supreme Court of the United States shall decide that a state of this Union cannot exclude slavery from its own limits will I submit to it? I am amazed that Lincoln should ask such a question. . . . Yes, a school boy does know better. Mr. Lincoln's object is to cast an imputation upon the Supreme Court. He knows that there never was but one man in America, claiming any degree of intelligence or decency, who ever for a moment pretended such a thing. It is true that the Washington *Union*, in an article published on the 17th of last December, did put forth that doctrine, and I denounced the article on the floor of the Senate. . . .

The fourth question of Mr. Lincoln is, are you in favor of acquiring additional territory in disregard as to how such acquisition may affect the Union on the slavery question. This question is very ingeniously and cunningly put. . . .

The Black Republican creed lays it down expressly, that under no circumstances shall we acquire any more territory unless slavery is first prohibited in the country. I ask Mr. Lincoln whether he is in favor of that proposition.

Are you (addressing Mr. Lincoln) opposed to the acquisition of any more territory, under any circumstances, unless slavery is prohibited in it? That he does not like to answer. When I ask him whether he stands up to that article in the platform of his party, he turns, Yankee-fashion, and without answering it, asks me whether I am in favor of acquiring territory without regard to how it may affect the Union on the slavery question. . . . I answer that whenever it becomes necessary, in our growth and progress to acquire more territory, that I am in favor of it, without reference to the question of slavery, and when we have acquired it, I will leave the people free to do as they please, either to make it slave or free territory, as they prefer. . . . It is idle to tell me or you that we have territory enough. Our fathers supposed that we had enough when our territory extended to the Mississippi River, but a few years' growth and expansion satisfied them that we needed more, and the Louisiana territory, from the west branch of the Mississippi, to the British possessions, was acquired. Then we acquired Oregon, then California and New Mexico. We have enough now for the present, but this is a young and a growing nation. It swarms as often as a hive of bees, and as new swarms are turned out each year, there must be hives in which they can gather and make their honey.

Questions

1. Which speaker in this exchange do you think was more consistent in his arguments? Why?

2. Does it seem that Lincoln was speaking primarily to one part of the country, and Douglas to the other? Explain.

3. Did Lincoln oppose slavery completely? If not, what was his position?

13-14   The Trial of John Brown (1859)

Lincoln and the Republicans tried to reassure the South that they did not want to disturb slavery where it existed but only to halt its spread. Then came John Brown's attempt to raid the government arsenal at Harpers Ferry and trigger a massive slave rebellion (see text p. 416). Although Republican leaders disavowed his action, private letters showed that he had had support from prominent abolitionists. Brown was tried and convicted of treason, and his statement before sentencing has become a classic. He was hanged on December 2, 1859, and abolitionists, as Emerson said, now had a "new saint." Slaveholders blamed Republican ideas for the raid and more than ever feared a Republican presidential victory.

Source: The Life, Trial and Execution of Captain John Brown . . . (New York: R. M. DeWitt, 1859), 94–95.

The clerk then asked Mr. Brown whether he had anything to say why sentence should not be pronounced upon him.

Mr. Brown immediately rose, and in a clear, distinct voice, said:

I have, may it please the Court, a few words to say. In the first place, I deny everything but what I have all along admitted, of a design on my part to free slaves. I intended certainly to have made a clean thing of that matter, as I did last winter when I went into Missouri, and there took slaves without the snapping of a gun on either side, moving them through the country, and finally leaving them in Canada. I designed to have done the same thing again on a larger scale. That was all I intended to do. I never did intend murder or treason, or the destruction of property, or to excite or incite the slaves to rebellion, or to make insurrection. I have another objection, and that is that it is unjust that I should suffer such a penalty. Had I interfered in the manner which I admit, and which I admit has been fairly proved—for I admire the truthfulness and candor of the greater portion of the witnesses who have testified in this case—had I so interfered in behalf of the rich, the powerful, the intelligent, the so-called great, or in behalf of any of their friends, either father, mother, brother, sister, wife, or children, or any of that class, and suffered and sacrificed what I have in this interference, it would have been all right, and every man in this Court would have deemed it an act worthy of reward rather than punishment. This Court acknowledges, too, as I suppose, the validity of the law of God. I see a book kissed, which I suppose to be the Bible, or at least the New Testament, which teaches me that all things whatsoever I would that men should do to me, I should do even so to them. It teaches me further to remember them that are in bonds as bound with them. I endeavored to act up to that instruction. I say I am yet too young to understand that God is any respecter of persons. I believe that to have interfered as I have done, as I have always freely admitted I have done in behalf of His despised poor, is no wrong, but right. Now, if it is deemed necessary that I should forfeit my life for the furtherance of the ends of justice, and mingle my blood further with the blood of my children and with the blood of millions in this slave country whose rights are disregarded by wicked, cruel, and unjust enactments, I say let it be done. Let me say one word further. I feel entirely satisfied with the treatment I have received on my trial. Considering all the circumstances, it has been more generous than I expected. But I feel no consciousness of guilt. I have stated from the first what was my intention, and what was not. I never had any design against the liberty of any person, nor any disposition to commit treason or excite slaves to rebel or make any general insurrection. I never encouraged any man to do so, but always discouraged any idea of that kind. Let me say also in regard to statements made by some of those who were connected with me, I fear it has been stated by some of them that I have induced them to join me, but the contrary is true. I do not say this to injure them, but as regretting their weakness. Not one but joined me of his own accord, and the greater part at their own expense. A number of them I never saw, and never had a word of conversation with till the day they came to me, and that was for the purpose I have stated. Now, I am done.

While Mr. Brown was speaking, perfect quiet prevailed, and when he had finished the Judge proceeded to pronounce sentence upon him. After a few primary remarks, he said, that no reasonable doubt could exist of the guilt of the prisoner, and sentenced him to be hung in public, on Friday, the 2d of December next.

Mr. Brown received his sentence with composure.

Questions

1. Do you think Brown really meant to free so many slaves without firing a shot? If so, why did he seize the arsenal?

2. Was Brown making a legal argument, or was he appealing to a "higher authority"?

3. Does it appear to you that Brown was seeking martyrdom? Why or why not?

13-15   Letter to His Parents (1859)

John A. Copeland Jr.

Five black men were with John Brown at Harpers Ferry in October 1859 (see text p. 416). One of the two taken captive, and nearly lynched before he could be tried for murder, conspiracy, and treason, was John A. Copeland Jr. a twenty-three-year-old Oberlin

College student who had once been jailed in Ohio for violating the fugitive slave law when he assisted in liberating a runaway from two slave catchers. There was little doubt about the outcome of Copeland's trial in Charlestown, Virginia. After Brown's conviction in a separate trial, the jury quickly found Copeland guilty of murder and conspiracy—the charge of treason having earlier been dropped by the prosecution—and the judge sentenced him to be hanged. Among the last letters written by Copeland prior to his execution on December 16 was the following to his parents.

Source: Excerpt from *The Black Abolitionist Papers*, ed. C. Peter Ripley, et al. (Chapel Hill: University of North Carolina Press, 1992), 5:43, 45. Used by permission of the publisher.

Charlesto[w]n, V[irgini]a
Nov[ember] 26, [18]59

Dear father & mother:

I now take my pen to address you for the first time since I have been in the situation that I am now in. My silence has not been occasioned by my want of love for you but because I wished to wait & find what my doom would be. I am well at this time & as happy as it is possible to be under the circumstances. I received your kind and affectionate letter, which brought much consolation to me, & the advice that you have therein given me. I thank God I can say I have accepted, & I have found that consolation which can only be found by accepting & obeying such advice.

Dear father & mother, happy am I that I can now truthfully say that I have sought the Holy Bible & have found that everlasting Life in its holy advice, which man can from no other source obtain. Yes, I have now in the eleventh hour sought for & obtained that forgiveness from my God, whose kindness I have outraged nearly all my life.

Dear Parents, my fate so far as man can seal it, is sealed, but let not this fact occasion you any misery; for remember the <u>cause</u> in which I was engaged; <u>remember it was a holy cause</u>, one in which men in every way better than I am, have suffered & died. Remember that if I must die, I die in trying to liberate a few of my poor & oppressed people from a condition of servitude against which God in his word has hurled his most bitter denunciations, a cause in which men, who though removed from its direct injurious effects by the color of their faces have already lost their lives, & more yet must meet the fate which man has decided I must meet. If die I must, I shall try to meet my fate as a man who can suffer in the glorious cause in which I have been engaged, without a groan, & meet my Maker in heaven as a christian man who through the saving grace of God has made his peace with Him.

Dear Parents, dear bros & sisters; miserable indeed would I be if I were confined in this jail awaiting the execution of the law for committing a foul crime; but this not being the case, I must say (though I know you all will feel deeply the fate I am to meet), that I feel more deeply on acc't of the necessity of myself or any other man having to suffer by the existence of slavery, than from the mere fact of having to die. It is true I should like to see you all once more on the earth, but God wills otherwise. Therefore I am content, for most certainly do I believe that God wills everything for the best good, not only of those who have to suffer directly, but of all, & this being the case I beg of you not to grieve about me. Now dear Parents I beg your forgiveness for every wrong I have done you, for I know that I have not at all times treated you as I ought to have done. Remember me while I shall live & forget me not when I am no longer in this world. Give my love to all friends. There are some little matters that I would give most anything to have settled & made right. There have been misrepresentations of things which I have said; & if I can I shall correct them.

Oh brothers, I pray you may never have to suffer as I shall have to do: stay at home contentedly, make your home happy not only to yourselves but to all with whom you may be connected.

Dear Brothers & sisters, love one another, make each other happy, love, serve & obey your God, & meet me in heaven. Now, dear father & mother, I will close this last—or at present I think last letter—I shall have the pleasure of writing to you.

Good-bye Mother & Father, Goodbye brothers & sisters, & by the assistance of God, meet me in heaven. I remain your most affectionate son,

John A. Copeland

Questions

1. Southerners and Northerners reacted differently to John Brown's raid and execution (see text pp. 416–417). How might they have responded to Copeland's participation and fate? Would their feelings have been more or less intense?

2. Compare Copeland's justification of his actions with the antislavery sentiments of Frederick Douglass (see text p. 403). In what ways were they similar? Dissimilar?

3. Compare Copeland's views with those of the leaders of the American Anti-Slavery Society (see text pp. 351–354). Would they have approved of his condemnation of slavery? Would they have approved of the actions he took against the institution?

Questions for Further Thought

1. From a political standpoint, why was Lincoln's election to the presidency in 1860 so threatening to southerners? If Calhoun (Document 13-6) had lived to witness the election, do you think that he would have seen the Republican victory as confirming his fear of the permanent inferiority of southerners within the Union? If so, why?

2. A school of historical thought has held that the slave plantation system was approaching its natural geographic limits by the 1850s, and it would not have become important in the western territories even if it had had free rein there. If so, what was the fuss about?

3. Whether in Thomas Jefferson's drafting of the Declaration of Independence, the debates at the Constitutional Convention, the Missouri Compromise (1820), or the Compromise of 1850, Americans in the North, South, and West had continually compromised on the issue of slavery to save the Union. Why, by 1860, had compromise for the Union become impossible?

CHAPTER FOURTEEN

Two Societies at War
1861–1865

Secession and Military Stalemate, 1861–1862, and *Toward Total War*

The election of Abraham Lincoln in 1860 represented a fundamental shift in the balance of power within the federal Union. For the first time in the history of the country, a president had been elected without any support from the slaveholding states; furthermore, Lincoln was the candidate of a party whose central ideology was *opposition* to the Slave Power. To be sure, Lincoln's election did not mean Republican control of the federal government: Democrats, including southern Democrats, still controlled the Congress, and the Supreme Court was still the same court that had less than four years earlier handed down the *Dred Scott* decision. But secessionists convincingly argued that the election, along with resistance to enforcement of the Fugitive Slave Act and widespread northern sympathy for John Brown, demonstrated that northerners could no longer be depended on to protect the South's "peculiar institution" (Document 14-1). South Carolina, long a hotbed of secessionist sentiment, led the way in leaving the Union, followed quickly by the rest of the Lower South: Georgia, Florida, Alabama, Mississippi, Louisiana, and Texas. In February 1861, the seven seceded states joined together as the new Confederate States of America (Document 14-2).

Lincoln took office on March 4, 1861, determined to face down the secessionists but seeking to proceed in a manner that would not spark further defections among the states of the Upper South (Document 14-3). The presence of a federal garrison at Fort Sumter in Charleston Harbor, however, became a flash point for Confederates who regarded it as an occupying force. Insistent on continuing the Union's sovereignty over the fort, Lincoln vowed to resupply the garrison, whereupon Confederate forces began an artillery bombardment that forced the garrison's surrender (Document 14-4). In Lincoln's eyes, secession was now rebellion, and he called for troops to suppress it—an action that sent Arkansas, Tennessee, North Carolina, and Virginia into the Confederate camp. The Civil War had begun.

At first, the war was makeshift. Although the first skirmish, the Battle of Bull Run (Manassas), was a disaster for the Union side, the Confederates were scarcely able to follow up on their victory. By 1862 both sides had successfully mobilized armies, and were also mobilizing their civilian populations to support the troops (Document 14-5). Furthermore, the Confederates had found a brilliant military leader in Robert E. Lee. Thanks largely to a remarkable string of victories by Lee's Army of Northern Virginia, the Confederacy successfully held off Union forces and even launched two counterstrikes into Union territory in the fall of 1862. To be sure, the Union was showing greater success than the Confederacy at mustering its resources. The Union government paid for the war with a balanced program of taxes, bond sales to a mass market, and a moderate issue of paper currency ("greenbacks"); the Confederacy, wedded to small and decentralized government and fearing to alienate the powerful planters, resorted to massive issues of paper money, sparking ruinous inflation. Nonetheless, many outside observers were convinced that the Confederacy would be successful in maintaining its independence and that the Union would lack the staying power to continue the struggle—an opinion bolstered by major Republican reverses in the 1862 elections.

14-1   South Carolina Secedes from the Union (1860)

Charles Memminger

The secession crisis was both a constitutional and a social problem in the eyes of white southerners (see text p. 424). Secessionists believed that the election of Lincoln threatened not only their slave property but also their freedom from a coercive central government in Washington. By exaggerating the policies of northern Republicans, secessionists convinced other white southerners that Republicans were revolutionaries bent on racial amalgamation and the destruction of southern society.

On December 20, 1860, three months before Lincoln was inaugurated, the South Carolina convention passed a terse Ordinance of Secession. The prominent Charleston lawyer and politician Charles Memminger was charged with writing a detailed explanation and defense of the state's action. Memminger argued that the North was wholly to blame, that the nonslaveholding states had violated the "constitutional compact" regarding slavery. (Memminger later served as chairman of the committee that drafted the Confederate constitution and as treasury secretary of the Confederacy.)

Sources: South Carolina State Archives, Columbia, South Carolina. Available in Henry Steele Commager and Milton Cramer, *Documents of American History*, 10th ed. (Englewood Cliffs, NJ: Prentice Hall, 1988), 1:372; *Declaration of the Immediate Causes Which Induce and Justify the Secession of South Carolina from the Federal Union* (Charleston, SC: Evans and Cogswell, 1860).

(a) South Carolina Ordinance of Secession December 20, 1860

An Ordinance to Dissolve the Union between the State of South Carolina and other States united with her under the compact entitled the Constitution of the United States of America:

We, the people of the State of South Carolina, in Convention assembled, do declare and ordain, and it is hereby declared and ordained, that the ordinance adopted by us in Convention, on the 23d day of May, in the year of our Lord 1788, whereby the Constitution of the United States of America was ratified, and also all Acts and parts of Acts of the General Assembly of this State ratifying the amendments of the said Constitution, are hereby repealed, and that the union now subsisting between South Carolina and other States under the name of the United States of America is hereby dissolved.

(b) Declaration of the Immediate Causes [for] the Secession of South Carolina

The People of the State of South Carolina, in Convention assembled, on the 2d of April, A.D., 1852, declared that the frequent violations of the Constitution of the United States, by the Federal Government, and its encroachments upon the reserved rights of the States, fully justified this State in then withdrawing from the Federal Union; but in deference to the opinions and wishes of the other slaveholding States, she forbore at that time to exercise this right. Since that time, these encroachments have continued to increase, and further forbearance ceases to be a virtue.

And now the State of South Carolina having resumed her separate and equal place among nations, deems it due to herself, to the remaining United States of America, and to the nations of the world, that she should declare the immediate causes which have led to this act.

In the year 1765, that portion of the British Empire embracing Great Britain, undertook to make laws for the government of that portion composed of the thirteen American Colonies. A struggle for the right of self-government ensued, which resulted, on the 4th July, 1776, in a Declaration by the Colonies, "that they are, and of right ought to be, FREE AND INDEPENDENT STATES; and that, as free and independent States, they have full power to levy war, conclude peace, contract alliances, establish commerce, and to do all other acts and things which independent States may of right do."

They further solemnly declared that whenever any "form of government becomes destruction of the ends for which it was established, it is the right of the people to alter or abolish it, and to institute a new government." Deeming the Government of Great Britain to have become destructive of these ends, they declared that the Colonies "are absolved from all allegiance to the British Crown, and that all political connection between them and the State of Great Britain is, and ought to be, totally dissolved."

In pursuance of this Declaration of Independence, each of the thirteen States proceeded to exercise its separate sovereignty; adopted for itself a Constitution, and appointed officers for the administration of government in all its departments—Legislative, Executive and Judicial. For purposes of defence, they united their arms and their counsels; and, in 1778, they entered into a league known as the Articles of Confederation, whereby they agreed to entrust the administration of their external relations to a common agent, known as the Congress of the United States, expressly declaring, in the first article, "that each State retains its sovereignty, freedom and independence, and every power, jurisdiction and right which is not, by this Confederation, expressly delegated to the United States in Congress assembled."

Under this Confederation the War of the Revolution was carried on, and on the 3d September, 1783, the contest ended, and a definitive Treaty was signed by Great Britain, in which she acknowledged the Independence of the Colonies in the following terms:

Article 1.—His Britannic Majesty acknowledges the said United States, viz: New Hampshire, Massachusetts Bay, Rhode Island and Providence Plantations, Connecticut, New York, New Jersey, Pennsylvania, Delaware, Maryland, Virginia, North Carolina, South Carolina and Georgia, to be FREE, SOVEREIGN AND INDEPENDENT STATES; that he treats them as such; and for himself, his heirs and successors, relinquishes all claims to the government, propriety and territorial rights of the same and every part thereof.

Thus were established the two great principles asserted by the Colonies, namely: the right of a State to govern itself; and the right of a people to abolish a Government when it becomes destructive of the ends for which it was instituted. And concurrent with the establishment of these principles, was the fact, that each Colony became and was recognized by the mother Country as a FREE, SOVEREIGN AND INDEPENDENT STATE.

In 1787, Deputies were appointed by the States to revise the Articles of Confederation, and on the 17th September, 1787, these Deputies recommended, for the adoption of the States, the Articles of Union, known as the Constitution of the United States.

The parties to whom this Constitution was submitted, were the several sovereign States; they were to agree or disagree, and when nine of them agreed, the compact was to take effect among those concurring; and the General Government, as the common agent, was then to be invested with their authority.

If only nine of the thirteen States had concurred, the other four would have remained as they then were—separate, sovereign States, independent of any of the provisions of the Constitution. In fact, two of the States did not accede to the Constitution until long after it had gone into operation among the other eleven; and during that interval, they each exercised the functions of an independent nation.

By this Constitution, certain duties were imposed upon the several States, and the exercise of certain of their powers were restrained, which necessarily implied their continued existence as sovereign States. But, to remove all doubt, an amendment was added, which declared that the powers of delegated to the United States by the Constitution, nor prohibited by it to the States, are reserved to the States, respectively, or to the people. On 23d May, 1788, South Carolina, by a Convention of her people, passed an Ordinance assenting to this Constitution, and afterwards altered her own Constitution, to conform herself to the obligations she had undertaken.

Thus was established, by compact between the States, a Government, with defined objects and powers, limited to the express words of the grant. This limitation left the whole remaining mass of power subject to the clause reserving it to the States or to the people, and rendered unnecessary any specification of reserved rights.

We hold that the Government thus established is subject to the two great principles asserted in the Declaration of Independence; and we hold further, that the mode of its formation subjects it to a third fundamental principle, namely: the law of compact. We maintain that in every compact between two or more parties, the obligation is mutual; that the failure of one of the contracting parties to perform a material part of the agreement, entirely releases the obligation of the other; and that where no arbiter is provided, each party is remitted to his own judgment to determine the fact of failure, with all its consequences.

In the present case, that fact is established with certainty. We assert, that fourteen of the States have deliberately refused for years past to fulfill their constitutional obligations, and we refer to their own Statutes for the proof.

The Constitution of the United States, in its 4th Article, provides as follows:

No person held to service or labor in one State, under the laws thereof, escaping into another shall, in consequence of any law or regulation therein, be discharged from such service or labor, but shall be delivered up, on claim of the party to whom such service or labor may be due.

This stipulation was so material to the compact, that without it that compact would not have been made. The greater number of the contracting parties held slaves, and they had previously evinced their estimate of the value of such a stipulation by making it a condition in the Ordinance for the government of the territory ceded by Virginia, which now composes the States north of the Ohio river.

The same article of the Constitution stipulates also for rendition by the several States of fugitives from justice from the other States.

The General Government, as the common agent, passed laws to carry into effect these stipulations of the States. For many years these laws were executed. But an increasing hostility on the part of the non-slaveholding States to the Institution of Slavery has led to a disregard of their obligations, and the laws of the General Government have ceased to effect the objects of the Constitution. The States of Maine, New Hampshire, Vermont, Massachusetts, Connecticut, Rhode Island, New York, Pennsylvania, Illinois, Indiana, Michigan, Wisconsin and Iowa, have enacted laws which either nullify the Acts of Congress or render useless any attempt to execute them. In many of these States the fugitive is discharged from the service or labor claimed, and in none of them has the State Government complied with the stipulation made in the Constitution. The State of New Jersey, at an early day, passed a law in conformity with her constitutional obligation; but the current of anti-slavery feeling has led her more recently to enact laws which render inoperative the remedies provided by her own law and by the laws of Congress. In the State of New York even the right of transit for a slave has been denied by her tribunals; and the States of Ohio and Iowa have refused to surrender to justice fugitives charged with murder, and with inciting servile insurrection in the State of Virginia. Thus the constitutional compact has been deliberately broken and disregarded by the non-slaveholding States, and the consequence follows that South Carolina is released from her obligation.

The ends for which this Constitution was framed are declared by itself to be "to form a more perfect union, establish justice, insure domestic tranquility, provide for the common defence, promote the general welfare, and secure the blessings of liberty to ourselves and our posterity."

These ends it endeavored to accomplish by a Federal Government, in which each State was recognized as an equal, and had separate control over its own institutions. The right of property in slaves was recognized by giving to free persons distinct political rights, by giving them the right to represent, and burthening them with direct taxes for three-fifths of their slaves; by authorizing the importation of slaves for twenty years; and by stipulating for the rendition of fugitives from labor.

We affirm that these ends for which this Government was instituted have been defeated, and the Government itself has been made destructive of them by the action of the non-slaveholding States. Those States have assumed the right of deciding upon the propriety of our domestic institutions; and have denied the rights of property established in fifteen of the States and recognized by the Constitution; they have denounced as sinful the institution of slavery; they have permitted the open establishment among them of societies, whose avowed object is to disturb the peace and to eloign [take away] the property of the citizens of other States. They have encouraged and assisted thousands of our slaves to leave their homes; and those who remain, have been incited by emissaries, books and pictures to servile insurrection.

For twenty-five years this agitation has been steadily increasing, until it has now secured to its aid the power of the Common Government. Observing the *forms* of the Constitution, a sectional party has found within that article establishing the Executive Department, the means of subverting the Constitution itself. A geographical line has been drawn across the Union, and all the States north of that line have united in the election of a man to the high office of President of the United States whose opinions and purposes are hostile to slavery. He is to be entrusted with the administration of the Common Government, because he has declared that that "Government cannot endure permanently half slave, half free," and that the public mind must rest in the belief that Slavery is in the course of ultimate extinction.

This sectional combination for the subversion of the Constitution, has been aided in some of the States by elevating to citizenship persons, who, by the Supreme Law of the land, are incapable of becoming citizens; and their votes have been used to inaugurate a new policy, hostile to the South, and destructive to its peace and safety.

On the 4th of March next, this party will take possession of the Government. It has announced, that the South shall be excluded from the common Territory; that the Judicial Tribunals shall be made sectional, and that a war must be waged against slavery until it shall cease throughout the United States.

The Guaranties of the Constitution will then no longer exist; the equal rights of the States will be lost. The slaveholding States will no longer have the power of self-government, or self-protection, and the Federal Government will have become their enemy.

Sectional interest and animosity will deepen the irritation, and all hope of remedy is rendered vain, by the fact that public opinion at the North has invested a great political error with the sanctions of a more erroneous religious belief.

We, therefore, the people of South Carolina, by our delegates, in Convention assembled appealing to the Supreme Judge of the world for the rectitude of our intentions, have solemnly declared that the Union heretofore existing between this State and the other States of North America, is dissolved, and that the State of South Carolina has resumed her position among the nations of the world, as a separate and independent State; with full power to levy war, conclude peace, contract alliances, establish commerce, and to do all other acts and things which independent States may of right do.

Questions

1. What similarities are there in tone and wording between the two South Carolina documents and the American Declaration of Independence (see text p. D-1)?

2. On what three fundamental principles did Memminger rest his argument?

3. It is often said that the Confederate states seceded to protest an overweening federal government. What (or who) was the principal target of the "Declaration of Causes," and why?

14-2   Constitution of the Confederate States (1861)

By early February of 1861 representatives from South Carolina, Mississippi, Florida, Alabama, Georgia, Louisiana, and Texas met in Montgomery, Alabama, to establish the foundations of government for the Confederate states. Quickly adopting a provisional constitution and electing a provisional president and vice president for the new federal Union, the convention assumed the role of an interim Congress while awaiting the report of a drafting committee assigned to work on a permanent frame of government. Finally, at the end of February, it received the committee's draft, and after ten days of debate adopted the Constitution of the Confederate States of America, portions of which are excerpted here.

Source: Paul Leicester Ford, ed., *The Federalist: A Commentary on the Constitution of the United States* (New York: Henry Holt, 1898), 720–721, 724–725, 727–732.

CONSTITUTION OF THE CONFEDERATE STATES OF AMERICA, 1861.

We, the people of the Confederate States, each State acting in its sovereign and independent character, in order to form a permanent federal government, establish justice, insure domestic tranquillity, and secure the blessings of liberty to ourselves and our posterity—invoking the favor and guidance of Almighty God—do ordain and establish this Constitution of the Confederate States of America.

ARTICLE I.

SECTION 1. [1]All legislative powers herein delegated shall be vested in a Congress of the Confederate States, which shall consist of a Senate and House of Representatives.

SEC. 2. [1]The House of Representatives shall be composed of members chosen every second year by the people of the several States; and the electors in each State shall be citizens of the Confederate States, and have the qualifications requisite for electors of the most numerous branch of the State Legislature: but no person of foreign birth, not a citizen of the Confederate States, shall be allowed to vote for any officer, civil or political, State or federal.

[2]No person shall be a Representative who shall not have attained the age of twenty-five years, and be a citizen of the Confederate States, and who shall not, when elected, be an inhabitant of that State in which he shall be chosen.

[3]Representatives and direct taxes shall be apportioned among the several States which may be included within this Confederacy, according to their respective numbers—which shall be determined by adding to the whole number of free persons, including those bound to service for a term of years, and excluding Indians not taxed, three-fifths of all slaves. . . .

SEC. 3. [1]The Senate of the Confederate States shall be composed of two Senators from each State, chosen for six years by the Legislature thereof at the regular session next immediately preceding the commencement of the term of service; and each Senator shall have one vote. . . .

[4]The Vice President of the Confederate States shall be President of the Senate; but shall have no vote, unless they be equally divided. . . .

SEC. 6. [3]No Senator or Representative shall, during the time for which he was elected, be appointed to any civil office under the authority of the Confederate States, which shall have been created, or the emoluments whereof shall have been increased during such time; and no person holding any office under the Confederate States shall be a member of either House during his continuance in office. But Congress may, by law, grant to the principal officer in each of the Executive Departments a seat upon the floor of either House, with the privilege of discussing any measure appertaining to his department.

SEC. 7. [1]All bills for raising revenue shall originate in the House of Representatives; but the Senate may propose or concur with amendments, as on other bills.

SEC. 8. The Congress shall have power—

[1]To lay and collect taxes, duties, imposts and excises for revenue necessary to pay the debts, provide for the common defense, and to carry on the government of the Confederate States; but no bounties shall be granted from the treasury; nor shall any duties or taxes on importations from foreign nations be laid to promote or foster any branch of industry; and all duties, imposts and excises shall be uniform throughout the Confederate States:

[2]To borrow money on the credit of the Confederate States:

[3]To regulate commerce with foreign nations, and among the several States, and with the Indian tribes; but neither this, nor any other clause contained in the Constitution, shall ever be construed to delegate the power to Congress to appropriate money for any internal improvement intended to facilitate commerce; except for the purpose of furnishing lights, beacons, and buoys, and other aids to navigation upon the coasts, and the improvement of harbors and the removing of obstructions in river navigation, in all which cases, such duties shall be laid on the navigation facilitated thereby, as may be necessary to pay the costs and expenses thereof:

[4]To establish uniform laws of naturalization, and uniform laws on the subject of bankruptcies, throughout the Confederate States, but no law of Congress shall discharge any debt contracted before the passage of the same:

[5]To coin money, regulate the value thereof and of foreign coin, and fix the standard of weights and measures:

[6]To provide for the punishment of counterfeiting the securities and current coin of the Confederate States:

[7]To establish post offices and post routes; but the expenses of the Post Office Department, after the first day of March, in the year of our Lord eighteen hundred and sixty-three, shall be paid out of its own revenues:

[8]To promote the progress of science and useful arts, by securing for limited times to authors and inventors the exclusive right to their respective writings and discoveries:

[9]To constitute tribunals inferior to the Supreme Court:

[10]To define and punish piracies and felonies committed on the high seas, and offenses against the law of nations:

[11]To declare war, grant letters of marque and reprisal, and make rules concerning captures on land and water:

[12]To raise and support armies; but no appropriation of money to that use shall be for a longer term than two years:

[13]To provide and maintain a navy:

[14]To make rules for the government and regulation of the land and naval forces:

[15]To provide for calling forth the militia to execute the laws of the Confederate States, suppress insurrections, and repel invasions:

[16]To provide for organizing, arming and disciplining the militia, and for governing such part of them as may be employed in the service of the Confederate States; reserving to the States, respectively, the appointment of the officers, and the authority of training the militia according to the discipline prescribed by Congress:

[17]To exercise exclusive legislation, in all cases whatsoever, over such district (not exceeding ten miles square) as may, by cession of one or two States and the acceptance of Congress, become the seat of the Government of the Confederate States; and to exercise like authority over all places purchased by the consent of the Legislature of the State in which the same shall be, for the erection of forts, magazines, arsenals, dockyards, and other needful buildings: and

[18]To make all laws which shall be necessary and proper for carrying into execution the foregoing powers, and all other powers vested by this Constitution in the government of the Confederate States, or in any department or officer thereof.

SEC. 9. [1]The importation of negroes of the African race, from any foreign country, other than the slaveholding States or Territories of the United States of America, is hereby forbidden; and Congress is required to pass such laws as shall effectually prevent the same.

[2]Congress shall also have power to prohibit the introduction of slaves from any State not a member of, or Territory not belonging to, this Confederacy.

[3]The privilege of the *habeas corpus* shall not be suspended, unless when in cases of rebellion or invasion the public safety may require it.

[4]No bill of attainder, *ex post facto* law, or law denying or impairing the right of property in negro slaves, shall be passed. . . .

[9]Congress shall appropriate no money from the treasury except by a vote of two-thirds of both Houses, taken by yeas and nays, unless it be asked and estimated for by some one of the heads of department, and submitted to Congress by the President; or for the purpose of paying its own expenses and contingencies; or for the payment of claims against the Confederate States, the justice of which shall have been judicially declared by a tribunal for the investigation of claims against the Government, which it is hereby made the duty of Congress to establish. . . .

[12]Congress shall make no law respecting an establishment of religion, or prohibiting the free exercise thereof; or abridging the freedom of speech, or of the press; or the right of the people peaceably to assemble and petition the Government for a redress of grievances.

[13]A well-regulated militia being necessary to the security of a free State, the right of the people to keep and bear arms shall not be infringed.

ARTICLE II.

SECTION 1. [1]The executive power shall be vested in a President of the Confederate States of America. He and the Vice President shall hold their offices for the term of six years; but the President shall not be re-eligible. . . .

[10]Before he enters on the execution of his office, he shall take the following oath or affirmation:

"I do solemnly swear (or affirm) that I will faithfully execute the office of President of the Confederate States, and will, to the best of my ability, preserve, protect, and defend the Constitution thereof."

Sec. 2. . . . [2]He shall have power, by and with the advice and consent of the Senate, to make treaties, provided two-thirds of the Senators present concur; and he shall nominate, and by and with the advice and consent of the Senate, shall appoint ambassadors, other public ministers and consuls, Judges of the Supreme Court, and all other officers of the Confederate States, whose appointments are not herein otherwise provided for, and which shall be established by law; but the Congress may, by law, vest the appointment of such inferior officers, as they think proper, in the President alone, in the courts of law, or in the heads of Departments. . . .

Sec. 4. [1]The President, Vice President, and all civil officers of the Confederate States, shall be removed from office on impeachment for, and conviction of, treason, bribery or other high crimes and misdemeanors.

ARTICLE III.

Section 1. [1]The judicial power of the Confederate States shall be vested in one Supreme Court, and in such Inferior Courts as the Congress may from time to time ordain and establish. The judges, both of the Supreme and Inferior Courts, shall hold their offices during good behavior, and shall, at stated times, receive for their services a compensation, which shall not be diminished during their continuance in office.

Sec. 2. [1]The judicial power shall extend to all cases arising under this Constitution, the laws of the Confederate States, and treaties made or which shall be made under their authority; to all cases affecting ambassadors, other public ministers and consuls; to all cases of admiralty and maritime jurisdiction; to controversies to which the Confederate States shall be a party; to controversies between two or more States; between a State and citizens of another State where the State is plaintiff; between citizens claiming lands under grants of different States, and between a State or the citizens thereof, and foreign States, citizens or subjects; but no State shall be sued by a citizen or subject of any foreign State.

ARTICLE IV.

. . . Section 2. . . . [3]No slave or other person held to service or labor in any State or territory of the Confederate States, under the laws thereof, escaping or lawfully carried into another, shall, in consequence of any law or regulation therein, be discharged from such service or labor; but shall be delivered up on claim of the party to whom such slave belongs, or to whom such service or labor may be due.

Sec. 3. [1]Other States may be admitted into this Confederacy by a vote of two-thirds of the whole House of Representatives, and two-thirds of the Senate, the Senate voting by States; but no new State shall be formed or erected within the jurisdiction of any other State; nor any State be formed by the junction of two or more States, or parts of States, without the consent of the Legislatures of the States concerned, as well as of the Congress.

[2]The Congress shall have power to dispose of and make all needful rules and regulations concerning the property of the Confederate States, including the lands thereof.

[3]The Confederate States may acquire new territory; and Congress shall have power to legislate and provide governments for the inhabitants of all territory belonging to the Confederate States, lying without the limits of the several States; and may permit them, at such times, and in such manner as it may by law provide, to form States to be admitted into the Confederacy. In all such territory, the institution of negro slavery as it now exists in the Confederate States, shall be recognized and protected by Congress, by the territorial government; and the inhabitants of the several Confederate States and Territories, shall have the right to take to such territory any slaves, lawfully held by them in any of the States or territories of the Confederate States.

[4]The Confederate States shall guarantee to every State that now is or hereafter may become a member of this Confederacy, a republican form of government, and shall protect each of them against invasion; and on application of the Legislature (or of the Executive, when the Legislature is not in session) against domestic violence.

ARTICLE V.

[1]Upon the demand of any three States, legally assembled in their several Conventions, the Congress shall summon a convention of all the States, to take into consideration such amendments to the Constitution as the said States shall concur in suggesting at the time when the said demand is made; and should any of the proposed amendments to the Constitution be agreed on by the said Convention—voting by States—and the same be ratified by the Legislatures of two-thirds of the several States, or by Conventions in two-thirds thereof—as the one or the other mode of ratification may be proposed by the general Convention—they shall thenceforward form a part of this Constitution. But no State shall, without its consent, be deprived of its equal representation in the Senate.

ARTICLE VI.

. . . [3]This Constitution, and the laws of the Confederate States, made in pursuance thereof, and all treaties made, or which shall be made, under the authority of the Confederate States, shall be the supreme law of the land; and the judges in every States shall be bound thereby, anything in the Constitution or laws of any State to the contrary notwithstanding. . . .

[5]The enumeration, in the Constitution, of certain rights, shall not be construed to deny or disparage others retained by the people of the several States.

[6]The powers not delegated to the Confederate States by the Constitution, nor prohibited by it to the States, are reserved to the States, respectively, or to the people thereof.

ARTICLE VII.

[1]The ratification of the conventions of five States shall be sufficient for the establishment of this Constitution between the States so ratifying the same.

Questions

1. The committee that drafted the Confederate Constitution used the U.S. Constitution as a model. Is this surprising?

2. What are some of the more notable differences between the U.S. Constitution and the Confederate Constitution? Why are these differences significant? What do they reveal?

3. Some of the more radical secessionists were disappointed by this Constitution. Why? How is slavery dealt with under this Constitution? What is the significance of the inclusion of a "necessary and proper" clause, and is this surprising? Was it possible for a nonslaveholding state to join the Confederacy under the terms of this Constitution?

4. There are no provisions for secession or nullification in this Constitution. Why not?

14-3   First Inaugural Address (1861)

Abraham Lincoln

Abraham Lincoln took the presidential oath of office with the nation in crisis. Although he made clear in the 1860 campaign that he did not intend to interfere with slavery in the states where it already existed, he had carried none of the southern states. Soon after his election, South Carolina seceded from the union (see Document 14-1). Three decades earlier, during the nullification crisis of 1832–1833 (see Document 10-8), South Carolina had failed to persuade any other state to join its cause. But the situation had changed in the intervening years; this time, six states—Mississippi, Florida, Alabama, Georgia, Louisiana, and Texas—chose to follow South Carolina's lead. Meeting in a southern convention in early 1861, these states proclaimed the establishment of the Confederate States of America, elected Jefferson Davis as its president, and began drafting a constitution for the Confederacy (see Document 14-2). At his inauguration in March 1861, therefore, Lincoln spoke to a divided nation on the brink of civil war.

Source: Reprinted courtesy of the Abraham Lincoln Association.

I hold, that in contemplation of universal law, and of the Constitution, the Union of these States is perpetual. Perpetuity is implied, if not expressed, in the fundamental law of all national governments. It is safe to assert that no government proper, ever had a provision in its organic law for its own termination. Continue to execute all the express provisions of our national Constitution, and the Union will endure forever—it being impossible to destroy it, except by some action not provided for in the instrument itself.

Again, if the United States be not a government proper, but an association of States in the nature of contract merely, can it, as a contract, be peaceably unmade, by less than all the parties who made it? One party to a contract may violate it—break it, so to speak; but does it not require all to lawfully rescind it?

Descending from these general principles, we find the proposition that, in legal contemplation, the Union is perpetual, confirmed by the history of the Union itself. The Union is much older than the Constitution. It was formed in fact, by the Articles of Association in 1774. It was matured and continued by the Declaration of Independence in 1776. It was further matured and the faith of all the then thirteen States expressly plighted and engaged that it should be perpetual, by the Articles of Confederation in 1778. And finally, in 1787, one of the declared objects for ordaining and establishing the Constitution, was "*to form a more perfect union.*"

But if destruction of the Union, by one, or by a part only, of the States, be lawfully possible, the Union is *less* perfect than before the Constitution, having lost the vital element of perpetuity.

It follows from these views that no State, upon its own mere motion, can lawfully get out of the Union,—that *resolves* and *ordinances* to that effect are legally void; and that acts of violence, within any State or States, against the authority of the United States, are insurrectionary or revolutionary, according to circumstances. . . .

. . . If the minority will not acquiesce, the majority must, or the government must cease. There is no other alternative; for continuing the government, is acquiescence on one side or the other. If a minority, in such case, will secede rather than acquiesce, they make a precedent which, in turn, will divide and ruin them; for a minority of their own will secede from them, whenever a majority refuses to be controlled by such minority. For instance, why may not any portion of a new confederacy, a year or two hence, arbitrarily secede again, precisely as portions of the present Union now claim to secede from it. All who cherish disunion sentiments, are now being educated to the exact temper of doing this. Is there such perfect identity of interests among the States to compose a new Union, as to produce harmony only, and prevent renewed secession?

Plainly, the central idea of secession, is the essence of anarchy. A majority, held in restraint by constitutional checks, and limitations, and always changing easily, with deliberate changes of popular opinions and sentiments, is the only true sovereign of a free people. Whoever rejects it, does, of necessity, fly to anarchy or to despotism. Unanimity is impossible; the rule of a minority, as a permanent arrangement, is wholly inadmissible; so that, rejecting the majority principle, anarchy, or despotism in some form, is all that is left. . . .

One section of our country believes slavery is *right*, and ought to be extended, while the other believes it is *wrong*, and ought not to be extended. This is the only substantial dispute. The fugitive slave clause of the Constitution, and the law for the suppression of the foreign slave trade, are each as well enforced, perhaps, as any law can ever be in a community where the moral sense of the people imperfectly supports the law itself. The great body of the people abide by the dry legal obligation in both cases, and a few break over in each. This, I think, cannot be perfectly cured; and it would be worse in both cases *after* the separation of the sections, than before. The foreign slave trade, now imperfectly suppressed, would be ultimately revived without restriction, in one section; while fugitive slaves, now only partially surrendered, would not be surrendered at all, by the other.

Physically speaking, we cannot separate. We cannot remove our respective sections from each other, nor build an impassable wall between them. A husband and wife may be divorced, and go out of the presence, and beyond the reach of each other; but the different parts of our country cannot do this. They cannot but remain face to face; and intercourse, either amicable or hostile, must continue between them. Is it possible then to make that intercourse more advantageous, or more satisfactory, *after* separation than *before*? Can aliens make treaties easier than friends can make laws? Can treaties be more faithfully enforced between aliens, than laws can among friends? Suppose you go to war; you cannot fight always; and when, after much loss on both sides, and no gain on either, you cease fighting, the identical old questions, as to terms of intercourse, are again upon you. . . .

My countrymen, one and all, think calmly and *well* upon this whole subject. Nothing valuable can be lost by taking time. If there be an object to *hurry* any of you, in hot haste, to a step which you would never take *deliberately*, that object will be frustrated by taking time; but no good object can be frustrated by it. Such of you as are now dissatisfied, still have the old Constitution unimpaired, and, on the sensitive point, the laws of your own framing under it; while the new administration will have no immediate power, if it would, to change either. If it were admitted that you who are dissatisfied, hold the right side in the dispute, there still is no single good reason for precipitate action. Intelligence, patriotism, Christianity, and a firm reliance on Him, who has never yet forsaken this favored land, are still competent to adjust, in the best way, all our present difficulty.

In *your* hands, my dissatisfied fellow countrymen, and not in *mine*, is the momentous issue of civil war. The government will not assail *you*. You can have no conflict, without being yourselves the aggressors. *You* have no oath registered in Heaven to destroy the government, while *I* shall have the most solemn one to "preserve, protect and defend" it.

I am loth to close. We are not enemies, but friends. We must not be enemies. Though passion may have strained, it must not break our bonds of affection. The mystic chords of memory, stretching from every battlefield, and patriot grave, to every living heart and hearthstone, all over this broad land, will yet swell the chorus of the Union, when again touched, as surely they will be, by the better angels of our nature.

Questions

1. Which portions of Lincoln's speech were aimed at those states that had already seceded? Which were intended for southern states that had not yet seceded? Which were directed at the northern states?

2. Compare Lincoln's views on the Union and the Constitution with those expressed by Frederick Grimké (Document 13-7). What are their major points of disagreement? Based on historical evidence, whose arguments are more compelling?

3. What did Lincoln mean by the "mystic chords of memory"? To what was he appealing?

14-4   The Crisis at Fort Sumter (April 1861)

Mary Boykin Chesnut

When South Carolina seceded from the United States on December 20, 1860, the construction of Fort Sumter, on an island in Charleston harbor, was not complete and the fort had not yet been occupied by federal troops. On December 26, however, the federal commander in Charleston, Major Robert Anderson, consolidated his forces (fewer than a hundred men) at the new fort. Anderson's force could not be easily defeated, but it also could not be easily reinforced or resupplied. On March 1, 1861, General P. G. T. Beauregard assumed command of Confederate forces at Charleston; on March 4 Lincoln became president of the United States. Throughout the month of March the crisis at Fort Sumter grew increasingly tense (see text p. 427). On April 6 Lincoln announced a "humanitarian" effort to resupply the fort. On April 9 the Confederate president, Jefferson Davis, ordered Beauregard to capture the fort. The Confederate bombardment began on April 12 at 4:30 A.M. Anderson surrendered on April 14, and on April 15 Lincoln called on the states to send seventy-five thousand troops to suppress the insurrection. The Civil War had begun.

The wife of James C. Chesnut, a wealthy planter and prominent southern politician, Mary Chesnut (see text p. 448), began her diary as the war clouds gathered and ended it when the Confederacy collapsed under the pressure of the advancing Union armies. Surrounded by the leaders of the Confederate cause, Mary Chesnut epitomized the aristocratic southern lady: charming in manners, clever in conversation, and modest in deferring to the public life of the men around her. In her diary, however, she revealed her independent cast of mind and deep misgivings about the Confederate cause.

Source: From C. Vann Woodward, ed., *Mary Chesnut's Civil War* (New Haven and London: Yale University Press, 1981), 35–53 passim. Used by permission of Yale University Press.

March 26, 1861. Charleston. Yesterday we came down here by rail, as the English say. . . .

March 31, 1861 . . . At church today, saw one of the peculiar local traits—old Negro maumeys going up to the communion in their white turbans.

Being the Lord's table—so-called. Even there—black, white, and brown, separate according to caste. . . .

No war yet, thank God. . . .

There stands Fort Sumter . . . and thereby hangs peace or war. . . .

April 6, 1861. The plot thickens. The air is red-hot with rumors. The mystery is to find out where these utterly groundless tales originate. . . .

April 7, 1861 . . . [Former] Governor [John Laurence] Manning walked in, bowed gravely, and seated himself by me.

Again he bowed low, in mock heroic style and, with a grand wave of his hand said, "Madame, your country is invaded."

When I had breath to speak, I asked, "What does he mean?"

"He means this. There are six men-of-war outside of the bar. . . . Governor [Francis Wilkinson] Pickens and [General P. G. T.] Beauregard are holding a council of war."

Mr. [James C.] Chesnut then came in. He confirmed the story.

[Louis Trezevant] Wigfall next entered in boisterous spirits. . . .

In any stir or confusion, my heart is apt to beat so painfully. Now the agony was so stifling—I could hardly see or hear. The men went off almost immediately. And I crept silently to my room, where I sat down to a good cry.

Mrs. Wigfall came in, and we had it out on the subject of civil war. We solaced ourselves with dwelling on all its known horrors, and then we added what we had a right to expect, with Yankees in front and negroes in the rear.

"The slave-owners must expect a servile insurrection, of course," said Mrs. Wigfall, to make sure that we were unhappy enough. . . . Ammunition wagons rumbling along the streets all night. Anderson burning blue lights—signs and signals for the fleet outside, I suppose.

Today at dinner there was no allusion to things as they stand in Charleston Harbor. There was an undercurrent of intense excitement. . . . In earnest, [former] Governor Means rummaged a sword and red sash from somewhere and brought it for Colonel Chesnut, who has gone to demand the surrender of Fort Sumter.

And now, patience—we must wait.

Why did that green goose Anderson go into Fort Sumter? Then everything began to go wrong. . . .

April 12, 1861. Anderson will not capitulate. . . .

I do not pretend to go to sleep. How can I? If Anderson does not accept terms—at four—the orders are—he shall be fired upon.

I count four—St. Michael chimes. I begin to hope. At half-past four, the heavy booming of a cannon.

I sprang out of bed. And on my knees—prostrate—I prayed as I never prayed before.

There was a sound of stir all over the house—pattering of feet in the corridor—all seemed hurrying one way. I put on my double gown and a shawl and went, too. It was to the housetop.

The shells were bursting. In the dark I heard a man say "waste of ammunition."

I knew my husband was rowing about in a boat somewhere in that dark bay. And that the shells were roofing it over—bursting toward the fort. If Anderson was obstinate—he [Chesnut] was to order the forts on our side to open fire. Certainly fire had begun. The regular roar of the cannon—there it was. And who could tell what each volley accomplished of death and destruction. . . .

April 13, 1861 . . . Not by one word or look can we detect any change in the demeanor of these negro servants. Laurence sits at our door, as sleepy and as respectful and as profoundly indifferent. So are they all. They carry it too far. You could not tell that they hear even the awful row that is going on in the bay, though it is dinning in their ears night and day. And people talk before them as if they were chairs and tables. And they make no sign. Are they stolidly stupid or wiser than we are, silent and strong, biding their time? . . .

April 15, 1861. I did not know that one could live such days of excitement. . . .

And so we took Fort Sumter.

Questions

1. Unlike the men around her, Chesnut appeared to be fearful of war. Why?

2. Did Chesnut seem confident and comfortable as part of the slaveholding elite? Explain why or why not.

3. Why were the slaves quiet and subdued during the bombardment of Fort Sumter?

14-5   The Work of the United States Sanitary Commission (1864)

The United States Sanitary Commission represented the largest and most successful volunteer wartime activity in the North (see text p. 435). The commission's founders intended to bring modern methods of sanitation to the treatment of sick and wounded soldiers and thereby avoid the devastating health problems that had plagued British and French troops during the Crimean War (1854–1856). In June 1861, the United States Sanitary Commission received official recognition from the War Department as a civilian agency supporting the Army Medical Bureau.

Sharply critical of traditional army methods, Sanitary Commission inspectors visited military encampments to direct latrine construction, food preparation, and the design of hospitals. Sanitary Commission activities dominated the home-front activities of northern women. Hundreds of volunteers organized "sanitary fairs" in northern cities to raise funds to supply soldiers with medical supplies, fresh fruits and vegetables, and nurses and doctors to assist in the care and evacuation of the wounded. Although the intrusion of civilians into military matters disturbed some commanders, the commission's popularity among the troops and its influence with Congress ensured the success of its efforts.

Source: [Linus P. Brockett], *The Philanthropic Results of the War in America: Collected from Official and Other Authentic Sources, by an American Citizen* (New York: Sheldon & Co., 1864), 32–42, 89–91.

The proclamation of the President [following the fall of Fort Sumter] . . . evoked the patriotic and earnest sympathies of the women of the nation, as well as those of the sterner sex. Everywhere fair hands were at work, and fair brows grew grave with thought, of what could be done for those who were going forth to fight the nation's battles. With the characteristic national fondness for organization, Ladies' Aid and Relief Societies were formed everywhere. One, "The Soldiers' Aid Society," at Cleveland, Ohio, bearing the date April 20, 1861, only five days after the President's proclamation; another at Philadelphia, "The Ladies' Aid Society," adopting its constitution on the 26th of April, and a third, "The Woman's Central Association of Relief, of New York," on the 30th of the same month. By the middle of May there were hundreds of these associations formed. As yet, however, they hardly knew what was to be done, or how, when, and where to do it. . . . The Woman's Central Association of Relief had among its officers some gentlemen of large experience in sanitary science, and of considerable knowledge of military hygiene, and they wisely gave a practical turn to its labors from the first. . . . Other organizations of gentlemen were attempting by . . . similar measures, to render assistance to the Government. . . . Fraternizing with each other . . . these associations resolved to send a joint delegation to Washington. . . .

On the 18th of May, 1861 . . . representatives of these . . . associations drew up and forwarded to the Secretary of War a communication setting forth the propriety of creating an organization which should unite the duties and labors of [these] associations, and co-operate with the Medical Bureau of the War Department . . . in securing the welfare of the army. For this purpose they asked that a mixed commission of civilians, military officers, and medical men, might be appointed by the Government, charged with the duty of methodizing and reducing to practical service the already active but undirected benevolence of the people. . . .

The President and Secretary of War were not at first disposed to look with any great favor upon this plan, which they regarded rather as a sentimental scheme concocted by women, clergymen, and humane physicians, than as one whose practical workings would prove of incalculable benefit to the army. . . . [But] when the Acting Surgeon-General asked for it, as a needed adjuvant to the Medical Bureau, likely soon to be overwhelmed by its new duties, they finally decided, though reluctantly, to permit its organization.

Accordingly the Secretary of War, on the 9th of June, decided on the creation of . . . "The United States Sanitary Commission." . . . After the Government had established its own permanent hospitals . . . a considerable number of the supplies were furnished by the Sanitary Commission. The value of these supplies furnished by private hands . . . has been carefully ascertained . . . [and] could not have been less in value than $2,200,000.

One of these hospitals, now under the charge of the Government, originated in the philanthropic spirit of the citizens of . . . Philadelphia. . . . After the great battles before Washington, in the summer of 1862 [the Second Battle of Bull Run/Manassas], trains, freighted with the wounded, poured into Philadelphia, and no provisions having been made for their quiet and speedy transfer to the hospitals, most of which were at considerable distance, they were temporarily placed in churches. . . . The citizens of the vicinity, a large portion of them mechanics, laboring by day in the busy manufactories of that vicinity, were greatly distressed at witnessing this suffering, and resolved . . . to erect near the station-house a hospital for the temporary accommodation of sick and wounded soldiers. A landowner generously gave them the use of some vacant lots . . . others contributed lumber, furniture, heating apparatus, bath-tubs, and some, money. One poor Irishman wheeled a half-worn stove to the new hospital. "He had nothing else to give," he said, "and must do something for the sogers." The hospital was erected, and furnished with five hundred beds in fifteen days. . . .

The feeling of sympathy and patriotism which has actuated the masses of the people, manifested itself in numberless instances of thoughtfulness and tenderness, even from classes, among whom it was hardly to be looked for.

Questions

1. Why do you think the president and the secretary of war were initially leery of civilian involvement in aiding sick and wounded soldiers?

2. Even if these volunteer activities were not absolutely necessary to the Union cause, were they important in maintaining home-front morale? Explain why or why not.

3. What class of people did the writer of this document expect to respond to the Sanitary Commission's philanthropic appeal? Why?

Questions for Further Thought

1. Why wasn't the Union better prepared for war? Considering the North's overwhelming superiority in resources and manpower, how can the Confederate victories in the war's first years be explained?

2. The passages from Mary Boykin Chesnut's diary of 1861 (Document 14-4) are striking in the way in which they speak of the slaves. What presuppositions about the nature of slaves underlie both these passages and the "Declaration of the Immediate Causes" (Document 14-1)?

3. Given the principles articulated by the secessionists (Documents 14-1 and 14-2), was there anything that Lincoln could have said in 1861 (Document 14-3) that would have restored the Union? Was the Civil War inevitable by then?

4. Compare Memminger's justification for secession (Document 14-1) with the Confederate Constitution (Document 14-2), which doesn't address the issue. What might account for this discrepancy?

The Turning Point: 1863

As the war progressed, its character and aims underwent fundamental change. Most important, for the Union it became not simply a war to quell a rebellion but a war to end slavery. At first Lincoln was careful to avoid addressing the issue of slavery. He had a conception of his own powers as president and commander in chief that limited his authority to enforcing the law and upholding federal authority. Moreover, he was eager to keep the remaining slave states in the Union, hoped to entice seceded slave states back in, and needed to pay heed to a northern white public opinion that was hardly as much opposed to slavery as he, let alone the Radical Republicans to his left.

The stalemate of 1861–1862, however, convinced more and more Northerners that winning the war required more than strictly military means. Slavery was a major prop to Confederate power, and it soon became apparent that the slaves themselves regarded Union troops, and the missionaries that came in their wake, as "liberators" (Documents 14-6 and 14-7). Given the racism prevalent among white Union soldiers, much of that grateful admiration was misplaced. Nonetheless, increasing numbers of northerners began to endorse the notion that at least a threatened strike against slavery might end the war more quickly and appeal to those slaves itching to forward insurrection within the Confederacy. Accordingly, on September 22, 1862, Lincoln issued a carefully worded preliminary Emancipation Proclamation, which was followed by the formal proclamation on January 1, 1863. The Confederacy reacted with outrage, and Lincoln's move also stirred hostility in the North (Document 14-8). The Republicans suffered major reverses in the fall elections of 1862, and the shift in war aims, along with resentment at the inequities of war mobilization, led to serious riots in New York City in July 1863 (Document 14-9). But the character of the war had shifted irreversibly; slaves increasingly undercut the Confederacy by fleeing to Union lines, with many of the men enlisting in the Union army to fight for their own and their people's freedom.

In the meantime, the Union's advantages in war mobilization made themselves felt. The Union naval blockade tightened; the army of Ulysses S. Grant scored a major strategic victory in the West at Vicksburg, breaking the Confederacy's supply lines to Texas and Mexico. Robert E. Lee's string of brilliant victories finally ended at Gettysburg (Document 14-10). By the end of the year, the Confederate cause was still potent, but it was now clearly on the defensive.

14-6   Slave Runaways in South Carolina (1861)

Many slaves did not wait for the Emancipation Proclamation to claim their freedom. Barely a month after the firing on Fort Sumter, three runaway slaves presented themselves to General Benjamin Butler at the Union command post in Virginia. Butler's refusal to return these runaways to the Confederates, claiming that they were "contraband of war," set a precedent for federal policy and encouraged thousands of other slaves to flee to Union lines. In the following article, which appeared in the *New York Tribune* in December of 1861, a reporter describes his firsthand account of this phenomenon, highlighting the danger slaves faced in fleeing their masters and their overwhelming thirst for freedom.

Source: New York Tribune, 23 December 1861.

There are now in Beaufort District alone, I am informed by official personages, nearly sixteen thousand slaves, whose masters have fled, and Beaufort District is but a small portion of the country at present in our hands. I have accompanied a number of the reconnoissances made in all directions from this post, both by sea and land; have witnessed the exploration of the country from Tybee Island on the south to North Edisto on the north, an extent of at least sixty miles, and have penetrated as far into the interior, on some of these excursions, as our troops have yet gone. Everywhere I find the same state of things existing: everywhere the blacks hurry in droves to our lines; they crowd in small boats around our ships; they swarm upon our decks; they hurry to our officers, from the cotton-houses of their masters, in an hour or two after our guns are fired. I am writing now not what I have heard, but what I have seen. I am not sending you opinions, or conclusions at which I have arrived, but facts that I have observed. I mean each statement I make to be taken literally; it is not garnished for rhetorical effect, but put into such a form as will most exactly convey to the mind of a reader the impression made on me. I have seen negroes who reported themselves as just escaped from their masters, who came breathless to our forces, and said they dared not go back, for their masters would kill them; who told that their masters were at that moment armed and threatening to shoot any slave that did not fly with them; who declared they had tricked their owners and came away in boats that they were bidden to take back to the whites. I have talked with drivers and field-hands, with house-maids, and coachmen, and body-servants, who were apparently as eager to escape as any. I have heard the blacks point out how their masters might be caught, where they were hidden, what were their forces. I have seen them used as guides and pilots. I have been along while they pointed out in what houses stores of arms and ammunition were kept, and where bodies of troops were stationed. In a few hours I have known this information verified. I have

asked them about the sentiment of the slave population, and been invariably answered that everywhere it is the same. . . .

The absurd attempts of Southern papers to pretend that the blacks are still loyal can only excite a compassionate smile. The poor wretches cling to this hope, the absence of which would present to them so appalling a future. The slaves not yet escaped of course pretend to be faithful, but some have told me how they said to their masters and mistresses on the day of the fight, "The Yankees will be whipped, Massa and Missus," but all the while they prayed and believed otherwise. So, casual allusions are made in Charleston papers to the fidelity of their "servants," as if it were a matter of course, but there is no laboured discussion of a subject too terrible for discussion. As for my own judgment—it may not be worth much—but I came hither prepared to find all the negroes attached to their masters, and I have gradually observed a feeling of bitterness displayed by the blacks; at first there was only elation at their own escape; of late this has been mingled with indignation at the insane attempt of the masters to fire on them. I have known of several instances where slaves asked for arms to fire on their own masters (this was the case with Colonel Whitmarsh Seabrook's live stock near Edisto); I have known where slaves assisted in the capture of their masters; I have sometimes asked myself whether the time might not come when arming the blacks and regularly drilling them as soldiers under white officers might not prove the only means of averting the odious horrors of a servile insurrection. That time appears to me not to have yet come even here; but it may be nearer than any of us suppose. The blacks fall to plundering as soon as their masters flee, and go by our lines confidently with their arms or their boats laden with plunder; and it is hardly the business of Federal troops to look after the property of rebels.

From pillaging within an hour after the master is gone, from firing on him as soon as he attempts to fly, from assisting in his capture, and informing us before of his designs—the step to absolute insurrection is not a wide one.

Questions

1. Coming five months after the war's first battle, that of Bull Run (Manassas), what effect would the *Tribune* report have had on northern readers?

2. How did this reporter explain slave owners' insistence that their slaves were still loyal?

3. Was the *Tribune* reporter in favor of fomenting a slave rebellion in the South? What solution did he suggest for avoiding rebellion?

14-7   A Northern Black Woman Teaches Contrabands in South Carolina (1862)

Charlotte Forten

In November 1861, federal gunboats forced the evacuation of the Confederate defenders of the Sea Islands region of South Carolina (between Charleston and Savannah on the Atlantic coast). The Sea Islands became a federal base in the Atlantic blockade of southern commerce. Confederate soldiers left the islands, as did the wealthy planters and their families. The slaves remained, sensing that the enemies of their masters would be their friends. With the federal government now in control of about 10,000 "contrabands" (see text pp. 439–440) and some of the most productive cotton land in the South, the future development of the plantations and the fate of the laborers attracted immediate attention. The Treasury Department took control of the plantations and appointed superintendents to direct their operations. Northern abolitionists sent teachers into the region to educate the former slaves and prove them worthy of emancipation. One of the teachers was Charlotte Forten (1838–1914) of Philadelphia. For generations the Fortens had been abolitionist leaders in the black community. Charlotte Forten had taught in the nonsegregated public schools of Salem, Massachusetts, before visiting the Sea Islands. Her light complexion and northern ways raised suspicions at first, but she deemed her labors on the islands a success. From her journal she drafted a narrative of her experience to share with her friends. One friend, the poet John Greenleaf Whittier, arranged to have the piece published in the *Atlantic Monthly* in May and June 1864.

Source: Charlotte Forten, "Life on the Sea Islands," *Atlantic Monthly* 13 (May 1864 and June 1864), 587–596, 666–676, in *Two Black Teachers during the Civil War* (New York: Arno Press and New York Times, 1969).

It was on the afternoon of a warm, murky day late in October that our steamer, the United States, touched the landing at Hilton head. A motley assemblage had collected on the wharf, — officers, soldiers, and "contrabands" of every size and hue: black was, however, the prevailing color. . . . It is wonderful with what ease they carry all sorts of things on their heads, — heavy bundles of wood, hoes and rakes, everything, heavy or light, that can be carried in the hands; and I have seen a woman, with a bucketful of water on her head, stoop down to take up another in her hand, without spilling a drop from either. We noticed that the people had much better taste in selecting materials for dresses than we had supposed. They do not generally like gaudy colors, but prefer neat, quiet patterns. They are, however, very fond of all kinds of jewelry. I once asked the children in school what their ears were for. "To put rings in," promptly replied one of the little girls.

These people are exceedingly polite in their manner towards each other, each new arrival bowing, scraping his feet, and shaking hands with the others, while there are constant greetings, such as, "Huddy? How's yer lady?" ("How d' ye do? How's your wife?"). The hand-shaking is performed with the greatest possible solemnity. There is never the faintest shadow of a smile on anybody's face during this performance. The children, too, are taught to be very polite to their elders, and it is the rarest thing to hear a disrespectful word from a child to his parent, or to any grown persons. They have really what the New-Englanders call "beautiful manners." . . .

In the evenings, the children frequently come in to sing and shout for us. These "shouts" are very strange, — in truth, almost indescribable. It is necessary to hear and see in order to have any clear idea of them. The children form a ring, and move around in a kind of shuffling dance, singing all the time. Four or five stand apart, and sing very energetically, clapping their hands, stamping their feet and rocking their bodies to and fro. These are the musicians, to whose performance the shouters keep perfect time. . . . We cannot determine whether it has a religious character or not. Some of the people tell us that it has, others, that it has not. But as the shouts of the grown people are always in connection with their religious meetings, it is probable that they are the barbarous expression of religion, handed down to them from their African ancestors, and destined to pass away under the influence of Christian teachings. . . . Prince, a large black boy from a neighboring plantation, was the principal shouter among the children. . . . His performances were most amusing specimens of Ethiopian gymnastics. Amaretta . . . a cunning, kittenish little creature of only six years old, had a remarkably sweet voice. . . .

Daily the long-oppressed people of these islands are demonstrating their capacity for improvement in learning and labor. What they have accomplished in one short year exceeds our utmost expectations. . . . An old freedman said to me one day, "De Lord make me suffer long time, Miss. 'Peared like we nebber was gwine to get troo. But now we's free. He bring us all out right at las'." In their darkest hours they have clung to Him, and we know He will not forsake them.

Questions

1. What did Forten find most surprising about the people of the Sea Islands?

2. What strengths and weaknesses did she discern in the culture she encountered?

3. At the very moment of emancipation why did Forten feel the need to demonstrate the African Americans' "capacity for improvement in learning and labor"?

14-8   Lincoln and Emancipation (1864)

Adalbert John Volck, J. F. Meeks

The Emancipation Proclamation redefined the Civil War by binding the struggle to save the Union with the liberation of southern slaves. Jefferson Davis promptly condemned it as the most despicable act in the "history of guilty man." There was also a tremendous backlash within the Union, especially from Democrats, who declared the proclamation unconstitutional and warned that it would instigate race warfare in the South.

Adalbert John Volck's 1864 etching "The Emancipation Proclamation" shows Lincoln drafting the proclamation amid satanic symbols. He has his foot on the Constitution, and the walls of his office are decorated with paintings of "St. Osawatomie" and "Santo Domingo."

By the time of the 1864 presidential election, even some moderate Republicans were voicing their disapproval of Lincoln's policies, especially his making abolition a precondition of any peace proposal. "Abraham Africanus I" was a satirical pamphlet

(A)   *Adalbert John Volck, "The Emancipation Proclamation"*

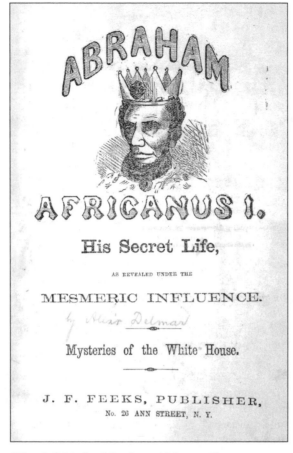

(B)   *J. F. Meeks, "Abraham Africanus I"*

that appeared in New York in 1864. Like Volck's etching, the imagery on the cover appealed to the political and racial fears of many whites.

Sources: Adalbert John Volck, "The Emancipation Proclamation," transfer lithograph, 1864. Courtesy of the National Portrait Gallery, Smithsonian Institution. Cover from J. F. Meeks, "Abraham Africanus I," 1864. Courtesy of the Huntington Library, San Marino, California.

Questions

1. Before his assault on Harpers Ferry (see text p. 416), John Brown earned the nickname Osawatomie Brown when he organized a mob that attacked and killed five proslavery settlers in a Kansas town by the same name. In Volck's etching, "St. Osawatomie," meant to represent Brown, is depicted with a halo and spear. Why did Volck include this image, and how did it play on whites' fears?

2. What is the "Santo Domingo" painting in Volck's etching supposed to depict? What happened on the island of Santo Domingo in the 1790s? What does this suggest will be the outcome of the Emancipation Proclamation?

3. What criticism of Lincoln is made in "Abraham Africanus I"? What do the crown and royal title represent? How might this view of Lincoln be related to his issuing the Emancipation Proclamation?

4. In what ways do both images represent a critique of Lincoln's expanding power?

14-9   The New York City Draft Riots (July 1863)

Anna Elizabeth Dickinson

When the Union instituted conscription in 1863, it allowed men to avoid the draft if they could provide a substitute or pay a $300 fee—more than half an average worker's annual income. Democratic opponents of Lincoln exploited resentment over the high fee to win support from recent immigrants and the urban poor. In July 1863, riots against the draft exploded in New York City. The following description of the riots is by Anna Dickinson, who was involved in the antislavery and women's rights movements. Her account is no exaggeration; the rioting was finally suppressed on the fourth day by troops from the Army of the Potomac.

Source: Anna Elizabeth Dickinson, *What Answer?* (Boston, 1868), 242–259.

On the morning of Monday, the thirteenth of July, began this outbreak, unparalleled in atrocities by anything in American history, and equalled only by the horrors of the worst days of the French Revolution. Gangs of men and boys, composed of railroad *employees*, workers in machine-shops, and a vast crowd of those who lived by preying upon others, thieves, pimps, professional ruffians,—the scum of the city,—jail-birds, or those who were running with swift feet to enter the prison-doors, began to gather on the corners, and in streets and alleys where they lived; from thence issuing forth they visited the great establishments on the line of their advance, commanding their instant clos[ing] and the companionship of the workmen,—many of them peaceful and orderly men,—on pain of the destruction of one and a murderous assault upon the other, did not their orders meet with instant compliance.

A body of these, five or six hundred strong, gathered about one of the enrolling-offices in the upper part of the city, where the draft was quietly proceeding, and opened the assault upon it by a shower of clubs, bricks, and paving-stones torn from the streets, following it up by a furious rush into the office. Lists, records, books, the drafting-wheel, every article of furniture or work in the room was rent in pieces, and strewn about the floor or flung into the street; while the law officers, the newspaper reporters,—who are expected to be everywhere,—and the few peaceable spectators, were compelled to make a hasty retreat through an opportune rear exit, accelerated by the curses and blows of the assailants.

A safe in the room, which contained some of the hated records, was fallen upon by the men, who strove to wrench open its impregnable lock with their naked hands, and, baffled, beat them on its iron doors and sides till they were stained with blood, in a mad frenzy of senseless hate and fury. And then, finding every portable article destroyed,—their thirst for ruin growing by the little drink it had had,—and believing, or rather hoping, that the officers had taken refuge in the upper rooms, set fire to the house, and stood watching the slow and steady lift of the flames, filling the air with demoniac shrieks and yells, while they waited for the prey to escape from some door or window, from the merci-less fire to their merciless hands. One of these, who was on the other side of the street, courageously stepped forward, and, telling them that they had utterly demolished all they came to seek, informed them that helpless women and little children were in the house, and besought them to extinguish the flames and leave the ruined premises; to disperse, or at least to seek some other scene.

By his dress recognizing in him a government official, so far from hearing or heeding his humane appeal, they set upon him with sticks and clubs, and beat him till his eyes were blind with blood, and he—bruised and mangled—succeeded in escaping to the handful of police who stood helpless before this howling crew, now increased to thousands. With difficulty and pain the inoffensive tenants escaped from the rapidly spreading fire, which, having devoured the house originally lighted, swept across the neighboring buildings till the whole block stood a mass of burning flames. The firemen came up tardily and reluctantly, many of them of the same class as the miscreants who surrounded them, and who cheered at their approach, but either made no attempt to perform their duty, or so feeble and farcical a one, as to bring disgrace upon a service they so generally honor and ennoble.

At last, when there was nothing more to accomplish, the mob, swollen to a frightful size, including myriads of wretched, drunken women, and the half-grown, vagabond boys of the pavements, rushed through the intervening streets, stopping cars and insulting peaceable citizens on their way, to an armory where were manufactured and stored carbines and guns for the government. In anticipation of the attack, this, earlier in the day, had been fortified by a police squad capable of coping with an ordinary crowd of ruffians, but as chaff before fire in the presence of these murderous thousands. Here, as before, the attack was begun by a rain of missiles gathered from the streets; less fatal, doubtless, than more civilized arms, but frightful in the ghastly wounds and injuries they inflicted. Of this no notice was taken by those who were stationed within; it was repeated. At last, finding they were treated with contemptuous silence, and that no sign of surrender was offered, the crowd swayed back,—then forward,—in a combined attempt to force the wide entrance-doors. Heavy hammers and sledges, which had been brought from forges and workshops, caught up hastily as they gathered the mechanics into their ranks, were used with frightful violence to beat them in,—at last successfully. The foremost assailants began to climb the stairs, but were checked, and for the moment driven back by the fire of the officers, who at last had been commanded to resort to their revolvers. A half-score fell wounded; and one, who had been acting in some sort as their leader,—a big, brutal, Irish ruffian,—dropped dead. . . .

Late in the afternoon a crowd which could have numbered not less than ten thousand, the majority of whom were ragged, frowzy, drunken women, gathered about the Orphan Asylum for Colored Children,—a large and beautiful building, and one of the most admirable and noble charities of the city. When it became evident, from the menacing cries and groans of the multitude, that danger, if not destruction, was meditated to the harmless and inoffensive inmates, a flag of truce appeared, and an appeal was made in their behalf, by the principal, to every sentiment of humanity which these beings might possess,—a vain appeal! Whatever human feeling had ever, if ever, filled these souls was utterly drowned and washed away in the tide of rapine and blood in which they had been steeping themselves. The few officers who stood guard over the doors, and manfully faced these demoniac legions, were beaten down and flung to one side, helpless and stunned, whilst the vast crowd rushed in. All the articles upon which they could seize—beds, bedding, carpets, furniture,—the very garments of the fleeing inmates, some of these torn from their persons as they sped by—were carried into the streets, and hurried off by the women and children who stood ready to receive the goods which their husbands, sons, and fathers flung to their care. The little ones, many of them, assailed and beaten; all,—orphans and care-takers,—exposed to every indignity and every danger, driven on to the street,—the building was fired. This had been attempted whilst the helpless children—some of them scarce more than babies—were still in their rooms. . . .

By far the most infamous part of these cruelties was that which wreaked every species of torture and lingering death upon the colored people of the city,—men, women, and children, old and young, strong and feeble alike. Hundreds of these fell victims to the prejudice fostered by public opinion, incorporated in our statute-books, sanctioned by our laws, which here and thus found legitimate outgrowth and action. . . .

It was absurd and futile to characterize this new Reign of Terror as anything but an effort on the part of Northern rebels to help Southern ones, at the most critical moment of the war,—with the State militia and available troops absent in a neighboring Commonwealth,—and the loyal people unprepared. These editors [of Democratic newspapers] and their coadjutors, men of brains and ability, were of that most poisonous growth,—traitors to the Government and the flag of their country,—renegade Americans. Let it, however, be written plainly and graven deeply, that the tribes of savages—the hordes of ruffians—found ready to do their loathsome bidding, were not of native growth, nor American born.

Questions

1. According to Dickinson, what kinds of people made up the mobs?

2. Why did the mob attack blacks, including black children?

3. Why were the police and firemen so ineffective in stopping the riots and arson?

14-10   The Gettysburg Address (1863)

Abraham Lincoln

The Battle of Gettysburg in July 1863 was the bloodiest of the Civil War. But the costly Union victory strengthened northern resolve and ended any hopes the Confederacy had of winning foreign recognition (see text pp. 440–444). Later that year, in a speech dedicating a cemetery at Gettysburg, Abraham Lincoln helped define the modern concept of the American nation.

Source: From Roy P. Basler et al., eds., *The Collected Works of Abraham Lincoln* (New Brunswick, NJ: Rutgers University Press, 1953), 7:23. Used by permission of Rutgers University Press.

Four score and seven years ago our fathers brought forth on this continent, a new nation, conceived in Liberty, and dedicated to the proposition that all men are created equal.

Now we are engaged in a great civil war, testing whether that nation, or any nation so conceived and so dedicated, can long endure. We are met on a great battlefield of that war. We have come to dedicate a portion of that field, as a final resting place for those who here gave their lives that that nation might live. It is altogether fitting and proper that we should do this.

But, in a larger sense, we can not dedicate—we can not consecrate—we can not hallow—this ground. The brave men, living and dead, who struggled here, have consecrated it, far above our poor power to add or detract. The world will little note, nor long remember what we say here, but it can never forget what they did here. It is for us the living, rather, to be dedicated here to the unfinished work which they who fought here have thus far so nobly advanced. It is rather for us to be here dedicated to the great task remaining before us—that from these honored dead we take increased devotion to that cause for which they gave the last full measure of devotion—that we here highly resolve that these dead shall not have died in vain—that this nation, under God, shall have a new birth of freedom—and that government of the people, by the people, for the people, shall not perish from the earth.

Questions

1. Why did Lincoln say in 1863 that the United States had been founded on the "proposition that all men are created equal"?

2. Why did Lincoln want to tie the Union's cause so closely to that of the founders? Was Lincoln attempting to redefine the Union cause with the Gettysburg Address? If so, in what way?

3. Lincoln concluded his address with the thought "that this nation, under God, shall have a new birth of freedom." What type of freedom did he mean?

Questions for Further Thought

1. Many historians have argued that at this point the Civil War changed character and became a struggle over fundamentally different issues than it had been concerned with before. Given these documents, would you agree? What or who was responsible?

2. As Documents 14-8 and 14-9 show, the turning point of the war was accompanied by considerable turmoil in the North. Were the two connected by more than coincidence? If so, how?

3. Compare the Gettysburg Address and Lincoln's 1861 inaugural address (Document 14-3). Had his ideas changed? Was his appeal fundamentally different?

The Union Victorious, 1864–1865

The war was hardly finished by the beginning of 1864. While the Confederacy could no longer hope to score a knockout punch, it had plenty of reason to hope it could simply outlast the Union side. Ulysses Grant's Virginia campaign of 1864 produced unprecedented Union advances in a theater that had seen previous commanders squander their opportunities, but his casualty rate was appalling. By fall Grant had pressed Lee's army to the outskirts of Petersburg, where both sides settled into grim, ugly trench warfare. War-weariness was a real threat to continuation of the war; 1864 was an election year, and the Democrats were gearing up to run against the "Republican war." Meanwhile, Lincoln faced challengers on another front—among black Americans who questioned his commitment to emancipation and racial equality (Document 14-12).

On September 2, though, a major break for the Union came when William Tecumseh Sherman's western army captured the then-small but strategic rail center of Atlanta; the lift to Union morale led to Republican victory in the fall elections. By the end of the year, the principal western Confederate army had disintegrated at Nashville and Sherman had completed his legendary March to the Sea, "making Georgia howl." The Confederate cause was now in such desperate straits that some leaders, including Jefferson Davis and Robert E. Lee, began to endorse proposals to arm and free slaves, suggestions that stirred violent opposition (Document 14-11). While some African Americans were enlisted in the Confederate army after being voluntarily freed by their masters, they were too few and too late. By April 1865, Sherman had swept through the Carolinas with little resistance, threatening Lee's rear, while Grant's forces had outflanked Lee, forcing him to abandon Richmond and Petersburg and retreat to Appomattox Court House, where he surrendered on April 9. The Confederacy was no more.

14-11   Confederates Debate Emancipation (1863–1864)

After the critical Confederate defeats at Gettysburg and Vicksburg in 1863, with emancipation now Union policy and African Americans flocking to Union colors, some Confederates began to think the previously unthinkable: that in order to attain independence, the Confederacy might have to enlist blacks in its own army. The ensuing debate got louder as the Confederate position deteriorated, and especially after President Jefferson Davis in November 1864 suggested the possibility of emancipation as a reward for service. In March 1865, after intervention by General Robert E. Lee, the Confederate Congress finally passed legislation permitting the enlistment of slaves, but without changing their status. Although the army recognized the impossibility of arming slaves, the most it could do was require that masters grant freedom to any slaves they sent into service. Few were recruited in the scant month remaining before Appomattox. Thus the debate was fatally inconclusive for the Confederacy; but it laid bare some of the basic contradictions underlying the Confederate cause.

Source: Robert F. Durden, *The Gray and the Black: The Confederate Debate on Emancipation* (Baton Rouge: Louisiana State University Press, 1972), 30–32, 97–99, 124–125, 141–142. Used by permission of the publisher.

(a) Excerpts from the *Jackson Mississippian,* Reprinted in *Montgomery* (AL) *Weekly Mail,* September 9, 1863

EMPLOYMENT OF NEGROES IN THE ARMY.

. . . We must either employ the negroes ourselves, or the enemy will employ them against us. While the enemy retains so much of our territory, they are, in their present avocation and status, a dangerous element, a source of weakness. They are no longer negative characters, but subjects of volition as other people. They must be taught to know that this is peculiarly the country of the black man—that in no other is the climate and soil so well adapted to his nature and capacity. He must further be taught that it is his duty, as well as the white man's, to defend his home with arms, if need be.

We are aware that there are persons who shudder at the idea of placing arms in the hands of negroes, and who are not willing to trust them under any circumstances. The negro, however, is proverbial for his faithfulness under kind treatment. He is an affectionate, grateful being, and we are persuaded that the fears of such persons are groundless.

There are in the slaveholding States four millions of negroes, and out of this number at least six hundred thousand able-bodied men capable of bearing arms can be found. Lincoln proposes to free and arm them against us. There are already fifty thousand of them in the Federal ranks. Lincoln's scheme has worked well so far, and if no[t] checkmated, will most assuredly be carried out. The Confederate Government must adopt a counter policy. It must thwart the enemy in this gigantic scheme, at all hazards, and if nothing else will do it—if the negroes cannot be made effective and trustworthy to the Southern cause in no other way, we solemnly believe it is the duty of this Government to forestall Lincoln and proceed at once to take steps for the emancipation or liberation of the negroes itself. Let them be declared free, placed in the ranks, and told to fight for their homes and country.

We are fully sensible of the grave importance of the question, but the inexorable logic of events has forced it upon us. We must deal with it, then, not with fear and trembling—not as timid, time-serving men—but with a boldness, a promptness and a determination which the exigency requires, and which should ever characterize the action of a people resolved to sacrifice everything for liberty. It is true, that such a step would revolutionize our whole industrial system—that it would, to a great extent, impoverish the country and be a dire calamity to both the negro and the white race of this and the Old World; but better this than the loss of the negroes, the country and liberty.

If Lincoln succeeds in arming our slaves against us, he will succeed in making them our masters. He will reverse the social order of things at the South. Whereas, if he is checkmated in time, our liberties will remain intact; the land will be ours, and the industrial system of the country still controlled by Southern men.

Such action on the part of our Government would place our people in a purer and better light before the world. It would disabuse the European mind of a grave error in regard to the cause of our separation. It would prove to them that there were higher and holier motives which actuated our people than the mere love of property. It would show that, although slavery is one of the principles that we started to fight for, yet it falls far short of being the chief one; that, for the sake of our liberty, we are capable of any personal sacrifice; that we regard the emancipation of slaves, and the consequent loss of property as an evil infinitely less than the subjugation and enslavement of ourselves; that it is not a war exclusively for the privilege of holding negroes in bondage. It would prove to our soldiers, three-fourths of whom never owned a negro, that it is not "the rich man's war and the poor man's fight," but a war for the most sacred of all principles, for the dearest of all rights—the right to govern ourselves. It would show them that the rich man who owned slaves was not willing to jeopardize the precious liberty of the country by his eagerness to hold on to his slaves, but that he was ready to give them up and sacrifice his interest in them whenever the cause demanded it. It would lend a new impetus, a new enthusiasm, a new and powerful strength to the cause, and place our success beyond a peradventure. It would at once remove all the odium which attached to us on account of slavery, and bring us speedy recognition, and, if necessary, intervention.

We sincerely trust that the Southern people will be found willing to make any and every sacrifice which the establishment of our independence may require. Let it never be said that to preserve slavery we were willing to wear the chains of bondage ourselves—that the very avarice which prompted us to hold on to the negro for the sake of the money invested in him, riveted upon us shackles more galling and bitter than ever a people yet endured. Let not slavery prove a barrier to our independence. If it is found in

the way—if it proves an insurmountable obstacle to the achievement of our liberty and separate nationality, away with it! Let it perish. We must make up our minds to one solemn duty, the first duty of the patriot, and that is, to save ourselves from the rapacious North, WHATEVER THE COST. . . .

(b) *Charleston Mercury*, November 3, 1864

Usurpation is ever prolific. When the Confederacy, by the Confederate Congress, claimed omnipotence over the States and its citizens, including the officers of the States in its military resources, by the Conscription Law, any one conversant with human nature must have known that this might not be the end of its usurpations. A Constitution is like a dyke keeping out the sea. Cut it and the influx of waters must be endless. This usurpation was soon followed by the Direct Tax Act, by which the Confederate Government claimed to be omnipotent and consolidated, in its taxing, as it was, by the Conscription Law, in its military powers. We are now at a third stage of its usurpations, soon to [be] accomplished, if not promptly met by the States—*the power to emancipate our slaves.*

. . . Now, if there was any single proposition that we thought was unquestionable in the Confederacy it was this—that the States, and the States alone, have the *exclusive* jurisdiction and mastery over their slaves. To suppose that any slaveholding country [*i.e.,* state] would voluntarily leave it to any other power than its own, to emancipate its slaves, is such an absurdity, that we did not believe a single intelligent man in the Confederacy could entertain it. Still less could we believe that after what had taken place under the United States, with respect to slavery in the Southern States, it was possible that any pretension to emancipate slaves could be set up for the Confederate States. It was because the exclusion of slaves from our Territories by the Government of the United States, *looked to their emancipation,* that we resisted it. The power to exercise it was never claimed by that Government. The mere agitation in the Northern States to effect the emancipation of our slaves largely contributed to our separation from them. And now, before a Confederacy which we established to put at rest forever all such agitation is four years old, we find the proposition gravely submitted that the Confederate Government should emancipate slaves in the States. South Caroline, acting upon the principle that she and she alone had the power to emancipate her slaves, has passed laws prohibiting their emancipation by any of her citizens, unless they are sent out of the State; and no free person of color already free, who leaves the State, shall ever afterwards enter it. She has laws now in force, prohibiting free negroes, belonging either to the Northern States, or to European powers, from entering the State, and by the most rigid provisions, they are seized and put into prison should they enter it. These were her rights, under the Union of the United States, recognized and protected by the Government of the United States, and acquiesced in by all foreign nations. And, now, here, it is proposed that the Government of the Confederate States, not only has the right to seize our slaves and to make them soldiers, but to emancipate them in South Carolina, and compel us to give them a home amongst us. We confess, that our indignation at such pretensions is so great, that we are at a loss to know how to treat them. To argue against them, is self-stultification. They are as monstrous as they are insulting.

The pretext for this policy is, that we want soldiers in our armies. This pretext is set up by the *Enquirer* in the face of the fact disclosed by the President of the Confederate States, that two-thirds of our soldiers, now in the army, are absentees from its ranks. The *Enquirer* is a devout upholder of President Davis and the Administration. It does not arraign the Government for such a state of things. It passes over the gross mismanagement which has produced them; and cries out, that negroes are wanted to fill the ranks of our armies. . . . It is vain to attempt to blink the truth. The freemen of the Confederate States must work out their own redemption, or they must be the slaves of their own slaves. The statesmanship, which looks to any other source for success, is contemptible charlatanry. It is worse — it is treachery to our cause itself. Assert the right in the Confederate Government to emancipate slaves, and it is stone dead.

(c) "Sydney" (a nonslaveholder), in the *Macon Telegraph and Confederate*, November 19, 1864

. . . Now there is [*sic*] in the Confederacy one or two hundred thousand able bodied negroes not engaged in agriculture. Many of them [are] refugees from the country overrun, and they consume just as much as if they were in the army and can be very well spared. While thousands of poor white men that have nothing but their country to defend, have bled and died, their families are left to the cold charities of the world. The rich planters can stay at home undisturbed, and if it is hinted [that] cuffey [the Negro] is wanted to help defend his country and property we see a great howl set up about it, and more fuss made than if 1000 white men were sacrificed. Try to hide it as much as we may, yet the question of negro slavery was the great leading cause of this war, and but for it we would have been recognized long ago by foreign powers, but in that particular the world is against us, and so we will remain until this war shall have placed it upon a basis too firm to be questioned.

Then why may not the negro help to establish the only government that looks to the Christianizing of the African and placing him in a condition far above his fellow countrymen in any part of the world, if the exigency demands men to the extent above referred to, in God's name, do not sacrifice every white man in the Confederacy in preference to taking a few negroes from their fondling masters.

(d) Rep. Henry C. Chambers (MS) in Confederate House of Representatives, November 10, 1864

. . . Sir, on what motive is he to fight our battles? He is after all a human being, and acts upon motives. Will you offer him his freedom? The enemy will offer him his freedom, and also as a deserter, immunity from military service. Will you offer him the privilege of return home to his family, a freeman, after the war? That you dare not do, remembering it was the free negroes of St. Domingo, who had been trained to arms, that excited the insurrection of the slaves. And the enemy would meet even that offer with the promise of a return free to his Southern home and the right of property in it. The amount of it all is, that in despair of achieving our independence with our own right arms, we turn for succor to the slave and implore him to establish our freedom and fix slavery upon himself, or at least upon his family and his race, forever. He, at least, after the expiration of his term of service, is to be banished to Liberia or other inhospitable shore, for the States could never permit an army of negroes to be returned home, either free or slave. . . .

. . . Sir, this scheme, if attempted, will end in rapid emancipation and colonization — colonization in the North by bringing up the slaves by regiments and brigades to the opportunity of escape to the enemy; emancipation and colonization abroad to those who render service to us for a specified period. I argue on the presumption that nothing of the kind will be attempted without the consent of the States, whether as to employing them on the promise of freedom, or as to returning them free and disciplined to their old homes. By means of the power of impressment or purchase, this Government could not safely be permitted, without the consent of the States, to inaugurate a system of emancipation that might end in the abolition of the institution, nor do I suppose that the President designed the contrary. In suggesting freedom as the motive to be offered to the slave, he performed a simple official duty, leaving to Congress if it adopted the suggestion, to provide by law all the conditions it might be proper to impose.

In any aspect of the case, this is a proposition to subvert the labour system, the social system and the political system of our country. Better, far, to employ mercenaries from abroad, if dangerous and impracticable expedients are to be attempted, and preserve that institution which is not only the foundation of our wealth but the palladium of our liberties. Make the experiment, of course, with negro troops as the last means to prevent subjugation; but when we shall be reduced to the extremity of exclaiming to the slave, "help us, or we sink," it will already have become quite immaterial what course we pursue!

Questions

1. Some historians have argued that the existence of this debate demonstrates that a fundamental change had occurred in Confederate, as well as Union, war aims after the turning point of the war. Do you agree?

2. On what grounds did the writer in the *Charleston Mercury* oppose the emancipation and arming of the slaves? What did his position reveal about the nature of the Confederacy and its ability to take united action for its own self-preservation?

3. Both the *Jackson Mississippian* and the *Macon Telegraph and Confederate* alluded to divisions among southern whites—specifically, between slaveholders and non-slaveholders—and suggested that arming slaves might restore white solidarity. How?

4. For what reasons did the author writing in the *Jackson Mississippian* believe that the slaves, once freed, would fight for the South?

14-12   Letters to the Editor (1864)

Weekly Anglo-African

Abraham Lincoln faced two competing challenges simultaneously in the presidential election of 1864 (see text pp. 448–449). On the one hand, the so-called Peace Democrats, mainly war-weary Northerners dismayed by the grisly casualty reports emanating from the battlefields of Virginia and convinced that the South would accept reunification if the issue of emancipation were abandoned, campaigned for a negotiated end to the war (see text, Chapter 14). On the other hand, disaffected Radical Republicans, who found Lincoln's plan of reconstruction too lenient and his commitment to equality too tepid, flirted with the idea of nominating John C. Fremont, the popular general whose 1861 emancipation proclamation had been countermanded by Lincoln. Northern advances spearheaded by Generals William Tecumseh Sherman in Georgia and Philip H. Sheridan in the Shenandoah Valley, the addition of Andrew Johnson, a "War Democrat," to the Republican ticket, and a party platform that called for a constitutional amendment to guarantee freed persons "absolute equality before the law" all but ensured Lincoln's reelection. Nevertheless, prominent reformers, including Frederick Douglass, expressed their dissatisfaction with Lincoln in 1864. The following letters to Robert Hamilton, the editor of the *Weekly Anglo-African*, are illustrative of the divided mind of black America. J. W. C. Pennington was a prominent black abolitionist; "Africano" was a soldier in the Fifth Massachusetts Cavalry. The Cleveland Convention, mentioned by "Africano," met in May 1864 and nominated Fremont for president. However, it was largely ignored by Republicans, who renominated Lincoln at their June convention in Baltimore.

Source: Excerpt from *The Black Abolitionist Papers*, ed. C. Peter Ripley, et al. (Chapel Hill: University of North Carolina Press, 1992), 5:276–278. Used by permission of the publisher.

New York, [New York]
June 9th, 1864

MR. EDITOR:

The prospect of having HIS EXCELLENCY ABRAHAM LINCOLN for our next President should awaken in the inmost soul of every American of African descent emotions of the most profound and patriotic enthusiasm. There was a kind and wise Providence in bringing Mr. Lincoln into the Presidential chair, and I believe that the same all-wise Providence has directed him in everything he has done as our President. I say OUR President, because he is the only American President who has ever given any attention to colored men as citizens. I believe that his renomination by the Convention is not only sound policy, but that it is equivalent to reelection, and especially if colored men will do their duty at the ballot box next November.

It lies with colored men now to decide this great issue. The wisest, the safest, and the soundest policy for colored Americans is to exert all our influence to keep our present Chief Magistrate where he is for four years from next March.

There are many reasons why we, as colored men, should prefer Mr. Lincoln for our next President. Among the many I may say: 1. He is an honest President. 2. He is faithful to the whole nation. 3. He commands the respect of the world. 4. He is more cordially hated by the Copperheads of the North and the rebels of the South than any other living man. 5. His reelection will be the best security that the present well-begun work of negro freedom and African redemption will be fully completed. May God grant us four long years more of the judicious administration of that excellent man, ABRAHAM LINCOLN, and when I speak thus I believe I speak the sentiments of nine-tenths of my colored fellow-citizens. What say you, Mr. Editor?

J. W. C. Pennington

Point Lookout, M[arylan]d
July 18, 1864

MR. EDITOR:

. . . I would say a few words as to the necessity of colored men, soldiers particularly, voting, if such is allowed, for the creator of the Emancipation proclamation. Many of our intelligent colored men believe in Mr. Lincoln; but *we*, who have studied him thoroughly, know him better, and as *we* desire to conglomerate in the land of our nativity, and not be severed from the ties we hold most dear, we hail the nomination of one of liberty's most radical sons—John C. Fremont. Mr. Lincoln's policy in regard to the elevation and inseparability of the negro race has always been one of a fickle-minded man—one who, holding anti-slavery principles in one hand and colonization in the other, always gave concessions to slavery when the *Union* could be preserved without touching the peculiar institution. Such a man is not again worthy the votes of the voting portion of the colored race, when the intrepid Fremont, explorer of the Mariposa Valley, the well-known freedom-cherishing, negro-equalizing patriot, is the competitor. The press, like Mr. Lincoln, has always been, and will ever be, in favor of negro colonization; for, like him, they fear competition, and it is not extraordinary if the press should now uphold Mr. Lincoln, though dissatisfied with his vacillating administration, to keep John C. Fremont from occupying the presidential chair. The loyal and truehearted people of the North will, no doubt, weigh the two men now before the public, and choose the one not found wanting. We are within ourselves satisfied that the Cleveland Convention will carry its object—that of electing Freedom's son—while the Baltimore Convention, with its nominee for reelection, will return to the plowshare.

While we thank Mr. Lincoln for what the exigencies of the times forced him to do, we also censure him for the non-accomplishment of the real good this accursed rebellion gave him the power to do, and which if he had done, instead of bartering human sinews and human rights with slaveholding Kentucky, the world would have looked upon him as the magnanimous regenerator of American institutions, and the benevolent protector of human freedom.

AFRICANO

Questions

1. Which of Pennington's reasons were most likely to appeal to black Americans? Which of Africano's arguments were most likely to appeal to white Americans?

2. How valid was Africano's assertion that the "exigencies of the times forced" Lincoln to do what he did for emancipation?

3. How were the sentiments expressed in Lincoln's second inaugural address (Document 14-13) consistent with the support provided by Pennington and the criticism lodged by Africano?

14-13   Second Inaugural Address (1865)

Abraham Lincoln

Abraham Lincoln's reelection in 1864 demonstrated the desire of Northerners to continue the war until the Confederacy was totally defeated and had yielded to all northern war aims. In his second inaugural address in March 1865, Lincoln presented the "causes" of a war that was in its fourth year and suggested that the Almighty had imposed "this terrible war" on the nation as punishment for the evils of slavery. Lincoln's reflections are reminiscent of the classic Puritan sermon and Frederick Douglass's "What to the Slave Is the Fourth of July?" speech (Document 11-7).

Source: James D. Richardson, ed., *A Compilation of the Messages and Papers of the Presidents* (Washington, DC: U.S. Government Printing Office, 1896–1899), 6:276ff.

At this second appearing to take the oath of the presidential office, there is less occasion for an extended address than there was at the first. Then a statement, somewhat in detail, of a course to be pursued, seemed fitting and proper. Now, at the expiration of four years, during which public declarations have been constantly called forth on every point and phase of the great contest which still absorbs the attention, and engrosses the energies of the nation, little that is new could be presented. The progress of our arms, upon which all else chiefly depends, is as well known to the public as to myself; and it is, I trust, reasonably satisfactory and encouraging to all. With high hope for the future, no prediction in regard to it is ventured.

On the occasion corresponding to this four years ago, all thoughts were anxiously directed to an impending civil-war. All dreaded it—all sought to avert it. While the inaugural address was being delivered from this place, devoted altogether to *saving* the Union without war, insurgent agents were in the city seeking to *destroy* it without war—seeking to dissolve the Union, and divide effects, by negotiation. Both parties deprecated war; but one of them would *make* war rather than let the nation survive; and the other would *accept* war rather than let it perish. And the war came.

One eighth of the whole population were colored slaves, not distributed generally over the Union, but localized in the Southern part of it. These slaves constituted a peculiar and powerful interest. All knew that this interest was, somehow, the cause of the war. To strengthen, perpetuate, and extend this interest was the object for which the insurgents would rend the Union, even by war; while the government claimed no right to do more than to restrict the territorial enlargement of it. Neither party expected for the war, the magnitude, or the duration, which it has already attained. Neither anticipated that the *cause* of the

conflict might cease with, or even before, the conflict itself should cease. Each looked for an easier triumph, and a result less fundamental and astounding. Both read the same Bible, and pray to the same God; and each invokes His aid against the other. It may seem strange that any men should dare to ask a just God's assistance in wringing their bread from the sweat of other men's faces; but let us judge not that we be not judged. The prayers of both could not be answered; that of neither has been answered fully. The Almighty has His own purposes. "Woe unto the world because of offences! for it must needs be that offences come; but woe to that man by whom the offence cometh!" If we shall suppose that American Slavery is one of those offences which, in the providence of God, must needs come, but which, having continued through His appointed time, He now wills to remove, and that He gives to both North and South, this terrible war, as the woe due to those by whom the offence came, shall we discern therein any departure from those divine attributes which the believers in a Living God always ascribe to Him? Fondly do we hope—fervently do we pray—that this mighty scourge of war may speedily pass away. Yet, if God wills that it continue, until all the wealth piled by the bond-man's two hundred and fifty years of unrequited toil shall be sunk, and until every drop of blood drawn with the lash, shall be paid by another drawn with the sword, as was said three thousand years ago, so still it must be said "the judgments of the Lord, are true and righteous altogether."

With malice toward none; with charity for all; with firmness in the right, as God gives us to see the right, let us strive on to finish the work we are in; to bind up the nation's wounds; to care for him who shall have borne the battle, and for his widow, and his orphan—to do all which may achieve and cherish a just, and a lasting peace, among ourselves, and with all nations.

Questions

1. What was Lincoln saying about the treatment of African Americans in the United States?

2. In this speech, did Lincoln view the Civil War and slavery as a tragedy, a sin, or a crime?

3. Which do you think Lincoln was emphasizing in this speech, the extraordinarily radical statement about race relations in America or the "with malice toward none" passage?

Questions for Further Thought

1. Compare Lincoln's second inaugural address (Document 14-13) to Douglass's "What to the Slave Is the Fourth of July?" speech (Document 11-7). Both speeches introduced a biblical quotation at a critical moment. Why?

2. Compare the arguments contained in the *Charleston Mercury* excerpt and the Chambers speech (Document 14-11, b and d) with the observations of the *New York Tribune* reporter (Document 14-6). According to these documents, under what illusions were the Confederates operating? How pragmatic were their demands?

3. Based on the powers granted under Article 1, Section 8, of the Confederate Constitution (Document 14-2), including the power to enact all laws deemed "necessary and proper," was the proposal to enlist and emancipate slaves (Document 14-11, a and c) constitutional? How realistic was this proposal?

CHAPTER FIFTEEN

Reconstruction

1865–1877

Presidential Reconstruction

Planning for Reconstruction began to take shape in December 1863, when President Lincoln laid out his ideas in a presidential proclamation. His pronouncement opened a debate that became the central issue in American politics for more than a decade. The power struggle that followed led to a collision between the executive and legislative branches of government, the displacement of presidential Reconstruction by congressional Reconstruction, and the first impeachment of a president of the United States.

Reconstruction involved fundamental questions. To begin with, who had the primary responsibility for Reconstruction—the president or Congress? Believing that rebuilding the Union was simply a matter of suppressing "rebels" under presidential war powers, Lincoln's successor, Andrew Johnson, took the early initiative, establishing provisional governments that were supposed to purge secessionists from southern leadership, repudiate secession and Confederate debts, and recognize the end of slavery (Document 15-1). Beyond these measures Johnson was unwilling to go: a former southern slaveholder himself, he had no sympathy for blacks; in addition, as a southern Democrat he was firmly devoted to states' rights. Although Johnson was satisfied with these measures, northerners were hearing increasingly alarming reports that white southerners were refusing to recognize their defeat; engaging in brutal reprisals against blacks, northern whites, and southern Unionists; and enacting "Black Codes" that appeared to be backdoor attempts to restore slavery (Documents 15-2, 15-3, and 15-4). A rising tide of northern outrage pushed the Republican-dominated Congress toward the views of the Republicans' radical wing; in 1866, over the violent opposition of President Johnson, Congress undertook an unprecedented extension of federal power. With the Civil Rights Act of 1866 (Document 15-5) and the Fourteenth Amendment, Congress declared for the first time that federal citizenship was not restricted by race and guaranteed all citizens the "equal protection of the laws," even if it required federal intervention into the affairs of a state. The outcome of the Civil War was beginning to force fundamental changes in the constitutional character of the American political system, with profound consequences for subsequent American history.

15-1   Plan of Reconstruction (1865)

Andrew Johnson

As the Civil War came to an end, Lincoln's successor, Andrew Johnson, moved quickly to implement his plan for Reconstruction, which differed little from Lincoln's plan (see text pp. 458–459). Johnson acted largely on his own, without much consultation with Congress. In particular, he ignored Congress's demand for a harsher policy toward the former Confederate states.

On May 29, 1865, President Johnson set forth his plan in two presidential proclamations. In the first he promised amnesty to all rebels who would swear an oath of future loyalty, except for certain high-ranking officials and officers of the Confederacy, who had to petition for a presidential pardon.

In the second proclamation, which appears below, Johnson announced the creation of a provisional government for North Carolina. After appointing William W. Holden, a North Carolina Unionist who had opposed secession, as the provisional governor, Johnson described the means by which that state could be restored to the Union. Johnson intended this plan to serve as a model for the other seceded states, hoping that all could be restored before Congress reconvened in December.

Johnson's approach to Reconstruction was very different from that proposed by the Wade-Davis Bill (see text p. 458), which stipulated that more than 50 percent of the voters who were qualified in 1860 in each southern state had to be able to prove their past loyalty and swear future loyalty to the Union. Johnson and Congress also differed about allowing former Confederate leaders to participate in Reconstruction and in government. Presidents Lincoln and Johnson envisioned temporary disqualification; Congress favored permanent exclusion.

Source: James D. Richardson, ed., *A Compilation of the Messages and Papers of the Presidents* (Washington, DC: U.S. Government Printing Office, 1896–1899), 6:312–313.

Whereas the fourth section of the fourth article of the Constitution of the United States declares that the United States shall guarantee to every State in the Union a republican form of government and shall protect each of them against invasion and domestic violence; and

Whereas the President of the United States is by the Constitution made Commander in Chief of the Army and Navy, as well as chief civil executive officer of the United States, and is bound by solemn oath faithfully to execute the office of President of the United States and to take care that the laws be faithfully executed; and

Whereas the rebellion which has been waged by a portion of the people of the United States against the properly constituted authorities of the Government . . . and

Whereas it becomes necessary and proper to carry out and enforce the obligations of the United States to the people of North Carolina in securing them in the enjoyment of a republican form of government:

Now, therefore, in obedience to the high and solemn duties imposed upon me by the Constitution of the United States and for the purpose of enabling the loyal people of said State to organize a State government whereby justice may be established, domestic tranquillity insured, and loyal citizens protected in all their rights of life, liberty, and property, I, Andrew Johnson, President of the United States and Commander in Chief of the Army and Navy of the United States, do hereby appoint William W. Holden provisional governor of the State of North Carolina, whose duty it shall be, at the earliest practicable period, to prescribe such rules and regulations as may be necessary and proper for convening a convention composed of delegates to be chosen by that portion of the people of said State who are loyal to the United States, and no others, for the purpose of altering or amending the constitution thereof, and with authority to exercise within the limits of said State all the powers necessary and proper to enable such loyal people of the State of North Carolina to restore said State to its constitutional relations to the Federal Government and to present such a republican form of State government as will entitle the State to the guaranty of the United States therefor and its people to protection by the United States against invasion, insurrection, and domestic violence: *Provided*, That in any election that may be hereafter held for choosing delegates to any State convention as aforesaid no person shall be qualified as an elector or shall be eligible as a member of such convention unless he shall have previously taken and subscribed the oath of amnesty as set forth in the President's proclamation of May 29, A.D. 1865, and is a voter qualified as prescribed by the constitution and laws of the State of North Carolina in force immediately before the 20th day of May, A.D. 1861, the date of the so-called ordinance of secession; and the said convention, when convened, or the legislature that may be thereafter assembled, will prescribe the qualification of electors and the eligibility of persons to hold office under the constitution and laws of the State—a power the people of the several States composing the Federal Union have rightfully exercised from the origin of the Government to the present time.

And I do hereby direct—

. . . That the military commander of the department and all officers and persons in the military and naval service aid and assist the said provisional governor in carrying into effect this proclamation; and they are enjoined to abstain from in any way hindering, impeding, or discouraging the loyal people from the organization of a State government as herein authorized.

Questions

1. According to President Johnson, what was his authority for this proclamation? Who was to be in charge of the process?
2. What steps did Johnson prescribe for restoring civil government in North Carolina?
3. Under Johnson's plan, would freedmen be able to vote? (*Hint:* See the section starting "*Provided.*")

15-2   Report on Conditions in the South (1865)

Carl Schurz

By December 1865, when Congress was gathering in Washington for a new session, Johnson had declared that all the Confederate states but Texas had met his requirements for restoration. Newly elected senators and congressmen from the former Confederacy had arrived to take seats in Congress.

Johnson's efforts to restore the South stalled. Congress exercised its constitutional authority to deny seats to delegations from the South and launched an investigation into conditions there. In response to a Senate resolution requesting "information in relation to the States of the Union lately in rebellion," Johnson painted a rosy picture: "In 'that portion of the Union lately in rebellion' the aspect of affairs is more promising than, in view of all the circumstances, could well have been expected. The people throughout the entire south evince a laudable desire to renew their allegiance to the government, and to repair the devastations of war by a prompt and cheerful return to peaceful pursuits. An abiding faith is entertained that their actions will conform to their professions, and that, in acknowledging the supremacy of the Constitution and the laws of the United States, their loyalty will be unreservedly given to the government, whose leniency they cannot fail to appreciate, and whose fostering care will soon restore them to a condition of prosperity. It is true, that in some of the States the demoralizing effects of war are to be seen in occasional disorders, but these are local in character, not frequent in occurrence, and are rapidly disappearing as the authority of civil law is extended and sustained."

Johnson's message to the Senate was accompanied by a report from Major General Carl Schurz. Among the subjects on which Schurz reported were whether southern whites had accepted defeat and emancipation, and whether ex-slaves and southern Unionists were safe in the South and were receiving fair treatment. Schurz's report was apparently largely ignored by President Johnson, who had assigned him to make the report but was not happy with what he said.

Schurz went to considerable lengths to get an accurate reading of attitudes in the South. He tried to get a representative sample of people to interview in his three-month tour of portions of South Carolina, Georgia, Alabama, Mississippi, and Louisiana and gathered documentary evidence as well as interviews. Then he tried to analyze his findings carefully and make recommendations on the basis of those findings. Clearly, he believed that Reconstruction in the South involved more than the restoration of civil government.

Source: U.S. Congress, Senate, 39th Cong., 1st sess., 1865, Ex. Doc. No. 2, 1–5, 8, 36–39, 41–44.

SIR: . . . You informed me that your "policy of reconstruction" was merely experimental, and that you would change it if the experiment did not lead to satisfactory results. To aid you in forming your conclusions upon this point I understood to be the object of my mission, . . .

CONDITION OF THINGS IMMEDIATELY AFTER THE CLOSE OF THE WAR

In the development of the popular spirit in the south since the close of the war two well-marked periods can be distinguished. The first commences with the sudden collapse of the confederacy and the dispersion of its armies, and the second with the first proclamation indicating the "reconstruction policy" of the government. . . . When the news of Lee's and Johnston's surrenders burst upon the southern country the general consternation was extreme. People held their breath, indulging in the wildest apprehensions as to what was now to come. . . . Prominent Unionists told me that persons who for four years had scorned to recognize them on the street approached them with smiling faces and both hands extended. Men of standing in the political world expressed serious doubts as to whether the rebel States would ever again occupy their position as States in the Union, or be governed as conquered provinces. The public mind was so despondent that if readmission at some future time under whatever conditions had been promised, it would then have been looked upon as a favor. The most uncompromising rebels prepared for leaving the country. The masses remained in a state of fearful expectancy. . . .

Such was, according to the accounts I received, the character of that first period. The worst apprehensions were gradually relieved as day after day went by without bringing the disasters and inflictions which had been vaguely anticipated, until at last the appearance of the North Carolina proclamation substituted new hopes for them. The development of this second period I was called upon to observe on the spot, and it forms the main subject of this report.

RETURNING LOYALTY

. . . [T]he white people at large being, under certain conditions, charged with taking the preliminaries of "reconstruction" into their hands, the success of the experiment depends upon the spirit and attitude of those who either attached themselves to the secession cause from the beginning, or, entertaining originally opposite views, at least followed its fortunes from the time that their States had declared their separation from the Union. . . .

I may group the southern people into four classes, each of which exercises an influence upon the development of things in that section:

1. Those who, although having yielded submission to the national government only when obliged to do so, have a clear perception of the irreversible changes produced by the war, and honestly endeavor to accommodate themselves to the new order of things. Many of them are not free from traditional prejudice but open to conviction, and may be expected to act in good faith whatever they do. This class is composed, in its majority, of persons of mature age—planters, merchants, and professional men; some of them are active in the reconstruction movement, but boldness and energy are, with a few individual exceptions, not among their distinguishing qualities.

2. Those whose principal object is to have the States without delay restored to their position and influence in the Union and the people of the States to the absolute control of their home concerns. They are ready, in order to attain that object, to make any ostensible concession that will not prevent them from arranging things to suit their taste as soon as that object is attained. This class comprises a considerable number, probably a large majority, of the professional politicians who are extremely active in the reconstruction movement. They are loud in their praise of the President's reconstruction policy, and clamorous for the withdrawal of the federal troops and the abolition of the Freedmen's Bureau.

3. The incorrigibles, who still indulge in the swagger which was so customary before and during the war, and still hope for a time when the southern confederacy will achieve its independence. This class consists mostly of young men, and comprises the loiterers of the towns and the idlers of the country. They persecute Union men and negroes whenever they can do so with impunity, insist clamorously upon their "rights," and are extremely impatient of the presence of the federal soldiers. A good many of them have taken the oaths of allegiance and amnesty, and associated themselves with the second class in their political operations. This element is by no means unimportant; it is strong in numbers, deals in brave talk, addresses itself directly and incessantly to the passions and prejudices of the masses, and commands the admiration of the women.

4. The multitude of people who have no definite ideas about the circumstances under which they live and about the course they have to follow; whose intellects are weak, but whose prejudices and impulses are strong, and who are apt to be carried along by those who know how to appeal to the latter. . . .

FEELING TOWARDS THE SOLDIERS AND THE PEOPLE OF THE NORTH

. . . [U]pon the whole, the soldier of the Union is still looked upon as a stranger, an intruder—as the "Yankee," "the enemy." . . .

It is by no means surprising that prejudices and resentments, which for years were so assiduously cultivated and so violently inflamed, should not have been turned into affection by a defeat; nor are they likely to disappear as long as the southern people continue to brood over their losses and misfortunes. They will gradually subside when those who entertain them cut resolutely loose from the past and embark in a career of new activity on a common field with those whom they have so long considered their enemies. . . . [A]s long as these feelings exist in their present strength, they will hinder the growth of that reliable kind of loyalty which springs from the heart and clings to the country in good and evil fortune.

SITUATION OF UNIONISTS

. . . It struck me soon after my arrival in the south that the known Unionists—I mean those who during the war had been to a certain extent identified with the national cause— were not in communion with the leading social and political circles; and the further my observations extended the clearer it became to me that their existence in the south was of a rather precarious nature. . . . Even Governor [William L.] Sharkey, in the course of a conversation I had with him in the presence of Major General Osterhaus, admitted that, if our troops were then withdrawn, the lives of northern men in Mississippi would not be safe. . . . [General Osterhaus said]: "There is no doubt whatever that the state of affairs would be intolerable for all Union men, all recent immigrants from the north, and all negroes, the moment the protection of the United States troops were withdrawn." . . .

NEGRO INSURRECTIONS AND ANARCHY

. . . [I do] not deem a negro insurrection probable as long as the freedmen were assured of the direct protection of the national government. Whenever they are in trouble, they raise their eyes up to that power, and although they may suffer, yet, as long as that power is visibly present, they continue to hope. But when State authority in the south is fully restored, the federal forces withdrawn, and the Freedmen's Bureau abolished, the colored man will find himself turned over to the mercies of those whom he does not trust. If then an attempt is made to strip him again of those rights which he justly thought he possessed, he will be apt to feel that he can hope for no redress unless he procure it himself. If ever the negro is capable of rising, he will rise then. . . .

There is probably at the present moment no country in the civilized world which contains such an accumulation of anarchical elements as the south. The strife of the antagonistic tendencies here described is aggravated by the passions inflamed and the general impoverishment brought about by a long and exhaustive war, and the south will have to suffer the evils of anarchical disorder until means are found to effect a final settlement of the labor question in accordance with the logic of the great revolution.

THE TRUE PROBLEM — DIFFICULTIES AND REMEDIES

In seeking remedies for such disorders, we ought to keep in view, above all, the nature of the problem which is to be solved. As to what is commonly termed "reconstruction," it is not only the political machinery of the States and their constitutional relations to the general government, but the whole organism of southern society that must be reconstructed, or rather constructed anew, so as to bring it in harmony with the rest of American society. The difficulties of this task are not to be considered overcome when the people

of the south take the oath of allegiance and elect governors and legislatures and members of Congress, and militia captains. That this would be done had become certain as soon as the surrenders of the southern armies had made further resistance impossible, and nothing in the world was left, even to the most uncompromising rebel, but to submit or to emigrate. It was also natural that they should avail themselves of every chance offered them to resume control of their home affairs and to regain their influence in the Union. But this can hardly be called the first step towards the solution of the true problem, and it is a fair question to ask, whether the hasty gratification of their desire to resume such control would not create new embarrassments.

The true nature of the difficulties of the situation is this: The general government of the republic has, by proclaiming the emancipation of the slaves, commenced a great social revolution in the south, but has, as yet, not completed it. Only the negative part of it is accomplished. The slaves are emancipated in point of form, but free labor has not yet been put in the place of slavery in point of fact. And now, in the midst of this critical period of transition, the power which originated the revolution is expected to turn over its whole future development to another power which from the beginning was hostile to it and has never yet entered into its spirit, leaving the class in whose favor it was made completely without power to protect itself and to take an influential part in that development. The history of the world will be searched in vain for a proceeding similar to this which did not lead either to a rapid and violent reaction, or to the most serious trouble and civil disorder. It cannot be said that the conduct of the southern people since the close of the war has exhibited such extraordinary wisdom and self-abnegation as to make them an exception to the rule.

In my despatches from the south I repeatedly expressed the opinion that the people were not yet in a frame of mind to legislate calmly and understandingly upon the subject of free negro labor. And this I reported to be the opinion of some of our most prominent military commanders and other observing men. It is, indeed, difficult to imagine circumstances more unfavorable for the development of a calm and unprejudiced public opinion than those under which the southern people are at present laboring. The war has not only defeated their political aspirations, but it has broken up their whole social organization. . . .

In which direction will these people be most apt to turn their eyes? Leaving the prejudice of race out of the question, from early youth they have been acquainted with but one system of labor, and with that one system they have been in the habit of identifying all their interests. They know of no way to help themselves but the one they are accustomed to. . . .

It is certain that every success of free negro labor will augment the number of its friends, and disarm some of the prejudices and assumptions of its opponents. I am convinced one good harvest made by unadulterated free labor in the south would have a far better effect than all the oaths that have been taken, and all the ordinances that have as yet been passed by southern conventions. But how can such a result be attained? The facts enumerated in this report, as well as the news we receive from the south from day to day, must make it evident to every unbiased observer that unadulterated free labor cannot be had at present, unless the national government holds its protective and controlling hand over it.... One reason why the southern people are so slow in accommodating themselves to the new order of things is, that they confidently expect soon to be permitted to regulate matters according to their own notions. Every concession made to them by the government has been taken as an encouragement to persevere in this hope, and, unfortunately for them, this hope is nourished by influences from other parts of the country. Hence their anxiety to have their State governments restored *at once*, to have the troops withdrawn, and the Freedmen's Bureau abolished, although a good many discerning men know well that, in view of the lawless spirit still prevailing, it would be far better for them to have the general order of society firmly maintained by the federal power until things have arrived at a final settlement. Had, from the beginning, the conviction been forced upon them that the adulteration of the new order of things by the admixture of elements belonging to the system of slavery would under no circumstances be permitted, a much larger number would have launched their energies into the new channel, and, seeing that they could do "no better," faithfully co-operated with the government. It is hope which fixes them in their perverse notions. That hope nourished or fully gratified, they will persevere in the same direction. That hope destroyed, a great many will, by the force of necessity, at once accommodate themselves to the logic of the change. If, therefore, the national government firmly and unequivocally announces its policy not to give up the control of the free-labor reform until it is finally accomplished, the progress of that reform will undoubtedly be far more rapid and far less difficult than it will be if the attitude of the government is such as to permit contrary hopes to be indulged in....

IMMIGRATION [AND CAPITAL]

[The south would benefit] from immigration of northern people and Europeans.... The south needs capital. But capital is notoriously timid and averse to risk.... Capitalists will be apt to consider—and they are by no means wrong in doing so—that no safe investments can be made in the south as long as southern society is liable to be convulsed by anarchical disorders. No greater encouragement can, therefore, be given to capital to transfer itself to the south than the assurance that the government will continue to control the development of the new social system in the late rebel States until such dangers are averted by a final settlement of things upon a thorough free-labor basis.

How long the national government should continue that control depends upon contingencies. It ought to cease as soon as its objects are attained; and its objects will be attained sooner and with less difficulty if nobody is permitted to indulge in the delusion that it will cease *before* they are attained. This is one of the cases in which a determined policy

can accomplish much, while a half-way policy is liable to spoil things already accomplished....

NEGRO SUFFRAGE

It would seem that the interference of the national authority in the home concerns of the southern States would be rendered less necessary, and the whole problem of political and social reconstruction be much simplified, if, while the masses lately arrayed against the government are permitted to vote, the large majority of those who were always loyal, and are naturally anxious to see the free labor problem successfully solved, were not excluded from all influence upon legislation. In all questions concerning the Union, the national debt, and the future social organization of the south, the feelings of the colored man are naturally in sympathy with the views and aims of the national government. While the southern white fought against the Union, the negro did all he could to aid it; while the southern white sees in the national government his conqueror, the negro sees in it his protector; while the white owes to the national debt his defeat, the negro owes to it his deliverance; while the white considers himself robbed and ruined by the emancipation of the slaves, the negro finds in it the assurance of future prosperity and happiness. In all the important issues the negro would be led by natural impulse to forward the ends of the government, and by making his influence, as part of the voting body, tell upon the legislation of the States, render the interference of the national authority less necessary.

As the most difficult of the pending questions are intimately connected with the status of the negro in southern society, it is obvious that a correct solution can be more easily obtained if he has a voice in the matter. In the right to vote he would find the best permanent protection against oppressive class-legislation, as well as against individual persecution. The relations between the white and black races, even if improved by the gradual wearing off of the present animosities, are likely to remain long under the troubling influence of prejudice. It is a notorious fact that the rights of a man of some political power are far less exposed to violation than those of one who is, in matters of public interest, completely subject to the will of others....

In discussing the matter of negro suffrage I deemed it my duty to confine myself strictly to the practical aspects of the subject. I have, therefore, not touched its moral merits nor discussed the question whether the national government is competent to enlarge the elective franchise in the States lately in rebellion by its own act; I deem it proper, however, to offer a few remarks on the assertion frequently put forth, that the franchise is likely to be extended to the colored man by the voluntary action of the southern whites themselves. My observation leads me to a contrary opinion. Aside from a very few enlightened men, I found but one class of people in favor of the enfranchisement of the blacks: it was the class of Unionists who found themselves politically ostracised and looked upon the enfranchisement of the loyal negroes as the salvation of the whole loyal element. But their numbers and influence are sadly insufficient to secure such a result. The masses are strongly opposed to colored suffrage; anybody that dares to advocate it is stigmatized as a dangerous fanatic; nor do I deem it probable that in the ordinary course of things prejudices will wear off to such an extent as to make it a popular measure. . . .

DEPORTATION OF THE FREEDMEN

. . . [T]he true problem remains, not how to remove the colored man from his present field of labor, but how to make him, where he is, a true freeman and an intelligent and useful citizen. The means are simple: protection by the government until his political and social status enables him to protect himself, offering to his legitimate ambition the stimulant of a perfectly fair chance in life, and granting to him the rights which in every just organization of society are coupled with corresponding duties.

CONCLUSION

I may sum up all I have said in a few words. If nothing were necessary but to restore the machinery of government in the States lately in rebellion in point of form, the movements made to that end by the people of the south might be considered satisfactory. But if it is required that the southern people should also accommodate themselves to the results of the war in point of spirit, those movements fall far short of what must be insisted upon.

Questions

1. Why did Schurz recommend keeping the Freedmen's Bureau and the army in the South? How did that differ from what Johnson wanted?

2. Why did Schurz suggest that it might be wise to give African Americans in the South the vote?

3. What did Schurz say about the Unionists in the South? About the emergence of a free labor system?

15-3 Reconstruction (1865)

Philip A. Bell

President Andrew Johnson's plan of reconstruction (see Document 15-1) was justly criticized by those who had anticipated far-reaching changes in the South after the Civil War, and none was more vocal in expressing his disgruntlement than Philip A. Bell. A leading African American journalist and abolitionist prior to the war, Bell founded *The Elevator* in 1865 to champion the rights of southern blacks. That emboldened ex-Confederates had resumed control of Johnson's state governments and enacted Black Codes (see Document 15-4) that aimed to reduce the newly freed population to plantation laborers under a system of quasi-slavery was simply unacceptable to Bell. In his September 15, 1865, *Elevator* editorial, Bell posed what was arguably the fundamental question pertaining to the status of the ex-Confederate states and, in no uncertain terms, articulated the Radical Republicans' opposition to the president's plan.

Source: Excerpt from *The Black Abolitionist Papers*, ed. C. Peter Ripley, et al. (Chapel Hill: University of North Carolina Press, 1992), 5:369–370. Used by permission of the publisher.

This is the most important subject which now engages the attention of the American people, for on it depends the future welfare of the nation, and the destinies of a race but partially redeemed from bondage. It is a question which absorbs the minds of all reflecting men, and all energies, all thoughts are now directed to that point. Not only in America, but in Europe, also, does this subject attract marked attention, as it involves other momentous subjects of civil, political, and philanthropic importance, as well as the theory of republican or representative government.

The whole subject seems to revolve itself into this: Have the rebel States ever lost or renounced their position as members of the Union? If they have not, as President Johnson avers, why threat them as territories or subjugated provinces by appointing officers which it is the prerogative of the State to elect? Why prescribe rules and regulations for their government, when they have their own State Constitution? All that is required, according to this theory, is for them to resume their former functions, acknowledge the supremacy of the General Government, and take their position again as States of the Union. They can establish slavery, for until the Constitutional Amendments are confirmed, Congress cannot prohibit slavery by virtue of the Proclamation, for the necessity which called for that is passed, and the States return to the "Union as it was and the Constitution as it is."

We must confess we were somewhat inclined to President Johnson's theory, but we cannot reconcile the idea of an appointing power for States which are members of the Union—integral portions thereof. We have seen the fallacy of that theory which the practice of the President contradicts, and are now convinced that the rebel States have no rights which the Government is bound to respect.

If the theory of the President is correct, he has overstepped the bounds of his authority by appointing Provisional Governors over sovereign States which had their fundamental laws intact, and had power to elect their own Governors. If he has that power, he should exercise it to its fullest extent—first, by appointing *all* the officers of State government, and, secondly, by appointing men of sound Union sentiments, not endeavor to coax and conciliate the rebels by appointing men of known secession proclivities, some of whom have taken an active part in the rebellion.

Again—it must be obvious to all that by allowing the rebel States to return to the Union without purgation, is but sowing seed for future difficulties.

We now come to the most important point, and to which Government has paid no attention whatever—the suffrage question. In his various proclamations, the President has declared what classes are not entitled to citizenship, but he has apparently lost sight of the negro population, which will ever be a disturbing element as long as they are an oppressed race. They form a large proportion of the Southern States, and will become as necessary to the Government in the future as they have been in the past, if they are treated like men and have the rights of citizens. But in their present anomalous position as freedmen, not freemen, they can render the Government no aid political, and in case of another outbreak, they would not render military service to a government which has once broken faith with them.

Considerable speculation is raised on qualifications for voters. We were never very democratic in our political opinions; we care not for universal suffrage—what we want is equal suffrage; and in reconstructing the States we only desire "Equality before the Law." The difficulty on this point is to make the qualifications such as to take in the most worthy and intelligent, and exclude the vicious and ignorant. No human judgment, nor laws framed by fallible man, could do that—hence we must expect, under any qualification, some who are worthy and capable would be excluded, and others the reverse, admitted. Still we will be content with any law which bears equally on all.

Questions

1. What was the basis of Bell's claim that the "rebel States have no rights which the [federal] Government is bound to respect"? What did he see as the principal shortcoming of the Johnson plan?

2. Given the southern defense of secession as a "constitutional" right (see Documents 13-7, 14-1, and 14-2), was Bell justified in his assertions about Reconstruction and the powers of the federal government?

3. Compare Bell's views on Reconstruction with those of Charles Sumner (Document 13-11) and Thaddeus Stevens (Document 15-6). Were they identical? Did they share the same priorities?

15-4 The Mississippi Black Codes (1865)

As Carl Schurz reported, after the Civil War whites in the South sought a system of race relations in which African Americans would be clearly subordinate to whites and would constitute a readily accessible and controllable workforce (see text p. 461).

Immediately after the Civil War southern whites wrote or revised vagrancy laws and the old slave codes as a means of establishing the system of race relations they wanted. Following is one of their most famous attempts to codify race relations, the Black Codes passed by the Mississippi legislature.

The Mississippi codes gave blacks rights they had not had before and clearly acknowledged that chattel slavery had ended. The codes recognized the right of African Americans to own property, though not in incorporated towns or cities. (Before the Civil War there were black property owners in Mississippi and even a few black slaveholders, but their legal standing was not clear.) The 1865 codes also recognized marriages among blacks as legal.

Not all the southern states passed comprehensive Black Codes, and some codes were much less stringent than those of Mississippi. South Carolina's codes differed in that they restricted blacks to buying property in cities or towns.

The creators of the codes drew their ideas from the world in which they lived. Slavery had just ended very abruptly, and the ravages of war were ever present. The men who drafted these codes used the old slave codes from the South, vagrancy laws from the North and the South, laws for former slaves in the British West Indies, and antebellum laws for free blacks. They were also aware that most northern states had laws that discriminated against African Americans and that very few northern states allowed African Americans to vote.

Most of these codes and similar measures were declared void by the Union army officials who were stationed in the former Confederate states. Subsequently, during Reconstruction, the rights of African Americans were greatly expanded (see text pp. 464–472).

Source: Laws of Mississippi, 1865, pp. 82ff.

---

1. CIVIL RIGHTS OF FREEDMEN IN MISSISSIPPI

. . . That all freedmen, free negroes, and mulattoes may sue and be sued . . . may acquire personal property . . . and may dispose of the same in the same manner and to the same extent that white persons may: [but no] freedman, free negro, or mulatto . . . [shall] rent or lease any lands or tenements except in incorporated cities or towns, in which places the corporate authorities shall control the same. . . .

All freedmen, free negroes, or mulattoes who do now and have herebefore lived and cohabited together as husband and wife shall be taken and held in law as legally married, and the issue shall be taken and held as legitimate for all purposes; that it shall not be lawful for any freedman, free negro, or mulatto to intermarry with any white person; nor for any white person to intermarry with any freedman, free negro, or mulatto; and any person who shall so intermarry, shall be deemed guilty of felony, and on conviction thereof shall be confined in the State penitentiary for life; and those shall be deemed freedmen, free negroes, and mulattoes who are of pure negro blood, and those descended from a negro to the third generation, inclusive, though one ancestor in each generation may have been a white person. . . .

[F]reedmen, free negroes, and mulattoes are now by law competent witnesses . . . in civil cases [and in criminal cases where they are the victims]. . . .

All contracts for labor made with freedmen, free negroes, and mulattoes for a longer period than one month shall be in writing, and in duplicate . . . and said contracts shall be taken and held as entire contracts, and if the laborer shall quit the service of the employer before the expiration of his term of service, without good cause, he shall forfeit his wages for that year up to the time of quitting.

. . . Every civil officer shall, and every person may, arrest and carry back to his or her legal employer any freedman, free negro, or mulatto who shall have quit the service of his or her employer before the expiration of his or her term of service without good cause; and said officer and person shall be entitled to receive for arresting and carrying back every deserting employee aforesaid the sum of five dollars. . . .

. . . If any person shall persuade or attempt to persuade, entice, or cause any freedman, free negro, or mulatto to desert from the legal employment of any person before the expiration of his or her term of service, or shall knowingly employ any such deserting freedman, free negro, or mulatto, or shall knowingly give or sell to any such deserting freedman, free negro, or mulatto, any food, raiment, or other thing, he or she shall be guilty of a misdemeanor. . . .

2. MISSISSIPPI APPRENTICE LAW

. . . It shall be the duty of all sheriffs, justices of the peace, and other civil officers of the several counties in this State, to report to the probate courts of their respective counties semi-annually, at the January and July terms of said courts, all freedmen, free negroes, and mulattoes, under the age of eighteen, in their respective counties, beats or districts, who are orphans, or whose parent or parents have not the means or who refuse to provide for and support said minors; . . . the clerk of said court to apprentice said minors to some competent and suitable person, on such terms as the court may direct, having a particular care to the interest of said minor: *Provided*, that the former owner of said minors shall have the preference when, in the opinion of the court, he or she shall be a suitable person for that purpose. . . .

. . . In the management and control of said apprentice, said master or mistress shall have the power to inflict such moderate corporal chastisement as a father or guardian is allowed to inflict on his or her child or ward at common law: *Provided*, that in no case shall cruel or inhuman punishment be inflicted. . . .

3. MISSISSIPPI VAGRANT LAW

... That all rogues and vagabonds, idle and dissipated persons, beggars, jugglers, or persons practicing unlawful games or plays, runaways, common drunkards, common nightwalkers, pilferers, lewd, wanton, or lascivious persons, in speech or behavior, common railers and brawlers, persons who neglect their calling or employment, misspend what they earn, or do not provide for the support of themselves or their families, or dependents, and all other idle and disorderly persons, including all who neglect all lawful business, habitually misspend their time by frequenting houses of ill-fame, gaming-houses, or tippling shops, shall be deemed and considered vagrants, under the provisions of this act, and upon conviction thereof shall be fined not exceeding one hundred dollars ... and be imprisoned at the discretion of the court, not exceeding ten days.

... All freedmen, free negroes and mulattoes in this State, over the age of eighteen years, found on the second Monday in January, 1866, or thereafter, with no lawful employment or business, or found unlawfully assembling themselves together, either in the day or night time, and all white persons so assembling themselves with freedmen, free negroes or mulattoes, or usually associating with freedmen, free negroes or mulattoes, on terms of equality, or living in adultery or fornication with a freed woman, free negro or mulatto, shall be deemed vagrants, and on conviction thereof shall be fined in a sum not exceeding, in the case of a freedman, free negro or mulatto, fifty dollars, and a white man two hundred dollars, and imprisoned at the discretion of the court, the free negro not exceeding ten days, and the white man not exceeding six months. ...

4. PENAL LAWS OF MISSISSIPPI

... That no freedman, free negro or mulatto, not in the military service of the United States government, and not licensed so to do by the board of police of his or her county, shall keep or carry fire-arms of any kind, or any ammunition, dirk or bowie knife. ...

... Any freedman, free negro, or mulatto committing riots, routs, affrays, trespasses, malicious mischief, cruel treatment to animals, seditious speeches, insulting gestures, language, or acts, or assaults on any person, disturbance of the peace, exercising the function of a minister of the Gospel without a license from some regularly organized church, vending spirituous or intoxicating liquors, or committing any other misdemeanor, the punishment of which is not specifically provided for by law, shall, upon conviction thereof in the county court, be fined not less than ten dollars, and not more than one hundred dollars, and may be imprisoned at the discretion of the court, not exceeding thirty days. ...

... If any freedman, free negro, or mulatto, convicted of any of the misdemeanors provided against in this act, shall fail or refuse for the space of five days, after conviction, to pay the fine and costs imposed, such person shall be hired out by the sheriff or other officer, at public outcry, to any white person who will pay said fine and all costs, and take said convict for the shortest time.

Questions

1. What was the intent of these laws?

2. Who was charged with enforcing them? ("Every civil officer shall, and every person may, arrest and carry back to his or her legal employer ...") Who was considered a "person"? Who was not a "person"?

3. How were vagrants defined? Were these laws based on the assumption that the only vagrants were African Americans? What restrictions were placed on the freedom of expression of African Americans? What restrictions were placed on their freedom of association? On whites in Mississippi?

15-5 The Civil Rights Act of 1866

When Congress reconvened in December 1865, it blocked President Johnson's attempts to restore the South quickly. It extended the life of the Freedmen's Bureau over the president's veto and passed another landmark law, the Civil Rights Act of 1866, again over the president's veto (see text p. 465). This act made African Americans citizens and countered the 1857 *Dred Scott* decision, in which the Supreme Court had declared that no African American who was descended from a slave was or could ever be a citizen (Document 13-12).

Doubts about the constitutionality and permanence of the Civil Rights Act of 1866 prompted Congress to pass the Fourteenth Amendment (see text pp. 465–466). Ratified in 1868, this amendment for the first time constitutionally defined citizenship and some of the basic rights of citizenship; it also embraced the Republican program for Reconstruction.

Source: U.S. Statutes at Large, 14 (1868?), 27ff.

An Act to protect all Persons in the United States in their Civil Rights, and furnish the Means of their Vindication.

Be it enacted, That all persons born in the United States and not subject to any foreign power, excluding Indians not taxed, are hereby declared to be citizens of the United States; and such citizens, of every race and color, without regard to any previous condition of slavery or involuntary servitude, except as a punishment for crime whereof the party shall have been duly convicted, shall have the same right, in every State and Territory in the United States, to make and enforce contracts, to sue, be parties, and give evidence, to inherit, purchase, lease, sell, hold, and convey real and personal property, and to full and equal benefit of all laws and proceedings for the security of person and property, as is enjoyed by white citizens, and shall be subject to like punishment, pains, and penalties, and to none other, any law, statute, ordinance, regulation, or custom, to the contrary notwithstanding.

SEC. 2. *And be it further enacted*, That any person who, under color of any law, statute, ordinance, regulation, or custom, shall subject, or cause to be subjected, any inhabitant of any State or Territory to the deprivation of any right secured or protected by this act, or to different punishment, pains, or penalties on account of such person having at any time been held in a condition of slavery or involuntary servitude, except as a punishment for crime whereof the party shall have been duly convicted, or by reason of his color or race, than is prescribed for the punishment of white persons, shall be deemed guilty of a misdemeanor, and, on conviction, shall be punished by fine not exceeding one thousand dollars, or imprisonment not exceeding one year, or both, in the discretion of the court.

SEC. 3. *And be it further enacted*, That the district courts of the United States, . . . shall have, exclusively of the courts of the several States, cognizance of all crimes and offences committed against the provisions of this act, and also, concurrently with the circuit courts of the United States, of all causes, civil and criminal, affecting persons who are denied or cannot enforce in the courts or judicial tribunals of the State or locality where they may be any of the rights secured to them by the first section of this act. . . .

SEC. 4. *And be it further enacted*, That the district attorneys, marshals, and deputy marshals of the United States, the commissioners appointed by the circuit and territorial courts of the United States, with powers of arresting, imprisoning, or bailing offenders against the laws of the United States, the officers and agents of the Freedmen's Bureau, and every other officer who may be specially empowered by the President of the United States, shall be, and they are hereby, specially authorized and required, at the expense of the United States, to institute proceedings against all and every person who shall violate the provisions of this act, and cause him or them to be arrested and imprisoned, or bailed, as the case may be, for trial before such court of the United States or territorial court as by this act has cognizance of the offence. . . .

SEC. 8. *And be it further enacted*, That whenever the President of the United States shall have reason to believe that offences have been or are likely to be committed against the provisions of this act within any judicial district, it shall be lawful for him, in his discretion, to direct the judge, marshal, and district attorney of such district to attend at such place within the district, and for such time as he may designate, for the purpose of the more speedy arrest and trial of persons charged with a violation of this act; and it shall be the duty of every judge or other officer, when any such requisition shall be received by him, to attend at the place and for the time therein designated.

SEC. 9. *And be it further enacted*, That it shall be lawful for the President of the United States, or such person as he may empower for that purpose, to employ such part of the land or naval forces of the United States, or of the militia, as shall be necessary to prevent the violation and enforce the due execution of this act.

SEC. 10. *And be it further enacted*, That upon all questions of law arising in any cause under the provisions of this act a final appeal may be taken to the Supreme Court of the United States.

Questions

1. What was the intent of the Civil Rights Act?

2. Who was responsible for enforcing this law, and what powers might they use? Was it necessary to wait until the law was violated before officers of the law could act?

3. According to the Fourteenth Amendment, who is a citizen of the United States? What rights does the amendment say citizens have? What does "equal protection of the laws" mean?

Questions for Further Thought

1. Compare President Johnson's description of conditions in the South (Document 15-1) with that of General Schurz (Document 15-2). Which do you find to be more accurate? Why?

2. Schurz reported that if Reconstruction meant that the social order of the former Confederate states had to be "constructed anew," then Johnson's program (Document 15-1) was a failure. Based on your reading of the Mississippi Black Codes (Document 15-4), to what extent was Shurz correct in his assessment?

3. Compare the Mississippi Black Codes (Document 15-4) with the Civil Rights Act of 1866 (Document 15-5). Why do you think Congress believed that it had to pass the Civil Rights Act and then adopt the Fourteenth Amendment?

Radical Reconstruction

When only Tennessee ratified the Fourteenth Amendment (and was readmitted to the Union), congressional Republicans, strengthened by their victories in the 1866 congressional elections, passed the Reconstruction Acts. These laws forced unreconstructed former Confederate states to meet Republican conditions for readmission, including granting African American men the vote. While these measures were called radical by their detractors (and this phase of Reconstruction referred to as "radical Reconstruction"), these measures actually fell far short of what some in Congress desired (Document 15-6). They fell even further short of the hopes of women's rights advocates that the vote might be extended to them as well as blacks—a frustration that seriously split the movement, but led ultimately to the creation of a new, and eventually successful, woman suffrage movement (Document 15-7).

During Reconstruction African Americans obtained a number of civil and political rights, most especially in the realm of politics. While no former Confederate state was controlled by blacks, a large group of African American politicians surged into prominence, seeking to use government power to help constituents who previously had not even been regarded as citizens (Document 15-8). While many of these new political rights were lost in the years following Reconstruction, other gains, especially in social and economic realms, were more enduring. At the insistence of the freed slaves, planters dismantled much of the old slave regime, replacing gang labor and the old slave quarters with a new system of individual plots worked by families for shares of the crops. Black marriages were formalized, and African Americans gained control over their family lives. They pursued education, built new institutions such as the black church, and began to acquire property. While white racism and white landlord power raised enormous barriers to black advancement, through the years increasing (though still small) numbers of African Americans became property holders.

15-6   Black Suffrage and Land Redistribution (1867)

Thaddeus Stevens

The Radical Republicans, including Congressman Thaddeus Stevens of Pennsylvania, believed that besides the vote, freedmen would need an economic basis for controlling their lives (see text p. 466). Below are excerpts from the remarks of Thaddeus Stevens and from a bill in which he proposed to alter the South drastically.

Source: Congressional Globe, 3 January 1867, 252; 19 March 1867, 203.

ON BLACK SUFFRAGE

Unless the rebel States, before admission, should be made republican in spirit, and placed under the guardianship of loyal men, all our blood and treasure will have been spent in vain. I waive now the question of punishment which, if we are wise, will still be inflicted by moderate confiscations. . . . Impartial suffrage, both in electing the delegates and ratifying their proceedings, is now the fixed rule. There is more reason why colored voters should be admitted in the rebel States than in the Territories. In the States they form the great mass of the loyal men. Possibly with their aid loyal governments may be established in most of those States. Without it all are sure to be ruled by traitors; and loyal men, black and white, will be oppressed, exiled, or murdered. There are several good reasons for the passage of this bill. In the first place, it is just. I am now confining my argument to negro suffrage in the rebel States. Have not loyal blacks quite as good a right to choose rulers and make laws as rebel whites? In the second place, it is a necessity in order to protect the loyal white men in the seceded States. The white Union men are in a great minority in each of those States. With them the blacks would act in a body; and it is believed that in each of said States, except one, the two united would form a majority, control the States, and protect themselves. Now they are the victims of daily murder. . . .

Another good reason is, it would insure the ascendency of the Union party. . . . I believe . . . that on the continued ascendency of that party depends the safety of this great nation. If impartial suffrage is excluded in the rebel States, then every one of them is sure to send a solid rebel representative delegation to Congress, and cast a solid rebel electoral vote. They, with their kindred Copperheads of the North, would always elect the President and control Congress. While slavery sat upon her defiant throne, and insulted and intimidated the trembling North, the South frequently divided on questions of policy between Whigs and Democrats, and gave victory alternately to the sections. Now, you must divide them between loyalists, without regard to color, and disloyalists, or you will be the perpetual vassals of the free-trade, irritated, revengeful South. . . . I am for negro suffrage in every rebel State. If it be just, it should not be denied; if it be necessary, it should be adopted; if it be a punishment to traitors, they deserve it.

BILL ON LAND REDISTRIBUTION

Whereas it is due to justice, as an example to future times, that some proper punishment should be inflicted on the people who constituted the "confederate States of America," both because they, declaring an unjust war against the United States for the purpose of destroying republican liberty and permanently establishing slavery, as well as for the cruel and barbarous manner in which they conducted said war, in violation of all the laws of civilized warfare, and also to compel them to make some compensation for the damages and expenditures caused by said war: Therefore,

Be it enacted by the Senate and House of Representatives of the United States of America in Congress assembled, That all the public lands belonging to the ten States that formed the government of the so-called "confederate States of America" shall be forfeited by said States and become forthwith vested in the United States. . . .

That out of the lands thus seized and confiscated the slaves who have been liberated by the operations of the war and the amendment to the Constitution or otherwise, who resided in said "confederate States" on the 4th day of March, A.D. 1861, or since, shall have distributed to them as follows, namely: to each male person who is the head of a family, forty acres; to each adult male, whether the head of a family or not, forty acres; to each widow who is the head of a family, forty acres—to be held by them in fee-simple, but to be inalienable for the next ten years after they become seized thereof. . . .

That out of the balance of the property thus seized and confiscated there shall be raised, in the manner hereinafter provided, a sum equal to fifty dollars, for each homestead, to be applied by the trustees hereinafter mentioned toward the erection of buildings on the said homesteads for the use of said slaves; and the further sum of $500,000,000, which shall be appropriated as follows, to wit: $200,000,000 shall be invested in United States six per cent securities; and the interest thereof shall be semi-annually added to the pensions allowed by law to pensioners who have become so by reason of the late war; $300,000,000, or so much thereof as may be needed, shall be appropriated to pay damages done to loyal citizens by the civil or military operations of the government lately called the "confederate States of America." . . .

That in order that just discrimination may be made, the property of no one shall be seized whose whole estate on the 4th day of March, A.D. 1865, was not worth more than $5,000, to be valued by the said commission, unless he shall have voluntarily become an officer or employé in the military or civil service of the "confederate States of America," or in the civil or military service of some one of said States.

Questions

1. On what grounds did Stevens justify granting African American men the vote?

2. What did Stevens want to do with land confiscated in the South?

3. Why do you think Congress rejected Stevens's land confiscation and redistribution proposal? Do you think that if Congress had adopted the proposal, it would have made a difference in the history of the South or the United States? Why or why not?

15-7 The Fourteenth Amendment and Woman Suffrage (1873, 1875)

As noted in the text, not only did the Fourteenth and Fifteenth Amendments ignore the demands of the women's rights movement for equal access to the ballot box, but the Fourteenth Amendment introduced the word *male* for the first time into the U.S. Constitution. Nonetheless, many suffragists continued to believe that the newly formalized and broadened definition of American citizenship established by the Fourteenth Amendment could be used to gain women the vote through a judicial ruling. In 1872 a number of suffragists, including Susan B. Anthony, voted in the presidential election; Anthony was indicted and brought to trial, providing her the opportunity she sought to make her case (Document 15-7a). Anthony was blocked from making her appeal, but another suffragist, Virginia Minor of Missouri, sued the official who blocked her from the ballot box and saw her case reach the Supreme Court. The Court's decision (Document 15-7b), handed down in 1875, effectively ended all hopes that gender relations as well as race relations had been "reconstructed" by the Fourteenth Amendment, and strengthened the movement for a constitutional woman suffrage amendment. Furthermore, by effectively separating the right to vote from fundamental citizenship rights, the Court also helped set the stage for the later movement to use "color-blind" laws to disfranchise African Americans.

Sources: From Ruth Barnes Moynihan, Cynthia Russett, and Laurie Crumpacker, eds., *Second to None: A Documentary History of American Women* (Lincoln: University of Nebraska Press, 1993), 2:16–19. Used by permission of the University of Nebraska Press. This selection first appeared in *The Life and Work of Susan B. Anthony*, vol. 3 (Indianapolis: Bowen-Merrill, 1898).

(a) I Stand Before You Under Indictment (1873)

Friends and Fellow-Citizens:—I stand before you under indictment for the alleged crime of having voted at the last presidential election, without having a lawful right to vote. It shall be my work this evening to prove to you that in thus doing, I not only committed no crime, but instead simply exercised my citizen's right, guaranteed to me and all United States citizens by the National Constitution beyond the power of any State to deny.

Our democratic-republican government is based on the idea of the natural right of every individual member thereof to a voice and a vote in making and executing the laws. We assert the province of government to be to secure the people in the enjoyment of their inalienable rights. We throw to the winds the old dogma that government can give rights. No one denies that before governments were organized each individual possessed the right to protect his own life, liberty and property. When 100 or 1,000,000 people enter into a free government, they do not barter away their natural rights; they simply pledge themselves to protect each other in the enjoyment of them through prescribed judicial and legislative tribunals. They agree to abandon the methods of brute force in the adjustment of their differences and adopt those of civilization. Nor can you find a word in any of the grand documents left us by the fathers which assumes for government the power to create or to confer rights. The Declaration of Independence, the United States Constitution, the constitutions of the several States and the organic laws of the Territories, all alike propose to *protect* the people in the exercise of their God-given rights. Not one of them pretends to bestow rights.

All men are created equal, and endowed by their Creator with certain inalienable rights. Among these are life, liberty and the pursuit of happiness. To secure these, governments are instituted among men, deriving their just powers from the consent of the governed.

Here is no shadow of government authority over rights, or exclusion of any class from their full and equal enjoyment. Here is pronounced the right of all men, and "consequently," as the Quaker preacher said, "of all women," to a voice in the government. And here, in this first paragraph of the Declaration, is the assertion of the natural right of all to the ballot; for how can "the consent of the governed" be given, if the right to vote be denied? Again:

Whenever any form of government becomes destructive of these ends, it is the right of the people to alter or abolish it, and to institute a new government, laying its foundations on such principles, and organizing its powers in such form, as to them shall seem most likely to effect their safety and happiness.

Surely the right of the whole people to vote is here clearly implied; for however destructive to their happiness this government might become, a disfranchised class could neither alter nor abolish it, nor institute a new one, except by the old brute force method of insurrection and rebellion. One-half of the people of this nation today are utterly powerless to blot from the statute books an unjust law, or to write there a new and just one. The women, dissatisfied as they are with this form of government, that enforces taxation without representation—that compels them to obey laws to which they never have given their consent—that imprisons and hangs them without a trial by a jury of their peers—that robs them, in marriage, of the custody of their own persons, wages and children—are this half of the people who are left wholly at the mercy of the other half, in direct violation of the spirit and letter of the declarations of the framers of this government, every one of which was based on the immutable principle of equal rights to all. By these declarations, kings, popes, priests, aristocrats, all were alike dethroned and placed on a common level, politically, with the lowliest born subject or serf. By them, too, men, as such, were deprived of their divine right to rule and placed on a political level with women. By the practice of these declarations all class and caste distinctions would be abolished, and slave, serf, plebeian, wife, woman, all alike rise from their subject position to the broader platform of equality.

The preamble of the Federal Constitution says:

We, the people of the United States, in order to form a more perfect union, establish justice, insure domestic tranquillity, provide for the common defence, promote the general welfare and secure the blessings of liberty to ourselves and our posterity, do ordain and establish this Constitution for the United States of America.

It was we, the people, not we, the white male citizens, nor we, the male citizens; but we, the whole people, who formed this Union. We formed it not to give the blessings of liberty but to secure them; not to the half of ourselves and the half of our posterity, but to the whole people—women as well as men. It is downright mockery to talk to women of their enjoyment of the blessings of liberty while they are denied the only means of securing them provided by this democratic-republican government—the ballot. . . .

For any State to make sex a qualification, which must ever result in the disfranchisement of one entire half of the people, is to pass a bill of attainder, an ex post facto law, and is therefore a violation of the supreme law of the land. By it the blessings of liberty are forever withheld from women and their female posterity. For them, this government has no just powers derived from the consent of the governed. For them this government is not a democracy; it is not a republic. It is the most odious aristocracy ever established on the face of the globe. An oligarchy of wealth, where the rich govern the poor; an oligarchy of learning, where the educated govern the ignorant; or even an oligarchy of race, where the Saxon rules the African, might be endured; but this oligarchy of sex which makes father, brothers, husband, sons, the oligarchs over the mother and sisters, the wife and daughters of every household; which ordains all men sovereigns, all

women subjects—carries discord and rebellion into every home of the nation. . . . The moment you deprive a person of his right to a voice in the government, you degrade him from the status of a citizen of the republic to that of a subject. It matters very little to him whether his monarch be an individual tyrant, as is the Czar of Russia, or a 15,000,000 headed monster, as here in the United States; he is a powerless subject, serf or slave; not in any sense a free and independent citizen. . . .

Though the words persons, people, inhabitants, electors, citizens, are all used indiscriminately in the national and State constitutions, there was always a conflict of opinion, prior to the war, as to whether they were synonymous terms, but whatever room there was for doubt, under the old regime, the adoption of the Fourteenth Amendment settled that question forever in its first sentence:

All persons born or naturalized in the United States, and subject to the jurisdiction thereof, are citizens of the United States, and of the State wherein they reside.

The second settles the equal status of all citizens:

No State shall make or enforce any law which shall abridge the privileges or immunities of citizens of the United States; nor shall any State deprive any person of life, liberty or property without due process of law, or deny to any person within its jurisdiction the equal protection of the laws.

The only question left to be settled now is: Are women persons? I scarcely believe any of our opponents will have the hardihood to say they are not. Being persons, then, women are citizens, and no State has a right to make any new law, or to enforce any old law, which shall abridge their privileges or immunities. Hence, every discrimination against women in the constitutions and laws of the several States is today null and void, precisely as is every one against negroes.

Is the right to vote one of the privileges or immunities of citizens? I think the disfranchised ex-rebels and ex-State prisoners all will agree that it is not only one of them, but the one without which all the others are nothing. Seek first the kingdom of the ballot and all things else shall be added, is the political injunction. . . .

If once we establish the false principle that United States citizenship does not carry with it the right to vote in every State in this Union, there is no end to the petty tricks and cunning devices which will be attempted to exclude one and another class of citizens from the right of suffrage. It will not always be the men combining to disfranchise all women; native born men combining to abridge the rights of all naturalized citizens, as in Rhode Island. It will not always be the rich and educated who may combine to cut off the poor and ignorant; but we may live to see the hardworking, uncultivated day laborers, foreign and native born, learning the power of the ballot and their vast majority of numbers, combine and amend State constitutions so as to disfranchise the Vanderbilts, the Stewarts, the Conklings and the Fentons. It is a poor rule that won't work more ways than one. Establish this precedent, admit the State's right to deny suffrage, and there is no limit to the confusion, discord, and disruption that may await us. There is and can be but one safe principle of government—equal rights to all. Discrimination against any class on account of color, race, nativity, sex, property, culture, can but embitter and disaffect that class, and thereby endanger the safety of the whole people. Clearly, then, the national government not only must define the rights of citizens, but must stretch out its powerful hand and protect them in every State of this Union.

(b) *Minor v. Happersett* (1875)

MR. CHIEF JUSTICE MORRISON R. WAITE DELIVERED THE OPINION OF THE COURT:

The question is presented in this case, whether, since the adoption of the fourteenth amendment, a woman, who is a citizen of the United States and of the State of Missouri, is a voter in that State, notwithstanding the provision of the constitution and laws of the State, which confine the right of suffrage to men alone. . . . The argument is, that as a woman, born or naturalized in the United States and subject to the jurisdiction thereof, is a citizen of the United States and of the State in which she resides, she has the right of suffrage as one of the privileges and immunities of her citizenship, which the State cannot by its laws or constitution abridge.

There is no doubt that women may be citizens. They are persons, and by the fourteenth amendment "all persons born or naturalized in the United States and subject to the jurisdiction thereof" are expressly declared to be "citizens of the United States and of the State wherein they reside." But, in our opinion, it did not need this amendment to give them that position . . . sex has never been made one of the elements of citizenship in the United States. In this respect men have never had an advantage over women. The same laws precisely apply to both. The fourteenth amendment did not affect the citizenship of women any more than it did of men . . . Mrs. Minor . . . has always been a citizen from her birth, and entitled to all the privileges and immunities of citizenship.

If the right of suffrage is one of the necessary privileges of a citizen of the United States, then the constitution and laws of Missouri confining it to men are in violation of the Constitution of the United States, as amended, and consequently void. The direction question is, therefore, presented whether all citizens are necessarily voters.

The Constitution does not define the privileges and immunities of citizens. For that definition we must look elsewhere. In this case we need not determine what they are, but only whether suffrage is necessarily one of them.

It certainly is nowhere made so in express terms. The United States has no voters in the States of its own creation. The elective officers of the United States are all elected directly or indirectly by state voters. . . . [I]t cannot for a moment be doubted that if it had been intended to make all citizens of the United States voters, the framers of the Constitution would not have left it to implication. . . .

It is true that the United States guarantees to every State a republican form of government. . . . No particular government is designated as republican, neither is the exact form to be guaranteed, in any manner especially designated. . . . When the Constitution was adopted . . . all the citizens of the States were not invested with the right of suffrage. In all, save perhaps New Jersey, this right was only bestowed upon men and not upon all of them. . . . Under these circumstances it is certainly now too late to contend that a government is not republican, within the meaning of this guaranty in the Constitution, because women are not made voters. . . . If suffrage was intended to be included within its obligations, language better adapted to express that intent would most certainly have been employed. . . .

. . . For nearly ninety years the people have acted upon the idea that the Constitution, when it conferred citizenship, did not necessarily confer the right of suffrage. If uniform practice long continued can settle the construction of so important an instrument as the Constitution of the United States confessedly is, most certainly it has been done here. Our province is to decide what the law is, not to declare what it should be.

We have given this case the careful consideration its importance demands. If the law is wrong, it ought to be changed; but the power for that is not with us. . . . No argument as to woman's need of suffrage can be considered. We can only act upon her rights as they exist.

Questions

1. What case did Anthony make for treating voting as an "inalienable right"?

2. What did Anthony see as the consequence of denying that the right to vote is intrinsic to citizenship? Is her view prophetic?

3. Compare the reasoning of Anthony and of Chief Justice Waite on the question of whether the right to vote is one of the "privileges and immunities" of citizenship. What sorts of evidence do they cite?

15-8   An Advocate of Federal Aid for Land Purchase (1868)

Richard H. Cain

With the enactment of the Reconstruction Act of 1867, the cast of political leadership in the South dramatically changed. One good example of the new men rising to prominence was Richard H. Cain (1825–1887). Born in Virginia of African American and Cherokee parents, Cain was raised in Ohio, attending Wilberforce University and becoming a minister in the African Methodist Episcopal (A.M.E.) Church. After spending the Civil War as pastor of a Brooklyn church, he went south in 1865 as a missionary; reorganizing the Emmanuel A.M.E. Church of Charleston, South Carolina, Cain built it into the largest A.M.E. congregation in the state and used it as a political base. He was a delegate to the South Carolina constitutional convention of 1868; served as a state senator from 1868 to 1870; unsuccessfully sought the Republican nomination for lieutenant governor in 1872; and served in the U.S. House of Representatives from 1873 to 1875 and again from 1877 to 1879. Cain left South Carolina in 1880 and spent the remainder of his life as a bishop and college president in the A.M.E. Church.

Like many successful African American preachers, Cain was an astute businessman, eager to lend his services to build up the black community. Like many other black politicians, he saw the issue of land for the freedmen as paramount. An early advocate of redistribution of confiscated lands à la Thaddeus Stevens (Document 15-6), at the constitutional convention Cain advocated petitioning the federal government to appropriate $1 million to finance land purchases by the freedmen. When his proposal was attacked by C. P. Leslie, a white Republican delegate, Cain defended it with the following remarks.

Source: Proceedings of the Constitutional Convention of South Carolina (Charleston: Denny and Perry, 1868), 378–382.

. . . *Mr. CAIN.* I offer this resolution with good intentions. I believe there is need of immediate relief to the poor people of the State. I know from my experience among the people, there is pressing need of some measures to meet the wants of the utterly destitute. The gentleman says it will only take money out of the Treasury. Well that is the intention. I do not expect to get it anywhere else. I expect to get the money, if at all, through the Treasury of the United States, or some other department. It certainly must come out of the Government. I believe such an appropriation would remove a great many of the difficulties now in the State and do a vast amount of good to poor people. It may be that we will not get it, but that will not debar us from asking. It is our privilege and right. Other Conventions have asked from Congress appropriations. Georgia and other States have sent in their petitions. One has asked for $30,000,000 to be appropriated to the Southern States. I do not see any inconsistency in the proposition presented by myself.

Mr. C. P. LESLIE. Suppose I should button up my coat and march up to your house and ask you for money or provisions, when you had none to give, what would you think of me?

Mr. CAIN. You would do perfectly right to run the chance of getting something to eat. This is a measure of relief to those thousands of freed people who now have no lands of their own. I believe the possession of lands and homesteads is one of the best means by which a people is made industrious, honest and advantageous to the State. I believe it is a fact well known, that over three hundred thousand men, women and children are homeless, landless. The abolition of slavery has thrown these people upon their own resources. How are they to live? I know the philosopher of the New York *Tribune* says, "root hog or die;" but in the meantime we ought to have some place to root. My proposition is simply to give the hog some place to root. I believe if the proposition is sent to Congress, it will certainly receive the attention of our friends. I believe the whole country is desirous to see that this State shall return to the Union in peace and quiet, and that every inhabitant of the State shall be made industrious and profitable to the State. I am opposed to this Bureau system. I want a system adopted that will do away with the Bureau, but I cannot see how it can be done unless the people have homes. As long as people are working on shares and contracts, and at the end of every year are in debt, so long will they and the country suffer. But give them a chance to buy lands, and they become steady, industrious men. That is the reason I desire to bring this money here and to assist them to buy lands. It will be the means of encouraging them to industry if the petition be granted by Congress. It will be the means of meeting one of the great wants of the present among the poor. It will lay the foundation for the future prosperity of the country as no other measure will at this time, because it will bring about a reconciliation in the minds of thousands of these helpless people, which nothing else can. This measure, if carried out, will bring capital to the State and stimulate the poor to renewed efforts in life, such as they never had before. Such a measure will give to the landholders relief from their embarrassments financially, and enable them to get fair compensation for their lands. It will relieve the Government of the responsibility of taking care of the thousands who now are fed at the Commissaries and fostered in laziness. I have gone through the country and on every side I was besieged with questions: How are we to get homesteads, to get lands? I desire to devise some plan, or adopt some measure by which we can dissipate one of the arguments used against us, that the African race will not work. I do not believe the black man hates work any more than the white man does. Give these men a place to work, and I will guarantee before one year passes, there will be no necessity for the Freedman's Bureau, or any measure aside from those measures which a people may make in protecting themselves.

But a people without homes become wanderers. If they possess lands they have an interest in the soil, in the State, in its commerce, its agriculture, and in everything pertaining to the wealth and welfare of the State. If these people had homes along the lines of railroads, and the lands were divided and sold in small farms, I will guarantee our railroads will make fifty times as much money, banking systems will be advanced by virtue of the settlement of the people throughout the whole State. We want these large tracts of land cut up. The land is productive, and there is nothing to prevent the greatest and highest prosperity. What we need is a system of small farms. Every farmer owning his own land will feel he is in possession of something. It will have a tendency to settle the minds of the people in the State and settle many difficulties. In the rural districts now there is constant discontent, constant misapprehension between the parties, a constant disregard for each other. One man won't make an engagement to work, because he fears if he makes a contract this year, he will be cheated again as he thinks he was last year. We have had petitions from planters asking the Convention to disabuse the minds of the freedmen of the thought that this Convention has any lands at its disposal, but I do desire this Convention to do something at least to relieve the wants of these poor suffering people. I believe this measure, if adopted and sent to Congress, will indicate to the people that this Convention does desire they shall possess homes and have relief.

Some of my friends say that the sum is too small, and ask why I do not make it more. I made it a million, because I thought there would be more probability of getting one million than five. It might be put into the hands of the Bureau, and I am willing to trust the Bureau. . . .

I do not desire to have a foot of land in this State confiscated. I want every man to stand upon his own character. I want these lands purchased by the government, and the people afforded an opportunity to buy from the government. I believe every man ought to carve out for himself a character and position in this life. I believe every man ought to be made to work by some means or other, and if he does not, he must go down. I believe if the same amount of money that has been employed by the Bureau in feeding

lazy, worthless men and women, had been expended in purchasing lands, we would to-day have no need of the Bureau. Millions upon millions have been expended, and it is still going on *ad infinitum*. I propose to let the poor people buy these lands, the government to be paid back in five years time. It is one of the great cries of the enemies of reconstruction, that Congress has constantly fostered laziness. I want to have the satisfaction of showing that the freedmen are as capable and willing to work as any men on the face of the earth. This measure will save the State untold expenses. I believe there are hundreds of persons in the jail and penitentiary cracking rock to-day who have all the instincts of honesty, and who, had they an opportunity of making a living, would never have been found in such a place. I think if Congress will accede to our request, we shall be benefited beyond measure, and save the State from taking charge of paupers, made such by not having the means to earn a living for themselves.

I can look to a part of my constituency, men in this hall, mechanics, plasterers, carpenters, engineers, men capable of doing all kind of work, now idle because they cannot find any work in the city. Poverty stares them in the face, and their children are in want. They go to the cotton houses, but can find no labor. They are men whose honesty and integrity has never been called in question. They are suffering in consequence of the poverty-stricken condition of the city and State. I believe the best measure is to open a field where they can labor, where they can take the hoe and the axe, cut down the forest, and make the whole land blossom as the Garden of Eden, and prosperity pervade the whole land.

Now, the report of Major General Howard gives a surplus of over seven millions in the Freedman's Bureau last year. Out of that seven millions I propose we ask Congress to make an appropriation of one million, which will be properly distributed and then leave several millions in that Department, my friend from Barnwell notwithstanding.

I think there could be no better measure for this Convention to urge upon Congress. If that body should listen to our appeal, I have no doubt we shall be benefited. This measure of relief, it seems to me, would come swiftly. It is a swift messenger that comes in a week's time after it is passed; so that in the month of February or March the people may be enabled to go to planting and raising crops for the ensuing year. One gentleman says it will take six months or a year, but I hope, with the assistance of the Government, we could accomplish it in less time.

Mr. C. P. LESLIE. Did you ever see the Government do anything quick?

Mr. R. H. CAIN. They make taxes come quick. If this measure is carried out, the results will be that we will see all along our lines of railroad and State roads little farms, log cabins filled with happy families, and thousands of families coming on the railroads with their products. There will also spring up depots for the reception of cotton, corn and all other cereals. Prosperity will return to the State, by virtue of the people being happy, bound to the Government by a tie that cannot be broken. The taxes, that are so heavy now that men are compelled to sell their horses, will be lightened. I want to see the State alive, to hear the hum of the spindle and the mills! I want to see cattle and horses, and fowls, and everything that makes up a happy home and family. I want to see the people shout with joy and gladness. There shall then be no antagonism between white men and black men, but we shall all realize the end of our being, and realize that we are all made to dwell upon the earth in peace and happiness. The white man and the black man may then work in harmony, and secure prosperity to all coming generations.

Questions

1. What arguments did Cain make in favor of his proposal? To what present policies, especially of the Freedmen's Bureau, did he object?

2. In certain respects, Cain's proposal can be characterized as *conservative*. How? Would you agree, or not?

3. How would you characterize Cain's intentions toward the *whites* of South Carolina?

Questions for Further Thought

1. Compare Cain's argument on land reform (Document 15-8) to that of Thaddeus Stevens (Document 15-6). To what degree did Cain, like Stevens, see land redistribution as a means of punishing "rebels"? What did each man see as the proper role of the federal government in "reconstructing" the South?

2. Susan B. Anthony's argument (Document 15-7a) rested on an analogy between the status of women in the pre-Reconstruction United States and the status of African Americans. How well did that analogy work?

3. In view of the preceding documents, just how "radical" would you say radical Reconstruction really was? Bear in mind the meaning of the word *radical*—to desire change not on the surface of society, but *at its roots*.

The Undoing of Reconstruction

Northern support for Reconstruction was never reliable. Because most white northerners feared that President Johnson's program threatened to undo the Union victory and place Confederates back in the saddle (Document 15-9a), they preferred the program of congressional Republicans. However, they were at best only slightly more liberal in their racial views than were southerners, and over time northerners were increasingly receptive to southern white arguments that blacks were not to be trusted to govern (Document 15-9b).

Most southern whites, of course, opposed congressional Reconstruction from the outset, though the vehemence of the opposition fluctuated. The animosity of southern whites toward Reconstruction, Republicans, and African Americans intensified when elections were contested or when sensitive issues were placed before the public. The Ku Klux Klan was especially active during such times, despite legislation passed against it.

The final undoing of Reconstruction came in the mid-1870s. A serious economic crisis struck the nation in 1873, plunging it into depression. New, economic issues, such as unemployment, labor conflict, and monetary policy, increasingly took precedence over the aging agenda of the sectional conflict, while northern lack of sympathy for blacks became increasingly important in shaping federal policy toward the South (Document 15-10). At the same time, southern whites got bolder, organizing paramilitary organizations to carry elections by whatever means were necessary. In such states as Mississippi and South Carolina, the end of Reconstruction resulted not so much from an election as from a white counterrevolution.

15-9   The Rise and Fall of Northern Support for Reconstruction (1868, 1874)

Thomas Nast

Evidence of broad northern support for the Republican program could be found in many places other than the ballot box. Illustrations from *Harper's Weekly*, such as the one in the text (p. 477) and the one here from 1868 titled "This Is a White Man's Government," reflected popular attitudes in the North in the 1860s. However, northern support for Reconstruction began to erode as early as 1868 and was exhausted by 1874 (see text pp. 478–479), the year the *Harper's Weekly* illustration presented here appeared. Both cartoons are by Thomas Nast.

The first cartoon satirizes the Democratic Party in 1868, with its platform rejecting the Congressional Reconstruction Acts as "unconstitutional, null, and void." Nathan

(A)   *Thomas Nast, "This Is a White Man's Government" (1868)*

Bedford Forrest — the Confederate general who became the first grand wizard of the Ku Klux Klan — is represented in the center, while to his right stands an Irish immigrant, depicted (as was common in Nast cartoons) as a barbaric hoodlum. The third figure (to Forrest's left) is the Democratic candidate for president in 1868, Governor Horatio Seymour — depicted here as the prosperous associate of New York financiers. This unholy alliance unites in what to Nast were the characteristic Democratic Party activities of racial oppression and treason, illustrated by scenes from the New York draft riots (see Document 14-9) and the postwar South, and by their trampling on the prostrate form of a black Union soldier.

The second cartoon shows a sharp shift in opinion on the part of both Nast and his audience. The cartoon illustrates a derisive news account of the black-majority

COLORED RULE IN A RECONSTRUCTED (?) STATE.—[SEE PAGE 242.]

(THE MEMBERS CALL EACH OTHER THIEVES, LIARS, RASCALS, AND COWARDS.)

COLUMBIA. "You are Aping the lowest Whites. If you disgrace your Race in this way you had better take Back Seats."

(B)   *Thomas Nast, "Colored Rule in a Reconstructed State" (1874)*

South Carolina House of Representatives, reprinted from the white conservative *Charleston News*. In 1868 the views of the *News* would have been dismissed as "disloyal" by Nast's employer, *Harper's Weekly*; by 1874 the magazine was allowing those views a respectful hearing, and its famous cartoonist was giving them his stamp of approval. Why?

Sources: Thomas Nast, "This Is a White Man's Government," *Harper's Weekly*, 5 September 1868; Thomas Nast, "Colored Rule in a Reconstructed State," *Harper's Weekly*, 14 March 1874. Art courtesy of the Research Libraries, New York Public Library.

Questions

1. Note the picture of African Americans presented here and in the illustration on text page 477. Contrast that with the portrayal of government by southern whites.

2. Compare the portrayal of African Americans in the last illustration with that in the earlier illustrations.

3. What do you think accounts for the change?

15-10 President Grant Refuses to Aid Republicans in Mississippi (1875)

As one of three southern states with a black-majority population, one whose black voters were well organized, Mississippi should logically have remained secure for the Republicans. However, in the state election year of 1875, white Democrats launched a campaign of systematic violent intimidation of black and Republican voters. Against the massive mobilization of white "Rifle Clubs," the government of Governor Adelbert Ames was helpless, and in September Ames sent President Grant a desperate plea for federal troops. Grant and his attorney general, Edwards Pierrepont, turned down Ames's request; Pierrepont's letter to Ames of September 14, quoting Grant, was subsequently released to the press (Document 15-10a). Thanks to a catastrophic decline in Republican votes and blatant ballot-box stuffing, Democrats "redeemed" the state in a landslide. One of the few survivors of the Democratic onslaught, African American congressman John R. Lynch, wrote some years later of a postelection encounter with President Grant, who explained to him the political considerations behind his abandonment of Mississippi Republicans (Document 15-10b).

Sources: *New York Times*, 17 September 1875, 1; John Roy Lynch, *The Facts of Reconstruction* (New York: Neale Publishing Co., 1913), 150–153.

(a) Pierrepont's Letter of Refusal

DEPARTMENT OF JUSTICE, WASHINGTON, SEPT. 14, 1875.

To Gov. Ames, Jackson, Miss.:

This hour I have had dispatches from the President. I can best convey to you his ideas by extracts from his dispatch: "The whole public are tired out with these annual Autumnal outbreaks in the South, and the great majority are ready now to condemn any interference on the part of the Government. I heartily wish that peace and good order may be restored without issuing the proclamation; but if it is not the proclamation must be issued, and if it is I shall instruct the commander of the forces to have *no child's play*. If there is a necessity for military interference, there is justice in such interference as shall deter evil-doers. . . . I would suggest the sending of a dispatch (or better, a private messenger,) to Gov. Ames, urging him to strengthen his own position by exhausting his own resources in restoring order before he receives Government aid. He might accept the assistance offered by the citizens of Jackson and elsewhere. . . .

Gov. Ames and his advisors can be made perfectly secure. As many of the troops in Mississippi as he deems necessary may be sent to Jackson. If he is betrayed by those who offer assistance, he will be in a position to defeat their ends and punish them."

You see by this the mind of the President, with which I and every member of the Cabinet who has been consulted are in full accord. You see the difficulties—you see the responsibilities which you assume. We cannot understand why you do not strengthen yourself in the way the President suggests, nor do we see why you do not call the Legislature together, and obtain from them whatever powers, money, and arms you need. The Constitution is explicit that the Executive of the State can call upon the President for aid in suppressing "domestic violence" only "when the Legislature cannot be convened," and the law expressly says: "In case of an insurrection in any State against the Government thereof, it shall be lawful for the President, on application of the Legislature of such State, or of the Executive, when the Legislature cannot be convened, to call," &c. It is the plain meaning of the Constitution and laws when taken together that the Executive of the State may call upon the President for military aid to quell "domestic violence" only in case of an insurrection in any State against the Government thereof when the Legislature cannot be called together. You make no suggestions even that there is any insurrection against the Government of the State, or that the Legislature would not support you in any measures you might propose to preserve the public order. I suggest that you take all lawful means and all needed measures to preserve the peace by the forces in your own State, and let the country see that the citizens of Mississippi, who are largely favorable to good order, and who are largely Republican, have the courage and the manhood to fight for their rights and to destroy the bloody ruffians who murder the innocent and inoffending freedmen. Everything is in readiness. Be careful to bring yourself strictly within the Constitution and the laws, and if there is such resistance to your State authorities as you cannot, by all the means at your command, suppress, the President will swiftly aid you in crushing those lawless traitors to human rights.

Telegraph me on receipt of this, and state explicitly what you need. Very respectfully yours,

EDWARDS PIERREPONT, Attorney General.

(b) Grant's Subsequent Explanation

. . . I then informed the President that there was another matter about which I desired to have a short talk with him, that was the recent election in Mississippi. After calling his attention to the sanguinary struggle through which we had passed, and the great disadvantages under which we labored, I reminded him of the fact that the Governor, when he saw that he could not put down without the assistance of the National Administration what was practically an insurrection against the State Government, made application for assistance in the manner and form prescribed by the Constitution, with the confident belief that it would be forthcoming. But in this we were, for some reason, seriously disappointed and sadly surprised. The reason for this action, or rather non-action, was still an unexplained mystery to us. For my own satisfaction and information I should be pleased to have the President enlighten me on the subject.

The President said that he was glad I had asked him the question, and that he would take pleasure in giving me a frank reply. He said he had sent Governor Ames' requisition to the War Department with his approval and with instructions to have the necessary assistance furnished without delay. He had also given instructions to the Attorney-General to use the marshals and the machinery of the Federal judiciary as far as possible in coöperation with the War Department in an effort to maintain order and to bring about a condition which would insure a peaceable and fair election. But before the orders were put into execution a committee of prominent Republicans from Ohio had called on him. (Ohio was then an October State,—that is, her elections took place in October instead of November.) An important election was then pending in that State. This committee, the President stated, protested against having the requisition of Governor Ames honored. The committee, the President said, informed him in a most emphatic way that if the requisition of Governor Ames were honored, the Democrats would not only carry Mississippi,—a State which would be lost to the Republicans in any event,—but that Democratic success in Ohio would be an assured fact. If the requisition were not honored it would make no change in the result in Mississippi, but that Ohio would be saved to the Republicans. The President assured me that it was with great reluctance that he yielded,—against his own judgment and sense of official duty,—to the arguments of this committee, and directed the withdrawal of the orders which had been given the Secretary of War and the Attorney-General in that matter.

This statement, I confess, surprised me very much.

"Can it be possible," I asked, "that there is such a prevailing sentiment in any State in the North, East or West as renders it necessary for a Republican President to virtually give his sanction to what is equivalent to a suspension of the Constitution and laws of the land to insure Republican success in such a State? I cannot believe this to be true, the opinion of the Republican committee from Ohio to the contrary notwithstanding. What surprises me more, Mr. President, is that you yielded and granted this remarkable request. That is not like you. It is the first time I have ever known you to show the white feather. Instead of granting the request of that committee, you should have rebuked the men,—told them that it is your duty as chief magistrate of the country to enforce the Constitution and laws of the land, and to protect American citizens in the exercise and enjoyment of their rights, let the consequences be what they may; and that if by doing this Ohio should be lost to the Republicans it ought to be lost. In other words, no victory is worth having if it is to be brought about upon such conditions as those, — if it is to be purchased at such a fearful cost as was paid in this case."

"Yes," said the President, "I admit that you are right. I should not have yielded. I believed at the time that I was making a grave mistake. But as presented, it was duty on one side, and party obligation on the other. Between the two I hesitated, but finally yielded to what was believed to be party obligation. If a mistake was made, it was one of the head and not of the heart. That my heart was right and my intentions good, no one who knows me will question. If I had believed that any effort on my part would have saved Mississippi I would have made it, even if I had been convinced that it would have resulted in the loss of Ohio to the Republicans. But I was satisfied then, as I am now, that Mississippi could not have been saved to the party in any event and I wanted to avoid the responsibility of the loss of Ohio, in addition. This was the turning-point in the case. . . ."

Questions

1. Do you think that Grant was correct in his argument against federal intervention? Was there really nothing that the federal government and the national Republican Party could have done to "save" Mississippi?

2. Had Governor Ames convened the Mississippi legislature to deal with "the bloody ruffians," how successful do you think he would have been?

3. What does Grant's decision illuminate about how Republicans, and many people in the North, had come to view the South and the progress of Reconstruction — especially in the Deep South — by the mid-1870s?

15-11   The Slaughterhouse Cases (1873)

The failure of Reconstruction might be traced to several causes: the readiness of southerners to engage in acts of violence and intimidation (Document 15-2); the unwillingness of the federal government to repel these actions and to intervene on behalf of freed blacks (Document 15-10); the fragmentation of the Republican Party; and the onset of economic depression, which deflected national attention away from the "old" problems of sectionalism and civil rights. But no less important were the actions of the U.S. Supreme Court. Beginning in the 1870s, the Court issued a series of crucial decisions that weakened the Fourteenth Amendment, limiting the legal basis for federal intervention in the South. The decision in the slaughterhouse cases, 1873, was the first and most important of these. In 1869 the Louisiana legislature granted the Crescent City Slaughterhouse Company a monopoly over the butchering business in New Orleans. Butchers not included in the monopoly filed suit, claiming that the monopoly deprived them of their property without due process and violated their rights as citizens under the Fourteenth Amendment. In a 5-to-4 majority decision, the Court ruled against the butchers, all of whom were white, by finding that they had no standing under the provisions of the amendment, whose "main purpose was to establish the citizenship of the negro." It then proceeded to define precisely what rights were protected by the Fourteenth Amendment.

Source: The Butchers' Benevolent Association of New Orleans v. The Crescent City Live-Stock Landing and Slaughter-House Company, 83 U.S. 36 (1873).

Mr. Justice Miller, now April 14th, 1873, delivered the opinion of the court.

The plaintiffs . . . allege that the statute is a violation of the Constitution of the United States in these several particulars:

That it creates an involuntary servitude forbidden by the thirteenth article of amendment;

That it abridges the privileges and immunities of citizens of the United States;

That it denies to the plaintiffs the equal protection of the laws; and,

That it deprives them of their property without due process of law; contrary to the provisions of the first section of the fourteenth article of amendment.

This court is thus called upon for the first time to give construction to these articles.

We do not conceal from ourselves the great responsibility which this duty devolves upon us. No questions so far-reaching and pervading in their consequences, so profoundly interesting to the people of this country, and so important in their bearing upon the relations of the United States, and of the several States to each other and to the citizens of the States and of the United States, have been before this court during the official life of any of its present members. . . .

The first section of the fourteenth article, to which our attention is more specially invited, opens with a definition of citizenship—not only citizenship of the United States, but citizenship of the States. No such definition was previously found in the Constitution, nor had any attempt been made to define it by act of Congress. It had been the occasion of much discussion in the courts, by the executive departments, and in the public journals. It had been said by eminent judges that no man was a citizen of the United States, except as he was a citizen of one of the States composing the Union. Those, therefore, who had been born and resided always in the District of Columbia or in the Territories, though within the United States, were not citizens. Whether this proposition was sound or not had never been judicially decided. But it had been held by this court, in the celebrated Dred Scott case, only a few years before the outbreak of the civil war, that a man of African descent, whether a slave or not, was not and could not be a citizen of a State or of the United States. This decision, while it met the condemnation of some of the ablest statesmen and constitutional lawyers of the country, had never been overruled; and if it was to be accepted as a constitutional limitation of the right of citizenship, then all the negro race who had recently been made freemen, were still, not only not citizens, but were incapable of becoming so by anything short of an amendment to the Constitution.

To remove this difficulty primarily, and to establish a clear and comprehensive definition of citizenship which should declare what should constitute citizenship of the United States, and also citizenship of a State, the first clause of the first section was framed.

"All persons born or naturalized in the United States, and subject to the jurisdiction thereof, are citizens of the United States and of the State wherein they reside."

The first observation we have to make on this clause is, that it puts at rest both the questions which we stated to have been the subject of differences of opinion. It declares that persons may be citizens of the United States without regard to their citizenship of a particular State, and it overturns the Dred Scott decision by making *all persons* born within the United States and subject to its jurisdiction citizens of the United States. That its main purpose was to establish the citizenship of the negro can admit of no doubt. The phase, "subject to its jurisdiction" was intended to exclude from its operation children of ministers, consuls, and citizens or subjects of foreign States born within the United States.

The next observation is more important in view of the arguments of counsel in the present case. It is, that the distinction between citizenship of the United States and citizenship of a State is clearly recognized and established. Not only may a man be a citizen of the United States without being a citizen of a State, but an important element is necessary to convert the former into the latter. He must reside within the State to make him a citizen of it, but it is only necessary that he should be born or naturalized in the United States to be a citizen of the Union.

It is quite clear, then, that there is a citizenship of the United States, and a citizenship of a State, which are distinct from each other, and which depend upon different characteristics or circumstances in the individual.

We think this distinction and its explicit recognition in this amendment of great weight in this argument, because the next paragraph of this same section, which is the one mainly relied on by the plaintiffs in error, speaks only of privileges and immunities of citizens of the United States, and does not speak of those of citizens of the several States. The argument, however, in favor of the plaintiffs rests wholly on the assumption that the citizenship is the same, and the privileges and immunities guaranteed by the clause are the same.

The language is, "No State shall make or enforce any law which shall abridge the privileges or immunities of citizens of *the United States*." It is a little remarkable, if this clause was intended as a protection to the citizen of a State against the legislative power of his own State, that the word citizen of the State should be left out when it is so carefully used, and used in contradistinction to citizens of the United States, in the very sentence which precedes it. It is too clear for argument that the change in phraseology was adopted understandingly and with a purpose.

Of the privileges and immunities of the citizen of the United States, and of the privileges and immunities of the citizen of the State, and what they respectively are, we will presently consider; but we wish to state here that it is only the former which are placed by this clause under the protection of the Federal Constitution, and that the latter, whatever they may be, are not intended to have any additional protection by this paragraph of the amendment.

If, then, there is a difference between the privileges and immunities belonging to a citizen of the United States as such, and those belonging to the citizen of the State as such, the latter must rest for their security and protection where they have heretofore rested; for they are not embraced by this paragraph of the amendment. . . .

The constitutional provision there alluded to did not create those rights, which it called privileges and immunities of citizens of the States. It threw around them in that clause no security for the citizen of the State in which they were claimed or exercised. Nor did it profess to control the power of the State governments over the rights of its own citizens.

Its sole purpose was to declare to the several States, that whatever those rights, as you grant or establish them to your own citizens, or as you limit or qualify, or impose restrictions on their exercise, the same, neither more nor less, shall be the measure of the rights of citizens of other States within your jurisdiction.

It would be the vainest show of learning to attempt to prove by citations of authority, that up to the adoption of the recent amendments, no claim or pretence was set up that those rights depended on the Federal government for their existence or protection, beyond the very few express limitations which the Federal Constitution imposed upon the States—such, for instance, as the prohibition against ex post facto laws, bills of attainder, and laws impairing the obligation of contracts. But with the exception of these and a few other restrictions, the entire domain of the privileges and immunities of citizens of the States, as above defined, lay within the constitutional and legislative power of the States, and without that of the Federal government. Was it the purpose of the fourteenth amendment, by the simple declaration that no State should make or enforce any law which shall abridge the privileges and immunities of *citizens of the United States*, to transfer the security and protection of all the civil rights which we have mentioned, from the States to the Federal government? And where it is declared that Congress shall have the power to enforce that article, was it intended to bring within the power of Congress the entire domain of civil rights heretofore belonging exclusively to the States? . . .

We are convinced that no such results were intended by the Congress which proposed these amendments, nor by the legislatures of the States which ratified them.

Having shown that the privileges and immunities relied on in the argument are those which belong to citizens of the States as such, and that they are left to the State governments for security and protection, and not by this article placed under the special care of the Federal government, we may hold ourselves excused from defining the privileges and immunities of citizens of the United States which no State can abridge, until some case involving those privileges may make it necessary to do so.

But lest it should be said that no such privileges and immunities are to be found if those we have been considering are excluded, we venture to suggest some which owe their existence to the Federal government, its National character, its Constitution, or its laws.

One of these is well described in the case of *Crandall v. Nevada*. It is said to be the right of the citizen of this great country, protected by implied guarantees of its Constitution, "to come to the seat of government to assert any claim he may have upon that government, to transact any business he may have with it, to seek its protection, to share its offices, to engage in administering its functions. He has the right of free access to its seaports, through which all operations of foreign commerce are conducted, to the subtreasuries, land offices, and courts of justice in the several States." . . .

Another privilege of a citizen of the United States is to demand the care and protection of the Federal government over his life, liberty, and property when on the high seas or within the jurisdiction of a foreign government. Of this there can be no doubt, nor that the right depends upon his character as a citizen of the United States. The right to peaceably assemble and petition for redress of grievances, the privilege of the writ of *habeas corpus*, are rights of the citizen guaranteed by the Federal Constitution. The right to use the navigable waters of the United States, however they may penetrate the territory of the several States, all rights secured to our citizens by treaties with foreign nations, are dependent upon citizenship of the United States, and not citizenship of a State. One of these privileges is conferred by the very article under consideration. It is that a citizen of the United States can, of his own volition, become a citizen of any State of the Union by a *bonâ fide* residence therein, with the same rights as other citizens of that State. To these may be added the rights secured by the thirteenth and fifteenth articles of amendment, and by the other clause of the fourteenth, next to be considered.

But it is useless to pursue this branch of the inquiry, since we are of opinion that the rights claimed by these plaintiffs in error, if they have any existence, are not privileges and immunities of citizens of the United States within the meaning of the clause of the fourteenth amendment under consideration.

Questions

1. On what basis did the Court rule that the Fourteenth Amendment distinguishes between state and federal citizenship?

2. What sort of rights qualified as the rights of federal citizens? What sort of rights qualified as rights of state citizens? Which set of rights would be more important in the everyday lives of most Americans?

3. Following the reasoning of the Court, to whom were blacks supposed to appeal in cases involving violations of their civil and political rights? Why might this not be in their best interest?

15-12   Susan Myrick Interviews Ex-Slave Catherine Beale (1929)

By the 1890s, as the bitterness of the Civil War was giving way to romantic myths about the Lost Cause and a reconciliationist literature was obligingly promoting the Southern "Redeemers" version of the "evils" of Reconstruction, a distorted image of plantation life began to take hold in the popular imagination. In this absurdly mawkish rendering of life in the Old South, kind masters and faithful slaves united to create an idyllic world. That world had disappeared with the defeat of the Confederacy, its promoters suggested, but not altogether. Survivors were still around, including former slaves. Partly out of a misdirected sense of nostalgia, then, but also in pursuit of human interest stories, newspapers and magazines between 1890 and 1940 featured interviews with former slaves. Often conducted with great skill by professional journalists, these interviews have since constituted a valuable source of information for historians seeking to complement white eyewitness accounts with those derived from the slaves themselves. The following interview first appeared in the Macon (Georgia) *Telegraph*, February 10, 1929.

Source: Excerpt from *Slave Testimony: Two Centuries of Letters, Speeches, Interviews, and Autobiographies*, ed. John W. Blasingame (Baton Rouge: Louisiana State University Press, 1977), 574–578. Used by permission of the publisher.

Aunt Catherine speaks in a high, rather shrill voice which paradoxically enough is soft. Except when she tries to walk, this voice is the main indication of her years, though her hair is snowy white and that is a pretty good sign of age in one of her race, for the Negro is not apt to grow gray, as is the white person. Her face is remarkably free from wrinkles and her mind is clear. She does not use the ordinary Negro dialect which is commonly found in old Negroes in general, speaks with pretty good English, occasionally relapsing into careless speech, but in the main only dropping her R's and G's as the average Southerner. . . .

"Do you remember about being sold as a slave?"

"Yessum, me an' my sister was brought from Virginia and sold here when I was eleven an' Miss Leila was one year old. I remember living with my mother and papa and my sister with a Mistuh Goode in Virginia. We belonged to them, they had a heap er Niggers. Mistuh Goode had a wife named Miss Annie and a sister named Miss Kate. Ole Master, he died an after he was buried a few weeks, Miss Kate took me and my sister out on the back steps and tol' us we would have to be sold. She said she hated it because she had to sell us and take us away from our mother and family but there wasn't any money an' they had to have some from some place and they had decided to sell us.

"She took us to Richmond an' sold us to a slave buyer an' he brought us to Macon. There was a whole drove of Niggers; the slave buyer brought us in droves like horses an' cows. . . .

There was in her patient old voice no hint of animosity toward the slave driver or the world in general for her hardships. She was merely reciting facts as she recalled them, with as impersonal [a] manner as if the people had been some others and she were not concerned at all with the affair.

"Do you remember being put on the block and sold when you arrived in Macon?" I shuddered a little at the words, thinking (even though I am Southern for many generations and my father was a Confederate soldier), how horrible it seemed that human beings had been bought and sold as cattle and horses, and wondering if it could be true that I was actually talking to one, seemingly so gentle and peaceful now, who had undergone this ordeal.

"Yessum, I was sold to Mistuh Joe Blackshear from Twiggs an' I lived with them most all the rest of my life. He was living at Oak Ridge then, close to what they called Fitzpatrick, when he bought me, but he moved to a place about two miles from Bullard Station."

"Do you remember much about the War? You must have been old enough to recall it?"

"Yessum, I was grown woman befo's I ever heard tell of the war. I didn't know much about it then. I know Mr. Tom Blackshear, he went to the Wah an' he got shot. But out on the plantation, we didn't know nothing about what was going on."

"But when Sherman's army came through, didn't they burn things and drive off horses and cows?" I insisted.

"No'm they didn't do no burnin' nor nothing like that at our house. You know where Ol' Marion wuz?"

I nodded, for I recalled hearing that Marion was at one time the county seat of Twiggs and that it was in what is now Pulaski county and not very far from Hawkinsville.

"Wellum, they dont a heap of burnin' over there an' er heap of damage, I hear em say. But they didn't hurt nuthin' at our place."

"Did they tell you were free?"

"Yessum, but we didn't know no difference. We stayed on with Ole Marster. Old Mistis was good to us an' we didn't have no where to go if we had er left. Ole Marster was sort er crabbed but he wasn't never mean an' there wasn't no slaves whipped on that place. I hear tell that fokes that had overseers, they would whup the niggers. But there aint no scar on me. All my bones is whole! I aint never been drove to work, I jest went myself. I never was treated mean. I can set up nights and think and I say to myself, 'Thank God! Thankee Jesus! I had a good life!'"

"Did you come to Macon with the Blackshears, Aunt Catherine?"

"Yessum, I lived with them most all my life. Old Marster's oldest son Dr. James Emmett Blackshear, he was a medicine doctor, he come to Macon. Old Mistis had six children. Albert come first an then James Emmett an I think the next one was Henry and then Tom and William[,] Miss Leila come in there some where, I forgot which one she was next to. Mr. Tom he come to Macon and took pictures here for a long time."

Many of Macon's oldest inhabitants will recall T. B. Blackshear, who was a photographer here for many years, with a studio at No. 13 Cotton avenue. . . .

"Who else did you work for in Macon?"

"I worked for Mrs. Cabiness a long time, I went there when Miss Emmie wasn't no moren so high (she raised her hand to indicate a girl of ten or eleven years and went on) I helped raise Mr. Emory Cabiness, he called me Mammy and I sho loved that chile. Many's the time I been down to the school ter git him an it would be raining an he would say, 'Here, Mammy, you take the umbrella, I can run fast and not get wet.'" . . .

"Aunt Catherine, can you remember anything about the plantation in Virginia, what games you played and how you worked and what you did? . . .

"No'm, I don't remember nuthin about games. We never did play none. We had tasks to do. We had little patches of cotton then an' the[re] wasn't no gins like the[re] was after the Wah, and we had to work in the field in the day an' at night we had to pick out the seed fo' we went to bed. An' we had to clean the wool, we had to pick the burrs an' sticks out so it would be clean an' could be carded an' spun an' wove. We had to spin our own thread then an' make our own cloth too. We had the geeses to drive in the barn an' pick."

She sighed a little at the recollection and said, "Them feather mattresses was the nicest! Not like these things fokes sleep on now!

Questions

1. Before using any bit of information as evidence, historians must answer questions pertaining to the reliability of the source from whence it came and the circumstances under which it was generated. How reliable is the information conveyed by Catherine Beale? Is the fact that the interview was conducted nearly sixty-five years after her emancipation significant?

2. What can you say about Susan Myrick, the interviewer? Do her editorial comments reveal anything about her? What was her family background? Is Myrick's background relevant in determining the reliability of the information she got from Catherine Beale?

3. Catherine Beale moved to Macon as a slave and was still living there at the time of the interview. Many of the descendants of her former master were also living in Macon. How might this circumstance have affected the answers she gave to Susan Myrick, the reporter for the *Telegraph*?

Questions for Further Thought

1. Compare and contrast northern and southern views of blacks (Documents 15-9a, 15-9b, and 15-12. How were they the same? How were they different? What impact did the northern view of blacks have on the progress of Reconstruction?

2. If the Republican Party had pressed ahead with Reconstruction, do you think that it could have achieved its goals?

3. According to the Supreme Court's decision in the slaughterhouse cases (Document 15-11), did the president have the authority to intervene in Mississippi (Document 15-10)? Does this justify his failure to intervene? Explain.